P9-CED-454

Schweiz

DEUTSCHLAND

Rhein
Schaffhausen
Bodensee
Basel
Winterthur
Baden
Zürich
St. Gallen
Solothurn
Zürichsee
Biel
Aare
ÖSTERREICH
Bieler See
Vaduz
LIECHTENSTEIN
Neuchâtel
Walensee
FRANKREICH
Lac de Neuchâtel
Bern
Luzern
Chur
Rhein
Davos
Fribourg
Vierwaldstätter
Schwyz
Inn
Yverdon-
Thun
See
les-Bains
Brienzer See
Thuner See
Interlaken
A   L   P   E   N
Genfer See
Lausanne
Jungfrau
4,158 m
St.
Gotthard-Tunnel
St. Moritz
Montreux
Rhône
Simplonpass
Locarno
A
Genf
Lugano
Zermatt
Lago Maggiore
Lago di Lugano
Matterhorn
4,478 m
Mont Blanc
4,807 m
ITALIEN

0   25   50   75 km
0   25   50 mi

Österreich

TSCHECHOSLOWAKEI

Donau
NIEDERÖSTERREICH
Schärding
Donau
Krems
Inn
Braunau
Linz
St. Pölten
WIENERWALD
Wien
OBERÖSTERREICH
Melk
Steyr
WIEN
Salzburg
Eisenstadt
St. Wolfgang
Wiener Neustadt
Neusiedler
Bad Ischl
See
DEUTSCHLAND
Wolfgangsee
Enns
Bodensee
Bregenz
Kitzbühel
Leoben
Dornbirn
Zugspitze
2,963 m
Zell am See
SALZBURG
Dachstein
2,995 m
STEIERMARK
Mur
SCHWEIZ
Inn
Salzach
P
Vaduz
VORARLBERG
Innsbruck
Badgastein
L
Graz
TIROL
A
E
N
BURGENLAND
LIECHTENSTEIN
Großglockner
3,798 m
Tauern-
Tunnel
Gurk
UNGARN
Brenner-Paß
TIROL
Lienz
Spittal
Wolfsberg
KÄRNTEN
Drau
Wörther
Klagenfurt
Mur
ITALIEN
Villach
See
Drau

0   50   100 km
0   25   50 mi

SLOWENIEN   KROATIEN

DEUTSCHLAND
LIECHTENSTEIN
SCHWEIZ
ÖSTERREICH

Deutsch heute

Grundstufe

DEUTSCH HEUTE
GRUNDSTUFE FIFTH EDITION

JACK MOELLER
Oakland University

HELMUT LIEDLOFF
Southern Illinois University

WINNIFRED R. ADOLPH
Florida State University

CONSTANZE KIRMSE
Goethe-Institut München

JOHN F. LALANDE, II
University of Illinois

Annotations by Barbara Beckman Sharon

HOUGHTON MIFFLIN COMPANY   BOSTON   TORONTO
Dallas   Geneva, Illinois   Palo Alto   Princeton, New Jersey

Cover photo: Graham Lawrence/Leo de Wys, Inc.

Senior Sponsoring Editor: Isabel Campoy-Coronado
Senior Development and Project Editor: Barbara Blaine Lasoff
Design Coordinator: Patricia Mahtani
Senior Production Coordinator: Renee Le Verrier
Manufacturing Coordinator: Holly Schuster
Marketing Manager: George Kane

Copyright © 1992 by Houghton Mifflin Company. All rights reserved.

No part of this work may be reproduced or transmitted in any form or by any means, electronic or mechanical, including photocopying and recording, or by any information storage or retrieval system without the prior written permission of Houghton Mifflin Company unless such copying is expressly permitted by federal copyright law. Address inquiries to College Permissions, Houghton Mifflin Company, One Beacon Street, Boston, MA 02108.

Printed in the U.S.A.

Library of Congress Catalog Card Number: 91-72096

Student's Edition ISBN: 0-395-47299-7

Instructor's Annotated Edition ISBN: 0-395-59143-0

DEFGHIJ-D-998765432

CONTENTS

v

KAPITEL 4   83

INTRODUCTION

Deutsch heute: Grundstufe, Fifth Edition is an introductory program in German designed for college students and other adult learners. The basic intention of *Deutsch heute* is to provide students with a sound basis for learning German as it is used in spoken and written communication today within the context of German-speaking culture. The *Deutsch heute* program offers systematic practice in the four basic language skills of listening, speaking, reading, and writing, along with materials geared to provide a firm foundation in the basic elements of German grammar. Building on the previous editions of *Deutsch heute,* the Fifth Edition provides more activities that guide students in employing their skills in active personal communication and offers them opportunities to experience authentic materials likely to be encountered in a German-speaking country—materials like schedules, menus, and movie listings.

By the end of the course, students should have mastered the basic features of the sound and writing system, be familiar with the communicative functions of the language, be able to role-play various situations with a partner, be able to grasp the gist of various types of authentic materials, be able to use actively many basic grammatical structures in everyday conversation and writing as well as understand material that contains grammatical features of lower frequency, and be in control of an active vocabulary of approximately 1200 words and understand a considerable number of additional words.

Another goal of the Fifth Edition of *Deutsch heute* is to familiarize students with contemporary life and culture in the three primary German-speaking countries. The dialogues and readings convey important information on everyday life and culture in Germany, Austria, and Switzerland, including many specific references to the changed situation created by the unification of the former German Democratic Republic with the Federal Republic. The readings are mature in content but simple in structure. Cultural notes throughout the textbook provide more in-depth information. In combination with the photographs, realia, and drawings included in the Fifth Edition of *Deutsch heute,* the readings help convey to students what life is like in the German-speaking countries today.

A further aim of *Deutsch heute, Fifth Edition* is to have students experience the relationship between culture and language, thereby making them more aware of their own native language and culture.

Organization of the Student Text

The student text contains fourteen chapters (*Kapitel*). *Kapitel 1* is designed to get students speaking and using German for active, personal communication from the very start. It introduces students to the German sound system by means of a short dialogue (*Bausteine für Gespräche*), the German alphabet, and numbers. Students learn to give information about themselves, to spell words, to use numbers in simple arithmetic, to give the day of the week, and to describe the contents of their rooms by size and color.

Each of the *Kapitel* centers on a cultural theme such as university life, shopping, German attitudes toward privacy, the social position of women, the German economy, leisure time, or the unified Germany. There are also specific readings on Austria and Switzerland.

A typical chapter is composed of the following sections:

1. *Lernziele* are chapter objectives that summarize the content of each chapter and provide the student with categorized learning goals in four areas: communicative functions (*Sprechakte*), grammar (*Grammatik*), vocabulary (*Vokabeln*), and culture (*Landeskunde*).

2. *Bausteine für Gespräche* introduce idiomatic and colloquial phrases presented in dialogue format. Communication practice and vocabulary development continue in the oral activities that follow, which include *Fragen* (questions on the dialogues), and partner/group activities offering choices so that students can formulate their own responses. A list of *Vokabeln* follows the *Bausteine*, and most chapters contain sections of vocabulary expansion exercises and activities (*Erweiterung des Wortschatzes*).

3. *Lesestücke*, the core cultural readings, present the cultural theme of each chapter, beginning in *Kapitel 3*. Each *Lesestück* is preceded by pre-reading activities to aid and direct students toward a successful experience in second language reading: *Zum Thema* (*About the Topic*) contains questions that help familiarize students with the topic of each reading by letting them discover what they may already know about the topic through brainstorming, and *Leitfragen* (*Questions to Consider While Reading*) give direction to students' reading by focusing on main points and asking students to search for specific information as indicated by key words and phrases (*Stichworte*). Readings are then followed by a number of written and oral exercises including *Fragen zum Lesestück, Erzählen Sie.* (*Talk About It!*), partner/group activities *Vokabeln*, and *Erweiterung des Wortschatzes*.

4. *Grammatik und Übungen* (*Grammar and Exercises*) explain grammatical concepts in concise, lucid terms and contain illustrative examples, often with equivalents in English. Grammar is explained in English to ensure immediate comprehension, and basic terms are regularly defined for the novice language learner. German structure is often contrasted with English to clarify the structure of both languages. The grammar exercises have German titles, and the direction lines set the scene and clearly state grammatical tasks to make the communicative purpose clearer. The exercises can be completed in writing or orally in class; they can also be used for review and additional practice in combination with the student audiocassettes for home or language lab study. Included in the grammar exercises are partner/group activities that provide opportunity to use "grammar" in a personal situation.

5. *Wiederholung* (*Review*) activities practice the content, structure, and vocabulary of the chapter in new formats and reintroduce material from earlier chapters.

6. *Grammatik: Zusammenfassung* (*Grammar: Summary*) provides grammatical tables, and, where useful, a brief summary of a grammatical feature introduced in the chapter. This is a reference section that is useful for review.

Partner/group activities occur throughout the chapter, in the *Bausteine* and *Lesestück* sections, as well as in the *Grammatik und Übungen* and *Wiederholung*. They are outlined and preceded by two facing arrows.

In the one type of partner/group activities, students are requested to respond to questions or statements in a way that reflects their personal opinions, attitudes, or experience. Often, varied responses are listed; these responses represent a variety of attitudes or moods. New vocabulary is marked with a raised degree mark (°). Students should realize that the printed variations do not represent all possible responses, but rather, that they are a selection of useful conversational tools covering a range of meanings. Students should choose the responses that actually express their own feelings—or their whims—and invent or recall other expressions from previous chapters.

In the second type of partner/group work students are given a situation that requires communication with a partner but no vocabulary or structures are suggested. Additional words and phrases to express notions such as skepticism, insecurity, and annoyance are found in the Supplementary Expressions of the Reference Section. Students may refer to these and to the Supplementary Word Sets to approach more closely what they want to say.

Authentic materials appear at various places throughout the text. Authentic materials or texts is a term used to indicate such common printed material as train schedules, menus, advertisements, classified ads, and movie and television listings. These materials are part of the experience in the daily life of a native speaker and many of them are also encountered by a visitor to a German-speaking country. Students are not expected to understand each word in such a text. Rather they should try to extract only the information that interests them. For example, it is not necessary to read the entire *TV Guide* to find out what program one wishes to see on a particular day at a particular time.

To help students learn to deal with such materials a variety of activities are provided that range from questions that help students get essential information and directions that help students guess meaning to opportunities to make use of the material in a role-playing situation. Definitions of all new words are provided in the Vocabulary for Authentic Text Activities in the Reference Section.

Deutsch heute, Fifth Edition is illustrated with numerous photographs, realia, and line drawings. Since many of the photographs and pieces of realia are closely related to the cultural notes and themes of the dialogues and core reading selections, they can be effectively used as the basis for many class activities or out-of-class assignments. The line drawings are used to introduce word sets and to demonstrate grammatical concepts and semantic differences explained in the grammar section. Maps of the German-speaking countries are found on the inside cover leaves at both the front and back of the book; a map of Europe precedes *Kapitel 1*.

The short stories by Helga Novak and Werner Schmidli introduce students to literary prose. In style and content, these selections offer students a change of pace from the regular chapters and the satisfaction of reading German as written by established authors. Side glosses and notes clarify unfamiliar vocabulary and structures, and questions aid student comprehension and discussion.

The Reference Section contains the following elements:

Pronunciation and Writing Guide: This sound-symbol section gives three or four key words and simplified phonetic symbols for each German sound. Each section provides hints on how to pronounce the sound, and where useful, contrasts it with English.

Grammatical Tables: The tables in the Reference Section include the following charts: (1) paradigms for pronouns, articles, adjectives, and nouns; (2) adjectives and adverbs that are irregular in their comparative and superlative forms; (3) lists of prepositions governing the accusative, dative, or genitive case; (4) special verb + preposition combinations; (5) dative verbs; (6) examples of regular and irregular weak verbs, modals, and strong verbs, including stem-changing verbs, in the various tenses of the indicative, passive, and subjunctive; and (7) a list of the strong and irregular weak verbs used in the Fifth Edition of *Deutsch heute* with principal parts and English meanings.

Supplementary Expressions: This reference list of supplementary expressions helps students increase the number of things they can say and write during the course of a chapter. The list of expressions is organized according to functions and notions, for example, stalling for time; expressing skepticism, regret, or admiration; asking for favors; and making requests.

Supplementary Word Sets: This reference list of supplementary word sets offers students another opportunity to personalize vocabulary. These word lists, arranged by theme and chapter, are helpful to students with special interest in a topic who wish to expand their vocabulary. Many of the partner/group activities indicate where these lists may be useful, and they are often correlated with topics presented in the *Erweiterung des Wortschatzes* sections.

Vocabulary for Authentic Text Activities: All words and abbreviations that appear in authentic materials and because of their special nature are not included in the German-English Vocabulary are listed in Vocabulary for Authentic Text Activities. Students may consult this section for help if they cannot guess the meaning of a word or phrase and are thus not able to get the gist of the message.

Supplementary Dialogues: This list of specific, functional phrases in dialogue format is useful for students traveling or living in German-speaking countries. These dialogues for "survival German" take place in settings such as the airport, the post office, and the hotel.

German-English Vocabulary: The German-English end vocabulary lists all words used in ***Deutsch heute, Fifth Edition*** except numbers. Numerals after the English definitions indicate the chapter in which words and phrases are introduced in the *Vokabeln* lists for the *Bausteine für Gespräche* and *Lesestücke*. Recognition vocabulary from readings and exercises not intended for active mastery is also included.

English-German Vocabulary: The English-German end vocabulary contains the words listed in the chapter *Vokabeln* lists. This list of approximately 1200 words constitutes the active vocabulary of a student who has successfully completed the ***Deutsch heute*** program.

Index: The index indicates the pages on which grammatical features and topics in the *Erweiterung des Wortschatzes* are introduced. References to the cultural notes are also included.

Arbeitsheft:
Workbook/Lab Manual/Video

The ***Arbeitsheft*** consists of five sections: (1) a lab manual that requires students to react orally or in writing to material on the recordings; (2) a workbook with writing exercises coordinated with each chapter of the text; (3) a video workbook, new to the Fifth Edition, that offers a number of pre- and post-viewing activities; (4) a set of self-tests with an answer key for correction; and (5) a set of proficiency cards, which provide tasks and problem-solving activities for in-class use. Exercises in both the Workbook and the Lab Manual parallel the presentation of content, structure, and vocabulary in the student text. Many Workbook chapters contain short reading passages based on familiar material to give students extra practice in reading German. The Fifth Edition of the ***Deutsch heute Arbeitsheft*** contains many communicative exercises that allow students greater freedom of expression, and a number of realia-based exercises.

The proficiency cards supplement the proficiency activities in the text. The cards are coordinated with each chapter and allow students to synthesize their acquired knowledge of communicative function, vocabulary, grammar, and culture in simulations of culturally authentic situations and to employ their creativity and spontaneity along with these acquired skills in the successful completion of a communication task. Intended as free activities for students in which the instructor refrains from correcting and providing any information or feedback until their completion, the proficiency cards allow students to employ their acquired knowledge and demonstrate to themselves and their peers their growing language proficiency and ability to use German for active and personal communication in creative, culturally relevant contexts.

Recordings

The audio recordings that accompany *Deutsch heute, Fifth Edition* were made to provide the best possible models of German speech. Using a cast of young adult and adult actors and actresses, the recordings provide recorded versions of printed material from *Kapitel 1*, the *Bausteine*, the *Lesestücke*, exercises from the *Grammatik und Übungen*, some with additional items appearing only in the recordings, and the two short stories in the textbook. In addition, the recordings include the listening comprehension exercises called *Übungen zum Hörverständnis* and the pronunciation sections called *Übungen zur Aussprache* from the Lab Manual.

Sentences from the *Bausteine* are spoken once at normal speed, then modeled phrase by phrase with pauses for student repetition, and finally modeled again with pauses for repetition of complete utterances. The core reading selections (*Lesestücke*) are recorded without pauses. The grammar exercises are recorded in three phases: cue, pause for student response, and confirmation response. Group/partner activities and activities from the *Wiederholung* section are not on tape. The *Übungen zum Hörverständnis* from the Lab Manual are followed by a pause to allow students to respond in writing. Longer reading passages are read twice. The *Übungen zur Aussprache* are recorded in two phases: cue and pause for response. The recordings are available for student purchase in boxed sets of cassettes.

Video Program

A video program entitled *Einfach toll!* is based upon some of the topics in *Deutsch heute*. The video program consists of eight modules and a brief prelude in which the main characters introduce themselves. The scenes were shot in Germany and show experiences in the lives of young German people. In addition, there are seven short cultural interludes to increase students' familiarity with the German scene. Pre-viewing and post-viewing activities in the Video Workbook section of the *Arbeitsheft* help students learn to view video material so that they get the most out of the experience.

Classroom Expressions

Below is a list of common classroom expressions in German (with English equivalents) which the instructor may use. Also provided are common expressions students can use to make comments or requests and ask questions.

Terms of praise and disapproval

Gut. Das ist (sehr) gut. Good. That is (very) good.
Schön. Das ist (sehr) schön. Nice. That is (very) nice.
Ausgezeichnet. Excellent.
Wunderbar. Wonderful.
Das ist schon besser. That's better.
Viel besser. Much better.
Nicht schlecht. Not bad.
Richtig. Right.
Natürlich. Of course.
Genau. Exactly.
Sind Sie/Bist du sicher? Are you sure?
Nein, das ist nicht (ganz) richtig. No, that's not (quite) right.
Ein Wort ist nicht richtig. One word isn't right.
Nein, das ist falsch. No, that's wrong.
Sie haben/Du hast mich nicht verstanden. Ich sage es noch einmal. You didn't understand me. I'll say it again.
Sie haben/Du hast den Satz (das Wort) nicht verstanden. You didn't understand the sentence (the word).
Sagen Sie/Sag (Versuchen Sie/Versuch) es noch einmal bitte. Say (Try) it again please.

General instructions

Nicht so laut bitte. Not so loud please.
Würden Sie/Würdet ihr bitte genau zuhören. Would you please listen carefully.

Stehen Sie/Steht bitte auf. Stand up please.

Bilden Sie/Bildet einen Kreis. Form a circle.

Arbeiten Sie/Arbeitet einen Moment mit Partnern. Work for a minute with partners.

Bringen Sie/Bringt (Bilder) von zu Hause mit. Bring (pictures) along from home.

(Morgen) haben wir eine Klausur. (Tomorrow) we're having a test.

Schreiben Sie/Schreibt jetzt bitte. Please write now.

Lesen Sie/Lest jetzt bitte. Please read now.

Ich fange (Wir fangen) jetzt an. I'll begin now.

Fangen Sie/Fangt jetzt an. Begin now.

Hören Sie/Hört bitte auf zu schreiben (lesen). Please stop writing (reading).

Könnte ich bitte Ihre/eure Aufsätze (Klassenarbeiten, Tests, Übungsarbeiten, Hausaufgaben) haben? Could I please have your essays (tests, tests, exercises, homework)?

Jeder verbessert seine eigene Arbeit. Everyone should correct his or her own work (paper).

Verbessern Sie Ihre/Verbessere deine Arbeit bitte. Please correct your work (paper).

Tauschen Sie mit Ihrem/Tausch mit deinem Nachbarn. Exchange with your neighbor.

Machen Sie/Macht die Bücher auf (zu). Open (Shut) your books.

Schlagen Sie/Schlagt Seite (11) in Ihrem/eurem Buch auf. Turn to page (11) in your book.

Schauen Sie/Schaut beim Sprechen nicht ins Buch. Don't look at your book while speaking.

Wiederholen Sie/Wiederholt den Satz (den Ausdruck). Repeat the sentence (the expression).

Noch einmal bitte. Once again please.

(Etwas) Lauter. (Deutlicher./Langsamer./Schneller.) (Somewhat) Louder. (Clearer./Slower./Faster.)

Sprechen Sie/Sprich bitte deutlicher. Please speak more distinctly.

(Jan), Sie/du allein. (Jan), you alone.

Alle zusammen. All (everybody) together.

Sprechen Sie/Sprecht mir nach. Repeat after me.

(Nicht) Nachsprechen bitte. (Don't) repeat after me.

Hören Sie/Hört nur zu./Nur zuhören bitte. Just listen.

Hören Sie/Hört gut zu. Listen carefully.

Lesen Sie/Lies den Satz (den Absatz) vor. Read the sentence (the paragraph) aloud.

Jeder liest einen Satz. Everyone should read one sentence.

Fangen Sie/Fang mit Zeile (17) an. Begin with line (17).

Nicht auf Seite (19), auf Seite (20). Not on page (19), on page (20).

Gehen Sie/Geh an die Tafel. Go to the board.

(Jan), gehen Sie/gehst du bitte an die Tafel? (Jan), will you please go to the board?

Wer geht an die Tafel? Who will go to the board?

Schreiben Sie/Schreib den Satz (das Wort) an die Tafel. Write the sentence (the word) on the board.

Schreiben Sie/Schreibt ab, was an der Tafel steht. Copy what is on the board.

Wer weiß es (die Antwort)? Who knows it (the answer)?

Wie sagt man das auf deutsch (auf englisch)? How do you say that in German (in English)?

Auf deutsch bitte. In German please.

Verstehen Sie/Verstehst du die Frage (den Satz)? Do you understand the question (the sentence)?

Ist es (zu) schwer (leicht)? Is it (too) difficult (easy)?

Sind Sie/Seid ihr fertig? Are you finished?

Kommen Sie/Komm (morgen) nach der Stunde zu mir. Come see me (tomorrow) after class.

Jetzt machen wir weiter. Now let's go on.

Jetzt machen wir was anderes. Now let's do something different.

Jetzt beginnen wir was Neues. Now let's begin something new.

Das ist genug für heute. That's enough for today.

Hat jemand Fragen? Does anyone have a question?

Haben Sie/Habt ihr Fragen? Do you have any questions?

Student responses and questions

Das verstehe ich nicht.   I don't understand that.

Das habe ich nicht verstanden.   I didn't understand that.

Ah, ich verstehe.   Oh, I understand.

Ich weiß es nicht.   I don't know (that).

Wie bitte? (*Said when you don't catch what someone said.*)   Excuse me?

Wie sagt man … auf deutsch (auf englisch)?   How do you say . . . in German (in English)?

Können Sie den Satz noch einmal sagen bitte?   Can you repeat that please?

Kann er/sie den Satz wiederholen bitte?   Can he/she repeat the sentence please?

Ich habe kein Papier (Buch).   I don't have any paper (a book).

Ich habe keinen Bleistift (Kuli).   I don't have a pencil (a pen).

Auf welcher Seite sind wir? Welche Zeile?   Which page are we on? Which line?

Wo steht das?   Where is that?

Ich habe eine Frage.   I have a question.

Was haben wir für morgen (Montag) auf?   What do we have due for tomorrow (Monday)?

Sollen wir das schriftlich oder mündlich machen?   Should we do that in writing or orally?

Wann schreiben wir die nächste Arbeit?   When do we have the next paper (written work)?

Wann schreiben wir den nächsten Test?   When do we have the next test?

Für wann (sollen wir das machen)?   For when (are we supposed to do that)?

Ist das so richtig?   Is that right this way?

(Wann) Können Sie mir helfen?   (When) Can you help me?

(Wann) Kann ich mit Ihnen sprechen?   (When) Can I see you?

Acknowledgments

The authors and publisher would like to thank Professors Renate Gerulaitis, Barbara Mabee, and Jack Barthel, Oakland University (Rochester, MI), and Mark Cadd, William Jewell College (Liberty, MO), for their suggestions for the Fifth Edition. Special thanks go to the following instructors for their thoughtful reviews of portions of the manuscript:

Reinhard Andress, Alfred University (Alfred, NY)

Ingeborg Baumgartner, Albion College (Albion, MI)

Leo M. Berg, California State Polytechnic University (Pomona, CA)

Phillip J. Campana, Tennessee Technological University (Cookeville, TN)

Jeannette Clausen, Indiana University-Purdue University at Fort Wayne (Fort Wayne, IN)

Alfred L. Cobbs, Wayne State University (Detroit, MI)

Virginia M. Coombs, Concordia College (Moorhead, MN)

Ronald W. Dunbar, West Virginia University (Morgantown, WV)

Annelise M. Duncan, Trinity University (San Antonio, TX)

Wilhelmine Hartnack, College of the Redwoods (Eureka, CA)

Claus Reschke, University of Houston (Houston, TX).

The authors would also like to express their appreciation of the following Houghton Mifflin editorial, art, and design staff and freelancers for their technical and creative contributions to the text: Harriet Dishman, Karen Hohner, Karen Rappaport, Margaret Tsao, Linda Hadley, Amy Davidson, Anne Mottier, Karen Storz, Bruce Carson, Julie Fair, Irene Sturam, and Kirk Smith. Finally, the authors wish to thank Barbara Lasoff who guided the fifth edition of *Deutsch heute* through the various phases of manuscript development and production. This new edition of *Deutsch heute* has been enhanced by her expertise and critical judgment and only her devotion to the project made the timely publication of the text possible.

Europa

Reykjavik
ISLAND

ATLANTISCHER
OZEAN

Europäisches
Nordmeer

FINNLAND

NORWEGEN
Oslo
SCHWEDEN
Helsinki

Stockholm
Tallinn
ESTLAND
RUSSLAND

Nordsee
Riga
Moskau
LETTLAND

IRLAND
Dublin
DÄNEMARK
Ostsee
LITAUEN

Kopenhagen
Wilna
Minsk

GROSSBRITANNIEN
NIEDERLANDE
BELARUS

London
Den Haag
Amsterdam
Berlin
POLEN

Brüssel
DEUTSCHLAND
Warschau

BELGIEN
Kiew

Luxemburg
Prag
UKRAINE

Paris
TSCHECHOSLOWAKEI

LUXEMBURG
MOLDAWIEN

FRANKREICH
Vaduz
Wien
Kischinew

Bern
ÖSTERREICH
Budapest

SCHWEIZ
UNGARN

LIECHTENSTEIN
SLOWENIEN
Zagreb
RUMÄNIEN

Ljubljana
KROATIEN
Wojwodina

PORTUGAL
ANDORRA
BOSNIEN-
Belgrad
Bukarest

HERZEGOWINA
Serbien
Schwarzes
Meer

Lissabon
Madrid
ITALIEN
Sarajevo
JUGOSLA-

SPANIEN
Monte-
WIEN
BULGARIEN

Rom
negro
Kosovo

Titograd
Sofia

Tirana
Skopje

Athen
MAKEDONIEN

ALBANIEN

Mittelmeer
GRIECHENLAND
TÜRKEI

MAROKKO
ALGERIEN
TUNESIEN

Diese Sportler kommen aus Köln.

Kapitel 1

BAUSTEINE FÜR GESPRÄCHE

(Building Blocks for Conversation)

The dialogues in this section will help you acquire a stock of idiomatic phrases that will enable you to participate in conversations on everyday topics.

Wie heißt du?   What is your name?

While at the art department to sign up for an excursion to Florence with her art history class, Gisela runs into Alex, who is in the same class but whom she has never really met. After chatting briefly, Gisela and Alex decide to meet before the trip. Then Gisela goes into the office to sign up for the trip to Florence.

Vorm Schwarzen Brett

In front of the bulletin board

Alex: Ich heiße Alex. Und du — Wie heißt du?

My name is Alex. How about you—What is your name?

Gisela: Ich heiße Gisela.

My name is Gisela.

Alex: Ach ja. Und deine Telefonnummer?

Oh yes. And your telephone number?

Gisela: 71 63 54. (Einundsiebzig, dreiundsechzig, vierund- fünfzig.) Und wie ist deine Nummer?

71 63 54. And what is your telephone number?

Alex: 34 79 01. (Vierunddreißig, neunundsiebzig, null, eins.)

34 79 01.

Gisela: Wie bitte?

I beg your pardon?

Alex: 34 79 01.

34 79 01.

Gisela: O.K. Also, tschüß, dann.

O.K. Well, so long then.

Wie heißen Sie?   What is your name?

Gisela is next in line. She goes into the office to sign up for the excursion to Florence.

Bei der Sekretärin

In the secretary's office

Sekretärin: Bitte? Wie heißen Sie?

Can I help you? What is your name?

Gisela: Gisela Riedholt.

Gisela Riedholt.

Sekretärin: Wie schreibt man das?	How do you spell (write) that?
Gisela: R-i-e-d-h-o-l-t.	R-i-e-d-h-o-l-t.
Sekretärin: Und Ihre Adresse?	And your address?
Gisela: Bahnhofstraße 10 (zehn), 7800 (siebentausendachthundert) Freiburg.	10 Bahnhofstraße, 7800 Freiburg.
Sekretärin: Danke, Frau Riedholt.	Thank you, Ms. Riedholt.
Gisela: Bitte.	You're welcome.

Activities in sections preceded by this symbol give you the opportunity to speak with a partner about your personal feelings and experiences and to learn how to exchange ideas and negotiate in German. Sometimes you will be asked to role-play a situation. Substitute your own words for those in brackets.

New vocabulary is indicated by a raised degree mark (°). The meaning of the words is found in the vocabulary lists in the sections called **Vokabeln.** In this chapter the **Vokabeln** section is on pages 16–17.

1. Wie heißt du?   Get acquainted with members of your class. Introduce yourself to your fellow students and ask what their names are.

Getting acquainted

Sie (You)	*Gesprächspartner/in (Partner)*
Ich heiße [Dieter]. Wie heißt du?	Ich heiße [Barbara].

2. Heißt du Inge?   See how well you remember the names of at least four fellow students. If you're wrong they will correct you.

Sie (You)	*Gesprächspartner/in (Partner)*
Heißt du [Mark Schmidt]?	Ja.°
Du heißt [Monika], nicht°?	Nein.° Ich heiße [Karin].

3. Wie heißen Sie?   Ask your instructor for her/his name.

Sie (You)	*Herr/Frau Professor*
Wie heißen Sie?	Ich heiße [Lange].

In a German address, the zip code **(Postleitzahl)** precedes the name of the city. Zip codes have a maximum of four numbers and indicate the geographic area within Germany. Hamburg, in northern Germany, has the zip code 2000; Bremen, also in northern Germany, has the zip 2800. The names of large cities are often followed by an additional number indicating the postal district: 6000 Frankfurt 1.

**Die Post: Briefmarken,
Telefon, Geld sparen (Berlin)**

Erweiterung des Wortschatzes (Vocabulary Expansion)

1 The subject pronouns *du* and *Sie*

Wie heißt **du?**	What is your name? (What are *you* called?)
Wie ist **deine** Telefonnummer?	What is *your* telephone number?

Du is equivalent to *you* and is used when addressing a relative, close friend, or person under approximately fifteen years of age. Members of groups such as students, athletes, laborers, and soldiers also address each other as **du.** It is used when talking to one person and is referred to as the familiar form. The word for *you* used to address more than one friend, relative, etc., will be explained in *Kapitel 2.*

   Dein(e) is equivalent to *your*. It is used with a person to whom you say **du.**

Wie heißen **Sie?**	What is your name? (What are *you* called?)
Wie ist **Ihre** Adresse?	What is *your* address?

Sie is also equivalent to *you* but is a more formal form of address, and is used when addressing a stranger or adult with whom the speaker is not on intimate terms. **Sie** is used when speaking to one person or to more than one person.

Ihr(e) is equivalent to *your* and is used with a person to whom you say **Sie**. In writing, **Sie** and **Ihr(e)** are capitalized.

Dein and **Ihr** modify masculine and neuter nouns. **Deine** and **Ihre** modify feminine nouns. See the section on Gender of nouns on pages 11–12 of this chapter.

2 Das Alphabet

The German alphabet has 26 regular letters and 4 special letters. They are pronounced as follows:

a ah	**g** geh	**l** ell	**q** kuh	**v** fau	**ä** äh (a-Umlaut)
b beh	**h** hah	**m** emm	**r** err	**w** weh	**ö** öh (o-Umlaut)
c tseh	**i** ih	**n** enn	**s** ess	**x** iks	**ü** üh (u-Umlaut)
d deh	**j** jot	**o** oh	**t** teh	**y** üppsilon	**ß** ess-tsett
e eh	**k** kah	**p** peh	**u** uh	**z** tsett	
f eff					

Capital letters are indicated by **groß: großes B, großes W.** Lower-case letters are indicated by **klein: kleines b, kleines w.**

Junge Leute sagen fast immer „du" zueinander.

1. Schreiben   Ask your instructor or a fellow student for her/his name. Then ask how to spell it.

▶ Wie heißt du?   *Mark Fischer.*
▶ Wie schreibt man das?   *Emm-ah-err-kah. Eff-ih-ess-tseh-hah-eh-err.*

2. Abkürzungen (Abbreviations)   Pronounce the following abbreviations and have your partner write them down.

1. VW (= Volkswagen)
2. USA (= U.S.A.)
3. BMW (= Bayerische Motorenwerke)
4. CDU (= Christlich-Demokratische Union)
5. FDP (= Freie Demokratische Partei)
6. SPD (= Sozialdemokratische Partei Deutschlands)
7. Pkw (Personenkraftwagen)
8. WC (Wasserklosett)

3. Wie schreibt man das?   Spell the name of your hometown for your partner. See if she/he can tell where you are from.

4. Schreiben   Spell several German words to a partner who will write them down. Then reverse roles. You may use the words listed or choose your own.

tschüß ◇ danke ◇ bitte ◇ Adresse ◇ Telefonnummer

5. A, B, C   Form groups of three. The first person says a letter, the second person adds one letter, the third another letter until a word has been spelled.

3 Die Zahlen von 1 bis 1.000

0 = null	10 = zehn	20 = zwanzig	30 = dreißig
1 = eins	11 = elf	21 = einundzwanzig	40 = vierzig
2 = zwei	12 = zwölf	22 = zweiundzwanzig	50 = fünfzig
3 = drei	13 = dreizehn	23 = dreiundzwanzig	60 = sechzig
4 = vier	14 = vierzehn	24 = vierundzwanzig	70 = siebzig
5 = fünf	15 = fünfzehn	25 = fünfundzwanzig	80 = achtzig
6 = sechs	16 = sechzehn	26 = sechsundzwanzig	90 = neunzig
7 = sieben	17 = siebzehn	27 = siebenundzwanzig	100 = hundert
8 = acht	18 = achtzehn	28 = achtundzwanzig	101 = hunderteins
9 = neun	19 = neunzehn	29 = neunundzwanzig	1.000 = tausend

Note the following irregularities:

1. **Eins** (*one*) becomes **ein** when it combines with the twenties, thirties, and so on: **einundzwanzig, einunddreißig.**
2. **Dreißig** (*thirty*) ends in **-ßig** instead of the usual **-zig.**
3. **Vier** (*four*) is pronounced with long [ī], but **vierzehn** (*fourteen*) and **vierzig** (*forty*) are pronounced with short [i].
4. **Sechs** (*six*) is pronounced [ṣeks], but **sechzehn** (*sixteen*) and **sechzig** (*sixty*) are pronounced [ṣeç-].
5. **Sieben** (*seven*) ends in **-en,** but the **-en** is dropped in **siebzehn** (*seventeen*) and **siebzig** (*seventy*).
6. **Acht** (*eight*) is pronounced [axt], but the final **t** fuses with initial **ts** in **achtzehn** (*eighteen*) and **achtzig** (*eighty*).
7. Numbers in the twenties, thirties, and so on follow the pattern of the nursery rhyme "four-and-twenty blackbirds":
   24 = **vierundzwanzig** (*four-and-twenty*)
   32 = **zweiunddreißig** (*two-and-thirty*)
8. German uses a period instead of a comma in numbers over 999. German uses a comma instead of a period to indicate decimals.

German	*English*
1.000 g (Gramm)	1,000 g
4,57 m (Meter)	4.57 m

9. Simple arithmetic:
   Addition (**+ = und**): **Fünf und drei ist acht.**
   Subtraction (**− = weniger**): **Fünf weniger drei ist zwei.**
   Multiplication (**×** or **· = mal**): **Fünf mal drei ist fünfzehn.**
   Division (**÷ = [geteilt] durch**): **Fünfzehn durch drei ist fünf.**

6. Rechnen (Doing arithmetic) Find a partner. On a piece of paper each of you writes out five simple mathematical problems. Read your five problems to your partner and let him/her solve them; then solve your partner's five problems.

Sie (You)	*Gesprächspartner/in (Partner)*
Wieviel° ist drei und zwei [3 + 2]?	*Drei und zwei ist fünf.*
Wieviel ist zehn weniger acht [10 − 8]?	*Zehn weniger acht ist zwei.*

7. Deine Adresse? Deine Telefonnummer? Rollenspiel (Role-play)
Imagine you have a job checking names for the telephone directory. Ask at least three of your fellow students for their names, phone numbers, and addresses. Then get the same information from your instructor. Remember to use **Ihre** with your instructor. Also be sure to say thank you.

Sie (You)	*Gesprächspartner/in (Partner)*
Wie heißt du?	[Julia Meier].
Wie ist deine Telefonnummer?	[652-9846].
Wie ist deine Adresse?	[Park Road zehn].
Danke.	Bitte.

8. Wie alt bist du? Find out the ages of four fellow students. Be sure you know their names. Write down the information.

Sie (You)	*Gesprächspartner/in (Partner)*
Wie alt bist du?	Ich bin [19] Jahre alt.

9. Wie ist die Telefonnummer von … ? At right is part of a page from the Bonn telephone directory. Ask your partner for the telephone numbers of three different people on this page.

10. Ich heiße … Introduce yourself to the class by giving the information mentioned in the model.

▶ Ich heiße _____ . Ich bin _____ Jahre alt. Meine° Adresse ist _____ .
Meine Telefonnummer ist _____ .

11. Gespräche (Conversations) With a partner express the following exchange of information in German. One of you should be student 1 (S1), the other, student 2 (S2). Once you have finished, exchange roles and start again from the beginning.

A

S1: Ask S2 for her/his name.
S2: Say in German: "My name is . . . "
S1: Ask S2 to repeat it.
S2: Repeat your name.
S1: Ask S2 how to spell it.
S2: Spell your last name.

B

S1: Find out S2's telephone number.
S2: Give your telephone number.
S1: Find out S2's address.
S2: Give your address, but remember to do it the German way.

Neubauer Harald	65 08 02
Rosental 25	
Neubauer Heinz	21 67 83
Ing.grad. Renoisstr.1	
Neubauer Heinz	32 38 87
(Bgo) Kantstr.8	
Neubauer Helmut	32 26 00
(Bgo) Tulpenbaumweg 10	
Neubauer Hermann	32 38 29
(Bgo) Akazienweg 21	
Neubauer Ines	61 22 25
1 Bahnhofstr.99	
Neubauer J.	61 45 74
Mohrstr.26	
Neubauer Josef	64 22 96
(Dui) Europaring 24	
Neubauer Karl	47 55 00
Beuel HeinrichHeineStr.27	
Neubauer Klaus	47 36 77
Beuel Geislarstr.124	
Neubauer Maria	45 00 68
(Ndk) Langgasse 91	
Neubauer Rainer	64 06 65
(Alf) Oberdorf 47	
Neubauer Sabine	67 41 70
Friedlandstr.62	
Neubauer Uwe Dr.	31 32 42
(Bgo) DechantHeimbachStr.21	
Neubauer Wilhelm	31 68 79
(Bgo) EltvillerStr.16	
Neubauer Wolf	69 14 28
1 Wolfstr.37	
Neubeck Hans Frhr.	32 35 13
von (Bgo) Rotdornweg 83	
Neuber Bruno Dr.	45 03 05
Zahnarzt	
(Ndk) Provinzia lstr.103	

C

S1: Ask S2 how old he/she is.

S2: Answer. (You may give a "creative" response if you like.) Ask S1 how old he/she is.

S1: Answer. (Feel free to give a "creative" response.)

The academic year at a German university has two terms: the **Wintersemester,** from mid-October to mid-February; and the **Sommersemester,** from mid-April to mid-July. Students must register each semester. The first time a student registers is called **Immatrikulation;** any subsequent registration is a **Rückmeldung.** Courses taken by the student are listed in an official transcript book **(Studienbuch),** which the student is responsible for, along with certificates signed by a professor to acknowledge the student's presence and success in the seminar **(Seminarscheine).** German students do not pay tuition, but they are required to have health insurance **(Krankenversicherung).** An ID card **(Studentenausweis)** enables a student to use university facilities such as the library and the cafeteria **(Mensa)** and to get reductions on theater and museum tickets, certain club memberships, and public transportation.

Studenten-Ausweis der Universität Karlsruhe: Jochen Grobholz studiert Informatik und ist im fünfzehnten Semester.

Public telephones in Germany are usually installed in bright yellow booths. They operate on a coin-operated message-unit system that automatically calculates charges for local or long-distance calls. Local calls cost a minimum of 30 Pfennig. Calls outside the immediate area require both an area code **(Vorwahl)** and additional 10 Pfennig, 50 Pfennig, or 1 Mark coins. The telephone system is a division of the Federal Post Office **(Bundespost).** Every post office maintains public telephones. These are either coin-operated, or one pays for the call at the counter. Phone numbers in Germany can vary in length. The following are examples of telephone numbers of two businesses in Munich: 52 60 96 and 2 18 36 75.

Recently, plastic, non-recyclable debit cards for a specific amount of telephone charges **(Telefonkarten)** have been introduced. These cards can be purchased at the post office or telephone office and used in special phones. Environmentalists have opposed these cards because their disposal adds to environmental problems. Yet, because of their varied designs, these cards have become collector's items and are traded like American baseball cards.

Germans usually identify themselves at once when they answer the phone. Callers also give their names before asking for the person they are trying to reach.

Whereas people who want to end a telephone conversation formally say **Auf Wiederhören** (literally: *Until we hear each other again*), friends typically use an informal **Tschüß** *(So long)* or **Bis dann** *(Till later)* to say good-by. For example:

Die Telefonzellen sind gelb. Gelb ist die Farbe der Bundespost.

— Ingrid Breimann.
— Hier ist Gerda. Kann ich bitte mit Thomas sprechen?
— Hallo, Gerda. Thomas ist nicht zu Hause. Er spielt heute Fußball.
— Ach ja, richtig. Ich rufe am Montag wieder an. Bis dann, Ingrid.
— Tschüß.

— Ingrid Breimann.
— This is Gerda. Can I speak to Thomas, please?
— Hi, Gerda. Thomas is not at home. He's playing soccer today.
— Oh, that's right. I'll call back on Monday. Till later, Ingrid.
— So long.

4 Die Wochentage

Welcher Tag ist heute?	What day is it today?
Heute ist Montag.	Today is Monday.
Dienstag	Tuesday
Mittwoch	Wednesday
Donnerstag	Thursday
Freitag	Friday
Samstag *(in southern Germany)*	Saturday
Sonnabend *(in northern Germany)*	
Sonntag	Sunday

12. Welcher Tag ist heute? Ask a fellow student what day it is today.

▶ Welcher Tag ist heute?   *Heute ist [Mittwoch].*

13. Nein, heute ist Montag. Practice correcting people who are always a day behind.

▶ Ist heute Dienstag?   *Nein, heute ist Mittwoch.*

1. Montag?
2. Sonntag?
3. Mittwoch?

4. Freitag?
5. Donnerstag?
6. Samstag?

5 Gender of nouns

Masculine	Neuter	Feminine
the man ← he	the baby ← it the word ← it	the woman ← she

Every English noun belongs to one of three genders: masculine, neuter, or feminine. The gender of a singular English noun shows up in the choice of the pronoun that is used to refer back to it.

The English type of gender system is one of natural gender. Nouns referring to male beings are masculine. Nouns referring to female beings are feminine. Nouns referring to young beings (if thought of as still undifferentiated as to sex) are neuter, and all nouns referring to inanimate objects are also neuter. (*Neuter* is the Latin word for *neither*, i.e., neither masculine nor feminine.)

Like English, German generally uses a system of natural gender for nouns that refer to living beings. Unlike English, however, German also makes gender distinctions in nouns that do not refer to living things. This type of gender system is one of grammatical gender.

Masculine	Neuter	Feminine
der Mann° ← er	das Kind° ← es	die Frau ← sie
der Tag ← er	das Wort° ← es	die Adresse ← sie

In German there are three groups of nouns: masculine (**der**-nouns), neuter (**das**-nouns), and feminine (**die**-nouns). The definite articles **der, das,** and **die** function like the English definite article *the*. Most nouns referring to males are **der**-nouns (**der Mann** = *man*), most nouns referring to females are **die**-nouns (**die Frau** = *woman*), and nouns referring to young beings are **das**-nouns (**das Kind** = *child*). Note that **der Junge**° (= *boy*) is a **der**-noun, but **das Mädchen**° (= *girl*) is a **das**-noun because all words ending in **-chen** are **das**-nouns. Other nouns may belong to any of the three groups: **der Tag, das Wort, die Adresse.**

◆ *Signals of gender*

Like English, German signals the gender of a noun in the choice of the pronoun that is used to refer back to it: **er** is masculine, **es** is neuter, and **sie** is feminine. Unlike English, however, German also signals gender in the choice of the definite article that precedes a noun: **der** is masculine, **das** is neuter, and **die** is feminine.

The article is the most powerful signal of gender. You should always learn a German noun together with its definite article, because there is no simple way of predicting the gender of a particular noun.

6 Ein Studentenzimmer (A student's room)

Learn the following nouns:

1. der Bleistift	7. das Bett	16. die Büchertasche
2. der Computer	8. das Bild	17. die Gitarre
3. der Fernseher	9. das Buch	18. die Lampe
4. der Kugel-	10. das Bücherregal	19. die Pflanze
schreiber	11. das Fenster	20. die Stereoanlage
(der Kuli)	12. das Heft	21. die Tür
5. der Stuhl	13. das Papier	22. die Uhr
6. der Tisch	14. das Poster	23. die Wand
	15. das Zimmer	

14. Groß oder klein?   Sabine is going to help you arrange your room. She asks whether certain pieces of furniture are large **(groß)** or small **(klein).** Respond.

▶   Ist das Zimmer groß oder klein?   *Das Zimmer ist [groß].*

1. Ist das Fenster groß oder klein?
2. Ist das Bett groß oder klein?
3. Ist der Fernseher groß oder klein?
4. Wie ist der Stuhl?
5. Ist die Pflanze groß oder klein?

6. Wie ist die Uhr?
7. Und die Lampe?
8. Und der Tisch?
9. Und das Bücherregal?
10. Wie ist die Stereoanlage?

15. Alt oder neu? Tell your partner whether various things in your room are new **(neu)** or old **(alt).**

▶ Computer   *Der Computer ist [neu].*

1. Fernseher
2. Bett
3. Lampe
4. Stereoanlage
5. Radio
6. Büchertasche
7. Buch
8. Kugelschreiber
9. Bild
10. Poster

16. Groß, klein, alt You and Erik are sitting in a snack bar watching people. Make comments about them using the cues.

▶ Kind / groß   *Das Kind da° ist groß!*

1. Mann / groß
2. Frau / groß
3. Mann / alt
4. Kind / klein
5. Junge / klein
6. Frau / alt
7. Mädchen / klein

7 Pronouns

Wie alt ist **Mark?**	How old is Mark?
Er ist zwanzig.	He is twenty.

A **pronoun** is a part of speech that designates a person, place, thing, or concept. It functions as nouns do. A pronoun is capable of replacing a noun or a noun phrase.

8 Noun-pronoun relationship

Der Mann ist groß.	**Er** ist groß.	He is tall.
Der Stuhl ist groß.	**Er** ist groß.	It is large.
Das Kind ist klein.	**Es** ist klein.	She/He is small.
Das Zimmer ist klein.	**Es** ist klein.	It is small.
Die Frau ist groß.	**Sie** ist groß.	She is tall.
Die Lampe ist groß.	**Sie** ist groß.	It is large.

In German the pronouns **er, es,** and **sie** may refer to persons or things. In English the singular pronoun referring to things *(it)* is different from those referring to persons *(she, he).*

17. Wie ist das Zimmer?   Tanja is seeing your room for the first time since you made some changes. She's trying to sort out which things are new and which are old. Respond, using a pronoun instead of the noun.

▶ Ist der Tisch neu?   *Ja, er ist neu.*

1. Ist der Stuhl alt?
2. Ist die Uhr neu?
3. Ist das Radio alt?
4. Ist die Pflanze neu?
5. Ist die Lampe alt?
6. Ist die Büchertasche neu?
7. Ist das Poster neu?
8. Ist der Computer neu?
9. Ist der Fernseher alt?
10. Ist die Stereoanlage neu?

9 Die Farben (Colors)

The following sentences should help you remember the colors.

	blau	Die See ist blau.
	braun	Die Schokolade ist braun.
	gelb	Die Banane ist gelb.
	grau	Die Maus ist grau.
	grün	Das Gras ist grün.
	rot	Die Tomate ist rot.
	schwarz	Die Kohle ist schwarz.
	weiß	Das Papier ist weiß.

18. Welche Farbe?   Describe the colors of various items in your room or in the classroom. You may want to refer to the Supplementary Word Sets in the Reference Section.

Describing

▶ Welche Farbe hat der Tisch?   *Der Tisch ist [braun].*

1. Stuhl
2. Lampe
3. Bett
4. Radio
5. Deutschbuch
6. Heft
7. Kugelschreiber
8. Bleistift
9. Wand

19. Die Büchertasche   Describe briefly several items in your book bag to your partner. Your partner will then describe items in her/his book bag.

▶ Das ist [der Kuli].   *Er ist [klein und schwarz].*

Vokabeln (Vocabulary)

In English, proper nouns like *Monday* or *America* are capitalized, but not common nouns like *address* or *street*. In German, all nouns are capitalized: proper nouns like **Montag** or **Amerika** as well as common nouns like **Adresse** and **Straße**. Unlike English, German does not capitalize proper adjectives.

Compare the following: **amerikanisch**   American
                                       englisch   English
                                       deutsch   German

The German pronoun **Sie** (you *formal*) and the possessive adjective **Ihr** (your *formal*) are capitalized in writing. The pronoun **ich** (I) is not capitalized.

___ Substantive (Nouns) _____

die **Adresse** address
das **Bett** bed
das **Bild** picture; photo
der **Bleistift** pencil
das **Bücherregal** bookcase
die **Büchertasche** book bag
das **Buch** book
der **Computer** computer
der **Dienstag** Tuesday
der **Donnerstag** Thursday
die **Farbe** color
das **Fenster** window
der **Fernseher** TV
die **Frau** woman; **Frau** Mrs., Ms.
  (*term of address for adult women*)
das **Fräulein** young lady; **Fräulein**
  Miss (*term of address for very
  young, unmarried women; also for
  waitresses*)
der **Freitag** Friday
der **Garten** garden
die **Gitarre** guitar
das **Heft** notebook
der **Herr** gentleman; **Herr** Mr.
  (*term of address*)
das **Jahr** year
der **Junge** boy
das **Kind** child
der **Kugelschreiber** (der **Kuli**, *colloquial*) ballpoint pen
die **Lampe** lamp

das **Mädchen** girl
der **Mann** man
der **Mittwoch** Wednesday
der **Montag** Monday
die **Nummer** number
das **Papier** paper
die **Pflanze** plant
das **Poster** poster
das **Radio** radio
der **Samstag** (*in southern Germany*)
  Saturday
der **Sekretär** (*m.*)/die **Sekretärin** (*f.*)
  secretary
der **Sonnabend** (*in northern Germany*) Saturday
der **Sonntag** Sunday
die **Stereoanlage** stereo unit, stereo
  system
die **Straße** street
der **Student** (*m.*)/die **Studentin** (*f.*)
  student
der **Stuhl** chair
der **Tag** day
das **Telefon** telephone
die **Telefonnummer** telephone
  number
der **Tisch** table
die **Tür** door
die **Uhr** clock, watch
die **Wand** wall
die **Woche** week

das **Wort** word
die **Zahl** number, numeral

das **Zimmer** room

Verben (Verbs)

bin / ist / sind am / is / are
hat / haben has / have

heißen to be named, to be called
schreiben to write

Andere Wörter (Other words)

ach oh
also well
alt old
bitte please; you're welcome (*after* **danke**)
blau blue
braun brown
da there
danke thanks
dann then
das that; the (*neuter*)
dein(e) your (*familiar*)
der the (*masculine*)
die the (*feminine*)
du you (*familiar*)
er he, it
es it
gelb yellow
[geteilt] durch divided by (*in division*)
grau gray
groß large, big; tall (*people*)
grün green
heute today
ich I

Ihr(e) your (*formal*)
ja yes
klein small; short (*people*)
mal times (*in multiplication*)
man one, people
mein(e) my
nein no
neu new
nicht? (*tag question*) don't you? isn't it? **Du heißt (Sie heißen) [Monika], nicht?** Your name is [Monika], isn't it?
rot red
schwarz black
sie she, it
Sie you (*formal*)
tschüß so long, good-by (*informal*)
und and; plus (*in addition*)
von of
weiß white
welch (-er, -es, -e) which
weniger minus (*in subtraction*)
wie how
wieviel how much

Besondere Ausdrücke (Special expressions)

Ich bin 19 Jahre alt. I'm 19 years old.
Du heißt (Sie heißen) [Mark], nicht? Your name is [Mark], isn't it?
Welche Farbe hat … ? What color is . . . ?
Welcher Tag ist heute? What day is today?
(Wie) bitte? (I beg your) pardon.
Wie alt bist du (sind Sie)? How old are you?

Wie ist deine (Ihre) Adresse? What's your address?
Wie heißt du (heißen Sie)? What's your name?
Wie schreibt man das? How do you spell that? (*literally:* How does one write that?)
Wie ist die Telefonnummer von [Clemens Neumann]? What is [Clemens Neumann's] telephone number?

Eine Studentin mit ihrem Professor
(Universität Wien)

Kapitel 2

LERNZIELE

SPRECHAKTE

Greeting people formally
Greeting friends
Saying good-by
Asking people how they are
Expressing likes and dislikes
Asking about personal plans
Asking what kind of person someone is
Expressing agreement and disagreement
Describing people
Telling time
Making plans

GRAMMATIK

Pronouns and nouns as subjects
Three forms for *you: du, ihr, Sie*
The verb *sein*
Regular verbs
Expressing likes and dislikes with *gern*
Negation with *nicht*
Expressing future time with the present
   tense
Asking specific and general questions
Tag questions

VOKABELN

Descriptive adjectives
Sports
Telling time

LANDESKUNDE

Regional greetings and farewells
The role of sports in Germany
Appropriate use of *du* and *Sie*

BAUSTEINE FÜR GESPRÄCHE

Wie geht's?

In der Bibliothek

Professor Lange: Guten Morgen, Frau Kluge. Wie geht es Ihnen?
Professor Kluge: Guten Morgen, Herr Lange. Gut, danke. Und Ihnen?
Professor Lange: Danke, ganz gut.

Im Hörsaal

Alex: Hallo, Gisela.
Gisela: Grüß dich, Alex. Wie geht's?
Alex: Ach, nicht so gut.
Gisela: Was ist los? Bist du krank?
Alex: Nein, ich bin nur furchtbar müde.

How are you?

In the library

Good morning, Mrs. Kluge. How are you?
Good morning, Mr. Lange. Fine, thanks. And you?

Thanks, not bad.

In the lecture hall

Hi, Gisela.
Hello, Alex. How are you?

Oh, not so well.
What's wrong? Are you sick?
No, I'm just terribly tired.

---

1. Guten Tag. Greet different people in the class. Choose a time of day and greet your partner, who responds appropriately.

Sie	*Gesprächspartner/in*
Guten Morgen.	Morgen.
Guten Tag.	Tag.°
Guten Abend.°	Abend.°
	Hallo.
	Grüß dich.

> Greeting someone

2. Wie geht's? Find a partner and role-play a scene between you and a friend or a professor. Assume you haven't seen your friend or the professor for several days and you run into her/him in the cafeteria. Say hello and ask how she/he is.

> Asking people how they are

Sie	*Gesprächspartner/in*
Hallo, [Tanja]. Wie geht's?	Gut, danke°. (Und dir?° / Und
Guten Tag, Herr/Frau Professor, wie	Ihnen?°)
geht es Ihnen?	Danke, ganz gut.
	Es geht.°
	Nicht so gut.
	Schlecht°.
	Ich bin krank.
	Ich bin müde.

3. Krank? It's Monday afternoon and your roommate is still in bed. Ask what's wrong and whether she/he is sick.

4. In der Bibliothek You see your German instructor in the library. Extend her/him a greeting and ask how she/he is doing.

> Greeting someone formally

Eine Professorin und eine Studentin: Sie sagen „Guten Tag" und geben einander die Hand. (Humboldt Universität, Berlin)

Adults in German-speaking countries often greet each other with a handshake. When one is first introduced or in a formal situation a handshake is expected. Greetings vary depending on the region and the speakers. **Tag** and **Morgen** are less formal than **Guten Tag** and **Guten Morgen**. To say good-by one says **Auf Wiedersehen** (which can be shortened to **Wiedersehen**). In some areas **Auf Wiederschauen** and **Adieu** are also used to say good-by. Both **(Auf) Wiedersehen** and **(Auf) Wiederschauen** mean literally *Until we see each other [meet] again.* **Tschüß** and **ciao** are reserved for friends and family. **Gute Nacht** *(good night)* is used at bedtime.

In southern Germany and in Austria one also hears **Grüß Gott** to say hello, and friends use **Grüß dich** or **Servus** when greeting each other or saying good-by. In these areas **Ade** is also used when parting. In Switzerland one often hears **Grüezi,** and among young people **Salut** is used to say hello and good-by.

Was machst du gern?

Lutz: Was machst du heute abend?

Ute: Nichts Besonderes. Musikhören oder so. Vielleicht gehe ich ins Kino.

Lutz: Hmm. Spielst du gern Schach?

Ute: Schach? Ja. Aber nicht so gut.

Lutz: Ach komm, wir spielen zusammen, ja?

Ute: Na gut! Wann?

Lutz: Um sieben?

Ute: O.K. Bis dann.

What do you like to do?

What are you doing tonight?

Nothing special. Listen to music or something like that. Maybe I'll go to the movies.

Hmm. Do you like to play chess?

Chess? Yes. But not so well.

Ah come on, we'll play together, O.K.?

All right. When?

At seven?

O.K. See you then.

When sample sentences have one or more words in **boldface type,** you should replace those words in subsequent sentences with the new words provided.

5. Was spielst du gern?   Find out which activities your partner likes to do. Then respond to his/her questions. You may want to refer to the Supplementary Word Sets in the Reference Section.

| Expressing likes and |
| dislikes |

Sie   *Gesprächspartner/in*

Spielst du	**gern**	**Schach?**	Ja. Und du?
	gut	Karten°?	Ja. Du auch°, nicht?
	oft°	Fußball°?	Nein. Und du?
	viel°	Tennis?	Nein. Aber du, nicht?
		Tischtennis°?	
		Basketball°?	
		Volleyball°?	
		Videospiele°?	

6. Treibst du gern Sport?   A fellow student asks whether you like to engage in sports. Respond as in the model.

Gesprächspartner/in   *Sie*

| Treibst du gern Sport°? | Ja. Ich | **schwimme° gern.** |
| | | wandere° gern. |

| Machst du viel Sport? | Nein. Ich mache nicht viel Sport. |
| | Nein, nicht viel. |

7. Was machst du?   Think about what you are going to do today. Ask a few classmates what they are going to do in their free time. They will ask you in turn.

Asking about personal plans

Sie   *Gesprächspartner/in*

Was machst du	**heute**	**morgen**°?	Ich	**arbeite**°.
		nachmittag°?		mache Deutsch°.
		abend°?		spiele Tennis.
	am [Montag]?			höre Musik.
				gehe ins Kino.
				gehe tanzen°.

8. Ich mache das.   Report to the class four things you do or don't do. Use **gern, viel, oft, nicht gern, nicht viel, nicht oft.**

Reporting

▶ *Ich spiele [nicht] viel Schach.*

9. Was machen Sie gern?   Your German instructor wants to know what you like to do in your spare time. How would you answer? And how would you ask your instructor what he/she likes to do?

Viele glauben, Radfahren ist gesund.

Many people in the German-speaking countries love to go hiking **(wandern)** and walking **(spazierengehen).** There are well-maintained trails everywhere. Some are no more than paths through local scenic spots or city parks, while others are part of a vast complex of trails.

Swimming is also a popular activity. In addition to seashore and lakeside beaches, town pools—both indoors and outdoors—provide ample opportunity for swimming. An outdoor pool **(Freibad),** with a nominal admission fee, is generally located on the outskirts of a city. It is often large and surrounded by grassy areas. People come with food and blankets to spend the day picnicking, swimming, and playing volleyball or badminton. Indoor pools **(Hallenbäder)** are becoming more and more elaborate. Cities are building them with cafés and may include a solarium **(Solarium),** saunas, bodybuilding room **(Bodybuildingraum),** and hot tubs **(Hot-Whirl-Pools).** Many are **Wellenbäder,** that is they can create artificial waves in the pools, and some have outdoor swimming areas that are heated in the winter.

Erweiterung des Wortschatzes

1 Was für ein Mensch sind Sie?

fleißig

faul

freundlich/nett

unfreundlich

froh

traurig

lustig

ernst

ruhig

nervös

1. Was für ein Mensch?   Ask three students what kind of person they are. Then report on your findings.

Asking what kind of person someone is

Sie

Was für ein Mensch bist du?
[Frank] ist lustig.

Gesprächspartner/in

Ich bin lustig.

Words that are related in spelling and meaning and are derived from the same source language are called cognates. There are hundreds of German-English cognates. Examples of adjectives that are cognates are **intelligent** *(intelligent)* and **dumm** *(dumb, stupid)*. Are there any other adjectives depicted that are cognates?

2. Und Sie, Frau/Herr Professor? Ask your instructor what kind of person she/he is.

▶ *Was für ein Mensch sind Sie?*

3. Ja oder nein? In groups of three, ask your partners whether they agree with your opinions of certain people. One of them agrees, but the other doesn't and corrects your opinions with an opposite adjective. You may want to refer to the Supplementary Word Sets in the Reference Section.

Expressing agreement and disagreement

Sie	*Gesprächspartner/in*
[Margit] ist sehr° ernst, nicht?	S1: Ja, sehr.
Ist [Margit] sehr ernst?	S2: Nein, ich glaube nicht°. Sie° ist sehr lustig.

4. So ist er/sie. Think of several adjectives that would describe a famous person. Then ask the class if they agree with your description.

▶ *Boris Becker ist groß und intelligent, nicht?*

2 Telling time

The following methods are used to express clock time.

Wieviel Uhr ist es?° ⎫
Wie spät ist es?° ⎬ What time is it?

	Method 1	Method 2
1.00 Uhr	Es ist eins.	Es ist eins.
	Es ist ein Uhr.	Es ist ein Uhr.
1.05 Uhr	Es ist fünf (Minuten) nach eins.	Es ist ein Uhr fünf.
1.15 Uhr	Es ist Viertel nach eins.	Es ist ein Uhr fünfzehn.
1.25 Uhr	Es ist fünf (Minuten) vor halb zwei.	Es ist ein Uhr fünfundzwanzig.
1.30 Uhr	Es ist halb zwei.	Es ist ein Uhr dreißig.
1.35 Uhr	Es ist fünf nach halb zwei.	Es ist ein Uhr fünfunddreißig.
1.45 Uhr	Es ist Viertel vor zwei.	Es ist ein Uhr fünfundvierzig.
1.55 Uhr	Es ist fünf (Minuten) vor zwei.	Es ist ein Uhr fünfundfünfzig.
2.00 Uhr	Es ist zwei Uhr.	Es ist zwei Uhr.

Note that German uses a period instead of a colon in time expressions.

German has two ways to indicate clock time. With a few exceptions, they parallel the two ways English indicates clock time.

| *Method 1* | Es ist Viertel nach acht. | It's a quarter past eight. |
| *Method 2* | Es ist acht Uhr fünfzehn. | It's eight-fifteen. |

In conversational German, method 1 is used to indicate time. Notice that the **-s** of **eins** is dropped before the word **Uhr.** The expression with **halb** indicates the hour to come, not the preceding hour: **halb zwei = 1.30 Uhr.**

In official time, such as train and plane schedules and concerts, method 2 is used.

Mein Zug fährt um **7.30 Uhr [7 Uhr 30].**	My train leaves at 7:30 A.M.
Das Konzert beginnt um **19.30 Uhr [19 Uhr 30].**	The concert begins at 7:30 P.M.

Official time is indicated on a 24-hour basis.

Um wieviel Uhr spielen wir Tennis?	(At) what time are we playing tennis?
Um halb neun.	At 8:30.

German uses **um** + a time expression to ask or speak about the specific hour that something will or did take place.

5. Wie spät ist es?   A friend asks you what time it is. Respond using the times listed below, in German.

▶   2.00 Uhr   *Es ist zwei.*

1. 3.00 Uhr	3. 11.45 Uhr	5. 4.55 Uhr
2. 6.15 Uhr	4. 1.20 Uhr	6. 2.30 Uhr

6. Nein, später°!   Say that it is ten minutes later than your friend thinks it is.

▶   Ist es 8 Uhr?   *Nein, später! Es ist zehn nach acht.*

1. 12.00 Uhr	4. 4.20 Uhr	6. 8.40 Uhr
2. 1.05 Uhr	5. 5.30 Uhr	7. 9.45 Uhr
3. 2.10 Uhr		

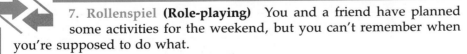

7. Rollenspiel (Role-playing)   You and a friend have planned some activities for the weekend, but you can't remember when you're supposed to do what.

Sie	*Gesprächspartner/in*
Um wieviel Uhr/Wann …	Wir [gehen] um [halb neun] …

1. gehen wir heute abend ins Kino?
2. gehen wir Samstag abend tanzen?
3. spielen wir Samstag nachmittag Tennis?
4. hören wir heute Musik?
5. gehen wir Sonntag wandern?
6. gehen wir schwimmen?

8. **Das machen wir zusammen.**   Below is a datebook with two entries. Write two more activities in your datebook. Then find a partner and compare your activities. Try to find a time when you can play tennis together.

Making plans

Sie

Ich bin um 9 Uhr in der Bibliothek. Und du?
Ich spiele um 8 mit Martin Schach. Und du?
Um wieviel Uhr spielen wir Tennis?
Ja, gut. Bis dann.

Gesprächspartner/in

Ich mache um 9 Uhr Deutsch.
Ich gehe ins Kino.
Um 2?
Tschüß.

Donnerstag 9. Mai	Freitag 10. Mai
7 Uhr	7 Uhr
8	8
9	9 *Bibliothek*
10	10
11	11
12	12
13	13
14	14
15	15
16	16
17	17
18	18
19	19
20	20 *Schach mit Martin*

9. Fahrplan (Train schedule) On a train schedule **Ankunft** indicates when a train arrives and **Abfahrt** when it departs. Using the train schedule, say when the trains arrive at: **Köln, Bonn, Nürnberg.**

IC 667
Meistersinger
Dortmund – Nürnberg

Ankunft	km	Abfahrt	Anschlüsse
	Dortmund Hbf	17.48	
18.09	**Hagen Hbf**	18.10	
18.25	**Wuppertal-**		
	Elberfeld	18.26	
18.54	**Köln Hbf**	18.58	intercity hotel ibis köln Tel 02 21/13 20 51
19.16	**Bonn Hbf**	19.18	
19.49	**Koblenz Hbf**	19.51	HOTEL **Hohenstaufen** 100 mv Hbf Tel (02 61) 3 70 81
20.40	**Mainz Hbf**	20.42	
20.58	**Frankfurt (Main)**		
	Flughafen	21.00	
21.13	**Frankfurt**		
	(Main) Hbf	21.21	
21.49	**Aschaffenburg**		
	Hbf	21.50	
22.39	**Würzburg Hbf**	22.41	
23.35	**Nürnberg Hbf**		hotel ibis nürnberg Tel. 09 11/23 71-0

Now say when the trains depart from: **Dortmund, Koblenz, Würzburg.**

10. Wann ist der Zug in [Köln]? Study the following exchanges, then continue on your own according to the models.

1. A: Wann ist der Zug in Frankfurt?
   B: Um 20.58 (zwanzig Uhr achtundfünfzig).
2. A: Wann ist der Zug in Mainz? Um 19.16?
   B: Nein. Um _____ .
3. A: Wann ist der Zug in _____ ?
   B: Um _____ .

Vokabeln

— Substantive

der **Abend**   evening
der **Basketball**   basketball
die **Bibliothek**   library
(das) **Deutsch**   German language
der **Fußball**   soccer
die **Karte**   card; postcard; die
   Karten *(pl.)*   (playing) cards
das **Kino**   movie theater
der **Mensch**   person, human being
die **Minute, die Minuten** *(pl.)*
   minute
der **Morgen**   morning

die **Musik**   music
der **Nachmittag**   afternoon
die **Nacht**   night
der **Professor** *(m.)*/die **Professorin**
   (f.)   professor
das **Schach**   chess
der **Sport**   sport
das **Tennis**   tennis
das **Tischtennis**   table tennis, Ping-
   Pong
das **Videospiel**   video game
der **Volleyball**   volleyball

— Verben

arbeiten   to work; to study
gehen   to go
glauben   to believe
hören   to hear
kommen   to come
machen   to do; to make

schwimmen   to swim
sein   to be
spielen   to play
tanzen   to dance
treiben   to engage in
wandern   to hike; to go walking

— Andere Wörter

aber   but, however
ach   oh
auch   also
bis   until, till
dumm   dumb, stupid
ein(e)   a, an
ernst   serious
faul   lazy
fleißig   industrious, hard-working
freundlich   friendly
froh   happy
furchtbar   terrible; very
ganz   complete, whole; very; **ganz**
   gut   not bad, O.K.
gern   gladly, willingly; *used with*
   verbs to indicate liking, as in **Ich**
   spiele *gern* **Tennis.**
gut   good, well; fine
halb   half

hallo   hello
heute abend   this evening
heute morgen   this morning
heute nachmittag   this afternoon
ihr   you *(familiar pl.)*
intelligent   smart, intelligent
krank   sick, ill
lustig   merry, cheerful
müde   tired
nach   after
nervös   nervous
nett   nice
nicht   not
nichts   nothing
nur   only
oder   or
oft   often
ruhig   calm, easy-going, quiet
schlecht   bad, badly

sehr   very (much)
sie   she, they
so   so
spät   late; **später**   later
traurig   sad
um   at; **um zehn Uhr**   at ten
   o'clock
unfreundlich   unfriendly
viel   much

vielleicht   maybe, perhaps
vor   before
wann   when
warum   why
was   what
was für (ein)   what kind of (a)
wer   who
wir   we
zusammen   together

___ Besondere Ausdrücke _____

am [Montag]   on [Monday]
Auf Wiedersehen   good-by
bis dann   see you then
Es geht.   O.K.; Not bad.; All right.
Grüß dich   hi
Gute Nacht   good night
Guten Abend/Abend   good evening
Guten Morgen/Morgen   good
   morning
Guten Tag/Tag   hello
halb   half; **halb zwei**   one-thirty
Ich glaube nicht.   I don't think so.
   Ich glaube ja.   I think so.
Ich mache Deutsch.   I'm doing
   German homework.
in der Bibliothek   in the library
ins Kino   to the movies
Musikhören   listening to music
Na gut!   All right.

nicht (wahr)?   *(tag question)*   don't
   you? isn't he? isn't that so?, etc.
nichts Besonderes   nothing special
O.K.   okay, O.K.
Um wieviel Uhr?   At what time?
um [sieben] Uhr   at [seven] o'clock
Und dir?   And you? (How about
   you?) *(familiar)*
Und Ihnen?   And you? (How about
   you?) *(formal)*
Was ist los?   What's wrong?
Wie geht's?   How are you? *(literally:*
   How's it going?)
Wie geht es Ihnen?   How are you?
Wie spät ist es?   What time is it?
Wieviel Uhr ist es?   What time is
   it?
Viertel nach   quarter after
Viertel vor   quarter of, quarter to

Doof bleibt doof, da helfen keine Pillen!

GRAMMATIK UND ÜBUNGEN

(Grammar and Exercises)

1 Subject pronouns

Singular *(sg.)*		Plural *(pl.)*	
1.	**ich** I	**wir** we	
2.	**du** you	**ihr** you	
	(familiar sg.)	*(familiar pl.)*	
3.	**er** he, it		
	es it	**sie** they	
	sie she, it		
	Sie you *(formal, sg. and pl.)*		

A personal pronoun is said to have "person," which indicates the identity of the subject.

1. First person refers to the one(s) speaking *(I, we).*
2. Second person refers to the one(s) spoken to *(you).*
3. Third person refers to the one(s) or thing(s) spoken about *(he/it/she, they).*

2 The subject pronouns *du, ihr, Sie*

Tag, Elke. ... Was machst **du?**
Tag, Inge. Tag, Gerd! ... Was macht **ihr?**

In *Kapitel 1* (p. 4) you learned when to use the familiar form **du. Du** is used to address one person. The familiar form used to address more than one person is **ihr.**

Tag, Herr Wagner. ... Was machen **Sie?**
Tag, Frau Braun. Tag, Fräulein Schneider! ... Was machen **Sie?**

In *Kapitel 1* (p. 5) you learned when to use the formal form **Sie.** Like the English *you,* **Sie** can be used to address one person or more than one.

3 The meanings and use of *sie* and *Sie*

Glaubt **sie** das?	Does she believe that?
Glauben **sie** das?	Do they believe that?
Glauben **Sie** das?	Do you believe that?

In spoken German, the meanings of **sie** *(she)*, **sie** *(they)*, and **Sie** *(you)* can be distinguished by the corresponding verb forms and by context. In written German, **Sie** *(you)* is always capitalized.

> **sie +** singular verb form = *she*
> **sie +** plural verb form = *they*
> **Sie +** plural verb form = *you* (formal)

Auf dem Markt sagt man „Sie" zueinander. (Bonn)

Historically speaking, **sie sind** *(they are)* and **Sie sind** *(you are)* are the same form. It was considered polite to address someone in the third person plural and to capitalize the pronoun in writing.

The development of formal pronouns to address a person was a phenomenon common to most European languages. English used to distinguish singular *thou/thee* from plural *ye/you;* *thou/thee* was restricted to informal usage, and *ye/you* was used both as informal plural and formal singular and plural. Today only *you* survives as our all-purpose pronoun. In German (as well as in other European languages such as French, Spanish, and Italian) there are still distinctions between the formal and informal pronouns for *you.*

The formal pronoun **Sie** is used for everyday communication outside the realm of family and friends. Even neighbors and coworkers address each other as **Sie** (they **siezen**). **Du** (along with its plural form **ihr**) is traditionally a form of address used among relatives or close friends. An older person usually decides on the appropriateness of this form in speaking to someone younger. Most young people address each other with **du** (they **duzen**) nowadays. A step somewhere between **du** and **Sie** is to use a first name and **Sie.** This form of address expresses intimacy and respect at the same time, and is often a "warm up" for the less formal, more friendly **duzen.**

1. Ich, du, er Give the subject pronouns you would use in the following situations.

▶ You're talking about a female friend. *sie*
▶ You're talking to a female friend. *du*

1. You're talking about a male friend.
2. You're talking to a male friend.
3. You're talking about yourself.
4. You're talking about yourself and a friend.
5. You're talking to your parents.
6. You're talking to a clerk in a store.
7. You're talking about your father.
8. You're talking about your sister.
9. You're talking about a child.
10. You're talking to your professor.
11. You're talking about your friends.

4 Present tense of *sein*

sein	
ich **bin**	wir **sind**
du **bist**	ihr **seid**
er/es/sie **ist**	sie **sind**
Sie **sind**	

to be	
I am	we are
you are	you are
he/it/she is	they are
you are	

The verb **sein,** like its English equivalent *to be,* is irregular in the present tense.

2. Intelligente Menschen Say that the persons listed below are intelligent in their political views.

▶ Ingrid *Ingrid ist intelligent.*

1. Gerd
2. du
3. Monika und Günter
4. Professor Schneider
5. ich
6. wir
7. Jens und Ute
8. Frau Müller
9. ihr
10. das Kind

3. Nein, so sind sie nicht.   Benno is talking about your friends. Say they're the opposite of what he thinks.

▶   Frank ist froh, nicht?   *Nein, er ist traurig.*

1. Gisela ist freundlich, nicht?
2. Alex ist ruhig, nicht?
3. Andrea ist intelligent, nicht?
4. Bruno ist lustig, nicht?
5. Beate und Christl sind dumm, nicht?
6. Dietmar und Mark sind nett, nicht?
7. Inge und Erika sind faul, nicht?

4. Nein, so bin ich nicht. Agree or disagree with the kind of person your partner suggests you may be.

ernst/lustig ◇ ruhig/nervös ◇ fleißig/faul ◇ freundlich/unfreundlich ◇ intelligent/dumm ◇ froh/traurig

Sie	*Gesprächspartner/in*
Was für ein Mensch bist du? Bist du ruhig?	Ja, ich bin ruhig.
	Nein, ich bin nervös.

5 Infinitive

Infinitive	Stem + ending	English equivalents
glauben	glaub + en	*to believe*
heißen	heiß + en	*to be named*
arbeiten	arbeit + en	*to work; study*
wandern	wander + n	*to hike; go walking*

The basic form of a German verb (the form listed in dictionaries and vocabularies) is the infinitive. German infinitives consist of a stem and the ending **-en** or **-n.**

6 The finite verb

Andrea **arbeitet** viel.   Andrea works a lot.
Arbeitest du viel?   Do you work a lot?

The term "finite verb" indicates the form of the verb that agrees with the subject.

7 Present tense of regular verbs

glauben	
ich glaub**e**	wir glaub**en**
du glaub**st**	ihr glaub**t**
er/es/sie glaub**t**	sie glaub**en**
Sie glaub**en**	

to believe	
I believe	we believe
you believe	you believe
he/it/she believes	they believe
you believe	

In the present tense, most English verbs have two different forms; most German verbs have four different forms.

The present tense of regular German verbs is formed by adding the endings **-e, -st, -t,** and **-en** to the infinitive stem. The verb endings change according to the subject. (Note that a few verbs like **wandern** add only **-n** instead of **-en: wir wandern.**) In informal spoken German, the ending **-e** is sometimes dropped from the **ich**-form: **Ich glaub' das wirklich nicht.**

Inge **spielt** gut Tennis.
Frank und Uwe **spielen** gut Basketball.

With a singular noun subject **(Inge)** the verb ending is **-t.** With a plural noun subject **(Frank und Uwe)** the verb ending is **-en.**

arbeiten: to study; work	
ich arbeite	wir arbeiten
du arbeit**est**	ihr arbeit**et**
er/es/sie arbeit**et**	sie arbeiten
Sie arbeiten	

In regular English verbs, the third-person singular ending is usually *-s: she works.* After certain verb stems, however, this ending expands to *-es: she teaches, he dances.*

German also has verb stems that require an expansion of the ending. If a verb stem ends in **-d** or **-t,** the endings **-st** and **-t** expand to **-est** and **-et.** The other endings are regular.

heißen: to be called, named	
ich heiße	wir heißen
du heiß**t**	ihr heißt
er/es/sie heißt	sie heißen
Sie heißen	

If a verb stem ends in a sibilant **(s, ss, ß, z),** the **-st** ending contracts to a **-t: du heißt, du tanzt.** The other endings are regular.

8 The construction verb + *gern*

Ich spiele **gern** Tennis. I like to play tennis.
Ich spiele **nicht gern** Golf. I don't like to play golf.

The most common way of saying in German that you like doing something is to use the appropriate verb + **gern.** To say that you don't like doing something, use **nicht gern.**

5. Ja, das mache ich. Sabine is trying to find out more about you and your plans. Answer her questions in the affirmative.

▶ Treibst du gern Sport? *Ja, ich treibe gern Sport.*

1. Arbeitest du heute morgen?
2. Arbeitest du gern?
3. Spielst du heute nachmittag Tennis?
4. Spielst du auch Volleyball?
5. Machst du viel Sport?
6. Schwimmst du gern?
7. Hörst du auch gern Musik?
8. Wanderst du viel?
9. Spielst du oft Videospiele?

6. Und du, Uwe? Uwe is telling about the things his friend Lore does. Ask whether he enjoys the same things. Begin your question with the verb.

▶ Lore treibt gern Sport. *Treibst du auch gern Sport?*

1. Sie macht viel Sport.
2. Sie spielt auch gern Volleyball.
3. Sie schwimmt gern.
4. Lore spielt gut Schach.
5. Und sie hört gern Musik.
6. Sie arbeitet auch viel.
7. Sie wandert gern.
8. Sie geht gern ins Kino.
9. Sie tanzt gern.

7. Machst du das auch gern? Choose four things that some people like to do. Find four students who like to do the activities—one for each activity. Report to the class. You may want to refer to the Supplementary Word Sets in the Reference Section.

> Expressing likes and dislikes

▶ Spielst du gern Schach? *Ja, sehr gern und oft.*
Nein, Schach ist dumm.

Die deutschen Frauen waren 1990 Europameisterinnen im Fußball.

German people of all ages engage in sports, and they especially enjoy **Fußball** (soccer) and **Gymnastik** (calisthenics and aerobic exercises). School sports are intramural rather than intermural. A person who wishes to participate in competitive sports can join a sports club **(Sportverein).**

Before unification there were more than 60 thousand such clubs in the Federal Republic, with more than 18 million members. In the former German Democratic Republic (GDR) approximately 600,000 people participated in soccer under the auspices of the Sports and Gymnastics Union of the GDR. Currently sports activities in eastern Germany are undergoing a restructuring process that will result in a system similar to that in western Germany. **Fußball** is played by over 3.5 million Germans, of whom approximately 75 thousand are women who play on more than a thousand women's teams. Germany also has a professional women's soccer league. Even the smallest village has its own **Verein,** which also plays an important part in the social life of the town.

Not only does the local **Sportverein** often sponsor a **Fußball** team that may compete at an international level, but it provides for many other popular sports like **Handball, Tischtennis, Turnen** (gymnastics), **Leichtathletik** (track and field), and **Schwimmen.**

9 Position of *nicht*

The position of **nicht** is determined by various elements in the sentence.

Herr Wagner *arbeitet* **nicht.**	Mr. Wagner doesn't work.
Mark glaubt *Inge* **nicht.**	Mark doesn't believe Inge.
Ich glaube *es* **nicht.**	I don't believe it.
Arbeitest du *heute* **nicht?**	Aren't you working today?

Nicht always follows:

1. the finite verb (e.g., er **arbeitet**)
2. nouns used as objects (e.g., **Inge**)
3. pronouns used as objects (e.g., **es**)
4. specific adverbs of time (e.g., **heute**)

Benno ist **nicht** *faul.*	Benno is not lazy.
Das ist **nicht** *Frau Wagner.*	That is not Ms. Wagner.
Wir wandern **nicht** *oft.*	We don't hike much.
Wir gehen heute **nicht** *ins Kino.*	We're not going to the movies today.

Nicht precedes most other kinds of elements:

1. predicate adjectives (a predicate adjective completes the meaning of a linking verb; the most frequently used linking verb is **sein,** *to be:* e.g., Mark ist nicht **faul.**)
2. predicate nouns (a predicate noun is a noun that completes the meaning of a linking verb: e.g., Das ist nicht **Frau Wagner.**)
3. adverbs, including general time adverbs (e.g., nicht **oft,** nicht **sehr,** nicht **gern**)
4. prepositional phrases (e.g., nicht **ins Kino**)

Ich gehe **nicht** *oft ins Kino.*	I don't often go to the movies.

If several of the elements occur in a sentence, **nicht** usually precedes the first one.

8. Ich nicht.   A new acquaintance has a number of questions about you and your friends. Unfortunately you have to answer all in the negative. Use **nicht** in the proper place.

▶   *Treibst du gern Sport?*   *Nein, ich treibe nicht gern Sport.*

1. Spielst du gern Schach?
2. Wanderst du viel?
3. Spielst du oft Fußball?
4. Gehst du oft ins Kino?
5. Gehst du heute abend ins Kino?
6. Bist du müde?
7. Ist das Klaus Braun?
8. Ist es Klaus Meier?
9. Arbeitet Frau Schmidt in Hamburg?

9. Wir nicht.   Jutta, a new acquaintance, has some questions for you and Hans-Dieter. Answer in the negative.

▶   *Macht ihr viel Sport?*   *Nein. Wir machen nicht viel Sport.*

1. Spielt ihr viel Basketball?
2. Spielt ihr oft Tennis?
3. Schwimmt ihr gern?
4. Arbeitet ihr viel?
5. Arbeitet ihr gern?
6. Hört ihr gern Musik?
7. Wandert ihr viel?
8. Spielt ihr gern Tischtennis?
9. Tanzt ihr gern?

10. Aber macht ihr es gern? Your friends tell you what they're doing today. Ask whether they like to do those things. Begin your questions with the verb.

▶ Wir spielen heute morgen Tennis. *Spielt ihr gern Tennis?*

1. Wir spielen auch Fußball.
2. Wir gehen heute schwimmen.
3. Wir arbeiten heute abend.
4. Wir spielen auch Karten.
5. Wir hören heute abend Musik.
6. Wir wandern heute nachmittag.
7. Wir gehen heute abend ins Kino.
8. Wir gehen auch tanzen.

11. Detlev aber nicht. Veronika makes some observations about Detlev and Inge. Say that she's right about Inge, but not Detlev.

▶ Detlev und Inge treiben gern Sport, nicht? *Inge treibt gern Sport, Detlev aber nicht.*

1. Detlev und Inge machen viel Sport, nicht?
2. Sie schwimmen gut, nicht?
3. Sie arbeiten viel, nicht?
4. Sie arbeiten gern, nicht?
5. Sie spielen oft Schach, nicht?
6. Sie spielen sehr viel Videospiele, nicht?
7. Sie hören gern Musik, nicht?
8. Sie machen auch Musik, nicht?
9. Sie tanzen gern, nicht?

12. Und das machen sie gern. Nicole and Gustav lead an active life. Say what they like to do.

▶ Arbeiten Nicole und Gustav viel in Bremen? *Ja, und sie arbeiten gern in Bremen.*

1. Treiben Nicole und Gustav viel Sport?
2. Sind sie oft in Basel?
3. Spielen sie viel Schach?
4. Hören sie viel Musik?
5. Hören sie oft Radio?
6. Spielen sie viel Tischtennis?
7. Tanzen sie oft?
8. Gehen sie viel ins Kino?
9. Spielen sie oft Videospiele?

13. Das ist gesund. (It's healthy.) Many Germans believe that fresh air is especially healthy. Say that the following people believe it.

▶ Wir glauben das. (Sie)   *Sie glauben das.*

1. ich
2. sie *(pl.)*
3. er
4. sie *(sg.)*

5. wir
6. Herr Müller
7. Frau Schneider
8. Gabi und Jürgen

14. Was machst du gern? With a partner, try to find two activities you both enjoy doing and two you both dislike doing. When you are ready, introduce your partner to the class and tell everyone a little about her/him.

Sie	*Gesprächspartner/in*
Ich schwimme gern. Schwimmst du auch gern?	[Ja.]
Das hier ist Inge. Sie schwimmt gern.	

Finding common likes and dislikes

10 Present-tense meanings

Sie **arbeitet** gut. = $\begin{cases} \text{She } \textit{works} \text{ well. (plain)} \\ \text{She } \textit{does work} \text{ well. (emphatic)} \\ \text{She } \textit{is working} \text{ well. (progressive)} \end{cases}$

German uses a single verb form to express ideas or actions that may require one of three different forms in English.

Du **gehst** heute nachmittag schwimmen, nicht?

Ich **mache** das morgen.

You*'re going* swimming this afternoon, aren't you?

I*'ll do* that tomorrow.

German, like English, may use the present tense to express action intended or planned for the future.

15. Wie sagt man das? (How do you say that?) Give the German equivalents of the following sentences.

▶ Frank does not work well.   *Frank arbeitet nicht gut.*

1. Karla does work a lot.
2. I do believe that.
3. Stefan does play soccer well.
4. You're working tonight, Ute.
5. You do that well, Ursula.
6. I'm playing tennis today.

7. We're playing basketball today.
8. I believe so.
9. Detlev is going to the movies.
10. I'm going dancing.

11 Specific questions

Wann gehst du schwimmen? ⌒   When are you going swimming?
Wer arbeitet heute nachmittag°? ⌒   Who is working this afternoon?

A specific question asks for a particular bit of information. It begins with an interrogative expression such as **wann** *(when)*, **was** *(what)*, **welch(-er, -es, -e)** *(which)*, **wer** *(who)*, **wie** *(how)*, and **was für (ein)** *(what kind of)*. The interrogative is followed by the verb. In a specific question in German, the finite verb is used. In English, a form of the auxiliary verb *to be* or *to do* is often used with a form of the main verb. In German, the voice normally falls at the end of a specific question, just as it does in English.

16. Wer? Was? Wann?   Your partner knows who is playing what and when. Ask your partner for the information.

▶   Peter spielt heute nachmittag Fußball.

Sie	*Gesprächspartner/in*
Wer spielt Fußball?	Peter.
Was spielt Peter?	Fußball.
Wann spielt Peter Fußball?	Heute nachmittag.

1. Barbara spielt heute Tennis.
2. Anne und Veronika spielen um drei Schach.
3. Heute abend spiele ich Hockey.
4. Professor Wagner spielt heute Basketball.
5. Karl spielt um acht Uhr Volleyball.
6. Um halb sechs spielen wir Fußball.

17. Wie? Wie alt?   Your partner makes several statements about people. You don't catch everything your partner says. Ask for the missing information.

Gesprächspartner/in	*Sie*
Gerhard spielt gut Fußball.	Wie spielt er?
Gut.	
Karla ist siebzehn.	Wie alt ist Karla?
Siebzehn.	

1. Der Professor heißt [Beck].
2. Herbert ist neunzehn.
3. Es geht Manfred gut.
4. Der Junge tanzt gut.

5. Frau Müller ist 39 Jahre alt.
6. Die Frau heißt Marianne.
7. Martin spielt sehr gut Schach.

12 General questions

Gehst du heute schwimmen? ⌄   Are you going swimming today?
Treiben Sie gern Sport? ⌄   Do you like to play sports?

A general question requires a yes-or-no answer. It begins with the verb. A general question in German uses the finite verb, whereas English often requires a form of the auxiliary verb *to do* or *to be* plus a form of the main verb. In German, the voice normally rises at the end of a general question, just as it does in English.

18. Und du? Comment on things you and your friends do. Then ask whether others also do those things.

▶ Ich arbeite heute abend. Und du?   *Arbeitest du auch heute abend?*

1. Ich schwimme gern. Und du?
2. Ich spiele oft Basketball. Und du?
3. Ich treibe gern Sport. Und du?
4. Klaus spielt gut Fußball. Und Viktor?
5. Petra spielt viel Volleyball. Und Antje?
6. Rita macht viel Sport. Und Sara?
7. Wir wandern gern. Und ihr?
8. Wir gehen heute abend ins Kino. Und ihr?

13 Tag questions

Du hörst gern Musik, **nicht wahr?**   You like to listen to music, don't you?

Mark geht heute abend ins Kino, **nicht?**   Mark is going to the movies tonight, isn't he?

A tag question is literally "tagged on" to the end of a statement. In English the tag equivalent to **nicht wahr?** or **nicht?** depends on the subject of the sentence: *don't you?*, *aren't you?*, *isn't he?*, and *doesn't she?*, etc.

19. Nicht? In a conversation with a friend, ask for confirmation that what you think is correct. Use the tag question **nicht?** or **nicht wahr?**

▶ Frau Meier ist sehr nett.   *Frau Meier ist sehr nett, nicht?*
                                 Frau Meier ist sehr nett, nicht wahr?

1. Professor Wagner arbeitet viel.
2. Sie und ihr Mann wandern gern.
3. Jürgen ist oft müde.
4. Rita macht viel Sport.
5. Sie schwimmt gut.
6. Sie ist auch sehr intelligent.
7. Wir gehen heute abend ins Kino.
8. Wir gehen um sieben.

20. Wie sagt man das?   You overhear someone on the phone talking with Ursula. Translate the questions for Dieter, your German friend.

▶   Ursula, how are you?   *Ursula, wie geht's?*

1. What are you doing, Ursula?
2. Are you working?
3. Are you going swimming today?
4. Is Rudi going also?
5. When are you playing tennis, Ursula?
6. Does Rudi play well?
7. What kind of person is Rudi?
8. Do you like to play chess?
9. Rudi likes to play, too, doesn't he?
10. You're coming at seven, aren't you?
11. When are Rudi and Beate going to the movies?

21. Ein Interview   You are looking for a new roommate. Write five questions you want to ask the person about his/her likes, dislikes, and activities. Then find a partner and conduct an interview.

WIEDERHOLUNG

1. Kurze Gespräche (Short conversations)   Read the conversations and answer the questions.

Lutz: Wie heißt der Junge?
Ute: Er heißt Klaus.
Lutz: Und das Mädchen?
Ute: Sie heißt Gabi.

1. Wie heißt der Junge?
2. Wie heißt das Mädchen?

Gabi: Wie geht's Jürgen?
Klaus: Gut.
Gabi: Spielt er heute morgen Fußball?
Klaus: Ich glaube ja.

3. Wie geht es Jürgen?
4. Wer spielt heute morgen Fußball?

Christel: Was machst du heute abend?
Michael: Ich spiele Tennis.
Christel: Um wieviel Uhr?
Michael: Um halb acht.

5. Was macht Michael heute abend?
6. Um wieviel Uhr spielt er?

2. Ja, Veronika. Confirm Veronika's information about you and your friends.

▶ Gabi arbeitet in Basel, nicht wahr?   *Ja, sie arbeitet in Basel.*

1. Du arbeitest in Zürich, nicht?
2. Wolf hört gern Musik, nicht wahr?
3. Renate und Paula spielen gut Rock, nicht?
4. Wir spielen gut Basketball, nicht?
5. Trudi macht viel Sport, nicht wahr?
6. Du und Regina, ihr spielt gern Tennis, nicht?

3. Was machen sie? Construct sentences using the following cues.

▶ was / machen / du / heute / ?   *Was machst du heute?*

1. er / heißen / Konrad
2. wie / heißen / du / ?
3. wie / arbeiten / er / ?
4. wann / gehen / Martha / ins Kino / ?
5. was / machen / Martha und er / heute abend / ?
6. Martha / schwimmen / gut und viel
7. ich / glauben / das / nicht
8. wer / treiben / gern / Sport / ?
9. Lore / spielen / gut / Fußball / nicht / ?

4. Ergänzen Sie. (Complete.) Complete the sentences below with appropriate words.

1. Wie _____ es Ihnen?
2. Arbeitest _____ heute nicht?
3. Ich _____ heute Tennis.
4. Arbeiten _____ heute abend?
5. _____ heißen Sie?
6. _____ geht Ulrich ins Kino?
7. _____ du viel Sport?
8. _____ spiele gern Volleyball.
9. _____ hört gern Musik?

5. Wie sagt man das? Give the German equivalents of the sentences below.

1. What's your name?
2. How are you?
3. What are you doing today?
4. Do you like to listen to music?
5. Do you play chess well?
6. Are you going to the movies tonight?
7. When do you work?

6. So sind wir. Fill out the chart by giving some information about yourself, your partner, and others.

Sie

Ich bin nervös. Bist du nervös?

Ist [Michael] nervös?

Gesprächspartner/in

Ja. Ich bin nervös.
Nein. Ich bin nicht nervös.
Ja. Er ist nervös.
Nein. Er ist nicht nervös.

	Ich bin	Mein(e) Partner/in ist	[Michael/Anne] ist	Herr Professor [Lange]/ Frau Professor [Kluge] ist
nervös				
faul				
alt				
oft krank				
intelligent				
ruhig				
freundlich				
dumm				
müde				
fleißig				
ernst				
froh				
lustig				
traurig				
unfreundlich				
nett				

7. Was sagen Sie? (What do you say?) Respond appropriately to the expressions or questions below in German.

1. Guten Tag!
2. Wie ist Ihre Telefonnummer?
3. Welcher Tag ist heute?
4. Wie spät ist es?
5. Wie geht's?
6. Was ist los?
7. Was machen Sie heute abend?
8. Hören Sie gern Musik?
9. Treiben Sie gern Sport?
10. Was für ein Mensch sind Sie?

8. **Anregung (Idea)** Introduce yourself to a classmate you don't know well. Be prepared to ask for and provide information in German that answers the questions below.

Describing yourself

Wie heißt du? ◇ Wie alt bist du? ◇ Wie ist deine Adresse? ◇ Wie ist deine Telefonnummer? ◇ Was für ein Mensch bist du? ◇ Was machst du gern?

9. **Partnersuche (Looking for a partner)** Talk to your fellow classmates until you find one with whom you have at least three things in common and three things you don't have in common. When you are finished, introduce the person to the class and tell the class what you have in common. Here are some ideas you may wish to use:

how old the person is
what kind of person she/he is
whether the person likes going to the movies
what game(s) the person likes to play
whether she/he plays a particular sport well
whether she/he likes to dance
(your suggestion)

GRAMMATIK: ZUSAMMENFASSUNG

(Grammar: Summary)

Subject pronouns

Singular	Plural
ich I	**wir** we
du you *(familiar)*	**ihr** you *(familiar)*
er he/it	
es it	**sie** they
sie she/it	
Sie you *(formal)*	

Present tense of *sein*

ich	**bin**	wir	**sind**
du	**bist**	ihr	**seid**
er/es/sie	**ist**	sie	**sind**
	Sie **sind**		

Infinitive and infinitive stem

Infinitive	Stem + ending
glauben	glaub + en
wandern	wander + n

The basic form of a German verb is the infinitive. Most German infinitives end in **-en;** a few end in **-n,** such as **wandern.** In vocabularies and dictionaries, verbs are listed in their infinitive form.

Present tense of regular verbs

	glauben	**arbeiten**	**heißen**
ich	glaub**e**	arbeit**e**	heiß**e**
du	glaub**st**	arbeit**est**	heiß**t**
er/es/sie	glaub**t**	arbeit**et**	heiß**t**
wir	glaub**en**	arbeit**en**	heiß**en**
ihr	glaub**t**	arbeit**et**	heiß**t**
sie	glaub**en**	arbeit**en**	heiß**en**
Sie	glaub**en**	arbeit**en**	heiß**en**

1. German verb endings change, depending on what the subject of the verb is. The verb endings are added to the infinitive stem. There are four basic endings in the present tense of most regular verbs: **-e, -st, -t, -en.**
2. If a verb stem ends in **-d** or **-t,** the endings **-st** and **-t** expand to **-est** and **-et.**
3. If a verb stem ends in a sibilant **(s, ss, ß, z),** the **-st** ending contracts to **-t.**

Position of *nicht*

The position of **nicht** is determined by the various elements in the sentence. Because of the great flexibility of **nicht,** its use is best learned by observing its position in sentences you hear and read. Here are several guidelines:

1. **Nicht** always follows the finite verb

   Bernd arbeitet **nicht.**   Bernd is not working.

2. **Nicht** generally follows:
   a. noun objects

   | Ich glaube *Bernd* **nicht.** | I don't believe Bernd. |

   b. pronoun objects

   | Ich glaube *es* **nicht.** | I don't believe it. |

   c. specific time expressions

   | Bernd spielt *heute* **nicht.** | Bernd is not playing today. |

3. **Nicht** precedes other elements:
   a. predicate adjectives

   | Uwe ist **nicht** *nett.* | Uwe isn't nice. |

   b. predicate nouns

   | Das ist **nicht** *Herr Schmidt.* | That isn't Mr. Schmidt. |

   c. adverbs

   | Er spielt **nicht** *gut* Tennis. | He doesn't play tennis well. |

   d. expressions of general time

   | Er spielt **nicht** *oft* Tennis. | He doesn't play tennis often. |

   e. prepositional phrases

   | Ute geht **nicht** *ins Kino.* | Ute isn't going to the movies. |

4. If several of the elements occur in a sentence, **nicht** usually precedes the first one.

   | Ich gehe **nicht** *oft ins Kino.* | I don't often go to the movies. |

Specific questions

1	2	3	
Wann	gehen	Sie?	When are you going?
Wo	arbeitest	du?	Where do you work?

A German speaker signals the meaning "specific question" by using an interrogative in first position and the finite verb in second position.

General questions

1	2	3	
Bist	du	müde?	Are you tired?
Spielt	Andrea	gut?	Does Andrea play well?
Arbeitest	du	heute?	Are you working today?

A German speaker signals the meaning "general question" by putting the finite verb in the first position.

Bei schönem Wetter ist man gern draußen.
(Sommerhausen am Main, bei Würzburg)

Kapitel 3

LERNZIELE

SPRECHAKTE

Talking about the weather
Inquiring about someone's birthday
Summarizing information
Stating one's nationality

GRAMMATIK

Simple past tense of *sein*
Present tense of *haben*
Position of the finite verb in statements
Nominative case
Plural of nouns
Indefinite article *ein*
Expressing negation by *kein* and *nicht*
Possession with proper names
Possessive adjectives
Demonstrative pronouns *der, das, die*

VOKABELN

Months and seasons
Weather expressions
Understanding the flavoring particle *aber*
Names of countries and nationalities
Suffixes *-er* and *-in*

LANDESKUNDE

Geography and climate of Germany
Birthday customs and greetings
Development of the standard German
    language

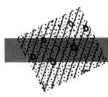

BAUSTEINE FÜR GESPRÄCHE

Wie ist das Wetter?	**How's the weather?**

Im Sommer

Frau Kümmel: Schönes Wetter, nicht?

Herr Althaus: Ja, aber es ist zu trocken.

Frau Kümmel: Vielleicht regnet es morgen.

Herr Althaus: Hoffentlich.

In the summer

Nice weather, isn't it?

Yes, but it's too dry.

Maybe it'll rain tomorrow.

I hope so.

Im Herbst

Herr Hofer: Heute ist es wirklich kalt, nicht?

Frau Vogel: Ja, sehr, und gestern war es noch so schön.

Herr Hofer: Jetzt bleibt es bestimmt kalt.

Frau Vogel: Leider.

In the fall

It's really cold today, isn't it?

Yes, very much so. And it was still so nice yesterday.
Now it'll stay cold for sure.

Unfortunately.

Im Winter

Dieter: Was für ein Wetter!

Ingrid: Der Wind ist furchtbar kalt. Ich glaube, es schneit bald.

In the winter

What weather!
The wind is awfully cold. I think it's going to snow soon.

---

1. Schönes Wetter, nicht?   A fellow student comments on the weather. Agree with her/him.

Discussing the weather

Gesprächspartner/in	*Sie*	
Schönes Wetter, hm?	Ja, es ist wirklich	schön.
Gutes		gut
Schlechtes		schlecht
Furchtbares		furchtbar
		warm°
		kalt

2. Das Wetter   Talk about the weather with two or three fellow students. Ask how it is now and then make a prediction about tomorrow. You may want to refer to the Supplementary Word Sets in the Reference Section.

Sie   *Gesprächspartner/in*

Wie ist das Wetter?   Es ist | **kalt.**
                                                 | schlecht
                                                 | naß°
                                                 | warm
                                                 | schön
                                                 | heiß

Vielleicht | **regnet es** morgen. | Ja, vielleicht.
           | schneit es | Ich glaube nicht.
           | scheint° die Sonne° | Hoffentlich nicht.

3. Was für ein Wetter!   A fellow student is unhappy with the weather. Respond by commenting on the weather yesterday.

Gesprächspartner/in   *Sie*

Was für ein | **Wetter!**   Ja, und gestern war es | **noch schön warm°.**
            | Wind | auch schlecht
            | Regen° | auch kalt
            | Schnee° | noch trocken

4. Was sagen Sie?   Make each of the comments below to a partner. After each comment, your partner will respond with an appropriate expression from the list. Your partner should avoid using the same expression each time.

Hoffentlich. ◇ Leider. ◇ Vielleicht. ◇ Jetzt bleibt es so. ◇ Vielleicht schneit es bald. ◇ Vielleicht regnet es. ◇ Ja, sehr. ◇ Nein, noch nicht.

1. Heute ist es schön warm.   5. Der Wind ist furchtbar kalt.
2. Heute ist es wirklich heiß.   6. Schneit es?
3. Es ist zu trocken.   7. Jetzt bleibt es bestimmt kalt.
4. Was für ein Wetter!

5. Rollenspiel   Act out a telephone conversation between two friends. One lives in Hamburg, the other in Venice. Talk about today's weather, yesterday's, and what you think tomorrow's weather will be.

Erweiterung des Wortschatzes

1 Die Monate

Januar	April	Juli	Oktober
Februar	Mai	August	November
März	Juni	September	Dezember

Der Mai war schön, nicht?   May was nice, wasn't it?

All the names of the months are **der**-words.

2 Die Jahreszeiten°

der Frühling spring

der Sommer summer

der Herbst autumn, fall

der Winter winter

1. Wann ist es … ? Tell in what months the following weather conditions occur.

▸ Wann ist es oft kalt? *Im Januar und im Februar.*

1. Wann regnet es viel?
2. Wann schneit es viel?
3. Wann ist es oft heiß?
4. Wann scheint die Sonne nicht viel?
5. Wann ist es schön warm?
6. Wann ist es sehr trocken?
7. Wann ist der Wind kalt? warm? heiß?
8. Wann ist das Wetter gut—nicht heiß und nicht kalt?

2. Wie heißen sie? Answer the following questions about the seasons.

1. Wie heißen die Wintermonate? die Sommermonate?
2. Wie heißen die Herbstmonate? die Frühlingsmonate?

3. Wie ist das Wetter … ? Respond to a fellow student's questions about the weather in different seasons or months. You may want to refer to the Supplementary Word Sets in the Reference Section.

Gesprächspartner/in	*Sie*
Wie ist das Wetter im [Herbst]?	Es ist [schön].
Wie ist das Wetter im [Juli]?	Es ist [sehr heiß].

Talking about seasonal weather

4. Wann hast du Geburtstag°? Interview four students to find out the month of their birthday.

Sie	*Gesprächspartner/in*
Wann hast du Geburtstag?	Im [Mai].

Inquiring about someone's birthday

5. Du auch? Find another student who has a birthday the same month you do.

Sie	*Gesprächspartner/in*
Ich habe im [März] Geburtstag. Und du?	Im [April].
	Auch im [März].

Vokabeln

— Substantive

der **Frühling** spring
der **Geburtstag** birthday
der **Herbst** autumn, fall
die **Jahreszeit, -en** season
der **Monat, -e** month
der **Regen** rain

der **Schnee** snow
der **Sommer** summer
die **Sonne** sun
das **Wetter** weather
der **Wind** wind
der **Winter** winter

— Verben

bleiben to remain, to stay
regnen to rain
scheinen to shine

schneien to snow
war was (*past tense of* **sein**)

— Andere Wörter

bald soon
bestimmt certain(ly)
furchtbar horrible, terrible
gestern yesterday
heiß hot
hoffentlich I hope so
jetzt now
kalt cold
leider unfortunately

morgen tomorrow
naß wet
noch still; in addition
schön nice, beautiful
trocken dry
warm warm
wirklich really
zu too

— Besondere Ausdrücke

Ich habe im [Mai] Geburtstag My
  birthday is in May.
im [Herbst] in the [fall]; **im [Mai]**
  in [May]
schön warm nice and warm

Wann hast du Geburtstag? When
  is your birthday?
Was für ein Wetter! What
  weather!

Sommer *in* **Frankfurt**

KÜHLE BARS + HEISSES EIS + WELT-THEATRE

KÜHL UND KLEIN? —JA UND NEIN!

Vorbereitung auf das Lesen

Before every reading **(Lesestück)** you will find series of questions or state-ments that will help you read and understand the text. This preparation is called **Vorbereitung auf das Lesen.** Questions included under the title **Zum Thema (On the topic)** will help you discover what you may already know about the topic, while **Leitfragen (Study questions)** give direction to your reading by suggesting things to look for as you work through the text. As preparation for this reading passage on the size of Germany and its weather, answer as many of the questions below as you can.

◆ *Zum Thema*

1. Large and small are relative terms. Name some other relative terms.
2. Do you think the concept of cold means the same thing to inhabitants of Florida as to those of Toronto, Canada?
3. Where do you think winters are colder: Minnesota, U.S.A.; Ontario, Can-ada; or northern Germany?
4. Where do you think winters are colder: in northern Germany (Hamburg) or in southern Germany (Munich)?
5. Locate the following countries and cities on the maps of the German-speaking countries and Europe at the front of this book:

Belgien	Erfurt	Magdeburg	die Schweiz
Berlin	Frankfurt	München	Schwerin
Bonn	Frankreich	die Niederlande	die Tschechoslowakei
Dänemark	Hamburg	Österreich	
Deutschland	Leipzig	Polen	
Dresden	Luxemburg	Potsdam	

◆ *Leitfragen*

1. Which is farther north: Berlin, the capital of Germany, or Washington, D.C.?
2. You will find data on the number of inhabitants of Germany, relative to its size. In order to establish a comparison, find out how many people live in Texas (or Alberta).
3. In order to compare distances, find out how many kilometers it is from Washington, D.C., to Los Angeles. How many kilometers is it from Min-neapolis to Miami?
4. How many countries border the U.S.A.? Canada?
5. How many countries border Germany? How many can you name?

In preparing the reading selection, you should read each selection twice. The first time try to get the gist of the material without looking up unfamiliar words. On the second reading, you will discover that you can guess some of the words you did not initially recognize, and you will understand some of the constructions that were unclear on the first reading. Many unfamiliar words are glossed in the margins; others are found in the vocabulary (**Vokabeln**) section following the reading selection. By reading the selection twice and using intelligent guessing, you will read more efficiently and develop a genuine skill in reading.

*E*in Deutscher in Deutschland sagt: „Heute ist es aber° heiß. Es ist schon   really
richtig Sommer." Ein Amerikaner hört das und denkt: „Heiß? Hier? Jetzt? Nein! Schön warm."

    Wörter wie „heiß" und „warm" sind also relativ. Denn in Deutschland ist
5 der Sommer anders. Deutschland liegt nämlich° weiter nördlich als Amerika.   after all
Nehmen wir° zum Beispiel die Hauptstädte. Berlin ist die deutsche   **nehmen wir:** let's take
Hauptstadt. Washington ist die amerikanische Hauptstadt. Berlin liegt circa°   approximately
1500 Kilometer weiter nördlich als Washington.

    Auch der Atlantische Ozean beeinflußt das Klima. Er beeinflußt es mehr
10 im Westen Deutschlands als im Osten. Und er beeinflußt es mehr im Norden
als im Süden. So ist das Wetter oft kühl im Sommer und nicht so kalt im
Winter.

Nach Leipzig sind es nur 12 Kilometer. Wie weit ist es nach Halle? (Schkeuditz bei Leipzig)

Auch die Wörter „groß" und „klein" sind relativ, wenigstens° in der   at least
Geographie. Für Deutsche ist Amerika sehr groß. Für Amerikaner ist
15 Deutschland ziemlich klein. Deutschland hat etwa achtundsiebzig Millionen
Einwohner, aber es ist nur etwa halb so groß wie Texas (oder Alberta). Von
Bonn im Westen nach Dresden im Osten sind es nur etwa fünfhundert Kilometer. Von Hamburg im Norden nach München im Süden sind es nur
sechshundert Kilometer. In Deutschland haben „groß" und „klein" also an-
20 dere Dimensionen als in Amerika.

    Deutschland liegt im Zentrum° Europas. Es hat neun Nachbarn: Das   center
Nachbarland im Norden ist Dänemark; die Nachbarländer im Süden sind
Österreich und die Schweiz; im Osten liegen Polen und die
Tschechoslowakei; im Westen Frankreich, Luxemburg, Belgien und die
25 Niederlande.

Fragen zum Lesestück (Questions on the reading passage)

1. Was sagt ein Deutscher in Deutschland im Sommer?
2. Was denkt der Amerikaner?
3. Welche Wörter sind relativ?
4. Warum ist der Sommer anders als in Amerika?
5. Wie ist der Sommer in Deutschland?
6. Wie heißt die deutsche Hauptstadt?
7. Welche Stadt liegt weiter nördlich — Berlin oder Washington?
8. Wo beeinflußt der Atlantische Ozean das Wetter mehr — im Westen oder im Osten?
9. Wie groß ist Deutschland?
10. Wie viele Einwohner hat Deutschland?
11. Wie viele Kilometer sind es von Bonn nach Dresden?
12. Wie viele Kilometer sind es von Hamburg nach München?
13. Wie viele Nachbarn hat Deutschland?

Erzählen Sie. (Talk about it.) Be prepared to talk briefly about Germany. If necessary, go back to the reading and make notes about the following:

Summarizing information

Klima
Größe°   size
Einwohner
Nachbarn

Vokabeln

Nouns are listed with their plural forms: die **Stadt,** ⸚e = die **Städte.**

— Substantive

(das) **Amerika** America
der **Amerikaner, -**/die
 Amerikanerin, -nen American
 person
das **Beispiel, -e** example
der **Deutsche** *(m.)*/die **Deutsche** *(f.)*/
 die **Deutschen** *(pl.)* German person
ein **Deutscher** *(m.)*/eine **Deutsche**
 (f.) a German person
(das) **Deutschland** Germany *(officially:* **Die Bundesrepublik
 Deutschland** The Federal Republic of Germany)
der **Einwohner, -**/die **Einwohnerin,
 -nen** inhabitant
das **Europa** Europe
die **Hauptstadt,** ⸚e capital
der **Kilometer, -** kilometer
das **Klima** climate

das **Land,** ⸚er country, land
die **Million, -en** million
der **Nachbar, -n**/die **Nachbarin,
 -nen** neighbor
das **Nachbarland,** ⸚er neighboring
 country
der **Norden** north
der **Osten** east
(das) **Österreich** Austria
der **Österreicher, -**/die
 Österreicherin, -nen Austrian
 person
der **Ozean** ocean
die **Schweiz** Switzerland
der **Schweizer, -**/die **Schweizerin,
 -nen** Swiss person
die **Stadt,** ⸚e city
der **Süden** south
der **Westen** west
das **Wort,** ⸚er word

— Verben

beeinflussen to influence
denken to think
erzählen to tell, narrate

haben to have
liegen to lie, be situated, be located
sagen to say, tell

— Andere Wörter

als than
also therefore, so
amerikanisch American *(adj.)*
andere other
anders different(ly)
denn *(conj.)* because
deutsch German *(adj.)*
etwa approximately, about
für for
halb half
hier here

in in
kühl cool
mehr more
nach to *(with cities and neuter countries, e.g.,* **nach Berlin; nach
 Deutschland**).
nördlich to the north
nur only
richtig correct, right; real; **richtig
 Sommer** really summer
schon already

so ... wie   as . . . as
von   from; of
warum   why
weiter   farther, further
wie   like; **ein Wort wie heiß**   a
  word like hot

wieder   again
wo   where
ziemlich   quite, rather; **ziemlich
  klein**   rather small

___ Besondere Ausdrücke _____

zum Beispiel (*abbrev.* **z.B.**)   for example (*abbrev.* e.g.)

Erweiterung des Wortschatzes

1 Flavoring particle *aber*

"Flavoring" particles are little words used to express a speaker's attitude
about an utterance. These flavoring particles relate the utterance to something
the speaker or the listener has said or thought. Depending on the choice of
the particle and sometimes on the tone of voice, the speaker expresses interest, surprise, impatience, denial, and so on. Because a particle has various
shades of meaning that depend on the context, a dictionary can give only the
approximate English meaning. With experience you will gain a "feel" for the
meaning and use of these words, which are very characteristic of colloquial
German.

Der Wind ist **aber** kalt.	The wind is really cold.
Heute ist das Wetter **aber** furchtbar.	I think the weather is horrible today, don't you?

In addition to its usual meaning of *but,* **aber** can be used as a flavoring particle. **Aber** often indicates a situation that is somewhat unexpected, or it gives
added emphasis to the speaker's feelings about an utterance.

1. Was bedeutet das? (What does that mean?)   How would you express the
following sentences in idiomatic English?

1. Das Wetter ist aber furchtbar.
2. Der Wind ist aber kalt.
3. Der Sommer ist aber schön.
4. Heute ist es aber heiß.
5. In Kanada ist der Winter aber kalt.
6. Der Wind ist aber furchtbar.

2 The suffix *-in*

Masculine	der Nachbar
Feminine	die Nachbar**in**
Feminine plural	die Nachbar**innen**

The suffix **-in** added to the singular masculine noun gives the feminine equivalent. The plural of a noun with the suffix **-in** ends in **-nen.**

2. Mann oder Frau? Give the other form—feminine or masculine—of the words listed below.

▶   die Professorin   *der Professor*

1. die Sekretärin
2. der Student

3. die Amerikanerin
4. der Einwohner

3 Names of countries

Wie groß ist **Deutschland?**
Existiert **das romantische Deutschland** noch?

How large is Germany?
Does romantic Germany still exist?

The names of most countries are neuter; for example **(das) Deutschland** and **(das) Amerika.** However, articles are not used with names of countries that are neuter, unless the name is preceded by an adjective.

Die Schweiz ist schön.   Switzerland is beautiful.
Die USA sind groß.   The United States is large.

The names of a few countries are feminine (e.g., **die Schweiz**); some names are used only in the plural (e.g., **die USA**). Articles are always used with names of countries that are feminine or plural.

3. Andere Länder Try to guess the English names for the countries listed below.

1. Italien
2. Spanien
3. Griechenland
4. Schweden

5. Rumänien
6. Frankreich
7. Norwegen
8. Bulgarien

9. die Türkei
10. die Niederlande

4 Nouns indicating citizenship and nationality

Berlin	der Berliner	die Berlinerin
England	der Engländer	die Engländerin
Spanien	der Spanier	die Spanierin
Norwegen	der Norweger	die Norwegerin

München	der Münchner	die Münchnerin
Kanada	der Kanadier	die Kanadierin
Deutschland	der Deutsche (Deutscher)	die Deutsche

Nouns indicating an inhabitant of a city or a citizen of a country follow several patterns. While you won't be able to predict the exact form, you will always be able to recognize it.

The noun suffix **-er** is added to the name of many cities, states, or countries to indicate a male citizen or inhabitant (**Berliner**). Some nouns take an umlaut (**Engländer**). To indicate a female citizen or inhabitant the additional suffix **-in** is added to the **-er** suffix (**Berlinerin**).

In some instances the **-er/-erin** is added to a modified form of the country (**Kanadier/Kanadierin**). Other countries have still other forms to indicate the citizen or inhabitant (**Deutscher/Deutsche**).

Mark ist Deutscher.	Mark is (a) German.

Note that to state a person's nationality, German uses the noun directly after a form of **sein.** The indefinite article **ein** is not used, whereas in English nouns of nationality may be preceded by an indefinite article.

Woher kommst du?	Where are you from?
Ich komme aus Frankfurt.	I am from Frankfurt.

To ask in German where someone is from, use the interrogative **woher** and a form of the verb **kommen.** To answer such a question, use a form of the verb **kommen** and the preposition **aus.**

Fluggesellschaften aus vielen Ländern

4. Wo? Woher? Was? Ask your partner several questions based on the chart below.

Sie	*Gesprächspartner/in*
Wo wohnt Anton?	Er wohnt in München.
Woher kommt Anton?	Er kommt aus Deutschland.
Was ist Anton?	Er ist Deutscher.

	Wo? wohnt in	Woher? kommt aus	Was? ist
Anton	München	Deutschland	Deutscher
Heidi	Luxemburg	Luxemburg	Luxemburgerin
Luigi	Florenz	Italien	Italiener
Sven	Oslo	Norwegen	Norweger
Carmen	Barcelona	Spanien	Spanierin
Herr Mozart	Salzburg	Österreich	Österreicher
Kristina	Leipzig	Deutschland	Deutsche
ich			
mein(e) Partner(in)			

5. Woher kommst du? Ask five classmates where they are from. Make notes so you can tell others where they are from.

> Stating one's nationality

Viele Köche verderben den Brei.

GRAMMATIK UND ÜBUNGEN

1 Simple past tense of *sein*

Present	Heute ist das Wetter gut.	The weather is good today.
Simple past	Gestern war es schlecht.	It was bad yesterday.

The simple past tense of **sein** is **war.**

ich **war**	wir waren
du warst	ihr wart
er/es/sie **war**	sie waren
Sie waren	

I was	we were
you were	you were
he/it/she was	they were
you were	

In the simple past, the **ich-** and **er/es/sie-**forms have no verb endings.

1. Nicht gut   Everybody had a bad day yesterday. Tell how the people mentioned below were. Use the past tense of **sein.**

▶   Günter / nervös   *Günter war nervös.*

1. Nicole / müde
2. ich / krank
3. wir / faul
4. Bernd und Eva / nicht sehr nett
5. du / sehr müde
6. ihr / wirklich dumm

2. Wie war das Wetter?   Ask a fellow student what the weather was like on four previous days. Record the answers. You may want to refer to the Supplementary Word Sets in the Reference Section.

Sie	*Gesprächspartner/in*
Wie war das Wetter [am Samstag]?	Es war [schön].
	[Am Samstag] war es [schön].

2 Present tense of *haben*

haben: to have	
ich habe	wir haben
du **hast**	ihr habt
er/es/sie **hat**	sie haben
Sie haben	

The verb **haben** is irregular in the **du-** and **er/es/sie**-forms of the present tense.

3. Wann hast du Geburtstag? Frank and his friends are comparing birthdays. Say that the people mentioned were born in the same months as their friends. Change the form of **haben** to agree with the subject. Add **auch,** as in the model.

▶ Du hast im März Geburtstag. (Jens) *Jens hat auch im März Geburtstag.*

1. Petra hat im Juni Geburtstag. (ich)
2. Wir haben im Februar Geburtstag. (Karin und Urs)
3. Jürgen hat im Mai Geburtstag. (ihr)
4. Ulrike und Thomas haben im September Geburtstag. (wir)
5. Anke hat im März Geburtstag. (du)
6. Ich habe im November Geburtstag. (Ellen)

3 Position of the finite verb in statements

1	2	3	4
Der Sommer	ist	in Deutschland	anders.
In Deutschland	ist	**der Sommer**	anders.

In a German statement, the finite verb is always in second position, even when an element other than the subject (for example, an adverb or a prepositional phrase) is in first position. When an element other than the subject is in first position, the subject follows the verb.

4. Morgen spielen wir Tennis. You and Sonja are talking about possibly playing tennis. Agree with her by restating her comments, beginning with the word in parentheses. Follow the model.

▶ Wir spielen morgen Tennis, nicht? (morgen) *Ja, morgen spielen wir Tennis.*

1. Es ist hoffentlich warm. (hoffentlich)
2. Das Wetter war gestern schlecht, nicht? (gestern)
3. Es ist heute schön, nicht? (heute)

4. Das Wetter war auch am Mittwoch gut, nicht? (am Mittwoch)
5. Das Wetter bleibt jetzt bestimmt gut, nicht? (jetzt)
6. Die Sonne scheint hoffentlich. (hoffentlich)

5. Wie sagt man das? Give the German equivalents of the following statements. Begin your responses with the adverbial element given in parentheses. Be sure the verb is in second position and the subject follows.

1. The sun is shining today. (heute)
2. The weather was also nice yesterday. (gestern)
3. I hope the weather remains nice. (hoffentlich)
4. In Germany the summer is often cold. (in Deutschland)
5. In America the summer is often warm. (in Amerika)
6. It was cold on Thursday. (am Donnerstag)
7. Maybe it'll rain tomorrow. (vielleicht)
8. We're playing tennis tomorrow, aren't we? (morgen)

In German-speaking countries birthdays are celebrated in different ways. The "birthday child" (**Geburtstagskind**) may have an afternoon coffee party (**Geburtstagskaffee**) with family members and friends or a more extensive birthday party in the evening. At the **Geburtstagskaffee** candles are placed around the edge of a birthday cake (**Geburtstagskuchen**) and blown out by the person whose birthday it is. Although the **Geburtstagskind** is often taken out by family members or friends, he or she usually invites friends to a party or brings a cake to work. Besides giving presents (**Geburtstagsgeschenke**), it is common to send a birthday card or make a phone call. Common greetings are: **Herzlichen Glückwunsch zum Geburtstag!** *(Happy Birthday!)* or **Alles Gute zum Geburtstag!** *(All the best on your birthday!)*, and **Ich gratuliere zum Geburtstag!** *(Congratulations on your birthday!)*

In Austria and the predominantly Catholic regions of Germany, name days (**Namenstage**) may be celebrated with as much excitement as a birthday. **Namenstage** commemorate the feast day of one's patron saint. Newspapers and florist shops in these areas typically remind people whose name day is being celebrated and announce the names of people celebrating birthdays.

Ein Geburtstagsfest: Kuchen mit Schlag

6. So ist das Wetter.   Tell when your birthday is and what the weather is usually like at that time of year. Make a brief report to a group of four or to the whole class.

Describing seasonal weather

▶ *Ich habe im Februar Geburtstag. Im Februar ist es kalt. Es schneit oft, und die Sonne scheint nicht viel.*

4 The nominative case

That woman plays tennis well.
She doesn't play volleyball very well.

English uses word order to signal different grammatical functions (e.g., subject) of nouns or pronouns. In a statement in English the subject precedes the verb.

Die Frau spielt gut Tennis.
Volleyball spielt **sie** aber nicht sehr gut.

German uses a different type of signal to indicate the grammatical function of nouns and pronouns. German uses a signal called *case*. When a noun or pronoun is used as the subject of a sentence, it is in the nominative case.

Masculine	Neuter	Feminine
der	das	die

In the nominative case, the German definite article has three forms. They are all equivalent to "the" in English.

Subject	Predicate Noun
Herr Lange ist **Professor.**
Das Mädchen heißt **Gabi Fischer.**
Das ist nicht **der Junge.**

Subject	Predicate Noun
Mr. Lange is *a professor.*
The girl's name is *Gabi Fischer.*
That is not *the boy.*

The nominative case is also used for a *predicate noun*. A predicate noun designates a person, concept, or thing that is equated with the subject. A predicate noun completes the meaning of linking verbs such as **sein** and **heißen**. In a negative sentence **nicht** precedes the predicate noun.

Herzlichen Glückwunsch

ZUM NAMENSTAG

16. Juni — allen Lesern, die Gebhard heißen.

17. Juni — allen Leserinnen, die Marina und Euphemia heißen.

7. Wie war das Wetter?   Practice making comments about the weather. Use the cues provided. Make the comments in the past tense.

▶   Wetter / schön   *Das Wetter war schön.*

1. Morgen / kalt
2. Tag / warm
3. Wind / warm
4. Sonne / heiß

5. Abend / kalt
6. Tag / naß
7. Sommer / trocken
8. Juli / heiß

8. Wie heißen sie?   Your friend can't keep people's names and objects straight. Say that she/he is wrong about each one. In your response use a pronoun and put **nicht** before the predicate noun.

▶   Heißt der Junge Mark?   *Nein, er heißt nicht Mark.*

1. Heißt die Frau Meier?
2. Heißt der Professor Schmidt?
3. Heißt die Professorin Nagel?

4. Heißt die Sekretärin Neumann?
5. Heißt das Mädchen Gisela?
6. Heißt das Kind Dieter?

▶   Ist das der Tisch?   *Nein, das ist nicht der Tisch.*

1. Ist das der Stuhl?
2. Ist das die Lampe?
3. Ist das das Radio?
4. Ist das das Buch?

5. Ist das die Uhr?
6. Ist das der Computer?
7. Ist das die Stereoanlage?

5 Plural of nouns

A thousand years ago English had a variety of ways to signal the plural of nouns. With some nouns it used stem change: *mann — menn (man, men); fōt — fēt (foot, feet);* with other nouns it used endings: *stān — stānas (stone, stones); oxa — oxan (ox, oxen);* and with still other nouns it used no signal at all: *scēap — scēap (sheep, sheep).* Over the centuries the ending *-as* gradually replaced most other plural endings, and its modern development *-(e)s* is now the almost universal signal for the plural of English nouns.

Type	Plural signal	Singular	Plural
1	-	das Fenster	die Fenster
	¨	der Garten	die G**ä**rten
2	**-e**	der Tisch	die Tisch**e**
	¨**e**	der Stuhl	die St**ü**hl**e**
3	**-er**	das Kind	die Kind**er**
	¨**er**	das Buch	die B**ü**ch**er**
4	**-en**	die Frau	die Frau**en**
	-n	die Lampe	die Lampe**n**
	-nen	die Studentin	die Studentin**nen**
5	**-s**	das Radio	die Radio**s**

German uses five basic types of signals to mark the plural of nouns: the endings **-, -e, -er, -(e)n,** and **-s.** Some of the nouns of types 1, 2, and 3 add umlaut in the plural. Nouns of type 4 that end in **-in** add **-nen** in the plural. German makes no gender distinctions in the plural; the definite article **die** is used with all plural nouns.

When you learn a German noun, you must also learn its plural form because there is no sure way of predicting to which plural-type the noun belongs. You will, however, gradually discover that there is a kind of system to the various types. This "system" depends partly on whether the noun is a **der-, das-,** or **die**-noun, and partly on how many syllables it has.

Die Kinder sind nett. **Sie** sind nett.
Die Lampen sind alt. **Sie** sind alt.

The personal pronoun **sie** (they) may refer to persons or things.

In the vocabularies of this book, the plural of most nouns is indicated after the singular forms. For example:

das Zimmer, - indicates that there is no change in the plural form of the noun: **das Zimmer, die Zimmer**

die Stadt, ⸚e indicates that an **-e** is added in the plural, and an umlaut is added to the appropriate vowel: **die Stadt, die Städte**

9. Alt oder neu?   Alex wants to know whether the things in your room are new or old. Tell him that the one is new and the other is old. Use the adverb **da** after the singular noun.

▶ Sind die Stühle neu?   *Der Stuhl da ist neu. Der da ist alt.*

1. Sind die Lampen neu?
2. Sind die Tische neu?
3. Sind die zwei Radios neu?
4. Sind die zwei Betten neu?
5. Sind die zwei Bücher neu?
6. Sind die zwei Uhren neu?

10. Der, das, die   State the noun with the definite article and then give the plural with the definite article.

▶ Tisch   *der Tisch / die Tische*

1. Stuhl
2. Buch
3. Bleistift
4. Kugelschreiber
5. Heft

6. Lampe
7. Radio
8. Computer
9. Gitarre
10. Sekretärin

A thousand years ago there was no standard form of the German language. The large central European area from the North Sea and the Baltic Sea to the Alps in the south was inhabited by many different types of "Germans" who spoke many different kinds of "German."

Martin Luther (1483–1546) played an important role in the development and refinement of German. For his Bible translation and other works, Luther used a form of the language spoken in east central Germany; eventually it became the spoken and written standard for all of Germany as well as Austria and Switzerland. This single standard language is called **Hochdeutsch.** It is used professionally and officially (e.g., in newspapers and on radio and TV).

A recent reaction to the standard use of **Hochdeutsch** in all domains of public life has been the revival of interest in local dialects in many regions. Realizing that dialects are often neglected and that a few of them are dying out, authors, journalists, and pop musicians are making local dialects popular again.

Seit Martin Luther gibt es eine deutsche Sprache.

Eine niederdeutsche Karte: Das tut mir aber leid, daß du krank bist. Werde schnell wieder gesund. Gute Besserung.

Dat deit mie oaver leed. dat Du krank büst.

Weer gau wear gesund.

Gode Bäterung.

Dialects are often incomprehensible to people from different regions and may even differ significantly from town to town. Complete words, intonation, and pronunciation can vary dramatically. (Different ways to say **sprechen,** for example, include **schwätzen** and **schnacken.**) Political borders also have an effect on language development. However, people from different areas within the German-speaking countries such as **Bayern, Sachsen, Burgenland,** or **Tirol** can always communicate with each other in **Hochdeutsch.** This way, German-speaking countries are linguistically unified.

An interesting recent phenomenon is the differences that developed in the two Germanys from 1949 to 1990. Studies show that people in the East tend to use more dialect and speak less formally. Words used in daily life also vary between the East and West. For instance, broiled chicken is called **Broiler** in the East and **gebratenes Hähnchen** in the West.

11. Machen Sie Sätze. (Form sentences.) Make up sentences in the singular and then in the plural. Be sure the subject and verb agree.

▶ Stadt / liegen / im Norden   *Die Stadt liegt im Norden.*
  Die Städte liegen im Norden.

1. Nachbarin / sein / nett
2. Straße / sein / schön
3. Frau / arbeiten / viel
4. Student / arbeiten / nicht viel
5. Mann / spielen / viel Fußball
6. Kind / spielen / gern Volleyball
7. Zimmer / sein / kalt
8. Garten / sein / klein
9. Bild / sein / schön

6 The indefinite article *ein*

Ist das **ein** Radio oder **eine** Uhr?   Is that a radio or a clock?

The German indefinite article **ein** is equivalent to English *a* or *an*.

Masculine	Neuter	Feminine
ein Mann	ein Kind	eine Frau

In the nominative case the German indefinite article has two forms: **ein** for masculine and neuter, and **eine** for feminine. The indefinite article has no plural form.

12. Was ist das? Jan is taking his first drawing course and is showing some of his first attempts to draw things. You're a little doubtful about the results. Use an indefinite article in the response.

▶ Das Kind ist nicht schlecht, nicht?   *Das ist ein Kind?*

1. Die Frau ist gut, nicht?
2. Der Mann ist nicht schlecht, nicht?
3. Das Kind ist schön, nicht?
4. Der Stuhl ist nicht schlecht, nicht?
5. Die Lampe ist lustig, nicht?
6. Die Uhr ist nicht schlecht, nicht?
7. Der Tisch ist schön, nicht?

7 The negative *kein*

Ist das **ein** Radio?	Is that a radio?
Nein, das ist **kein** Radio.	No, that's not a radio.
Sind die Studenten Amerikaner?	Are the students Americans?
Nein, sie sind **keine** Amerikaner.	No, they are not Americans.

The negative form of **ein** is **kein.** It is equivalent to English *not a, not any,* or *no.* It negates a noun that in the positive would be preceded by a form of **ein** or no article at all.

Masculine	Neuter	Feminine	Plural
kein Tisch	**kein** Radio	**keine** Uhr	**keine** Radios

In the nominative case **kein** has two forms: **kein** for masculine and neuter, and **keine** for feminine and plural.

13. Das ist es nicht.   To get back at you Jan pretends he can't figure out what you have drawn. Tell him his guesses are wrong. Use a form of **kein** in your responses.

▶   Ist das eine Frau?   *Nein, das ist keine Frau.*

1. Ist das ein Mann?
2. Ist das ein Mädchen?
3. Ist das ein Kind?
4. Ist das eine Lampe?
5. Ist das ein Zimmer?
6. Ist das ein Tisch?
7. Ist das ein Computer?
8. Ist das eine Pflanze?

14. Das ist es aber nicht.   Gabi compliments you on your drawings, but unfortunately she mistakes what they represent. Use a form of **kein** in the response.

▶   Der Mann ist gut.   *Das ist aber kein Mann.*

1. Die Frau ist gut.
2. Das Kind ist schön.
3. Die Uhr ist gut.
4. Die Tür ist gut.
5. Der Stuhl ist gut.
6. Das Zimmer ist schön.
7. Der Fernseher ist gut.

8 *Kein* vs. *nicht*

Ist das **eine** Uhr?	Nein, das ist **keine** Uhr.
Ist das **die** Uhr?	Nein, das ist **nicht die** Uhr.
Sind sie Amerikaner?	Nein, sie sind **keine** Amerikaner.

Kein is used to negate a noun that in an affirmative sentence would be preceded by **ein** or no article at all. **Nicht** is used when negating a noun preceded by a definite article.

15. Nicht oder kein? Answer the following questions in the negative. Use **nicht** or **kein** before the predicate noun, as appropriate.

▶ *München ist die Hauptstadt von Deutschland, nicht?* *Nein, München ist nicht die Hauptstadt von Deutschland.*

▶ *Das ist ein Kugelschreiber, nicht?* *Nein, das ist kein Kugelschreiber.*

1. Ist das ein Stuhl?
2. Ist das die Gartenstraße?
3. Ist das das Buch?
4. Ist Hamburg die Hauptstadt von Deutschland?
5. Ist das eine Straße?

16. Kein oder nicht? Gerd is reviewing with Tanja some basic German words. With a partner complete the following exchanges in German. Then continue on your own using the models. You may point to objects in the classroom or in the drawing of a student's room in *Kapitel 1*, or use information from the **Lesestück.**

1. *Gerd:* Ist das ein Tisch?
   Tanja: Nein. Das ist _____ . Das ist ein Stuhl.
2. *Gerd:* Die Lampe ist schön, nicht?
   Tanja: Das ist aber _____ . Das ist eine Gitarre.
3. *Gerd:* Ist Dresden die Hauptstadt von Deutschland?
   Tanja: Nein, Dresden ist _____ . Berlin ist _____ .

9 Proper names showing possession

Das ist **Giselas** Buch.	That is Gisela's book.
Das ist **Jens'** Kuli.	That is Jens's ballpoint pen.

A proper name is a word that designates a specific individual or place (e.g., Ingrid, Berlin). In German as in English, possession and other close relationships are expressed by adding **-s** to the proper names. If the name already ends in a sibilant, no **-s** is added. In written German, an apostrophe is used only when no **-s** is added (e.g., Jens' Kuli).

17. Ist das Gerds Buch? After a club meeting you and a friend are straightening up. Tell your friend to whom the various things belong. Use the possessive form of the proper name.

▶ Gerd / Buch   *Das ist Gerds Buch.*

1. Beate / Kuli
2. Bruno / Lampe
3. Franz / Radio
4. Regina / Heft
5. Thomas / Büchertasche
6. Sylvia / Uhr

10 Possessive adjectives

Mein Zimmer ist groß.	My room is large.
Ist **dein** Zimmer groß?	Is your room large?
Ist **sein** Zimmer groß?	Is his room large?
Ist **ihr** Zimmer groß?	Is her room large?
Unser Zimmer ist groß.	Our room is large.
Ist **euer** Zimmer groß?	Is your room large?
Ist **ihr** Zimmer groß?	Is their room large?
Ist **Ihr** Zimmer groß?	Is your room large?

German possessive adjectives are equivalent in meaning to the English possessive adjectives, such as *my, his,* and *her.* Context usually makes clear whether **ihr** is the subject pronoun *you,* the adjective *her* or *their,* or the adjective *your.* Note that **Ihr** *(your)* is capitalized, just as the corresponding subject pronoun **Sie** *(you)* is.

der Bleistift	Wo ist ein Bleistift?
	Wo ist **mein** Bleistift?
das Heft	Wo ist ein Heft?
	Wo ist **mein** Heft?
die Uhr	Wo ist eine Uhr?
	Wo ist **meine** Uhr?
die Bücher	Wo sind **meine** Bücher?

Since possessive adjectives take the same endings as **ein,** they are frequently called **ein-**words.

Wo ist **euer** Radio? Wo sind **eure** Bücher?

When **euer** has an ending, the **-e-** preceding the **-r-** is usually omitted.

18. So ist es.   You are discussing several persons' things. Say that the things are similar. Use the cued possessive adjectives.

▶ Ingrids Zimmer ist groß. (dein)   *Dein Zimmer auch.*

1. Daniels Lampe ist schön. (dein)
2. Ingrids Stühle sind neu. (euer)
3. Ingrids Tisch ist sehr alt. (sein)
4. Daniels Garten ist klein. (mein)
5. Brunos Bilder sind furchtbar. (unser)
6. Brunos Poster sind anders. (ihr)

19. Wie sagt man das?   Complete the sentences with the German equivalents of the cued words.

▶ _____ Mann arbeitet nicht. *(her)*   *Ihr Mann arbeitet nicht.*

1. _____ Kind heißt Dieter. *(their)*
2. _____ Frau ist lustig. *(his)*
3. Barbara, Frank, was für ein Mensch ist _____ Nachbar? *(your)*
4. Wo sind _____ Kinder, Frau Neumann? *(your)*
5. Ich glaube, das ist _____ Kuli. *(my)*
6. Ist das _____ Uhr, Gisela? *(your)*

◆ *Negating nouns preceded by possessive adjectives*

Ist das dein Heft?   Nein, das ist nicht mein Heft.

Nicht is used to negate a noun that is preceded by a possessive adjective.

11 Demonstrative pronouns *der, das, die*

Lore spielt viel Tischtennis, nicht?   Lore plays a lot of table tennis, doesn't she?

Ja, **die** spielt wirklich gut.   Yes, she plays really well.

Mark spielt viel Fußball.   Mark plays a lot of soccer.
Ja, **der** spielt aber schlecht.   Yes, but he plays poorly.

Franz und Kurt spielen heute gut.   Franz and Kurt are playing well today.
Ja, **die** spielen wirklich gut.   Yes, they are playing really well.

Der, das, and **die** are often used as demonstrative pronouns to replace nouns. A demonstrative pronoun is used instead of a personal pronoun (**er, sie, es**) when the pronoun is to be emphasized. Demonstrative pronouns usually occur at or near the beginning of a sentence. The English equivalent is usually a personal pronoun (*he, she, it, they*).

20. Ja, so sind die. Dieter is speaking on the phone with Renate. They're discussing friends and agreeing with each other. Use a demonstrative pronoun as the subject.

▶ Barbara ist intelligent, nicht? *Ja, die ist wirklich intelligent.*

1. Thomas war gestern traurig, nicht?
2. Professor Müller ist freundlich, nicht?
3. Die Kinder sind heute lustig, nicht?
4. Gerd und Dieter sind faul, nicht?
5. Frau Professor Dörflinger ist nett, nicht?
6. Max und Christine waren gestern froh, nicht?

WIEDERHOLUNG

1. Singular, Plural Give the singular and plural forms of each noun. Give the appropriate form of the definite article with each noun.

▶ Einwohner *der Einwohner, die Einwohner*

1. Mädchen
2. Stadt
3. Wort
4. Student
5. Tag
6. Woche
7. Mann
8. Frau
9. Nachbarin
10. Stuhl
11. Kugelschreiber
12. Fenster

2. Machen Sie Sätze. Form sentences, using the cues provided.

▶ du / gehen / morgen / ? *Gehst du morgen?*

1. warum / ihr / spielen / heute / wieder / Tennis / ?
2. Jens / arbeiten / heute abend / nicht /
3. er / glauben / das / nicht
4. wer / sagen / das / ?
5. sie (*pl.*) / schwimmen / gern
6. ich / sagen / nichts
7. wo / liegen / Deutschland / ?
8. Deutschland / liegen / weiter nördlich / als Amerika
9. vielleicht / es / regnen / morgen
10. hoffentlich / die Sonne / scheinen

3. Wer, wie, wo, was? Form questions that elicit the responses given. Begin the questions with the cued words.

▶ Danke, gut. *(Wie)*   *Wie geht es Ihnen?*

1. Das Wetter ist schön. *(Wie)*
2. In Deutschland ist das Wetter im Sommer oft kühl. *(Wo)*
3. Nein, es regnet heute nicht. *(Regnet)*
4. Ja, der Tag war schön. *(War)*
5. Herr Braun sagt das oft. *(Wer)*
6. Die Studenten gehen heute abend. *(Wann)*
7. Dieter spielt gern Tennis. *(Was)*
8. Gabi arbeitet in München. *(Wo)*
9. Nadja kommt aus Wien. *(Woher)*
10. Anton ist lustig. *(Was für ein Mensch)*
11. Valerie ist 20. *(Wie alt)*

4. Wie sagt man das? Give the German equivalents of the sentences below.

▶ It's raining.   *Es regnet.*

1. It's not raining.
2. Does she believe that?
3. What do you think?
4. Is she saying that?
5. Do you swim well?
6. What are you saying?
7. Who's going tomorrow?
8. How often does he do that?
9. Is Dieter working today?
10. We play a lot of tennis.
11. Where do you come from?
12. Where are we playing chess tomorrow?

5. So sind sie. Pick people known locally, nationally, or internationally and say two or three things about them.

▶ Steffi Graf ist groß und ernst. Sie spielt gut Tennis.

Steffi Graf und Boris Becker — Tennis-Profis aus Deutschland

6. Wo? Wann? Wie?   Exchange information with a partner about where you were on your last vacation, when, and what the weather was like.

▶ Ich war im Juli in Alaska. Das Wetter war sehr schön.

7. Woher kommst du?   Assume the role of either student 1 (S1) or student 2 (S2). When you have completed the conversation, exchange roles and try it again.

S1: Find out where your partner is from.
S2: Answer by giving your hometown.
S1: Ask what the weather is like there at this time of year.
S2: Respond.

8. Anregung   Imagine you have just arrived in Germany. Write a short paragraph (4–5 sentences) in German about Germany. You may want to mention weather, size, and population.

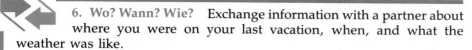

GRAMMATIK: ZUSAMMENFASSUNG

Simple past tense of *sein*

ich **war**	wir waren
du warst	ihr wart
er/es/sie **war**	sie waren
Sie waren	

Present tense of *haben*

ich habe	wir haben
du **hast**	ihr habt
er/es/sie **hat**	sie haben
Sie haben	

Position of the finite verb in statements

	1	2	3	4
	Subject	**Verb**	**Adverb**	**Adjective**
Normal	**Der Sommer**	ist	in Deutschland	anders.
	Adverb	**Verb**	**Subject**	**Adjective**
Inverted	In Deutschland	ist	**der Sommer**	anders.

In a German statement, the verb is always in second position. In so-called normal word order, the subject is in first position. In so-called inverted word order, something other than the subject (for example, an adverb, an adjective, or indirect object) is in first position, and the subject follows the verb.

Plural of nouns

Type	Plural signal	Singular	Plural
1	- *(no change)*	das Zimmer	die Zimmer
	∺	der Garten	die G**ä**rten
2	**-e**	das Heft	die Heft**e**
	∺e	die Stadt	die St**ä**dt**e**
3	**-er**	das Kind	die Kind**er**
	∺er	der Mann	die M**ä**nn**er**
4	**-en**	die Tür	die Tür**en**
	-n	die Lampe	die Lampe**n**
	-nen	die Studentin	die Studentin**nen**
5	**-s**	das Radio	die Radio**s**

Nominative case of definite articles, indefinite articles, and *kein*

	Masculine	**Neuter**	**Feminine**	**Plural**
Definite article	der ⎫	das ⎫	die ⎫	die ⎫
Indefinite article	ein ⎬Stuhl	ein ⎬Radio	eine ⎬Lampe	— ⎬Bücher
kein	kein ⎭	kein ⎭	keine ⎭	keine ⎭

Kein vs. nicht

Ist das **eine** Uhr?	Nein, das ist **keine** Uhr.
Ist das **die** Uhr?	Nein, das ist **nicht die** Uhr.
Ist das **deine** Uhr?	Nein, das ist **nicht meine** Uhr.

Kein is used to negate a noun that would be preceded by **ein** or no article at all in an affirmative sentence. **Nicht** is used in a negative sentence when the noun is preceded by a definite article (**die**) or a possessive adjective (**meine**). (For positions of **nicht**, see *Kapitel 2*, Grammatik und Übungen, section 8.)

Possessive adjectives

◆ Forms and meanings

Singular			Plural		
ich:	**mein**	my	wir:	**unser**	our
du:	**dein**	your	ihr:	**euer**	your
er:	**sein**	his, its			
es:	**sein**	its	sie:	**ihr**	their
sie:	**ihr**	her, its			
	Sie:	**Ihr** your			

◆ Nominative of possessive adjectives

Masculine		Neuter		Feminine		Plural	
ein		ein		eine		—	
mein	Tisch	**mein**	Radio	**meine**	Uhr	**meine**	Bücher
unser		**unser**		**unsere**		**unsere**	

Demonstrative pronouns and personal pronouns

	Masculine	Neuter	Feminine	Plural
Personal Pronouns	er	es	sie	sie
Demonstrative Pronouns	der	das	die	die

Zum Einkaufen braucht man
eine Einkaufstasche.

Kapitel 4

LERNZIELE

SPRECHAKTE

Talking about shopping and buying groceries
Expressing and inquiring about need
Discussing meals
Inquiring about personal habits
Offering advice and making requests
Giving directives
Expressing likes and dislikes

GRAMMATIK

Verbs with stem-vowel change *e > i*
Word order: time and place expressions
Imperatives
Direct objects
Accusative case
Expressing likes and dislikes with *gern*
Es gibt

VOKABELN

Flavoring particles: *denn, ja,* and *doch*
Common foods
Noun compounds
Days of the week as adverbs
Units of weight, capacity, measurement, and
quantity

LANDESKUNDE

Apotheke and *Drogerie*
Types of bread
Shopping for groceries
Specialty stores vs. supermarkets
Typical German breakfast
Outdoor markets
Currency in German-speaking countries
Shopping hours

BAUSTEINE FÜR GESPRÄCHE

Was brauchst du?

Jochen: Gibt es hier eine Apotheke?
Heike: Ja, was brauchst du denn?
Jochen: Ich brauche etwas gegen Kopfschmerzen.
Heike: Nimmst du Aspirin? Das habe ich.

What do you need?

Is there a pharmacy (around) here?
Yes, what do you need?
I need something for a headache.

Do you take aspirin? I have that.

Gehst du heute einkaufen?

Jürgen: Gehst du heute nicht einkaufen?
Petra: Doch. Warum fragst du?
Jürgen: Wir haben keinen Kaffee mehr.
Petra: Ein Pfund ist genug, nicht? Sonst noch etwas?
Jürgen: Ja, ein Brot. Kauf das doch bei Rischart. Da ist das Brot besser.

Are you going shopping today?

Aren't you going shopping today?

Of course. Why do you ask?
We don't have any more coffee.

One pound is enough, right? Anything else?
Yes, a loaf of bread. But buy that at Rischart's. The bread is better there.

Aus dem Hause  *Dallmayr in München*

An **Apotheke** sells both prescription and non-prescription drugs. In every town and in each section of a large city, one **Apotheke** offers emergency service (**Notdienst**) at night and on Sunday. An **Apotheke** is staffed by a pharmacist (**Apotheker/in**). A **Drogerie** sells a wide variety of toiletries and often herbal remedies as well as many other items found in American drugstores. The **Drogerie** is gradually being replaced by the larger, self-service drugstore (**Drogeriemarkt**). A druggist (**Drogist**) is trained in a three-year apprenticeship.

Im Drogeriemarkt bedient man sich selbst.

In der Apotheke kann man Medikamente kaufen.

There are generally fewer over-the-counter drugs in Germany than in the U.S. Some drugs, such as aspirin, which are non-prescription, are, nevertheless, **apothekenpflichtig** in Germany, that is, to purchase them, one must go to an **Apotheke.** They cannot be found in supermarkets or **Drogerien.**

1. Rollenspiel   While staying in a hotel, you develop a splitting headache on Sunday afternoon. You ask the desk clerk to direct you to a drugstore. The desk clerk consults the **Notdienst** *(emergency service)* newspaper listing and tells you the name, address, and telephone number of a few drugstores open on the weekend. Be sure to note the information you are given.

Notdienste

Von Samstag, 13 Uhr, bis Sonntag, 8.30 Uhr, haben folgende Apotheken Notdienst.

Victoria-Apotheke, Thomas-Mann-Str. 52, Tel. 63 25 06. Flora-Apotheke, Clemens-August-Straße 42, Tel. 22 24 85. Lessing-Apotheke, Beuel, Hermannstr. 72, Tel. 47 56 20. Hardt-Apotheke, Medinghoven, Europaring 42, Tel. 64 38 62. Apotheke am Römerplatz, Bad Godesberg, Rheinstr. 3, Tel. 36 41 04 u. 35 51 68. Martin-Apotheke, Bad Godesberg/Muffendorf, Hopmannstr. 7, Tel. 32 33 06

Von Sonntag, 8.30 Uhr, bis Montag, 8.30 Uhr, haben folgende Apotheken Notdienst.

Einhorn-Apotheke, Poststr. 34, Tel. 65 28 33 u. 63 63 57. Adler-Apotheke, Bonner Talweg/Ecke Weberstr., Tel. 21 05 87. Apotheke im Tannenbusch, Tannenbusch, Paulusplatz 13, Tel. 66 24 56. Kreuz-Apotheke, Oberkassel, Königswinterer Str. 673, Tel. 44 12 11. Engel-Apotheke, Duisdorf, Rochusstr. 192, Tel. 62 26 18. Robert-Koch-Apotheke, Bad Godesberg, Beethovenallee 19, Tel. 35 36 69.

Sie

Welche Apotheken sind offen°?

Gesprächspartner/in

Die Adler-Apotheke, Bonner Talweg/Ecke Weberstraße, 21 05 87.

---

2. Was suchen Sie?   Think of three things you need to buy. A fellow student or your instructor asks what kind of store you're looking for. Respond. You may want to refer to the Supplementary Word Sets in the Reference Section for names of specialty shops.

> Inquiring about shopping possibilities

Gesprächspartner/in

Was suchst° du?
Was suchen Sie?

Sie

Ich brauche	Brot. Gibt es hier	eine Bäckerei°?
	Aspirin.	eine Apotheke?
	Wurst°.	eine Metzgerei°?
	Spaghetti°.	einen Supermarkt°?
	einen Kamm°.	eine Drogerie°?

3. Geh doch. Your friend needs some things. Tell her/him to go to the store that sells them.

Expressing needs

Gesprächspartner/in		Sie	
Ich brauche	**etwas gegen Kopfschmerzen.**	Geh doch°	**in die Apotheke.**
	Brot für morgen.		zum Bäcker.
	Wurst für heute abend.		zum Metzger.
	Spaghetti.		in den Supermarkt.
	ein Heft.		ins Kaufhaus°.
	ein Buch über° Schach.		in die Buchhandlung°.

4. Sonst noch etwas? You've been telling a friend what you need, but there's something you've forgotten. What is it? When she/he asks whether there's anything else you need, say what it is.

Gesprächspartner/in	Sie	
Brauchst du sonst noch etwas?	Ja, wir haben	**kein Brot** mehr.
		keine Spaghetti
		kein Bier°
		keinen Kaffee
		keine Butter°

5. Kopfschmerzen Your instructor or fellow student asks you whether you have a headache. Respond appropriately.

Gesprächspartner/in	Sie
Haben Sie Kopfschmerzen?	Ja, furchtbar.
Hast du	Ja, ich brauche Aspirin.
	Ja, leider.
	Nein, warum fragst du/fragen Sie?
	Nein, ich habe keine Kopfschmerzen.

6. Gespräche Construct two dialogues based on the elements provided. Remember to add words where they are needed and to use the proper word order. A double slash (//) indicates that you should begin a new sentence.

1. **Michael:** wo / sein / hier / Apotheke / ?
   Lore: warum / fragen / ?
   Michael: brauchen / etwas / gegen / Kopfschmerzen
2. **Frau Schmidt:** Wetter / sein / furchtbar
   Herr Braun: ja / leider // hoffentlich / scheinen / Sonne / morgen
   Frau Schmidt: glauben / nicht // regnen / bestimmt / wieder

Vokabeln

Starting in *Kapitel 4* vowel changes in the present tense will be noted in parentheses following the infinitive of the verb, e.g., **essen (ißt)**.

— Substantive

das **Abendessen, -** evening meal
die **Apotheke, -n** pharmacy
das **Aspirin** aspirin
der **Bäcker, -** baker
die **Bäckerei, -en** bakery
das **Bier, -e** beer
das **Brot, -e** bread
die **Buchhandlung, -en** bookstore
die **Butter** butter
die **Drogerie, -n** drugstore
das **Essen, -** meal; prepared food
das **Frühstück** breakfast
das **Haus, ⁼er** house
der **Kaffee** coffee
der **Kamm, ⁼e** comb

das **Kaufhaus, ⁼er** department
  store
die **Kopfschmerzen** *(pl.)* headache
der **Metzger, -** butcher
die **Metzgerei, -en** butcher shop,
  meat market
das **Mittagessen** midday meal
das **Pfund, -e** pound (= 1.1 U.S.
  pounds; *abbrev. Pfd.*)
die **Spaghetti** *(pl.)* spaghetti
der **Supermarkt, ⁼e** supermarket
die **Tasche, -n** bag; pocket
die **Torte, -n** fancy multi-layer cake
die **Wurst ⁼e** sausage, lunch meat

— Verben

brauchen to need
einkaufen to shop
essen (ißt) to eat
fragen to ask

kaufen to buy
nehmen (nimmt) to take
suchen to look for
trinken to drink

— Andere Wörter

bei at; at a place of business (**beim
  [Metzger]**); at the home of (**bei
  [Ingrid]**)
besser better
doch yes *(after a negative question or
  statement)*

ein paar a few
gegen against
genug enough
kein not a, not any
sonst otherwise
über about

— Besondere Ausdrücke

beim Bäcker at the baker's (bakery)
beim Metzger at the butcher's
  (butcher shop)
es gibt there is; there are
in die Apotheke to the pharmacy

in den Supermarkt to the super-
  market
kein ... mehr no more . . .
Sonst noch etwas? Anything else?
Was gibt's zum [Abendessen]
  What's for [dinner/supper]?

zum Abendessen   for the evening
  meal, for dinner
zum Bäcker   to the baker's (bakery)
zum Frühstück   for breakfast

zum Metzger   to the butcher's
  (butcher shop)
zum Mittagessen   for the midday
  meal, for lunch

Erweiterung des Wortschatzes

1 Flavoring particle *denn*

Detlev: Was brauchst du **denn**?
Ute: Spaghetti.
Detlev: Machst du **denn** wieder
  Spaghetti?

Tell me, what do you need?
Spaghetti.
You mean you're making spaghetti
  again?

Denn is used frequently in questions to show the personal interest of the
speaker. It softens the speaker's question and makes it less abrupt. **Denn** also
refers back to a previous utterance of the speaker or listener or to a topic
familiar to both.

**Hier kann man viele verschiedene
Brotsorten kaufen. (Bäckerei in Wien)**

Approximately 200 sorts of bread, 30 types of
rolls, and 1200 types of cookies (**Kleingebäck**),
pastries, and cakes (**Kuchen** and **Torten**) are
baked in the German-speaking countries. Names
and shapes vary from region to region. The bread
has a firmer and sometimes coarser texture than
American bread, and is used at almost every
meal. Open-faced sandwiches (**belegte Brote**)
are popular for breakfast, the evening meal, and
as a light lunch and are usually eaten with a knife
and fork. The typical breakfast would not be complete without a crisp **Brötchen** or **Semmel,** as
rolls are called in many areas. Bread is made
from a wide variety of grains, including rye
(**Roggen**) and wheat (**Weizen**). **Vollkornbrot** is
made of unrefined, crushed grain. Other types of
bread have linseed (**Leinsamenbrot**) and sun-
flower (**Sonnenblumenbrot**) added to them.
  There are bread museums in Ulm,
Mollenfelde, and Detmold which often feature
Gebildbrote, "picture breads", in the shapes of
animals, wreaths, even violins.

2 Flavoring particle *doch*

The flavoring particle **doch** is used to express several shades of meaning.

Du machst **doch** heute Spaghetti, nicht?	You're making spaghetti today, aren't you?
Das glaubst du **doch** nicht.	{ You surely don't believe that. { You can't really believe that.

The speaker uses **doch** to ask the listener for corroboration. "This is really true, isn't it?"

Geh **doch** in den Supermarkt!	Why don't you go to the supermarket?
Machen Sie es **doch**!	Go ahead and do it.

The speaker uses **doch** to persuade the listener to do something.

Das ist **doch** dumm.	You must know that that's stupid.

The speaker uses **doch** to express slight impatience: "Come on, really . . . ."

3 *Doch* as a way to correct negative false assumptions

Jochen: Es regnet heute nicht.	It's not going to rain today.
Heike: **Doch.**	But it is.

In addition to its function as a flavoring particle, **doch** may be used to contradict the assumption contained in a previous negative assertion.

4 *Doch* as a positive response to a negative question

Jürgen: Gehst du heute nicht einkaufen?	Aren't you going shopping today?
Petra: **Doch.**	Of course I am.

Doch may be used as a positive response to a negative question.

1. Doch oder ja?   Respond in the positive, using **doch** or **ja** as appropriate.

▶   Arbeitest du heute nicht?   *Doch.*
▶   Gehst du um sieben?   *Ja.*

1. Brauchen wir Brot?
2. Gehst du nicht zum Bäcker?
3. Hast du kein Aspirin?
4. Gibt es hier eine Apotheke?
5. Klaus spielt gut Tennis, nicht?
6. Treibst du auch viel Sport?
7. Andrea spielt nicht gut Tennis.
8. Du glaubst das nicht.

5 Lebensmittel

1. der Fisch, -e	8. das Brot, -e	14. die Butter
2. der Kaffee	9. das Brötchen, -	15. die Kartoffel, -n
3. der Käse	10. das Ei, -er	16. die Limonade
4. der Kuchen, -	11. das Fleisch	17. die Margarine
5. der Saft	12. das Gemüse	18. die Milch
6. der Tee	13. das Obst	
7. der Wein, -e		

2. Was ißt du? Interview fellow students to learn what they eat at various meals.

| Talking about meals and food |

Sie   *Gesprächspartner/in*

Was	ißt du	**zum Frühstück°?**	Ich esse [zwei Brötchen].
	trinkst° du	zum Mittagessen°?	Ich trinke [Orangensaft]°
		zum Abendessen°?	

3. Wo? Wann? Was? Your partner has invited you over to eat. Find out more information, such as your partner's address, what time you will be eating, and what you will be eating.

Im Supermarkt muß man seine Sachen selbst einpacken.

Traditionally, Germans would do their food shopping in small stores (**Tante-Emma-Läden**). However, their popularity has decreased in the last 25 years. In 1972 there were 160,400 small food stores in the Federal Republic. By 1990 there were only 67,000 and the number is expected to decrease to 55,000 by the year 2000. Today Germans do most of their food shopping in supermarkets, which tend to be smaller than American ones and are located within walking distance of residential areas. But there are also huge markets on the outskirts of cities which sell not only groceries, but a wide variety of items ranging from clothing to electronic equipment, even pre-fabricated houses. Many people go shopping several times a week. Although the markets are self-service stores, fresh food such as cheeses, sausages and cold cuts, bread, and vegetables may be sold by shop assistants at separate counters.

Customers carry their own shopping bags (**Einkaufstaschen**) to the supermarkets or buy plastic bags (**Plastiktüten**) at the check-out counter. Customers pack their own groceries and generally pay for their purchases with cash (**Bargeld**), not by check.

EINKAUFEN IN DEUTSCHLAND

Vorbereitung auf das Lesen

◆ *Zum Thema*

1. Where do you think people in your area do most of their food shopping? In supermarkets? Or in small stores (for example, buying bread at a bakery, meat at a butcher shop, fish at a fish market)? How about you?
2. Do most people in your area open a can of coffee or grind their own coffee beans? How about you?
3. Would people in your area be likely to buy cut flowers every weekend? How about you?
4. Name some other shopping habits you think are common in your area.

◆ *Leitfragen*

1. What is the role of small specialty stores in Germany (die **Bäckerei,** bakery / die **Metzgerei,** butcher shop) versus supermarkets (der **Supermarkt**)?
2. Many Germans shop at open-air markets. Are they more like supermarkets or specialty stores?
3. Would Germans be likely to buy cut flowers for the weekend?
4. How does the German pharmacy (die **Apotheke**) differ from the drugstore (die **Drogerie**)?

---

*E*s ist Samstag. Monika macht Frühstück. Sie macht es besonders schön, denn Diane und Joan aus° Amerika sind da. Ihre Schwester Andrea kommt in die Küche°, und Monika sagt: „Du, Andrea, wir haben keinen Kaffee und keine Marmelade mehr. Geh bitte zu Meiers und kauf Kaffee und
5 Marmelade." Andrea nimmt Einkaufstasche und Geld und geht. Nebenan° ist noch ein Tante-Emma-Laden°. Da kauft sie manchmal morgens ein°. Da kennt man sie. Hoffentlich schließt der nicht auch bald, denkt Andrea. Viele Leute gehen jetzt in den Supermarkt, denn da ist es natürlich billiger. Aber hier ist es viel persönlicher°.
10   Herr Meier sagt: „Guten Morgen, Frau Stamer. Was bekommen Sie denn heute?"
    „Ich brauche Kaffee, ein Pfund."
    „Ungemahlen°, wie immer?"
    „Ja, natürlich. Und dann brauche ich noch Marmelade. Ich nehme zwei
15 Sorten°."

Margin glosses:
from
kitchen

next door
mom-and-pop store / **kauft ein** = shops

more personal

unground

kinds

Einige Leute kaufen immer noch gern im Tante-Emma-Laden ein.

„Haben Sie denn Besuch?"

„Ja, Freundinnen aus Amerika sind da. — Gut, das ist alles für heute."
Andrea nimmt noch eine Morgenzeitung und bezahlt.

„Auf Wiedersehen, Frau Stamer, und schönes Wochenende!"

20 „Danke. Tschüß, Herr Meier."

Der Bäcker ist gegenüber°. Da riecht es immer so gut. Andrea kauft   across from here
Brötchen. Die sind noch ganz warm. Und ein Vollkornbrot° von gestern   wholemeal bread
nimmt sie auch noch.

Das Frühstück ist wirklich sehr gut. Joan und Diane finden die Brötchen
25 und den Kaffee besonders gut. Monika sagt: „Wir mahlen° ihn° ja auch selbst   grind / it
und kochen ihn dann gleich. So verliert er kein Aroma." Joan denkt:
Wirklich?

Später gehen die Vier zusammen auf° den Markt. Sie kaufen Erbsen° und   to / peas
zwei Kilo Kartoffeln fürs° Mittagessen. Der Fischmann ist auch da. Hier   = für das
30 kaufen sie frischen Fisch. Den essen sie zum Abendessen. Joan sagt: „Das
Einkaufen° hier ist nicht schlecht. Nur die Einkaufstaschen sind etwas   shopping
schwer." Dann gehen sie auf den Blumenmarkt. Für wenig Geld bekommen
sie einen sehr schönen Strauß°. Monika kommt oft samstags mit Blumen nach   bouquet
Hause.

35 Auf dem Weg nach Hause gehen sie noch in eine Drogerie. Monika
braucht einen Kamm und Andrea einen Lippenstift°. Diane fragt: „Wo ist   lipstick
denn hier das Aspirin? Ich brauche Aspirin und Vitamintabletten." Monika
fragt: „Bist du denn krank?" — „Nein, ich nehme immer Vitamintabletten."
Monika denkt: Wirklich? Und sie sagt: „Hier, die Vitamintabletten stehen
40 hier. Aber Aspirin hat eine Apotheke." So gehen sie noch in die Apotheke.
Dann haben sie endlich alles, wenigstens bis Montag.

Fragen zum Lesestück

1. Welcher Tag ist es?
2. Warum macht Monika das Frühstück besonders schön?
3. Was brauchen Monika und Andrea?
4. Was für ein Laden ist nebenan?
5. Warum schließen Meiers vielleicht bald?
6. Wo ist es persönlicher, bei Meiers oder im Supermarkt?
7. Und wo ist es billiger?
8. Warum kauft Andrea zwei Sorten Marmelade?
9. Was kauft Andrea noch?
10. Von wann ist das Vollkornbrot? Und die Brötchen?
11. Was finden Joan und Diane besonders gut? Warum?
12. Was glaubt Monika — warum verliert der Kaffee kein Aroma?
13. Was machen die Vier später?
14. Was gibt es auf dem Markt?
15. Für wann kaufen sie den Fisch?
16. Joan findet das Einkaufen nicht schlecht. Warum findet sie es dann doch nicht so gut?
17. Was kauft Monika oft samstags?
18. Wer hat Vitamintabletten, die Drogerie oder die Apotheke?
19. Wer hat Aspirin?

1. Erzählen Sie. How do Monika and Andrea's shopping habits differ from Joan and Diane's—or your own? Be prepared to say one or two sentences in class. Use the following topics to get you started.

Kaffee ◇ Supermarkt ◇ Einkaufstasche ◇ Blumen ◇ Vitamintabletten

2. Machen wir das amerikanisch. You and your roommate are expecting a guest from Germany for the weekend. Discuss your shopping plans. Will you buy items to make the guest feel at home or introduce her to American shopping and eating habits?

Sie	*Gesprächspartner/in*
Monika kommt morgen. Wir müssen Brötchen und Marmelade zum Frühstück kaufen.	Nein. Machen wir das amerikanisch.

A German breakfast (**Frühstück**) can be quite extensive, especially on weekends or holidays. Usually it consists of a hot beverage, fresh rolls (**Brötchen**) or bread, butter and jam; often there are cold cuts, an egg, cheese or perhaps yogurt, whole grain granola (**Müsli**), and juice or fruit. Pancakes are not a common breakfast food. Eggs for breakfast are usually soft-boiled (**weichgekocht**). Scrambled eggs (**Rühreier**) and fried eggs (**Spiegeleier**) are more often served for a light meal either for lunch or in the evening. Traditionally, the main warm meal of the day was eaten at noon (**Mittagessen**). Recently, however, more and more people prefer to eat their warm meal in the evening (**Abendessen**).

Zum Frühstück gibt es Brötchen, Marmelade, Kaffee und Milch.

Vokabeln

— Substantive

der **Besuch, -e** visit; **wir haben Besuch** we have company
die **Blume, -n** flower
das **Brötchen, -** roll
die **Einkaufstasche, -n** shopping bag
der **Freund, -e**/die **Freundin, -nen** friend
das **Geld** money
das **Glas, ⁼er** glass
das **Gramm** gram (*abbrev.* **g**)
das **Kilo(gramm)** kilogram (*abbrev.* **kg**)
der **Laden, ⁼** store
die **Lebensmittel** (*pl.*) food; groceries

die **Leute** (*pl.*) people
der **Liter, -** liter (*abbrev.* **l** = 1.056 U.S. quarts)
die **Mark, -** mark; die **Deutsche Mark (DM)** German currency
der **Markt, ⁼e** market
die **Marmelade** marmalade, jam
die **Schwester, -n** sister
das **Stück, -e** piece
die **Tablette, -n** tablet, pill
die **Tasse, -n** cup
der **Weg, -e** way
das **Wochenende, -n** weekend
die **Zeitung, -en** newspaper

— Verben

bekommen to receive
bezahlen to pay (for); **sie bezahlt das Essen** she pays for the meal
finden to find; **wie findest du das Brot?** how do you like the bread?
geben (gibt) to give

kennen to know, be acquainted with
kochen to cook
riechen to smell
schließen to close
stehen to stand, be located
verlieren to lose

— Andere Wörter

alles everything, all
besonders especially, particularly
billig cheap; **billiger** cheaper
endlich finally
etwas some, somewhat
frisch fresh
gleich immediately; same; similar
immer always
manchmal sometimes

morgens mornings, every morning
natürlich natural(ly); of course
samstags (on) Saturdays
schwer heavy; difficult
selbst oneself, myself [etc.]
viele many
wenig little; **wenige** few
wie as
zu to

— Besondere Ausdrücke

auf dem Weg on the way
Besuch haben to have company
nach Hause (to go) home
Nimmst du Kaffee oder Tee? Are you having coffee or tea?

Schönes Wochenende! Have a nice weekend!
wie immer as always
zu Abend essen to have dinner
zu Mittag essen to have lunch

Erweiterung des Wortschatzes

1 Flavoring particle *ja*

Wir mahlen ihn **ja** selbst. 　　We grind it ourselves, of course [as we both know].

Ja may be used by a speaker to express the belief that an utterance is related to a condition that both the speaker and the listener are aware of, or should be aware of.

2 Noun compounds

die **Blumen** + der **Markt** = der **Blumenmarkt**
flowers + market = flower market

kaufen + das **Haus** = das **Kaufhaus**
to buy + building = department store

A characteristic of German is its ability to form noun compounds easily. Where German uses compounds, English often uses separate words. Your vocabulary will increase rapidly if you learn to analyze the component parts of compounds.

der Kopf + **die** Schmerzen = **die** Kopfschmerzen
der Fisch + **der** Mann = **der** Fischmann

The last element of a compound determines its gender.

1. Was bedeutet das? (What does that mean?)   The compounds listed below are made up of cognates and familiar nouns. Give the English equivalent of each.

1. der Winterabend
2. der Sommertag
3. die Marktfrau
4. der Sonnenschein

5. die Tischlampe
6. die Morgenzeitung
7. die Zimmertür

3 Days of the week and parts of days as adverbs

Noun	Adverb	English equivalent
Montag	montags	Mondays
Samstag	samstags	Saturdays
Morgen	morgens	mornings
Abend	abends	evenings

A noun that names a day of the week or a part of a day may be used as an adverb to indicate repetition or habitual action. An **-s** is added to the noun. In writing, adverbs are not capitalized.

2. Ein Interview   Interview a partner. Record her/his responses.

Wann ißt du mehr — mittags oder abends?
Wann bist du sehr müde — morgens oder abends?
Wann arbeitest du mehr — samstags oder sonntags?
Wann gehst du einkaufen — freitags, samstags, oder wann?
Gehst du morgens oder abends einkaufen?

> Inquiring about personal habits

In towns and cities of the German-speaking countries it is very common to shop at an outdoor market (**Markt**). Some markets are held daily, others once or twice a week, still others, like the famous **Viktualienmarkt** in Munich have become permanent and are open the same hours as regular stores. At the **Markt** farmers from the region sell fresh vegetables, fruit, flowers, eggs, herbs, and teas. There may also be stands (**Stände**) with bread, fish, and sausages. In smaller towns, these markets are often integrated into the medieval town architecture (e.g., in Freiburg). In bigger cities Turkish or Italian markets, which have sprung up with the presence of foreign workers, sell their specialties from home. Hamburg's famous **Fischmarkt** in the St. Pauli harbor district opens very early on Sunday mornings and sells not only fish but a great variety of products from all over the world.

Auf dem Markt sind die Sachen frisch, und die Auswahl ist groß. (Weimar)

4 Units of weight and capacity

```
1 Kilo(gramm) (kg) = 1000 Gramm
1 Pfund (Pfd.)      =  500 Gramm
1 Liter (l)
```

In the United States a system of weight is used in which a pound consists of 16 ounces. In German-speaking countries the metric system is used: the basic unit of weight is the **Gramm,** and a thousand grams are a **Kilo(gramm).** German speakers also use the older term **Pfund** for half a **Kilo(gramm),** or **500 (fünfhundert) Gramm.** The American *pound* equals **454 Gramm.** The basic unit of capacity in the German-speaking countries is the liter. A liter equals 1.056 quarts.

5 Units of measurement and quantity

Geben Sie mir zwei **Pfund** Kaffee.	Give me two pounds of coffee.
Ich nehme zwei **Glas** Milch.	I'll take two glasses of milk.
Er kauft zwei **Liter** Milch.	He's buying two liters of milk.
Sie ißt zwei **Stück** Kuchen.	She's eating two pieces of cake.

In German, masculine and neuter nouns expressing measure, weight, or number are in the singular. Note that feminine nouns are in the plural: **Sie trinkt zwei Tassen Kaffee.** *(She drinks two cups of coffee.)*

3. Einkaufen   Answer the questions affirmatively, as in the model.

▶ Wieviel Pfund Kaffee kaufen Sie? zwei?   *Ja, ich kaufe zwei Pfund Kaffee.*

1. Wieviel Pfund Fisch kaufen Sie? drei?
2. Wieviel Pfund Butter kaufen Sie? zwei?
3. Wieviel Liter Milch kaufen Sie? vier?
4. Wieviel Gramm Tee kaufen Sie? 250?
5. Wieviel Gramm Käse kaufen Sie? 200?
6. Wieviel Kilo Kartoffeln kaufen Sie? fünf?
7. Wieviel Glas Marmelade kaufen Sie? zwei?

Wieviel Geld bekommt der junge Mann? (Bank in Hannover)

Germany's basic monetary unit is the **Deutsche Mark (DM),** referred to as the **Mark** when speaking. There are 100 **Pfennig** in a **Mark.** Switzerland's basic unit, the **Franken (sFr.)** is roughly equal in value to the **Mark.** There are 100 **Rappen (Rp.)** in a **Franken.** Austria's basic unit is the **Schilling (S).** The **Schilling** is a much smaller unit than the **Mark:** a piece of cake costs about 28 **Schilling,** the equivalent of 4**DM.** There are 100 **Groschen** in a **Schilling.** In order to make identification of the different denominations clearer, each of the German-speaking countries prints the bills in various colors, and their size increases with their value. For example, the green 20**DM** bill (**Schein**) is larger than the blue 10**DM** bill.

4. Essen und Trinken Ask your partner how much he/she drinks and eats of certain things.

Trinkst du Kaffee oder Tee zum Frühstück? Wie viele Tassen?
Trinkst du Milch oder Limonade zum Mittagessen? Wieviel Glas?
Trinkst du Orangensaft zum Frühstück? Wieviel Glas?
Ißt du Kuchen zum Abendessen? Wieviel Stück?

5. Einkaufen You and a partner plan to go grocery shopping. You are on a tight budget and are planning to buy only the items advertised at **Preisring-Markt.** You have 25 Marks to spend. Make a list of the items you need, how much of each item you need, and what the cost of each item is. If you need help, see Vocabulary for Authentic Text Activities in the Reference Section.

> Buying groceries

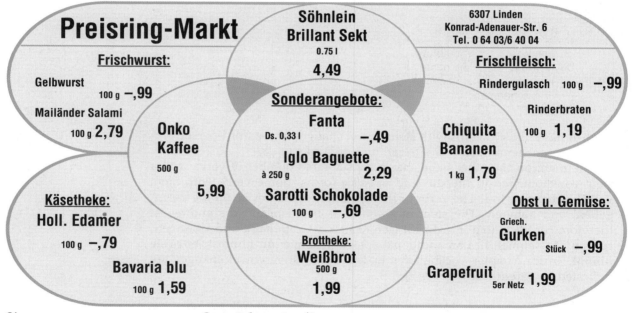

Preisring-Markt

6307 Linden
Konrad-Adenauer-Str. 6
Tel. 0 64 03/6 40 04

Söhnlein Brillant Sekt
0.75 l
4,49

Frischwurst:
Gelbwurst 100 g **−,99**
Mailänder Salami 100 g **2,79**

Onko Kaffee
500 g
5,99

Sonderangebote:
Fanta Ds. 0,33 l **−,49**
Iglo Baguette à 250 g **2,29**
Sarotti Schokolade 100 g **−,69**

Frischfleisch:
Rindergulasch 100 g **−,99**
Rinderbraten 100 g **1,19**

Chiquita Bananen
1 kg **1,79**

Käsetheke:
Holl. Edamer 100 g **−,79**
Bavaria blu 100 g **1,59**

Brottheke:
Weißbrot 500 g **1,99**

Obst u. Gemüse:
Griech. **Gurken** Stück **−,99**
Grapefruit 5er Netz **1,99**

Sie	*Gesprächspartner/in*
Wir brauchen Kaffee, nicht?	Ja. Wieviel?
500 Gramm.	Gut. Wieviel kostet der?
Fünf Mark neunundneunzig.	
	Wir brauchen Bananen, nicht?
Ja. Wieviel?	2 Kilo.
Gut. Wieviel macht das?	Drei Mark achtundfünfzig.

GRAMMATIK UND ÜBUNGEN

1 Verbs with stem-vowel change *e > i*

essen: to eat	
ich esse	wir essen
du **ißt**	ihr eßt
er/es/sie **ißt**	sie essen
Sie essen	

geben: to give	
ich gebe	wir geben
du **gibst**	ihr gebt
er/es/sie **gibt**	sie geben
Sie geben	

nehmen: to take	
ich nehme	wir nehmen
du **nimmst**	ihr nehmt
er/es/sie **nimmt**	sie nehmen
Sie nehmen	

English has only two verbs with stem-vowel changes in the third-person singular, present tense: *say > says (sezz)*, and *do > does (duzz)*.

German, on the other hand, has a considerable number of verbs with a stem-vowel change in the **du-** and **er/es/sie**-forms. Some verbs with stem vowel **e** change **e** to **i**. The verbs of this type that you know so far are **essen, geben,** and **nehmen.** The stem of **essen** ends in a sibilant; the ending **-st** therefore contracts to a **-t = du ißt** (see *Kapitel 2, Grammatik und Übungen,* section 7). **Nehmen** has an additional spelling change: **du nimmst, er/es/sie nimmt.** In the chapter vocabularies in this book, stem-vowel changes are indicated in parentheses: **geben (gibt).**

1. Was geben wir Inge? Inge needs things for her room at college. Tell what various friends are giving her. Use the proper form of **geben.**

▶ Walter / zwei alte Stühle   *Walter gibt Inge zwei alte Stühle.*

1. Claudia / zwei Hefte
2. Dietmar und Jens / ein Radio
3. wir / eine Lampe
4. ihr / eine Uhr
5. Frau Hauff / eine Büchertasche
6. du / ein Buch über Musik
7. ich / zwei Kugelschreiber

2. Was nehmen wir? You're in a restaurant with a group of friends. Indicate what you think each person will have. Use the proper form of **nehmen.**

▶ Grete / Kaffee   *Grete nimmt Kaffee, nicht?*

1. du / Tee
2. Franz / Milch
3. ihr / etwas Obst
4. wir / Wurst und Brot
5. Volker und Inge / Käse und Brot
6. Tanja / Kuchen

3. Was essen sie gern? You are planning a picnic. Ask what the people listed below would like to eat. Use the proper form of **essen.**

▶ Frank   *Was ißt Frank gern?*

1. du
2. Barbara
3. Alex und Dieter

4. ihr
5. Paula
6. Sie

4. Was ißt du? A friend asks questions about your eating habits.

Answering questions about eating habits

Gesprächspartner/in		*Sie*	
Nimmst du	Vitamintabletten?	Ja,	**viel.**
			immer
Nimmst du	oft Aspirin?	Ja, aber nicht viel.	
Ißt du viel	**Brot?**	Nein, nicht sehr	**oft.**
	Kuchen		viel
	Obst		gern
	Gemüse	Was ißt du gern?	
	Käse		

5. Wir haben Hunger. You and your roommate have been studying until two o'clock in the morning and you are suddenly very hungry. You decide to raid the refrigerator (**Kühlschrank**). Since the selection is limited, you have to agree on who will get what to eat.

▶ *Wir haben keine Wurst. Wir haben nur noch Käse. Was nimmst du?*

2 Word order with expressions of time and place

Time Place
Sie geht heute in die Buchhandlung.

Place	**Time**
She's going to the bookstore today.	

When a German sentence contains both a time expression and a place expression, the time expression precedes the place expression.

6. Wann gehst du? Your friend is trying to guess when you're going to do various errands. Confirm the guesses.

▶ Wann gehst du in die Stadt? Heute morgen?   *Ja, ich gehe heute morgen in die Stadt.*

1. Wann gehst du in den Supermarkt? Um neun?
2. Wann gehst du in die Buchhandlung? Morgen?
3. Wann gehst du zum Bäcker? Später?
4. Wann gehst du in die Apotheke? Heute morgen?
5. Wann gehst du ins Kaufhaus? Jetzt?

3 Imperatives

The imperative forms are used to express commands, offer suggestions and encouragement, give instructions, and try to persuade people. In both German and English, the verb is in the first position.

Infinitive	**Imperative**		
	du-**Form**	*ihr*-**Form**	*Sie*-**Form**
fragen	frag(e)	fragt	fragen Sie
arbeiten	arbeite	arbeitet	arbeiten Sie
geben	gib	gebt	geben Sie
sein	sei	seid	seien Sie

◆ **du-***imperative*

Erna. { **Frag(e)** Frau List.
Arbeite jetzt, bitte.
Gib mir bitte das Brot.
Nimm doch zwei Aspirin.

Erna. { Ask Mrs. List.
Work now, please.
Give me the bread, please.
Why don't you take two aspirin?

The **du**-imperative consists of the stem of a verb plus **-e,** but the **-e** is often dropped in informal usage: **frage** > **frag.** If the stem of the verb ends in **-d** or **-t,** the **-e** may not be omitted in written German: **arbeite.** If the stem vowel of a verb changes from **e** to **i,** the imperative has this vowel change and never has final **-e: geben** > **gib, essen** > **iß, nehmen** > **nimm.**

◆ **ihr-***imperative*

Günter. Peter. { **Fragt** Frau List.
Gebt mir bitte
das Brot.

Günter. Peter. { Ask Mrs. List.
Give me the
bread, please.

The **ihr**-imperative is identical with the **ihr**-form of the present tense.

◆ **Sie-***imperative*

Herr Hahn. { **Fragen Sie** Frau List.
Geben Sie mir
bitte das Brot.

Mr. Hahn. { Ask Mrs. List.
Give me the
bread, please.

The **Sie**-imperative is identical with the **Sie**-form of the present tense. The pronoun **Sie** is always stated and follows the verb directly. In speech, one differentiates a command from a general question by the inflection of the voice. As in English, the voice rises at the end of a general question and falls at the end of a command.

◆ *Imperative of* **sein**

Anton, **sei** nicht so nervös!   Anton, don't be so nervous!
Kinder, **seid** jetzt ruhig!   Children, be quiet now!
Frau Weibl, **seien Sie** bitte   Mrs. Weibl, please be
    so gut und …   so kind and . . .

Note that the **du**-imperative (**sei**) and **Sie**-imperative (**seien Sie**) are different from the present tense forms: **du bist, Sie sind.**

7. Auf einer Party: Frau Berg und Julia The Bergs have guests. Below are some things Frau Berg says to Sarah and Martin, two people she knows well. She also knows Julia well. How would she say the same things to her?

> Offering advice and
> making requests

▶   Sarah und Martin, nehmt noch etwas Käse.   *Julia, nimm noch etwas Käse.*

1. Trinkt doch noch ein Glas Wein.
2. Sagt mal, wie findet ihr die Musik?
3. Seid so nett und spielt etwas Gitarre.
4. Eßt noch etwas.
5. Kommt, hier sind unsere Fotos von Berlin.
6. Bleibt noch ein wenig hier.
7. Seid so gut und gebt mir eure Telefonnummer.

8. Auf einer Party: Frau Berg und Herr Fromme   Herr Fromme is an acquaintance but not a personal friend of Frau Berg. Frau Berg uses **Sie** when speaking with him. How would she say the same things to him she said to Sarah and Martin in *exercise 7*?

9. Macht das.   Volker and Inge are planning a surprise party for Jürgen. They need your help for the final decisions. Give them your advice. Use the **ihr**-imperative.

Offering advice

▶   Geben wir Jürgen ein Buch oder ein Radio? (Radio)   *Gebt Jürgen ein Radio.*

1. Machen wir die Party bei Inge oder bei Volker? (Inge)
2. Kochen wir Spaghetti oder Gulasch? (Spaghetti)
3. Essen wir Brot oder Gemüse dazu? (Brot)
4. Kaufen wir das Brot im Supermarkt oder beim Bäcker? (beim Bäcker)
5. Trinken wir Wein oder Mineralwasser? (Mineralwasser)
6. Machen wir eine große oder eine kleine Party? (eine kleine Party)

10. Wie sagt man das?   Give the German equivalents of the commands below. Use the **du-** or **ihr**-imperative as appropriate with first names and the **Sie**-imperative with last names.

▶   Stay here, Sylvia.   *Bleib hier, Sylvia.*
▶   Don't ask, Mr. Braun.   *Fragen Sie nicht, Herr Braun.*

1. Don't work too much, Inge.
2. Say something, Udo.
3. Go to the supermarket, Gisela and Tanja.
4. Don't believe that, Jörg and Thomas.
5. Please buy bread and sausage, Mr. Jahn.
6. Eat the bread now, Tanja.
7. Take aspirin, Alex.
8. Be so kind, Mrs. Schulz, and stay here.
9. Alex, be quiet.
10. Please have some cake, Mrs. Holz. (use **nehmen**)

   11. Mach das.   Say the following things in German to your partner.

Giving directives

Take my book.
Say the days of the week.
Ask me something.
Say hello to [Paul].
Give me your pen.

4 Direct object

Kennst du **Lotte Schneider**?	Do you know Lotte Schneider?
Frank ißt gern **Kuchen**.	Frank likes to eat cake.

The direct object is the noun or pronoun that receives or is affected by the action of the verb. The direct object answers the question whom (**Lotte**) or what (**Kuchen**).

5 Accusative of the definite articles *der, das, die*

	Nominative	Accusative
Masculine	**Der** Kaffee ist billig.	Nehmen Sie **den** Kaffee.
Neuter	**Das** Brot ist frisch.	Nehmen Sie **das** Brot.
Feminine	**Die** Marmelade ist gut.	Nehmen Sie **die** Marmelade.
Plural	**Die** Blumen sind schön.	Nehmen Sie **die** Blumen.

The direct object of a verb is in the accusative case. In the accusative case, the definite article **der** changes to **den.** The articles **das** and **die** do not show case change in the accusative.

12. Einkaufen gehen   A friend is shopping for things for her/his room. Ask whether she/he intends to buy the things. The things become direct objects in your questions.

▶   Die Lampe ist lustig.   *Kaufst du die Lampe oder nicht?*

1. Das Radio ist gut.
2. Der Stuhl ist billig.
3. Der Tisch ist schön.
4. Das Bett ist groß.
5. Die Uhr ist billig.
6. Die Blumen sind schön.

In der Kürze liegt die Würze.

6 Word order and case as signals of meaning

Subject	Verb	Direct object
The man	asks	the professor something.
The professor	asks	the man something.

English usually uses word order to signal the difference between a subject and a direct object. The usual word-order pattern in statements is *subject, verb,* and *direct object.* The two sentences above have very different meanings.

Subject (nom.)	Verb	Direct object (acc.)
Der Mann	fragt	den Professor etwas.

Direct object (acc.)	Verb	Subject (nom.)
Den Professor	fragt	der Mann etwas.

German generally uses case to signal the difference between a subject and a direct object. The different case forms of the definite article (e.g., **der, den**) signal the grammatical function of the noun. **Der,** in the example above, indicates that the noun **Mann** is in the nominative case and functions as the subject. **Den** indicates that the noun **Professor** is in the accusative case and functions as the direct object. The word-order pattern in statements may be *subject, verb, direct object,* or *direct object, verb, subject.* The two sentences above have the same meaning.

Since German uses case to signal grammatical function, it can use word order for another purpose: to present information from different perspectives. A speaker may use "normal" word order *(subject, verb, direct object)* or inverted word order *(direct object, verb, subject).* The English equivalents vary, depending on context and the meaning the speaker wishes to convey. The sentence **Der Mann fragt den Professor etwas** is equivalent to *The man asks the professor something.* The sentence **Den Professor fragt der Mann etwas** is equivalent to saying something like *It's **the professor** the man is asking something.*

Der Professor fragt **die** Studentin etwas.	The professor asks the student something.

When only one noun or noun phrase shows case, it may be difficult at first to distinguish meaning. In the example above, **der Professor** has to be the subject, since the definite article **der** clearly shows nominative case. By the process of elimination, therefore, **die Studentin** has to be the direct object.

Die Frau fragt **das** Mädchen etwas.

Sometimes neither noun contains a signal for case. In an example like the one above, one would usually assume normal word order: *The woman asks the girl something.* Depending on context, however, it is possible to interpret it as inverted word order: *It's **the woman** the girl is asking something.*

13. Das Subjekt?   Identify the subject of the sentences below; then give their English equivalents.

▶   Das Mädchen findet der Junge nett.   *der Junge / It's the girl the boy finds nice.*

1. Den Kuchen kauft die Frau morgen.
2. Der Mann kocht den Kaffee.
3. Den Mann hört die Frau aber nicht.
4. Der Junge fragt das Mädchen etwas.
5. Den Kuchen essen die Kinder gern.
6. Die Amerikaner kennt die Frau nicht.
7. Das Mädchen kennt die Frau gut.

7 Direct object vs. predicate noun

| **Predicate noun** | Der **Mann** ist [heißt] **Dieter Müller.** | The man is Dieter Müller. |
| **Direct object** | Ich kenne **den Mann** gut. | I know the man well. |

The predicate noun designates a person, concept, or thing that is equated with the subject. A predicate noun completes the meaning of linking verbs such as **sein** and **heißen** and is in the nominative.

The direct object is the noun or pronoun that receives or is related to the action of the verb. The direct object noun or pronoun is in the accusative case.

| **Predicate noun** | Das ist **nicht** Gisela Meier. |
| **Direct object** | Ich kenne Gisela Meier **nicht.** |

Nicht precedes a predicate noun and usually follows a noun or pronoun used as a direct object.

14. Nominativ oder Akkusativ?   Identify the direct object or predicate noun.

▶   Das ist **Frau Schmidt.**   *predicate noun*
▶   Fragen Sie **Frau Schmidt.**   *direct object*

1. Ißt du viel Obst?
2. Das ist kein Obst.
3. Der Junge heißt Max.
4. Kennst du Max gut?
5. Kaufst du das Bild von Hamburg?
6. Das ist doch kein Bild von Hamburg.

Geschäftszeiten

Mo, Di, Mi + Fr	8⁰⁰ – 18³⁰ h	
Do	8⁰⁰ – 19³⁰ h	
Sa	8³⁰ – 14⁰⁰ h	
1.Sa von April- September	8³⁰ – 16⁰⁰ h	
1.Sa von Oktober - März	8³⁰ – 18⁰⁰ h	

CITY APOTHEKE ZUM LÖWEN

Im Winter ist diese Apotheke am langen Samstag bis 18 Uhr geöffnet.

For many people in the German-speaking countries, shopping is an integral part of daily life. Going shopping several times a week and walking to a store are very common. Although most food shopping is done in supermarkets, specialty stores (**Fachgeschäfte**) like the bakery, butcher shop, or fruit and vegetable store are still frequently patronized. Some customers enjoy the more personal atmosphere and the convenient location of these neighborhood stores, where they are often known and greeted by name.

Business hours for stores are regulated by law. In Germany, stores may be open from 7:00 A.M. to 6:30 P.M. on weekdays except Thursdays, when stores may be open until 8:30 P.M. Stores close no later than 2:00 P.M. on Saturday; however, on the first Saturday of each month (**langer Samstag**) and the four Saturdays before Christmas they may stay open until 6:00 P.M. Many neighborhood stores close during the early afternoon (**Mittagspause**) from about 1:00 to 3:00. On Sundays most stores are closed. Exceptions are made for flower shops (**Blumenläden**) and pastry shops (**Konditoreien**) which often open for a few hours on Sunday morning. Another exception are stores which serve the traveling public in train stations and airports.

The shop closing law (**Ladenschlußgesetz**) has been a controversial topic for the last few years, and various arrangements for lengthening shopping hours have been suggested. Business-people and consumers generally support longer hours, but the unions strictly oppose further changes because the present law allows employees to work regular hours and have a full weekend with their families.

15. Was kaufst du? You are selling things in your room or apartment. Several people ask the price. After you tell them, they decide whether to buy it. You may wish to refer to the **Studentenzimmer** in *Kapitel 1*.

Gesprächspartner/in	*Sie*
Was kostet [der Stuhl]?	[Zwanzig] Mark.
Gut. Ich kaufe/nehme [den Stuhl]./	
Das ist zuviel. Ich kaufe/nehme [den Stuhl] nicht.	

8 Demonstrative pronouns in the accusative case

Wie findest du **den** Kaffee?	How do you like the coffee?
Den finde ich gut.	This is (really) good!
Wie findest du **das** Fleisch?	How do you like the meat?
Das finde ich gut.	That's (really) good!
Wie findest du **die** Torte?	How do you like the cake?
Die finde ich gut.	That is (really) good!
Wie findest du **die** Eier?	How do you like the eggs?
Die finde ich gut.	Those are (really) good!

The accusative forms of the demonstrative pronouns are identical to the accusative forms of the definite articles.

16. Nein, das finde ich nicht. You and Gabi are shopping in a department store. Disagree with all of her opinions.

▶ Ich finde das Musikheft billig. Du auch? *Nein, das finde ich nicht billig.*

1. Ich finde das Buch über Schach schlecht. Du auch?
2. Ich finde die Buchhandlung zu klein. Du auch?
3. Ich finde den Kugelschreiber billig. Du auch?
4. Ich finde die Lampe schön. Du auch?
5. Ich finde das Radio gut. Du auch?
6. Ich finde den Tisch richtig fürs Zimmer. Du auch?
7. Ich finde die Stühle furchtbar. Du auch?
8. Ich finde die Uhr zu groß. Du auch?

17. Im Tante-Emma-Laden You run a small store. A customer has come to you with a shopping list. Unfortunately, your store doesn't carry these items. Send her/him to the appropriate store. You may want to refer to the Supplementary Word Sets in the Reference Section for names of specialty shops.

Giving directives

Gesprächspartner/in		*Sie*		
Ich brauche	**Kaffee.**	Kaufe	**den**	**bei Müller.**
	Butter	Kaufen Sie	die	im Supermarkt.
	Käse		das	beim Metzger.
	Wurst			beim Bäcker.
	Brot			im Kaufhaus.
	Tee			
	Papier			

9 Accusative of *wer*?

Nominative	Accusative
Wer fragt?	**Wen** fragt sie?

The accusative case form of the interrogative pronoun **wer?** *(who?)* is **wen?** *(whom?)*.

18. Wen? You keep missing the ends of people's statements at a party. Ask who they are talking about. Replace the direct object with **wen?** to pose your questions.

▶ Ich frage den Professor morgen.   *Wen fragst du morgen?*

1. Thomas fragt Birgit heute abend.
2. Martina findet Detlev lustig.
3. Ich finde Stefan intelligent.
4. Ich frage Professor Ulmer morgen.
5. Ulrike kennt die Amerikaner gut.

10 The construction *haben + gern*

Ich **habe** Inge **gern.**   I like Inge.
Ich **habe** Mark **nicht gern.**   I don't like Mark.

In *Kapitel 2,* you learned how to say you liked to do something by using a verb plus **gern: Ich schwimme gern.** A common way of expressing fondness for someone in German is to use **haben + gern. Nicht gern** is used to express dislike.

19. Wen hast du gern? Tell your partner about people you know or about famous people, such as musicians, politicians, and athletes you like or don't like and why.

> Expressing likes and dislikes

▶ *Ich habe Boris Becker gern. Er spielt gut Tennis.*
▶ *Ich habe Inge nicht gern. Sie ist unfreundlich.*

11 Accusative of *ein* and *kein*

	Nominative	Accusative
Masculine	Wo ist **ein** Bleistift?	Haben Sie **einen** Bleistift?
	Da ist **kein** Bleistift.	Ich habe **keinen** Bleistift.
Neuter	Wo ist **ein** Heft?	Haben Sie **ein** Heft?
	Da ist **kein** Heft.	Ich habe **kein** Heft.
Feminine	Wo ist **eine** Uhr?	Haben Sie **eine** Uhr?
	Da ist **keine** Uhr.	Ich habe **keine** Uhr.
Plural	Sind das Kulis?	Haben Sie Kulis?
	Da sind **keine** Kulis.	Ich habe **keine** Kulis.

The indefinite article **ein** and the negative **kein** change to **einen** and **keinen** before masculine nouns in the accusative singular. The neuter and feminine indefinite articles and their corresponding negatives do not show case changes in the accusative singular. **Ein** has no plural forms. **Kein,** however, does have a plural form: **keine.**

20. Was brauchst du? You're moving into an apartment with two other students. Tell your friends what you need in the way of furniture. Use **ein** with the direct object.

▶ ein Tisch   *Ich brauche einen Tisch.*

1. ein Stuhl
2. eine Lampe
3. ein Bett
4. eine Uhr
5. ein Radio
6. ein Bücherregal
7. ein Fernseher

21. Nein, das brauche ich nicht. You have changed your mind and decided you don't need what your friends suggest. Repeat Ex. 20 using **kein** with the direct object.

▶ ein Tisch   *Ich brauche keinen Tisch.*

12 Accusative of possessive adjectives

	Nominative	Accusative
Masculine	Ist das **mein** Bleistift?	Ja, ich habe **deinen** Bleistift.
Neuter	Ist das **mein** Heft?	Ja, ich habe **dein** Heft.
Feminine	Ist das **meine** Uhr?	Ja, ich habe **deine** Uhr.
Plural	Sind das **meine** Kulis?	Ja, ich habe **deine** Kulis.

The possessive adjectives (**mein, dein, sein, ihr, unser, euer, Ihr**) have the same endings as the indefinite article **ein** in both the nominative and accusative cases.

22. Wie, bitte? Restate, using the cued possessive adjective. The possessive adjective modifies the direct object.

▶ Freitags bekomme ich Geld. (mein)   *Freitags bekomme ich mein Geld.*

1. Brauchst du einen Kuli? (dein)
2. Er findet die Arbeit furchtbar. (sein)
3. Frank gibt Anja ein Radio. (sein)
4. Gabi gibt Andreas ein Buch. (ihr)
5. Die Studenten fragen den Professor viel. (ihr)
6. Wir sehen die Freunde oft und gern. (unser)
7. Warum ißt du den Kuchen nicht? (dein)

13 Impersonal expression *es gibt*

Gibt es hier einen   Is there a supermarket here?
  Supermarkt?
Es gibt heute Butterkuchen.   There's [We're having] butter cake today.

Es gibt is equivalent to English *there is* or *there are*. It is followed by the accusative case.

23. Was gibt's? Form sentences, using the cues below.

▶ es / geben / heute / kein Kuchen   *Es gibt heute keinen Kuchen.*

1. es / geben / auch / kein Kaffee
2. geben / es / noch / Brötchen / ?
3. nein, es / geben / keine Brötchen
4. es / geben / heute / bestimmt / Schnee
5. nein, es / geben / kein Schnee
6. es / geben / aber / Regen

24. Wie sagt man das? Give the German equivalents of the sentences below. Material in parentheses is not to be translated.

▶ Where are you buying the fish?   *Wo kaufst du den Fisch?*

1. We're cooking the fish this evening.
2. Do you like to eat cake? (Use the verb **essen** + **gern.**)
3. How do you like the cheese? Good? (Use the verb **finden.**)
4. Give Mrs. Schneider the coffee, Michael.
5. Who's paying (for) everything? (Use the verb **bezahlen.**)
6. Whom are you asking?
7. Who is buying the wine?
   —That [is what] I'm buying.

14 Prepositions

Margot kauft die Uhr **für ihren Freund.** Margot is buying the watch for her friend.

Margot kauft die Uhr **für ihn.** Margot is buying the watch for him.

A preposition (e.g., **für**–*for*) is used to show the relation of a noun (e.g., **Freund**–*friend*) or pronoun (e.g., **ihn**–*him*) to some other word in the sentence (e.g., **kauft**–*buying*). The noun or pronoun following the preposition is called the object of the preposition.

15 Accusative prepositions

durch	through	Sie geht **durch** die Buchhandlung.
für	for	Sie kauft es **für** das Haus.
gegen	against	Sie hat nichts **gegen** den Mann.
ohne	without	Sie geht **ohne** das Kind.
um	around	Sie geht **um** den Tisch.

The objects of the prepositions **durch, für, gegen, ohne,** and **um** are always in the accusative case.

Er geht **durchs** Zimmer.	durch das = **durchs**
Er kauft es **fürs** Haus.	für das = **fürs**
Er geht **ums** Haus.	um das = **ums**

The prepositions **durch, für,** and **um** often contract with the definite article **das** to form **durchs, fürs,** and **ums.** These contractions are common in colloquial German, but are not required.

25. Etwas anderes Substitute the cued words for the italicized words in the sentences below. Make any other necessary changes.

▶ Ursel geht durch die *Buchhandlung.* (Supermarkt) *Ursel geht durch den Supermarkt.*

1. Walter geht durch das *Zimmer.* (Stadt, Garten)
2. Volker sagt etwas gegen die *Frau.* (Mann, Mädchen)
3. Trudi kauft es für *Frau Hof.* (Kind, ihr Freund, ihre Freundin)
4. Wir gehen um die *Stadt.* (Haus)
5. Susanne geht ohne *Frau Wagner.* (ihre Kinder, ihr Mann)

16 Accusative of masculine *N*-nouns

Nominative	Accusative
Der Herr sagt etwas.	Hören Sie **den** Her**rn?**
Der Student sagt etwas.	Hören Sie **den** Student**en?**

German has a class of masculine nouns that have signals for case. Not only the article, but the noun itself ends in **-n** or **-en** in the accusative. This class of nouns may be referred to as masculine **N**-nouns or "weak nouns." In the vocabularies of this book, masculine **N**-nouns will be followed by two endings: **der Herr, -n, -en.** The first ending is the singular accusative and the second is the plural ending. The masculine **N**-nouns you know so far are **der Herr, der Junge, der Mensch, der Nachbar,** and **der Student.**

26. Wie sagt man das? Give the German equivalents of the conversational exchanges below.

1. Do you like the gentleman there, Mrs. Kluge?
   —Yes. He's a neighbor.
2. Why is the neighbor going around the house?
   —Ask Mr. Heidemann.
3. Why is Mr. Leber coming without the children?
   —He's buying books for the children.
4. I have nothing against Mr. Knecht.
   —Who's Mr. Knecht?

17 Accusative of personal pronouns

Nominative	Accusative		
Subject	**Object**	**Subject**	**Object**
Er braucht	**mich.**	*He* needs	*me.*
Ich arbeite für	**ihn.**	*I* work for	*him.*

Pronouns used as direct objects or objects of accusative prepositions are in the accusative case.

Subject pronouns	I	you	he	she	it	we	you	they
Object pronouns	me	you	him	her	it	us	you	them

Some English pronouns have different forms when used as subject or as object.

Nominative	ich	du	er	es	sie	wir	ihr	sie	Sie
Accusative	**mich**	**dich**	**ihn**	**es**	**sie**	**uns**	**euch**	**sie**	**Sie**

Some German pronouns also have different forms in the nominative and accusative.

27. Nein danke! Mark wants to lend you all his things. Say you don't need them. Use a pronoun in each answer.

▶ Brauchst du mein Buch über Schach? *Nein, danke, ich brauche es nicht.*

1. Brauchst du meinen Fußball?
2. Brauchst du mein Musikheft?
3. Brauchst du meinen Kugelschreiber?

4. Brauchst du meine Lampe?
5. Brauchst du meine Stühle?
6. Brauchst du meinen Tisch?

28. Wie sagt man das? Give the German equivalents of the conversational exchanges below.

1. Who is working for us?
   —We're working for you.
2. Are you asking me?
   —Yes, I'm asking you.
3. What do you have against me?
   —I have nothing against you, Herr Schuhmacher.
4. Do you know Uwe and Barbara?
   —Yes. I like them.

WIEDERHOLUNG

1. Noch einmal (Once more) Restate the sentences below, beginning with the words in italics. Make the necessary changes in word order.

▶ Andrea und Monika essen Brötchen *zum Frühstück.*   *Zum Frühstück essen Andrea und Monika Brötchen.*

1. Monika geht *heute morgen* einkaufen.
2. Viele Leute gehen *jetzt* in den Supermarkt.
3. Es ist aber *im Supermarkt* nicht so persönlich.
4. Monika kauft *den Kaffee* ungemahlen.
5. Sie geht *dann* auf den Blumenmarkt.
6. Sie bekommt *für wenig Geld* einen schönen Blumenstrauß.

2. Machen Sie Sätze.   Form sentences, using the cues below.

▶   heute / es / geben / kein Kuchen   *Heute gibt es keinen Kuchen.*

1. du / essen / kein Fisch / ?
2. du / nehmen / der Käse / ?
3. Frank / geben / Rita / der Kaffee
4. was / du / bekommen / zum Frühstück / ?
5. wie / du / finden / der Wein / ?
6. Margot / kaufen / Obst / für / die Kinder
7. warum / du / bezahlen / alles / für / die Jungen / ?
8. was / du / haben / gegen / der Junge / ?

3. Wie sagt man das?   Give the German equivalents of the conversational exchanges below.

1. Who needs a table?
   —Ask Mr. Falk, Elly.
2. Erika, give Peter the coffee.
   —I don't have any coffee.
3. I'm not buying the table.
   —Why not?
   —It's too small.
4. Whom do you know here, Ingrid?
   —I know Mr. Schubert.
5. Are there many supermarkets in Germany?
   —Of course, Michael. Why do you ask?

4. Doch, Helga.   Helga is making a number of incorrect assumptions. Correct her, using **doch** in each of your responses.

▶   Gehst du heute nicht einkaufen?   *Doch. Ich gehe heute einkaufen.*

1. Kaufst du kein Obst?
2. Ißt du heute kein Brot zum Frühstück?
3. Arbeitest du heute nicht?
4. Gehst du nicht ins Kino?
5. Du glaubst das nicht.
6. Das ist nicht richtig.

5. Nicht oder kein?   Answer in the negative, using **nicht** or a form of **kein.**

▶   Kauft Erika heute Kartoffeln?   *Nein, sie kauft heute keine Kartoffeln.*

1. Kauft sie Kuchen?
2. Geht sie heute zum Bäcker?
3. Kauft sie das Fleisch im Supermarkt?
4. Kauft Gerd heute Käse?
5. Kauft er das Brot beim Bäcker?
6. Kauft er heute Milch?
7. Gibt es hier einen Supermarkt?

6. Elfi hat viele Fragen. Your German friend Elfi is visiting you. She has a number of questions. Use one of the responses supplied or provide your own to answer those questions (listed below).

Wirklich? ◇ Heute morgen. ◇ Morgen. ◇ Warum fragst du? ◇ Kauf es bei Müller. ◇ Sonst noch etwas? ◇ Ja, was brauchst du denn? ◇ Jetzt. ◇ Ich glaube ja. ◇ Vielleicht. ◇ Wir haben keine Butter mehr.

1. Gibt es hier eine Apotheke?
2. Was brauchst du denn?
3. Wann gehst du einkaufen?
4. Machst du morgen Spaghetti?
5. Wir haben kein Brot mehr.
6. Wir brauchen Butter.
7. Was machst du jetzt?

7. Wie sagt man das? Give the German equivalents of the conversational exchanges below.

1. What color are the flowers?
   —They're red and white.
2. How are you, Mrs. Driesbach?
   —I'm fine, thanks.
3. What are you doing tonight, Iris?
   —I'm working.
4. Horrible weather today, isn't it?
   —Yes, the wind is cold. It'll certainly rain again.

8. Was ißt du gern? Work through the following conversational exchange with a partner. Once you have completed the exchange, reverse roles and do it again.

S1: Ask your partner what he/she likes to eat.
S2: Mention at least two to three of your favorite foods.

S1: Ask your partner what he/she normally buys each week at the grocery store/supermarket.
S2: Mention three to five different foods. Use the modifiers **viel(e)** and **etwas** in your reply.

S1: Tell your partner you need one of the items he/she just mentioned and ask him/her to buy it for you.
S2: Respond that you will be glad to do so.

9. **Am Wochenende**   Exchange information with your partner about what you will do this weekend (**am Wochenende**). English equivalents of verbs you have already had and which may be useful are listed below:

study	eat	dance	listen (to)
play	drink	stay	be
buy	have	cook	go
work	look for	take	go shopping

10. **Eine Party**   In preparation for a party this weekend tell one or more of your friends what to buy for the party and what to make.

11. **Diät essen**   Give your friend a list of items she/he should or should not eat.

▶   *Iß Vollkornbrot, _____ …*
▶   *Iß keinen Käse, kein _____ …*

12. **Anregung**

1. You've just returned from Germany. A friend asks you about German shopping customs. Prepare a brief dialogue you might have with your friend in German.
2. Your friend Erik prefers to shop in **Supermärkte,** but Inge prefers **Tante-Emma-Läden.** Write a paragraph in German in which you state your personal preference and your reasons for it.

GRAMMATIK: ZUSAMMENFASSUNG

Verbs with stem-vowel change *e > i*

essen	
ich esse	wir essen
du **ißt**	ihr eßt
er/es/sie **ißt**	sie essen
Sie essen	

geben	
ich gebe	wir geben
du **gibst**	ihr gebt
er/es/sie **gibt**	sie geben
Sie geben	

nehmen	
ich nehme	wir nehmen
du **nimmst**	ihr nehmt
er/es/sie **nimmt**	sie nehmen
Sie nehmen	

Several verbs with the stem vowel **e** (including **essen**, **geben**, **nehmen**) change **e > i** in the **du-** and **er/es/sie**-forms of the present tense.

Word order with expressions of time and place

	Time	Place
Monika geht	heute abend	ins Kino.
Robert war	gestern	nicht hier.

In German, place expressions generally follow time expressions.

The imperative forms

	Infinitive	Imperative	Present
du	sagen	**Sag(e)** etwas bitte.	Sagst du etwas?
ihr		**Sagt** etwas bitte.	Sagt ihr etwas?
Sie		**Sagen Sie** etwas bitte.	Sagen Sie etwas?
du	nehmen	**Nimm** das Brot bitte.	Nimmst du das Brot?
ihr		**Nehmt** das Brot bitte.	Nehmt ihr das Brot?
Sie		**Nehmen Sie** das Brot bitte.	Nehmen Sie das Brot?

◆ *Imperative of* **sein**

du	**Sei** nicht so nervös.
ihr	**Seid** ruhig.
Sie	**Seien Sie** so gut.

Accusative case of nouns

Nominative	Accusative
Subject	**Direct Object**
Der Kuchen ist frisch.	Er nimmt **den Kuchen**
Die Uhr ist schön.	Sie kauft **die Uhr.**

A noun that is used as a direct object of a verb is in the accusative case.

Accusative case of masculine *N*-nouns

Nominative	der Herr	der Junge	der Mensch	der Nachbar	der Student
Accusative	den Herr**n**	den Junge**n**	den Mensch**en**	den Nachbar**n**	den Student**en**

A number of masculine nouns add **-n** or **-en** in the accusative singular.

Accusative case of the definite articles *der, das, die*

	der	**das**	**die**	**Plural**
Nominative	**der** } Käse	**das** } Brot	**die** } Butter	**die** } Eier
Accusative	**den**	**das**	**die**	**die**

Accusative case of demonstrative pronouns

Accusative nouns	**Accusative pronouns**
Ich finde den Käse gut.	**Den** finde ich auch gut.
Ich finde das Brot trocken.	**Das** finde ich auch trocken.
Ich finde die Butter frisch.	**Die** finde ich auch frisch.
Ich finde die Eier schlecht.	**Die** finde ich auch schlecht.

Accusative case of *wer*

Nominative	**Accusative**
Wer fragt?	**Wen** fragt er?

Accusative of *ein, kein,* and possessive adjectives

	Masculine	**Neuter**	**Feminine**	**Plural**
	(der Kuli)	**(das Heft)**	**(die Uhr)**	**(die Kulis)**
Nominative	**ein** **kein** } Kuli **dein**	**ein** **kein** } Heft **dein**	**eine** **keine** } Uhr **deine**	**keine** } Kulis **deine**
Accusative	**einen** **keinen** } Kuli **deinen**	**ein** **kein** } Heft **dein**	**eine** **keine** } Uhr **deine**	**keine** } Kulis **deine**

Kein and the possessive adjectives (**mein, dein, sein, ihr, unser, euer, Ihr**) have the same endings as the indefinite article **ein**.

Accusative case of personal pronouns

Nominative	ich	du	er	es	sie	wir	ihr	sie	Sie
Accusative	**mich**	**dich**	**ihn**	**es**	**sie**	**uns**	**euch**	**sie**	**Sie**

Prepositions with the accusative case

durch	through	Sie geht **durch** das Zimmer. [durchs Zimmer]
für	for	Sie kauft die Uhr **für** das Haus. [fürs Haus]
gegen	against	Sie hat nichts **gegen** den Mann.
ohne	without	Sie geht **ohne** Herrn Bauer.
um	around	Sie geht **um** das Haus. [ums Haus]

The construction *haben + gern*

Hast du Lore **gern?**   Do you like Lore?
Ich **habe** sie nicht **gern.**   I don't like her.

A common way of expressing fondness for someone in German is to use **haben + gern. Nicht gern** is used to express dislike.

Impersonal expression *es gibt*

Es gibt keinen Kaffee mehr.   There is no more coffee.
Gibt es auch keine Brötchen?   Aren't there any rolls, either?

Es gibt is equivalent to English *there is* or *there are*. It is followed by the accusative case.

HÖRSAAL

Eberhard-Karls-Universität Tübingen
Sachgebiet Arbeitssicherheit
und Umweltschutz

Gmelinstrasse 6

Studenten sprechen über ihre Arbeit.
(Tübingen)

Kapitel 5

BAUSTEINE FÜR GESPRÄCHE

Notizen für die Klausur

Andreas: Hallo, Michael. Kannst du mir bitte deine Notizen leihen?
Michael: Ja, gern.
Andreas: Das ist nett. Für die Klausur muß ich noch viel lernen.
Michael: Klar, hier hast du sie. Kannst du die morgen wieder mitbringen?

Ist das dein Hauptfach?

Ursel: Grüß dich. Seit wann gehst du denn in die Brecht-Vorlesung? Studierst du nicht Geschichte?
Sabine: Nein, nicht mehr. Ich mache jetzt Germanistik.
Ursel: Ah ja? Als Nebenfach?
Sabine: Nein, als Hauptfach.
Ursel: So? Aha. Du, möchtest du nachher Kaffee trinken gehen?

Sabine: Ich kann leider nicht, muß noch etwas lesen. Morgen habe ich ein Referat und bin nicht besonders gut vorbereitet.

Notes for the test

Hi, Michael. Can you please lend me your notes?

Yes, glad to.
That's nice [of you]. I still have to study a lot for this test.

Of course, here they are. Can you bring them back tomorrow?

Is that your major?

Hi! Since when have you been taking the Brecht course? Aren't you studying history?

No, not any more. I'm taking German now.
Oh yes? As a minor?
No, as a major.
Is that so? Aha. Say, would you like to go out for coffee afterwards?
Unfortunately I can't. I still have to read something. Tomorrow I have an oral report and am not especially well prepared.

Fragen

1. Warum möchte Andreas Michaels Notizen leihen?
2. Warum muß Andreas noch viel lernen?
3. Wann möchte Michael seine Notizen wiederhaben?
4. Warum geht Sabine jetzt in die Brecht-Vorlesung?
5. Was ist Sabines Hauptfach?
6. Was möchte Ursel nachher machen?
7. Warum kann Sabine nicht mitgehen?

Bertolt Brecht

Bertolt Brecht (1898–1956) is one of the most important figures of the twentieth-century theater. His dramatic theories have influenced many playwrights and theater directors throughout the world. As a young playwright during the twenties, Brecht took the German theater by storm with "The Threepenny Opera" *(Die Dreigroschenoper);* it shocked and fascinated audiences with its depiction of London's criminal underworld, and the social and political forces underlying it. Brecht's critical focus on society and his dramatic theories revolutionized the German stage and made him a celebrity.

As an outspoken opponent of National Socialism, however, Bertolt Brecht had to flee Germany in 1933. He lived temporarily in several European countries until he settled down in California. Like many other German emigrants, he found refuge in the United States until the end of World War II and the end of the National Socialist regime. Brecht wrote some of his major plays in exile: *Mutter Courage und ihre Kinder* (1941), *Der gute Mensch von Sezuan* (1942), *Leben des Galilei* (1943).

In 1947, after he had been called before the House Committee on Un-American Activities, he moved back to Europe and eventually chose the German Democratic Republic as his home. With his wife Helene Weigel, he founded the *Berliner Ensemble,* a theater in former East Berlin that continues to perform Brecht's plays and tries to put his theories into practice.

Das Berliner Ensemble spielt *Der gute Mensch von Sezuan.* (Theater am Schiffbauerdamm)

1. Leihen   Try to borrow something from a fellow student. She/he responds with *yes* or *no*. Then, out of curiosity, she/he asks why you want the item you requested. You may use the questions and responses provided or make up your own. When you have finished, ask another student.

Borrowing objects/lending objects

Sie		*Gesprächspartner/in*
Kannst du mir	**deine Notizen** leihen?	Ja, gern.
	dein Referat	Klar.
	deine Seminararbeit°	Natürlich.
	deinen Kugelschreiber	Ja, ich bringe ihn [es/sie] mit.
	deine Software	Geht leider nicht. Ich brauche den [das/die] selbst.
	deine Disketten	Tut mir leid.°

Gesprächspartner/in		*Sie*			
Warum brauchst du	**meine Notizen** denn?	Ich muß	noch	**viel**	**lernen.**
Warum brauchst du	sie			etwas	vorbereiten.
	es				arbeiten.
	ihn			eine Klausur schreiben.	

2. Hauptfach, Nebenfach   Interview four students. Find out their major and minor subjects; then ask what they like to read. To find the names of other academic disciplines, you may want to refer to the Supplementary Word Sets in the Reference Section.

Discussing college majors and minors

Sie		*Gesprächspartner/in*	
Was ist dein	**Hauptfach?**	Ich studiere	**Germanistik.**
	Nebenfach		Anglistik.
		Mein	**Nebenfach** ist **Psychologie.**
			Hauptfach Philosophie.
			Chemie.
			Physik.
			Mathematik.
			Deutsch.
			Englisch.
			Informatik.
Was liest du gern?		Artikel° über	Sport/Musik/Schach.
		Bücher über	Psychologie.
		Krimis°.	
		Liebesromane°.	

3. Es tut mir leid. You run into a friend in the library who wants to make plans for later. Respond that you are sorry but you can't. Explain why you are busy.

Offering explanations/ excuses

Gesprächspartner/in		*Sie*	
Willst du nachher	**Kaffee trinken** gehen?	Ich kann nicht. Ich	**bereite mein Referat vor.**
	einkaufen		schreibe meine Seminararbeit.
	schwimmen		lerne für die Klausur.
	ins Kino		lese einen Artikel über Brecht.
			mache heute abend Deutsch.
			muß wieder in die Bibliothek°.
Was [müssen/können/sollen] wir heute abend machen?		Wir müssen	unser Referat vorbereiten, nicht?
		Wir sollen	**unsere Notizen** durcharbeiten°.
			die letzte° Vorlesung durcharbeiten.
		Wir können	Deutsch machen.

Vokabeln

___ Substantive _____

die **Anglistik** English studies (language and literature)
die **Arbeit, -en** work; paper
der **Artikel, -** article
die **Bibliothek, -en** library
die **Chemie** chemistry
die **Diskette, -n** disk
(das) **Englisch** English (language)
die **Germanistik** German studies (language and literature)
die **Geschichte, -n** story; history
das **Hauptfach, ˸er** major (subject)
die **Informatik** computer science
die **Klausur, -en** test; **eine Klausur schreiben** to take a test
der **Krimi, -s** mystery (novel or film)

die **Liebe** love; der **Liebesroman** romance (novel)
die **Mathematik** mathematics
das **Nebenfach, ˸er** minor (subject)
die **Notiz, -en** note
die **Philosophie, -n** philosophy
die **Physik** physics
die **Psychologie** psychology
das **Referat, -e** report
der **Roman, -e** novel
das **Seminar, -e** seminar
die **Seminararbeit, -en** seminar paper
die **Software** software
die **Vorlesung, -en** lecture

— Verben —

bringen to bring
durch·arbeiten to work through; to study
dürfen (darf) to be permitted to, to be allowed to; may
können (kann) to be able to; can
leihen to lend; to borrow
lernen to learn; to study
lesen (liest) to read

mit·bringen to bring along
möchten (*subjunctive of* **mögen**) would like
müssen (muß) to have to; must
sollen (soll) to be supposed to
studieren to study; to go to college
vor·bereiten to prepare
wollen (will) to want to, intend to

— Andere Wörter —

immer wieder again and again
klar clear; of course, naturally
letzt last
nachher afterwards

nicht mehr no longer, not anymore
seit since

— Besondere Ausdrücke —

Deutsch machen to do/study German (as homework)
Du, ... Hey, . . . (used to get someone's attention)
(es) tut mir leid I'm sorry

ich bin (nicht) gut vorbereitet I am (not) well prepared
seit wann since when, (for) how long
So? Is that so? Really?

STUDENTEN IN DEUTSCHLAND

Vorbereitung auf das Lesen

◆ *Zum Thema*

A German asks you to give her/him some idea of what life as a student in a college or university in this country is like. List the things that seem to you to be characteristic.

◆ *Leitfragen*

1. Wenn man studiert, braucht man Geld. Was kostet viel, wenig, nichts? Wie bekommen Studenten Geld?
2. Es gibt nicht genug Studienplätze° in Deutschland. Wie reguliert man die Studentenzahlen?

   Stichworte°: Abitur° ◇ Numerus clausus° ◇ Zensuren° ◇ Regelstudienzeit°

available space to study a major

key words / **Gymnasium** diploma / closed or limited number (Latin) / grades / limit on time spent at the university

In einem Seminar arbeiten Studenten enger mit einem Professor zusammen als in einer Vorlesung. (Universität Tübingen)

The university system in Germany is different from that in the United States. Because students are expected to have gained a good general education in high school (**Gymnasium**), they concentrate on one major field at the university. The German university system does not have an equivalent to a Bachelor's degree. In the arts and humanities, students usually take one major and two minor subjects, or two majors, and complete their studies with a Master of Arts (**Magister**). In natural and social sciences, students earn a di-

ploma (**Diplom**), which is equivalent to the M.A. If students intend to become teachers, lawyers, or medical doctors, they finish with state certification after passing a special examination (**Staatsexamen**). The Ph.D. (**Doktor**) is an advanced degree that requires a **Dissertation. Professor** is an advanced academic title, which requires writing a postdoctoral thesis (**Habilitationsschrift**).

University students bear the major responsibility for their own progress. There are fewer exams, papers, and daily assignments, and for many courses there are no exams. At the beginning of the semester students choose classes according to type and subject matter. A **Vorlesung** is a lecture with little discussion and no exams. An **Übung** is a course often with daily assignments, discussion, and a test (**Klausur**) at the end. In a **Seminar,** students write papers and discuss the material. They have to write term papers (**Seminararbeiten**) as well.

After the successful completion of a **Seminar** or **Übung,** students receive a certificate (**Schein**), which includes a grade. A minimum number of **Scheine** is necessary before a student may take the intermediate qualifying exam (**Zwischenprüfung**), which is usually taken after four to six semesters at the university. A number of **Scheine** are also required before a student can take a final comprehensive examination such as the **Staatsexamen,** which is taken at the end of the university studies.

3. Der amerikanische Student hat zwei Hauptfächer und macht außerdem Englisch und Mathematik. Warum macht er Englisch und Mathematik?
4. In Deutschland sind fast alle Universitäten staatlich°. Warum findet die deutsche Studentin das gut?   state-owned
5. Wo gibt es mehr Prüfungen°, an deutschen oder amerikanischen Universitäten?   tests

*D*avid ist Amerikaner. Er macht eine Reise durch Deutschland und sieht auch einige Universitätsstädte an.

In einem Café in Hamburg lernt er eine junge Frau kennen. Sie ist Studentin und heißt Nicole. Sie sprechen über dies und das, natürlich auch
5 über die Universität. David fragt: „Ich höre und sehe immer wieder das Wort BAFöG. Was ist das eigentlich?" Nicole erklärt: „Also mit BAFöG ist das so: Wir bekommen Geld vom° Staat, aber nur ein Darlehen°. Später sollen wir das ganze Geld zurückzahlen. Das möchten wir natürlich nicht. Viele Studenten glauben, daß wir ein Recht° auf° dieses Geld haben." David kann
10 das nicht verstehen: „Ja, arbeitet ihr denn nicht auf dem Campus, im Studentenheim zum Beispiel?"
Nicole: Nein, an° unseren Unis gibt es wenige Studentenjobs. Und einen anderen Job findet man auch nur schwer.
David: Aber ihr bezahlt doch keine Studiengebühren°.
15 *Nicole:* Natürlich nicht, aber Wohnen° und Essen° sind teuer. Viele Studenten hier haben keine reichen Eltern. Wir brauchen das Geld vom° Staat. Nur so kann jeder studieren. Das ist Chancengleichheit°.
David: Aber will dann nicht jeder studieren?
Nicole: Vielleicht. Wie du weißt, muß man Abitur haben. Aber es gibt
20 immer noch zuwenig Studienplätze. Daher haben viele Fächer N.C., den Numerus clausus. Das heißt°, nur mit sehr guten Zensuren im Gymnasium bekommt man da einen Studienplatz°. Und Glück muß man auch haben.
David bestellt noch einen Kaffee. Er sieht Nicole an und sagt: „Es gibt
25 also zuwenig Studienplätze, nicht?"
Nicole: Genau. Daher gibt's die Regelstudienzeit. Die meisten Studenten müssen in acht Semestern fertig sein. So wird Platz frei für neue Studenten. Ich muß auch in acht Semestern fertig werden.
David: Was studierst du denn?
30 *Nicole:* Politik° und Geschichte. Und du?
David: Wirtschaftswissenschaft° und Deutsch. Aber ich bin erst im zweiten° Semester und muß noch Kurse nehmen in Englisch, Mathe und Geschichte, zum Beispiel.
Nicole: Warum das denn?
35 *David:* Na, das muß doch jeder. Du nicht? Machst du denn nur deine beiden Fächer?
Nicole: Ja, natürlich. Deshalb gehe ich doch auf° die Uni. Fremd-sprachen° und Mathe usw.°, das machen wir doch in der Schule.
David findet das alles sehr interessant. Er hat noch eine Frage: „Ist die
40 Uni Hamburg privat oder staatlich?"
Nicole: Staatlich natürlich. Private Unis gibt es hier eigentlich kaum. Das ist bei euch° anders, nicht?
David: Aber klar. Wir haben die ganz großen Namen, die Privatuniversitäten. Und es gibt enorme° Unterschiede.

Margin glosses:

from the / loan

right / to

at

tuition
room / board

from the / equal opportunity

das heißt: that is
bekommt ... Studienplatz: does one get admitted

political science
economics
second

auf ... Uni: to college
foreign languages / **usw. (= und so weiter):** etc.

bei euch: in your country

enormous

BAFöG — Informationen in der Mensa der Universität Bonn

45 *Nicole:* Aber das ist doch unsozial°!   socially unjust

  David: Vielleicht. Aber einige Privatuniversitäten sind eben sehr gut. Einige Privatcolleges auch.

  Nicole: Das ist ja interessant. In Amerika kann also jeder Mensch eine Universität aufmachen, wie einen Supermarkt?

50 *David:* Ja, warum denn nicht?

Nicole steht auf: „Du, es tut mir leid, aber ich muß jetzt gehen. Nächste Woche habe ich meine Zwischenprüfung°. Die ist nicht leicht, und ich muß noch sehr viel lernen."   qualifying exam

  David: Ja, das kenne ich. Wir haben auch für jeden Kurs eine Prüfung, 55 und das jedes Semester.

  Nicole: Was? Wir haben nur wenige Kurse mit Prüfungen. Dafür° haben wir aber die Zwischenprüfung nach° vier Semestern und dann DAS EXAMEN am Ende.   instead / after

  David: Dann mußt du wirklich gehen und lernen. Viel Glück!

60 David bleibt noch ein bißchen und trinkt seinen Kaffee aus.° Er überlegt°: Möchte er wohl° gern in Deutschland studieren?   **trinkt ... aus:** finishes / reflects / possibly

---

Fragen zum Lesestück

1. Was für Städte sieht David auf seiner Reise an?
2. Welches Wort sieht er immer wieder?
3. Wen lernt David in einem Café kennen?
4. Warum weiß er nicht, was BAFöG ist?

5. Wer bekommt ein Darlehen vom Staat?
6. Was haben die Studenten gegen Darlehen?
7. Warum arbeiten wenige deutsche Studenten auf dem Campus?
8. Warum brauchen sie Geld vom Staat?
9. Was muß jeder Student natürlich haben?
10. Warum haben viele Fächer N.C.?
11. Wer bekommt einen Studienplatz?
12. Warum gibt es die Regelstudienzeit?
13. In wie vielen Semestern muß Nicole fertig werden?
14. Warum muß David Kurse nehmen wie Englisch und Mathe?
15. Wo macht man diese Kurse in Deutschland?
16. Welche Fächer studiert Nicole?
17. Warum findet Nicole Privatuniversitäten nicht so gut?
18. Warum muß Nicole gehen?
19. Wie viele Prüfungen muß Nicole machen?

1. Erzählen Sie. Write down a few useful words about the following topics. Then react to the German university system by making one or two statements about the topics.

▶ BAFöG *(Geld vom Staat, zurückzahlen)*   *BAFöG ist Geld vom Staat für Studenten. Ich finde das gut. Die Studenten sollen das Geld zurückzahlen.*

Studentenjobs ◇ Studienplätze ◇ staatliche Universitäten ◇ Prüfungen

Vokabeln

Substantive

das **Abitur** diploma from college-track high school [**Gymnasium**]
das **Café, -s** café
die **Eltern** *(pl.)* parents
das **Ende, -n** end, conclusion; **am Ende** at (in) the end
das **Examen** examination
das **Fach, ̈er** (academic) subject
der **Film, -e** film
die **Frage, -n** question
das **Glück** luck; **Glück haben** to be lucky; **viel Glück** good luck
das **Gymnasium** *(pl.* **Gymnasien)** college-track high school

der **Job, -s** job
der **Kurs, -e** course
der **Name** *(acc.* **-n), -n** name
das **Picknick, -s** picnic
der **Platz, ̈e** space; place; seat
die **Prüfung, -en** examination, test
die **Reise, -n** trip
die **Schule, -n** school
das **Semester, -** semester
das **Studentenheim, -e** dormitory
die **Universität, -en** university; die **Uni, -s** *(abbreviation)*
der **Unterschied, -e** difference
die **Zensur, -en** grade, mark

Verben

an·sehen (sieht an) to look at, watch
auf·machen to open
auf·stehen to stand up; to get up (out of bed)
bestellen to order
erklären to explain
holen to get
kennen·lernen to get to know, make the acquaintance of

sehen (sieht) to see
sprechen (spricht) to speak
verstehen to understand
werden (wird) to become
wissen (weiß) to know (a fact)
wohnen to live, reside
zahlen to pay
zurück·zahlen to pay back

Andere Wörter

beide both; two
bißchen: ein bißchen a little
daher therefore, for that reason
deshalb therefore, for that reason
dies (-er, -es, -e) this, these
eben just
eigentlich actually
einige some, several
erst only, just; not until
fertig finished; ready
frei free, available
genau exactly; careful
interessant interesting
jed (-er, -es, -e) each, every; **jeder** everyone
jung young

kaum hardly, scarcely
leicht easy; light
meist- most; **die meisten (Leute)** most of (the people)
na well *(interjection)*
nächst- next
noch ein another, additional
privat private
reich rich
so [ein] such [a], that kind of
staatlich public, government-owned
teuer expensive
zurück back, in return
zuwenig too little, too few

Besondere Ausdrücke

genau exactly, that's right
immer noch still
viel Glück good luck

Erweiterung des Wortschatzes

1 Flavoring particle *eben*

Einige Privatuniversitäten sind **eben** sehr gut.	Some private universities are after all very good.
Du mußt es **eben** machen.	You'll simply have to do it. [No argument, please.]

Eben may be used by a speaker to support or strengthen a previous statement or idea. It can also be used by a speaker in a discussion in a final or closing statement to imply that she/he has no desire or need to discuss the point further.

Ich glaube, wir müssen gehen.	I think we have to leave.
Ja, **eben.**	Yes, right.

Eben is often used to express agreement with what someone has said.

2 Stating one's profession or nationality

Anton ist Student.	Anton is a student.
Barbara wird Ingenieurin.	Barbara is going to be an engineer.
Barbara ist Kanadierin.	Barbara is (a) Canadian.
Anton ist Deutscher.	Anton is (a) German.

Herr Becker ist **nicht (kein)** Ingenieur.	Mr. Becker is not an engineer.
Marga ist **nicht (keine)** Österreicherin; sie ist Deutsche.	Marga is not (an) Austrian; she's (a) German.

Either **nicht** or **kein** may be used to negate a sentence about someone's profession, nationality, or membership in a group. Remember that no indefinite article (**ein**) is used in the positive statement (see *Kapitel 3*). For names of additional professions, refer to the Supplementary Word Sets in the Reference Section.

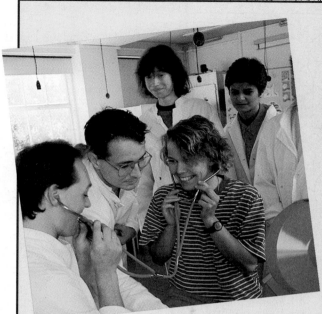

Diese Medizinstudenten haben einen Studienplatz bekommen. (Hannover)

More than 1.5 million students are enrolled in Germany's 129 universities and other institutions of higher learning and more than 350 polytechni-cal institutes and colleges.* Admission is limited under a system called **Numerus clausus (N.C.)** in about 60 percent of the subjects. In these disciplines, among which are medicine, law, pharmacy, and psychology, admissions (**Studienplätze**) are limited and distributed mainly on the basis of high school grades (**Zensuren**) received during the last years of the **Gymnasium** and grades on the final comprehensive examination (**das Abitur**). There can be a waiting period of up to five years for admission in some disciplines.

The national law to provide financial support for students (**Bundesausbildungsförderungsgesetz,** or **BAFöG**) was passed in 1971 to give everyone an equal chance to study at a university. Today approximately 50 percent of all students are subsidized to some extent. The amount of financial support is dependent on parents' income. Since 1983, students have been required to pay back the full amount of the state loan, but they pay no interest. The **Regelstudienzeit,** in effect in some states, requires that students finish their studies within a required number of semesters. (This regulation is a response to overcrowding at the universities.)

---

*The number of colleges and enrollment is the combined figure for western and eastern Germany.

1. Wie sagt man das?

1. David is a Canadian.
2. He is a student.
3. Brigitte is not a Canadian.
4. She is also not an American; she's a German.
5. She is going to be an engineer.
6. Her brother Helmut lives in Frankfurt; he's a Frankfurter.
7. He is a butcher.

2. Persönliche Informationen   Prepare a brief autobiography. Give: **Name, Nationalität, Adresse und Telefonnummer, Hauptfach, Nebenfach. Was wollen Sie werden?**

> Describing one's nationality and profession

3 Die Familie

Willi Clausen	Käthe Clausen
Ernst Hoppe	Johanna Hoppe
Hans Pfeiffer	Kersten Clausen-Pfeiffer
Gabriele Clausen-Hoppe	Volker Hoppe
Angelika Pfeiffer	Jürgen Pfeiffer
Regina Hoppe	Jens Hoppe
Tina Hoppe	Jonas Hoppe

die Mutter, ⸚ (die Mutti)   der Vater, ⸚ (der Vati)
                = die Eltern *(pl.)*

die Tochter, ⸚   der Sohn, ⸚e
die Schwester, -n   der Bruder, ⸚
                = Geschwister *(pl.)*

die Tante, -n   der Onkel, -
die Kusine, -n   der Vetter, -n
die Nichte, -n   der Neffe, -n, -n

die Großmutter, ⸚ (die Oma, -s)   der Großvater, ⸚ (der Opa, -s)
                = die Großeltern *(pl.)*

die Schwägerin, -nen   der Schwager, ⸚

Refer to the Supplementary Word Sets in the Reference Section for names of additional family members.

3. Die Familie   Answer the following questions based on the family tree (**der Stammbaum**).

1. Wie heißen Jürgen Pfeiffers Vettern?
2. Wer ist Tina Hoppes Kusine? Wie heißt Tinas Tante?
3. Wie heißen Jens Hoppes Großeltern?
4. Wie viele Geschwister hat Regina Hoppe?
5. Wie heißt Angelika Pfeiffers Onkel?

4. Erzählen Sie über Ihre Familie.   Give a brief account of your family. You may include answers to the questions below.

| Describing one's family |

1. Wie heißt Ihre Mutter? Ihr Vater?
2. Haben Sie Schwestern? Brüder? Wie viele? Wie heißen sie? Wie alt sind sie?
3. Wie alt sind Ihre Großeltern? Wo wohnen sie?
4. Haben Sie Tanten und Onkel? Wie viele? Wo wohnen sie?
5. Wie viele Kusinen und Vettern haben Sie? Sind sie noch jung?

An den deutschen Universitäten studieren auch ausländische Studenten.

Many foreign students are enrolled in German universities. In western Germany alone there are more than seventy thousand. Even in the **Numerus clausus** disciplines, some places are reserved for foreigners. Like a German student, a foreigner pays no tuition (**Studiengebühren**), but all students pay thirty to eighty marks in semester fees plus about seventy marks a month for health insurance. To be admitted for study in Germany, an American must usually have had at least two years of college and must pass a language examination.

To study at a Swiss university, an American needs a Bachelor's degree and a working knowledge of the language of instruction, which may be German, French, or Italian.

GRAMMATIK UND ÜBUNGEN

1 Present tense of *werden*

werden: to become	
ich werde	wir werden
du **wirst**	ihr werdet
er/es/sie **wird**	sie werden
Sie werden	
du-*imperative:* werde	

Werden is irregular in the **du-** and **er/es/sie-**forms in the present tense.

1. Sie werden anders. People are changing. Say how.

▶ Erik / leider / müde   *Erik wird leider müde.*

1. ich / auch / müde
2. Petra / besser / in Mathe
3. die Kinder / groß
4. du / leider / faul

5. wir / nervös
6. ihr / sehr / froh
7. Hans und Karin / besser / in Deutsch

2 Verbs with stem-vowel change *e > ie*

sehen: to see	
ich sehe	wir sehen
du **siehst**	ihr seht
er/es/sie **sieht**	sie sehen
Sie sehen	
du-*imperative:* **sieh**	

lesen: to read	
ich lese	wir lesen
du **liest**	ihr lest
er/es/sie **liest**	sie lesen
Sie lesen	
du-*imperative:* **lies**	

Several verbs with the stem-vowel **e** change the **e** to **ie** in the **du-** and **er/es/sie-**forms of the present tense and in the **du-**imperative. Since the stem of **lesen** ends in a sibilant, the **du-**form ending contracts from **-st** to **-t** (see *Kapitel 2*, Grammatik und Übungen, section 7).

2. Lesen und sehen Say what kind of films and reading matter the people mentioned below like.

▶ Erik / ernste Filme *Erik sieht gern ernste Filme.*

1. Ingrid / lustige Filme
2. Gabi und Jürgen / leichte Filme
3. du / Schwarzweißfilme / ?
4. Christine / Bücher / über Sport
5. Detlev / Bücher / über Musik
6. du / Bücher / über Politik / ?
7. ihr / Bücher / über Geschichte / ?

3. Filme und Bücher Interview three students to find out what kinds of movies they like and what they like to read about. Then report back to the class. Refer to the Supplementary Word Sets in the Reference Section for additional descriptions of film and literature.

Talking about personal interests

Sie	*Gesprächspartner/in*
Was für Filme siehst du gern?	Ich sehe [lustige] Filme gern.
Über was liest du gern?	Ich lese gern über [Musik].

[Bill] sieht [lustige] Filme gern.
[Judy und Jack] lesen gern über [Geschichte].

3 Present tense of *wissen*

wissen: to know	
ich **weiß**	wir wissen
du **weißt**	ihr wißt
er/es/sie **weiß**	sie wissen
Sie wissen	

Wissen is irregular in the singular forms of the present tense. Note that the **du**-form ending contracts from **-st** to **-t**.

4. Ein Picknick You and your friends are going to drive in different cars to a picnic spot in the country. Inform Klaus that the people mentioned know where the picnic is. Use pronouns in your responses.

▶ Weiß Jutta, wo das Picknick ist? *Ja, sie weiß es.*
▶ Und Jürgen? *Ja, er weiß es.*

1. Und Benno?
2. Und du?
3. Und Christine?
4. Und Ulf und Jochen?
5. Und ihr?

4 *Wissen* and *kennen*

Sie **weiß,** wer Professor Schmidt ist.

She knows who Professor Schmidt is.

Sie **kennt** Professor Schmidt gut.

She knows Professor Schmidt well.

The English equivalent of **wissen** and of **kennen** is *to know*. **Wissen** means *to know something as a fact*. **Kennen** means *to be acquainted with a person, place, or thing*.

Kennen was used as a verb in Middle English and is still used in Scottish. The noun *ken* means perception or understanding: "That is beyond my ken."

5. Kennen oder wissen? Complete the sentences below with a form of **kennen** or of **wissen,** as appropriate.

▶ _____ du, wo Bonn liegt?   *Weißt du, wo Bonn liegt?*
▶ Dirk _____ die Stadt gut.   *Dirk kennt die Stadt gut.*

1. _____ ihr den Mann da?
2. Ich _____ , wie er heißt.
3. Petra _____ , wo er arbeitet.
4. _____ Sie Professor Reimanns Buch über Musik?
5. Wir _____ nicht viel über Musik.
6. Aber wir _____ Frau Professor Reimann gut.
7. _____ du Heidelberg gut?
8. _____ du, wo die Bibliothek ist?

5 *Der*-words

Diese Klausur ist schwer.

This test is hard.

Jede Klausur ist schwer.

Every test is hard.

Welche Klausur hast du?

Which test do you have?

Manche Klausuren sind doch leicht.

Some tests are easy.

Solche Klausuren sind nicht interessant.

Those kinds of tests aren't interesting.

In the singular, **so ein** is usually used instead of **solcher: So eine Uhr ist sehr teuer.** *That kind of/such a watch/clock is very expensive.*

	Masculine	**Neuter**	**Feminine**	**Plural**
	der	**das**	**die**	**die**
Nominative	dies**er**	dies**es**	dies**e**	dies**e**
Accusative	dies**en**	dies**es**	dies**e**	dies**e**

The words **dieser, jeder, welcher?, mancher,** and **solcher** are called **der**-words because they follow the same pattern in the nominative and accusative cases as the definite articles. **Jeder** is used in the singular only. **Welcher?** is an interrogative adjective, used at the beginning of a question. **Solcher** and **mancher** are used almost exclusively in the plural.

Der Stuhl (**da**) ist neu.   That chair is new.

The equivalent of *that (those)* is expressed by the definite article (**der, das, die**). **Da** is often added for clarity.

6. Welcher? Dieser?   You're shopping with a friend who comments on various items. Ask which things she/he is referring to. Use the nominative of **welcher** and **dieser.**

▶   Der Kuli ist teuer.   *Welcher Kuli ist teuer? Dieser hier?*

1. Das Buch über Sport ist interessant.
2. Die Lampe ist schön.
3. Der Stuhl ist zu schwer.
4. Das Radio ist zu teuer.
5. Der Tisch ist zu klein.
6. Die Bleistifte sind billig.
7. Die Hefte sind teuer.

7. Kannst du mir etwas leihen?   A friend needs to borrow a few things for his/her apartment temporarily. Be generous and tell him/her to take them. Use the accusative of **dieser** in your responses.

▶   Kannst du mir einen Kuli leihen?   *Ja. Nimm diesen.*

1. Kannst du mir auch einen Bleistift leihen?
2. Hast du auch ein Heft?
3. Kannst du mir vielleicht eine Lampe leihen?
4. Hast du ein Buch über Schach?
5. Kannst du mir einen Tisch leihen?
6. Du, kannst du mir eine Wanduhr leihen?
7. Hast du noch einige Stühle?
8. Hast du vielleicht drei oder vier Poster für mich?

8. Wie finden Sie diese Bilder?   You are showing pictures of Switzerland and Austria to your friends. Restate the questions and comments, using the cued **der**-word in place of the italicized words.

▶   Finden Sie *die* Städte schön? (dieser)   *Finden Sie diese Städte schön?*

1. Kennen Sie *die* Städte schon? (mancher)
2. *Die* Städte möchten Sie kennenlernen? (welcher?)
3. Im Fenster gibt es immer *diese* Blumen. (solcher)
4. Wie heißt *die* Straße? (dieser)
5. *Die* Universitäten sind alt. (dieser)
6. Wie finden Sie *die* Bilder? (dieser)
7. *Das* Bild ist wirklich schön. (jeder)
8. *Die* Bilder möchten Sie haben? (welcher?)

6 Modal auxiliaries

Ich **muß** jetzt arbeiten.	I *have to* work now.
Erika **kann** es machen.	Erika *can* do it.
Du **darfst** nichts sagen.	You *are not allowed* to say anything.

Both English and German have a group of verbs called *modal auxiliaries*. Modal verbs (**muß, kann, darfst**) indicate an attitude about an action; they do not express the action itself. In German, the verb that expresses the action is in the infinitive form (**arbeiten, machen, sagen**) and is in last position.

Modals are irregular in the present-tense singular. They lack endings in the **ich-** and **er/es/sie-**forms, and five of the six modals show stem-vowel change, e.g., **können > kann.**

können: can, to be able to	
ich **kann** es erklären	wir **können** es erklären
du **kannst** es erklären	ihr **könnt** es erklären
er/es/sie **kann** es erklären	sie **können** es erklären
Sie **können** es erklären	

9. Was können diese Leute?   Say what the following people can do.

▶   Mark schwimmt gut.   *Mark kann gut schwimmen.*

1. Karla spielt gut Tennis.
2. Wir kochen Spaghetti.
3. Ich verstehe dich.
4. Du tanzt gut.
5. Herr Professor, Sie schreiben schön.
6. Karin und Peter tanzen wunderbar.
7. Ihr kocht gut.

10. Was kannst du?   Find out from several fellow students whether they can do certain activities. You may use the suggestions given and think of some of your own.

> Inquiring about abilities

Sie	*Gesprächspartner/in*
Kannst du Fußball spielen?	Ja, ich kann Fußball spielen.
	Nein, ich kann nicht Fußball spielen.

1. schwimmen
2. Tennis spielen
3. gut tanzen
4. den Professor verstehen

5. italienisch kochen
6. Basketball spielen
7. schön schreiben

wollen: to want, wish; to intend to	
ich **will** arbeiten	wir **wollen** arbeiten
du **willst** arbeiten	ihr **wollt** arbeiten
er/es/sie **will** arbeiten	sie **wollen** arbeiten
Sie **wollen** arbeiten	

11. Was wollen diese Leute?   Say what the following people want to do or intend to do.

▶   Erich trinkt Kaffee.   *Erich will Kaffee trinken.*

1. Beatrice macht Musik.
2. Du gehst heute abend tanzen, nicht?
3. Paul geht einkaufen.
4. Ich tue nichts.
5. Die Kinder essen ein Stück Kuchen.
6. Ihr macht Mathe.
7. Frau Kaiser studiert Geschichte.

12. Willst du?   You and your partner are planning things to do tonight and tomorrow. Suggest two things. Your partner can or cannot do them.

Sie	*Gesprächspartner/in*
Willst du heute abend/morgen [ins Kino gehen]?	Ja gern. Nein, ich kann nicht.

sollen: to be supposed to	
ich **soll** morgen gehen	wir **sollen** morgen gehen
du **sollst** morgen gehen	ihr **sollt** morgen gehen
er/es/sie **soll** morgen gehen	sie **sollen** morgen gehen
Sie **sollen** morgen gehen	

13. Wir planen ein Fest.   You and some friends are planning a party. Tell what each person is supposed to do for it.

▶   Gabi und Moritz: Musik mitbringen   *Gabi und Moritz sollen Musik mitbringen.*

1. wir: Käse kaufen
2. du: Salat machen
3. ich: Brot holen
4. Corinna: Wein mitbringen
5. ihr: Bier kaufen

14. Wie wird das Wetter? Write down weather predictions for three days. Ask your partner about his/her predictions, then reverse roles.

Describing possibilities and probabilities

Sie	*Gesprächspartner/in*
Wie wird das Wetter morgen?	Morgen soll es [regnen].
Und am [Mittwoch]?	Am [Mittwoch] soll [die Sonne scheinen].

müssen: must, to have to	
ich **muß** jetzt arbeiten	wir **müssen** jetzt arbeiten
du **mußt** jetzt arbeiten	ihr **müßt** jetzt arbeiten
er/es/sie **muß** jetzt arbeiten	sie **müssen** jetzt arbeiten
Sie **müssen** jetzt arbeiten	

15. Was müssen diese Leute tun? Say what all these people have to do.

▶ Frau Professor Kluge: in die Vorlesung gehen.

Frau Professor Kluge muß in die Vorlesung gehen.

1. wir: noch zwei Kapitel durcharbeiten
2. Karin: ein Buch lesen
3. ich: eine Klausur schreiben
4. ihr: in die Bibliothek gehen
5. Lukas und Lutz: ein Referat schreiben
6. du: für die Klausur lernen

16. Was mußt du machen? Write a schedule for the rest of the week showing what you must do. Then ask a fellow student what she/he must do in the next few days. Use a form of the verb **müssen.**

Discussing duties and requirements

Sie	*Gesprächspartner/in*
Ich muß heute arbeiten. Was machst du?	Ich muß heute auch arbeiten.
Ich muß morgen in die Bibliothek. Was machst du morgen?	Ich muß morgen ein Buch über Politik lesen.

dürfen: may, to be permitted to	
ich **darf** es sagen	wir **dürfen** es sagen
du **darfst** es sagen	ihr **dürft** es sagen
er/es/sie **darf** es sagen	sie **dürfen** es sagen
Sie **dürfen** es sagen	

17. Das darf man nicht. Say what these people are not allowed to do or what is not permitted.

▶ wir: hier nicht schwimmen *Wir dürfen hier nicht schwimmen.*

1. ich: keinen Kaffee trinken
2. du: hier nicht rauchen°   smoke
3. Eckhard: nicht so viel arbeiten
4. ihr: bei Rot nicht über die Straße gehen
5. Paul und Paula: kein Fleisch essen
6. man: hier nicht parken

18. Kannst du mir dein Buch leihen? Try to borrow something from your partner. Your partner will agree to lend it to you or express regrets and explain why she/he can't, e.g., "I need it," "I only have one," "I can't find it."

Sie	*Gesprächspartner/in*
Kannst du mir [dein Buch] leihen?	Gern.
	Es tut mir leid. [Ich muß es diese Woche selbst lesen.]

7 *Mögen* and the *möchte*-forms

mögen: to like	
ich **mag** keine Tomaten	wir **mögen** Erik nicht
du **magst** keine Eier	ihr **mögt** Inge nicht
er/es/sie **mag** kein Bier	sie **mögen** Schmidts nicht
Sie **mögen** keinen Kaffee	

Mögen Sie Frau Lenz?   Nein, ich **mag** sie nicht.

The modal **mögen** is often used to express a fondness or dislike for someone or something, much like the construction **haben** + **gern.** With this meaning it usually does not take a dependent infinitive.

19. **Was magst du?** You are raising questions about various people's likes and dislikes. Use a form of **mögen**.

▶ du: Fisch   *Magst du Fisch?*

1. Mark: deutsches Bier
2. Ilse und Erik: Rockmusik
3. Frank: Shakespeare
4. du: moderne Musik
5. Professor Schneider: Vollkornbrot
6. ihr: Rotwein
7. Herr und Frau Braun: Österreich

ich **möchte** gehen	wir **möchten** gehen
du **möchtest** gehen	ihr **möchtet** gehen
er/es/sie **möchte** gehen	sie **möchten** gehen
Sie **möchten** gehen	

Möchte and **mögen** are different forms of the same verb. The meaning of **mögen** is *to like;* the meaning of **möchte** is *would like (to).*

20. **Ja, das möchten wir.** It's going to be a busy evening, and everything sounds good to everyone. Say what the people mentioned below would like to do.

▶ Dirk: heute abend ins Kino gehen   *Dirk möchte heute abend ins Kino gehen.*

1. wir: heute nachmittag einkaufen gehen
2. du: mehr arbeiten
3. ihr: bestimmt hier bleiben
4. Gabi: im Café essen
5. Lotte und Erika: Musik hören
6. ich: ein interessantes Buch lesen
7. Rolf: am Wochenende wandern

21. Was möchtet ihr machen? Ask three fellow students what they would like to do. Use a **möchte**-form in each question.

Inquiring about future plans

▶ Was möchtest du [am Wochenende/heute abend/im Sommer] machen?   *Ich möchte [einkaufen gehen].*

8 Omission of the dependent infinitive with modals

Ich **kann** das nicht.	= Ich **kann** das nicht **machen.**
Ich **muß** in die Bibliothek.	= Ich **muß** in die Bibliothek **gehen.**
Das **darfst** du nicht.	= Das **darfst** du nicht **tun.**

Modals may occur without a dependent infinitive if a verb of motion (e.g., **gehen**) or the idea of *to do* (**machen, tun**) is clearly understood from the context.

Ich **kann** Deutsch.   I know German.

Können is used to say that someone knows a language.

22. Was bedeutet das?   Give the English equivalents.

1. Wollen Sie jetzt nach Hause?
2. Ich muß in die Apotheke.
3. Peter kann es nicht. Er ist sehr müde.
4. Was soll ich da?
5. Ich muß noch heute zum Bäcker.
6. Darf das Kind heute in die Stadt?
7. Was will Christine denn hier?
8. Können Sie Deutsch?
9. Möchten Sie noch etwas Fisch?

23. Wie sagt man das?

1. Can you work this afternoon?
   —No, I have to go home.
2. May I pay (for) the coffee?
   —No, you may not. [Add **das.**]
3. Dirk wants to go to the movies tonight.
   —What would he like to see?
4. Barbara intends to study German.
   —Good. She already knows German well.
5. It's supposed to rain tomorrow.
   —Really? That can't be.

Exklusiv
neuform

granoVita
Vollkorn-Knusper-Frühstück
gibt es in vier Sorten:

Apfel-Rosinen. Nuß-Mandel.
Beeren. Ohne Rosinen.

granoVita

„Das mag ich!"

24. Kino-Programm Study the movie ads from a Munich paper and answer the following questions. If you need help, see Vocabulary for Authentic Text Activities in the Reference Section.

1. Was gibt es im Mathäser Filmpalast zu essen?
2. Der Film *Zurück in die Zukunft III* ist nur für Personen „ab 12" Jahren. Wie alt muß man sein, um den Film *Hexen Hexen* zu sehen?
3. Wo können Sie den Film *Zurück in die Zukunft III* auf englisch sehen?
4. Welchen Film kann ein 7-jähriges Kind im Royal-Filmpalast sehen? Um wieviel Uhr?
5. Welchen Film oder welche Filme in dieser Anzeige kennen Sie?

25. Möchtest du den Film sehen? Choose a movie from the ads. Tell a friend that it is supposed to be super (**super**)/great (**toll**) and ask if she/he would like to see it. Decide which theater you'll go to and at what time.

The German movie industry flourished during the era of silent films and early "talkies" (1919–1932). Directors like Fritz Lang, F. W. Murnau, and F. W. Pabst were considered among the finest in the world, and the German use of the "moving camera" influenced many directors.

During the Nazi era (1933–1945), many great German and Austrian filmmakers emigrated to the United States and other countries. Some of them never returned; this loss led to a period of mediocrity in German filmmaking that lasted until the mid-sixties. At that point a generation of young filmmakers began to introduce the New German Cinema (**Neuer deutscher Film**). Many of those directors are now famous, including the late Rainer Werner Fassbinder, Werner Herzog, Wim Wenders, and Wolfgang Petersen. Since then other directors such as Margarethe von Trotta, Volker Schlöndorff, Doris Dörrie, and Percy Adlon have gained international recognition.

Oscar (Kategorie: Kurzfilme) für zwei deutsche Filmemacher: Christoph und Wolfgang Lauenstein.

9 Separable-prefix verbs

to get up   I get up early.
to throw away   Don't throw away all those papers!

English has a large number of two-word verbs, such as *to get up, to throw away.* These two-word verbs consist of a verb, such as *get,* and a particle, such as *up.*

aufmachen   Sie **macht** das Fenster **auf.**
mitbringen   **Bringen** Sie bitte Blumen **mit.**

German has a large number of "separable-prefix verbs" that function like certain English two-word verbs. Examples are **ansehen, aufmachen, einkaufen,** and **mitbringen.** In present-tense statements and questions, and in imperative forms, the separable prefix (**an-, auf-, ein-, mit-**) is separated from the base form of the verb and is in the last position.

Sie möchte das Fenster **auf**machen.

In the infinitive form, the prefix is attached to the base form of the verb.

| **Basic verb** | Er **steht** da. | He's standing there. |
| **Separable-prefix verb** | Er **steht** um sechs **auf.** | He gets up at six. |

The meaning of a separable-prefix verb, such as **aufstehen,** is often different from the sum of the meanings of its parts: **stehen** (stand), **auf** (on).

Er will nicht **auf'**stehen.   Er steht nicht **auf'**.

In spoken German, the stress falls on the prefix of separable-prefix verbs. In vocabulary lists in this textbook, separable prefixes are indicated by a raised dot between the prefix and the verb: **an·sehen, auf·machen, ein·kaufen, mit·bringen.**

26. Das mache ich.   Andreas is telling Michael what he plans for the day. Using the cued words, repeat what Andreas says.

▶ heute nachmittag einkaufen   *Ich kaufe heute nachmittag ein.*

1. Großmutter Blumen mitbringen
2. unsere Notizen durcharbeiten
3. mein Referat vorbereiten
4. Kapitel fünf ansehen
5. morgen spät aufstehen

27. Mach das.   Tell your partner to do certain things in German.

▶ Stand up.   *Steh auf.*

Open the door.
Open your book.
Open the window.
Look at me.

28. Was ist hier los?   Describe the activities of the people mentioned below, using the cued modal verbs.

▶ Tanja steht um sechs Uhr auf. (möchte)   *Tanja möchte um sechs Uhr aufstehen.*

1. Erik macht das Fenster auf. (wollen)
2. Bringst du Tante Inge Blumen mit? (können)
3. Wir bereiten unsere Seminararbeit vor. (sollen)
4. Wir arbeiten unsere Notizen durch. (müssen)
5. Ich kaufe Samstag ein. (möchte)
6. Peter zahlt das Geld nicht zurück. (wollen)

WIEDERHOLUNG

1. Elke muß zu Hause bleiben. Elke wants to go to the movies but should stay home. Form sentences, using the cues below.

1. Elke / (möchte) / gehen / heute abend / ins Kino
2. sie / müssen / lernen / aber / noch viel
3. sie / können / verstehen / ihre Notizen / nicht mehr
4. sie / müssen / schreiben / morgen / eine Klausur
5. sie / müssen / vorbereiten / auch noch / ein Referat
6. sie / wollen / studieren / später / in Deutschland

2. Mach das. Tell Thomas what he must do this morning, using **du**-form imperatives.

▶ aufstehen / jetzt   *Steh jetzt auf.*

1. aufmachen / Fenster
2. essen / Ei / zum Frühstück
3. gehen / einkaufen / dann
4. kaufen / alles / bei Meiers
5. kommen / gleich / nach Hause
6. vorbereiten / dein Referat
7. durcharbeiten / deine Notizen

3. Wer arbeitet für wen? You and your friends work for members of the family. Say who works for whom. Use a possessive adjective.

▶ Annette / Großmutter   *Annette arbeitet für ihre Großmutter.*

1. Felix / Tante
2. ich / Vater
3. du / Mutter / ?
4. Jürgen / Onkel
5. Karin und Sonja / Schwester
6. wir / Eltern
7. ihr / Großvater / ?

4. Wie sagt man das? Construct a dialogue between Ingrid and Christine, based on the English cues provided below.

Christine: Ingrid, may I ask something?
Ingrid: Yes, what would you like to know?
Christine: What are you reading?
Ingrid: I'm reading a book. It's called *A Trip Through Germany*.
Christine: Do you have to work this evening?
Ingrid: No, I don't think so.
Christine: Do you want to go to the movies?
Ingrid: Can you lend me money?
Christine: Certainly. But I would like to pay for you.

5. Viele Fragen   Ask several people the questions below. They will reply as they wish, using the following cues as needed: work, study, play, go to the movies, swim, write a paper, go shopping, take an exam.

1. Was möchtest du heute machen?
2. Was darfst du heute nicht machen?
3. Was kannst du gut?
4. Was mußt du heute oder morgen machen?

6. Verwandte (Relatives)   Find out information about a relative of your partner by asking her/him the following questions. She/he will then ask you the same questions. Find out:

her/his name, age, and birthday month
what she/he likes to do in her/his spare time
if she/he plays sports
if she/he has a hobby (**das Hobby**)
what type of person she/he is
what she/he likes to eat and drink

Großeltern, Eltern und Enkelkinder

7. Anregung

1. In 6–8 German sentences give your opinion about the following features of higher education in Germany: **BAFöG, keine Studiengebühren, Numerus clausus.**
2. Describe in German a typical Friday at your college or university. You might want to discuss your classes, where you eat, your shopping habits, and your plans for the evening.

 GRAMMATIK: ZUSAMMENFASSUNG

Present tense of *werden*

werden	
ich werde	wir werden
du **wirst**	ihr werdet
er/es/sie **wird**	sie werden
Sie werden	

Verbs with stem-vowel change *e > ie*

sehen	
ich sehe	wir sehen
du **siehst**	ihr seht
er/es/sie **sieht**	sie sehen
Sie sehen	
du-*imperative:* **sieh**	

lesen	
ich lese	wir lesen
du **liest**	ihr lest
er/es/sie **liest**	sie lesen
Sie lesen	
du-*imperative:* **lies**	

Present tense of *wissen*

wissen	
ich **weiß**	wir wissen
du **weißt**	ihr wißt
er/es/sie **weiß**	sie wissen
Sie wissen	

Der-words

	Masculine	**Neuter**	**Feminine**	**Plural**
	der	das	die	die
Nominative	dies**er** Mann	dies**es** Kind	dies**e** Frau	dies**e** Leute
Accusative	dies**en** Mann	dies**es** Kind	dies**e** Frau	dies**e** Leute

Der-words follow the same pattern in the nominative and accusative as the definite articles.

Meanings and uses of *der*-words

dieser	this; these *(pl.)*
jeder	each, every *(used in the singular only)*
mancher	many a, several, some *(used mainly in the plural)*
solcher	that kind of (those kinds of), such *(used mainly in the plural)*
welcher	which *(interrogative adjective)*

Modal auxiliaries

	dürfen	**können**	**müssen**	**sollen**	**wollen**	**mögen**	**(möchte)**
ich	**darf**	**kann**	**muß**	**soll**	**will**	**mag**	(möchte)
du	**darfst**	**kannst**	**mußt**	**sollst**	**willst**	**magst**	(möchtest)
er/es/sie	**darf**	**kann**	**muß**	**soll**	**will**	**mag**	(möchte)
wir	dürfen	können	müssen	sollen	wollen	mögen	(möchten)
ihr	dürft	könnt	müßt	sollt	wollt	mögt	(möchtet)
sie	dürfen	können	müssen	sollen	wollen	mögen	(möchten)
Sie	dürfen	können	müssen	sollen	wollen	mögen	(möchten)

German modals are irregular in that they lack endings in the **ich**- and **er/es/ sie**-forms, and most modals show stem-vowel changes.

Carmen muß jetzt **gehen.**   Carmen has to leave now.

Modal auxiliaries in German are often used with dependent infinitives. The infinitive is in last position.

Meanings of modals

Infinitive	Meaning	Examples	English equivalents
dürfen	permission	Ich **darf** arbeiten.	I'm allowed to work.
können	ability	Ich **kann** arbeiten.	I can (am able to) work.
mögen	liking	Ich **mag** es nicht.	I don't like it.
müssen	compulsion	Ich **muß** arbeiten.	I must (have to) work.
sollen	obligation	Ich **soll** arbeiten.	I'm supposed to work.
wollen	wishing, wanting, intention	Ich **will** arbeiten.	I want (intend) to work.

Ich **mag** Paul nicht.	I don't like Paul.
Mögen Sie Tee?	Do you like tea?
Möchten Sie Tee oder Kaffee?	Would you like tea or coffee?

Mögen and **möchte** are different forms of the same verb. The meaning of **mögen** is *to like*; the meaning of **möchte** is *would like (to)*.

Separable-prefix verbs

mitbringen	**Bring** Blumen **mit.**	Bring flowers.
aufmachen	Ich **mache** das Fenster **auf.**	I'll open the window.

Many German verbs begin with prefixes such as **mit** or **auf**. Some prefixes are "separable," that is, they are separated from the base form of the verb in the imperative and in the present tense. The prefix generally comes at the end of the sentence. The separable-prefix verbs you have had are **ansehen, aufmachen, aufstehen, durcharbeiten, einkaufen, mitbringen, kennenlernen, vorbereiten, zurückzahlen.** (Kennen, in **kennenlernen,** is a verb and not a separable prefix, but it behaves just like a separable prefix.)

Warum **kauft** er heute **ein?**	Warum möchte er heute **einkaufen?**
Stehst du um sechs **auf?**	Mußt du um sechs **aufstehen?**

The separable prefix is attached to the base form of the verb when the verb is used as an infinitive.

Innsbruck — Olympische Winterspiele
1964 und 1976

KAPITEL 6

BAUSTEINE FÜR GESPRÄCHE

Fährst du morgen zur Uni?

Paul: Fährst du morgen mit dem Auto zur Uni?
Birgit: Ja. Willst du mitfahren?
Paul: Ja, gern. Ich hab' so viele Bücher für die Bibliothek. Kannst du mich vielleicht abholen?
Birgit: Ja, kein Problem. Ich komme dann um halb neun bei dir vorbei. Geht das?
Paul: Ja, klar. Ich warte dann unten.

Fragen

1. Wer fährt mit dem Auto zur Uni?
2. Warum möchte Paul mitfahren?
3. Wann holt Birgit Paul ab?
4. Wo wartet Paul?

In den Ferien

Gerhard: Wohin fährst du in den Ferien?
Rita: Nach Dänemark.
Gerhard: Fährst du allein?
Rita: Nein, ich fahre mit meiner Freundin. Die kann Dänisch.
Gerhard: Echt? Und wie fahrt ihr?
Rita: Mit der Bahn. Wir wollen viel wandern.
Gerhard: Und wo wollt ihr schlafen?
Rita: In Kopenhagen schlafen wir bei Freunden, wenn die zu Hause sind. Sonst zelten wir.

Are you driving to the university tomorrow?

Are you going by car to the university tomorrow?
Yes. Do you want to ride along?
Yes, I'd like to. I've got so many books for the library. Can you pick me up maybe?
Yes, no problem. I'll come by your place at eight-thirty. Is that OK?

Yes, of course. I'll be waiting downstairs then.

On vacation

Where are you going on vacation?

To Denmark.
Are you going alone?
No, I'm going with my friend. She knows Danish.
Really? And how are you going?
By train. We want to hike a lot.

And where do you intend to spend the night/stay/sleep?
In Copenhagen we'll sleep/stay/ spend the night at our friends' house if they're at home. Otherwise we'll camp out.

Fragen

1. Wohin fährt Rita in den Ferien?
2. Warum ist es gut, daß Ritas Freundin mitfährt?
3. Wie kommen Rita und ihre Freundin nach Dänemark?
4. Wo schlafen sie in Kopenhagen?
5. Was machen sie, wenn Ritas Freunde nicht zu Hause sind?

1. Interview   Your car has broken down and you're looking for a ride. Ask three students how they get to school or work, when they leave, and when they return home.

| Discussing transportation |

Sie	*Gesprächspartner/in*
Fährst du mit dem Auto zur | **Uni?**	Ja, willst du mitfahren?
| Arbeit?	Nein, | **mein Auto ist kaputt°.**
	| ich nehme den Bus°.
	| ich gehe immer zu Fuß°.
	| ich laufe°.
	| ich fahre mit dem Rad°.
Wann | **gehst** du zur | **Uni?**	Um | **acht.** Ist das zu | **früh?**
| fährst | Arbeit?	| halb neun. | spät?
Wann kommst du wieder nach Hause?	Um vier. Soll ich auf dich warten?
	Gegen sechs.

2. Was machst du in den Ferien?   A friend is looking for someone to go on vacation with and asks what you're going to do during the summer vacation. Respond.

| Discussing travel plans |

Gesprächspartner/in	*Sie*
Hast du schon Pläne° für die Ferien?	Ja, | ich fahre nach Österreich.
	| ich möchte | **wandern.**
	| zelten.
	| viel schwimmen.
	| Wasserski fahren°.
	| schlafen.
	| Ski laufen°.
	Nein, ich habe keine.
	Ich muß arbeiten.
	Nein, meine Ferien sind zu kurz°.

3. Rollenspiel   You and your roommate are discussing plans for tomorrow. Tell her/him what time you have to get up and what you plan to do. Find out the same information from your roommate.

Away from home, young Germans and foreigners can stay at one of over 600 youth hostels (**Jugendherbergen**). Originally established in the early twentieth century, **Jugendherbergen** were located not more than a day's hike apart. They are found not only near vacation spots and national parks, but also in cities and towns. The appearance of **Jugendherbergen** varies greatly from one to another. Some are found in modern buildings while others are in small country houses or even in old fortresses. All serve breakfast and provide bedding, if needed. Many have curfews and some even require their guests to help with various chores.

Traveling to other European countries is very common among German students, particularly since there are special railway fares for young people under the age of 26. (North Americans in that age group can also obtain reduced fares.)

Stahleck am Rhein, eine Jugendherberge in einer alten Burg

Vokabeln

Substantive

das **Auto, -s** automobile, car
die **Bahn, -en** train; railroad
der **Bus, -se** bus
die **Ferien** (*pl.*) vacation
das **Flugzeug, -e** airplane
der **Fuß, ⸚e** foot
das **Motorrad, ⸚er** motorcycle
der **Plan, ⸚e** plan
das **Problem, -e** problem

das **Rad, ⸚er** (*short for* **Fahrrad**) bike, bicycle
das **Schiff, -e** ship
der **Ski, -er** (**Ski** *is pronounced* **Schi**) ski
der **Wagen, -** car
der **Wasserski, -er** water ski
der **Zug, ⸚e** train

Verben

ab·holen to pick up
fahren (fährt) to drive, to travel;
  mit (dem Auto) fahren to go by (car)
fliegen to fly

laufen (läuft) to run; to go on foot; to walk
mit·fahren (fährt mit) to drive (go) along
Ski laufen (läuft Ski) to ski

schlafen (schläft) to sleep
vorbei·kommen to come by
warten (auf + *acc.***)** to wait (for)

Wasserski fahren (fährt Wasserski)
to water ski
zelten to camp in a tent

— Andere Wörter

allein alone
dir *(dat.)* (to *or* for) you
echt really, very *(slang)*
früh early
kaputt broken; exhausted *(slang)*

kurz short, brief
unten downstairs; below
wem *(dat.* of **wer)** (to *or* for) whom
wenn *(conj.)* when; if
wohin where (to)

— Besondere Ausdrücke

bei dir at your place
bei mir vorbeikommen to come by
my place
Geht das? Is that OK?
in den Ferien on vacation; during
vacation

mit (dem Auto) by (car)
zu Fuß on foot; **Ich gehe immer
zu Fuß.** I always walk.
zu Hause (at) home

Erweiterung des Wortschatzes

1 *Wo?* and *wohin?*

Wo ist Dieter?
Where is Dieter?

Wohin geht Erika?
Where is Erika going?

English uses the single word *where* for the two meanings *in what place* and *to what place*. German always distinguishes these two meanings: **wo?** for *in what place* (position) and **wohin?** for *to what place* (direction).

1. Wie bitte? You don't understand what Nicole is saying. Ask her to repeat her statements.

▶ Cornelia fährt zur Uni.   *Wohin fährt Cornelia?*
▶ Erik arbeitet im Supermarkt.   *Wo arbeitet Erik?*

1. Dieter fährt in die Schweiz.
2. Bärbel fährt nach Österreich.
3. Mark geht nach Hause.
4. Tanja arbeitet beim Bäcker.
5. Schmidts wandern in Dänemark.
6. Fischers kaufen immer im Supermarkt ein.

The **Kaffeehaus** was first introduced to the German-speaking areas in the seventeenth century. The Viennese **Kaffeehäuser** in the late nineteenth and early twentieth centuries were especially famous as gathering places for artists, writers, and even revolutionaries like Leon Trotsky. Today, **Cafés** are still popular meeting places throughout the German-speaking countries and often provide newspapers and magazines for their customers. Business people, students, and people from all walks of life enjoy taking a break for coffee and perhaps a piece of cake. In addition to **Kaffee** and a wide variety of **Kuchen** and **Torten,** most **Cafés** offer a small selection of meals (hot and cold), ice cream treats, and other beverages.

A cup of coffee costs around 24 **Schilling** in Austria and 3 **Mark** in Germany, and there are no free refills. In most Viennese **Kaffeehäuser** coffee is served with a small glass of water on a small wooden or silver tray. A spoon is placed upside down across the top of the water glass. Coffee with **Schlagobers** (whipped cream) is a favorite in Vienna.

Cafés are usually not open evenings, but they are open six or seven days per week. The day on which a **Café** or restaurant is closed is called its **Ruhetag.** Most **Cafés** have a sign posted in a prominent place indicating their **Ruhetag.**

In einem Café in Wien

2 Wie fährt man? Man fährt ...

das Fahrrad (das Rad)

mit dem Fahrrad/Rad

das Auto, der Wagen

mit dem Auto/mit dem Wagen

das Motorrad

mit dem Motorrad

der Bus

mit dem Bus

die Straßenbahn

mit der Straßenbahn

die U-Bahn

mit der U-Bahn

die Bahn/der Zug

mit der Bahn/mit dem Zug

das Schiff

mit dem Schiff

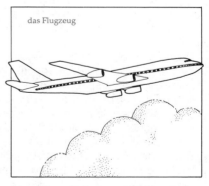

das Flugzeug

Man fliegt (mit dem Flugzeug).

2. Wie fahren Sie?   Answer the following questions. For additional transportation terms, refer to the Supplementary Word Sets in the Reference Section.

Talking about transportation

Haben Sie ein Fahrrad? einen Wagen? ein Motorrad?
Ist es/er neu oder alt?
Wie fahren Sie zur Uni? Mit dem Bus? Mit dem Auto? Mit dem Rad? Mit der
   U-Bahn?
Fliegen Sie gern? viel?

**In Wien kann man mit der
Straßenbahn in die Oper fahren.**

Public transportation is efficient and much utilized by the people in German-speaking countries. Buses, streetcars, subways, and trains are owned either by the federal or local government. While the popularity of the car continues to grow, governments subsidize public transportation because public transportation is better for the environment (**umweltfreundlich**) and ensures that everyone has access to transportation. Reduced rates are available for senior citizens (**Seniorenkarten**) and for students at all levels (**Schüler-/Studentenkarten**). In towns, villages, and suburbs there is convenient bus and sometimes streetcar (**Straßenbahn**) service. Major cities have a subway (**Untergrundbahn** or **U-Bahn**) and/or a modern commuter rail system (**Schnellbahn/Stadtbahn** or **S-Bahn**). The German, Austrian, and Swiss post offices provide extensive bus service between towns. If needed, even ferries are included in the public transportation network, such as the ferry on the Alster Lake (**Alsterfähre**) in Hamburg.

Trains are still a major part of the transportation system in German-speaking countries for both long and short distance travel. Larger cities have more than one train station (**Bahnhof**), but the main train station (**Hauptbahnhof**) is usually located in the center of town. In addition to transportation facilities, larger train stations may also have a variety of restaurants and shops to serve the traveling public. To commute, people often use short-distance trains (**Nahverkehrszüge**). Fast, comfortable **Inter-City Express** trains run hourly between major cities. This system is being supplemented with the **Interregio-Züge,** which depart every two hours. The slightly slower "through" trains (**D-Züge**) also make long distance runs, but stop more frequently than the **ICE** trains. A network of trains known as the **Euro-City Express** connects the major cities throughout Europe.

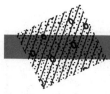

ÖSTERREICH

Vorbereitung auf das Lesen

◆ Zum Thema

Was wissen Sie schon über Österreich? Was meinen° Sie?   think

1. Wie groß ist Österreich? Größer als New York oder Ontario oder so groß wie Maine oder Neubraunschweig?
2. Wie viele Einwohner hat Österreich? 7,5 Millionen oder 15 Millionen?
3. Wo liegen die Alpen? Im Westen oder im Osten von Österreich?
4. Wo liegt Wien? Im Westen oder im Osten?
5. Wie viele Nachbarn hat Österreich? Drei oder sieben?
6. Wie heißen die Nachbarländer?

Suchen Sie die folgenden Städte und Länder auf der Landkarte.

Länder: Bulgarien ◇ Italien ◇ Jugoslawien ◇ Österreich ◇ Polen ◇ Rumänien ◇ die Sowjetunion ◇ die Tschechoslowakei ◇ Ungarn
Städte: Budapest ◇ Prag ◇ Belgrad ◇ Wien

◆ Leitfragen

1. Warum kommen die Wiener aus vielen verschiedenen° Ländern?   various

   Stichworte: vor 1918 ◇ Vielvölkerstaat°   multi-ethnic state

2. Welche Rolle spielte° Österreich im Ost-West-Konflikt?   played

   Stichworte: neutral ◇ vermitteln° ◇ Flüchtlinge°   mediate / refugees

3. Welche Rolle spielt Österreich heute?

   Stichworte: internationale Zusammenarbeit ◇ Tor° zu Osteuropa   gate

4. Was sind einige Grundlagen° für Österreich heute?   basic elements

   Stichworte: Geschichte ◇ neutral ◇ Vermittler° ◇ Konflikt (nicht) mediator
   mögen ◇ Dinge (nicht) ernst nehmen

The reading on Austria contains references to historical events. These events are expressed in the past tense. You will find the following verbs in the past tense: **lag (liegen)** *lay, was located;* **gehörte(n) (gehören)** *belonged;* **lebte(n) (leben)** *lived;* **kam(en) (kommen)** *came;* **versuchte (versuchen)** *tried;* **nahm auf (aufnehmen)** *accepted;* **schrieb (schreiben)** *wrote.*

**Wien —
Innenstadt mit Stephansdom**

Austria has a very rich and diverse cultural tradition. In the late eighteenth and early nineteenth centuries, Vienna (**Wien**) was the center of a musical culture associated with such names as Haydn, Mozart, Beethoven, and Schubert. In the second half of the nineteenth century the **Operette** reached its prime with composers like Johann Strauß the Younger and Franz Lehar. At the turn of the century (referred to in French as **Fin de Siècle**), Vienna was a major artistic and intellectual center of Europe. All at about the same time, Sigmund Freud established psychoanalysis; Arthur Schnitzler, Hugo von Hofmannsthal, and Stefan Zweig wrote important dramas and novels; and Gustav Mahler continued the city's great musical tradition.

83.855 qkm°; 7,5 Millionen Einwohner
etwa so groß wie Maine (86.027 qkm)
etwas größer° als Neubraunschweig° (72.000 qkm)
Bundesstaat° mit 9 Bundesländern°
5 Hauptstadt: Wien
parlamentarische Demokratie
7 Nachbarn: I, FL, CH, D, ČS, H, YU*

qkm = Quadratkilometer:
square kilometers

larger / New Brunswick, Canada

a federation / federal states

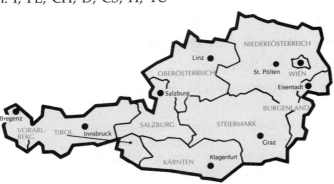

*I = Italien, FL = Fürstentum Liechtenstein, CH = die Schweiz, D = Bundesrepublik Deutschland, ČS = die Tschechoslowakei, H = Ungarn, YU = Jugoslawien

Österreich ist vor allem ein Alpenland. Die Berge sind im Westen. Nur der Osten ist Flach- oder Hügelland°. Daher leben hier die meisten Menschen.
10 Die Hauptstadt liegt fast am Rande° des° Landes. Das erscheint° wenig praktisch. Wenn man aber das Österreich von vor° 1918 ansieht, findet man, daß Wien mehr im Westen des° Landes lag. Zu diesem Land der Habsburger° gehörten nämlich° Gebiete°, die° heute in der Tschechoslowakei, in der Sowjetunion, in Rumänien, Ungarn, Jugoslawien und Italien liegen. In
15 diesem Österreich lebten also viele verschiedene Völker zusammen. Es war ein Vielvölkerstaat°. In Wien kamen Menschen aus allen diesen Völkern zusammen.

Eine Österreicherin aus Kärnten° sagt dazu°: „Für alle Teile des Landes war Wien das Zentrum°. Das kann man schon an den Namen im Telefonbuch
20 sehen. Da gibt es z.B. mehrere Seiten Dvorak oder Svoboda, beides tschechische Namen. In vielen Familien ist es ganz normal, daß der Vater z.B. aus Prag ist, eine Tante in Budapest verheiratet war, daß ein Onkel aus Triest kommt und daß die Mutter gute Freunde in Jugoslawien hat.

„Auf diese Weise° ist Österreich ganz anders als die anderen
25 deutschsprachigen° Länder. Die Geschichte ist ganz anders. Für Österreicher ist es eben ganz natürlich, daß wir auch gute Kontakte zu unseren Nachbarn im Osten haben."

So überrascht es nicht, daß Österreich in der Zeit des° Ost-West-Konflikts neutral war. Es versuchte, kulturell, wirtschaftlich° und politisch zu
30 vermitteln°. Es war auch neutral, wenn es Flüchtlinge° aufnahm: Es war egal, aus welchem Land sie kamen. Seit dem Zweiten Weltkrieg hat dieses kleine Land 1,75 Millionen Flüchtlinge aufgenommen°. Viele von ihnen leben noch heute in Österreich.

Die neunziger Jahre° bringen Österreich eine neue geopolitische Lage°.
35 Österreich liegt nicht mehr an der Grenze von Osten und Westen, sondern mehr oder weniger im Zentrum Europas. Es kennt die Sprachen und Kulturen seiner° östlichen Nachbarn schon seit langer Zeit. Es hat Erfahrung° im Ost-West-Handel. Daher haben viele internationale Firmen Büros in Wien (1990 waren es 700). Wien ist eine logische Ausgangsbasis° für die neuen
40 Märkte in Osteuropa. So sieht Österreich sich° als Tor° oder als Brücke zu Osteuropa.

Wien ist auch der Sitz° wichtiger° internationaler Organisationen. UNO° und OPEC haben in Wien Büros. Eine neue internationale Organisation ist die Pentagonale. Seit 1990 verbindet° diese Organisation Österreich, Italien,
45 Jugoslawien, Ungarn und die Tschechoslowakei, fünf Staaten aus dem alten Land der Habsburger. Sie wollen auf Gebieten wie Umweltschutz° und Transport zusammenarbeiten.

---

low and hilly country
am Rande: on the edge / of the / appears / before
of the / of the Hapsburgs
you see / areas / which

multi-ethnic state

Carinthia (state in Austria) / to that / center

auf ... Weise: in this way
German-speaking

of the
economically
mediate / refugees

hat aufgenommen: accepted

Die ... Jahre: the 1990s / position

of its / experience

starting point
itself / gate

seat / of important / United Nations

links

environmental protection

Für viele Menschen im heutigen° Österreich gehören die lange Geschichte, Neutralität und Vermittlerfunktion° zu den Grundlagen° ihres°
50 Landes. Der österreichische Schriftsteller Gerhard Roth schrieb über die Österreicher, daß sie den offenen° Konflikt nicht mögen. Vielleicht haben sie in dem engen Kontakt mit anderen Kulturen während° ihrer langen Geschichte gelernt°, die Dinge nicht so ernst zu nehmen wie z.B. die Deutschen. In Deutschland sagt man eher°: „Die Lage° ist ernst, aber nicht
55 hoffnungslos°.“ In Österreich sagt man dagegen° eher: „Die Lage ist hoffnungslos, aber nicht ernst.“

present day
mediating function / basic elements / of their

public
during
haben gelernt: learned
rather / situation
hopeless / on the other hand

Fragen zum Lesestück

1. Wie viele Nachbarn hat Österreich? Welche liegen im Süden? Im Westen? Im Norden? Im Osten?
2. Wo in Österreich liegen die Berge? Wie ist das Land im Osten?
3. Wo in Österreich liegt Wien? Erklären Sie.
4. Bis wann war Österreich ein Vielvölkerstaat?
5. Was für Namen sind Dvorak und Svoboda?
6. Wie kommen z.B. tschechische Namen ins Wiener Telefonbuch?
7. Zu wem haben die Österreicher gute Kontakte?
8. In welchem Konflikt war Österreich neutral?
9. Wie viele Flüchtlinge hat Österreich seit 1945 aufgenommen?
10. Warum ist Österreichs geopolitische Lage neu?
11. Warum kann Österreich im Ost-West-Handel eine besondere Rolle spielen?
12. Warum ist Wien für viele internationale Firmen so attraktiv?
13. Wie sieht Österreich sich heute?
14. Welche internationalen Organisationen haben Büros in Österreich?
15. Welche Länder gehören zur Pentagonale?
16. Was gehört zu den Grundlagen Österreichs heute? Nennen Sie drei Dinge.
17. Warum sagt man in Österreich eher „Die Lage ist hoffnungslos, aber nicht ernst“?

Erzählen Sie.   Tell something about Austria. Use some of the cued words below and add some words of your own.

die Hauptstadt Wien im Osten ◊ Namen aus vielen Ländern ◊ Ost-West-Konflikt: neutral ◊ neue geopolitische Lage ◊ neue Märkte ◊ internationale Organisationen ◊ Dinge nicht so ernst nehmen

A very significant period in Austria's history is the era under the rule of the House of Habsburg. In 1273 Rudolf von Habsburg was the first member of the Habsburg family to be elected emperor of the Holy Roman Empire (**Heiliges Römisches Reich**), which existed from 962 until 1806. In the first 400 years of Habsburg rule, the empire expanded greatly. The expansion was due to wars and to a successful **Heiratspolitik,** which deliberately aimed at advantageous marriages with the ruling European houses. The success of Napoleon's wars at the beginning of the nineteenth century led to the end of the empire in 1806. Members of the House of Habsburg continued to rule the Austro-Hungarian empire until 1918, however, when Austria was declared a republic.

Wien — Schloß Schönbrunn, die Sommerresidenz der Habsburger Kaiser

Vokabeln

Substantive

die **Alpen** *(pl.)* Alps
der **Berg, -e** mountain
das **Büro, -s** office
das **Ding, -e** thing
die **Firma, Firmen** *(pl.)* company, firm
die **Grenze, -n** border
der **Handel** trade
der **Kontakt, -e** contact
der **Krieg, -e** war; **der Weltkrieg, -e** World War
die **Landkarte, -n** map

die **Rolle, -n** role
der **Schriftsteller, -/die Schriftstellerin, -nen** writer, author
die **Seite, -n** page; side
die **Sprache, -n** language
der **Staat, -en** country; state
der **Teil, -e** part
das **Volk, ⸚er** people, folk
die **Welt, -en** world
Wien Vienna
die **Zeit, -en** time

— Verben —

danken (+ *dat.*) (**für**) to thank (for)	**schenken** to give (as a gift)
gehören (+ *dat.*) to belong to	**überraschen** to surprise
leben to live	**versuchen** to try, attempt

— Andere Wörter —

aus (+ *dat.*) out of; from	**ob** (*conj.*) whether, if
beides both	**seit** (+ *dat.*) since (*time*)
besonder particular	**sondern** (*conj.*) but, on the contrary
daß (*conj.*) that	**verheiratet (mit)** married (to)
egal equal; the same; **Das ist mir egal.** It's all the same to me.	**verschieden** different, various
eng close; tight; narrow	**wichtig** important
fast almost	**weil** (*conj.*) because
lang long	

— Besondere Ausdrücke —

mehr oder weniger more or less	**eine Rolle spielen** to play a role
nicht nur … sondern auch not only . . . but also	**vor allem** above all; most important(ly)

UNO-Gebäude in Wien

After the end of World War II, Austria's sovereignty was restored in 1955. In the same year, Austria declared its policy of permanent neutrality (**immerwährende Neutralität**)—which it has always interpreted as a commitment to armed neutrality. During the Cold War, Austria was not a member of NATO or the Warsaw Pact. From the end of World War II until the end of the Cold War, Austria granted temporary or permanent asylum to about two million people from more than thirty countries. In fact, its decision to allow East German refugees to enter through its border with Hungary was a contributing factor to the fall of the government of the East German state.

Austria continues to play an important role in Europe and serves as an important link between western and eastern Europe. Austria expects to join the European Community (**Europäische Gemeinschaft**) without surrendering its neutrality. It is an active member of the United Nations and serves as the site of many international congresses and conferences. Vienna ranks among the leading convention cities in the world.

GRAMMATIK UND ÜBUNGEN

1 Verbs with stem-vowel change *a* > *ä*

fahren: to drive	
ich fahre	wir fahren
du **fährst**	ihr fahrt
er/es/sie **fährt**	sie fahren
Sie fahren	

laufen: to run; to go on foot, walk	
ich laufe	wir laufen
du **läufst**	ihr lauft
er/es/sie **läuft**	sie laufen
Sie laufen	

Some verbs with stem-vowel **a** or **au** change **a** to **ä** in the **du-** and **er/es/sie-** forms of the present tense.

1. Wohin fährst du?   You are discussing travel plans for the summer with a friend. Tell who is going where. Use a form of **fahren.**

▶   Paula / Italien   *Paula fährt nach Italien.*

1. Frank / auch / Italien
2. meine Großeltern / Spanien
3. ich / Dänemark

4. meine Schwester / Ungarn
5. wir / auch / Schweden
6. du / Österreich / ?

2. Wir laufen gern.   You are discussing how and when people you know like to run or walk. Use a form of **laufen.**

▶   Erika / morgens   *Erika läuft morgens.*

1. Gisela / abends
2. ich / zur Uni
3. mein Vater / auch gern

4. wir / gern zusammen
5. du / viel / ?
6. Bärbel / meistens / morgens

Wer zuletzt lacht, lacht am besten.

3. Restop Altea Tell what one can learn about the Restop Altea Motel from its ad by answering the questions. If you need help, see Vocabulary for Authentic Text Activities in the Reference Section.

RESTOP
ALTEA
— M O T E L —
MONDSEE

Tel. 0 62 32/28 76–28 79, Telex 63 33 57 altea
Telefax 06 2 32/28 76/5

DER MONDSEE LIEGT IHNEN ZU FÜSSEN

Idealer Ausgangspunkt für jung und alt in äußerst ruhiger Lage. Das ist unser Motel mit 46 Komfortzimmern, erreichbar von beiden Fahrtrichtungen der A-1-Autobahn. In unserem Panorama-Restaurant überraschen wir Sie mit kulinarischen Spezialitäten.
Hoteleigener Badestrand!
Es lädt Sie ein:

Der Mondsee:	zum Segeln, Surfen, Wasserschilaufen und zu Schiffsrundfahrten.
Die Bergwelt:	zum Bergwandern und Bergsteigen.
Mondsee:	zum Besuch von Kulturstätten und Veranstaltungen.
Die Umgebung:	zum Tennisspielen, zum Golfen auf zwei Plätzen mit neun bzw. 18 Löchern, zu Ausflugsfahrten ins Salzkammergut.
Unser Haus:	mit dem Weekend-Hit, zahle 2 Nächte und bleibe 3!

Gute Erholung und viel Vergnügen!

1. Wie viele Zimmer hat das Motel?
2. Welchen Sport kann man treiben?
3. Was ist der Weekend-Hit?

4. Rollenspiel Work with a partner. You have just come across the ad for Altea Motel and want to spend a weekend there. Convince your partner to go with you and plan your activities for your time at the resort.

> Making plans for the weekend

2 Word order with expressions of time

	General Time	Specific Time	
Ich stehe	morgens	um sieben	auf.

When a sentence contains two time expressions, the more specific time element (e.g., **um sieben**) is stressed and comes after the more general time element (e.g., **morgens**).

5. Was machst du jeden Tag?   You feel you have very busy days and wonder what it's like for others. Ask a fellow student about her/his daily schedule. Use two time expressions in the response.

> Talking about daily routines

Sie   *Gesprächspartner/in*

Wann stehst du morgens auf?   *Ich stehe morgens um [sieben] auf.*

Wann fährst du morgens zur Uni?
Wann gehst du nachmittags zur Vorlesung?
Um wieviel Uhr gehst du nachmittags wieder nach Hause?
Um wieviel Uhr gehst du samstags zu Bett?
Um wieviel Uhr ißt du sonntags zu Mittag?

3 Independent clauses and coordinating conjunctions

Wir wollen am Wochenende zelten. Es soll regnen.
Wir wollen am Wochenende zelten, **aber** es soll regnen.

An independent (or main) clause can stand alone as a complete sentence. Two or more independent clauses may be connected by coordinating conjunctions (e.g., **aber**). Because coordinating conjunctions are merely connectors and not part of either clause, they do not affect word order. The coordinating conjunctions you know are **aber, denn, oder, sondern,** and **und.**

Erika kommt morgen, **und** Christel kommt am Montag.
Erika kommt morgen **und** Christel am Montag.
Erika kommt morgen **und** bleibt eine Woche.

In written German, coordinating conjunctions are generally preceded by a comma. **Oder** and **und** are not preceded by a comma when either the subject or the verb is omitted in the second clause.

6. **Erika und Sabine**   Tell what Sabine and Erika are going to do this week. Combine each pair of sentences below, using the coordinating conjunctions indicated.

▶   *Die Studentin heißt Erika. Ihre*   *Die Studentin heißt Erika, und*
     Freundin heißt Sabine. (und)   *ihre Freundin heißt Sabine.*

1. Erika wohnt bei einer Familie. Sabine wohnt bei ihren Eltern. (aber)
2. Erika arbeitet zu Hause. Sabine muß in die Bibliothek gehen. (aber)
3. Erika arbeitet schwer. Am Mittwoch hat sie eine Klausur. (denn)
4. Sabine hat ihre Klausur nicht am Mittwoch. Sie hat sie am Freitag. (sondern)
5. Was machen die Mädchen in den Ferien? Wissen sie es nicht? (oder)

◆ Sondern *and* aber

Paul fährt morgen nicht mit dem   Paul isn't going by car tomorrow,
    Auto, **sondern** geht zu Fuß.   but (rather) is walking.

Sondern is a coordinating conjunction that expresses a contrast or contradiction. It connects two ideas that are mutually exclusive. It is used only after a negative clause and is equivalent to *but, on the contrary, instead, rather.* When the subject is the same in both clauses, it is not repeated. This is also true of a verb that is the same; it is not repeated.

Cordelia tanzt nicht nur viel,   Cordelia not only dances a lot,
    sondern auch gut.   but also well.

The German construction **nicht nur … sondern auch** is equivalent to *not only . . . but also.*

Er fährt nicht mit dem Auto, **aber**   He isn't going by car, but his father
    sein Vater fährt mit dem Auto.   is.

Aber as a coordinating conjunction is equivalent to *but* or *nevertheless.* It may be used after either positive or negative clauses.

7. **Was macht Annette?**   Complete the sentences about Annette's activities with **aber** or **sondern,** as appropriate.

▶   *Annette steht nicht früh, _____ spät auf.*   *Annette steht nicht früh,*
                                                 sondern spät auf.

1. Sie spielt heute nicht Fußball, _____ Tennis.
2. Sie spielt Tennis nicht gut, _____ sie spielt es sehr gern.
3. Sie geht nicht zur Vorlesung, _____ in die Bibliothek.
4. Im Café bestellt sie Bier, _____ sie trinkt Eriks Kaffee.
5. Sie möchte den Kaffee bezahlen, _____ sie hat kein Geld.

8. Meine Freunde Your friends are all very active people. Tell what they do using **nicht nur ... sondern auch.**

Showing connections and relationships

▶ Karola studiert Musik. Sie studiert auch Sport. *Karola studiert nicht nur Musik, sondern auch Sport.*

1. Adrian lernt Deutsch. Er lernt auch Spanisch.
2. Sabine arbeitet im Café. Sie arbeitet auch im Supermarkt.
3. Bettina besucht° einen Tanzkurs. Sie besucht auch einen Karatekurs.   attends
4. Bernd spielt Fußball und Hockey. Er spielt auch Tennis.
5. Jan macht Informatik. Er macht auch Geschichte und Mathematik.

ítallíngua

Italienisch in München
Italienisch in Italien
Oster- und Sommerkurse
in der Toscana am Meer
Franz-Joseph-Str. 48 · 8000 Mü 40
☎ *2716438*

Intensiv-Wochenendkurs im April und Mai Informationen bitte anfordern!

luisenstr. 62
8000 münchen 40
tel. 089/2 72 21 95

mo.–fr. 16⁰⁰–19⁰⁰

step in dance studio
susanne stortz

Jazz · Ballett · Modern Dance · Aerobic · Stretching

TAEKWON-DO BLACK-BELT-CENTER
SELBSTVERTEIDIGUNG
ZEN-KUNST
tägl. ANFÄNGERKURSE
Berduxstr. 30, 8000 München 60 (Pasing), Telefon 83 03 60
Berg am Laim, Neumarkter Str. 75 Telefon 4 31 45 88
Training: tägl. vormittags u. abends

4 Dependent clauses and subordinating conjunctions

Independent Clause	Conjunction	Dependent Clause
Rita sagt,	**daß**	sie nach Dänemark **fährt.**
Sie schläft bei Freunden,	**wenn**	die zu Hause **sind.**

A dependent clause is a clause that cannot stand alone; it must be combined with a main clause to express a complete idea. Two signals distinguish a dependent clause from an independent clause: (1) it is introduced by a subordinating conjunction (**daß, wenn**) and (2) the finite verb (**fährt, sind**) is at the end. In writing, a dependent clause is separated from the main clause by a comma. A few common subordinating conjunctions are: **daß,** *that;* **ob,** *if,* *whether;* **obwohl,** *although;* **weil,** *because;* **wenn,** *if, when.*

Paul fragt Birgit, **ob** sie zur Uni fährt.

Er möchte mitfahren, **wenn** sie zur Uni fährt.

Paul asks Birgit *whether* she is driving to the university.

He would like to go along, *if* she is driving to the university.

Both **wenn** and **ob** are equivalent to English *if.* However, they are not interchangeable. **Ob** can always be translated with *whether* and is used with main clauses such as **er fragt, ob ...** and **ich weiß nicht, ob ...**

9. Deutsche Studenten   Answer the questions. Use **wenn** to answer questions beginning with **wann.** Use **weil** to answer questions beginning with **warum.**

▶   Wann bekommen Studenten Geld   *Wenn sie zuwenig Geld haben.*
   vom Staat? (Sie haben zuwenig Geld.)

1. Warum arbeiten die Studenten nicht? (Es gibt wenige Studentenjobs.)
2. Warum brauchen sie soviel Geld? (Wohnen und Essen sind teuer.)
3. Wann bekommt man einen Studienplatz? (Man hat gute Zensuren im Gymnasium.)
4. Warum müssen Studenten in acht Semestern fertig sein? (Es gibt zuwenig Studienplätze.)
5. Wann ist es billiger zu studieren? (Man wohnt bei den Eltern.)

10. Was weißt du über Birgit?   Practice asking someone for information. Begin your sentences with **Weißt du, ob ... ?**

Asking for specific information

▶   Fährt Birgit morgen zur Uni?   *Weißt du, ob Birgit morgen zur Uni fährt?*

1. Fährt sie mit dem Bus?
2. Ist ihr Auto kaputt?
3. Kommt sie um drei wieder nach Hause?
4. Wohnt sie noch im Studentenheim?
5. Arbeitet sie heute abend zu Hause?
6. Geht sie mit Paul ins Kino?

◆ *Dependent clauses and separable-prefix verbs*

Statement	Gisela **kauft** im Supermarkt **ein.**
Dependent clause	Gisela sagt, **daß** sie im Supermarkt **einkauft.**

In a dependent clause, the separable prefix is attached to the base form of the verb, which is in final position.

11. Was sagt Gabi?   You want to tell a friend about Gabi's plans. Begin each sentence with **Gabi sagt, daß ...**

Reporting on actions

▶   Sie steht früh auf.   *Gabi sagt, daß sie früh aufsteht.*

1. Sie kauft in der Stadt ein.
2. Renate kommt mit.
3. Renate kommt um neun bei ihr vorbei.
4. Das Kaufhaus macht um zehn auf.
5. Sie sehen alles an.
6. Sie bereitet zu Hause ein Referat vor.

◆ *Dependent clauses and modal auxiliaries*

Statement	Rita **möchte** in die Schweiz fahren.
Dependent clause	Rita sagt, **daß** sie in die Schweiz fahren **möchte**.

In a dependent clause, the modal auxiliary follows the dependent infinitive and is in final position.

12. Andreas sagt das. A friend wants to know if Andreas really has to do or have certain things. Respond that Andreas says he does.

▶ Andreas muß die Notizen von Michael haben, nicht?   *Ja, er sagt, daß er die Notizen haben muß.*

1. Er muß die Notizen heute haben, nicht?
2. Andreas will sie durcharbeiten, nicht?
3. Er muß einen Artikel über Brecht lesen, nicht?
4. Er soll eine Seminararbeit schreiben, nicht?
5. Er will in die Bibliothek gehen, nicht?
6. Er will heute abend viel arbeiten, nicht?

13. Warum? Answer the questions for yourself. Then ask your partner the same questions. Be sure to use the **du**-form with your partner.

1. Warum arbeiten Sie am Wochenende [nicht]?
2. Warum gehen Sie nicht mit ins Kino?
3. Warum laufen Sie [nicht] zur Uni?
4. Warum essen Sie [keinen] Salat?
5. Warum leihen Sie Ihren Freunden [kein] Geld?
6. Warum schlafen Sie so wenig?
7. Warum fliegen Sie in den Ferien [nicht] nach Deutschland?
8. Warum sind Sie so still?

◆ *Dependent clauses beginning a sentence*

	1	2	
	Paul	**fährt**	mit dem Bus.
1		2	
Weil sein Auto kaputt ist,		**fährt**	er mit dem Bus.

In a statement, the finite verb is in second position. If a sentence begins with a dependent clause, the entire clause is considered a single element, and the finite verb of the independent clause is in second position, followed by the subject.

14. Wenn es so ist.   Combine each pair of sentences. Begin the new sentence with the conjunction indicated.

▶   (wenn) Das Wetter ist gut. Gerhard   *Wenn das Wetter gut ist, wollen*
     und Paul wollen nach Dänemark.   *Gerhard und Paul nach Dänemark.*

1. (weil) Sie haben wenig Geld. Sie fahren mit dem Rad.
2. (wenn) Sie fahren mit dem Rad. Sie sehen mehr vom Land.
3. (wenn) Es ist nicht zu kalt. Sie zelten.
4. (wenn) Das Wetter ist sehr schlecht. Sie schlafen bei Freunden.
5. (obwohl) Sie haben wenig Geld. Sie können vier Wochen bleiben.
6. (weil) Sie haben nur vier Wochen Ferien. Sie müssen im August wieder zu Hause sein.

◆ *Question words as subordinating conjunctions*

Direct specific question		**Wann** kommt Birgit heute?
Indirect specific question	Ich weiß nicht, Thomas fragt,	**wann** Birgit heute kommt.

Question words (**wer, was, wann, wie lange, warum,** etc.) function as subordinating conjunctions when they introduce indirect questions.

15. Lia hat einen neuen Freund.   Barbara and Gerd are talking about Lia's new friend. Continue their conversation using the model below.

▶   Barbara: Wie heißt er?   *Gerd: Ich weiß nicht, wie er heißt.*

1. Was macht er?   5. Wo arbeitet er?
2. Wie lange kennt sie ihn schon?   6. Warum findet sie ihn so toll°?   great
3. Wo wohnt er?   7. Wann sieht sie ihn wieder?
4. Wie alt ist er?

16. Warum? Weil ...   Role-play a conversation with a partner in which you make some requests or suggestions (e.g., to lend you notes/map, to ride along, to come to your place tonight, to play [tennis] with you, to go [to the movies/shopping] with you, to go for coffee, to stay for a minute, to eat lunch together, to inquire whether he/she wants to buy [your bicycle]. Your partner responds in the negative. Ask why and your partner will give a reason.

	Giving reasons

Sie	*Gesprächspartner/in*
Kannst du mir deine Notizen leihen?	Nein. Es tut mir leid.
Warum nicht?	Weil ich sie heute selbst brauche.

5 Dative case

Nominative	**Der** Kaffee ist billig.
Accusative	Kaufst du **den** Kaffee?
Dative	Was hältst du von **dem** Kaffee?

In addition to nominative and accusative, German has a case called *dative*.

Masculine	Neuter	Feminine	Plural
de**m** Mann	de**m** Kind	de**r** Frau	de**n** Freunden
dies**em** Mann	dies**em** Kind	dies**er** Frau	dies**en** Freunden
ein**em** Mann	ein**em** Kind	ein**er** Frau	kein**en** Freunden
ihr**em** Mann	unser**em** Kind	sein**er** Frau	mein**en** Freunde**n**

The definite and indefinite articles, **der**-words and **ein**-words change their form in the dative case. The plural form of a noun in the dative case adds **-n,** unless the plural already ends in **-n** or **-s: meine Freunde > meinen Freunden:** but **die Frauen > den Frauen; die Autos > den Autos.**

6 Masculine *N*-nouns in the dative

Nominative	der Herr	der Student
Accusative	den Herr**n**	den Student**en**
Dative	dem Herr**n**	dem Student**en**

Masculine **N**-nouns, which add **-n** or **-en** in the accusative, also add **-n** or **-en** in the dative singular. The masculine **N**-nouns you know so far are: **der Herr, der Junge, der Mensch, der Nachbar, der Name,** and **der Student.**

7 Demonstrative pronouns in the dative

Masculine	Neuter	Feminine	Plural
dem	dem	der	denen

The dative forms of the demonstrative pronouns are identical to the dative forms of the definite articles, except that in the dative plural **den** becomes **denen.**

8 Dative of *wer?*

Nominative	**Wer** sagt das?	Who says that?
Dative	**Wem** sagen Sie das?	To whom are you saying that?

The dative form of the interrogative **wer?** (*who?*) is **wem?** (*[to] whom?*).

9 Dative verbs

Erika **dankt ihrem** Freund für die Blumen.	Erika thanks her friend for the flowers.
Das Haus **gehört meinen** Eltern.	The house belongs to my parents.

Most German verbs take objects in the accusative. However, a few verbs take objects in the dative. The dative object is usually a person. Such verbs can be classified as "dative verbs." The dative verbs in this chapter are **danken, glauben,** and **gehören.** A more complete list of dative verbs is found in section 17 of the Grammatical Tables in the Reference Section.

Sie **glaubt ihrem** Freund.	She believes her friend.
Erik **glaubt es** nicht.	Erik doesn't believe it.

The verb **glauben** always takes personal objects (e.g., **ihrem Freund**) in the dative case. However, impersonal objects (e.g., **es**) after **glauben** are in the accusative case.

17. Glauben, danken, gehören Answer the questions, using the cued words.

▶ Wem glaubt Thea? (ihr Freund) *Thea glaubt ihrem Freund.*

1. Wem glaubt Inge? (ihr Bruder)
2. Wem glaubt Frank? (seine Freundin)
3. Wem dankt Gerd für alles? (seine Eltern)
4. Wem dankt Lore für das Musikheft? (ihr Freund)

▶ Wem gehört das Fahrrad? (der Junge) *Es gehört dem Jungen.*

5. Wem gehört das Auto? (der Herr)
6. Wem gehört die Stereoanlage? (das Mädchen)
7. Wem gehört der Computer? (die Frau)

18. Was gehört wem? You have borrowed a number of things from various people and are having a hard time remembering what belongs to whom. Ask your partner, who will tell you.

▶ Buch Professor
Wem gehört das Buch? *Das gehört meinem Professor.*

1. Kuli Freund
2. Radio Schwester
3. Gitarre Bruder
4. Kassetten Eltern

5. Landkarte Nachbarn
6. Tasche Mutter
7. Bleistift Bruder

10 Indirect object

	Indirect object	Direct object
Inge schenkt	ihrem Freund	ein Radio.
Inge is giving	her friend	a radio.

In both English and German some verbs take two objects, which are traditionally called the direct object (e.g., **Radio**—*radio*) and the indirect object (e.g., **Freund**—*friend*). The indirect object is usually a person and answers the question *to whom* or *for whom* the direct object is intended. Some verbs that can take both direct and indirect objects are **bringen, erklären, geben, kaufen, leihen, sagen, schenken,** and **schreiben**.

11 Signals for indirect object and direct object

	Indirect (dative) object	Direct (accusative) object
Inge schenkt	ihren Eltern	ein Radio.
Inge is giving	her parents	a radio.

English signals the indirect object by putting it before the direct object or by using the preposition *to* or *for*. To determine in English whether a noun or pronoun is an indirect object, add *to* or *for* before it: Inge is giving a radio *to* her parents.

 German uses case to signal the difference between a direct object and an indirect object. The direct object is in the accusative, and the indirect object is in the dative. Since the case signals are clear, **German never uses a preposition to signal the indirect object.**

19. Was bedeutet das? Identify the indirect (dative) object and direct (accusative) object and give the English equivalent of the sentences below.

1. Ich muß meinem Freund meine Notizen leihen.
2. Ich möchte meiner Großmutter diese Blumen schenken.
3. Was kaufst du deiner Freundin zum Geburtstag?
4. Den Plan mußt du meinem Freund genauer erklären.
5. Wem soll ich das schreiben?
6. Ich möchte dem Mädchen etwas sagen.

20. Was macht Dieter? Answer the questions below about Dieter's activities. Replace **wem** with the dative possessive adjective and the nouns in parentheses.

▶ Wem kauft Dieter neue Weingläser? (seine Eltern) *Seinen Eltern.*

1. Wem bringt er Blumen mit? (seine Großmutter)
2. Wem gibt er seinen Fußball? (sein Freund Erik)
3. Wem gibt er sein Radio? (sein Bruder)
4. Wem leiht er etwas Geld? (seine Schwester)
5. Wem leiht er kein Geld? (seine Freunde Gerd und Alex)
6. Wem schenkt er den Fußball? (sein Bruder)
7. Wem schenkt er die Tasche? (seine Tante)
8. Wem erklärt er die Geschichte? (das Kind)
9. Wem schreibt er eine Karte? (der Junge)

21. Wie sagt man das?

1. What are you giving your mother for her birthday?
   —Flowers and a book.
2. Who are you writing the card to?
   —[To] my cousin Achim.
3. Are you lending your girlfriend Lore money?
   —Yes. She's buying her parents flowers.
4. I have to thank my aunt and my uncle for the radio.
   —Bring your aunt flowers.

22. Geburtstagsgeschenke You need some ideas for birthday presents for your family. Ask four fellow students what they would like to give members of their families for their birthdays.

▶ Was möchtest du [deiner Mutter] zum Geburtstag schenken?

Discussing ideas for birthday presents

12 Dative prepositions

aus	out of	Er geht früh **aus** dem Haus.
	(to come) from *[cities and countries]*	Sie kommt **aus** Deutschland.
außer	besides, except for	Wer ist **außer** den Studenten hier?
bei	with *(at the home of)*	Er wohnt **bei** einer Familie.
	at *(a place of business)*	Sie arbeitet **bei** Siemens.
	near *(in the proximity of)*	Die Bäckerei ist **bei** der Universität.
mit	with	Sie fährt **mit** ihrem Freund zur Uni.
	by means of *(transportation)*	Fährst du **mit** dem Auto zur Uni?
nach	to *(with cities and masculine and neuter countries)*	Sie fährt im Sommer **nach** Österreich.
	after	Er kommt **nach** dem Essen.
seit	since *(time)*	Sie ist **seit** Mittwoch in Wien.
von	from	Was hören Sie **von** Ihrem Freund?
	of	Österreich ist ein Land **von** 7.500.000 Einwohnern.
	by	Das Drama ist **von** Brecht
zu	to *(with people and some places)*	Wir gehen gern **zu** unseren Nachbarn.
		Wann fährst du **zur** Uni?

The prepositions **aus, außer, bei, mit, nach, seit, von,** and **zu** are always followed by the dative. Some common translations are provided in the chart above.

◆ **bei**

In addition to the meanings listed above, **bei** has many uses that are hard to translate exactly. It is used, in a general way, to indicate a situation: **beim Lesen** (while reading), **bei der Arbeit** (at work), **bei diesem Wetter** (in weather like this).

◆ **bei/mit**

Sie wohnt **bei** ihren Eltern.   She lives with her parents.
Sie fährt morgen **mit** ihren Eltern.   She's driving with her parents tomorrow.

One meaning of both **bei** and **mit** is *with*. However, they are not interchangeable. **Bei** indicates location. **Bei ihren Eltern** means at the home of her parents. **Mit** expresses the idea of doing something together (**mit ihren Eltern**).

◆ nach/zu

Schmidts fahren morgen **nach** Salzburg.	The Schmidts are going to Salzburg tomorrow.
Ich muß **zum** Bäcker.	I have to go to the bakery.

One meaning of both **zu** and **nach** is *to*. **Zu** is used to show movement toward people and many locations. **Nach** is used with cities and countries.

◆ seit

Tanja ist **seit** Montag in Hamburg.	Tanja has been in Hamburg since Monday.
Jürgen wohnt **seit** drei Wochen in Wien.	Jürgen has been living in Vienna for three weeks.

Seit plus the present tense is used to express an action or condition that started in the past but is still continuing in the present. Note that English uses the present perfect tense (e.g., *has been living*) with *since* or *for* to express the same idea.

Brot kaufen wir nur **beim** Bäcker.	bei dem = **beim**
Er kommt jetzt **vom** Markt.	von dem = **vom**
Sie geht **zum** Supermarkt.	zu dem = **zum**
Sie geht **zur** Schule.	zu der = **zur**

The prepositions **bei, von,** and **zu** often contract with the definite article **dem,** and **zu** also contracts with the definite article **der.** While contractions are generally optional, they are required in certain common phrases such as:

zum Beispiel
zum Geburtstag
beim Bäcker
zum Arzt gehen
zum Bäcker gehen
zur Schule gehen
vom Arzt kommen

Contractions are not used when the noun is stressed or modified: **Gehen Sie immer noch zu dem Bäcker in der Bahnhofstraße?** (*Do you still go to the bakery on Bahnhofstraße?*)

23. Nein, das ist nicht richtig. A friend has some wrong information about Christine. Correct it. Replace the object of the preposition with the words in parentheses.

▶ Christine kommt aus Österreich, nicht? (Schweiz)   *Nein, aus der Schweiz.*

1. Sie kommt doch aus Wien, nicht? (Basel)
2. Wohnt sie bei ihren Eltern? (eine Familie)
3. Wohnt sie seit einem Monat da? (zwei Monate)
4. Sie arbeitet bei einem Bäcker, nicht? (ein Metzger)
5. Fährt sie mit ihrem Freund Erik nach Dänemark? (ihre Freundin Petra)
6. Sie fährt mit dem Auto, nicht? (die Bahn)
7. Hörst du oft von Christine? (ihre Familie)

24. Eine Reise nach Budapest The ad below offers a trip from Vienna to Budapest. Tell about some of the conditions by answering the questions. If you need help see Vocabulary for Authentic Text Activities in the Reference Section.

1. Um wieviel Uhr fährt der Bus von Wien ab?
2. Wo treffen° sich die Touristen in Wien?   meet
3. Wie lange dauert° die Rückfahrt von Budapest nach Wien?   lasts
4. Was kostet die Reise nach Budapest?
5. Wieviel mehr kostet ein Einbettzimmer?

25. Rollenspiel Work with a partner. While in Vienna you have decided to visit Budapest. Call a travel agent and ask for details about a short trip to the capital of Hungary. You will want to inquire about cost, length of trip, departure time, and what is included in the tour.

> Making plans for a vacation

26. Verkehrsmittel° Using the drawing below, ask your partner for the most convenient means of transportation to get from place to place. Use the questions below to get you started.

means of transportation

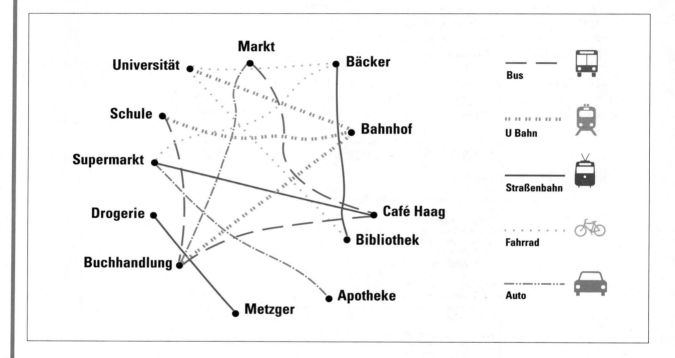

Sie

Wie komme ich am besten von der Uni zur Bibliothek?

Gesprächspartner/in

Am besten fährst du mit dem Fahrrad.

1. Wie komme ich am besten von der Schule zum Bahnhof°?
2. Wie komme ich am besten vom Markt zum Café Haag?
3. Wie komme ich am besten vom Metzger zur Drogerie?
4. Wie komme ich am besten von der Buchhandlung zum Markt?
5. Wie komme ich am besten von der Uni zum Bäcker?

train station

27. **Wie sagt man das?**

1. Mondays Ilse does not go out of the house.
2. Tuesdays she sleeps at her friend's.
3. Wednesdays she goes to the university early.
4. For breakfast she eats nothing except a roll.
5. She goes [*fahren*] to the university by streetcar.
6. I believe her friend is from Frankfurt.
7. She has been living here for a year.

WIEDERHOLUNG

1. **Eine Reise nach Österreich**   Tell about David's trip to Austria by forming sentences, using the cues below.

1. David / sein / Amerikaner
2. er / machen / Reise / durch / Österreich
3. er / ansehen / einige Universitätsstädte
4. er / fahren / mit / Zug / nach / Wien
5. er / kennenlernen / einige Studenten
6. sie / erzählen / von / diese Universität
7. nach / zwei Tage / David / fahren / nach / Salzburg

2. **Was macht Monika?**   Complete the account of Monika's day by using the cued nouns in the proper case.

1. Monika geht aus _____ . (das Haus)
2. Sie geht zu _____ . (der Bäcker)
3. _____ Andrea arbeitet bei _____ . (ihre Freundin / der Bäcker)
4. Monika arbeitet für _____ . (ihr Onkel)
5. Sie fährt mit _____ zur Arbeit. (das Fahrrad)
6. Nach _____ geht sie zu _____ . (die Arbeit / die Buchhandlung)
7. Sie kauft _____ über Österreich. (ein Buch)
8. _____ bringt sie Blumen mit. (ihre Mutter)
9. Morgen schenkt sie _____ das Buch zum Geburtstag. (ihr Vater)
10. Nächstes Jahr fährt sie mit _____ nach Österreich. (die Familie)

3. Wie sagt man das?

1. —Can we work together tonight? I have to prepare my report.
   —Of course. Come at seven thirty. We can go to the movies afterwards.
2. —Would you like to go to Austria this summer?
   —Yes. Gladly. Do you want to go by car or by train?
   —By bike. If the weather stays nice.

4. Jetzt weiß er es.   Dieter Meier sits down at Petra Müller's table in a café and they become acquainted. Read the conversation. Then summarize all the information Dieter learns about Petra. Begin each sentence with **Er weiß, daß ...**

Petra: Ich bin Österreicherin.
Dieter: Kommst du aus Wien?
Petra: Nein, aus Salzburg.
Dieter: Wohnst du in einem Studentenheim?
Petra: Nein, bei einer Familie.
Dieter: Was studierst du denn?
Petra: Wirtschaftswissenschaft ist mein Hauptfach und Englisch mein Nebenfach. Ich möchte in Amerika arbeiten.
Dieter: Warst du schon in Amerika?
Petra: Leider noch nicht.

5. Fragen über Österreich   You are helping organize a contest for German language students. You are responsible for making up several questions on Austria. Once you have them formulated ask a partner the questions. Possible questions can deal with the size of the country, the number of inhabitants, its location, neighbors, capital city, and international organizations located there.

6. Anregung

1. Your friend Rita wants to study in Europe, but doesn't know whether to go to Germany or Austria. Give her some facts in German about one of the countries. You may wish to include information on the following:

   wie groß das Land ist; wie viele Einwohner es hat; wie viele Nachbarn es hat; ob es viele Berge hat; ob es viel Industrie hat; was die Hauptstadt ist.

2. You are studying in Munich and wish to convince a friend to study there also. Write a short letter in German in which you state the advantages of a German university. Begin the letter with **Liebe** *(Dear)* [Barbara] or **Lieber** [Paul], and end with **Mit herzlichen Grüßen** *(With cordial greetings)*, **Deine** or **Dein** [your name]. In a German letter, the words **Du, Dein, Dich, Dir** are always capitalized.

GRAMMATIK: ZUSAMMENFASSUNG

Verbs with stem-vowel change *a* > *ä*

fahren	
ich fahre	wir fahren
du **fährst**	ihr fahrt
er/es/sie **fährt**	sie fahren
Sie fahren	

laufen	
ich laufe	wir laufen
du **läufst**	ihr lauft
er/es/sie **läuft**	sie laufen
Sie laufen	

Word order in independent clauses

Erik **kommt** morgen, aber Christl **muß** morgen arbeiten.

In independent (main) clauses the finite verb (**kommt, muß**) is in second position. A coordinating conjunction (**aber**) does not affect word order. The five common coordinating conjunctions are **aber, denn, oder, sondern,** and **und.**

Word order in dependent clauses

Ich weiß, daß Frank morgen **kommt.**
       daß Petra morgen **mitkommt.**
       daß Helmut nicht **kommen kann.**

In dependent (subordinate) clauses:

1. The finite verb (**kommt**) is in final position.
2. The separable prefix (**mit**) is attached to the base form of the verb (**kommt**) in final position.
3. The modal auxiliary (**kann**) follows the infinitive (**kommen**) and is in final position.

Some common subordinating conjunctions are **daß, ob, obwohl, weil,** and **wenn.** Question words (e.g., **wann, warum, wer, wie, wie lange**) function like subordinating conjunctions.

Wenn du mit dem Rad fährst, **siehst** du mehr vom Land.

When a dependent clause begins a sentence, it is followed directly by the finite verb (**siehst**) of the independent clause.

Articles, *der-* and *ein-*words in the dative case

	Masculine	Neuter	Feminine	Plural
Nominative	der Mann	das Kind	die Frau	die Freunde
Accusative	den Mann	das Kind	die Frau	die Freunde
Dative	**dem** Mann	**dem** Kind	**der** Frau	**den** Freunde**n**
	diesem Mann	**diesem** Kind	**dieser** Frau	**diesen** Freunde**n**
	einem Mann	**einem** Kind	**einer** Frau	**keinen** Freunde**n**
	ihrem Mann	**unserem** Kind	**seiner** Frau	**meinen** Freunde**n**

Nouns in the dative plural

Nominative	die Männer	die Frauen	die Radios
Dative	den Männer**n**	den Frauen	den Radios

Nouns in the dative plural add **-n** unless the plural already ends in **-n** or **-s**.

Masculine *N*-nouns in the dative case

Nominative	der Herr	der Mensch
Accusative	den Herrn	den Menschen
Dative	**dem** Herr**n**	**dem** Mensch**en**

For the masculine **N**-nouns used in this book, see the Grammatical Tables in the Reference Section.

Dative case of demonstrative pronouns

	Masculine	Neuter	Feminine	Plural
Nominative	der	das	die	die
Accusative	den	das	die	die
Dative	**dem**	**dem**	**der**	**denen**

Dative case of *wer*

Nominative	wer
Accusative	wen
Dative	**wem**

Dative verbs

Inge **dankt** ihrer Freundin.
Das Fahrrad **gehört** meinem Bruder.

Most German verbs take objects in the accusative. A few verbs take objects in the dative. The dative object is usually a person. For convenience such verbs can be classified as "dative verbs."

For dative verbs used in this book, see the Grammatical Tables in the Reference Section.

Dative prepositions

aus	out of; from (= *is a native of*)
außer	except for, besides
bei	with *(at the home of)*; at *(a place of business)*; near *(in the proximity of)*; while or during *(indicates a situation)*
mit	with; by means of *(transportation)*
nach	after; toward; to *(with cities, and with masculine and neuter countries)*
seit	since, for *(referring to time)*
von	from; of; by *(the person doing something)*
zu	to *(with people and some places)*

Contractions of dative prepositions

bei dem	=	**beim**
von dem	=	**vom**
zu dem	=	**zum**
zu der	=	**zur**

GEMÜSE
aus
kontrolliert biologischem
Anbau
Demeter
Bioland
Nature et Progrès
Biodyn

Hier kann man biologisch angebautes Gemüse kaufen.

KApiTel 7

BAUSTEINE FÜR GESPRÄCHE

Es hat geschmeckt.

Christine: Wo warst du gestern abend?

Klaus: Warum?

Christine: Ich hab' bei dir ange-rufen, aber da war niemand da. Ich hab' nämlich meine Notizen bei dir vergessen.

Klaus: Ach, die hab' ich ge-funden. — Ja, ich war gestern mit Petra im Café an der Uni. Wir haben ihren Geburtstag gefeiert.

Christine: Ah. Wie findest du das Café an der Uni?

Klaus: Ganz gut. Besonders der Nachtisch war lecker. Die machen das Eis selbst. Das hat ganz toll geschmeckt.

Christine: Hör auf, ich kriege gleich Hunger!

It tasted good.

Where were you last night?

Why?

I called you, but there was no one there. You see, I forgot my notes at your house.

Oh, I found them.—Yes, I was with Petra at the *Café an der Uni* yesterday. We were celebrating her birthday.

Uh. What do you think of the Café an der Uni?

Quite good. The dessert was espe-cially delicious. They make their own ice cream. It tasted really great.

Stop! I'm getting hungry!

Fragen

1. Warum hat Christine bei Klaus angerufen?
2. Warum war Klaus nicht zu Hause?
3. Warum haben Klaus und Petra im Café an der Uni gegessen?
4. Was hat Klaus zum Nachtisch gegessen?
5. Wie hat der Nachtisch geschmeckt?

Ruf doch mal an!

Die Telefon-Information für Österreich-Reisende

So einfach ist es, zu Hause anzurufen:
Von allen öffentlichen Telefonen. Ausgenom-men sind Ortsmünztelefone.

1. Hast du Hunger oder Durst? In groups of four, practice the questions and responses below. One person asks the question. Each of the others gives a different response. Then change roles and practice again. Ask whether a friend is hungry or thirsty.

Sie	*Gesprächspartner/in*
Hast du Hunger?	Ja, großen Hunger.
	Nein, ich habe keinen Hunger.
	Nein, ich habe schon gegessen.
Hast du Durst°?	Ja, großen Durst.
	Nein, ich habe keinen Durst.
	Nein, danke. Ich habe eben eine Cola° getrunken.

2. Gegessen und getrunken Answer the questions about a meal you ate yesterday. Possible answers are suggested. Then ask your partner the same questions. Note her/his answers and share them with a third person (or the class).

> Talking about food and dining out

1. Wo hast du gestern zu Abend gegessen?
   zu Hause ◇ im Café an der Uni ◇ in …
2. Was hast du gegessen?
   Steak° und Pommes frites° ◇ Spaghetti ◇ Wurst und Brot
3. Was hast du getrunken?
   eine Cola ◇ ein Mineralwasser°
4. Hat es geschmeckt?
   Danke, gut. ◇ Ganz toll. ◇ Nicht besonders. ◇ Nein, leider nicht.

JE FACHINGER -
DESTO GESÜNDER

ORIGINAL STAATL. FACHINGEN JETZT
Mit Schraubverschluß und neuem Etikett
In neuer Flasche und 12er Kasten

3. Ein Rollenspiel Use the menu from **Café an der Uni** to create a dialogue between a diner (**Gast**) and a waiter (**Ober**) or waitress (**Kellnerin**). You may want to follow the pattern of the model below. If you need help in reading the menu, see Vocabulary for Authentic Text Activities in the Reference Section.

Reading and ordering from a menu

Café an der Uni

Getränke

Große Tasse Kaffee mit Sahne		3,80
Große Tasse Schokolade mit Sahne		3,80
Große Tasse frisch gebrühter Tee		3,80
Cappuccino		3,20
Espresso		3,00
Schweppes Sodawasser	0,2l	2,60
Schweppes Bitter Lemon	0,2l	3,50
Schweppes Ginger Ale	0,2l	3,50
Apfelsaft	0,25l	2,80
Coca-Cola	0,25l	2,80
Fanta	0,25l	2,80
Johannisbeersaft	0,2l	3,80
Pils vom Faß	0,3l	3,30
Export vom Faß	0,3l	3,10

Kuchen und Gebäck

Bitte treffen Sie an unserer Schauvitrine Ihre Wahl und bestellen Sie bei Ihrer Bedienung!

Torten	3,50
Kuchen	3,00
Croissant	1,80
Portion Schlagsahne	1,20

Eis

kleines Eis (drei Kugeln nach Wahl)	4,20
mit Sahne	5,40
großes Eis (fünf Kugeln nach Wahl)	7,00
mit Sahne	8,20
Eiskaffee	5,50

Toasts

„Hawaii" mit Schinken, Käse und Ananas	7,50
„Spezial" mit Schinken, Käse und Pilzen	8,50
„Farmer"-Toast mit Truthahnbrust und Spiegelei	9,50

Kalte Speisen

Baguette „Café an der Uni"	7,50
Baguette mit Thunfisch und Ei	7,50
Wurstsalat mit Brot	6,50
Käsebrot, Emmentaler oder Camembert	5,50
Wurstbrot, Salami, Bierschinken oder Leberwurst	5,50

Salate

Griechischer Salat mit Brot	9,50
Salatschüssel mit frischen Saisonsalaten, Ei, Dressing und Brot	8,50
Große Salatplatte mit Schinken, Käse, Pepperoni, Oliven, frischen Salaten und Brot	12,50

Warme Gerichte

Gebackener Camembert mit Preiselbeeren, Salatbeilage und Brot	7,50
Spaghetti „Bolognese"	8,50
Tortellini in Sahnesauce mit Salat	10,50
Pizza mit Schinken, Käse, Salami, Oliven, Pepperoni und Champignons	9,50
Schnitzel Wiener Art mit Kartoffelsalat	12,50

Geöffnet:
Montag bis Freitag 8 bis 22 Uhr
Samstag und Feiertage 9 bis 22 Uhr

Alle Preise sind Inklusivpreise und enthalten Bedienungsgeld und Mehrwertsteuer.

Ober: Bitte sehr?° Was darf es sein?°   Yes, please. / May I help you?
Gast: Ich möchte gern [das Wiener Schnitzel].
Ober: Und zum Trinken°?   to drink
Gast: [Ein Pils° / eine Cola / ein Mineralwasser], bitte.   Pilsner beer
Ober: Sonst noch etwas?
Gast: Nein, danke, das ist alles.
Ober: Bitte schön.
Gast: Zahlen, bitte.°   The check, please.
Ober: Hat's geschmeckt?
Gast: Ja, sehr gut.
Ober: Das macht 15 Mark 80.
Gast: Machen Sie es 17.
Ober: Danke.

**Was gibt es heute
im Uni-Café in Würzburg?**

Although a growing number of Germans eat their main meal in the evening (**Abendessen**), many Germans still eat their main meal at noon (**Mittagessen**). It may consist of two or three courses. Dessert (**Nachtisch** or **Dessert**) is usually fruit, pudding, or ice cream. Cakes and pastries are served at afternoon coffee time (**Kaffee**). Before a meal, it is customary to say **Guten Appetit** or **Mahlzeit,** and others may wish you the same by responding **Danke, gleichfalls.** Even in a restaurant, when sharing a table with a stranger who has asked **Ist hier frei?,** one wishes the stranger **Guten Appetit** when the meal arrives.

Most restaurants post their menus outside. At the conclusion of the meal, one pays the waiter (**Ober**) or waitress (**Kellnerin**). A service charge (**Bedienung**) or tip (**Trinkgeld**) is included in the bill, although it is customary to add a little extra by rounding off the bill.

When people are invited to a friend's house for dinner or for **Kaffee** it is customary to bring a small gift. Most often the guest will bring a small bouquet, a box of chocolates, or a bottle of wine.

4. Im Restaurant Based on the information in the cultural note on eating in a restaurant, act out a scene with three people. One person is sitting at a table alone, when a second arrives. The second person asks if he or she can sit down and then orders something to eat from the third person who plays a waiter or waitress. Continue the skit until the food has arrived, and one person pays for a meal.

Vokabeln

__ Substantive _____

die **Cola, -** cola drink
der **Durst** thirst
das **Eis** ice; ice cream
der **Hunger** hunger
der **Nachtisch** dessert

die **Pommes frites** (*pl.*) French fries
das **Steak, -s** steak
das **Wasser** water; das **Mineralwasser** mineral water

__ Verben _____

an·rufen, angerufen to phone
auf·hören to stop (an activity)
feiern to celebrate
kriegen to get
schmecken (+ *dat.***)** to taste; **der
Käse schmeckt** the cheese tastes
good

vergessen (vergißt), vergessen to
forget

__ Andere Wörter _____

allein alone
gestern abend last night
lecker delicious, tasty
nämlich namely; that is (to say);
you know, you see

niemand nobody
toll great, fantastic

__ Besondere Ausdrücke _____

bei dir an·rufen to phone you
Durst haben to be thirsty
Hunger haben to be hungry

Hunger kriegen (*or*** bekommen)** to
get hungry

NATÜRLICHKEIT UND UMWELT

Vorbereitung auf das Lesen

◆ *Zum Thema*

1. Viele Kuchen sind mit künstlichen Farben dekoriert. Essen Sie solche
   Kuchen?
2. Welche Lebensmittel haben chemische Zusätze°? Sind Sie dafür°,   additives / for it
   dagegen° oder neutral?   against it

3. Gibt es viele Geschäfte, wo man „natürliche" Produkte kaufen kann?
4. Kaufen Sie nur natürliche Produkte: Lebensmittel ohne Pestizide, natürliche Seife, chemiefreie Shampoos, Kleidung aus natürlichen Stoffen°? — materials
5. Gibt es bei Ihnen eine Umweltbewegung°? Was tun Sie für die Umwelt? — environmental movement

◆ *Leitfragen*

1. Frau Fischer hat einen schönen Kuchen gebacken. Warum mögen ihn die deutschen Gäste nicht?
2. Warum gehen viele Deutsche zur Kur°? — **zur Kur gehen:** to go to a health spa
3. Warum gibt es in Deutschland viele Bio-Läden und Reformhäuser?
4. Welches Wort findet man in vielen deutschen Reklamen?
5. Wer sind und was wollen die Grünen?
6. Wie reduziert man den Müll°, und wie macht man den Müll weniger gefährlich°? — garbage / dangerous

Die Fischers aus Amerika leben erst seit einigen Wochen in Deutschland. Sie arbeiten bei einer amerikanischen Firma in Hamburg. Die Kinder haben schon Freunde gefunden, und den Eltern gefällt es auch schon besser als zuerst.

5   Eines Tages laden Fischers einige Bekannte zum Kaffee ein. Frau Fischer hat einen leckeren Kuchen gebacken. Sie hat ihn rot, grün und blau dekoriert, so daß er besonders schön aussieht. Fischers bieten also Kaffee und Kuchen an°. Der Kaffee schmeckt allen ausgezeichnet, aber von dem Kuchen probiert — **bieten an:** offer
jeder nur ein Stück und sagt dann: „Nein, danke; es tut mir furchtbar leid,
10 aber ich kann wirklich nicht mehr." Oder: „Danke, wirklich. Ich muß auf meine schlanke Linie achten°." Fischers denken: Merkwürdig! Was haben wir — **auf ... achten:** watch my figure
nur falsch gemacht? Der Kuchen kann es doch wirklich nicht sein. Der hat unseren Gästen zu Hause doch immer gut geschmeckt. Oder haben wir vielleicht etwas Dummes gesagt? Aber das kann es doch auch nicht sein, denn
15 die Gespräche waren lebhaft° und interessant. — lively
    Man spricht über Politik, die Kinder und die Schulen. Eine junge Frau erzählt von ihren letzten Ferien: „So ganz richtige Ferien waren es ja nicht. Ich war zur Kur° in Bad* Salzuflen." Herr Fischer fragt: „Zur Kur? Waren Sie — **Ich ... Kur:** I went for a cure
denn krank?" — „Ja, der Arzt hat mir eine Kur verschrieben°. Das tägliche — prescribed
20 Baden in den natürlichen Quellen° hat doch sehr gut getan. Außerdem hilft ja — springs
auch die Ruhe° sehr — mal ganz weg von Familie und Arbeit. Es hat wirklich — rest
sehr geholfen." Frau Fischer hat noch eine Frage: „Ist so was° denn nicht sehr — **so was:** something like that
teuer?" — „Na ja, einen Teil habe ich bezahlt, aber einen großen Teil hat ja die Krankenkasse° bezahlt." Alle finden eine solche Kur ganz normal, denn „die — health insurance
25 Kräfte° der Natur sind doch am besten°". — powers / **am besten:** the best

---

*Towns where spas are located often have names that begin with **Bad** (*bath*). There are 250 registered spas in western Germany alone. In the former GDR, **Kurorte** in the western tradition were phased out. Instead, people were generally sent to vacation homes or resorts run by the state.

**Im Reformhaus gibt es
natürliche Lebensmittel.
(Stuttgart)**

Ein junger Mann erzählt, daß er gerade in einem Bio-Laden° eingekauft
hat. Er fragt Frau Fischer, ob sie schon in so einem Geschäft gewesen ist.
„Nein, was ist denn ein Bio-Laden?" Der junge Mann erklärt: „Da gibt es
biologisch angebautes° Gemüse und Obst, überhaupt natürliche Lebensmit-
30 tel. Das sind Lebensmittel ohne Pestizide, ohne künstliche Farben, ohne
Kunstdünger°. Sie sind also chemiefrei. Diese Sachen sind auf natürlichem
Mist° gewachsen." Seine Mutter erklärt: „Vielleicht kennen Sie die
Reformhäuser°. Die sind ähnlich. Es gibt sie nur schon viel länger. Ich kaufe
ziemlich viel da, Lebensmittel und auch andere Sachen, Seife z.B. und
35 Hautcreme°. Wir kaufen viel Tee, Kamille°, Lindenblüte° und so weiter." Frau
Fischer antwortet: „Das ist ganz ähnlich wie die Bio-Ecke° in unserem Supermarkt, nicht?" — „Da haben Sie recht."
Nach diesen Gesprächen fangen Fischers an, ihre Umwelt genauer° anzusehen. Sie haben vorher nie bemerkt, wie wichtig der Begriff° der° Natür-
40 lichkeit in den Reklamen ist. Da gibt es „Shampoos garantiert aus Pflanzen",
„natürliche Hemden und Hosen: 100% reine Baumwolle" oder „Kopfschmerztabletten aus Pflanzenextrakt."

organic food store

biologisch angebaut:
 organically grown
chemical fertilizer

manure

health-food stores

skin cream / chamomile tea /
 linden tea
health-food section

more carefully
concept / of (*gen.*)

Fischers können nun auch verstehen, warum die Grünen° hier in vielen Parlamenten° sitzen. Sie sind die Umweltpartei. Sie protestieren gegen tech-
45 nische Großprojekte. Sie plädieren° für mehr Fahrradwege, für reine Luft und reines Wasser. Sie wollen die Müll-Lawine° reduzieren. Und hier beginnt auch schon vieles anders zu werden. Der Umweltminister° will, daß Kunden° überflüssige° Verpackungen° gleich im Geschäft lassen können. Von den Geschäften gehen diese dann an die Produzenten° zurück. Diese produzieren
50 dann, so hofft man, bald weniger überflüssige Verpackungen. In den Bio-Läden gibt es Milch und Saft nicht mehr in Kartons° oder Einwegflaschen°. Sie kommen in Mehrwegflaschen° mit Pfand°.

Wenn ein Geschäft Batterien verkauft, muß es alte Batterien zurücknehmen. Apotheken nehmen alte Medikamente zurück. Wenn jemand Motoröl
55 verkauft, dann muß er auch Altöl zurücknehmen. So hofft man, den Müll nicht nur zu reduzieren, sondern auch weniger gefährlich zu machen. So hofft man, die Umwelt wieder ein wenig natürlicher zu machen.

Nun wissen Fischers genau, warum der Kuchen ihren Gästen nicht geschmeckt hat. Die Farben waren nicht natürlich, sie waren künstlich. Frau
60 Fischer lächelt und sagt zu ihrem Mann: „Da haben wir wieder etwas gelernt: *Schön* ist eben nicht immer *schön*."

environmentalist political party / legislatures

plead

avalanche (mountains) of garbage / Secretary for the Environment / customers / superfluous / packing manufacturers

cartons / disposable bottles
returnable bottles / deposit

Fragen zum Lesestück

1. Wie lange leben Fischers schon in Deutschland?
2. Wer kommt eines Tages zum Kaffee?
3. Warum sieht Frau Fischers Kuchen schön aus?
4. Wie viele Stücke ißt jeder von dem Kuchen?
5. Von was erzählt die junge Frau?
6. Warum war sie zur Kur?
7. Wer bezahlt die Kur?
8. Warum finden alle eine solche Kur ganz normal?
9. Wo hat der junge Mann eingekauft?
10. Was für Sachen kann man da kaufen?
11. Was sehen Fischers oft in den Reklamen?
12. Aus was sind viele natürliche Hemden und Hosen?
13. Aus was sind einige Kopfschmerztabletten?
14. Wer sind die Grünen?
15. Gegen was sind die Grünen? Und für was?
16. Was wollen sie reduzieren?
17. Was für Flaschen gibt es in den Bio-Läden? Warum?
18. Warum nehmen die Apotheken alte Medikamente zurück?
19. Warum hat der Kuchen den Gästen nicht geschmeckt?
20. Was haben Fischers gelernt?

2.7t

**Durch Recycling
wird die Müll-Lawine kleiner.**

Protection of the environment has become increasingly important for the German-speaking countries. Water and air pollution (**Wasser- und Luftverschmutzung**) have caused serious damage to forests and rivers and threaten their actual survival. The Germans speak of the dying forests and rivers (**Waldsterben/Flußsterben**). More than one third of the forests in the western part of Germany suffers some damage and 15.9 percent is seriously damaged. The damage in the **neue Bundesländer** (the ''new'' states composed of the former German Democratic Republic) is twice as high as in the other states.

People in all the German-speaking countries have become more aware of the necessity for environmental protection (**Umweltschutz**) in recent years. There is strong sentiment among some groups against atomic power-plants, and many people use bicycles instead of cars, try to conserve water, and use products that are friendly to the environment (**umweltfreundlich**). In cities, almost every neighborhood provides several containers for recycling (**Recycling**) glass and paper. Of growing concern is the disposal (**Entsorgung**) of hazardous and non-degradable materials. Thus businesses that sell batteries must also accept the used ones for proper disposal. Many health-food stores (**Naturläden** or **Bioläden**) sell products that have been produced with minimal damage to the environment—products like organically grown vegetables and grains produced without insecticides or chemical fertilizers, recycled-paper products, and even ''natural'' cosmetic products.

1. Erzählen Sie. Select one of the topics below to talk about the reading selection. Use the cued words.

A *Kaffee*
   Fischers in Hamburg
   Bekannte beim Kaffee
   Kuchen mit Farben
   natürliche und künstliche Farben
B *Natürlichkeit in Deutschland*
   Kur: nicht teuer / Krankenkasse
   Bio-Laden
   natürliche Lebensmittel
   Shampoos
   Kleidungsstücke

2. Interview You and your partner have just resolved to lead a "more natural" life style that is also better for the environment. Discuss what actions you will take and why. You may use the following list to get you started.

natürliche Lebensmittel kaufen ◇ Batterien zurückgeben ◇ mehr mit dem Fahrrad fahren ◇ für die Grünen arbeiten

> Talking about current issues

Wissen Sie,
wie Energiesparen geht?

Wir schon!
Und wir helfen Ihnen daher auch gerne dabei!

Rufen Sie uns doch am besten an
und vereinbaren einen kostenlosen
Beratungstermin (0732 / 593-3490).

OKA
Energie für Oberösterreich

Vokabeln

Starting in *Kapitel 7* the past participles of strong verbs will be listed after the infinitive, e.g. **sitzen, gesessen.**

— Substantive

der **Anfang, ⁼e** beginning
der **Arzt, ⁼e**/die **Ärztin, -nen** doctor, physician
die **Baumwolle** cotton
der **Bekannte, -n, -n** (ein **Bekannter**)/die (eine) **Bekannte, -n** acquaintance
die **Ecke, -n** corner
der **Gast, ⁼e** guest
das **Geschäft, -e** store; business
das **Gespräch, -e** conversation
das **Hemd, -en** shirt

die **Hose, -n** pants
die **Jacke, -n** jacket
das **Leben** life
die **Luft** air
das **Medikament, -e** medicine
die **Natur** nature
die **Reklame, -n** advertisement, commercial
die **Sache, -n** thing
die **Seife, -n** soap
das **Shampoo, -s** shampoo
die **Umwelt** environment

__ Verben _____

an·fangen (fängt an), angefangen
to begin; **mit der Arbeit anfangen** to begin work

aus·sehen (sieht aus), ausgesehen
to look like, seem

backen, gebacken to bake

baden to bathe; swim

bemerken to notice

dekorieren to decorate

ein·laden (lädt ein), eingeladen to
invite

gefallen (gefällt), gefallen (+ *dat.*)
to please, be pleasing to

halten (hält), gehalten to hold;
halten von to think of, have an
opinion

helfen (hilft), geholfen (+ *dat.*) to
help; **bei [der Arbeit] helfen** to
help with [work]

hoffen to hope

kosten to cost

lächeln (über + *acc.*) to smile
(about)

lassen (läßt), gelassen to leave; to
let, permit

probieren to try; to taste something; **Probier mal den Käse.**
Try the cheese.

sitzen, gesessen to sit; to be located

tragen (trägt), getragen to carry; to
wear

tun (tut), getan to do

verkaufen to sell

wachsen (wächst), ist gewachsen
to grow

__ Andere Wörter _____

ähnlich similar

alle all

ausgezeichnet excellent

außerdem in addition; as well

bekannt well-known, familiar

falsch wrong

gerade just; straight

gesund healthy

jemand someone, anyone

künstlich artificial

lecker delicious, tasty

mal (= einmal) once, sometime

merkwürdig strange

nie never

nun now; well (*interjection*)

rein clean; pure

täglich daily

überhaupt in general; at all

vorher before

weg away, gone

zuerst first

__ Besondere Ausdrücke _____

eines Tages one day

etwas Dummes something dumb

na ja well now

recht haben to be right; **Du hast
recht.** You're right.

und so weiter (*abbrev.* **usw.**) and
so on, etc.

zum Kaffee for (afternoon) coffee

Erweiterung des Wortschatzes

1 *Gefallen*

Dein Freund **gefällt** mir.	I like your friend. [I think your friend is O.K.]
Ich habe deinen Freund gern.	I like your friend. [I'm fond of him.]
Deine Freunde **gefallen** mir nicht.	I don't like your friends. [I don't care for them.]
Deine Freunde mag ich nicht.	I don't like your friends. [I dislike them.]

Gefallen, mögen, and **gern haben** are all equivalent to English *like*. However, they express different degrees of liking. **Mögen** and **gern haben** usually express stronger feelings of liking than **gefallen.**

Das Bild gefällt mir. ⎫ Mir gefällt das Bild. ⎭	I like the picture.
Mir gefällt es nicht, daß Mark so wenig liest.	I don't like (the fact) that Mark reads so little.

When using the verb **gefallen,** what one likes is the subject and thus in the nominative case. The person who likes something is in the dative. Note that sentences with **gefallen** often begin with the dative.

1. Was bedeutet das?

1. Wie gefällt deinem Freund Mark Hamburg?
2. Dem gefällt es sehr.
3. Diese Vorlesungen gefallen Mark auch.
4. Was gefällt deinem Freund nicht so gut?
5. Dem gefällt es nicht, daß es so viel regnet.
6. Es gefällt Mark auch nicht, daß es soviel Autos gibt.

2. Wie gefällt dir [das Auto]? Find out if your partner likes a certain color, car, politician, singer, TV show, college, or university. Then reverse roles. Use the verb **gefallen.**

Expressing likes and dislikes

2 Noun suffixes *-heit* and *-keit*

die **Gesundheit**	health	die **Natürlichkeit**	naturalness
gesund	healthy	**natürlich**	natural

Nouns ending in **-heit** or **-keit** are feminine nouns. Many nouns of this type are related to adjectives. The suffix **-keit** is used instead of **-heit** with adjectives ending in **-ig** or **-lich.**

3. **Wörter mit** *-heit*   Complete the second sentence in each pair with a noun ending in **-heit** related to the boldfaced adjective.

1. Das finde ich **dumm** von dir. Da sieht man wieder deine große _____ .
2. Der Garten ist sehr **trocken.** Wie lange dauert diese _____ noch?
3. Baumwolle ist **gesund.** Hosen aus Baumwolle sind gut für die _____ .
4. Ingrid findet die Natur **schön.** Mir gefällt die _____ der Natur auch.
5. Sie liegt **krank** im Bett. Sie hat eine schwere _____ .

4. **Wörter mit** *-keit*   Complete the second sentence in each pair with a noun ending in **-keit** related to the boldfaced adjective.

1. Bei vielen Deutschen muß alles **natürlich** sein. Denen gefällt _____ in Essen und Trinken.
2. Die Frage ist **richtig.** Oder glaubst du nicht an ihre _____ ?
3. Das Kind sieht seiner Mutter **ähnlich.** Siehst du nicht die _____ ?
4. Wir machen eine **wichtige** Reise nach Basel. Es ist von großer _____ , daß wir nach Basel fahren.

3 Infinitives used as nouns

Wandern ist gesund.   Hiking is healthy.
Das Schlafen in frischer Luft ist   Sleeping in fresh air is
  gesund.   healthy.

German infinitives may be used as nouns. An infinitive used as a noun is always neuter. The English equivalent is often a gerund, that is, the *-ing* form of a verb used as a noun.

5. **Was bedeutet das?**

1. Laufen ist schön.
2. Reinheit und Natürlichkeit in Essen und Trinken gefallen den Deutschen.
3. Es gehört zum Einkaufen am Wochenende, daß man Blumen mitbringt.
4. Schwimmen ist ein schöner Sport.
5. Viele Leute finden Fliegen furchtbar.

Erdgarten
Naturkost
Tengstr. 31 · 8000 München 40 · Tel. 089 / 271 91 52

Öffnungszeiten:
Montag – Freitag 9.30 – 18.30 Uhr
Samstag 9.30 – 13 Uhr

4 Kleidungsstücke

1. der Anzug, ⸚e	10. das Hemd, -en	13. die Bluse, -n
2. der Handschuh, -e	11. das Kleid, -er	14. die (Hand)tasche, -n
3. der Hut, ⸚e	12. das T-Shirt, -s	15. die Hose, -n
4. der Pulli, -s		16. die Jacke, -n
5. der Regenmantel, ⸚		17. die Jeans (*pl.*)
6. der Rock, ⸚e		18. die Shorts (kurze Hose, -n)
7. der Sakko, -s		19. die Socke, -n
8. der Schuh, -e		20. die Strumpfhose, -n
9. der Sportschuh, -e		

For additional articles of clothing see the Supplementary Word Sets on clothing for *Kapitel 7* in the Reference Section.

6. Was tragen Sie?   Answer the questions below for yourself and then ask your partner. Remember to use **du** with your partner.

Discussing clothes

1. Was tragen Sie im Winter? Im Sommer?
2. Was tragen Sie, wenn Sie in die Vorlesung gehen?
3. Was tragen Sie, wenn Sie tanzen gehen?
4. Was möchten Sie zum Geburtstag haben?
5. Welche Farben tragen Sie gern?

7. Wie gefällt es dir?   Choose a picture in this text with articles of clothing and ask several fellow students their opinion about some of the items.

Expressing opinions and likes and dislikes.

Sie	*Gesprächspartner/in*
Was hältst° du von [dem Kleid]?	[Das] muß furchtbar teuer sein. Was kostet° [es]?
	[Das] ist schön/toll/praktisch.
	[Das] sieht billig aus.
	[Das] ist nichts Besonderes.

8. Wer ist das?   With a partner, choose a person and describe what she or he is wearing, including the color. Your classmates will try to guess whom you are describing.

Wenn die Katze aus dem Haus ist, tanzen die Mäuse.

GRAMMATIK UND ÜBUNGEN

1 The perfect tense

Ich **habe** mit Karin **gesprochen.**   I *have spoken* with Karin.
                                          I *spoke* with Karin.

Sie **ist** nach Hause **gegangen.**   She *has gone* home.
                                        She *went* home.

German has several past tenses. One of them is the perfect tense, which is commonly used in conversation to refer to past actions or states.

The perfect tense is made up of the present tense of the auxiliary **haben** or **sein** and the past participle of the verb. In independent clauses, the past participle is the last element in the sentence.

2 Past participles of regular weak verbs

Infinitive	Past participle	Perfect tense
machen	ge + mach + t	Er **hat** es nicht **gemacht.**
arbeiten	ge + arbeit + et	Sie **hat gearbeitet.**

German verbs may be classified as weak or strong according to the way in which they form their past tenses. A regular weak verb is a verb whose infinitive stem remains unchanged in the past tense forms.

The past participle of a weak verb is formed by adding **-t** to the unchanged stem. The **-t** expands to **-et** in verbs whose stem ends in **-d** (**baden** > **gebadet**) or **-t** (**arbeiten** > **gearbeitet**), and in some verbs whose stem ends in **-n** or **-m** (**regnen** > **geregnet**). Most weak verbs also add the prefix **ge-** in the past participle.

3 Auxiliary *haben* with past participles

ich **habe** etwas **gefragt**	wir **haben** etwas **gefragt**
du **hast** etwas **gefragt**	ihr **habt** etwas **gefragt**
er/es/sie **hat** etwas **gefragt**	sie **haben** etwas **gefragt**
Sie **haben** etwas **gefragt**	

The chart above shows how the perfect tense of a weak verb is formed, using the auxiliary **haben.**

1. Wir haben es schon gehört.   Your friend is eager to pass on a bit of gossip to various persons. However, you tell your friend that you and they have already heard it.

▶   Frau Fischer   *Frau Fischer hat es schon gehört.*

1. Klaus	4. unsere Freunde
2. ich	5. wir
3. Professor Weber	6. Karin

2. Ich hab's schon gemacht.   Heidi wants you to do all sorts of things. Tell her you've already done what she wants.

▶   Koch jetzt Kaffee.   *Den Kaffee habe ich doch schon gekocht.*

1. Mach die Arbeit.	5. Kauf das Buch.
2. Frag den Professor.	6. Such das Geld.
3. Hörst du die Vorlesung?	7. Spiel heute abend Tennis.
4. Lern die Vokabeln.	

4 Past participles of irregular weak verbs

Infinitive	Past participle	Perfect tense
bringen	ge + brach + t	Wer **hat** die Blumen **gebracht?**
denken	ge + dach + t	Jens **hat** an den Wein **gedacht.**
kennen	ge + kann + t	Sie **hat** Thomas gut **gekannt.**
wissen	ge + wuß + t	Wir **haben** es **gewußt.**

A few weak verbs, including **bringen, denken, kennen,** and **wissen,** are irregular. The past participle has the prefix **ge-** and the ending **-t,** but the verb also undergoes a stem change. The past participles of irregular weak verbs are noted in the vocabularies as follows: **denken, gedacht.**

3. Alles vorbereiten.   Gerd and his friends are getting ready for a party. Restate each sentence below in the perfect tense.

▶   Gerd denkt an Christine.   *Gerd hat an Christine gedacht.*

1. Christine denkt an den Wein.
2. Gerd weiß den Namen.
3. Klaus weiß den Namen nicht.
4. Gerd kennt das Weingeschäft.
5. Klaus kennt es nicht.
6. Kennst du den Namen?
7. Wer bringt das Essen?
8. Was bringst du?

4. Was wollen Sie sagen? The verbs listed below are most of the regular weak verbs you have learned so far. Choose ten of these verbs and use them in the perfect tense.

arbeiten ◇ brauchen ◇ danken ◇ fragen ◇ glauben ◇ hören ◇ kaufen ◇
kochen ◇ kosten ◇ lächeln ◇ leben ◇ lernen ◇ machen ◇ regnen ◇
sagen ◇ schenken ◇ schmecken ◇ schneien ◇ spielen ◇ suchen ◇
tanzen ◇ warten ◇ wohnen ◇ zahlen ◇ zelten

**Vera Wollenberger
ist eine Abgeordnete
der Grünen im Bundestag. (1990)**

The "Green" political party has its roots in many diverse movements in West Germany of the mid-1970s. **Die Grünen** integrated many groups of that time, such as citizens' action groups (**Bürgerinitiativen**), ecologists (**Ökologen**), peace groups (**Friedensgruppen**), and women's groups (**Frauengruppen**) into a viable political alternative. **Die Grünen** first gained prominence as an environmental party through such issues as their opposition to nuclear power and support of a speed limit on German expressways (**Autobahnen**). Today their efforts encompass working for protection of the ozone layer, elimination of chemical and nuclear weaponry, international cooperation to save the environment, and reshaping the market economy so that ecological concerns become a major priority.

The Greens were first elected to the **Bundestag** in 1983; however the western German party did not gain representation in the first all-German parliament elected in December 1990, although their counterparts from the new states did win election. Nonetheless, the Greens remain a legitimate political force on the local and state levels in Germany. The movement is also active in other European countries and is represented in many governmental bodies. Recently, Green parties have also been established in North America.

5 Use of the perfect tense

In English, the present perfect tense and the simple past tense have different meanings.

Where are you going?
Gerd has invited me to dinner (and we're going this evening).

The present perfect tense (e.g., has invited) refers to a period of time that continues into the present and is thus still uncompleted.

What did you do today?
Gerd invited me to dinner (and we went).

The simple past tense (e.g., invited), on the other hand, refers to a period of time that is completed at the moment of speaking.

Gerd hat mich zum Essen eingeladen. ⎰Gerd has invited me to dinner.
⎱Gerd invited me to dinner.

In German, the perfect tense (e.g., **hat eingeladen**) refers to all actions or states in the past, whereas in English the past is used for completed actions and the present perfect for uncompleted actions. Context usually makes the meaning clear.

In German, the perfect tense is most frequently used in conversation to refer to past actions or states, and is therefore often referred to as the "conversational past." German also has a simple past tense (see *Kapitel 11*) that is used to narrate connected events in the past, and which is, therefore, frequently called the "narrative past."

5. Ich hab' das nicht gewußt.   Answer the following questions for yourself and then ask your partner the same questions. Remember to use **du.**

Talking about the past

1. Wo haben Sie als Kind gewohnt?
2. Wie lange haben Sie dort gewohnt?
3. Wie viele Bücher haben Sie für Ihre Kurse gekauft?
4. Wieviel haben die Bücher gekostet?
5. Haben Sie schon viel Deutsch gelernt?
6. Bis wann haben Sie gestern abend gearbeitet?
7. Wie hat das Essen gestern abend geschmeckt?

6. Wie sagt man das? Give the German equivalents of the conversational exchanges below, using the perfect tense.

▶ What did Erik say? *Was hat Erik gesagt?*
▶ —I didn't hear it. *— Ich habe es nicht gehört.*

1. Christel bought a jacket.
   —What did it cost?
2. Why didn't the men work yesterday?
   —It rained.
3. Why didn't Barbara buy the purse?
   —She didn't have any money.
4. Markus cooked the meal.
   —Really? I didn't know that.
5. Who brought the wine?
   —I don't know. I didn't ask.

Hier gibt es Sachen für den *Neuen Mann*. (Stuttgart)

KARSTADT

Kapuzen-T-Shirt
langer Arm,
Superfarben **19.90**

Kapuzen-Sweatshirt
mod.
Farben **39.90**

Slot Maschine
Jeans
versch.
Farben,
stonewashed
oder black **49.90**

Marshal
Jeans-Jacke
stonewashed **49.-**

Marshal, His
Aktuelle Hosen
Baumwolle oder
Viskose,
für Sie und Ihn **79.-**

Wendeblouson
mit Kapuze,
Top-Farben **129.-**

Gut einkaufen
schöner leben

Donnerstag
Do
geöffnet bis
20.³⁰

**Riesenauswahl
in unserer
»Jeans-Box«
im Erdgeschoß.**

7. Einkaufen bei Karstadt Answer the following questions about the ad from the German department store chain **Karstadt.**

1. Welche englischen Wörter finden Sie?
2. Wo ist die „Jeans-Box"?
3. Wann macht Karstadt am Donnerstag zu?
4. Finden Sie die Jeans teuer?

8. Rollenspiel You meet a friend (your partner) who is wearing some new clothes. You like them very much and want to know where your friend got them, how much they cost, and what other articles of clothing the store has. It turns out that your friend was shopping at **Karstadt.** Have a conversation with him/her using the following questions and comments to get started. You may want to refer to the Vocabulary for Authentic Text Activities and the Supplementary Word Sets in the Reference Section for additional vocabulary.

Sie	*Gesprächspartner/in*
Du, das T-Shirt ist toll!	Die Kapuze gefällt mir auch.
Wieviel hat es gekostet?	Neunzehn Mark neunzig.
Hast du sonst noch etwas gekauft?	Ja, […].

6 Past participles of strong verbs

Infinitive	Past participle	Perfect tense
sehen	ge + seh + en	Ich **habe** es **gesehen**.
finden	ge + fund + en	Ich **habe** es **gefunden**.
nehmen	ge + nomm + en	Ich **habe** es nicht **genommen**.

The past participle of a strong verb is formed by adding **-en** to the participle stem. (Note the exception **getan**.) Most strong verbs also add the **ge-** prefix in the past participle. Many strong verbs have a change in the stem vowel of the past participle (**gefunden**) and some verbs also have a change in the consonants (**genommen**). Past participles of strong verbs are noted in the vocabularies as follows: **helfen, geholfen**.

For a list of strong verbs, see #23 of the Grammatical Tables in the Reference Section.

Infinitive	Past participle
backen	gebacken
halten	gehalten
lassen	gelassen
schlafen	geschlafen
tragen	getragen
tun	getan

9. Kuchen backen   Tell about Peter's cake-baking experience. Restate in the perfect tense.

▶   Warum schläft Peter heute so lange?   *Warum hat Peter heute so lange geschlafen?*

1. Er tut heute nicht viel.
2. Er backt nur einen Kuchen.
3. Was halten die Freunde von seinem Plan?
4. Sie backen auch einen Kuchen.
5. Dann tragen sie die Kuchen zu den Nachbarn.
6. Was tun die Nachbarn dann?

Infinitive	Past participle
geben	gegeben
liegen	gelegen
lesen	gelesen
sehen	gesehen
essen	gegessen
sitzen	gesessen

10. Im Café   You and Klaus start out in the café and end up at the movies. Restate the sentences below in the perfect tense.

▶   Wir sitzen im Café.   *Wir haben im Café gesessen.*

1. Ein Buch über die Schweiz liegt da.
2. Ich gebe Klaus das Buch.
3. Zuerst liest er das Buch.
4. Dann essen wir ein Wurstbrot.
5. Ich esse auch ein Ei.
6. Später sehen wir einen Film.

Infinitive	Past participle
helfen	geholfen
nehmen	genommen
sprechen	gesprochen
finden	gefunden
trinken	getrunken
leihen	geliehen
schreiben	geschrieben

11. Was haben sie getan?   Restate the conversational exchanges below in the perfect tense.

▶   Nehmen Gerd und Serge den Zug?   *Haben Gerd und Serge den Zug*
   — Nein, sie leihen ein Auto.   *genommen?*
                                                   — Nein, sie haben ein Auto
                                                   geliehen.

1. Trinken Sie Kaffee?
   — Nein, ich nehme Tee.
2. Schreibst du die Karte?
   — Nein, ich finde sie nicht.
3. Sprechen Gerd und Susi gut Englisch?
   — Ja, aber David hilft ihnen.

12. Mein Tag war langweilig°/interessant.   With a partner or in ~boring~ a group discuss your activities in the last 24 hours using the following questions as a guide. Then decide whose day was interesting and whose boring. You may want to exaggerate a bit to make your day more interesting. Then report to the class on your activities.

Sie   *Gesprächspartner/in*
Hast du gut geschlafen?   Ja.
                           Nein, ich habe die ganze Nacht getanzt.

1. Bis wann hast du geschlafen?
2. Was hast du zum Frühstück gegessen?
3. Was hast du zum Frühstück getrunken?
4. Wie viele Seiten hast du gestern abend gelesen?
5. Mit wem hast du telefoniert?
6. Hast du [deinem Freund/deiner Freundin] etwas geliehen?
7. Wen hast du heute auf der Uni gesehen?
8. Mit wem hast du heute gesprochen?

13. Wie sagt man das?   Give German equivalents of each of the two-line dialogues below.

▶ Have you taken my ballpoint, Gabi?
—No, I haven't seen it.

Hast du meinen Kuli genommen, Gabi?
— Nein, den habe ich nicht gesehen.

1. Have you eaten already, Susanne?
   —No, I haven't had time.
2. Did you sleep well, Benno?
   —No, I drank too much coffee last night.
3. Have you spoken with Mrs. Danziger, Tanja?
   —No, but I wrote her daughter.

7 Separable-prefix verbs in the perfect tense

Infinitive	Past participle	Perfect tense
anfangen	an + **ge** + fangen	Kirstin **hat** gestern **angefangen**.
einkaufen	ein + **ge** + kauft	Ingrid **hat** heute **eingekauft**.

The prefix **ge-** of the past participle comes between the separable prefix and the stem of the participle. Some separable-prefix verbs are weak; others are strong. In spoken German the separable prefix receives stress: **an'gefangen.** A list of some separable-prefix verbs you have encountered follows.

Infinitive	Past participle
anfangen	angefangen
anrufen	angerufen
ansehen	angesehen
aussehen	ausgesehen
einladen	eingeladen
mitnehmen	mitgenommen

14. Studentenleben Restate the conversational exchanges below in the perfect tense.

▶ Denkst du an dein Referat? *Hast du an dein Referat gedacht?*
— Klar. Ich fange heute an. *— Klar. Ich habe heute angefangen.*

1. Hört Gisela mit Geschichte auf?
   — Ja, sie fängt mit Mathematik an.
2. Lädt Klaus für Samstag einige Freunde ein?
   — Natürlich. Er lädt alle seine Freunde ein.
3. Kauft er auch Wein ein?
   — Na klar. Er kauft auch Käse, Wurst und Brot ein.
4. Bringen seine Freunde etwas mit?
   — Natürlich. Sie bringen viel mit.
5. Wann hörst du mit deiner Arbeit auf?
   — Um acht. Dann rufe ich Sigrid an.

**Viele Studenten essen
in der Mensa.
(Universität Würzburg)**

8 Past participles without the *ge-* prefix

◆ *Verbs ending in* **-ieren**

Infinitive	Past participle	Perfect tense
studieren	studiert	Dirk **hat** in München **studiert.**
probieren	probiert	**Hast** du den Wein **probiert?**

Verbs ending in **-ieren** do not have the prefix **ge-** in the past participle. They are always weak verbs whose participle ends in **-t**. These verbs are generally based on words borrowed from French and Latin; they are often similar to English verbs.

15. Was hat man diskutiert?   Restate the conversational exchanges below in the perfect tense.

▶   Wo studierst du?   *Wo hast du studiert?*
    — Ich studiere in München.   *— Ich habe in München studiert.*

1. Probiert Gerd von dem Kuchen?
   — Nein, er probiert nur den Kaffee.
2. Frau Fischer dekoriert den Kuchen rot und grün.
   — Warum dekoriert sie den Kuchen mit solchen Farben?
3. Die Professoren plädieren für mehr Mathematik.
   — Die Studenten protestieren gegen diesen Plan, nicht?

◆ *Verbs with inseparable prefixes*

Infinitive	Past participle	Perfect tense
bekommen	bekommen	Ich **habe** nichts **bekommen.**
bemerken	bemerkt	**Hast** du das **bemerkt?**
bestellen	bestellt	Wer **hat** die Wurst **bestellt?**
bezahlen	bezahlt	Wer **hat** das **bezahlt?**
erklären	erklärt	Ich **habe** es schon **erklärt.**
erzählen	erzählt	Erik **hat** es **erzählt.**
gefallen	gefallen	**Hat** es dir **gefallen?**
gehören	gehört	Wem **hat** diese alte Uhr **gehört?**
vergessen	vergessen	Ich **habe** seine Adresse **vergessen.**
verlieren	verloren	Ich **habe** meinen Kuli **verloren.**
verstehen	verstanden	Inge **hat** es nicht **verstanden.**

Some prefixes are never separated from the verb stem. These prefixes are **be-, emp-, ent-, er-, ge-, ver-,** and **zer-**. Inseparable-prefix verbs do not add the prefix **ge-** in the past participle. Some inseparable-prefix verbs are weak; others are strong.

An inseparable prefix is not stressed in spoken German: **bekom'men**.

16. Das versteht er nicht.   Klaus doesn't understand Inge's report. That makes him and her unhappy. Restate the sentences below in the present tense.

▶   Inge hat ein Bier für Klaus bestellt.   *Inge bestellt ein Bier für Klaus.*

1. Sie hat von ihrem Referat erzählt.
2. Klaus hat es nicht verstanden.
3. Inge hat es noch einmal erklärt.
4. Das hat Klaus nicht gefallen.
5. Inge hat das bemerkt.
6. Sie hat daher Klaus' Bier nicht bezahlt.
7. Das hat er auch nicht verstanden.

17. Petra erzählt von ihrer Reise.   Petra went to Switzerland. Tell about her trip. Restate each sentence in the perfect tense.

▶   Petra erzählt von ihren Ferien.   *Petra hat von ihren Ferien erzählt.*

1. Sie bezahlt die Reise selbst.
2. Die Schweiz gefällt Petra sehr.
3. Sie bemerkt viel Interessantes.
4. Sie bekommt da auch leckeren Käse.
5. Sie versteht die Schweizer ziemlich gut.
6. Ein Schweizer erklärt ihr vieles.
7. Er erzählt viel Lustiges.
8. Leider verliert sie ihre Handtasche in Zürich.

18. Ich habe es vergessen.   You have arrived in class, but you left everything you need (pen, paper, book, notes) at home. Ask your partner to lend you what you need. Finally, your partner loses patience with your forgetfulness. (You may want to refer to *#3: Expressing annoyance* in the Supplementary Expressions in the Reference Section.)

Sie	*Gesprächspartner/in*
Ich habe meinen Kuli vergessen.	Ja gern. Nimm diesen.
Kannst du mir einen leihen?	Ich habe leider keinen.

9 Auxiliary *sein* with past participles

ich **bin gekommen**	wir **sind gekommen**
du **bist gekommen**	ihr **seid gekommen**
er/es/sie **ist gekommen**	sie **sind gekommen**
Sie **sind gekommen**	

Some verbs use **sein** instead of **haben** as an auxiliary in the perfect.

Warum **ist** Erika so früh **aufge-standen**?	Why did Erika get up so early?
Sie **ist** nach Freiburg **gefahren**.	She drove to Freiburg.

Verbs that require **sein** must meet two conditions. They must:

1. be intransitive verbs (verbs without a direct object) and
2. indicate a change of condition (e.g., **aufstehen**) or location (e.g., **fahren**).

Infinitive		Past participle
aufstehen		aufgestanden
fahren		gefahren
fliegen	ist	geflogen
gehen		gegangen
kommen		gekommen

Infinitive		Past participle
laufen		gelaufen
schwimmen		geschwommen
wachsen	ist	gewachsen
wandern		gewandert
werden		geworden

Wer **ist** wieder so lange bei Helmut **geblieben**?	Who stayed so late at Helmut's again?
Ich **bin** es nicht **gewesen**.	It wasn't I.

The verbs **bleiben** and **sein** require **sein** as an auxiliary in the perfect, even though they do not indicate a change of location or condition.

Wie **war** der Kaffee?	How was the coffee?
Der Kuchen **war** gut.	The cake was good.

The simple past tense of **sein (war)** is used more commonly than the perfect tense of **sein (ist gewesen),** even in conversation.

19. So war es. Restate the conversational exchanges below in the perfect tense.

▶ Fahrt ihr mit dem Auto?   *Seid ihr mit dem Auto gefahren?*
  — Nein, wir fliegen.   *— Nein, wir sind geflogen.*

1. Fahrt ihr nach Österreich?
  — Nein, wir bleiben auch in den Ferien zu Hause.
2. Gehen Müllers auch schwimmen?
  — Ja, aber sie kommen erst später.
3. Schwimmt ihr viel?
  — Nein, wir schwimmen nicht. Wir wandern viel.
4. Stehst du heute früh auf?
  — Ja. Ich laufe um acht zur Uni.

20. Was haben Sie gemacht?   Tell about some of your recent activities by answering the questions. Then compare notes with your partner by asking her/him the same questions. Remember to use **du** with your partner.

1. Wann sind Sie gestern aufgestanden? Am Sonntag?
2. Wohin sind Sie nach dem Frühstück gegangen? Oder sind Sie zu Hause geblieben?
3. Wo haben Sie gestern abend gegessen?
4. Was haben Sie gestern abend getrunken?
5. Wann sind Sie heute zur Uni gefahren?
6. Wie viele Vorlesungen haben Sie gehabt?
7. Wann sind Sie gestern wieder nach Hause gegangen?
8. Welches Buch haben Sie zuletzt gelesen?
9. Was haben Sie letzte Woche gekauft?
10. Wann sind Sie ins Bett gegangen?

Talking about past activities

10 Dependent clauses in the perfect tense

Ich möchte wissen, was sie gestern abend gemacht **haben.**
Ich möchte wissen, ob sie ins Kino gegangen **sind.**

In a dependent clause, the auxiliary verb **haben** or **sein** follows the past participle and is the last element in the clause.

21. Ich weiß nicht.   A friend asks about David's and Nicole's college experiences. Say you don't know.

▶   Hat Nicole im Sommer gearbeitet?   *Ich weiß nicht, ob sie im Sommer gearbeitet hat.*

1. Hat Nicole einen Studentenjob gefunden?
2. Hat sie Geld vom Staat bekommen?
3. Ist alles teuer gewesen?
4. Hat David an einer staatlichen Uni studiert?
5. Haben seine Eltern alles bezahlt?
6. Hat David in Amerika Englisch und Mathematik studiert?

22. Kurze Gespräche   Restate the conversational exchanges below in the perfect tense.

1. Fährst du mit dem Rad zur Uni?
   — Nein, ich laufe.

2. Rufst du Erika an?
   — Nein, sie geht einkaufen.
   — Wer sagt denn das?

3. Bestellst du Fisch?
   — Nein, ich esse Fisch am Samstag.

4. Denkst du an den Wein?
   — Ja, ich kaufe ihn heute.
   — Bringst du auch Gläser mit?

23. Wer hat was gemacht? Find six fellow students who have done any one of the activities listed below in the past week.

▶ arbeiten *Hast du letzte Woche gearbeitet?*

einkaufen gehen	[Tennis] spielen	zu Hause bleiben
Referat vorbereiten	mit Freunden wandern	zuviel essen
Notizen durcharbeiten	ins Kino gehen	neue Schuhe kaufen
viel schlafen	schwimmen gehen	Buch lesen
Deutsch machen	Videospiele spielen	Geburtstag feiern

WIEDERHOLUNG

1. Renate hat einen Kuchen gebacken. Write a paragraph about Renate's experience baking a cake. Use the perfect tense, and the cues provided below.

1. Renate / einladen / am Sonntag / Freunde / zum Kaffee
2. am Samstag / sie / backen / ein Kuchen
3. sie / anfangen / sehr früh
4. sie / haben / keine Butter // und / ihre Schwester Monika / laufen / zu / Lebensmittelgeschäft
5. Kuchen / aussehen / nicht richtig
6. das / gefallen / Renate / natürlich / nicht
7. Monika / helfen / dann / ihre Schwester

2. Der Kuchen hat nicht geschmeckt. Now tell about Frank's experience with a cake by supplying the missing prepositions.

1. Frank lebt _____ zwei Monaten in Bremen.
2. Er arbeitet _____ einer amerikanischen Firma.
3. _____ Sonntag hat er einige Bekannte _____ Kaffee eingeladen.
4. Die Gäste sind _____ vier gekommen.
5. Frank hat _____ seine Bekannten einen Kuchen gebacken — rot, grün und gelb dekoriert.
6. Der Kaffee hat den Gästen geschmeckt, aber _____ dem Kuchen hat jeder nur ein Stück probiert.
7. „Was können die nur _____ meinen Kuchen haben?" denkt Frank.
8. _____ seinem Freund hört er dann, daß viele Deutsche nur Kuchen _____ künstliche Farben essen.

3. Was bedeutet das? The sentences below contain some unfamiliar words that are either compounds of familiar words or related to familiar words. Guess the meaning of the words in boldface, and then give the English equivalent.

1. Das Essen steht auf° dem **Eßtisch** im **Eßzimmer.**   on
2. Sie trinkt oft **Getränke** wie Bier und Wein.
3. Sie bringt ihren kranken Mann im **Krankenwagen** ins **Krankenhaus.**
4. Bei Regen trägt Herr Roth Regenmantel, Handschuhe und **Überschuhe.**

4. Wie sagt man das?

1. —Why did you come by bus?
   —My car is broken down.
   —I'm sorry.
2. —Did you like Denmark?
   —Yes. We hiked a lot.
   —Did you camp (in a tent)?
   —No. It rained too much. We slept at friends' (houses).
3. —Are you hungry?
   —Yes. May I try this cake?
   —Of course. How does it taste?
   —It's excellent. Very tasty.

5. Fragen über die Uni Tell what David discovered about going to a German university; combine the sentences with the conjunction indicated.

1. David hat viele Fragen. (weil) Er möchte in Deutschland studieren.
2. Er möchte wissen … (ob) Ist die Uni sehr teuer?
3. Nicole sagt … (daß) Es kostet überhaupt nichts.
4. Er fragt … (ob) Ist es leicht, einen Studentenjob zu bekommen?
5. Nicole sagt … (daß) Es ist nicht leicht. (denn) Es gibt wenige Studentenjobs.

6. Eine Reise You and a partner exchange information about a trip or vacation you each have taken. Find out about his/her trip and tell about yours. Some ideas for your conversation are:

Where did you go? With whom? By what means of transportation?
How long did you stay?
Whom or what did you see?
Did you buy anything? If so, what? If not, why not?
What did you do?
Would you like to return (**wieder hinfahren**)?

Schrebergarten: Ein Stückchen Land für Stadtbewohner.

7. Anregung

1. Two students, Michael and Sabine, are discussing various topics. Select one of the topics below and write the dialogue that takes place between them.

    das Wetter ◇ einkaufen ◇ die Vorlesung ◇ eine Seminararbeit vorbereiten ◇ das Essen ◇ das Wochenende ◇ Ferien

2. Write a paragraph or conversation on the topic *Natürlich ist natürlich besser*.

3. **Ein Werbespot°.** Using the ad from **Karstadt** on page 216, write copy for a radio advertisement. Below are some phrases you may want to use.　　　short ad

    heute bei Karstadt … ◇ Top Jeans … ◇ gut einkaufen … ◇ jeden Donnerstag bis 20.30 geöffnet

GRAMMATIK: ZUSAMMENFASSUNG

The perfect tense

Hast du das Referat endlich **geschrieben?**	Have you finally written the report?
Petra **ist** im Bett **geblieben.**	Petra has stayed in bed.

The German perfect tense, like the English present perfect, is a compound tense. It is made up of the present tense of the auxiliary **haben** or **sein** and the past participle. The past participle is in final position, except in a dependent clause.

Past participles of regular weak verbs

Infinitive	Past participle	Perfect tense
sagen	ge + sag + t	Er **hat** es **gesagt.**
arbeiten	ge + arbeit + et	Sie **hat** schwer **gearbeitet.**
baden	ge + bad + et	Er **hat** gestern nicht **gebadet.**
regnen	ge + regn + et	Es **hat** gestern **geregnet.**

The past participle of a weak verb is formed by adding **-t** to the unchanged stem. The **-t** expands to **-et** in verbs like **arbeiten, baden,** and **regnen.** In the past participle, most weak verbs also have the prefix **ge-.**

Past participles of irregular weak verbs

Infinitive	Past participle	Perfect tense
bringen	ge + brach + t	Wer **hat** das **gebracht?**
denken	ge + dach + t	Sie **hat** nicht an die Zeit **gedacht.**
kennen	ge + kann + t	Sie **hat** deinen Freund gut **gekannt.**
wissen	ge + wuß + t	Sie **hat** es **gewußt.**

A few weak verbs are irregular. The past participle has the prefix **ge-** and the ending **-t;** there is also a change in the stem vowel and in the consonants of several verbs.

Past participles of strong verbs

Infinitive	Past participle	Perfect tense
nehmen	ge + nomm + en	Ich **habe** das Brot **genommen**.
sitzen	ge + sess + en	Ich **habe** dort **gesessen**.
tun	ge + ta + n	Ich **habe** das nicht **getan**.

The past participle of a strong verb is formed by adding **-en** to the participle stem. Most strong verbs also add the **ge-** prefix in the past participle. Many strong verbs have a change in the stem vowel of the past participle, and some verbs also have a change in the consonants.

For a list of strong verbs, see #23 of the Grammatical Tables in the Reference Section.

Past participles of separable-prefix verbs

Infinitive	Past participle	Perfect tense
anfangen	an + **ge** + fangen	Gerd **hat** mit der Arbeit **angefangen**.
aufhören	auf + **ge** + hört	Inge **hat** mit der Arbeit **aufgehört**.

The prefix **ge-** of the past participle comes between the separable prefix and the stem of the participle. Some separable-prefix verbs are weak; others are strong.

Past participles without the *ge-* prefix

◆ *Verbs ending in* -ieren

Present tense	Perfect tense
Jutta **studiert** in Heidelberg.	Jutta **hat** in Heidelberg **studiert**.
Alle **probieren** von dem Kuchen.	Alle **haben** von dem Kuchen **probiert**.

Verbs ending in **-ieren** do not have the prefix **ge-** in the past participle. They are always weak verbs whose participle ends in **-t**. These verbs are generally based on words borrowed from French and Latin; they are often similar to English verbs.

◆ *Verbs with inseparable prefixes*

Present tense	Perfect tense
Birgit **erklärt** alles.	Sie **hat** alles **erklärt.**
Martin **versteht** uns nicht.	Er **hat** uns nicht **verstanden.**

Some prefixes are never separated from the verb stem. These prefixes are **be-, emp-, ent-, er-, ge-, ver-,** and **zer-.** Inseparable-prefix verbs do not add the prefix **ge-** in the past participle. Some inseparable-prefix verbs are weak; others are strong.

Use of the auxiliary *haben*

Christine **hat** heute **gearbeitet.**	Christine worked today.
Gerd **hat** seiner Freundin **geholfen.**	Gerd helped his friend.

Haben is used to form the perfect tense of most verbs.

Use of the auxiliary *sein*

Schmidts **sind** spät nach Hause **gekommen.**	The Schmidts came home late.
Sie **sind** dann spät **aufgestanden.**	Then they got up late.

The auxiliary **sein** is used to form the perfect tense of intransitive verbs (i.e., verbs that do not have a direct object) when these verbs denote a change in location (e.g., **kommen**) or condition (e.g., **aufstehen**).

Warum **bist** du so lange **geblieben?**	Why did you stay so long?
Es **ist** so schön **gewesen.**	It was so nice.

The intransitive verbs **bleiben** and **sein** require the auxiliary **sein,** even though they do not indicate change of location or condition.

Verbs using the auxiliary *sein*

You have already encountered some verbs that take the auxiliary **sein** in the perfect tense. They are shown in the table below.

Infinitive	Auxiliary	Past participle
aufstehen	ist	aufgestanden
bleiben	ist	geblieben
fahren	ist	gefahren
gehen	ist	gegangen
kommen	ist	gekommen
laufen	ist	gelaufen
schwimmen	ist	geschwommen
sein	ist	gewesen
wachsen	ist	gewachsen
wandern	ist	gewandert
werden	ist	geworden

Use of the perfect tense in dependent clauses

Klaus möchte wissen, ob David nach Österreich gefahren **ist**.
Karin möchte wissen, ob er da viel gesehen **hat**.

In a dependent clause, the auxiliary **haben** or **sein** follows the past participle and is the last element in the clause.

Freunde und Verwandte kommen oft am Nachmittag zum Kaffee.

Kapitel 8

BAUSTEINE FÜR GESPRÄCHE

Was machst du nach dem Seminar?

Alex: Was machst du nach dem Seminar?
Bärbel: Ich treffe Claudia im Altstadtcafé.
Alex: In der Fußgängerzone?
Bärbel: Ja. Gehst du mit?
Alex: Nein, nicht so gern, danke. Im Altstadtcafé ist immer so schlechte Luft. Da ist alles voll Rauch.
Bärbel: Wie wär's mit einem Biergarten? Im Waldcafé sitzt man schön draußen.
Alex: Aber du, ich bin pleite.
Bärbel: Macht nichts. Ich lade dich ein.

What are you doing after the seminar?

What are you doing after the seminar?
I'm meeting Claudia at the Altstadtcafé.
In the pedestrian zone?
Yes. Want to come along?
No, not really, thanks. At the Altstadtcafé the air is always so bad. Everything is full of smoke.
How about a beer garden? At the Waldcafé we can sit outside.

But you know, I'm broke.
That doesn't matter. I'll treat you.

Fragen

1. Wen trifft Bärbel? Wann? Wo?
2. Wo ist das Altstadtcafé?
3. Warum möchte Alex nicht mitgehen?
4. Warum findet Alex einen Biergarten bestimmt besser?
5. Leiht Bärbel Alex Geld? Warum (nicht)?

1. Was machst du?   A fellow student would like to do something later and asks what your plans are at various times.

Making plans

Gesprächspartner/in

Was machst du | **nach dem Seminar?**
nach der Vorlesung?
heute nachmittag?
am Wochenende?

Sie

Ich treffe [Alex] | **im Café.**
in der Mensa°.
in der Bibliothek.
Ich gehe nach Hause.
Ich sehe fern°.

2. Wohin möchtet ihr? Form a group of three. One asks where you can go. Another suggests a place, and the third responds.

S1: Wohin möchtet ihr [Samstag] abend?

S2: Wie wär's mit | einem Café?
                 | einem Biergarten?

S3: Nein, da sind zu viele Leute.
    Nein, da ist es zu laut°.
    Nein, da ist alles voll Rauch.
    Gern, das macht immer Spaß°.
    Gern, da kann man schön draußen sitzen.
    Gern, da trifft man viele nette Leute.

3. Interview Fragen Sie eine Gesprächspartnerin bzw. einen Gesprächspartner:

1. was sie/er nach der Vorlesung macht
2. ob sie/er oft fernsieht
3. wo sie/er oft Freunde trifft
4. ob sie/er oft pleite ist
5. ob sie/er manchmal von Freunden Geld leihen muß
6. ob sie/er Freunden Geld leihen muß

**Fußgängerzone —
Hier gehört die Straße
den Fußgängern. (Heidelberg)**

The physical layout of cities in the German-speaking countries is generally different from that of cities in the United States. The concept of building large suburbs and shopping malls around a city is uncommon in most of Europe. A city (**Großstadt**) or town (**Stadt**) in German-speaking countries has a center containing office buildings as well as apartment houses, stores, and places for cultural events. Many downtown areas have been converted to traffic-free pedestrian zones (**Fußgängerzonen**). A typical pedestrian zone has many stores, restaurants, and outdoor cafés. The streets are often lined with plants and trees and sometimes lead into small squares, where people can rest on benches. The downtown shopping areas are used not only by people who live in the city, but also by people who live in the outskirts or in nearby villages.

Freitag, 10. August

1. Programm

9.00 **Heute**
9.03 **Dallas.** Angst um Miss Ellie (1)
9.45 **Sport treiben – fit bleiben** (4)
10.00 **Heute**
10.03 **Die Reportage**
11.00 **Heute**
11.03 **„. . . die Post ist das!"** Geschichten aus 500 Jahren. Erzählt von S.D. Fürst von Thurn und Taxis u. a.
12.35 **Umschau**
12.55 **Presseschau**
13.00 **ZDF-Mittagsmagazin**
13.45 **Wirtschafts-Telegramm**
14.00 **Sesamstraße**
14.30 **„. . . und das Leben geht weiter"** (6). Fernsehserie in acht Teilen von Giorgio Arlorio, Dino Risi und Bernardino Zapponi
15.30 **Tagesschau**
15.35 **Die Zauberfischgräte.** Zeichentrickfilm von A. Munova nach einer Erzählung von Charles Dickens
17.15 **Tagesschau**
17.25 **BR Regional: Bayernstudio – Heute in Bayern / 17.35 Forstinspektor Buchholz / 18.30 Bayernstudio – Tagesthema / 18.45 Zwei alte Damen geben Gas / 19.10 Bayernstudio / 19.20 Mich laust der Affe / 19.50 Bayernstudio**

19.58 **Heute im Ersten**
20.00 **Tagesschau**
20.15 Die Freitagspremiere. **Zwei Italiener mögens heiß.** Ital. Spielfilm (1987) Regie: Enrico Oldoini
21.45 **Plusminus**
22.30 **Tagesthemen**
23.00 **Golden girls.** Die Macht des Käsekuchens
23.25 **Sportschau**
23.50 ARD-Gruselkabinett. **Ausgeliefert.** Amerik. Spielfilm (1972)
1.20 **Tagesschau**
1.25 **Nachtgedanken**

3. Programm

12.20 **Das Gespensterhaus.** Schweizer Spielfilm (1942)
14.00 **Englisch für Anfänger** (11)
14.30 **Der Schritt in die Marktwirtschaft.** Betriebswirtschaftslehre (10)
15.00 BFS Sport aktuell. **Golf.** Ladies German Open am Wörthsee

17.00 **Rundschau**
17.05 **Fit und frisch.** Gymnastik für die ganze Familie
17.20 **Spielmobil – Das Haus mit der Nummer 30**
17.50 **Floris von Rosemund**
18.15 **Abendschau**
18.42 **Der Abend im Bayerischen Fernsehen**
18.45 **Rundschau**
19.00 **Unser Land**
19.45 **Super-Grips.** Das schnelle Spiel
20.15 **François Cuvilliés d.Ä.** Baumeister des bayerischen Rokoko 1695–1768
21.05 **Polizeiinspektion 1.** 86. Das Jubiläum
21.30 **Rundschau**
21.45 **Sport heute**
22.00 **Nix für ungut!** Der Wochenkommentar
22.05 **Auweia! Alas Smith & Jones.** Comedy-Serie
22.35 **Von der Sommerfrische zum Massentourismus.** 100 Jahre Tourismus in Bayern
23.20 **Rundschau**
23.25 **Der explosive Koffer.** Amerik. Spielfilm (1937)

4. Fragen Answer the following questions based on the listings for the German channels 1 and 3. If you need help in reading the listings, see the Vocabulary for Authentic Text Activities in the Reference Section.

1. In den verschiedenen Programmen gibt es auch amerikanische Sendungen. Welche sind das?
2. Welchen Fernsehfilm für Kinder gibt es am Nachmittag im 1. Programm?
3. In Deutschland heißen die Nachrichtensendungen „Tagesschau" und „Heute". Wie viele Nachrichtensendungen gibt es? Wann kommen sie? In welchen Programmen?
4. Wo und wann gibt es Sportsendungen?
5. Wo und wann kann man am Morgen eine Fitness-Sendung ansehen?

5. Fernsehen   Look at the TV guide and find a program for each category and what time it airs. If there is no program for a particular category, give an example of a local program. You will find the meanings of the categories in the Supplementary Word Sets for *Kapitel 8* in the Reference Section.

Seifenoper	Nachrichten
Fernsehserie	Spielfilm
Musiksendung	Sportsendung

In Germany, each community has access to two national television channels and one regional channel. These are referred to respectively as **ARD (Arbeitsgemeinschaft der öffentlich-rechtlichen Rundfunkanstalten Deutschlands)** or **Erstes Programm, ZDF (Zweites Deutsches Fernsehen)** or **Zweites Programm,** and **Drittes Programm (Regionalprogramm).** These three channels are run as non-profit public corporations and supervised by broadcasting councils. Their programming is financed primarily by quarterly fees collected from viewers for every TV set they own. Commercials are usually shown in two to three clusters per evening and are restricted to a maximum of twenty minutes per workday. There are no commercials after 8 P.M. or on Sundays. Private television was introduced into then West Germany in the mid-1980s. Today cable television is available by subscription in most cities, and the new private stations have become strong competitors to the public TV stations. The two major cable TV stations are **SAT 1** and **SAT 2** or **3.** Their programs are found in virtually all German newspaper TV listings.

The regular broadcast-day of the public TV stations begins in the afternoon, although the broadcasts may begin earlier on weekends. In the morning, the **Erstes Programm** or the **Zweites Programm** repeats shows that were broadcast previously. Popular programs include news shows (**Nachrichten**), game shows, sports (**Sportsendungen**), movies (**Spielfilme**), and series (**Serien**) such as situation comedies or detective shows (**Krimis**)—many of which are co-productions with Swiss and Austrian television or imported from the United States. American and other foreign films are usually broadcast with dubbed in voices rather than subtitles. For many programs, stereo broadcasting makes it possible to hear the soundtrack either in the original language or in German. People who live close to a border sometimes receive broadcasts from a neighboring country.

Die Tagesschau ist eine Nachrichtensendung im ersten Programm.

6. Was gibt's im Fernsehen? Choose a program from the TV guide and describe it, and have your partner or the class guess which program you are describing.

▶ *Diese Sendung ist für Kinder. Sie kommt um 14.00 Uhr.*

7. Deine Lieblingssendung Find out from three people how often they watch TV, what their favorite programs are, which programs they don't like and why.

▶ Wie oft siehst du fern? Einmal (zweimal, dreimal) die Woche? Was ist deine Lieblingssendung?   *Ich sehe gern [...], weil es [lustig] ist.*

Vokabeln

__ Substantive __

der **Biergarten, -̈** beer garden
das **Fernsehen** television; der **Fernseher, -** TV set
die **Fußgängerzone, -n** pedestrian zone
der **Liebling, -e** favorite; die **Lieblingssendung, -en** favorite program
die **Mensa, -s** or **Mensen** college cafeteria
die **Nachrichten** (*pl.*) news

das **Programm, -e** program; TV channel; **im (ersten) Programm** on channel (1); das **Fernsehprogramm** TV guide
der **Rauch** smoke
die **Sendung, -en** broadcast, TV program
der **Spaß** fun; **Späße** (*pl.*) jokes
der **Wald, -̈er** forest
der **Wetterbericht, -e** weather report

__ Verben __

ein·laden (lädt ein), eingeladen to invite; to treat (pay for someone)
fern·sehen (sieht fern), ferngesehen to watch TV

treffen (trifft), getroffen to meet

__ Andere Wörter __

draußen outside
laut loud
mal time; **einmal** one time; once; **zweimal** two times; **dreimal** three times

pleite broke, out of money
voll full; complete(ly)

— Besondere Ausdrücke —————————————

Das macht Spaß.	That's fun.	**im Fernsehen** on TV
einmal die Woche	once a week	**wie wär's mit …** how about . . .
(Es) macht nichts.	(It) doesn't matter.	

TYPISCH DEUTSCH? TYPISCH AMERIKANISCH?

Vorbereitung auf das Lesen

◆ *Zum Thema*

1. Ein paar Ausländer° wollen etwas über die USA, Kanada oder Deutschland wissen. Beschreiben° Sie Land und Leute für sie.
2. Denken Sie an ein Land — Kanada, Deutschland, die USA. Was assoziieren Sie mit diesem Land?
3. Was ist für viele Amerikaner typisch deutsch? Was ist für viele Ausländer typisch amerikanisch?

°foreigners

°describe

◆ *Leitfragen*

1. Welche Ähnlichkeiten gibt es zwischen Deutschland und den USA?
2. In welchen Situationen benutzen die Deutschen Vornamen? Die Amerikaner?
3. Was hat Peter in Deutschland anders gefunden als zu Hause?
4. Welche Schwierigkeiten hat Peter in Deutschland gehabt?
5. Was gefällt Monika an Amerika? Was gefällt ihr weniger?
6. Warum hat jede Nation die Tendenz, das eigene System besser zu finden?

Zwischen den USA und Deutschland gibt es enge kulturelle, wirtschaftliche° und auch politische Beziehungen°. So überrascht es nicht, daß es zwischen den Ländern viele Ähnlichkeiten gibt. Aber es gibt auch Unterschiede. Viele Deutsche sehen im Fernsehen jede Woche amerikanische Sendungen.
5 Da sehen sie, daß Amerika anders ist als Bayern° oder Niedersachsen°. Einige Amerikaner dagegen° verbinden° Deutschland mit Qualitätsarbeit, andere mit klassischer Musik und wieder andere mit dem Weihnachtsbaum und Weihnachtsliedern. Die Frage ist nur: Sind beliebte° amerikanische Fernseh-

°economic / relations

°Bavaria / Lower Saxony
°on the other hand / associate

°popular

sendungen typisch für Amerika? Und sind Qualitätsarbeit, Weihnachten und
10 die Klassiker typisch für Deutschland? Und was ist das überhaupt: „Typisch"
für ein Land?

Da kommt zum Beispiel die Austauschstudentin° Monika Berger in ihrer | exchange student
amerikanischen Universitätsstadt an. Der Vater der° Gastfamilie holt sie vom | of the (gen.)
Flughafen ab: „Hallo, Monika! Herzlich° willkommen! Ich heiße Bob." | cordially
15 Monika findet diese Begrüßung° merkwürdig. Ihr Vater in Deutschland | greeting
benutzt den Vornamen nur unter guten Freunden. Und was bedeutet diese
Begrüßung nun? Sind die Amerikaner einfach freundlicher°, offener°, kon- | friendlier / more open
taktfreudiger°? Oder sind sie unkultiviert°, plump°, ohne Gefühl für feine | better mixers / uncultured / unrefined
Unterschiede?

20 Nach einiger Zeit sitzt Monika mit einem Freund, Peter, in einer Studentenkneipe. Peter ist ein Jahr in Deutschland gewesen. Mit ihm kann man gut
über solche Fragen reden. Monika fragt Peter: „Du, sag mal, was hast du
eigentlich so bemerkt, als du in Deutschland warst? Was hast du beobachtet?
Was war anders?"

25 *Peter:* Vieles° war ja genauso° wie hier. Aber vieles war doch auch anders. Da | many things / exactly
war zum Beispiel meine erste Fahrt auf der Autobahn. Furchtbar, sag' ich
dir. Die fahren wie die Wilden, hab' ich gedacht. Danach° bin ich richtig | afterwards
gern mit dem Zug gefahren. Die Bahnhöfe sind angenehm. Einige sind
sogar großartig. Außerdem macht es ja wirklich Spaß, mit dem Zug zu
30 fahren. Es gibt genug Züge. Sie sind sauber. Und sie fahren pünktlich ab,
und sie kommen pünktlich an. Andere Sachen, die° anders waren, ja, was | that
war da noch? Vielleicht die Parks in jeder Stadt, die vielen Blumen in den
Fenstern, auf den Märkten, in den Restaurants. Und dann das Essen.
Erstens° ist das Essen selbst anders — mehr Wurst, anderes Bier und so°. | first of all / and such things
35 Dann wie man ißt — wie man Messer und Gabel benutzt, meine ich. Und
schließlich hab' ich auch gefunden, daß das Essen mehr ein Ereignis° ist. | event
Man sitzt länger° am Tisch und redet miteinander. | for a longer time

Monika: Und womit hast du Schwierigkeiten gehabt?

Peter: Da war vor allem die Bürokratie. Ich weiß, wir Amerikaner haben auch
40 eine schreckliche Bürokratie. Die deutsche Variante hat mich wohl vor
allem deswegen so gestört, weil° sie an ungewohnten° Stellen° existiert, | **deswegen ... weil:** bothered me so much just because / unusual / places
d.h. für uns Amerikaner ungewohnt. Z.B. braucht man eine Aufent-
haltserlaubnis°. Die gibt's auf der Polizei. Die bekommt man aber nur, | residence permit
wenn man vorher beim Ausländerarzt gewesen ist. Dafür muß man aufs
45 Gesundheitsamt°. Und wenn man endlich eine Wohnung hat, muß man | public health office
aufs Einwohnermeldeamt°. Und überall muß man natürlich Formulare | residence registration office
ausfüllen. Aber nun mal was anderes. Was hast du denn hier so beobach-
tet?

Monika: Einige Sachen gefallen mir ausgesprochen° gut. Zum Beispiel kann | clearly
50 ich hier auch abends und am ganzen Wochenende einkaufen gehen. Das
finde ich gut. In Deutschland gibt es den Donnerstagabend und dann nur
einmal im Monat den langen Samstag.

Zwischen Deutschland
und den USA gibt es
viele persönliche Bezie-
hungen: Eine amerika-
nische Austauschstudentin
bei ihrer deutschen
Familie.

Peter: Und was hat dir weniger gefallen?

Monika: Na ja, also bitte, sei mir nicht böse. Ich finde die Amerikaner
55 unglaublich freundlich. Das mag ja zunächst° sehr schön sein. Aber diese   at first
Freundlichkeit erscheint mir doch sehr oberflächlich°. Sie kann einfach   superficial
nicht echt sein.

Peter: Das sehen wir eben anders. Ein nettes Lächeln im Alltag° macht das   daily life
Leben eben einfacher.

60 *Monika:* Das mag wohl sein.

    Wer hat nun recht, Monika oder Peter? Beide haben die Tendenz, erst
einmal° die eigene Seite besser zu finden. Und das ist sicher eine allgemeine   **erst einmal:** right away
Tendenz. Aber oft sind *andere* Dinge nur neu. Und neue Dinge machen uns
Angst. Daher werten wir sie ab°. Außerdem hat die Gruppenpsychologie   **abwerten:** discredit
65 vielleicht eine Erklärung: Die Sprecher° einer° Sprache sind eine Gruppe.   speakers / of a *(gen.)*
Damit° die Gruppe zusammenhält, muß sie *besser* sein als andere Gruppen.   so that
Daher hat jede Nation mehr oder weniger die Tendenz, das eigene System,
die eigene Art besser zu finden als die anderen.

Fragen zum Lesestück

1. Wie sind die kulturellen, wirtschaftlichen und politischen Beziehungen zwischen den USA und Deutschland?
2. Was sehen viele Deutsche jede Woche im Fernsehen?
3. Womit verbinden viele Amerikaner Deutschland?
4. Warum findet Monika Bobs Begrüßung am Flughafen merkwürdig?
5. Warum kann man mit Peter gut darüber reden?
6. Wie hat Peter seine erste Fahrt auf der Autobahn gefunden?
7. Warum macht es in Deutschland Spaß, mit dem Zug zu fahren?
8. Was hat Peter sonst noch beobachtet? Was war anders?
9. Was alles ist beim Essen anders?
10. Womit hat Peter vor allem Schwierigkeiten gehabt? Warum?
11. Wo bekommt man die Aufenthaltserlaubnis?
12. Warum muß ein Ausländer aufs Gesundheitsamt?
13. Wohin muß man, wenn man eine Wohnung hat?
14. Was gefällt Monika gut an Amerika?
15. Was hat Monika gegen die Freundlichkeit in Amerika?
16. Welche Tendenz haben Monika und Peter?
17. Warum werten wir neue Dinge oft ab?
18. Warum muß eine Gruppe „besser" sein als andere Gruppen?
19. Welche Tendenz findet man in fast allen Nationen?

Sagt man hier „du" oder „Sie"?

Adult Germans use **du** and first names only with close friends. They do not use the word **Freund(in)** as freely as Americans use *friend*. A **Freund(in)** is a person with whom one is on intimate terms, a person who is often called "a very good friend" by Americans. Germans tend to have fewer **Freunde** and a larger circle of acquaintances (**Bekannte**). Even acquaintances of years' standing do not necessarily become **Freunde**. The change from **Bekannte(r)** to **Freund(in)** has traditionally been accompanied by a change from **Sie** to **du**. Although students use **du** with each other immediately, it is still prudent in most situations for an American visitor to let a German-speaking person propose the use of the familiar **du**. Also, in German-speaking countries, friends and acquaintances do not just "drop in" for a visit, but wait until they receive an invitation for a specific time and date.

1. **Erzählen Sie.** Talk about three or four of the similarities and differences between Germany and the United States. Use the cues below.

Fernsehen ◇ Musik ◇ Vornamen ◇ Autofahren ◇ Züge ◇ Blumen ◇ Essen ◇ Einkaufen ◇ Freundlichkeit ◇ Bürokratie

2. **Eine Podiumsdiskussion** **(Panel discussion)** Choose several members of the class to play the roles of an American/Canadian, an Austrian, and a German. The other members of the class ask them questions about stereotypes and life in their countries and what they especially like or dislike about life in the different countries. Below are some questions to get you started. Remember to use the proper form of address when asking your questions.

> Discussing cultural differences

1. Bei wem benutzen Sie/benutzt du Vornamen — bei den Nachbarn? Bei Ihren/deinen Professoren? Bei Ihren/deinen Freunden?
2. Welches Transportmittel benutzen die meisten Leute? (Fahren Sie/ Fährst du oft mit dem Zug?)
3. Gehen die Amerikaner/Kanadier zuwenig zu Fuß?
4. Was halten Sie/hältst du von der Bürokratie in Amerika/Kanada?
5. Finden Sie/Findest du die Amerikaner/Kanadier zu freundlich?

Vokabeln

— Substantive

die **Angst, ⸚e** fear
die **Art, -en** way, manner
der **Ausländer, -**/die **Ausländerin, -nen** foreigner
die **Autobahn, -en** freeway, expressway
der **Bahnhof, ⸚e** train station
der **Baum, ⸚e** tree
der **Brief, -e** letter
die **Erklärung, -en** explanation
die **Fahrt, -en** trip
der **Flughafen, ⸚** airport
die **Freundlichkeit** friendliness
die **Gabel, -n** fork
das **Gefühl, -e** feeling
die **Kneipe, -n** pub

das **Lied, -er** song
der **Löffel, -** spoon
das **Messer, -** knife
der **Park, -s** park
die **Polizei** *(sing. only)* the police
das **Restaurant, -s** restaurant
die **Schwierigkeit, -en** difficulty
die **Serviette, -n** napkin
die **Sprache, -n** language
die **USA** *(pl.)* U.S.A.
der **Vorname, -n, -n** first name
das **Weihnachten** Christmas; *(used often in pl.)* **Fröhliche Weihnachten!** Merry Christmas!
die **Wohnung, -en** dwelling; apartment

__ Verben _____

ab·fahren (fährt ab), ist abgefahren to depart, leave by some means of transportation

**an·kommen, ist angekommen (in + ** *dat.*) to arrive (in)

bedeuten to mean, imply; **was bedeutet das?** what does that mean?

benutzen to use

beobachten to observe

erscheinen, ist erschienen to appear

hängen to hang [*something*], put

hängen, gehangen to be hanging

legen to lay, put

meinen to mean; to think, have an opinion; **was meinst du?** what do you think?

reden (über + ** *acc.*/von**) to talk (about)

setzen to set, put

stecken to stick, put into, insert

stellen to place, put

stören to disturb, bother

__ Andere Wörter _____

allgemein general

**an (+ ** *acc.* or *dat.*) on; at; to

angenehm pleasant

**auf (+ ** *acc.* or *dat.*) on, on top of; at; to

**böse (auf + ** *acc.*) angry (at)

echt genuine

eigen (*adj.*) own; **mein eigenes Auto** my own car

einander one another, each other

einfach simple, simply

erst first

fein fine

genug enough

großartig first-rate, splendid, great

klassisch classic; classical

lange (*adv.*) for a long time

offen open

pünktlich punctual(ly), on time

sauber clean

schließlich finally; after all

schrecklich terrible, frightful

sicher safe; certain(ly), for sure

typisch typical(ly)

überall everywhere

unglaublich unbelievable

**unter (+ ** *acc.* or *dat.*) under; among

wohl probably, indeed

**zwischen (+ ** *acc.* or *dat.*) between; among

__ Besondere Ausdrücke _____

**Angst haben (vor + ** *dat.*) to be afraid (of)

Angst machen to frighten

etwas anderes something different

Das mag wohl sein. That could be, that may well be.

sei [mir] nicht böse don't get mad [at me]

Erweiterung des Wortschatzes

1 Flavoring particle *mal*

Sag **mal**, schreiben wir nächste Woche wieder eine Klausur?

Schreib doch **mal**!

Say, are we having a test again next week?

Do write. (Why don't you write sometime?)

Mal is frequently used to soften the intensity of expressed needs—wishes, obligations, or commands—and leaves the time for carrying out the needs vague. **Mal** and **doch** are often used together.

2 Word families

die **Arbeit**   the work
arbeiten   to work
der **Arbeiter**/die **Arbeiterin**   the worker

Like English, German has many words that belong to families and are derived from a common root.

1. Noch ein Wort Add a familiar word to each group of related words below, and give the meanings for all of the words.

1. wohnen, der Einwohner, _____
2. sprechen, das Gespräch, die Sprecherin, _____
3. der Koch, die Köchin, das Kochbuch, _____
4. die Wanderung, der Wanderer, die Wanderlust, der Wanderweg, _____
5. das Flugzeug, die Flugkarte, der Flughafen, _____
6. die Bäckerei, backen, _____

3 The suffix *-ung*

wandern to hike   **die Wanderung** hike
wohnen   to live   **die Wohnung** dwelling; apartment

The suffix **-ung** may be added to a verb stem to form a noun. All nouns ending in **-ung** are feminine.

2. Was bedeutet das? Complete the sentences by forming nouns from the boldfaced verbs. Give the English equivalents of the nouns.

1. Mark kann es nicht gut **erklären.** Verstehen Sie seine _____?
2. Was **meinen** Sie zu diesem Problem? Was ist Ihre _____?
3. Gabi kann gut **erzählen.** Ihre _____ sind immer lustig.
4. Die Autoren **lesen** heute einige von ihren Geschichten. Kommst du zu ihrer _____?
5. Brauns haben mich zum Kaffee **eingeladen.** Habt ihr auch eine _____ bekommen?
6. Jans Besuch hat uns alle **überrascht.** Es war eine große _____, daß er gekommen ist.

4 The verbs *legen/liegen, stellen/stehen, setzen/sitzen, hängen, stecken*

Inge **legt** das Buch auf den Tisch.

Das Buch **liegt** auf dem Tisch.

Paul **stellt** die Lampe in die Ecke.

Die Lampe **steht** in der Ecke.

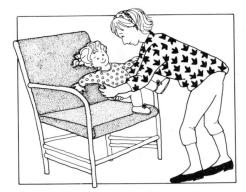

Marta **setzt** das Kind auf den Stuhl.

Das Kind **sitzt** auf dem Stuhl.

Achmed **hängt** die Uhr an die Wand.   Die Uhr **hängt** an der Wand.

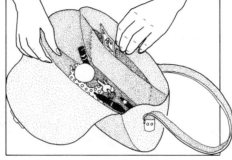

Monika **steckt** das Geld in die Tasche.   Ihr Geld **steckt** in der Tasche.

In English, the all-purpose verb for movement to a position is *to put*, and the all-purpose verb for the resulting position is *to be*. German uses several verbs to express the meanings *put* and *be*.

Ich habe das Buch auf den Tisch **gelegt.**

To express *put*, German uses **legen (gelegt),** *to lay*; **stellen (gestellt),** *to stand upright*; **setzen (gesetzt),** *to set*; **hängen (gehängt),** *to hang*; and **stecken (gesteckt),** *to stick, insert*. These verbs all take direct objects and are weak.

Das Buch **hat** auf dem Tisch **gelegen.**

To express position, German uses **liegen (gelegen),** *to be lying*; **stehen (gestanden),** *to be standing*; **sitzen (gesessen),** *to be sitting*; **hängen (gehangen),** *to be hanging*; and **stecken (gesteckt),** *to be (inserted)*. These verbs do not take direct objects and, except for **stecken,** are strong.

3. Welches Verb?   Indicate which of the following verbs would be used in the German equivalents of the sentences below: **legen, liegen, stellen, stehen, setzen, sitzen, hängen, stecken.**

▶   Put the lamp on the table.   *stellen*

1. The vase of flowers is on the table.
2. My shoes are under the bed.
3. Her books are on the floor again.
4. Put the pot on the stove.
5. He put his hat on his head.
6. The wine glasses are on the table.
7. Mark, put the stamps in the drawer.
8. The car is (parked) behind the house.
9. Put your coat in the closet.
10. Why is the umbrella under the chair?
11. Put the newspaper on the chair.
12. The lamp was over the table.
13. The guests are at the table.
14. He put the money in his pocket.

GRAMMATIK UND ÜBUNGEN

1 *Hin* and *her*

Meine Tante wohnt nicht hier.	My aunt doesn't live here.
Sie wohnt in Hamburg.	She lives in Hamburg.
Wir fahren einmal im Jahr **hin.**	Once a year we go *there*.
Und zweimal im Jahr kommt sie **her.**	And twice a year she comes *here*.

Hin and **her** are used to show direction. **Hin** shows motion away from the speaker, and **her** shows motion toward the speaker. **Hin** and **her** occupy last position in the sentence.

Er war letztes Jahr in Europa. Er möchte wieder **dorthin.**	He was in Europe last year. He wants to go there again.
Kommen Sie mal **herauf.**	Come on up here.

Hin and **her** may be combined with several parts of speech, including adverbs, prepositions, and verbs.

Woher kommen Sie?	**Wo** kommen Sie **her?**	Where are you from?
Wohin fahren Sie?	**Wo** fahren Sie **hin?**	Where are you going?

In spoken German, **hin** and **her** are often separated from **wo**. **Hin** and **her** occupy last position in the sentence.

1. Ilse und Axel Ask questions about Ilse and Axel, using **wo, wohin,** or **woher.**

▶ Ilse und Axel wohnen bei München.   *Wo wohnen sie?*
▶ Sie fahren jeden Morgen nach   *Wohin fahren sie? / Wo fahren*
    München.   *sie hin?*

1. Sie arbeiten in einer Buchhandlung.
2. Sie gehen am Samstag in den Supermarkt.
3. Die Blumen kommen vom Markt.
4. Sie fahren am Sonntag in die Berge.
5. Sie wandern gern in den Bergen.
6. Nach der Wanderung gehen sie in ein Restaurant.
7. Sie essen gern im Restaurant.
8. Nach dem Essen fahren sie wieder nach Hause.
9. In den Ferien fahren sie in die Schweiz.
10. Axel kommt aus der Schweiz.

2 Two-way prepositions

Dative: ***wo?***   *Accusative:* ***wohin?***

Jürgen sitzt **am** Tisch.
Jürgen is sitting at the table.

Corinna setzt sich **an den** Tisch.
Corinna sits down at the table.

German has nine prepositions that take either the dative or the accusative. The dative is used when position *(place where)* is indicated, answering the question **wo?** The accusative is used when a change of location (*place to which*) is indicated, answering the question **wohin?**

In their basic meanings, the two-way prepositions are "spatial," referring to positions in space (dative) or movements through space (accusative). To distinguish place *where* from place *to which*, German uses different cases; English sometimes uses different prepositions (e.g., *in* vs. *into*).

an	at (the side of)	Ute steht **am** (**an dem**) Fenster. *(dat.)*
	to	Benno geht **ans** (**an das**) Fenster. *(acc.)*
	on (vertical surfaces)	Das Bild hängt **an der** Wand. *(dat.)*
		Sabine hängt das Bild **an die** Wand. *(acc.)*
auf	on top of (horizontal surfaces)	Kurts Buch liegt **auf dem** Tisch. *(dat.)*
		Sabine legt ihr Buch **auf den** Tisch. *(acc.)*
	to	Ich gehe **auf den** Markt. *(acc.)*
hinter	in back of/behind	Inge arbeitet **hinter dem** Haus. *(dat.)*
		Nils geht **hinter das** Haus. *(acc.)*
in	in, inside (of)	Paula arbeitet **im** (**in dem**) Wohnzimmer. *(dat.)*
	into	Jürgen geht **ins** (**in das**) Wohnzimmer. *(acc.)*
	to	Wir gehen **ins** Kino. *(acc.)*
neben	beside, next to	Ritas Stuhl steht **neben dem** Fenster. *(dat.)*
		Jan stellt seinen Stuhl **neben das** Fenster. *(acc.)*
über	over, above	Eine Lampe hängt **über dem** Tisch. *(dat.)*
		Hugo hängt eine andere Lampe **über den** Tisch. *(acc.)*
	across	Ich gehe **über die** Straße. *(acc.)*
unter	under	Kurts Fahrrad steht **unter dem** Balkon. *(dat.)*
		Elly stellt ihr Fahrrad **unter den** Balkon. *(acc.)*
vor	in front of	Ilses Auto steht **vor dem** Haus. *(dat.)*
		Armin fährt sein Auto **vor das** Haus. *(acc.)*
zwischen	between	Eine Blume liegt **zwischen den** Büchern. *(dat.)*
		Judith legt noch eine Blume **zwischen die** Bücher. *(acc.)*

3 Prepositional contractions

Er geht **ans** Fenster.	an das = **ans**
Er steht **am** Fenster.	an dem = **am**
Sie geht **ins** Zimmer.	in das = **ins**
Sie ist **im** Zimmer.	in dem = **im**

The prepositions **an** and **in** often contract with **das** and **dem**. Other possible contractions are **aufs, hinters, hinterm, übers, überm, unters, unterm, vors,** and **vorm.**

4 *An* and *auf* = on

Die Uhr hängt **an der Wand.**	The clock is hanging on the wall.
Mein Buch liegt **auf dem Tisch.**	My book is lying on the table.

An and **auf** can both be equivalent to *on.* **An** = *on (the side of)* is used in reference to vertical surfaces. **Auf** = *on (top of)* is used in reference to horizontal surfaces.

5 *An, auf,* and *in* = to

Veronika geht **an** die Tür.	Veronika goes to the door.
Bernd geht **auf** den Markt.	Bernd goes to the market.
Lore geht **in** die Stadt.	Lore goes to town.

The prepositions **an, auf,** and **in** can be equivalent to the English preposition *to.*

2. *An* **oder** *auf?*   Answer the questions below, using the cued words and the prepositions **an** or **auf** as appropriate.

▶   Wohin geht Albert? (Tür)   *Er geht an die Tür.*

 1. Wo steht er jetzt? (Tür)
 2. Wohin geht Astrid? (Fenster)
 3. Wo steht sie jetzt? (Fenster)
 4. Wohin stellt Anton die Blumen? (Tisch)
 5. Wo stehen die Blumen? (Tisch)
 6. Wohin legt Elke ihren Pulli? (Bett)
 7. Wo liegt der Pulli jetzt? (Bett)
 8. Wohin hängt Andreas die Uhr? (Wand)
 9. Wo sitzt das Kind? (Stuhl)
10. Wo steht der Stuhl? (Tisch)

3. Ein Jahr in Deutschland Susan is spending a year in Germany. Form sentences to tell about the things she does during her first days there, using the cues below.

▶ sie / gehen / auf / Polizei   *Sie geht auf die Polizei.*

1. auf / Polizei / sie / bekommen / eine Aufenthaltserlaubnis
2. sie / gehen / dann / auf / Markt
3. auf / Markt / sie / kaufen / Blumen / für / ihr Zimmer
4. dann / sie / gehen / in / Buchhandlung
5. Erika / arbeiten / in / Buchhandlung
6. Susan / müssen / in / Drogerie
7. in / Drogerie / sie / wollen / kaufen / Vitamintabletten
8. sie / gehen / dann / in / Café
9. in / Café / sie / treffen / Erika
10. sie / sitzen / an / Tisch / in / Ecke

4. Ziemlich dumm Your house guest isn't too bright. Answer his/her questions, using the cued expressions in accusative or dative.

▶ Wohin stell' ich das Radio? (auf / Tisch)   *Auf den Tisch.*

1. Wohin leg' ich die Bücher? (neben / Radio)
2. Wo sind meine Schuhe? (hinter / Bett)
3. Wohin soll ich sie stellen? (unter / Bett)
4. Wo hängt meine Jacke? (hinter / Tür)
5. Wohin stell' ich diesen Stuhl? (an / Tisch)
6. Wohin stell' ich die Blumen? (auf / Tisch)
7. Wohin stecke ich die Zeitung? (in / Tasche)
8. Wir sind jetzt fertig. Wohin fahren wir? (in / Stadt)
9. Wo steht mein Auto? (vor / Haus)

5. Mach das bitte. Take turns giving instructions to a member of the class. For example: **Geh bitte an die Tür.** You may use the instructions cued below and think of your own.

an die Tür gehen / die Tür aufmachen (zumachen)
an das Fenster gehen
[Karlas] Buch nehmen / es auf den Schreibtisch legen
den Mantel an die Wand hängen
[Pauls] Kuli nehmen / ihn in die Tasche stecken

6 Special meanings of prepositions

In addition to their basic meanings, prepositions have special meanings when combined with specific verbs (**halten von**) or with certain nouns (**Angst vor**). Each combination should be learned as a unit, because it cannot be predicted which preposition is associated with a particular verb or noun. The accusative prepositions (**durch, für, gegen, ohne, um**) and the dative prepositions (**aus, außer, bei, mit, nach, seit, von, zu**) take the accusative and dative respectively. The case of the noun following two-way prepositions must be learned. When **über** means *about/concerning*, it is always followed by the accusative case. A few combinations are given below.

denken an (+ *acc.*)
Ich **denke** oft **an** meine Freunde.

to think of/about
I often *think of* my friends.

schreiben an (+ *acc.*)
Martina **schreibt an** ihren Vater.

to write to
Martina *is writing to* her father.

studieren an/auf (+ *dat.*)
Mark **studiert an/auf** der Universität München.

to study at
Mark *is studying at* the University of Munich.

warten auf (+ *acc.*)
Wir **warten auf** den Bus.

to wait for
We're *waiting for* the bus.

helfen bei
Hilf mir bitte **bei** meiner Arbeit.

to help with
Please *help* me *with* my work.

fahren mit
Wir **fahren mit** dem Auto nach Ulm.

to go by (means of)
We're *going* to Ulm *by* car.

reden/sprechen über (+ *acc.*)
Sie **reden über** das Wetter.

to talk/speak about
They're *talking about* the weather.

reden/sprechen von
Er **redet** wieder **von** seinem Porsche.

to talk/speak about/of
He's *talking about* his Porsche again.

schreiben über (+ *acc.*)
Sie **schreibt über** ihre Arbeit.

to write about
She's *writing about* her work.

halten von
Sie **hält** nicht viel **von** dem Plan.

to think of, have an opinion of
She doesn't *think* much *of* the plan.

Angst haben vor (+ *dat.*)
Leslie **hat Angst vorm** Fliegen.

to be afraid of
Leslie *is afraid of* flying.

6. Mein Bruder   Your friend Daniel is telling you about his brother. Give the English equivalent of his statements. Note especially the preposition combinations.

1. Mein Bruder geht auf die Universität.
2. Oft schreibt er Briefe an mich und meine Eltern.
3. Ich denke oft an ihn, weil er mir oft bei meinen Schularbeiten geholfen hat.
4. Wie oft haben wir stundenlang über Politik, Sport und Frauen gesprochen!
5. In seinem letzten Brief hat er mir von seiner Freundin Cornelia erzählt.
6. Soll ich ihm auch von meiner Freundin erzählen?

7. Welches Verb?   Make up sentences from the phrases below by adding subjects and verbs. Vary the verbs as much as possible.

▶   in diesem Geschäft   *Er arbeitet in diesem Geschäft.*

1. ins Geschäft
2. auf dem Markt
3. im Restaurant
4. auf die Polizei
5. mit dem Auto
6. in die Berge
7. im Café
8. auf der Autobahn
9. an der Universität
10. über Musik

8. Eine Reise nach Deutschland   Below are some statements about Peter's visit to Germany. Give the German equivalents.

1. Peter lives behind a supermarket.
2. There are parks in every city.
3. In the restaurants there are flowers on every table.
4. Peter goes to the university by bus.
5. He doesn't like to drive on the freeway.
6. One can buy aspirin only in the pharmacy.
7. His friends sit at the table a long time after the meal.
8. They talk about sports, books, and their seminar reports.

9. So bin ich.   Your partner wishes to know you better and will ask you five questions about your interests and reactions (e.g., **Woran denkst du oft?**). To prepare for this conversation complete the sentences below. Your partner will then tell a third person about your answers.

1. Ich denke oft an _____ .
2. Ich spreche gern über _____ .
3. Ich weiß viel/wenig über _____ .
4. Ich halte nicht viel von _____ .
5. Ich rede oft mit _____ .
6. Ich schreibe oft an _____ .
7. Ich habe oft Probleme mit _____ .
8. Ich muß oft über _____ lächeln.
9. Ich habe Angst vor _____ .

7 Time expressions in the dative

Am Montag bleibt sie immer zu Hause.	On Monday she always stays home.
Er kommt **in** einer Woche.	He's coming in a week.
Ich lese gern **am** Abend.	I like to read in the evening.
Er arbeitet **vor** dem Essen.	He works before dinner.
Sie war **vor** einer Woche hier.	She was here a week ago.

With time expressions, **an, in,** and **vor** take the dative case. The use of **am** + a day may mean *on that one day* or *on all such days.*

10. Wann machst du das? A friend is making comments about your activities. Correct her/him, using the cues provided in dative time expressions.

▶ Du arbeitest nur am Morgen, nicht? (Abend)   *Nein, nur am Abend.*

1. Frank kommt in fünf Minuten, nicht? (zwanzig Minuten)
2. Sollen wir vor dem Seminar Kaffee trinken gehen? (Vorlesung)
3. Du gehst am Donnerstag schwimmen, nicht? (Wochenende)
4. Du fährst am Samstag nachmittag nach Hause, nicht? (Sonntag abend)
5. Rita kommt in zwei Wochen, nicht? (eine Woche)
6. Du mußt die Arbeit vor dem Wintersemester fertig haben, nicht? (Sommersemester)
7. Im Sommer fahrt ihr in die Berge, nicht? (Herbst)
8. Du gehst nur einmal im Monat in die Bibliothek, nicht? (Woche)

8 Time expressions in the accusative

Definite point	Er arbeitet **jeden Abend.**	He works every evening.
Duration	Sie bleibt **einen Tag.**	She's staying one day.

Nouns expressing a definite point of time or a duration of time are in the accusative.

11. Wann und wie lange? Michael wants to know details about the visit of a pianist. Complete the answers, using the English cues.

▶ Wann war die Pianistin in Hamburg? — Sie war *letzten Mittwoch* in Hamburg. *(last Wednesday)*

1. Wann kommt sie zu uns? — Sie kommt _____ zu uns. *(this weekend)*
2. Wie lange bleibt sie? — Sie bleibt _____ . *(a day)*
3. Wie oft übt° sie? — Sie übt _____ . *(every morning)*   practice
4. Wann fährt sie wieder weg? — Sie fährt _____ wieder weg. *(next Monday)*
5. Wann kommt sie wieder? — Sie kommt _____ wieder. *(next year)*
6. Wie lange bleibt sie dann? — Dann bleibt sie _____ . *(a month)*

12. **Pläne** Discuss weekend or vacation plans with a partner. A few suggestions for times and activities are given.

Times: am Wochenende ◊ am Mittwoch ◊ nach dem Abendessen ◊ im Sommer ◊ in den Ferien

Activities: ins Kino gehen ◊ mit Freunden kochen ◊ lesen ◊ auf ein Fest gehen ◊ Freunde treffen ◊ tanzen gehen ◊ Briefe schreiben

Gesprächspartner/in	*Sie*
Was machst du [am Wochenende]?	Ich will [nichts tun].

9 *Da*-compounds

Erzählt Lisa **von ihrem Freund?**	Ja, sie erzählt viel **von ihm.**
Erzählt Lisa **von ihrer Reise?**	Ja, sie erzählt viel **davon.**

In German, pronouns used after prepositions normally refer only to persons (**Freund**). To refer to things and ideas (**Reise**), a **da**-compound consisting of **da** + a preposition is generally used: **dadurch, dafür, damit. Da-** expands to **dar-** when the preposition begins with a vowel: **darauf, darin, darüber.**

13. **Was hält Monika von Amerika?** Assure Gerd that Monika's activities and reactions in the United States are as he thinks. Use a **da**-compound or a preposition + a pronoun.

▶ Gefällt es Monika bei den amerikanischen Freunden?   *Ja, es gefällt Monika bei ihnen.*

▶ Hat sie Spaß an ihren Vorlesungen?   *Ja, sie hat Spaß daran.*

1. Hat sie Hunger auf deutsches Brot?
2. Redet sie gern mit Peter?
3. Reden sie oft über kulturelle Unterschiede?
4. Hilft sie Peter oft bei seinem Deutsch?
5. Geht sie gern mit ihren Freunden essen?
6. Denkt Monika oft an zu Hause?
7. Erzählt sie gern von ihrem Leben in Deutschland?
8. Fährt sie oft mit dem Fahrrad?
9. Erzählt sie oft von ihren Freunden?

10 *Wo*-compounds

Von wem spricht Lisa?   Sie spricht **von ihrem Freund.**
Wovon (Von was) spricht Lisa? Sie spricht **von ihrer Reise.**

The interrogative pronouns **wen** and **wem** are used with a preposition to refer only to persons. The interrogative pronoun **was** refers to things and ideas. As an object of a preposition, **was** may be replaced by a **wo**-compound consisting of **wo** + a preposition: **wofür, wodurch, womit. Wo-** expands to **wor-** when the preposition begins with a vowel: **worauf, worin, worüber.** A preposition + **was** (**von was, für was**) is colloquial.

Karl wohnt seit September in   **Seit wann** wohnt er in München?
  München.

Wo-compounds are not used to inquire about time. To inquire about time, **wann, seit wann,** or **wie lange** is used.

14. Wie, bitte?   Rolf mumbles because he's tired, so you don't hear about what or whom he is speaking. Ask what he said, using a **wo**-compound or a preposition + a pronoun to replace the boldfaced words, as appropriate.

▶ Klaus hat die Arbeit **mit dem**   *Womit hat er sie geschrieben?*
   Kugelschreiber geschrieben.
▶ Er hat sie **mit Annette** geschrieben.   *Mit wem hat er sie geschrieben?*

1. Susanne hat **von ihrer Vorlesung** erzählt.   _____ hat sie erzählt?
2. Sie hat auch **von Professor Weiß** erzählt.   _____ hat sie erzählt?
3. Udo arbeitet **für Frau Schneider.**   _____ arbeitet er?
4. Sabine ist **mit Gerd** essen gegangen.   _____ ist sie essen gegangen?
5. Beim Essen hat sie **von ihrer Arbeit** erzählt.   _____ hat sie beim Essen erzählt?
6. Nachher hat sie **mit Udo** Tennis gespielt.   _____ hat sie nachher Tennis gespielt?
7. Sie hat nur **über das Tennisspiel** geredet.   _____ hat sie geredet?
8. Sie denkt nur **an Tennis.**   _____ denkt sie nur?
9. Sie wohnt jetzt wieder **bei ihren Eltern.**   _____ wohnt sie jetzt wieder?
10. Sie denkt nicht mehr **an eine eigene Wohnung.** _____ denkt sie nicht mehr?

11 Dative personal pronouns

	Singular					
Nominative	ich	du	er	es	sie	Sie
Accusative	mich	dich	ihn	es	sie	Sie
Dative	**mir**	**dir**	**ihm**	**ihm**	**ihr**	**Ihnen**

	Plural			
Nominative	wir	ihr	sie	Sie
Accusative	uns	euch	sie	Sie
Dative	**uns**	**euch**	**ihnen**	**Ihnen**

Dative personal pronouns have different forms from the accusative pronouns, except for **uns** and **euch**.

15. *Mir* oder *mich?*   Say that Bärbel is referring to you; use **mir** or **mich**.

▶ Wen hat Bärbel gemeint?   *Sie hat mich gemeint.*
Wem glaubt Bärbel?   *Sie glaubt mir.*

1. Wen hat sie zum Essen eingeladen?
2. Mit wem fährt sie in die Stadt?
3. Wen holt Bärbel später ab?
4. Wem hat sie ihre Notizen geliehen?
5. Wem hat sie geholfen?
6. Mit wem arbeitet sie gern?
7. Für wen hat sie den Pulli gekauft?
8. Von wem hat Bärbel das Buch bekommen?

16. *Dir* oder *dich?*   Jochen asks whether you are referring to him. Say you are, using **dir** or **dich**.

▶ Meinst du mich?   *Ja, ich meine dich.*
Glaubst du mir?   *Ja, ich glaube dir.*

1. Willst du mich etwas fragen?
2. Hast du an mich gedacht?
3. Kannst du mir helfen?
4. Hast du das Hemd für mich gekauft?
5. Kommst du später zu mir?
6. Holst du mich um sieben ab?
7. Bleibst du bei mir?
8. Willst du mit mir Schach spielen?

17. Eine Diskussion You and your friends are having a discussion. Answer the questions negatively, using the pronoun **euch** or **uns** as in the model.

▶ Kannst du mit uns Tennis spielen?   *Mit euch? Leider nein.*

1. Bleibst du heute bei uns?
2. Kannst du mit uns arbeiten?
3. Kommst du später zu uns?

▶ Habe ich euch die Bücher geliehen?   *Uns? Nein, ich glaube nicht.*

4. Habe ich euch von dem Plan erzählt?
5. Habe ich euch wirklich geholfen?
6. Habe ich euch das nicht gesagt?

18. Viele Fragen Answer the questions below; use **Ihnen** or **Sie**.

▶ Für wen machen Sie das?   *Ich mache das für Sie, Frau Braun.*
▶ Mit wem sprechen Sie?   *Ich spreche mit Ihnen, Frau Braun.*

1. Wen meinen Sie?
2. Wen möchten Sie fragen?
3. Für wen haben Sie die Uhr gekauft?
4. Wem schenken Sie diese Blumen?
5. Wem sagen Sie das?
6. Von wem sprechen Sie?
7. Mit wem fahren Sie?

Reden ist Silber, Schweigen ist Gold.

19. Deutschland gefällt ihnen. Say that people like the features of Germany mentioned below. Use **ihm, ihr,** or **ihnen,** as appropriate.

▶ Gefallen Robert die vielen Parks? *Ja, sie gefallen ihm.*

1. Gefallen Barbara die vielen Blumen?
2. Gefallen den Ausländern die Märkte?
3. Gefallen deinem Freund die Bäckereien?
4. Gefallen den Amerikanern die Autobahnen?
5. Gefällt deiner Freundin das Essen?
6. Gefällt den Deutschen das Fernsehen?

20. Was machst du denn? Answer in the affirmative. Use nominative, accusative, and dative pronouns in your answers.

▶ Hat dir der Wein geschmeckt? *Ja, er hat mir geschmeckt.*
▶ Kaufst du den Wein? *Ja, ich kaufe ihn.*

1. Kommst du heute zu uns?
   Fährst du morgen zu Thomas?
2. Hast du deine Freunde im Biergarten getroffen?
   Hast du Erik eingeladen?
3. Hat Michael dich gemeint?
   Geht er morgen mit dir schwimmen?
4. Hast du das für Gabi getan?
   Tust du auch etwas für Erika und Christine?
5. Hast du mit Hans und Erich gesprochen?
   Arbeiten die Jungen zusammen?

21. Was gefällt dir (nicht)? Assume you have met a German at a party who is thinking of going to your university for a year. He/she wants to know what you like or dislike about your school and its environs. Your partner will play the role of the German student. Possible questions and topics are provided to get you started.

Gesprächspartner/in		*Sie*
Gefällt dir	**die Uni?**	Ja, [sehr].
	die Bibliothek?	Nein, [nicht wirklich].
	die Mensa?	[...]
	das Wetter?	
	die Stadt?	
Gefallen dir	**die Vorlesungen?**	
	die Professoren?	
	die Studenten?	

12 Word order of direct and indirect objects

	Indirect Object	Direct Object Noun
Inge leiht	*ihrem Freund*	**ihr Radio.**
Inge leiht	*ihm*	**ihr Radio.**

The direct (accusative) object determines the order of objects. If the direct object is a noun, it usually follows the indirect (dative) object.

	Direct Object Pronoun	Indirect Object
Inge leiht	**es**	*ihrem Freund.*
Inge leiht	**es**	*ihm.*

If the direct (accusative) object is a personal pronoun, it always precedes the indirect (dative) object. Note that a pronoun, whether accusative or dative, always precedes a noun.

22. Wer bekommt das?   You are cleaning out your room, closet, and drawers and a friend wants to know to whom you're giving the things. Answer the questions, using accusative pronouns as in the model.

▶   Wem schenkst du den Pulli? Deiner Schwester?   *Ja, ich schenke ihn meiner Schwester.*

1. Wem schenkst du das Messer? Deinem Bruder?
2. Wem schenkst du das Poster? Deiner Tante?
3. Wem schenkst du die Kassetten? Deinem Vetter?
4. Wem schenkst du die Jacke? Patrizia?
5. Wem schenkst du den Kuli? Erwin?
6. Wem schenkst du das Bild? Mir?

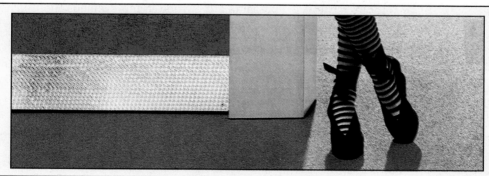

Girloon
Teppichboden

WIR LEGEN IHNEN QUALITÄT ZU FÜSSEN.

23. Zum Geburtstag Say what you would like to give four people—relatives and friends—for their birthdays or other holidays.

> Talking about giving gifts

▶ *[Zum Geburtstag] möchte ich [meinem Bruder] [ein Hemd] schenken.*

Ist dieser Weihnachtsmann typisch deutsch? (Kaufhaus des Westens in Berlin)

Christmas (**Weihnachten**) in the German-speaking countries is celebrated on Christmas Eve (**Heiliger Abend**) and the two following days. The Christmas season starts with the first day of Advent, the fourth Sunday before Christmas. In many homes, an Advent wreath (**Adventskranz**) and Advent calendar (**Adventskalender**) are displayed until Christmas. In many town squares, special markets create a festive Christmas atmosphere. On December 6, St. Nicholas (**Sankt Nikolaus**) brings small gifts such as candies, nuts, and fruits to good children and places them in the shoes and boots which the children put in front of their doors. Naughty children may receive a switch (**Rute**).

On December 24, a half-day holiday, shops and businesses close early. Christmas Eve is usually celebrated with the immediate family. The Christmas tree (**Weihnachtsbaum**) is not usually set up and decorated until December 24, and presents are opened in the evening. The Christmas tree was introduced to the United States in the eighteenth century by German immigrants; their **Weihnachtsmann** was transformed into Santa Claus by Thomas Nast, a German cartoonist who had come to the United States in 1846.

WIEDERHOLUNG

1. Das hat Nadja beobachtet.   Form sentences in the perfect tense. Tell about Nadja's experiences in the United States, using the cues below.

1. der Vater der Gastfamilie / abholen / sie / von / Flughafen
2. er / benutzen / gleich / den Vornamen
3. sie / verstehen / das / nicht
4. das Einkaufen / gefallen / sie
5. sie / finden / die Amerikaner / sehr freundlich
6. viele Leute / nehmen / Vitamintabletten
7. man / dekorieren / Kuchen / mit / Farben
8. man / essen / zuwenig / biologisch angebautes Gemüse
9. die Leute / gehen / wenig / zu Fuß

2. Das hat Mark in Deutschland beobachtet.   Now tell about Mark's experiences in Germany, using the cued words in the perfect tense.

1. Mark / fahren / nicht gern / auf / Autobahn
2. Leute / fahren / wie die Wilden
3. viele Kinder / sehen / im Fernsehen / *Sesamstraße*
4. die vielen Blumen und Parks / gefallen / er
5. viele Leute / trinken / an / Sonntag / um vier / Kaffee
6. man / benutzen / Messer und Gabel / anders
7. man / sitzen / nach / Essen / lange / an / Tisch
8. er / sehen / viel Reklame / mit / Wort / natürlich

3. Ferien   Complete the sentences about vacations in Germany and Switzerland, using one of the cued prepositions.

1. Im Sommer kommen viele Ausländer _____ Deutschland. (an, nach, zu)
2. Viele kommen _____ ihre Kinder. (mit, ohne, von)
3. Sie fahren natürlich _____ der Autobahn. (an, über, auf)
4. Junge Leute wandern gern _____ Freunden. (bei, ohne, mit)
5. Einige fahren _____ dem Fahrrad. (bei, an, mit)
6. Engländer fahren gern _____ die Schweiz. (an, in, nach)
7. _____ den Märkten kann man schöne Sachen kaufen. (auf, an, in)
8. Zu Hause erzählen die Engländer dann _____ ihrer Reise. (über, von, um)

4. Etwas über Musik   Answer the questions according to the cues. Use pronouns—alone or with prepositions—or **da**-compounds, as appropriate.

▶ Hast du gestern mit deiner   *Ja, ich habe gestern mit ihr gegessen.*
   Freundin gegessen? (Ja)

   1. Habt ihr viel über Musik geredet? (Ja)
   2. Kennst du viel von Schönberg? (Ja)
   3. Hältst du viel von seiner Musik? (Nein)
   4. Möchtest du Frau Professor Koepke kennenlernen? (Ja)
   5. Sie weiß viel über Schönberg, nicht? (Ja)
   6. Liest sie° dieses Semester über seine Musik? (Ja)   **Liest sie:** Is she lecturing
   7. Meinst du, ich kann die Vorlesung verstehen? (Nein)

5. Wie sagt man das?   Erik Schulz goes to the University of Zürich. Tell a little about his experiences there.

   1. Erik Schulz goes to the University of Zürich°.   **Universität Zürich**
   2. In the summer he works for his neighbor.
   3. On the weekend he goes with his girlfriend Karin to the mountains.
   4. They drive her car.
   5. They like to hike.
   6. Afterwards they are hungry and thirsty.
   7. They go to a café, where they have coffee and cake. (Use **trinken** and **essen.**)

6. Rollenspiel   Assume that your partner is an Austrian friend who comments on some things that strike him/her in the United States. Agree or express some doubts about his/her views, using some of the words and phrases below.

Discussing cultural differences

   Richtig. ◇ Genau. ◇ Natürlich. ◇ Eben. ◇ Du hast recht. ◇
   Wirklich? ◇ Meinst du? ◇ Ja, vielleicht. ◇ Vielleicht hast du recht. ◇
   Das finde ich gar nicht. ◇ Was hast du gegen [Freundlichkeit]? ◇
   Ich sehe das ganz anders. ◇ Das siehst du ganz falsch.

Amerikaner sind zu freundlich. Das kann nicht echt sein.
Das amerikanische Fernsehen ist prima.
Rock ist besser als klassische Musik.
Kuchen mit Farben wie rot, grün und blau sehen furchtbar aus.

7. Mein Zimmer   Have a partner make a rough sketch of your room based solely on your description. Name 3–5 items and be sure to explain where they are in relation to other things (e.g., the plant is in front of the window).

8. Anregung

1. Write three sentences in German about **Deutschland** and **Österreich**.
2. Choose one of the following topics and write several sentences in German, relating them to **Deutschland** and to your country.

   Musik ◇ Weihnachten ◇ Blumen ◇ Wetter ◇ Autofahren ◇ Bürokratie ◇ Fernsehen

GRAMMATIK: ZUSAMMENFASSUNG

Two-way prepositions and their English equivalents

an	at; on; to
auf	on, on top of; to
hinter	behind, in back of
in	in, into; to
neben	beside, next to
über	above, over; across; about
unter	under; among
vor	in front of; before; ago
zwischen	between

Nine prepositions take either the dative or the accusative. The dative is used for the meaning *place where,* in answer to the question **wo?** The accusative is used for the meaning *place to which,* in answer to the question **wohin?** The English equivalents of these prepositions may vary, depending on the object with which they are used. For example, English equivalents of **an der Ecke** and **an der Wand** are *at the corner* and *on the wall.*

Prepositional contractions

am = an dem	**im** = in dem
ans = an das	**ins** = in das

The prepositions **an** and **in** may contract with **das** and **dem.** Other possible contractions are **aufs, hinters, hinterm, übers, überm, unters, unterm, vors,** and **vorm.**

Special meanings of prepositions

Prepositions have special meanings when combined with specific verbs (e.g., **halten von**) or with certain nouns (e.g., **Angst vor**).

denken an (+ *acc.*)	*to think of/about*
schreiben an (+ *acc.*)	*to write to*
studieren an/auf (+ *dat.*)	*to study at*
warten auf (+ *acc.*)	*to wait for*
helfen bei	*to help with*
fahren mit	*to go by (means of)*
reden/sprechen über (+ *acc.*)	*to talk/speak about*
reden/sprechen von	*to talk/speak about/of*
schreiben über (+ *acc.*)	*to write about*
halten von	*to think of, have an opinion of*
Angst haben vor (+ *dat.*)	*to be afraid of*

Time expressions in the dative

am Montag	on Monday, Mondays
am Abend	in the evening, evenings
in der Woche	during the week
in einem Jahr	in a year
vor dem Essen	before the meal
vor einem Jahr	a year ago

In expressions of time, the prepositions **an, in,** and **vor** are followed by the dative case.

Time expressions in the accusative

Definite point	Er arbeitet **jeden Abend.**	He works every evening.
Duration	Sie bleibt **einen Tag.**	She's staying one day.

Nouns expressing a definite point in time or a duration of time are in the accusative. Note that words such as **nächst** and **letzt** have endings like the endings for **dies: diesen / nächsten / letzten Monat; dieses / nächstes / letztes Jahr.**

Da-compounds

Spricht Sabrina gern **von ihrem Freund?**	Ja, sie spricht gern **von ihm.**
Spricht Sabrina oft **von der Reise?**	Ja, sie spricht oft **davon.**

In German, pronouns after prepositions normally refer only to persons. German uses a **da**-compound, consisting of **da** + preposition, to refer to things or ideas.

Wo-compounds

Von wem spricht Sabrina?   Sie spricht **von ihrem Freund.**
Wovon (Von was) spricht Sabrina?   Sie spricht **von der Reise.**

The interrogative pronoun **wen** or **wem** is used with a preposition to refer to persons. The interrogative pronoun **was** refers to things and ideas. As an object of a preposition, **was** may be replaced by a **wo**-compound consisting of **wo** + a preposition. A preposition + **was** is colloquial: **von was.**

Patrick wohnt seit September in   **Seit wann** wohnt er in München?
  München.

Wo-compounds are not used to inquire about time. To inquire about time, **wann, seit wann,** or **wie lange** is used.

Dative personal pronouns

	Singular					**Plural**			
Nominative	ich	du	er	es	sie	wir	ihr	sie	Sie
Accusative	mich	dich	ihn	es	sie	uns	euch	sie	Sie
Dative	**mir**	**dir**	**ihm**	**ihm**	**ihr**	**uns**	**euch**	**ihnen**	**Ihnen**

Word order of direct and indirect objects

	Indirect Object	**Direct Object Noun**
Inge schenkt	*ihrer Schwester*	**den Kugelschreiber.**
Inge schenkt	*ihr*	**den Kugelschreiber.**

The direct (accusative) object determines the order of objects. If the direct object is a noun, it follows the indirect (dative) object.

	Direct Object Pronoun	**Indirect Object**
Inge schenkt	**ihn**	*ihrer Schwester.*
Inge schenkt	**ihn**	*ihr.*

If the direct (accusative) object is a personal pronoun, it precedes the indirect (dative) object.

Auf den Balkons kann man die Menschen nicht oder nicht leicht sehen. (Berlin)

Kapitel 9

BAUSTEINE FÜR GESPRÄCHE

Vorbereitung auf ein Geburtstagsfest

Elfi: Sag, willst du nicht endlich mal das Wohnzimmer aufräumen? Da liegen überall deine Bücher herum.

Arno: Muß das sein?

Elfi: Klar. In einer Stunde kommen die Leute.

Arno: Was? Schon in einer Stunde? Du meine Güte! Und wir müssen noch Staub saugen, abwaschen, abtrocknen, die Küche sieht aus wie …

Elfi: Jetzt red nicht lange, sondern mach schnell. Ich helf' dir ja.

Preparation for a birthday party

Say, don't you want to finally straighten up the living room? Your books are lying around everywhere.

Do I have to?

Of course. People are coming in an hour.

What? In an hour? Good heavens! And we still have to vacuum, wash dishes, dry them, the kitchen looks like . . .

Now stop talking so much and hurry up. You know I'm going to help you.

Das Geburtstagsgeschenk

Moritz: Jetzt mach' ich erst mal das Geschenk von euch auf.

Bea: Na, ich bin ja neugierig, was du sagst.

Konrad: Vielleicht kannst du es gar nicht gebrauchen.

Moritz: He, Mann, ein Kassettenrecorder! Das ist ja toll.

Konrad: Gefällt er dir?

Moritz: Na klar, und wie! Vielen, vielen Dank! Mein alter Recorder ist doch kaputt, und den kann man nicht mehr reparieren. Ihr seid wirklich nett!

The birthday present

Now first I'll open your present.

Hey, I'm curious what you're going to say.

Maybe you can't even use it.

Hey, man, a cassette recorder. That's great.

Do you like it?

Of course! And how! Thanks very, very much. My old recorder is broken and you can't repair it any more. You are really nice!

Fragen

1. Warum soll Arno das Wohnzimmer aufräumen?
2. Wann kommen die Gäste?
3. Was müssen Elfi und Arno noch machen?
4. Wer hat Geburtstag?
5. Was bekommt Moritz von seinen Freunden?
6. Wie findet er das Geschenk?
7. Warum braucht er einen neuen Recorder?

1. Geburtstage   Ask a fellow student all about her/his birthday. You may wish to refer to the Supplementary Word Sets on clothing for *Kapitel 7* and audio/stereo equipment for *Kapitel 9,* in the Reference Section.

| Talking about birthdays |

Sie	*Gesprächspartner/in*
Wann hast du Geburtstag?	Im [Mai].
Was hast du letztes Jahr zum Geburtstag bekommen?	Einen CD-Spieler°.
Was möchtest du dieses Jahr zum Geburtstag haben?	Ein Buch über Schach.
	Ein paar° CDs.

Das ist ja | **toll.**
         | phantastisch.

2. Ein Fest   A friend has invited you to a party. Ask about the plans and what you should bring.

| Making plans |

Sie	*Gesprächspartner/in*
Was macht ihr auf dem Fest?	Wir	**tanzen.**

                                               hören Musik.
                                               essen viel.
                                               trinken etwas.
                                               reden viel.

Was soll ich zu dem Fest mitbringen?   Bring doch die **Bilder von deiner Ferienreise** mit.

                   etwas zu | **essen**
                               | trinken
                   ein paar | **Flaschen° Cola**
                               | CDs
                               | Kassetten
                   einen Kassettenrecorder

3. **Was sagen Sie?** Respond to comments from your partner, using responses from the list below and adding a few of your own.

Gesprächspartner/in		*Sie*
Was für eine tolle	**CD!**	Möchtest du sie hören?
	Kassette!	Ich habe sie gestern gekauft.
Ich habe heute Geburtstag.		Herzlichen Glückwunsch!°
		Gratuliere.°
		Wie alt bist du denn?

4. **Rollenspiel** Invite a friend (**Gesprächspartner/in**) to a party, telling time, place, and what will happen at the party. Your friend is reluctant to come. Try to convince her/him to come.

5. **Hausarbeit** Find out from several fellow students which chores they do or don't do at home. You may wish to refer to the Supplementary Word Sets in the Reference Section for additional chores.

> Talking about household chores

Sie		*Gesprächspartner/in*
Welche Arbeiten machst du zu Hause?	Ich	**wasche ab.**
Welche Arbeiten machst du nicht?		trockne ab.
		mach' [die Küche] sauber.
		räume nicht auf.
		koche nicht.
		putze° das Bad° nicht.

6. **Wer macht was?** Two or three friends are going to share a house. Using the schedule below, negotiate who will be responsible for which chores. You may want to refer to the Supplementary Expressions, #10: Expressing agreement and disagreement and #11: Responding to requests, in the Reference Section.

> Negotiating

	Mo.	Di.	Mi.	Do.	Fr.	Sa.	So.
Abwaschen							
Garten							
Einkaufen							
Staub saugen							
Bad putzen							
Kochen							
Aufräumen							

auf dem Herd natürlich

nein, mit dem Geschirrspüler

mit dem Mikrowellenherd

mit der Waschmaschine

mit der Küchenmaschine

im Kühlschrank

7. Was benutzen Sie in der Küche? Find the right answers for yourself. Then ask your partner several questions. You may use several of the suggestions.

1. Wo kochen Sie Spaghetti?
2. Wie waschen Sie Ihre Wäsche?
3. Wo stehen Milch und Saft?
4. Wie wärmen Sie Essen von gestern auf?
5. Spülen Sie das Geschirr von Hand?

8. Fragen an den/die Gesprächspartner/in

1. Was kochst du gern?
2. Was steht in deinem Kühlschrank?
3. Spülst du das Geschirr von Hand?
4. Was machst du gern mit der Küchenmaschine?

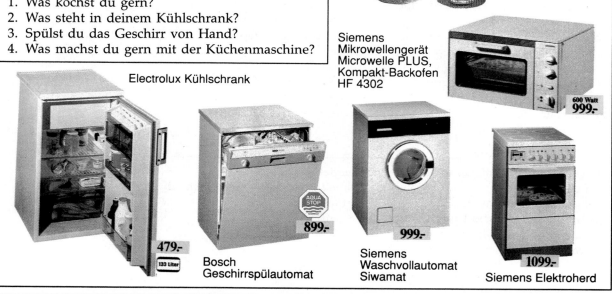

KARSTADT

Philips
Storemaster
»HR 2808«

Siemens
Mikrowellengerät
Microwelle PLUS,
Kompakt-Backofen
HF 4302

600 Watt
999.-

Electrolux Kühlschrank

479.-
133 Liter

Bosch
Geschirrspülautomat

AQUA STOP

899.-

Siemens
Waschvollautomat
Siwamat

999.-

1099.-
Siemens Elektroherd

Vokabeln

— Substantive

das **Bad, ⸚er** bath, bathroom
die **CD (Compact Disk), -s** CD (compact disc)
der **CD-Spieler, -** CD player
der **Dank** thanks; **vielen Dank** many thanks, thanks a lot
das **Fest, -e** party; celebration; feast; **auf dem Fest** at the party
die **Flasche, -n** bottle; **eine Flasche Mineralwasser** a bottle of mineral water
das **Gerät, -e** appliance; tool; utensil
das **Geschenk, -e** present; gift
das **Geschirr** dishes
der **Geschirrspüler, -** dishwasher
die **Hausarbeit** housework; chore; homework
der **Herd, -e** kitchen range

die **Kassette, -n** cassette (audio or video)
das **Kassettendeck, -s** cassette deck
der **Kassettenrecorder, -** cassette recorder
die **Küche, -n** kitchen
die **Küchenmaschine, -n** mixer and food processor combined
der **Kühlschrank, ⸚e** refrigerator
der **Mikrowellenherd, -e** microwave oven
die **Stunde, -n** hour; lesson; class; die **Deutschstunde** German class
die **Wäsche** laundry
die **Waschmaschine, -n** washing machine
das **Wohnzimmer, -** living room

— Verben

ab·trocknen to dry dishes; to wipe dry
ab·waschen (wäscht ab), abgewaschen to wash up (dishes)
auf·räumen to straighten up (a room)
gebrauchen to use

gratulieren (+ *dat.*) to congratulate, **[Ich] gratuliere zum Geburtstag.** Happy Birthday.
putzen to clean
reparieren to repair
spülen to rinse; to wash; **Geschirr spülen** to wash dishes
Staub saugen to vacuum

— Andere Wörter

ein paar a few, some; **ein Paar, -e** a pair
gar: gar nicht not at all
herum around; **Überall liegen Bücher herum.** Books are lying around everywhere.

neugierig curious
schnell fast, quick; **mach schnell** hurry up

Besondere Ausdrücke

Du meine Güte!   Good Heavens!,
   Good gracious!
Herzlichen Glückwunsch [zum
   Geburtstag]   Happy Birthday
He, Mann!   Hey, man!

TÜREN

Vorbereitung auf das Lesen

◆ *Zum Thema*

1. Welche Türen schließt man bei Ihnen —
   a. Schlafzimmertüren, wenn Sie im Schlafzimmer arbeiten oder schlafen?
      Wenn Sie nicht im Zimmer sind?
   b. Bürotüren, wenn man im Büro arbeitet?
2. Stört es Sie, wenn eine Schlafzimmertür oder eine Bürotür offen ist?
   Wenn sie geschlossen ist?
3. Kann man von der Haustür in Ihr Wohnzimmer oder Eßzimmer sehen?
   Stört Sie das?
4. Haben die Einfamilienhäuser bei Ihnen einen Zaun oder eine Hecke?

◆ *Leitfragen*

1. Was macht die Österreicherin nach Meinung° der Amerikanerin „falsch"?   opinion
2. Was ist der Unterschied zwischen vielen amerikanischen Türen und
   österreichischen Türen?
3. Warum sind die Türen in Österreich, in Deutschland und in der Schweiz
   meistens geschlossen?
4. Warum haben die Einfamilienhäuser in deutschsprachigen Ländern oft
   eine Hecke oder einen Zaun?
5. Was halten die Österreicher von offenen Türen?
6. Was halten die Amerikaner von geschlossenen Türen?

*J*utta Gruber, eine Österreicherin, studiert zwei Jahre an einer amerikanischen Universität. Während ihres ersten Jahres hat sie ein Zimmer bei einer Familie. Sie spricht gut Englisch. Das Zimmer gefällt ihr. Die Familie ist nett. Da fragt die Mutter der Familie sie eines Tages:

5 „Haben Sie etwas gegen uns?" Die Österreicherin ist erstaunt:

„Nein, natürlich nicht. Aber bitte, warum fragen Sie?"

„Wegen der Tür, wegen der geschlossenen Tür! Ich meine, weil Ihre Tür immer geschlossen ist, wenn Sie in Ihrem Zimmer sind."

Die Österreicherin ist sprachlos. Sie kann nur sagen: „Aber … aber das
10 bedeutet doch nichts. Ich mache das ganz automatisch. In Österreich tun wir das immer."

„Wirklich?" antwortet die Amerikanerin und denkt: Das muß ja ein eigenartiges° Land sein, wo die Türen immer geschlossen sind!   strange

Die Österreicherin geht langsam in ihr Zimmer und schließt trotz des
15 Gesprächs wieder die Tür. Sie muß an einen Satz denken, den° sie oft von   that
ihrer Mutter gehört hat: „Jeder Mensch braucht ein Plätzchen°, wo er die Tür   little place
hinter sich° zumachen kann."   oneself

Was für eine Zimmertür hält unsere Studentin denn immer geschlossen? Nun, sie ist leicht, nicht so schwer wie eine Zimmertür in Österreich, in
20 Deutschland oder in der Schweiz. Auch muß man wissen, daß die österreichischen Türen ein Schloß mit einem Schlüssel haben.* Sie passen auch besser in den Türrahmen°. Und unten° haben sie anstatt eines kleinen freien   door frame / below
Zwischenraumes° auch heute noch oft eine Schwelle°.   space / door sill

In Amerika sind die Türen nicht nur in einer Privatwohnung meistens
25 offen, sondern auch in Büros. Manchmal haben sie eine klare Glasscheibe°.   glass pane
Wenn eine österreichische Bürotür eine Glasscheibe hat, dann ist sie meistens aus Milchglas, d.h. sie ist nicht durchsichtig°.   transparent

Jutta Gruber ist die Häuser in Österreich gewohnt°. Da hat das   accustomed to
Grundstück° eines Einfamilienhauses z.B. fast immer einen Zaun, oft auch   property
30 eine undurchsichtige Hecke. Wenn man die Haustür öffnet, kommt man in größeren° Häusern zuerst in einen Flur. Von da geht man durch die   larger
eigentliche Wohnungstür in einen zweiten Flur, den Flur der Wohnung. Von diesem Flur führen die Türen ins Wohnzimmer und Eßzimmer, in die Schlafzimmer, in die Küche und ins Badezimmer. Da diese Türen fast immer
35 geschlossen sind, kann der Besucher von hier nicht in die Zimmer sehen. Auch kleine Mietwohnungen° haben immer einen solchen Flur.   rental apartments

Während ihres zweiten° Jahres hat Jutta Gruber eine kleine moderne   second
Wohnung. Es stört sie, daß sie hier keinen Flur hat. Nach einigen Wochen hat sie eine Idee: Sie baut einen Flur aus Bücherregalen. Jetzt kann man von der
40 Wohnungstür nicht mehr direkt ins Wohnzimmer sehen.

---

*Doors in Austria, Germany, and Switzerland generally have door handles (**Klinken**) rather than knobs.

Die Türen vom Flur in die Zimmer sind meistens geschlossen.

Die Österreicher nehmen ihre private Sphäre also sehr ernst. Ihre private Sphäre ist schon verletzt, wenn man sie sehen kann. Daher sind auch ihre Balkons und Terrassen anders gebaut als in Amerika. Man kann die Menschen darauf nicht oder nicht leicht sehen.

45 E.T. Hall *(The Hidden Dimension)* zeigt, wie „die Tür" zu ernsten Schwierigkeiten führen kann, wenn amerikanische Firmen Büros in Österreich haben. Wenn die Türen offen sind, stört das die Österreicher der Firma. Auch bedeuten offene Türen für sie Unordnung°. Und wer will schon in einer unordentlichen Firma arbeiten? Die Türen müssen also geschlossen bleiben.

50 Das stört aber die Amerikaner dieser Firma. Sie glauben nun, daß sie ausgeschlossen° sind, daß man vor ihnen etwas verheimlichen° will. Beide Seiten müssen also lernen, daß eine offene Tür und eine geschlossene Tür etwas bedeuten. Und sie müssen lernen, daß sie in Österreich etwas anderes bedeuten als in Amerika.

disorder

excluded / keep secret

Fragen zum Lesestück

1. Wo wohnt Jutta Gruber?
2. Kann sie gut Englisch?
3. Wie gefällt ihr ihr Zimmer?
4. Wie gefällt ihr ihre amerikanische Familie?
5. Was fragt die Mutter der Familie Jutta eines Tages?
6. Warum glaubt die Mutter, daß Jutta etwas gegen die Familie hat?

7. Warum ist Jutta erstaunt?
8. Warum schließt sie immer ihre Tür?
9. Wer hat gesagt, daß jeder Mensch ein Plätzchen braucht, wo er die Tür hinter sich zumachen kann?
10. Wie ist eine österreichische Tür? Eine amerikanische Tür?
11. Welche Tür hat manchmal eine durchsichtige Glasscheibe, die österreichische oder die amerikanische?
12. Wohin kommt man, wenn man durch die Wohnungstür eines österreichischen Hauses geht?
13. Warum kann man nicht in die Zimmer sehen?
14. Was hat Jutta aus Bücherregalen gebaut? Warum?
15. In welchem Land arbeitet man hinter geschlossenen Bürotüren?
16. Wer glaubt, daß man vor ihnen etwas verheimlichen will, wenn die Bürotüren geschlossen sind?

1. Erzählen Sie.   Tell about single-family homes in Austria. Use the cues below in addition to your own sentences.

Einfamilienhäuser in Österreich ◇ Zaun und Hecke ◇ Balkon und Terrasse ◇ Flur ◇ Zimmer mit geschlossenen Türen ◇ offene Türen

2. Meine Privatsphäre   In a group of three discuss how you maintain your own privacy. You may want to compare your idea of privacy with the ideas in the reading. Use the following questions as a guide.

Wo wohnen Sie? (allein, in einem Studentenheim, bei Ihrer Familie?)
Wann machen Sie Ihre Tür zu?
Welche Türen sind bei Ihnen meistens geschlossen?
Hat Ihr Haus eine Terrasse oder einen Balkon?
Können Sie die Nachbarn sehen, wenn sie auf der Terrasse sind?
Was machen Sie gern allein? Was machen Sie gern mit anderen Leuten?
Wo möchten Sie wohnen — in einer Wohnung oder in einem Einfamilienhaus? Warum?

Vokabeln

Substantive

das **Badezimmer, -** bathroom
der **Balkon, -s** balcony
der **Besucher, -**/die **Besucherin, -nen**
  visitor, guest

das **Einfamilienhaus, ⸚er**
  single-family home
das **Eßzimmer, -** dining room
der **Flur, -e** (entrance) hall

die **Hecke, -n** hedge
die **Idee, -n** idea
die **Meinung, -en** opinion;
  [meiner] Meinung nach in [my]
  opinion
der **Satz, ⸚e** sentence
das **Schlafzimmer, -** bedroom

das **Schloß,** *pl.* **Schlösser** lock;
  castle
der **Schlüssel, -** key
der **Stock,** *pl.* **Stockwerke** floor
  (story) of building
die **Terrasse, -n** terrace, patio
der **Zaun, ⸚e** fence

— Verben —————————

antworten (+ *dat.*) to answer (*as in*
  **ich antworte der Frau); antworten
  auf** (+ *acc.*) to answer (*as in* **ich
  antworte auf die Frage**)
bauen to build
führen to lead

öffnen to open
passen (+ *dat.*) to fit; to suit
verletzen to injure
zeigen to show; **zeigen auf** (+ *acc.*)
  to point to
zu·machen to close

— Andere Wörter —————————

(an)statt (+ *gen.*) instead of
da (*conj.*) since, because
dunkel dark
erstaunt astonished
hell bright
langsam slow(ly)

meistens mostly, most of the time
modern modern
sprachlos speechless
trotz (+ *gen.*) in spite of
während (+ *gen.*) during
wegen (+ *gen.*) on account of

Erweiterung des Wortschatzes

1 The prefix *un-*

Viele Deutsche glauben, daß
  Kuchen mit künstlichen Farben
  ungesund ist.

Many Germans believe that cake
  with artificial colors is *unhealthy.*

As in English, the prefix **un-** causes a word to have a negative or an opposite
meaning. The prefix **un-** is stressed: **un'gesund.**

2 The suffix *-los*

Jutta war **sprachlos,** als sie das
  gehört hat.

Jutta was *speechless* when she heard
  that.

The German suffix **-los** is used to form adjectives and adverbs from nouns.
The suffix **-los** is often equivalent to the English suffix *-less,* denoting *a lack of.*

3 Das Haus

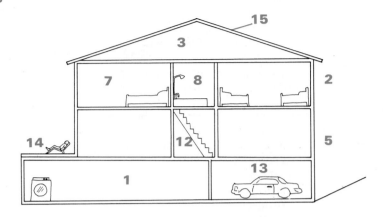

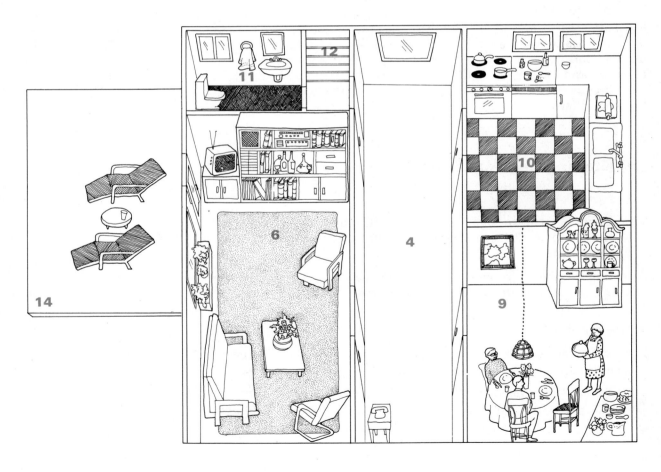

1. der Keller, - *garage*
2. der erste Stock
3. der Dachboden, ⸚
4. der Flur, -e

5. das Erdgeschoß
6. das Wohnzimmer, -
7. das Schlafzimmer, -
8. das Badezimmer, -
9. das Eßzimmer, -

10. die Küche, -n
11. die Toilette, -n
12. die Treppe, -n
13. die Garage, -n
14. die Terrasse, -n
15. das Dach, ⸚er

The second floor is called **der erste Stock,** the third floor **der zweite Stock,** and so on, because the first floor is called **das Erdgeschoß.**

1. Antworten Sie.

1. Wo kocht man?
2. In welchem Zimmer schläft man?
3. Wo badet man?
4. In welchem Zimmer sitzt man abends und liest?
5. In welchem Zimmer hört man Musik oder sieht fern?
6. In welchem Zimmer ißt man, wenn Gäste da sind?

2. Interview Answer the questions below. Then find students whose answers correspond to yours.

Describing the place you live

1. Wohnen Sie zu Hause, bei einer Familie oder im Studentenheim?
2. Wo wohnt Ihre Familie? In einem Einfamilienhaus? In einer Mietwohnung?
3. Wie viele Stockwerke hat Ihr Haus?
4. Hat Ihr Haus einen Keller? Einen Balkon? Eine Terrasse? Eine Hecke oder einen Zaun?
5. Wo schlafen Sie? Im Erdgeschoß? Im ersten Stock?
6. Was für eine Farbe haben Ihre Schlafzimmerwände — eine helle° oder eine dunkle°?
7. Im welchem Zimmer essen Sie?
8. In welchem Zimmer sehen Sie fern?

DAS MAGAZIN FÜR INTERNATIONALES WOHNEN GIBT'S JETZT ALLE ZWEI MONATE. BESONDERS GÜNSTIG IM ABONNEMENT.

Wohnlandschaft mit Garten

4½ Zimmer und 101 familienfreundliche Quadratmeter

– da gibt's Platz für alle und für jeden Einzelnen. Dazu der eigene Gartenanteil. –

Sowas mag die Familie! Besonders zu diesem günstigen Preis: DM 397.500,–

Moosach liegt im Trend. Am besten gleich informieren!

Im Erdgeschoß eigene Gartenanteile

<u>4-Zi.-Whg., ca. 94 m²,</u>
<u>DM 379.800,–</u>

<u>3½-Zi.-Whg., ca. 83 m²,</u>
<u>DM 339.900,–</u>

<u>2-Zi.-Whg., ca. 51 m²,</u>
<u>DM 232.400,–</u>

– im Dachgeschoß großzügige Loggien.
(Baubeginn Herbst '88)

NEUES WOHNEN

M2000

MOOSACH

gerade jetzt beraten lassen:

am Baugrundstück Thorner-/ Merseburgerstraße (Hinweispfeile)
Sa. + So. 13–17 Uhr
Mittw. 15.30–18 Uhr

Baywobau ◇ 230 320
Königinstraße 25 · 8000 München 22 (am Englischen Garten)

3. Neubauwohnungen° Using the advertisement above, answer the following questions. If you need help reading the ad, refer to the Vocabulary for Authentic Text Activities in the Reference Section.

new apartments

1. Diese Wohnungen liegen in Moosach. Moosach ist ein Stadtteil° von welcher Großstadt?
2. Wieviel kostet eine 4-Zimmer-Wohnung?
3. Wie groß ist die Küche? Das Wohnzimmer?
4. Wieviel kostet eine 2-Zimmer-Wohnung?
5. Finden Sie diese Wohnungen teuer?

district

4. Mit dem Hauseigentümer° reden   Act out a scene in which a   owner of the apartments
young married couple, Martin and Heike, meet the owner of the
apartments in Moosach to make inquiries about buying one. You may want
to include some of the following questions.

1. How expensive are the apartments in Moosach?
2. How large are the apartments?
3. How many rooms do the apartments have?
4. Are there any furnished° apartments?   möbliert-
5. Is Moosach near° schools and shopping?   in der Nähe von

**Nicht alle Deutschen wohnen
in Mietwohnungen. (Am Rhein bei Koblenz)**

Although many people in German-speaking countries live in apartments, either rented (**Mietwohnung**) or owned (**Eigentumswohnung**), many others live in single- and two-family homes. A typical house has stucco-coated walls and a tile or slate roof. Normally there is a full basement that is used primarily for storage or as a work area. The first floor (**erster Stock** or **erste Etage**) is what is usually considered the second story in American homes. Privacy is assured not only by closed doors but also by window curtains (**Gardinen**) and drapes (**Vorhänge**). Many homes and apartments are equipped with attractive outdoor shutters (**Rolläden**) that unfold vertically over the windows.

In addition to the modern houses, each region of Germany has its own traditional architecture. Many old **Fachwerkhäuser** (half-timbered houses) have been restored. Especially in rural areas these colorful houses lend charming character to small towns and their market squares.

GRAMMATIK UND ÜBUNGEN

1 Genitive case

◆ *Showing possession and close relationships*

Ich habe mit dem Sohn **des Bäckers** gesprochen.	I talked to the baker's son.
Das ist die Frage **eines Kindes.**	That is a child's question.
Der Flur **der Wohnung** ist nicht sehr groß.	The entrance hall of the apartment is not very large.

English shows possession or other close relationships by adding '*s* to a noun or by using a phrase with *of*. English generally uses the '*s* form only for persons. For things and ideas, English uses the *of*-construction.

German uses the genitive case to show possession or other close relationships. The genitive is used for things and ideas as well as for persons. The genitive generally follows the noun it modifies.

die Freundin **von meinem Bruder** (meines Bruders)
zwei **von ihren Freunden** (ihrer Freunde)
ein Freund **von Thomas** (Thomas' Freund)

In spoken German the genitive of possession is frequently replaced by **von** + *dative*.

ein Freund **von mir**
ein Freund **von Nicole**

Von + *dative* is also used in phrases similar to the English *of mine, of yours*, etc.

◆ *Masculine and neuter nouns*

Das ist die Meinung **meines Professors.**	That is my professor's opinion.
Hast du den Namen **des Kindes** verstanden?	Did you understand the child's name?

Masculine and neuter nouns of one syllable generally add **-es** in the genitive; nouns of two or more syllables add **-s**. The corresponding articles, **der**-words, and **ein**-words end in **-es** in the genitive.

◆ Masculine N-nouns

Die Frau **des Herrn** da kommt aus Österreich.	The wife of the man there is from Austria.
Haben Sie die Frage **des Jungen** verstanden?	Did you understand the boy's question?

Masculine nouns that add **-n** or **-en** in the accusative and dative singular also add **-n** or **-en** in the genitive. A few masculine nouns add **-ns: des Namens.**

1. Wie sagt man das?   Give the German equivalents, using the genitive case.

1. the man's plan
2. the entrance hall of the house
3. the car of the year
4. the child's bicycle
5. the boy's story
6. Mr. Schmidt's car
7. the name of the country
8. the color of the shirt

◆ Feminine and plural nouns

Die Farbe **der Bluse** gefällt mir.	I like the color of the blouse.
Frau Genscher ist eine Bekannte **meiner Eltern.**	Mrs. Genscher is an acquaintance of my parents.

Feminine and plural nouns do not add a genitive ending. The corresponding articles, **der**-words, and **ein**-words end in **-er** in the genitive.

2. Hast du die Adresse?   Your friend is getting settled near where you live and needs the addresses of various places. Help her/him.

▶   Kennst du eine Apotheke?   *Hier ist die Adresse einer Apotheke.*

1. Kennst du eine Bäckerei?
2. Und eine Metzgerei?
3. Wo ist eine Drogerie?
4. Gibt es hier eine Buchhandlung?
5. Wo ist die Bibliothek?

◆ The interrogative pronoun wessen?

Wessen Plattenspieler ist das?	Whose record player is that?
Wessen Platten sind das?	Whose records are those?

The question word to ask for nouns or pronouns in the genitive is **wessen**. It is the genitive form of **wer** and is equivalent to English *whose*.

◆ *Possessive adjectives*

Gerda ist die Freundin **meines Bruders.**	Gerda is my brother's girlfriend.
Frau Genscher ist eine Bekannte **seiner Eltern.**	Mrs. Genscher is an acquaintance of his parents.

Possessive adjectives take the case of the noun they modify. Even though a possessive adjective already shows possession (**mein** = my, **sein** = his), it must itself be in the genitive case when the noun it goes with is in the genitive (**meines Bruders** = of my brother). Thus a phrase like **die Freundin meines Bruders** shows *two* possessive relationships.

3. Wessen Telefonnummer ist das? Answer the questions using the genitive case. Follow the model.

▶ Wessen Telefonnummer ist das? (meine Eltern) *Das ist die Telefonnummer meiner Eltern.*

1. meine Tante
2. sein Bruder
3. ihr Freund Mark

4. seine Schwester
5. ihre Großeltern
6. unser Nachbar

4. Neue Sätze Restate the sentences below, replacing the genitive expressions with the genitive form of the cued words.

▶ Das Referat dieser Studentin war sehr interessant. (dieser Student) *Das Referat dieses Studenten war sehr interessant.*

1. Das ist die Telefonnummer meiner Frau. (mein Mann)
2. Der Flur unseres Hauses ist klein. (diese Wohnung)
3. Haben Sie die Antwort seiner Freundin gehört? (unser Nachbar)
4. Das ist die Sprache eines Kindes. (ein Student)
5. Kennen Sie den Namen dieser Firma? (dieses Geschäft)
6. Haben Sie die Adresse des Biergartens? (das Café)
7. Wie heißen die Bekannten seiner Tante? (ihre Eltern)

5. Familie und Freunde How much do you know about your family, relatives, and friends?

> Discussing friends and family

1. Wo wohnt der Freund Ihrer Schwester?
2. Wo wohnt die Freundin Ihres Bruders?
3. Wie ist die Telefonnummer Ihres Freundes? Ihrer Freundin?
4. Haben Sie die Adresse Ihrer Tante? Ihres Onkels? Ihrer Großeltern?
5. Was für ein Auto hat der Freund Ihrer Schwester? die Freundin Ihres Bruders?
6. Wie heißen die Bekannten Ihrer Eltern?

Das Grundstück eines Einfamilienhauses hat fast immer einen Zaun oder eine Hecke.

2 Genitive of time

Indefinite past	**Eines Tages** hat mir Jutta alles erklärt.	*One day* Jutta explained everything to me.
Indefinite future	**Eines Tages** mache ich das vielleicht.	*Someday* maybe I'll do that.

Nouns expressing an indefinite point in time are in the genitive.

3 Prepositions with the genitive

(an)statt	instead of	Kommt Inge **(an)statt** ihrer Schwester?
trotz	in spite of	**Trotz** des Wetters fahren wir in die Berge.
während	during	**Während** des Sommers bleiben wir nicht in Hamburg.
wegen	on account of	**Wegen** des Wetters gehen wir nicht schwimmen.

The prepositions **anstatt** or **statt, trotz, während,** and **wegen** require the genitive case.

wegen **dem Wetter** (des Wetters)
trotz **dem Regen** (des Regens)

In colloquial usage many people use the prepositions **statt, trotz, wegen,** and sometimes **während** with the dative.

trotz **ihm**
wegen **dir**

In colloquial usage dative pronouns are frequently used with the prepositions: **statt ihr, trotz ihm, wegen mir.**

6. Eine Wanderung   The company your father works for occasionally sponsors a hike. Your friend asks how the last one was. Answer the questions using the cues.

▶   Bist du auch mitgegangen?   *Ja, trotz des Wetters.*
    (ja, trotz / das Wetter)

1. Warum ist dein Bruder zu Hause geblieben? (wegen / seine Arbeit)
2. Ist deine Schwester mitgegangen? (ja, statt / mein Bruder)
3. Sind die Leute lange gewandert? (nein, nur während / der Nachmittag)
4. Sind viele Leute gekommen? (nein, wegen / das Wetter)
5. Wann macht ihr Pläne für die nächste Wanderung? (während / diese Woche)
6. Warum gehen die Leute eigentlich wandern? (wegen / das Café)

4 Adjectives

◆ *Predicate adjectives*

Die Schallplatte° ist **toll.**   record
Der Wein wird sicher **gut.**

Predicate adjectives are adjectives that follow the verbs **sein** or **werden** and modify the subject. Predicate adjectives do not take endings.

◆ *Attributive adjectives*

Das ist eine **tolle** Schallplatte.
Das ist ein **guter** Wein.

Attributive adjectives are adjectives that precede the nouns they modify. Attributive adjectives have endings.

5 Preceded adjectives

◆ *Adjectives preceded by a definite article or* **der-** *word*

	Masculine	Neuter	Feminine	Plural
Nom.	der alt**e** Mann	das klein**e** Kind	die jung**e** Frau	die gut**en** Freunde
Acc.	den alt**en** Mann	das klein**e** Kind	die jung**e** Frau	die gut**en** Freunde
Dat.	dem alt**en** Mann	dem klein**en** Kind	der jung**en** Frau	den gut**en** Freunden
Gen.	des alt**en** Mannes	des klein**en** Kindes	der jung**en** Frau	der gut**en** Freunde

	M.	N.	F.	Pl.
Nom.	e	e	e	en
Acc.	en	e	e	en
Dat.	en	en	en	en
Gen.	en	en	en	en

Adjectives preceded by a definite article or **der**-word have the endings **-e** or **-en.**

Das Zimmer ist zu **dunkel.**	Wer kann in diesem **dunklen** Zimmer lesen?
Diese Handschuhe sind **teuer.**	Willst du diese **teuren** Handschuhe wirklich kaufen?

Adjectives ending in **-el** omit the **-e** when the adjective takes an ending. Adjectives ending in **-er** may follow the same pattern.

7. Noch einmal. Restate the model sentences, using the cued adjectives in the nominative singular.

▶ Ist dieser Pulli noch gut? (alt)   *Ist dieser alte Pulli noch gut?*

1. rot
2. grün
3. schwer
4. leicht

▶ Wem gehört dieses Radio? (klein)   *Wem gehört dieses kleine Radio?*

5. toll
6. neu
7. kaputt
8. teuer

▶ Hoffentlich war die Platte° nicht sehr teuer. (neu)   *Hoffentlich war die neue Platte nicht sehr teuer.*   record

9. furchtbar
10. schlecht
11. amerikanisch
12. kaputt

8. Welche meinst du? In a department store Ingrid comments on a number of items; ask which she is referring to. Use adjectives in the accusative singular.

▶ Der rote Pulli ist toll, nicht? *Meinst du diesen roten Pulli?*

1. Der leichte Regenmantel ist praktisch, nicht?
2. Der helle Rock ist schön, nicht?
3. Das grüne Kleid ist sehr lang, nicht?
4. Das gelbe Hemd ist toll, nicht?
5. Die kleine Handtasche ist praktisch, nicht?
6. Die weiße Bluse ist wirklich schön, nicht?
7. Die schwarzen Schuhe sind furchtbar, nicht?
8. Die kurzen Handschuhe sind billig, nicht?

9. Woher hast du das? Ask four students or your instructor where they got a particular thing (e.g., a piece of clothing, a book bag). Be sure to identify it (color, size, etc.).

| Describing things |

Sie	*Gesprächspartner/in*
Woher hast du/haben Sie [die schöne braune Büchertasche]?	[Die] habe ich [von meiner Mutter]. [Die] habe ich [in einem kleinen Geschäft gekauft].

10. Bist du gern da? A friend wonders whether you like to do things in various places. Say he/she is correct. Use adjectives in the dative singular.

▶ Wo ißt du gern? In dem Café an der Uni? Es ist billig. *Ja, in dem billigen Café an der Uni.*

1. Wo läufst du gern? In dem Park? Er ist groß.
2. Wo sitzt du gern? In dem Biergarten? Er ist schön.
3. Wo kaufst du gern Bücher? In der Buchhandlung? Sie ist modern.
4. Wo sitzt du gern? In dem Café am Markt? Es ist klein.
5. Wo ißt du gern? In der Kneipe? Sie ist gemütlich°. cozy
6. Wo arbeitest du gern? In dem Musikgeschäft? Es ist bekannt.
7. Wo liest du gern? In der Bibliothek? Sie ist ruhig.

11. Viele Fragen   Peter has lots of questions. Rephrase them by combining the sentences in each pair below. Use the boldfaced adjectives with the plural nouns.

▶ Warum trägst du immer noch diese   *Warum trägst du immer noch*
   Schuhe? Sie sind schon **alt**.   *diese alten Schuhe?*

1. Wer hat diese Handschuhe gekauft? Sie sind schön **warm**.
2. Was hast du mit den Jeans gemacht? Sie sind zu **eng**.
3. Wann hast du diese Hemden bekommen? Sie sind wirklich **toll**.
4. Warum hast du diese Schuhe gekauft? Sie sind wirklich **furchtbar**.
5. Was hältst du von diesen Kassetten? Sie sind **neu**.
6. Wohin hängst du diese Poster? Sie sind **lustig**.
7. Wer hat dir diese Bücher geliehen? Sie sind sehr **interessant**.

12. Hier ist alles klein.   Add the adjective **klein** with the correct ending to each noun.

▶ Das Haus steht in der Sonnenstraße.   *Das kleine Haus steht in der*
                                          kleinen Sonnenstraße.

Der Junge wohnt in dem Haus. Hinter dem Haus ist der Garten. In dem Garten steht die Bank°. Auf der Bank sitzt der Junge. Unter der Bank liegt der   bench
Ball von dem Jungen. Er will mit dem Ball spielen. Er nimmt den Ball in die Hände und kickt ihn durch das Fenster. Peng! Da ist das Fenster kaputt.

◆ *Adjectives preceded by an indefinite article or **ein**-word*

	Masculine	Neuter	Feminine	Plural
Nom.	ein alt**er** Mann	ein klein**es** Kind	eine jung**e** Frau	meine gut**en** Freunde
Acc.	einen alt**en** Mann	ein klein**es** Kind	eine jung**e** Frau	meine gut**en** Freunde
Dat.	einem alt**en** Mann	einem klein**en** Kind	einer jung**en** Frau	meinen gut**en** Freunden
Gen.	eines alt**en** Mannes	eines klein**en** Kindes	einer jung**en** Frau	meiner gut**en** Freunde

	M.	N.	F.	Pl.
Nom.	er	es	e	en
Acc.	en	es	e	en
Dat.	en	en	en	en
Gen.	en	en	en	en

Adjectives preceded by an indefinite article or an **ein-**word have the same endings as those preceded by **der-**words, except when the **ein-**word itself has no ending: masculine nominative (**-er**) and neuter nominative and accusative (**-es**). Note the following table.

Nom.	ein alt**er** Mann	ein klein**es** Kind
Acc.	—	ein klein**es** Kind

13. Du hast recht. Regina comments on class work. Agree with her. Use adjectives in the nominative case.

▶ Professor Schmidts Musikvorlesung war trocken, nicht?   *Ja, das war wirklich eine trockene Vorlesung.*

1. Das Buch ist auch trocken, nicht?
2. Aber das Bier nachher war gut, nicht?
3. Die Klausur in Deutsch war lang und schwer, nicht?
4. Professor Langes Seminar ist interessant, nicht?
5. Eriks Referat war ziemlich kurz, nicht?
6. Das Referat war auch ziemlich schlecht, nicht?
7. Professor Memmels Kurs ist leicht, nicht?

14. Ein neues Zimmer Your friend Robert, who is a student at a Swiss university, has moved to a new room. Describe his new surroundings. Use the cued adjectives in the accusative case.

▶ Robert hat ein Zimmer. (groß, hell)   *Robert hat ein großes, helles Zimmer.*

1. Das Zimmer hat einen Balkon. (schön, privat)
2. Es hat eine Tür. (schwer)
3. Robert hat eine Lampe. (modern, lustig)
4. Er hat ein Bücherregal. (klein, praktisch)
5. Er hat einen Stuhl. (teuer, unpraktisch)
6. Er hat ein Bild. (groß, furchtbar)

15. Ich habe gewonnen. You just won some money in the lottery and you're feeling generous. Tell four people what you're going to buy for yourself and ask what you can buy for them.

▶ *Ich kaufe mir einen neuen, teuren CD-Spieler. Was kann ich dir kaufen?*

Dinge: Auto ◇ Fahrrad ◇ CD ◇ Kassette ◇ Radio ◇ Buch ◇ Jacke ◇ Pullover

Adjektive: besser ◇ gut ◇ interessant ◇ neu ◇ rot ◇ schnell ◇ schön ◇ teuer ◇ toll ◇ warm

16. Alles ist neu. In Andrea's life there are at the moment many new things and people. Ask for more details about them.

▶ Ich hab' ein neues Auto.   *Erzähl mal von deinem neuen Auto.*

1. Ich hab' eine neue Freundin.
2. Ich hab' einen neuen Kassettenrecorder.
3. Ich hab' neue Bekannte.
4. Ich hab' ein neues Fahrrad.
5. Ich hab' eine neue Wohnung.
6. Ich hab' neue Freunde.
7. Ich hab' einen neuen Deutschprofessor.

17. Wo möchtest du leben? Ask four students or your instructor in what kind of house and/or city they would like to live.

Sie	*Gesprächspartner/in*
In was für einem Haus möchtest du/möchten Sie leben?	Ich möchte in einem kleinen, weißen Haus leben, mit einem großen Wohnzimmer.

> Inquiring about preferences

18. Träume° Form a group of four. One person begins by telling what he/she is dreaming about having or doing and asks the next person what he/she is dreaming of. A few possibilities are given.

> Stating wants/desires

dreams

Träume: Reise ◇ Auto ◇ Frau ◇ Haus ◇ Mann ◇ Motorrad ◇ Wochenende
Adjektive: schnell ◆ klein ◆ reich ◆ schön ◆ interessant ◆ weiß ◆ groß ◆ toll ◆ lang

▶ *Ich träume° von einem schönen Wochenende. Wovon träumst du?*

dream

*Wer anderen eine Grube gräbt,
fällt selbst hinein.*

6 Unpreceded adjectives

	Masculine	Neuter	Feminine	Plural
Nom.	gut**er** Wein	gut**es** Brot	gut**e** Wurst	gut**e** Brötchen
Acc.	gut**en** Wein	gut**es** Brot	gut**e** Wurst	gut**e** Brötchen
Dat.	gut**em** Wein	gut**em** Brot	gut**er** Wurst	gut**en** Brötchen
Gen.	gut**en** Weines	gut**en** Brotes	gut**er** Wurst	gut**er** Brötchen

	M.	**N.**	**F.**	**Pl.**
Nom.	er	es	e	e
Acc.	en	es	e	e
Dat.	em	em	er	en
Gen.	en	en	er	er

Adjectives not preceded by a definite article, a **der**-word, an indefinite article, or an **ein**-word have the same endings as **der**-words, except the masculine and neuter genitive, which have the ending **-en**.

19. **Peter ißt gern.**   Make each of Peter's comments more descriptive by using the appropriate unpreceded form of the cued adjective.

▶ Brötchen schmecken gut. (frisch)   *Frische Brötchen schmecken gut.*

1. Bier schmeckt auch gut. (deutsch)
2. Ich trinke gern Wein. (trocken)
3. Blumen auf dem Tisch gefallen mir. (frisch)
4. In vielen Städten kann man Fisch kaufen. (frisch)
5. Ich koche gern mit Wein. (deutsch)
6. Ich habe Hunger. (groß)
7. Zum Mittagessen esse ich gern Steak. (amerikanisch)
8. Zum Abendessen esse ich gern Wurst. (deutsch)

7 Ordinal numbers

1. erst-	**6.** sechst-	**21.** einundzwanzig**st**-
2. zweit-	**7.** sieb**t**-	**32.** zweiunddreißig**st**-
3. dritt-	**8.** ach**t**-	**100.** hundert**st**-
		1000. tausend**st**-

An ordinal number is a number indicating the position of something in a sequence (e.g., the first, the second). In German, the ordinal numbers are formed by adding **-t** to numbers 1–19 and **-st** to numbers beyond 19. Exceptions are **erst-, dritt-, siebt-,** and **acht-.**

Die neue Wohnung ist im **dritten** Stock.
Am **siebten** Mai habe ich Geburtstag.

The ordinals take adjective endings.

8 Dates

Den wievielten haben wir heute?   What is the date today?
Heute haben wir **den 1.** März.
Heute haben wir **den ersten** März. }   Today is March first.

In German, dates are expressed with ordinal numbers preceded by the masculine form of the definite article referring to the noun **Tag.** A period after a number indicates that it is an ordinal. The day always precedes the month: **5. 2. 93. = den fünften Februar 1993.**

Hamburg, **den 2. März 1993.**

Dates in letter headings or news releases are in the accusative.

20. Zwei Tage später   Frank has forgotten the exact date of his friends' birthdays. The birthdays are two days later than he thinks. Correct him.

▶   Hat Inge am neunten Mai Geburtstag?   *Nein, am elften.*

1. Hat Gisela am dreizehnten Juli Geburtstag?
2. Hat Willi am ersten Januar Geburtstag?
3. Hat Uwe am zweiten März Geburtstag?
4. Hat Elke am sechsten November Geburtstag?
5. Hat Claudia am achtundzwanzigsten April Geburtstag?
6. Hat Gerd am fünfundzwanzigsten Dezember Geburtstag?

21. Zwei Fragen   Find out from four fellow students when their birthdays are and in what year or semester they are.

	Asking for personal information

Sie   *Gesprächspartner/in*

Wann hast du Geburtstag?   Am [siebten Juni].
In welchem Semester/Jahr bist du?   [Im zweiten.]

WIEDERHOLUNG

1. Ein Amerikaner in Deutschland Complete the paragraph by supplying the correct adjective ending where necessary.

Ein amerikanisch _____ Student studiert an einer deutsch _____ Universität. Er wohnt in einem klein _____, modern _____ Zimmer bei einer nett _____ Familie. In der erst _____ Woche ist er sehr erstaunt. Etwas versteht er nicht. Wenn er von seinen Vorlesungen nach Hause kommt, sieht er immer eine geschlossen _____ Zimmertür, aber ein offen _____ Fenster. Endlich erklärt ihm die Mutter der Familie, wie das ist. „Das Fenster ist wegen der frisch _____ Luft offen. Die geschlossen _____ Tür bedeutet, daß es Ihr privat _____ Zimmer ist."

2. Eine Schweizerin in Deutschland Tell where Susanne studies and what she does during the summer vacation by completing the sentences. Use the cued words.

1. Susanne studiert an _____ . (die Universität Göttingen)
2. Sie wohnt in _____ . (ein großes Studentenheim)
3. Sie denkt oft an _____ . (ihre Freunde zu Hause)
4. Sie kommt aus _____ . (die Schweiz)
5. In _____ fährt sie nach Hause. (die Sommerferien)
6. Sie arbeitet bei _____ . (ihre Tante)
7. Sie fährt mit _____ zur Arbeit. (der Bus)
8. Am Sonntag macht sie mit _____ eine kleine Wanderung. (ihr Freund)
9. Nach _____ gehen sie in ein Café. (die Wanderung)
10. Leider vergißt sie oft _____ zu Hause. (ihr Geld)
11. Ihr Freund muß _____ etwas Geld leihen. (sie)
12. Nachher gehen sie zu _____ . (ein Fest)

3. Vorbereitungen Form sentences to tell about the arrangements for getting the house in shape before guests arrive, using the cues below.

1. du / wollen / abwaschen / jetzt / ?
2. ich / können / abtrocknen / dann
3. ich / müssen / saubermachen / Küche / nachher
4. du / möchten / aufräumen / Wohnzimmer / ?
5. wer / sollen / saubermachen / Badezimmer / ?

Für Studenten ist es oft schwer, eine Wohnung zu finden.

4. Wie sagt man das?

1. —My friend Karin is studying at the University of Göttingen.
   —Does she live with a family?
   —Yes. The family is nice, and she likes her large room.
2. —What's the date today?
   —It's February 28.
   —Oh oh. Karin's birthday was yesterday.
3. —Are you going swimming in spite of the cold weather?
   —Yes, the cold weather doesn't bother me.

5. Letzte Woche   Tell what various people did last week.

▶ Ute macht Hausarbeit.   *Ute hat Hausarbeit gemacht.*

1. Sie räumt ihr Schlafzimmer auf.
2. Gerd wäscht jeden Tag ab.
3. Ute trocknet manchmal ab.
4. Ich kaufe ein.
5. Ich fahre mit dem Fahrrad auf den Markt.
6. Gerd kocht am Wochenende.
7. Ute backt für das Wochenende zwei Kuchen.

6. Was bedeutet das?   Context alone will often tell you the meaning of a new word. Try to guess the meanings of the boldfaced words in the sentences below.

1. Wie viele Familien wohnen in einem **Zweifamilienhaus?**
2. Zehn Wohnungen sind in diesem **Wohnhaus** frei.
3. Jede Uhr hat einen **Stundenzeiger** und einen **Minutenzeiger.** Der Stundenzeiger zeigt die Stunden an; der Minutenzeiger zeigt die Minuten an.
4. Ich komme immer zu spät. Meine Uhr **geht nach.** Gerd kommt immer zu früh. Seine Uhr **geht vor.**
5. War deine **Geburtstagsfeier** schön? Ja, wir haben auch den Geburtstag meiner Freunde gefeiert.
6. Die **Reparatur** meines Kassettenrecorders war letztes Mal zu teuer. Hoffentlich kannst du ihn diesmal reparieren.
7. Ich muß zum Arzt. Weißt du, wann Dr. Ortner **Sprechstunden** hat?

7. Ein Spiel   Form groups of four. Each person takes a turn giving clues about what is found in a room or part of a house. The others guess which room.

▶   Hier findet man alte Kleidung von   *Auf dem Dachboden*
    Großmutter.   *oder im Keller.*

8. Ein Geburtstagsfest   You are giving a birthday party for a friend. Role-play the following situations.

1. Invite several friends to attend and ask them to bring something to eat or drink or to provide entertainment.
2. Use adjectives to describe the gifts.
3. After the party the house is a mess. You and your friends must clean up. Negotiate who will do what.

9. Anregung

1. Hans-Jürgen, a student in Munich, plans to study for a year at an American university. Write him a letter in German telling him what to expect in the way of housing and courses at the university as well as American customs that differ from German customs. Draw on your knowledge about the sense of privacy, eating habits, cars and public transportation, natural foods, or the lack of a requirement for an *Aufenthaltserlaubnis.*
2. Rewrite the episode in lines 1–17 of the reading selection on page 276 from the point of view of an American visiting her/his relatives in a German-speaking country. She/he always leaves the door to her/his bedroom open.

GRAMMATIK: ZUSAMMENFASSUNG

Forms of the genitive

◆ *Forms of articles,* **der-**words *and* **ein-**words

	Masculine	Neuter	Feminine	Plural
Definite article	des Mann**es**	des Kind**es**	de**r** Frau	de**r** Freunde
Der-words	dies**es** Mann**es**	dies**es** Kind**es**	dies**er** Frau	dies**er** Freunde
Indefinite article	ein**es** Mann**es**	ein**es** Kind**es**	ein**er** Frau	—
Ein-words	ih**res** Mann**es**	uns**eres** Kind**es**	sein**er** Frau	mein**er** Freunde

◆ *Forms of nouns*

Masculine/Neuter	Feminine/Plural
der Name **des Mannes**	der Name **der Frau**
ein Freund **des Mädchens**	ein Freund **der Kinder**

Masculine and neuter nouns of one syllable generally add **-es** in the genitive; masculine and neuter nouns of two or more syllables add **-s.** Feminine and plural nouns do not add a genitive ending.

◆ *Forms of masculine* **N-**nouns

Nom.	der Herr	der Student
Acc.	den Herr**n**	den Student**en**
Dat.	dem Herr**n**	dem Student**en**
Gen.	des Herr**n**	des Student**en**

◆ *The interrogative pronoun* **wessen?**

Nom.	wer?
Acc.	wen?
Dat.	wem?
Gen.	**wessen?**

Uses of the genitive

◆ *Possession and other relationships*

das Buch **meines Freundes**   my friend's book
die Mutter **meines Freundes**   my friend's mother
die Farbe **der Blumen**   the color of the flowers

◆ *Prepositions*

(an)statt	instead of	Kommt Erika **(an)statt** ihrer Freundin?
trotz	in spite of	**Trotz** des Wetters wandern wir.
während	during	**Während** der Ferien wandern wir.
wegen	on account of	**Wegen** des Wetters bleiben sie zu Hause.

◆ *Genitive of time*

| **Indefinite past** | **Eines Tages** hat mir Jutta alles erklärt. | *One day* Jutta explained everything to me. |
| **Indefinite future** | **Eines Tages** mache ich das vielleicht. | *Someday* maybe I'll do that. |

Adjectives

◆ *Adjectives preceded by a definite article or* **der**-*word*

	Masculine	Neuter	Feminine	Plural
Nom.	der alt**e** Mann	das klein**e** Kind	die jung**e** Frau	die gut**en** Freunde
Acc.	den alt**en** Mann	das klein**e** Kind	die jung**e** Frau	die gut**en** Freunde
Dat.	dem alt**en** Mann	dem klein**en** Kind	der jung**en** Frau	den gut**en** Freunden
Gen.	des alt**en** Mannes	des klein**en** Kindes	der jung**en** Frau	der gut**en** Freunde

	M.	**N.**	**F.**	**Pl.**
Nom.	e	e	e	en
Acc.	en	e	e	en
Dat.	en	en	en	en
Gen.	en	en	en	en

◆ Adjectives preceded by an indefinite article or *ein-word*

	Masculine	Neuter	Feminine	Plural
Nom.	ein alt**er** Mann	ein klein**es** Kind	eine jung**e** Frau	meine gut**en** Freunde
Acc.	einen alt**en** Mann	ein klein**es** Kind	eine jung**e** Frau	meine gut**en** Freunde
Dat.	einem alt**en** Mann	einem klein**en** Kind	einer jung**en** Frau	meinen gut**en** Freunden
Gen.	eines alt**en** Mannes	eines klein**en** Kindes	einer jung**en** Frau	meiner gut**en** Freunde

	M.	N.	F.	Pl.
Nom.	er	es	e	en
Acc.	en	es	e	en
Dat.	en	en	en	en
Gen.	en	en	en	en

◆ Unpreceded adjectives

	Masculine	Neuter	Feminine	Plural
Nom.	gut**er** Wein	gut**es** Brot	gut**e** Wurst	gut**e** Brötchen
Acc.	gut**en** Wein	gut**es** Brot	gut**e** Wurst	gut**e** Brötchen
Dat.	gut**em** Wein	gut**em** Brot	gut**er** Wurst	gut**en** Brötchen
Gen.	gut**en** Weines	gut**en** Brotes	gut**er** Wurst	gut**er** Brötchen

	M.	N.	F.	Pl.
Nom.	er	es	e	e
Acc.	en	es	e	e
Dat.	em	em	er	en
Gen.	en	en	er	er

Ordinal numbers

1.	erst-	6.	sechst-	21.	einundzwanzigst-
2.	zweit-	7.	siebt-	32.	zweiunddreißigst-
3.	dritt-	8.	acht-	100.	hundertst-
				1000.	tausendst-

The ordinals (numbers indicating position in a sequence) are formed by adding **-t** to the numbers 1–19 and **-st** to numbers beyond 19. Exceptions are **erst-, dritt-, siebt-,** and **acht-**.

Dies ist mein **drittes** Semester.   This is my third semester.

The ordinals take adjective endings.

Auf dem Markt vor dem Rathaus von Basel ist Markt.

KApitel 10

BAUSTEINE FÜR GESPRÄCHE

Hast du dich erkältet?	**Have you caught a cold?**

Elisabeth: Du hustest ja fürchterlich.

Rainer: Ja, ich habe mich erkältet. Der Hals tut mir furchtbar weh.

Elisabeth: Hast du Fieber?

Rainer: Ein bißchen — 38.

Elisabeth: Du siehst ganz schön blaß aus.

Rainer: Ich fühle mich auch krank. Vielleicht ist es besser, wenn ich zum Arzt gehe.

Elisabeth: Ja, wir wollen doch am Sonntag zusammen Ski laufen.

You're coughing terribly.

Yes, I've caught a cold. My throat's hurting me a lot.

Do you have a fever?

A little—38 *[= 100.4°F].*

You look pretty pale.

I do feel pretty sick. Maybe I'd better go to the doctor.

Yes, after all we do want to go skiing together on Sunday.

Fragen

1. Beschreiben° Sie Rainers Krankheit°.
2. Warum ist es besser, daß er zum Arzt geht?

Wer in diesen Wochen in deutschen Landen unterwegs ist, sollte sich vorsehen: Erkältungskrankheiten drohen an verschiedenen Plätzen.

1. Was hast du? A fellow student looks pale. Ask what the matter is.

Inquiring about someone's health

Sie	*Gesprächspartner/in*
Du siehst blaß aus. Was hast du°?	Mir geht es nicht gut.
	Ich fühle mich nicht wohl°.
	Mir ist schlecht.°
	Ich habe | **Kopfschmerzen.**
	Zahnschmerzen°.
	Magenschmerzen°.
	Ich bin erkältet.
	Ich habe etwas Fieber.
	Mir tut der Hals° weh.

2. Geht es dir besser? Ask a friend about her/his cold.

Sie	*Gesprächspartner/in*
Was macht deine Erkältung?	Es geht mir | **besser.**
	schon besser.
	schlechter.
	Ich fühle mich | **krank.**
	schwach°.
	schwächer als gestern.

3. Das tut mir leid. You can't join in various plans because of a cold. Your friend expresses regret.

Sie	*Gesprächspartner/in*
Ich bin furchtbar erkältet.	Ach, wie dumm!
Ich kann heute nicht | **Ski laufen.**	Schade°.
zum Fest kommen.	Das tut mir leid.
ins Kino gehen.	Hoffentlich fühlst du dich morgen besser.

4. Wie fühlst du dich? Ask a fellow student about health matters.

1. Fühlst du dich nicht wohl?
2. Hast du dich erkältet?
3. Hast du Fieber?
4. Was machst du, wenn du Fieber hast?
5. Gehst du zum Arzt, wenn du dich erkältet hast?
6. Wie oft gehst du zum Zahnarzt?

Vokabeln

— Substantive —

die **Erkältung** cold (*illness*)
das **Fieber** fever
der **Hals** throat, neck
der **Kopf, ⁻e** head
die **Krankheit, -en** illness
der **Magen** stomach; die
   Magenschmerzen (*pl.*)
   stomachache

der **Schmerz, -en** pain
der **Zahn, ⁻e** tooth; die
   Zahnschmerzen (*pl.*) toothache

weg – gone

— Verben —

beschreiben, beschrieben to describe
sich erkälten to catch a cold;
   erkältet: ich bin erkältet I have
   a cold

sich fühlen to feel (*ill, well etc.*)
husten to cough

— Andere Wörter —

bißchen: ein bißchen a little bit
blaß pale
fürchterlich horrible, horribly
schade that's too bad, a pity, a
   shame

schwach weak; **schwächer** weaker
wohl well

— Besondere Ausdrücke —

ganz schön really quite; **ganz
   schön blaß** pretty pale
Mir ist schlecht. I feel nauseated.
Was macht deine Erkältung?
   How's your cold?

Was hast du? What is wrong with
   you? What's the matter?
weh tun (+ *dat.*) to hurt; **Die Füße
   tun mir weh.** My feet hurt.

Erweiterung des Wortschatzes

1 Körperteile

1. der Arm, -e
2. der Finger, -
3. der Fuß, ⸚e
4. der Kopf, ⸚e
5. der Mund, ⸚er
6. der Hals, ⸚e
7. der Magen, -
8. das Auge, -n
9. das Bein, -e
10. das Gesicht, -er
11. das Haar, -e
12. das Ohr, -en
13. die Nase, -n
14. die Hand, ⸚e

15. der Rücken -
16. das Knie -

1. Was tut dir weh?   Your hypochondriac friend asks whether something hurts. Respond.

Gesprächspartner/in	*Sie*
Tut dir | **der Kopf** weh? \ der Hals	Ja, mir tut [der Kopf] furchtbar weh. \ Nein, [der Kopf] tut mir (gar) nicht weh.
Tun dir die | **Füße** weh? \ Augen \ Ohren

2. Zeig auf deinen Kopf.   Assume you are helping someone (**Gesprächspartner/in**) learn the parts of the body in German. Tell him/her to point to the part you name.

3. Wie sieht er/sie aus? Your friend (**Gesprächspartner/in**) is talking about someone that he/she recently brought to a party. You can't recall the person. Ask your friend the following questions.

Ist er/sie groß oder klein?
Hat er/sie blonde/schwarze/braune/rote Haare?
Und die Nase? Ist sie klein oder groß?
Und die Beine? Sind sie lang oder kurz?

2 Wann macht man was?

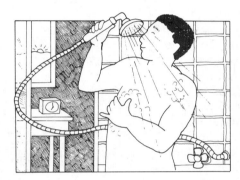

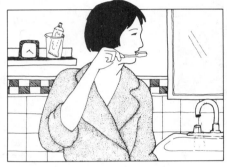

Wann duschst du dich?
Ich dusche mich morgens.

Wann putzt du dir die Zähne?
Ich putze mir morgens die Zähne.

Wann rasierst du dich?
Ich rasiere mich morgens.

Wann ziehst du dich an?
Ich ziehe mich morgens an.

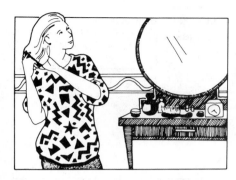

Wann kämmst du dich?
Ich kämme mich morgens.

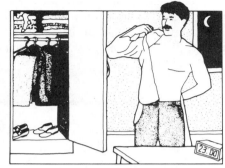

Wann ziehst du dich aus?
Ich ziehe mich abends aus.

Wann wäschst du dir Gesicht und
Hände?
Ich wasche mir abends Gesicht und
Hände.

Wann putzt du dir wieder die Zähne?
Ich putze mir abends wieder die
Zähne.

◆ Verben

sich an·ziehen, angezogen to get dressed, **ich ziehe mich an** I get dressed;
to put on, **ich ziehe mir die Schuhe an** I put on my shoes

sich aus·ziehen, ausgezogen to get undressed, **ich ziehe mich aus** I get
undressed; to take off, **ich ziehe mir die Schuhe aus** I take off my shoes

sich duschen to shower; **ich dusche mich** I take a shower

sich kämmen to comb; **ich kämme mich** I comb my hair; **ich kämme mir die
Haare** I comb my hair

sich rasieren to shave; **er rasiert sich** he shaves

sich waschen (wäscht), gewaschen to wash; **ich wasche mich** I wash myself; **ich wasche mir die Hände** I wash my hands

4. Der Tagesablauf°   Describe your daily routine: when you get   daily routine
up, when you shower, and so on. Then ask your partner ques-
tions about her/his routine.

Describing morning routines

▶   *Um [sieben] stehe ich auf. Danach [dusche ich mich]. Dann [ziehe ich mich
an]. Zum Frühstück esse ich [Toast].*

As a consequence of its location bordering France, Italy, and German-speaking countries, Switzerland has four official languages (**Amtssprachen**). Approximately 1% of the population speaks a language related to French and Italian, Rhaeto-Romanic (**Rätoromanisch**), 5% speak Italian, and 20% French. The majority of the population (74%) speaks German. Although **Schriftdeutsch** is taught in the schools, the primary language of German-speaking Swiss in both public and private life is Swiss German (**Schwyzerdütsch**).

Deutsch, Französisch und Italienisch sind in der Schweiz Amtssprachen.

DIE SCHWEIZ

Vorbereitung auf das Lesen

◆ *Zum Thema*

Was wissen Sie über die Schweiz? Was meinen Sie?

1. Wie groß ist die Schweiz? Größer als Österreich oder nur halb so groß?
2. Wie viele Einwohner hat die Schweiz? 6,5 Millionen oder 12 Millionen?

3. Was ist die Hauptstadt der Schweiz?
4. Wie viele Nachbarländer hat die Schweiz? Acht oder fünf?
5. Wie heißen die Nachbarländer?

Suchen Sie die folgenden Städte auf der Landkarte.

Basel ◇ Bern ◇ Chur ◇ Genf ◇ Lugano ◇ Luzern ◇ St. Moritz ◇ Zermatt ◇ Zürich

◆ *Leitfragen*

1. CH bedeutet „Confoederatio Helvetica". Was hat das mit der Autonomie der Kantone zu tun?
2. Wie wird man Schweizer Bürger(in)?

   Stichworte: Gemeinde ◇ **ein** Ort ◇ kosten ◇ Bern ◇ politische Einstellung

3. Warum ist die Qualität der Produkte aus der Schweiz so wichtig?

   Stichworte: Rohstoffe ◇ bezahlen ◇ Lebensstandard ◇ Neutralität

4. Wie kann es in einem so kleinen Land 26 verschiedene Kantone geben?

   Stichworte: Geschichte ◇ 13. bis 19. Jahrhundert ◇ besondere Mischung ◇ Schweizerdeutsch

5. Was sind die Unterschiede zwischen der Schweiz und den anderen deutschsprachigen Ländern?

   Stichworte: Mentalität ◇ Geschichte ◇ Sprache

Mit dem Zug fährt man sicher, schnell und bequem. (Glacier Express, Disentis, Schweiz)

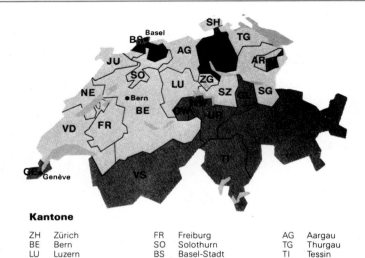

Kantone

ZH	Zürich	FR	Freiburg	AG	Aargau
BE	Bern	SO	Solothurn	TG	Thurgau
LU	Luzern	BS	Basel-Stadt	TI	Tessin
UR	Uri	BL	Basel-Land	VD	Waadt
SZ	Schwyz	SH	Schaffhausen	VS	Wallis
OW	Obwalden	AR	Appenzell A.-Rh.	NE	Neuenburg
NW	Nidwalden	AI	Appenzell I.-Rh.	GE	Genf
GL	Glarus	SG	St. Gallen	JU	Jura
ZG	Zug	GR	Graubünden		

41.228 qkm
6,4 Millionen Einwohner
etwa halb so groß wie Österreich oder Maine
etwas kleiner als Neuschottland° (52.841 qkm)   Nova Scotia
5 Bundesstaat° mit 26 Kantonen°   Federal State / cantons
parlamentarische Demokratie
Hauptstadt: Bern
5 Nachbarn: F, D, A, FL, I*

*D*er offizielle Name für die Schweiz ist „Schweizerische Eidgenossen-
10 schaft°", auf lateinisch „Confoederatio Helvetica". Daher das internationale   confederation
Autokennzeichen° CH. Dieser Name deutet an°, daß die Schweiz weniger *ein*   abbr. for country of registry /
Land ist als eine Sammlung° von autonomen Kantonen.   **deutet an:** indicates
    Die 26 Kantone nehmen ihre Autonomie sehr ernst. Zum Beispiel wird   collection
ein Ausländer nicht in der Hauptstadt Schweizer Bürger, sondern der Prozeß
15 beginnt in der Gemeinde°. Eine junge Schweizerin — sie ist gerade Bürgerin   community
geworden — erzählt: „Um Bürger zu werden, muß man erst einmal lange, 12
Jahre, an *einem* Ort wohnen. Diese Gemeinde muß mich also als Bürgerin
akzeptieren. Das Ganze hat zweitausend Franken gekostet. Das kann auch

---

*Autokennzeichen: F = Frankreich, D = Bundesrepublik Deutschland, A = Österreich, FL =
Fürstentum Liechtenstein, I = Italien

viel mehr sein. Wenn eine Gemeinde Leute und Steuerzahler° braucht, ist es   taxpayers
20 billiger. Wenn nicht, ist es teurer. Nach diesem ersten Schritt gehen die
Papiere zum Bund°, also nach Bern. Danach geht's weiter an den Kanton.   Federal Government
Irgendwann° überprüft° man auch die politische Einstellung°. Da gibt's   at some point / test / orienta-
Fragen wie: ‚Welche Zeitungen lesen Sie? Welche Fernsehsendungen sehen   tion
Sie?' So kompliziert ist der ganze Prozeß."
25   Bei einem Gespräch in einer amerikanischen Deutschklasse fragten° die   asked
Studenten zwei Besucherinnen, Helena aus Chur und Marta aus Luzern:
„Wenn ihr an die Schweiz denkt, welche Stichwörter fallen euch ein?"

Marta: Also zuerst einmal Qualität, Präzision, Zuverlässigkeit° und Pünkt-   dependability
    lichkeit. Dann eine starke Wirtschaft.
30 *Helena:* Und ganz bestimmt Neutralität. Vielleicht dann noch Fremden-
    verkehr°, also Tourismus.   tourism
Marta: Mir fallen auch noch die Unterschiede zwischen den Kantonen ein.
Studentin: Könnt ihr mal erklären, was ihr mit Qualität meint?
Helena: Wir sind ein kleines Land, fast ohne Rohstoffe. Wir müssen
35   Rohstoffe und Lebensmittel importieren. Um die bezahlen zu können,
    müssen wir auf den Weltmärkten° konkurrieren können. Das können wir   world markets
    nur mit Qualität. Wir machen also Qualitätsprodukte, Maschinen z.B.,
    chemische Produkte, Instrumente und Apparate. Die sind die Basis für
    unsere starke Wirtschaft. Und die starke Wirtschaft ist wiederum° die Basis   in turn
40   für unseren hohen Lebensstandard.
Marta: Die starke Wirtschaft ist auch die Basis für unsere Neutralität. Nur
    wenn wir wirtschaftlich stark sind, können wir unabhängig° sein. Und nur   independent
    wenn man unabhängig ist, kann man neutral sein. Neutralität ist für die
    Schweiz ein zentraler Wert°.   value
45 *Student:* Warum eigentlich?
Marta: Wir haben in zwei Weltkriegen die Erfahrung gemacht°, daß   **Erfahrung gemacht:** learned
    Neutralität gute Politik ist.
Student: Ich möchte noch wissen, warum ihr die Unterschiede zwischen den
    Kantonen erwähnt habt. Schließlich ist die Schweiz doch nur ein sehr
50   kleines Land. Und in diesem Land soll es 26 verschiedene Kantone geben?
Helena: Ja, das hängt wieder mit der Geschichte zusammen. Das Land hat
    sich eben langsam entwickelt. Mit drei Kantonen hat es im dreizehnten
    Jahrhundert angefangen. Erst im neunzehnten Jahrhundert war die
    Schweiz komplett, sozusagen°. Man muß sich klar machen, daß jeder   so to speak
    Kanton zu° einer bestimmten Zeit, unter bestimmten Umständen° und mit   at / circumstances
55   ganz bestimmten Menschen Teil der Schweiz geworden ist. So hat jeder
    Kanton seine besondere Mischung aus Menschenart, Religion, Geschichte
    und Sprache. Zum Beispiel gibt es im Schweizerdeutsch noch Unter-
    schiede. Die sind zum Teil so stark, daß die Leute manchmal Schwierig-
    keiten haben, einander zu verstehen.

CERN bei Genf ist das größte Zentrum der Welt für subatomare Forschung.

60 *Studentin:* Nun noch einmal eine ganz andere Frage: Wo oder wie seht ihr eigentlich die Unterschiede zu den anderen deutschsprachigen Ländern?

Marta: Gegenüber° Deutschland sehe ich eigentlich nicht so große Unterschiede. In beiden Ländern ist die Wirtschaft gleich stark. Und ich sehe oft eine ähnliche Mentalität°. Dagegen° scheint mir die Mentalität in 65 Österreich anders zu sein. Da sehe ich mehr Nonchalance.

Helena: Zu der Frage muß man vielleicht auch noch sagen, daß die Schweizer sich durch ihre Geschichte von den Deutschen unterscheiden und vor allem durch ihre Sprache. Die Umgangssprache°, die Alltagssprache° ist eben Schweizerdeutsch. Und das unterscheidet sich doch ganz enorm vom 70 Hochdeutschen. Mir fällt da gerade ein berndeutsches Chanson° von Mani Matter ein. Es heißt „Heidi" und beginnt so:

in contrast to

mentality / in contrast

colloquial language / everyday language

song

Är wont a dr glyche gass
und i bin mit dir i d'klass
so ischs cho, das mir grad beidi
75   ds härz a di verlore hei.
   Heidi, mir wei di beidi,
   beidi, Heidi, hei di gärn.

Die hochdeutsche Übersetzung ist:

Er wohnt in der gleichen Gasse°,   street
80   und ich bin mit dir in der Klasse.
So ist es, daß wir gerade beide
das Herz an dich verloren haben.
   Heidi, wir wollen dich beide,
   beide, Heidi, haben dich gern.

Mit den Kantonen Schwyz, Uri und Unterwalden begann im Jahre 1291 die Schweiz. (Bild im Bundeshaus in Bern)

Switzerland's roots reach back more than 2,000 years, when a Celtic people called the Helvetians lived in the area that is now Switzerland. Over the course of several hundred years, the Alemanni, the Burgundians, and the Franks settled there as well. When the Holy Roman Empire came into existence in A.D. 962, most of this area became part of it. Soon after the Habsburg family, as the rulers of the Empire, had gained control over these regions, the cantons (**Kantone**) Schwyz, Uri, and Unterwalden started the Swiss Confederation (1291) and fought together for their independence. Between 1315 and 1388 Switzerland defeated Austria in three different wars and finally gained independence from the Holy Roman Empire in 1499. A period of expansion and integration of more cantons followed.

Today Switzerland is composed of 23 cantons, three of which are divided into half-cantons. It does not have a strong central government. The cantons function with a large degree of political autonomy.

Fragen zum Lesestück

1. Was deutet der Name „Confoederatio Helvetica" an?
2. Wie lange muß man an *einem* Ort wohnen, wenn man Bürger werden will?
3. Was hat es für die junge Schweizerin gekostet, Bürgerin zu werden?
4. Was will man wissen, wenn man die politische Einstellung überprüft?
5. Nennen Sie fünf Stichwörter zum Thema Schweiz.
6. Warum müssen die Schweizer Qualitätsprodukte exportieren?
7. Warum ist die starke Wirtschaft für die Neutralität wichtig?
8. Warum ist Neutralität für die Schweiz so zentral?
9. Wie viele Kantone gibt es in der Schweiz?
10. Wie viele Kantone hat es im 13. Jahrhundert gegeben?
11. Warum ist jeder Kanton anders?
12. Warum haben Schweizer manchmal Schwierigkeiten, einander zu verstehen?
13. Warum sieht Marta keine großen Unterschiede zwischen der Schweiz und Deutschland?
14. Was sieht sie in der österreichischen Mentalität?
15. Was unterscheidet die Deutschen von den Schweizern?
16. In welchem Dialekt ist Matters Chanson?

Although political life in Switzerland is essentially based in the cantons, federal affairs are represented by several constitutional bodies.

Abstimmung über das Wahlrecht im Kanton Glarus

Swiss citizens who are more than twenty years old have the right to vote for the National Council (**Nationalrat**). Each citizen can vote for a party and a candidate. Elections for the Council of States (**Ständerat**) vary according to cantonal law. The National Council and the Council of States form the Federal Assembly (**Bundesversammlung**), which elects a cabinet of Federal Ministers (**Bundesrat**) and the Federal President (**Bundespräsident**). Although the President is the head of state, his duties are largely ceremonial and he does not hold special power within the government.

Usually several times a year the Swiss voters take part in binding referenda on initiatives that propose new federal or cantonal laws. Despite its long democratic tradition, it was not until 1971 that women gained the right to vote in federal elections, and not until 1990 did women in Appenzell, a half-canton, receive the right to vote in local elections.

1. Rollenspiel In a group of four assume that one of you is a German, one an Austrian, one a Swiss, and the fourth an American making his or her first trip to Europe. You are all sitting in the same compartment on a train. The American wants to learn more about the German-speaking countries. You may want to include information about the geography (location, size, population, neighbors), economy, or history.

Vokabeln

— Substantive

der **Apparat, -e** apparatus, appliance

der **Bürger, -/die Bürgerin, -nen** citizen

das **Herz, -ens, -en** heart

das **Hochdeutsch** High German, standard German

das **Jahrhundert, -e** century

die **Klasse, -n** class; die **Deutschklasse** German class

der **Lebensstandard** standard of living

der **Ort, -e** place

das **Produkt, -e** product

der **Rohstoff, -e** raw material

der **Schritt, -e** step

die **Steuer, -n** tax

die **Übersetzung, -en** translation

die **Wirtschaft** economy

— Verben

akzeptieren to accept

beginnen, begonnen to begin

ein·fallen (fällt ein), ist eingefallen to occur (in one's mind)

(sich) entwickeln to develop

konkurrieren to compete

scheinen, geschienen to appear, seem

(sich) unterscheiden, unterschieden to differ; to distinguish

— Andere Wörter

hoch (höher, höchst) high; (**hoh-** before nouns, as in **ein hoher Preis**)

irgendwann at some time

stark (ä) strong

unabhängig independent

— Besondere Ausdrücke

erst einmal first of all

um ... zu (+ *infinitive*) (in order) to; **um Bürger zu werden** in order to become a citizen

zum Teil in part

Erweiterung des Wortschatzes

1 Adjectives used as nouns

Herr Schmidt ist **ein Bekannter** von mir.	Mr. Schmidt is an acquaintance of mine.
Frau Schneider ist **eine Bekannte** von mir.	Ms. Schneider is an acquaintance of mine.
So ein Auto ist nur für **die Reichen.**	Such a car is only for the rich.

Many adjectives can be used as nouns. They retain the adjective endings as though a noun were still there: **ein Deutscher (Mann), eine Deutsche (Frau).** In writing, adjectives used as nouns are capitalized.

1. Was bedeutet das?

1. Kennen Sie den Alten da?
2. Das ist Herr Wolf, ein guter Bekannter von mir.
3. Meine Eltern haben gute Bekannte in der Schweiz.
4. Mein Vater erzählt oft von einem Bekannten in Luzern.
5. Die Deutschen arbeiten nicht gern bei offener Tür.
6. Ein freundlicher junger Deutscher hat mir das gesagt.

Das Gute daran ist, daß es billig ist.	The good thing about it is that it is cheap.
Hast du **etwas Neues** gehört?	Have you heard anything new?
Ja, aber **nichts Gutes.**	Yes, but nothing good.

Adjectives expressing abstractions (**das Gute,** the good; **das Schöne,** the beautiful) are considered neuter nouns. They frequently follow words such as **etwas, nichts, viel,** and **wenig,** and take the ending **-es (etwas Schönes).** Note **etwas anderes,** where **anderes** is not capitalized.

2. Was bedeutet das?

1. In den Ferien haben wir viel Schönes gesehen.
2. Christl hat etwas Tolles zu erzählen.
3. Gestern haben wir nichts Besonderes gemacht.
4. Jetzt verstehe ich dich. Das ist etwas anderes.
5. Oliver hat etwas Merkwürdiges gesagt.

2 The adjectives *viel* and *wenig*

Wir haben **wenig** Geld, aber **viel** Zeit.	We have little money but lots of time.

When used as adjectives, **viel** and **wenig** usually have no endings in the singular.

Dieter hat **viele** Freunde.	Dieter has lots of friends.
Das kann man von **vielen** Menschen sagen.	You can say that about many people.

In the plural, **viel** and **wenig** take regular adjective endings.

---

3. Viel oder wenig? Choose several words from the list below. Ask your partner about the quantity she/he has (**Wieviel?/Wie viele?**). Then depending on the answer, ask for details (**Warum? Welche?**).

Freunde ◇ Freundinnen ◇ Kurse dieses Semester ◇ CDs ◇ Kassetten ◇ Freizeit° ◇ Geld

°free time

4. Eine Wohnung im Tessin A Swiss family living in Zürich would like to have a home in another part of Switzerland. In the newspaper they find three ads that interest them, one in French, one in German, and one in Italian. Because they want to be where it is warmer, they are attracted to the place in Tessin, a canton on the Italian border. Show what one can learn from the ad by answering the questions. If you need help, see Vocabulary for Authentic Text Activities in the Reference Section.

1. An welchem See liegt die Wohnung?
2. Wie groß ist die Wohnung?
3. Wo hat man Platz für Boot und Auto?
4. Was kann man in der Freizeit machen?
5. Wie teuer ist die Wohnung?
6. Was nimmt der Verkäufer° in Zahlung?
7. Wie kann man den Eigentümer° erreichen°?

°seller

°owner / reach

Westschweiz (inkl. Wallis) EL

Occasion unique à Yverdon

Une villa de maître, début XIXe, comprenant propriété attenante de 16 317 m², ainsi qu'une ferme à rénover. Situation dominante avec vue imprenable sur la ville et sur le lac de Neuchâtel, à 2 minutes en voiture du centre ville.
Pour plus de renseignements, écrire sous chiffre 22-120-5843, Est Vaudois, 1820 Montreux.

ELX977 855M

Tessin EE

Bootsgarage am Luganersee

in **Maroggia,** direkt am See, 3½-Zimmer-Wohnung inkl. Bootsgarage mit Aufzug, Parkplatz in Einstellhalle, Lift, Anteil an Aussenbad, Hallenbad, Sauna, Pergola mit Cheminée. Fr. 720 000.–. Nehme Ferrari oder Porsche in Zahlung.

Tel. (045) 21 71 77
(045) 51 25 43
Fax (045) 21 67 07

EEX977 676L

Pian San Giacomo/ San Bernardino GR, 1000 s/m

Vendo

Chalet

composto da:
1 appartamento con grande soggiorno, camino, 3 camere, servizi, grande terrazza
1 appartamento con soggiorno, camera, servizi, legnaia, lavanderia, riscaldamento elettrico
Grazioso giardino con tavolo in granito, posteggi, tranquillità, soleggiato, vista aperta, completamente arredato.
5 min. dalle piste di S. Bernardino, 40 min. di autostrada N 13 da Lugano o Locarno.
Prezzo Fr. 395 000.–. Tel. sera (091) 54 20 21.

EKX977 509G

5. Rollenspiel   Assume you and your partner are members of the Swiss family who want the place in Tessin. Discuss the pros and cons of buying it and decide whether you will make an offer.

> Stating advantages and disadvantages

GRAMMATIK UND ÜBUNGEN

1 Reflexive constructions

Accusative	Ich habe **mich** gewaschen.	I washed (myself).
Dative	Kaufst du **dir** einen neuen Farbfernseher?	Are you buying (yourself) a new color TV?

A reflexive pronoun indicates the same person or thing as the subject. A reflexive pronoun may be in either the accusative or the dative case, depending on its function in the sentence.

2 Forms of reflexive pronouns

	ich	**du**	**er/es/sie**	**wir**	**ihr**	**sie**	**Sie**
Accusative	mich	dich	**sich**	uns	euch	**sich**	**sich**
Dative	mir	dir	**sich**	uns	euch	**sich**	**sich**

Reflexive pronouns differ from personal pronouns only in the **er/es/sie, sie** (*pl.*), and **Sie** forms, which are all **sich.**

◆ *Use of accusative reflexive pronouns*

Direct object	Ich habe **mich** schnell gewaschen.	I washed (myself) in a hurry.
Object of preposition	Er macht es für **sich** selbst.	He's doing it for himself.

A reflexive pronoun is in the accusative case when it functions as a direct object or as the object of a preposition that requires the accusative.

**Kapellbrücke mit
Wasserturm (1333) in
Luzern**

1. Sie duschen sich abends. Say that the people mentioned below shower at night. Use the appropriate accusative reflexive pronoun in each instance.

▶ Veronika duscht sich abends. (Andreas) *Andreas duscht sich abends.*

1. Gabi und Rolf
2. du
3. ich
4. wir
5. ihr
6. Uwe

◆ *Use of dative reflexive pronouns*

Indirect object	Kaufst du **dir** einen neuen Computer?	Are you going to buy yourself a new computer?
Dative verb	Ich kann **mir** nicht helfen.	I can't help myself.
Object of preposition	Sprichst du von **dir?**	Are you talking about yourself?

A reflexive pronoun is in the dative case when it functions as an indirect object, the object of a dative verb, or the object of a preposition that requires the dative case.

◆ *mich/mir; dich/dir*

Accusative	Dative
Ich wasche **mich.**	Ich wasche **mir** die Haare.
Zieh **dich** an.	Zieh **dir** einen warmen Pulli an.

Look at the chart on page 320 again. Note that only two reflexive pronouns differ in the accusative and dative forms:

Accusative	mich	dich
Dative	mir	dir

All other reflexive pronouns are the same in both cases:

Accusative	Dative
Er wäscht **sich.**	Er wäscht **sich** die Haare.
Wir ziehen **uns** an.	Wir ziehen **uns** einen warmen Pulli an.

2 Was kaufen sie sich? Say what the people mentioned would like to buy for themselves on their next shopping trip. Use the dative reflexive pronoun.

▶   Margot / ein neues Fahrrad   *Margot möchte sich ein neues Fahrrad kaufen.*

1. Schmidts / einen neuen Computer
2. ich / eine gute Stereoanlage
3. wir / einen kleinen Farbfernseher
4. Paul / einen neuen Kassettenrecorder
5. Brauns / einen neuen Küchentisch
6. ich / einen teuren CD-Spieler
7. du / ein amerikanisches Auto
8. ihr / einige CDs
9. du / ein lustiges Poster

3. Was möchtest du dir kaufen? You would like to buy some new piece of clothing. What will it be? Ask four other persons what they would like to buy.

	Discussing wants

▶   *Ich möchte mir [eine neue Jacke] kaufen. Was möchtest du dir kaufen?*

3 Reflexive verbs in German vs. English

Setz dich.	Sit down.
Fühlst du **dich** nicht wohl?	Don't you feel well?
Hast du **dich** gestern **erkältet?**	Did you catch a cold yesterday?
Hast du **dich** zu leicht **angezogen?**	Did you dress too lightly?
Mark hat **sich** heute nicht **rasiert.**	Mark didn't shave today.

In German, some verbs regularly have a reflexive pronoun as part of the verb pattern. The English equivalents of these verbs do not have reflexive pronouns. In general, the reflexive construction is used more frequently in German than in English. In the vocabularies of this book, reflexive verbs are listed with the pronoun **sich: sich fühlen.**

 4. Noch einmal   Restate the sentences below with the cued subjects.

► Ich fühle mich nicht wohl. (Heike)   *Heike fühlt sich nicht wohl.*

1. Fühlt Heike sich heute besser? (du)
2. Inge hat sich gestern erkältet. (ich)
3. Wie hast du dich erkältet? (Dieter)
4. Paul zieht sich später an. (wir)
5. Wann ziehst du dich an? (ihr)
6. Wir haben uns an den Tisch gesetzt. (die Gäste)
7. Warum setzt Sonja sich nicht zu uns? (du)

5 Wie sagt man das?

1. Do you feel better today, Mr. Meier?
   —No, I don't feel well.
2. How did Astrid catch cold?
   —I don't know. Did she catch cold again?
3. Lotte, why haven't you dressed yet?
   —It's still early. I'll get dressed later.
4. Please sit down, Erna.
   —Thanks, I'll sit on this chair.
5. Why haven't you bathed yet?
   —I'll shower later.

4 Definite article with parts of the body

Ich habe **mir die** Hände gewaschen.	I washed *my* hands.
Hast du **dir die** Zähne geputzt?	Did you brush *your* teeth?

The reflexive pronoun in the dative often indicates that the accusative object belongs to the subject of the sentence. This is especially common with parts of the body. German uses a definite article and a dative pronoun where English uses a possessive adjective.

Ich muß **mir die** Schuhe anziehen.   I have to put on *my* shoes.

In German the definite article is also often used with clothing.

6. **Schon fertig.**   Say that you have washed and dressed and are ready to go out.

▶ Gesicht waschen   *Ich habe mir das Gesicht gewaschen.*

1. Hände waschen
2. Haare waschen
3. Haare kämmen

4. Zähne putzen
5. saubere Jeans anziehen
6. ein sauberes Hemd anziehen

7. Was mache ich?   With a partner take turns miming an action. One partner says what the other is doing.

▶ *Du putzt dir die Zähne.*

8. Was sagen Sie?   Answer the following questions for yourself and then compare your answers to those of a classmate.

1. Wann duschen oder baden Sie sich?
2. Waschen Sie sich abends oder morgens die Haare?
3. Mit was für einem Shampoo waschen Sie sich die Haare?
4. Wann putzen Sie sich die Zähne?
5. Mit welcher Zahnpasta° putzen Sie sich die Zähne?   toothpaste
6. Ziehen Sie sich die Schuhe aus, wenn Sie arbeiten?
7. Ziehen Sie sich alte Sachen an, wenn Sie abends nach Hause kommen?

5 Infinitives with *zu*

Infinitives with *zu*	Ich brauche heute nicht **zu** arbeiten.	I don't have to [need to] work today.
Modal and infinitive	Mußt du morgen arbeiten?	Do you have to work tomorrow?

In English, dependent infinitives used with most verbs are preceded by *to*. In German, dependent infinitives used with most verbs are preceded by **zu**. Dependent infinitives used with modals are not preceded by **zu**.

Das Kind versucht auf**zu**stehen.   The child tries to get up.
Vergiß nicht, Kuchen mit**zu**bringen.   Don't forget to bring cake.

When a separable-prefix verb is in the infinitive form, the **zu** comes between the prefix and the base form of the verb.

If an infinitive phrase contains **zu** + an infinitive and modifiers (e.g., **Kuchen**), it is set off by commas in writing. Note that an infinitive phrase after **brauchen** (e.g., **Ich brauche heute nicht zu arbeiten**) is not set off by commas.

Some verbs you know that can be followed by **zu** + an infinitive are **anfangen, aufhören, brauchen, scheinen, vergessen,** and **versuchen.**

9. Das macht man in Österreich. Tell about some of David's experiences in Austria and what he has learned or not learned.

▶ Er gibt jedem die Hand. (Er hat gelernt …)   *Er hat gelernt, jedem die Hand zu geben.*

1. Er macht die Tür zu. (Er vergißt oft …)
2. Er ißt mit Messer und Gabel. (Er versucht …)
3. Er bringt Blumen mit. (Er vergißt nicht …)
4. Er läuft mehr. (Er versucht …)
5. David geht am Sonntag spazieren. (Er kann …)
6. Er kauft im Bio-Laden ein. (Er hat angefangen …)
7. Er fährt eines Tages zur Kur. (Er möchte …)
8. Man sitzt lange im Café und liest Zeitung. (Man kann …)

10. Hausarbeit You and a friend are comparing notes about all the housework you do. Use the list of chores below to continue your conversation.

| Talking about household chores |

einkaufen ◇ kochen ◇ das Bett machen ◇ [bei der Hausarbeit] helfen ◇ abwaschen ◇ abtrocknen ◇ aufräumen ◇ [die Küche] sauber machen ◇ Fenster putzen ◇ [die Wäsche/das Auto] waschen ◇ [im Garten] arbeiten ◇ [das Auto] reparieren

Sie	*Gesprächspartner/in*
Ich muß [jeden Tag] [abwaschen], und du?	Ja, ich muß auch [abwaschen].
	Ich brauche nicht [abzuwaschen].
	Du meine Güte! Ich habe vergessen [abzuwaschen].

Jakob kann beim Zähneputzen
seine Paste nicht benutzen;

aus der Tube kommt nichts raus.
Doch dafür gibt's ja im Haus

einen Schraubstock – immerhin
zeigt der bald: noch ist was drin!

Aber löst man ein Problem,
ist das oft nicht angenehm.

◆ *Expressions requiring infinitives with **zu***

Es macht Spaß, mit dem Zug zu fahren.	It's fun to go by train.
Es ist schwer, früh aufzustehen.	It's hard to get up early.

Infinitives with **zu** are used after a number of expressions, such as **es ist Zeit, es ist schön, es ist schwer,** and **es macht Spaß.**

11. Nicole studiert in Hamburg.   Tell about some of Nicole's experiences at the University of Hamburg.

▶   Sie steht früh auf. Es ist schwer.   *Es ist schwer, früh aufzustehen.*

1. Sie fährt mit dem Zug. Es macht Spaß.
2. Sie versteht die Vorlesungen. Es ist nicht leicht.
3. Sie sitzt mit Freunden im Biergarten. Es ist gut.
4. Sie findet einen Studentenjob. Es ist schwer.
5. Sie wandert am Wochenende mit Freunden. Es ist schön.

12. Es macht Spaß …   You and your partner can get better acquainted by telling each other what you find to be fun, difficult, easy, good, and nice.

▶   Es ist schön, [am Sonntag nichts zu tun].
▶   Es ist schwer [zu schlafen].

Es macht Spaß …
Es ist schön …
Es ist schwer …
Es ist leicht …
Es ist gut …
Ich habe keine Zeit …

6 The construction *um … zu* + infinitive

Um Bürger **zu** werden, muß man 12 Jahre an einem Ort wohnen.	*(In order) to* become a citizen one must live 12 years in one place.

The German construction **um … zu** + infinitive is equivalent to the English construction *(in order) to* + infinitive.

13. Was meinen Sie? Complete the sentences and compare your ideas with those of your partner. Then make up one or two of your own sentences using **um ... zu.**

▶ *Um gesund zu bleiben, [muß man viel Sport treiben].*

Um schöne Ferien zu haben, ...
Um gute Zensuren zu bekommen, ...
Um viele Freunde zu haben, ...
[Um ... zu ... , ...]

7 Comparison of adjectives and adverbs

◆ Comparison of equality

Ute ist **so** groß **wie** Christel.	Ute is as tall as Christel.
Erik schwimmt nicht **so** gut **wie** Klaus.	Erik doesn't swim as well as Klaus.
Diese Reise ist genau**so** schön **wie** die letzte.	This trip is just as nice as the last one.

The construction **so ... wie** is used to express the equality of a person, thing, or activity to another. It is equivalent to English *as ... as*.

14. Ich kann das auch. Say that you have some of the same qualities as your friends and can do things as well.

▶ *Franz ist intelligent.* *Ich bin genauso intelligent wie er.*

1. Klaus ist freundlich.
2. Martha arbeitet viel.
3. Johann singt schön.
4. Frank spielt gut Gitarre.
5. Rita kann schnell schwimmen.
6. Christian kann lecker kochen.
7. David spricht gut Deutsch.

◆ Comparative forms

Base form	**klein**	Österreich ist **klein.**	Austria is small.
Comparative	**kleiner**	Die Schweiz ist noch **kleiner.**	Switzerland is even smaller.

The comparative of an adjective or adverb is formed by adding **-er** to the base form.

Lore arbeitet **schwerer als** Kai. Lore works harder than Kai.
Lore ist **fleißiger als** Kai. Lore is more industrious than Kai.

The comparative form plus **als** is used to compare people, things, or activities. **Als** is equivalent to English *than*.

Base form	dunkel	teuer
Comparative	**dunkler**	**teurer (teuerer)**

Adjectives ending in **-el** drop the final **-e** of the base form before adding **-er**. Adjectives ending in **-er** may follow the same pattern.

15. Meine neue Wohnung   Describe your new apartment to a friend by comparing it to the old one that she/he knew. Use the comparative form of the predicate adjective. Replace the italicized words with **noch**.

▶   Deine alte Wohnung war *sehr* schön. *Meine neue ist noch schöner.*

1. Deine alte war *schön* hell.
2. Die alte war *sehr* praktisch.
3. Deine alte Wohnung war *aber* klein.
4. Die war *aber* modern.
5. Deine alte war *wirklich* toll.
6. Die alte war *auch* teuer.

Base form	**groß**	Hamburg ist **groß**.
Comparative	**größer**	Hamburg ist **größer** als Bremen.

Many common one-syllable words with stem vowel **a**, **o**, or **u** add an umlaut in the comparative form, including **alt, dumm, jung, kalt, kurz, lang, oft, rot**, and **warm**. Adjectives and adverbs of this type are indicated in the vocabularies of this book as follows: **kalt (ä)**.

16. Erik ist anders.   Your parents have met your new friend Andreas, but not your friend Erik. Tell them Erik is just the opposite of what they think.

▶   Ist Erik kleiner als Andreas? *Nein, er ist größer.*

1. Ist er älter?
2. Sind seine Haare kürzer?
3. Ist er intelligenter?

▶   Ist er nervöser? *Nein, er ist ruhiger.*

4. Ist er fleißiger?
5. Ist er lustiger?
6. Ist er freundlicher?

17. Ist sie/er anders? You are describing someone (a friend, a roommate, a sister, or a brother) to your partner. Your partner asks several questions to gain a clearer picture of how this person differs from you.

Making comparisons

Sie	*Gesprächspartner/in*
Mein Bruder ist groß und hat braune Haare.	Ist er größer als du?
[…]	

Base form	gern	gut	hoch	viel
Comparative	**lieber**	**besser**	**höher**	**mehr**

A few adjectives and adverbs have irregular comparative forms.

Jörg sieht **gern** fern.	Jörg likes to watch TV.
Karin liest **lieber.**	Karin prefers [likes more] to read.

The English equivalent of **lieber** is *to prefer*, or *preferably*, or *rather* with a verb.

18. In einem Geschäft You and a friend are browsing in a store, comparing items you see.

▶ Der Kühlschrank ist groß. *Aber dieser Kühlschrank ist größer.*

1. Die Waschmaschine ist billig.
2. Der Kassettenrecorder kostet viel.
3. Die Küchenmaschine sieht gut aus.
4. Das Radio ist teuer.
5. Der Kühlschrank ist hoch.
6. Der Fernseher sieht gut aus.
7. Die Preise sind hoch.

Morgen, morgen, nur nicht heute,
sagen alle faulen Leute.

19. Was machst du lieber? Your partner tells you what he/she likes to do. Say what you prefer to do. Some suggestions are given below.

Gesprächspartner/in	*Sie*
Ich spiele gern Fußball.	Ich spiele lieber Hockey.
Ich trinke gern Kaffee.	…
Ich esse gern Steak.	
Ich gehe gern ins Kino.	
Ich spiele gern Volleyball.	
Ich fahre gern mit der Bahn.	
Ich lese gern Zeitung.	
Ich tanze gern Tango.	
Ich lerne gern Deutsch.	

Eishockey ◇ Kuchen ◇ Rock 'n' Roll ◇ ins Theater ◇ Krimis ◇ mit dem Auto ◇ Chinesisch ◇ Tee ◇ Hockey

20. Was machst du lieber? Your partner asks which chores and leisure activities you prefer.

Gesprächspartner/in		*Sie*
Was machst du lieber?	**Laufen oder radfahren?**	Ich [laufe] lieber.
	Zeitungen lesen oder Bücher?	
	Klassische Musik hören oder Rock?	
	Das Badezimmer saubermachen oder das Wohnzimmer aufräumen?	
	Abwaschen oder abtrocknen?	
	Gartenarbeit oder Hausarbeit?	
	Ins Kino gehen oder zu einer Party gehen?	

◆ *Preceded comparative adjectives*

Das ist ein besser**er** Plan.	That's a better plan.
Hast du eine besser**e** Idee?	Do you have a better idea?

Preceded comparative adjectives take the same adjective endings as those in the base form.

21. Es ist alles besser. Two friends are talking about things they have or experience. One tries to outdo the other.

▶ Ich habe ein großes Auto.   *Ich habe ein größeres Auto.*

1. Ich habe eine schöne Wohnung.
2. Ich wohne in einem hohen Haus.
3. Ich kaufe ein teures Kleid.
4. Ich habe einen guten Professor.
5. Ich habe einen Freund/eine Freundin mit einem großen Auto.
6. Ich wohne in einem alten Haus.
7. Ich trage einen warmen Pulli.

◆ *Superlative forms*

Base form	alt	Trier ist sehr **alt**.	Trier is very old.
Superlative	ältest-	Es ist die **älteste** Stadt in Deutschland.	It is the oldest city in Germany.

The superlative of an adjective is formed by adding **-st** to the base form. The **-st** is expanded to **-est** if the adjective stem ends in **-d, -t,** or a sibilant. The superlative of **groß** is an exception: **größt-**. The words that add umlaut in the comparative also add umlaut in the superlative. Preceded superlative adjectives take the same endings as those of the base form.

22. Was weißt du über Deutschland? Your friend is checking on her/his facts about Germany. Tell your friend that the places she/he asks about are actually the oldest, largest, and so on.

▶ Trier ist eine alte Stadt, nicht?   *Ja, Trier ist die älteste Stadt Deutschlands.*

1. Heidelberg ist eine alte Universität, nicht?
2. Herdecke in Nordrhein-Westfalen ist eine junge Universität, nicht?
3. Bayern ist ein großes Land, nicht?
4. Bremen ist ein kleines Land, nicht?
5. Berlin ist sicher eine sehr große Stadt.
6. Der Rhein ist bestimmt ein langer Fluß°.   river

Im Winter arbeitet Frau Greif **am schwersten**.	In the winter Mrs. Greif works *(the) hardest*.
Im Winter sind die Tage **am kürzesten**.	In the winter the days are *(the) shortest*.

The superlative of adverbs (e.g., **am schwersten**) is formed by inserting the word **am** in front of the adverb and adding the ending **-(e)sten** to the adverb. The superlative of predicate adjectives (e.g., **am kürzesten**) is formed according to the same pattern.

23. Alles ist am größten. Claudia speaks in superlatives. When someone says something, she repeats it and makes it the greatest, coldest, slowest, etc. Take her role.

▶ Im Sommer sind die Tage lang.   *Im Sommer sind die Tage am*
    längsten.

1. Im Herbst sind die Bäume interessant.
2. Im Frühling sind die Blumen schön.
3. Im Winter sind die Tage kalt.
4. Regina fährt langsam.
5. Hans-Jürgen arbeitet schwer.
6. Ingrid und Thomas tanzen schön.

Erich ist der jüngste Sohn und   Erich is the youngest son and
    Hans ist **der älteste (Sohn).**   Hans is *the oldest (son).*

The superlative of attributive adjectives (with a following noun expressed or understood) is formed by inserting **der/das/die** in front of the adjective and adding an ending to the superlative form of the adjective.

**Ein Paradies für
Skiläufer und
Bergsteiger: Zermatt
mit Matterhorn (4.477
Meter)**

> 1. Im Sommer sind die Blumen **am schönsten.**
> 2. Diese Blume ist **die schönste.**
>   Diese Blumen sind **die schönsten.**

The above chart shows the two patterns of superlative predicate adjectives. The adjectives preceded by **der/das/die** have **-e** in the singular and **-en** in the plural.

24. Die schönsten, neuesten Sachen Like Claudia, Peter finds everything the greatest. Take his role.

▶ Diese Schuhe sind sehr billig. *Diese Schuhe sind die billigsten.*

1. Diese Blumen sind sehr schön.
2. Dieses Auto ist sehr teuer.
3. Diese Jacke ist sehr praktisch.
4. Dieser Fernseher ist ganz neu.
5. Dieser CD-Spieler ist billig.
6. Diese Stereoanlage ist ziemlich teuer.

Base form	gern	gut	hoch	viel
Comparative	**lieber**	**besser**	**höher**	**mehr**
Superlative	**liebst-**	**best-**	**höchst-**	**meist-**

The adjectives and adverbs that are irregular in the comparative are also irregular in the superlative. Irregular forms are indicated in the vocabularies of this book as follows: **gern (lieber, liebst-).**

25. Viele Fragen Answer the questions below, using the superlative.

▶ Heike trinkt lieber Bier als Kaffee. Und Wein? *Wein trinkt sie am liebsten.*

1. Frank spielt lieber Tennis als Basketball. Und Fußball?
2. Peter schreibt besser als Erik. Und Heidi?
3. Inge kocht besser als Erik. Und Mark?
4. Ein großer Opel kostet mehr als ein kleiner Volkswagen. Und ein Mercedes?
5. Klaus spricht mehr als seine Schwester. Und sein Bruder?
6. Heidi arbeitet lieber nachmittags als abends. Und morgens?
7. Am Nachmittag ist das Fieber höher als am Morgen. Und am Abend?

26. Ihre Meinung   Answer the questions for yourself and then compare your answers with those of your partner.

1. Was trinken Sie am liebsten?
2. Was essen Sie am liebsten?
3. An welchem Tag gehen Sie am spätesten ins Bett?
4. Welche Sprache sprechen Sie am besten?
5. Was studieren Sie am liebsten?
6. Wer arbeitet in Ihrer Familie am schwersten?
7. Welchen Sport treiben Sie am liebsten?
8. Welchen Teil Amerikas finden Sie am schönsten?
9. Welcher amerikanische Politiker spricht am besten?
10. Welche amerikanische Stadt ist die schönste?

WIEDERHOLUNG

1. Was machen Sie lieber?   Answer each of the questions below.

1. Schlafen Sie lieber bei offenem oder geschlossenem Fenster?
2. Stehen Sie lieber früh oder spät auf?
3. Duschen Sie sich lieber morgens oder abends?
4. Was trinken Sie am liebsten, Milch, Kaffee, Wein oder Bier?
5. Wo kaufen Sie lieber ein, im Supermarkt oder in kleinen Geschäften?
6. Fahren Sie lieber mit dem Auto, oder gehen Sie lieber zu Fuß?
7. Wo arbeiten Sie lieber, in der Bibliothek oder zu Hause?
8. Was lesen Sie lieber, Bücher oder Zeitungen?
9. Was machen Sie am liebsten, fernsehen, lesen oder Musik hören?

2. Wie sagt man das?

Inge: Why did you get up so late?
Erik: I don't feel well.
Inge: Do you have a fever?
Erik: No. I caught a cold. My throat hurts.
Inge: You look pale. Maybe it's better if you go to the doctor.
Erik: You're right. I do feel weak.

3. So beginnt mein Tag. Describe the beginning of your day. You may use the expressions provided below and add some of your own.

aufstehen ◊ sich baden oder duschen ◊ sich anziehen ◊ tragen ◊ etwas trinken und essen ◊ sich die Zähne putzen ◊ sich die Haare kämmen

4. Zeit und Ort Answer the questions below in complete sentences that contain both time expressions and place expressions.

1. Wann gehen Sie in Ihre erste Vorlesung? Um 8? Um 9?
2. Wann gehen Sie nach Hause? Um 3? Um 5?
3. Wann arbeiten Sie in der Bibliothek? Am Mittwoch? Jeden Tag?
4. Wie oft gehen Sie ins Kino? Einmal in der Woche? Einmal im Monat?
5. Wann möchten Sie in die Ferien gehen? Im Juli? Im August?

5. In Deutschland ist es anders. Join the sentences below, using a conjunction from the list.

aber ◊ da ◊ daß ◊ denn ◊ ob ◊ oder ◊ und ◊ weil ◊ wenn

▶ Diane Miller studiert in Deutschland. Sie möchte mehr Deutsch lernen.

Diane Miller studiert in Deutschland, denn sie möchte mehr Deutsch lernen.

1. Sie geht mit ihrer Freundin Nicole. Ihre Freundin geht einkaufen.
2. Diane ist erstaunt. Nicole geht jede Woche zweimal einkaufen.
3. Nicole kauft fast alles im Supermarkt. Die Sachen sind da oft billiger.
4. Sie kauft Tabletten in der Apotheke. Sie kauft Brot beim Bäcker.
5. Sie kauft frischen Kuchen. Sie kauft Brot von gestern.
6. Diane ist erstaunt. Nicole geht in so viele Geschäfte.

6. Bei Beckers in Zürich Robert is an American student staying with the Becker family in Zürich. The following dialogue reflects some of his experiences. Complete each sentence with an appropriate possessive adjective.

Anja: Du, Robert, _____ Mutter sieht das nicht gern, daß _____ Zimmertür immer offen steht.

Robert: Ich soll _____ Zimmertür schließen?

Anja: Ja, bitte. Es sieht besser aus.

Robert: Ach, jetzt verstehe ich. Ich hab' bemerkt, wie deine Mutter _____ Tür immer zumacht. Ihr macht alle _____ Türen zu.

Anja: Klar. Deshalb hat man Türen! Aber genug von Türen. Wir machen _____ Ferienpläne. Wir fahren nach Österreich zu _____ Freunden. Du kommst doch mit, nicht?

Robert: Gern. Wie lange bleibt ihr denn bei _____ Freunden?

Anja: Eine Woche. Du kannst _____ Arbeit mitnehmen.

Robert: Ja, das muß ich. Ich muß _____ Referat vorbereiten.

7. **Was bedeutet das?** The sentences below contain new words that are related to words you already know. Give the English equivalents of the sentences.

1. Ich danke Ihnen für Ihre *Hilfe.* Sie haben mir wirklich sehr geholfen.
2. Wenn man in Deutschland fahren will, muß man eine *Fahrschule* besuchen. Der *Fahrschulkurs* ist natürlich sehr teuer.
3. Es gefällt dem *Arbeitgeber,* wenn seine Arbeitnehmer gut arbeiten.
4. Auf dem Land fährt Susanne mit dem Motorrad; auf dem Wasser fährt sie im *Motorboot.*
5. Mein Freund Richard *reist* im Sommer nach Deutschland. So eine Reise ist sehr schön.
6. Wir haben uns ein neues *Zelt* gekauft. Im August zelten wir.
7. Die Übersetzung dieses Artikels über Brecht ist ausgezeichnet. Wer hat ihn *übersetzt?*

8. **Er/Sie geht mir auf die Nerven.** **(He/She is getting on my nerves.)** Your roommate's faults are getting on your nerves. Write a letter to **Tante Margo,** who gives advice in the newspaper. Tell her the problem. Your partner will play **Tante Margo** and give you advice orally or in writing.

Some problems could be that your roommate watches TV all day or never:

> washes ◇ combs his/her hair ◇ brushes his/her teeth ◇ cleans up the room ◇ has time

9. **Wie sagt man das?**

1. Dietmar is taller than his brother.
   —Yes, but still shorter than his father.
2. I work best in the mornings.
   —Really? I prefer to work evenings.
3. Today is the coldest day of the year.
   —Yes. It simply won't get warmer.
4. Do you like to work with younger people?
   —Yes. But I like to work with older people most of all.

10. **Anregung**

1. Based on your reading in this chapter prepare a short paragraph in German on one of the following topics.
   (a) „Ich möchte Schweizer Bürger/in werden."
   (b) Deutschland und die Schweiz: Ein Vergleich°   comparison
   (c) Die Sprachen in der Schweiz.

2. Germany has a national *Trimm dich!°* campaign, urging its citizens *„Halt dich fit!"°* Write one or two public-service ads for TV or radio that could be used in this campaign. For example: urge people to walk or ride bikes rather than using their cars; encourage people to get out and enjoy sports such as hiking, camping, swimming. You may wish to incorporate ideas on *Umweltprobleme*, such as pollution from traffic.

fitness
keep in shape

Trimm Dich.

Die schönste Freizeit.

GRAMMATIK: ZUSAMMENFASSUNG

Reflexive constructions

◆ Forms of reflexive pronouns

	ich	**du**	**er/es/sie**	**wir**	**ihr**	**sie**	**Sie**
Accusative reflexive	mich	dich	sich	uns	euch	sich	sich
Dative reflexive	mir	dir	sich	uns	euch	sich	sich

Use of reflexive constructions

◆ Accusative reflexive pronouns

Direct object	Ich habe **mich** gewaschen.	I washed (myself).
Object of preposition	Hast du das für **dich** gemacht?	Did you do that for yourself?

◆ Dative reflexive pronouns

Indirect object	Hast du **dir** ein neues Auto gekauft?	Did you buy yourself a new car?
Dative verb	Ich kann **mir** nicht helfen.	I can't help myself.
Object of preposition	Spricht Edith von **sich** selbst?	Is Edith talking about herself?

Definite articles with parts of the body

Ich habe **mir die** Hände gewaschen.	I washed *my* hands.
Sie hat **sich die** Haare gekämmt.	She combed *her* hair.

In referring to parts of the body, German often uses a definite article and a dative pronoun. English uses a possessive adjective.

Infinitives with *zu*

Er versucht, alles **zu** verstehen.	He tries to understand everything.
Er kann alles verstehen.	He can understand everything.

Dependent infinitives used with most verbs are preceded by **zu.** Dependent infinitives used with modals are not preceded by **zu.**

Sie hat keine Zeit, die Arbeit **zu** machen.	She has no time to do the work.
Es war schwer, die Vorlesung **zu** verstehen.	It was difficult to understand the lecture.

Infinitives with **zu** are also used after a large number of expressions like **es ist Zeit** and **es ist schwer.** If an infinitive phrase contains **zu** + infinitive and modifiers, it is set off by commas in writing.

Es ist schwer, so früh auf**zu**stehen.
Es ist Zeit, jetzt auf**zu**hören.

When a separable prefix is in the infinitive form, the **zu** comes between the prefix and the base form of the verb.

The construction *um ... zu* + infinitive

Amerikaner kommen oft nach Deutschland, **um** dort **zu** studieren.	Americans often come to Germany *in order to* study there.

The German construction **um ... zu** + infinitive is equivalent to the English construction *(in order) to* + infinitive.

Comparison of adjectives and adverbs

◆ *Forms of the comparative and superlative*

Base form	**laut**	loud	**schön**	beautiful
Comparative	**lauter**	louder	**schöner**	more beautiful
Superlative	**lautest-**	loudest	**schönst-**	most beautiful

German forms the comparative by adding the suffix **-er** to the base form. It forms the superlative by adding the suffix **-st** to the base form. The ending **-est** is added to words ending in **-d (gesündest-), -t (leichtest-)**, or a sibilant **(kürzest-).** An exception is **größt-.**

Base form	alt	groß	jung
Comparative	**älter**	**größer**	**jünger**
Superlative	**ältest-**	**größt-**	**jüngst-**

Many one-syllable adjectives and adverbs with stem vowel **a, o,** or **u** add an umlaut in the comparative and the superlative.

Base form	gern	gut	hoch	viel
Comparative	**lieber**	**besser**	**höher**	**mehr**
Superlative	**liebst-**	**best-**	**höchst-**	**meist-**

A few adjectives and adverbs are irregular in the comparative and superlative forms.

◆ *Special constructions and uses*

Bernd ist nicht **so groß wie** Jens.	Bernd is not *as tall as* Jens.
Es ist heute **so kalt wie** gestern.	Today it is just *as cold as* yesterday.

In German the construction **so ... wie** is used to make comparisons of equality. It is equivalent to English *as . . . as.*

Erika ist **größer als** ihre Mutter.	Erika is *taller than* her mother.
Es ist **kälter als** gestern.	It is *colder than* yesterday.

The comparative form of an adjective or adverb is used to make comparisons of inequality. **Als** is equivalent to English *than.*

Sie singt **am schönsten.**	She sings the best.
Im Frühling ist das Wetter hier **am schönsten.**	The weather here is nicest in the spring.
Die kleinsten Blumen sind **die schönsten.**	The smallest flowers are the prettiest (flowers).

The pattern **am** + superlative with the ending **-en** is used for adverbs (as in the first example above), and for predicate adjectives (as in the second example). The superlative of attributive adjectives, with a following noun that is expressed or understood, is preceded by the article **der/das/die** (as in the third example). The superlative form of the adjective has an ending.

Ist diese Frau die Personalchefin?

Kapitel 11

BAUSTEINE FÜR GESPRÄCHE

Ein Ferienjob

Personalchefin: Herr Ohrdorf, Sie sind jetzt im achten Semester Informatik und wollen im Sommer drei Monate bei uns arbeiten.

Herr Ohrdorf: Ja, richtig.

Personalchefin: Haben Sie schon als Informatiker gearbeitet?

Herr Ohrdorf: Ja, ich hatte letztes Jahr auch einen Ferienjob und konnte da ganz gute praktische Erfahrungen sammeln.

Personalchefin: Und was wollen Sie später damit machen?

Herr Ohrdorf: Ich möchte eine Stelle bei einer Bank, eine Aufgabe mit viel Verantwortung, hoffe ich.

A summer job

Mr. Ohrdorf, you're in your eighth semester of computer science and want to work here for three months.

Yes, that's right.

Have you already worked as a computer specialist?

Yes, I also had a summer job last year and was able to get some good practical experience.

And what do you want to do with it later on?

I would like a position with a bank, an assignment with lots of responsibility, I hope.

Fragen

1. Was studiert Herr Ohrdorf? Warum?
2. Was für einen Ferienjob hat er schon einmal gehabt?
3. Wie hat der Job ihn auf die neue Stelle vorbereitet?
4. Wo möchte er später eine Stelle finden?
5. Was erwartet° er von dieser Stelle?

Der Computer ist nur die Maschine. Erst die Software ist das Werkzeug, das den Computer zum Arbeitsgerät macht.

Wir führen Programme für die meisten Einsatzgebiete eines Personalcomputers.

HANNES KELLER
COMPUTERZENTRUM **AG**
EIDMATTSTRASSE 36
8032 ZÜRICH
TELEFON 01 69 36 33

1. Eine neue Stelle Take the part of one of the participants in a job interview. The interviewee should decide beforehand what he/she knows.

| Talking about one's qualifications for a job |

Sie (Personalchef/in)	*Gesprächspartner/in (Bewerber/in°)*	applicant
Können Sie | **Schreibmaschine schreiben°?** mit Wortprozessoren° arbeiten? mit dem Computer arbeiten?	Ja. Sehr gut. Ich kenne BASIC und ein bißchen Pascal. Nein, tut mir leid.	
Haben Sie schon praktische Erfahrung als Informatiker/in?	Ja, | **ich habe bei einer kleinen Firma gearbeitet.** ich hatte letztes Jahr einen Ferienjob.	
Warum wollen Sie die Stelle wechseln°?	Ich möchte | **neue Erfahrungen sammeln.** mehr Verantwortung bekommen. mehr verdienen°. bei einer größeren Firma arbeiten.	
	Ich suche eine neue Herausforderung°. Ich finde die Arbeit nicht mehr interessant.	challenge

2. Berufspläne° Ask four fellow students what profession they would like to pursue.

Sie	*Gesprächspartner/in*
Was möchtest du werden?	Ich möchte | **Lehrer/in° werden.** Professor/in Jurist/in° Geschäftsmann°/Geschäftsfrau° Musiker/in° Programmierer/in° Arzt/Ärztin Zahnarzt/Zahnärztin° Ingenieur/in°

3. **Die beste Stelle**   Answer the following questions for yourself and then compare your answers with those of another classmate.

1. Was studieren Sie?
2. Arbeiten Sie lieber allein oder mit anderen Menschen zusammen?
3. Würden Sie lieber in einem Büro oder im Freien° arbeiten?   outdoors
4. Wie soll die Arbeit sein? Interessant? Leicht? Schwer?
5. Wie wichtig ist Ihnen das Geld? Ein sicherer Arbeitsplatz?
6. Können Sie mit einem Computer arbeiten?
7. Was machen Sie in Ihrer Freizeit?

Using the information from your answers to the above questions, choose professions you might like to pursue and tell your classmate why you think your choices are appropriate.

4. **Stellenangebote**   Look through the ads for jobs and answer the questions. If you need help to get the gist, see Vocabulary for Authentic Text Activities in the Reference Section.

1. Welche Stellen wären für einen Studenten/eine Studentin gut?
2. Welche Stelle ist nicht in Deutschland?
3. Welche Stellen sind nur für eine Frau, für einen Mann, für eine Frau oder einen Mann? Woher wissen Sie das? Was halten Sie davon?

Kindermädchen
f. 3jhr. Zwillingsmädchen von italienischer Familie auf dem Lande gesucht. Separates Zimmer mit Bad. Bewerbung mit Lebenslauf, Foto und Zeugnissen an **G. Vrafino, 10034 Boschetto-Chivasso (Turin)**

Wir suchen im Raum Südosten einen tüchtigen u. aufgeschlossenen
Elektroinstallateur
der selbständig arbeiten kann und dem es Spaß macht, im Kundenbereich tätig zu werden.
Elektro Hiering, ☎ 6116659

Studentenjob
Taxifahren auch Festfahrer/Aushilfen. Gute Konditionen, Aushbildung im Schnellkurs.   ☎ **4484770,17-19U.**

Exportfirma sucht ab sofort
Sekretärin
mit Sprachkenntnissen in Italienisch u. Englisch. Zuschr. u. ✉ ZS9800194

Wir su. in unser Fotofachlabor eine/n
Fotolaborant/in
ganz- od. halbtags, auf Wunsch Schichtdienst. ☎**472091**

When Germany introduced new bank notes (1990–1992), it chose to honor four great women of its history: one musician, one scientist, and two authors. Clara Schumann (1819–1896), whose portrait is on the 100 DM-note, performed her first concert at the age of nine, and in the course of her career her interpretation of classical and romantic piano pieces (including works by her husband Robert Schumann) set the standard for several decades. She also gained fame as a composer and teacher. On the 500 DM-note is the portrait of the artist and biologist, Maria Sibylla Merian (1647–1717). Merian wrote and illustrated several volumes of natural history; her main interest was the insect world. Two writers, Bettina von Arnim (1785–1859) and Annette von Droste-Hülshoff (1797–1848) are represented on the 5 DM-note and 20 DM-note, respectively. Von Arnim was a writer in the Romantic period who was also active in the political life of her time. Droste-Hülshoff wrote poems and novellas (**Novellen**) which are recognized as among the best of the nineteenth-century realist literature.

**Annette von Droste-Hülshoff
(1797–1848)**

**Clara Schumann
(1819–1896)**

5. Eine neue Stelle Work in two groups of three. One group works in an employment agency, that has been asked to interview applicants for the positions advertised. Choosing one ad from the ones in this chapter, the group decides which skills and qualifications are important for the job and develops questions for a job interview, using the questions in exercises 1 and 3 but developing its own questions as well. The group then holds interviews with three people from the other group, who act as applicants. The employment agency group decides whom it will hire and why.

Vokabeln

— Substantive

die **Aufgabe, -n** assignment; task, set of duties; die **Hausaufgaben** homework

die **Bank, -en** bank

der **Beruf, -e** profession, occupation

der **Chef, -s**/die **Chefin, -nen** boss

die **Erfahrung, -en** experience

die **Geschäftsfrau, -en** businesswoman/der **Geschäftsmann, -leute** businessman

die **Informatik** computer science

der **Informatiker, -**/die **Informatikerin, -nen** computer specialist

der **Ingenieur, -e**/die **Ingenieurin, -nen** engineer

der **Jurist, -en, -en**/die **Juristin, -nen** lawyer

der **Lehrer, -**/die **Lehrerin, -nen** teacher

der **Musiker, -**/die **Musikerin, -nen** musician

der **Programmierer, -**/die **Programmiererin, -nen** programmer

die **Schreibmaschine, -n** typewriter; ~ **schreiben können** to be able to type

die **Stelle, -n** position, job; place

die **Verantwortung** responsibility

der **Wortprozessor, -en** word processor; **mit dem ~ arbeiten** to do word processing

der **Zahnarzt, ⁼e**/die **Zahnärztin, -nen** dentist

— Verben

erwarten to expect
hoffen to hope
sammeln to collect

verdienen to earn
wechseln to change

— Besondere Ausdrücke

mit dem Computer arbeiten to work (on) a computer

FRAUEN IN DEUTSCHLAND

Vorbereitung auf das Lesen

◆ *Zum Thema*

1. Was sind einige Ziele° der berufstätigen° Frauen in diesem Land?   goals / working

   Stichworte (in der Wirtschaft): Geld ◇ Verantwortung
   (in der Politik): Politikerin ◇ Abgeordnete° ◇ Senatorin   Representative
   ◇ Präsidentin/Ministerpräsidentin°   Prime Minister

2. Gibt es typische Männer- und typische Frauenarbeit? In der Wirtschaft?
   In der Politik? Zu Hause?
3. Was für Probleme gibt es für berufstätige Frauen?

   Stichworte: Beruf ◇ Hausarbeit ◇ Kinder

◆ *Leitfragen*

1. Was garantiert die Verfassung°?   constitution
2. Was macht Anja Dörner bei der Lufthansa°? Wo hatte sie Probleme und   German airline
   wo nicht?

   Stichworte: Streß ◇ Ausbildung° ◇ dumme Reden ◇ Passagiere   training

3. Welchen Beruf hat Frau Wieland? Wie half ihre Familie? Was hielten ihre
   Nachbarn von ihrer Arbeit?

   Stichworte: Wäsche waschen ◇ einkaufen ◇ Rabenmutter°   unfit mother

4. Inwiefern° ist Frau de Haas' Rolle traditionell? Inwiefern nicht?   in what way

   Stichworte: Beruf aufgeben° ◇ Demonstrationen   give up

---

*I*n der deutschen Verfassung heißt° es: „Männer und Frauen sind gleichbe-   says
rechtigt°.“ (ARTIKEL 3, 2) Die Verfassung ist also absolut klar und eindeutig°.   **sind gleichberechtigt:** have
Da gibt es kein Wenn und Aber. Und die Wirklichkeit? Nun, die ist etwas   equal rights / unequivocal
komplizierter.

5   Sicher gibt es heute mehr Gleichberechtigung als vor zehn oder zwanzig
Jahren. Die Lufthansa bildet z.B. seit einigen Jahren nicht mehr nur Männer,
sondern auch Frauen als Piloten aus. Anja Dörner gehörte zu den ersten
Frauen in einem Pilotenlehrgang° bei der Lufthansa. Sie war unter den fünf   course for pilots

Ariane Kall ist die jüngste Pilotin bei der Lufthansa.

bis zehn Prozent, die nach Interview und erstem Test am Ende von allen
10 Männern und Frauen übrig bleiben. Die Ausbildung ist anstrengend°. Piloten   strenuous
müssen lernen, Streß-Situationen zu meistern°. Sie müssen lernen, trotz   master
Sonne, Lärm und schlechtem Wetter ruhig zu bleiben. Sie dürfen auch nicht
nervös werden, wenn z.B. Instrumente plötzlich nicht funktionieren oder ein
Triebwerk°. Auf die Frage, ob sie nervös wird, wenn sie an solche   engine
15 Möglichkeiten denkt, antwortete Anja Dörner bei einem Interview: „Nein, ich
glaube, ich bin dann auf jeden Notfall° vorbereitet." Die Männer in ihrem   emergency
Lehrgang° haben die Frauen voll akzeptiert. Die dummen Reden, die ab   course of instruction
und zu von den Männern kommen, stören Anja Dörner nicht. Der
Lehrgangsleiter° sagt, daß die Ausbildung für die Frauen kein Problem ist.   course director
20 Ein Problem ergibt° sich vielleicht später, wenn die Passagiere eine   arises
Frauenstimme aus dem Cockpit hören: „Aber daran müssen sie sich eben
gewöhnen."

Ein anderes Beispiel ist Frau Wieland. Sie ist Elektroingenieurin. Und da
ist sie etwas Besonderes, denn als sie studierte, gab es unter den In-
25 genieurstudenten nur etwa fünf Prozent Frauen. Seit ein paar Jahren ist sie
voll berufstätig und erinnert sich sehr gut an die Kritik ihrer Nachbarn und
Bekannten, als sie mit der Arbeit anfing. Als Ingenieurin war sie jede Woche
vier Tage und vier Nächte von zu Hause weg. Sie sagt: „Kaum jemand fand
das toll, was wir da versuchten. Man nannte mich eine Rabenmutter°und   unfit mother
30 eine Karrieremacherin°. Plötzlich tat allen möglichen Leuten mein Mann leid.   a woman interested only in a career

Das Interessante war, daß unser Nachbar etwa zur gleichen Zeit auch vier Tage pro Woche weg war. Der war kein Rabenvater, und seine Frau tat niemandem leid. Da konnte man schon den Mut° und die Geduld verlieren. Aber meine Familie hat mir sehr geholfen." Klaus, ihr sechzehnjähriger Sohn,
35 sagt: „Als Mutter zu arbeiten anfing, mußten wir alle viel lernen. Ich hatte z.B. vorher noch nie die Wäsche gewaschen. Zum Einkaufen war ich auch noch nicht oft gegangen. Aber man lernt ja alles." Frau Wieland sagt: „Ich höre immer wieder von Kolleginnen, daß sie die ganze Hausarbeit neben ihrem Beruf auch noch machen. Das ist bei uns nicht so. Meine Familie hilft
40 mir sehr."

    Es gibt also eine Entwicklung zu mehr Gleichberechtigung. Das ist gar keine Frage. Aber es bleibt noch sehr viel zu tun. Das glaubt auch die Frauenbeauftragte° des Landes Sachsen, Friederike de Haas. Sie ist gelernte° Krankenschwester. Ihr Mann ist Arzt. Sie haben vier Kinder. Als die Kinder
45 kamen, gab sie ihren Beruf auf. Als sie die Schulbücher ihrer Kinder studierte, ärgerte sie sich darüber, wie die Rolle der Frau und des Mannes dort aussah. Das Mädchenbild paßte dazu und war anders als das Jungenbild. Die Mädchen sahen z.B. meistens zu°, wenn die Jungen etwas bauten oder Fußball spielten. Sie waren passiver als die Jungen und machten
50 weniger gefährliche Sachen. 1989 wollten viele Bürger die DDR reformieren. Sie demonstrierten, und bei den Demonstrationen ging Friederike de Haas mit auf die Straße. Als es dann klar wurde, daß die Vereinigung kommen würde, gab es wieder Demonstrationen und dann Verhandlungen°. Friederike de Haas war wieder dabei°, denn „die Männer demonstrierten und
55 verhandelten°, die Frauen kochten Kaffee und paßten auf die Kinder auf."

    In ihrem Amt° will sie unter anderem dafür sorgen, daß es Frauenhäuser° gibt: „Die Gewalt in den Familien nimmt durch die Arbeitslosigkeit immer mehr zu°." Sie möchte erreichen, daß in den Hochschulen° und in den großen Firmen Frauenbeauftragte° arbeiten. Sie sagt: „Das schiefe Frauenbild fängt
60 schon in den Schulbüchern an."

    Bis zur wirklichen Gleichberechtigung ist es also noch ein weiter Weg. Aber viele Deutsche glauben, daß Emanzipation und Gleichberechtigung wichtige und gute Ziele sind.

Glossen (Randspalte):
- courage
- commissioner for women's affairs / trained
- **sahen zu:** watched
- negotiations
- **war ... dabei:** was again part of it / negotiated
- office / safe houses for women
- **nimmt zu:** is increasing / institutions of higher learning / officers for women's affairs

Fragen zum Lesestück

1. Was steht in der deutschen Verfassung?
2. Was ist bei der Lufthansa in den letzten zehn bis zwanzig Jahren anders geworden?
3. Warum ist die Pilotenausbildung so anstrengend?
4. Was ist z.B. eine Streß-Situation?
5. Warum machen technische Probleme Anja Dörner nicht nervös?
6. Machen die Männer den Frauen in ihrem Lehrgang Schwierigkeiten? Begründen° Sie Ihre Antwort.

support

7. Gibt es für die Pilotinnen Schwierigkeiten? Begründen Sie Ihre Antwort.
8. Frau Wieland ist Elektroingenieurin. Warum ist das etwas Besonderes?
9. Warum tat Herr Wieland den Nachbarn leid?
10. Warum haben die Leute Frau Wielands Nachbarn nicht kritisiert?
11. Was hat Klaus gelernt, als seine Mutter zu arbeiten anfing?
12. Was müssen viele Frauen neben ihrer Berufsarbeit machen?
13. Warum hat Frau de Haas ihren Beruf aufgegeben?
14. Worüber ärgerte sie sich?
15. Was machten die Jungen in den Schulbüchern? Und was machten die Mädchen?
16. Warum ging Frau de Haas bei den Demonstrationen auf die Straße?
17. Was sind ihre Ziele als Frauenbeauftragte? Nennen Sie zwei Ziele.

**Kinderkrippe
in Offenbach am Main: Eine
Mutter bringt ihre Kinder.**

A few milestones in the progress of women toward equality:

1901   German universities begin to admit women.
1919   German women receive the right to vote.
1949   The Basic Law of the Federal Republic (**Grundgesetz**) guarantees the right of a person to decide on her or his role in society.
1955   The Federal Labor Court (**Bundesarbeitsgericht**) states that there should be no discrimination on the basis of sex in compensation for work performed.
1977   Women and men are judged by law to be equal in a marriage. Either can take the surname of the other, or a combination of both names.
1979   Women gain the right to a six-month leave from work to care for a newborn child. By 1990 the leave-time had increased to 12 months and was available to women or men.
1986   Child-raising years are included in the calculation of retirement pensions; long-term, financially supported child-rearing leaves are introduced for women and men.

1. Erzählen Sie. Summarize the account about one of the women in the reading. Use the following cues.

Anja Dörner: Ausbildung ◇ Streß-Situationen ◇ die Passagiere

Frau Wieland: Elektroingenieurin ◇ Kritik der Nachbarn und Bekannten ◇ ihre Familie ◇ Hausarbeit

Fredericke de Haas: Beruf aufgeben ◇ Schulbücher ◇ die Demonstrationen 1989 ◇ Frauenhäuser

2. Eine Talkshow Frau Dörner, Frau Wieland, Frau de Haas and a local woman are guests on a talk show about women's issues. The audience is allowed to ask them questions and comment on the issues. Choose members of the class to play the roles of the guests and the host. The other members of the class play the audience. Here are some questions to get you started.

1. Welches Mädchen- und Jungenbild geben Kinderbücher bei Ihnen?
2. Was für Probleme haben Pilotinnen bei der Lufthansa?
3. Soll eine Mutter mit kleinen Kindern in den Beruf gehen?
4. Wer macht in den Familien bei Ihnen die Hausarbeit?
5. Warum sind Frauenhäuser wichtig?
6. Was wollten die Männer und Frauen bei den Demonstrationen 1989 in der DDR erreichen?
7. Welche Probleme haben Frauen bei Ihnen? In der Wirtschaft? Zu Hause?
8. Verdienen bei Ihnen Frauen und Männer für die gleiche Arbeit gleich viel?
9. Gibt es „Männerberufe" und „Frauenberufe" oder ist das Geschlecht° unwichtig für den Beruf? gender
10. Haben Frauen bei Ihnen volle Gleichberechtigung?

Ärztin ist ein beliebter Frauenberuf.

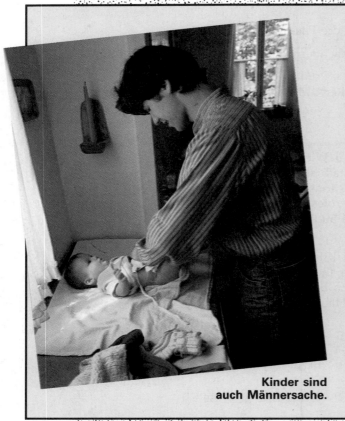

Kinder sind auch Männersache.

In Germany federal legislation concerning women (**Frauenpolitik**) covers a number of areas in women's lives. One aim is to help both women and men reconcile their professional and personal lives. In recent years opportunities for flexible work hours, part-time work (**Teilzeitbeschäftigung**) with full benefits, or sharing jobs have improved. Many single mothers receive financial aid, and every woman has the right to a maternity leave of six weeks preceding and eight weeks after the birth of the child while receiving her full salary (**Mutterschutz**), the cost of which is shared by the government and her employer. Another benefit is the child-rearing leave (**Erziehungsurlaub**), which allows either parent to stay home with a baby for up to twelve months. During that time the parent on leave receives her/his salary and an additional DM 600 monthly (**Erziehungsgeld**) for the first six months. These benefits are available for up to twelve months, although the amount after the sixth month may vary depending on the income level. Mothers with no outside job are also entitled to receive this support. Beginning in 1992 mothers-to-be receive a "family benefit" (**Familiengeld**) of DM 1,000, of which the mother receives DM 500 six weeks before the birth of the child and an additional DM 500 after the birth.

Vokabeln

— Substantive —

die **Ahnung** hunch; idea **keine Ahnung!** no idea!
die **Entwicklung, -en** development
die **Geduld** patience
die **Gleichberechtigung** equal rights
der **Kollege, -n, -n**/die **Kollegin, -nen** colleague
die **Krankenschwester, -n** nurse

das **Land, ̈er** state (of Germany or Austria)
der **Lärm** noise
das **Prozent, -e** percent
die **Regierung, -en** government
die **Stimme, -n** voice; vote
der **Streß** stress
die **Vereinigung** unification
das **Ziel, -e** goal

Verben

(sich) **ärgern (über** + *acc.*) to feel angry (about)

auf·geben (gibt auf), gab auf, auf-gegeben to give up

auf·passen to watch out; **auf·passen (auf** + *acc.*) to take care of

aus·bilden to train, educate

sich erinnern (an + *acc.*) to remember *(someone or something)*

erreichen to reach, attain

sich gewöhnen (an + *acc.*) to become accustomed (to)

kritisieren to criticize

nennen, nannte, genannt to name; to call

sorgen für to see to it, to arrange for *(a thing to be done)*; to care for

Andere Wörter

ab und zu now and then
berufstätig employed
dort there
gefährlich dangerous
möglich possible
nachdem *(conj.)* after

plötzlich suddenly
pro per; **pro Woche** per week
schief distorted, false; sloping; crooked
übrig left over, remaining
weit far

Besondere Ausdrücke

immer mehr more and more
zur gleichen Zeit at the same time

GRAMMATIK UND ÜBUNGEN

1 Simple past tense

Als Frau Wieland **anfing** zu arbeiten, **mußte** Klaus zu Hause mehr helfen. Er **wusch** die Wäsche, **räumte auf** und **ging** oft einkaufen.

When Mrs. Wieland started to work, Klaus had to help more at home. He did the laundry, straightened up the house, and often went shopping.

The simple past tense, like the perfect (see *Kapitel 7*), is used to refer to events in the past. However, the simple past and the perfect are used in different circumstances. The simple past tense is often called the narrative past because it is used to narrate a series of connected events in the past.

Monika: **Hast** du gestern abend **ferngesehen?**	Did you watch TV last night?
Dieter: Nein, ich **habe** ein paar Briefe **geschrieben.**	No, I wrote a few letters.

The perfect tense (**hast ferngesehen, habe geschrieben**) is often called the conversational past because it is used in a two-way exchange to talk about events in the past. English expresses the same ideas by using forms of the past *(did watch, wrote)*. Note that a question in the past in English often requires the past of the auxiliary verb *do (did)* (See *Kapitel 2*).

Monika: Jürgen **konnte** am Freitag nicht kommen.
Dieter: **War** er krank, oder **hatte** er keine Zeit?

The simple past tense forms of the modals **können** (**konnte**), **sein** (**war**), and **haben** (**hatte**) are used more frequently than the perfect tense, even in conversation.

2 *Sein* and *haben* in the simple past tense

sein			haben	
ich war	wir war**en**		ich hatte	wir hatte**n**
du war**st**	ihr war**t**		du hatte**st**	ihr hatte**t**
er/es/sie war	sie war**en**		er/es/sie hatte	sie hatte**n**
Sie war**en**			Sie hatte**n**	

You learned in *Kapitel 3* that the simple past tense of **sein** is **war.** The simple past tense of **haben** is **hatte.** In the simple past, all forms except the **ich-** and **er/es/sie-**forms add verb endings.

1. Noch einmal Restate the conversational exchanges below in the simple past.

▶ Wie ist deine Erkältung? *Wie war deine Erkältung?*
— Ach, die ist nicht so schlimm. *— Ach, die war nicht so schlimm.*

1. Bist du in den Ferien zu Hause?
— Nein, ich bin bei meinem Onkel.
2. Seid ihr heute in der Bibliothek?
— Ja, wir sind den ganzen Tag da.
3. Ist das Buch interessant?
— Nein, es ist furchtbar langweilig.

2) In den Bergen Tell a friend why you and various people didn't go on the mountain climbing excursion.

▶ Dennis / keine Zeit   *Dennis hatte keine Zeit.*

1. Irma / kein Geld
2. ich / viel Arbeit
3. Simon / Angst
4. wir / schlechtes Wetter
5. Nils und Anke / eine Vorlesung
6. ich / kein Auto

The unification of Germany has vast implications for the women's policies (**Frauenpolitik**) of Germany. In 1990 approximately 50 percent of the women worked outside the home in West Germany, while in East Germany 90 percent of the women worked outside the home. Women in the GDR made up about one-half of the work force and held one-third of the supervisory positions. Unification brought soaring unemployment to the new federal states, and at least in the short term women were the hardest hit.

Many women in eastern Germany not only lost their employment, but many of the job-site daycare centers were closed. East Germany had provided child care for virtually all pre-school children with an extensive system of government supported day care (**Kinderkrippen, Kindergärten**), while in West Germany there were spaces for only about 5 percent of the pre-school children in daycare facilities. The closing of many of these facilities in eastern Germany made it difficult for some mothers to re-enter the job market and forced others to stay at home to care for their children. While the immediate effect is a lowering of the family income, the social ramifications of their unemployment could have a long-term impact. Yet, the outlook is not entirely bleak. Some action has already been taken to improve child care in the unified Germany, and women in eastern Germany have banded together to learn about entrepreneurial possibilities and to work for needed legislation.

Birgit Breuel ist Direktorin der Treuhandanstalt.

3. Rollenspiel   Assume a friend (**Gesprächspartner/in**) did not call you yesterday as promised. Ask where he/she was. If appropriate ask a follow-up question such as **Wie war es denn?**

Sie	*Gesprächspartner/in*
Wo warst du gestern?	Ich war | **im Kino.**
	auf einem Fest.
	bei Freunden.
	in der Stadt.
	in der Bibliothek.
	in einer Vorlesung.

3 Modals in the simple past

Infinitive	Past stem	Tense marker	Simple past	English equivalent
dürfen	durf-	-te	**durfte**	was allowed to
können	konn-	-te	**konnte**	was able to
mögen	moch-	-te	**mochte**	liked
müssen	muß-	-te	**mußte**	had to
sollen	soll-	-te	**sollte**	was supposed to
wollen	woll-	-te	**wollte**	wanted to

In the simple past tense, most modals undergo a stem change. The past tense marker **-te** is added to the simple past stem. Note that the past stem has no umlaut.

Though most English modals have past-tense forms, they are confusing because they are commonly used with conditional meanings. For example, the past of *may* is *might*. But since that form is used in conditional sentences (*I might go*), *was allowed to* is generally used to express the simple past of *may* (*I was allowed to go*). Similarly, the past of *can* is *could*. But since *could* is used in conditional sentences (*I could go*), *was able to* (*I was able to go*) is often substituted to distinguish it from the conditional use.

können	
ich konnte	wir konnte**n**
du konnte**st**	ihr konnte**t**
er/es/sie konnte	sie konnte**n**
Sie konnte**n**	

In the simple past, all forms except the **ich-** and **er/es/sie**-forms add verb endings to the **-te** tense marker.

4. Auf einem Geburtstagsfest You and your friends planned a birthday party. Recall what happened, using the simple past of the modals.

▶ Ich will meine Freunde einladen. *Ich wollte meine Freunde einladen.*

1. Klaus kann die Kassetten nicht mitbringen.
2. Katja muß noch abwaschen.
3. Frank will abtrocknen.
4. Michael soll das Wohnzimmer saubermachen.
5. Die Gäste sollen in zwei Stunden kommen.
6. Wir müssen daher schnell aufräumen.
7. Jens kann leider nicht lange bleiben.

5. Meine Kindheit Compare your childhood with that of your partner. Answer the following questions for yourself. Then, using the questions, have a conversation with your partner. Finally, tell the class about your childhood experiences and your partner's.

1. Mußten Sie Ihren Eltern viel helfen?
2. Durften Sie viel fernsehen?
3. Mußten Sie sonntags für die Schule lernen?
4. Wollten Sie ein bekannter Star werden?
5. Wie lange durften Sie abends wegbleiben?
6. Konnten Sie ein Instrument spielen?
7. Um wieviel Uhr mußten Sie ins Bett gehen?
8. Durften Sie viel Sport treiben?
9. Konnten Sie machen, was Sie wollten?
10. Was durften Sie nicht machen?

6. Das wollte ich. Think of something you wanted to be as a child and what you would now like to be. Tell this to your partner and tell why.

▶ *Als Kind wollte ich [Pilot/in] werden. Jetzt möchte ich [Informatiker/in] werden. Ich [arbeite gern mit dem Computer].*

Wer sich noch auf seinen Traumjob vorbereitet, fährt mit der Juniorkarte so günstig wie noch nie. Zur Uni oder zur Ausbildung.

4 Regular weak verbs in the simple past

Infinitive	Stem	Tense marker	Simple past
machen	mach-	-te	machte
sagen	sag-	-te	sagte
reden	re**d**-	-ete	redete
arbeiten	arbei**t**-	-ete	arbeitete
regnen	re**gn**-	-ete	regnete

In the simple past tense, regular weak verbs add the past-tense marker **-te** to the infinitive stem. Regular weak verbs with a stem ending in **-d** (**reden**) or **-t** (**arbeiten**) and verbs like **regnen** and **öffnen** insert an **-e** before the tense marker. The addition of the **-e** ensures that the **-t**, as a signal of the past, is audible. This is parallel to the insertion of the extra **-e** in the present tense (**er arbeitet;** past tense **er arbeitete**).

machen	
ich machte	wir machte**n**
du machte**st**	ihr machte**t**
er/es/sie machte	sie machte**n**
Sie machte**n**	

reden	
ich redete	wir redete**n**
du redete**st**	ihr redete**t**
er/es/sie redete	sie redete**n**
Sie redete**n**	

All forms except the **ich-** and **er/es/sie-**forms add verb endings to the **-te** tense marker.

7. **So war es früher.** Prepare a report about what you and your friends did a few years ago. Use the simple past tense.

▶ Ich arbeite in einem Supermarkt.   *Ich arbeitete in einem Supermarkt.*

1. Ich verdiene natürlich sehr wenig.
2. Mein Freund Michael lernt nicht genug Mathe.
3. Aber er baut die besten Flugzeugmodelle.
4. Ihm gehört eine ganze Sammlung davon.
5. Ein Lehrer bildet ihn im Motorenbau° aus.   engine building
6. Der Vater kritisiert Michael oft.
7. Die beiden reden nicht wirklich miteinander.
8. Michael und ich machen nicht genug Hausaufgaben.
9. Wir hören zuviel Rockmusik.

8. **Wir fahren zelten.** Report on an outing. Use the simple past.

▶ Am Samstag regnet es nicht.   *Am Samstag regnete es nicht.*

1. Gerd arbeitet nur bis 12 Uhr.
2. Gerd und Klaus zelten in den Bergen.

3. Alle baden im See°.   lake
4. Susi und Alex warten auf ihre Freunde.
5. Am Abend öffnen sie eine Flasche Bier.
6. Sie reden über dies und das.

5 Irregular weak verbs in the simple past

Infinitive	Past stem	Tense marker	Simple past	Examples
bringen	brach-	-te	**brachte**	Peter brachte die Blumen nach Hause.
denken	dach-	-te	**dachte**	Jutta dachte an ihre Arbeit.
kennen	kann-	-te	**kannte**	Wir kannten ihre Chefin.
nennen	nann-	-te	**nannte**	Sie nannten das Kind nach dem Vater.
wissen	wuß-	-te	**wußte**	Du wußtest das schon, nicht?

German has a few weak verbs that have a stem vowel change in the simple past. (For this reason they are called *irregular* weak verbs.) The verbs **bringen** and **denken** also have a consonant change. The tense marker **-te** is added to the simple past stem. Several of the most common irregular weak verbs are listed above.

bringen	
ich brachte	wir brachte**n**
du brachte**st**	ihr brachte**t**
er/es/sie brachte	sie brachte**n**
Sie brachte**n**	

In the simple past, all forms except the **ich-** and **er/es/sie-**forms add verb endings to the **-te** tense marker.

9. Vor Jahren   This report tells how people regarded the role of women a few years ago. Restate it in the simple past.

▶ Viele Leute haben wenig über die Emanzipation gewußt.

    Viele Leute wußten wenig über die Emanzipation.

1. Sie haben nur typische Rollen von Mann und Frau gekannt.
2. Viele Frauen haben aber anders gedacht.
3. Sie haben neue Ideen gehabt.
4. Wir haben auch die Probleme gekannt.
5. Die Frau hat oft nur die Hausarbeit gekannt.
6. Die Kinder haben natürlich wie die Eltern gedacht.
7. Sie haben berufstätige Frauen „Rabenmütter" genannt.

10. Eine Reise in die USA   Tell about Monika's experiences. Use the simple past.

1. Last summer Monika made a trip to the U.S.A.
2. She traveled to Boston. [use **reisen**]
3. She thought Boston was [use **ist**] fantastic.
4. She could speak English well.
5. She wanted to study at a university there.
6. The semester cost a lot of money.
7. At a party, she talked with a German student. [use **reden**]
8. They talked about life in America. [use **reden**]
9. He knew a lot about Boston.
10. Monika had many questions.

6 Separable-prefix verbs in the simple past

Present	Simple past
Wolf **kauft** für seine Freunde **ein.**	Wolf **kaufte** für seine Freunde **ein.**
Er **bringt** für alle etwas zu trinken **mit.**	Er **brachte** für alle etwas zu trinken **mit.**

In the simple past, as in the present, the separable prefix is separated from the base form of the verb and is in final position.

11. Eine Party   Tell how three friends prepared for a party by using the cues. Use the simple past.

▶   Lilo / aufmachen / alle Fenster   *Lilo machte alle Fenster auf.*

1. sie / aufräumen / die Wohnung
2. Ralf / einkaufen
3. er / mitbringen / vom Markt / Blumen
4. Theo / vorbereiten / das Essen
5. erst um sechs / sie / aufhören / zu arbeiten

7 Strong verbs in the simple past

Infinitive	Simple past stem
sprechen	sprach
gehen	ging

A strong verb undergoes a stem change in the simple past. The tense marker **-te** is not added to a strong verb in the simple past tense.

sprechen	
ich sprach	wir sprach**en**
du sprach**st**	ihr sprach**t**
er/es/sie sprach	sie sprach**en**
Sie sprach**en**	

In the simple past, all forms except the **ich-** and **er/es/sie-**forms add verb endings to the simple past stem. The stem change of strong verbs cannot always be predicted, but you will probably not have trouble guessing the infinitive form and thus the meaning of most of the verbs. While there are thousands of weak verbs, the number of strong verbs in German is fortunately relatively small. This book uses approximately 60 strong verbs. The list of these verbs is found in the Grammatical Tables in the Reference Section. However, most of these you will only need to recognize in your reading. In the vocabularies of this book, the simple past stem is printed after the infinitive, followed by the past participle: **liegen, lag, gelegen.**

12. Ein Gespräch mit der Nachbarin   Say that the people mentioned below spoke with a neighbor. Use the cued subjects and the simple past.

▶   Frau Berger spricht oft mit der Nachbarin.   *Frau Berger sprach oft mit der Nachbarin.*

1. Herr Wagner
2. Michael und Anja
3. ich
4. du
5. unsere Großeltern
6. Katja

13. Frau Wieland   Reread the information about Frau Wieland's experience as an electrical engineer (lines 23–40, pages 348–349). Note each verb in the simple past, give the English equivalent, and then give the German infinitive.

INGENIEURBÜRO
THOR
· **ELEKTROBAU** ·

wenn's um Strom geht ...
BERATUNG · PROJEKTIERUNG
AUSFÜHRUNG

Offenbach, Bettinastraße 69,
✆ 88 47 98

Am besten sind wir zu erreichen:
mo - fr 8-9, mo 19-22

◆ *Verbs with past-tense vowel long* ā *and short* ă

Infinitive	Simple past stem *(ā)*
essen	aß
geben	gab
kommen	kam
lesen	las
liegen	lag
nehmen	nahm
sehen	sah
sitzen	saß
sprechen	sprach
treffen	traf
tun	tat
vergessen	vergaß

Infinitive	Simple past stem *(ă)*
finden	fand
helfen	half
stehen	stand
trinken	trank

14. Die Sommerarbeit   Peggy, an American, has written to a German friend about her summer job. Read the account and answer the questions.

Samstag, den 1. Oktober

Liebe Marga,

Du wolltest etwas über meinen Sommerjob wissen. Also, ich kam am 5. Juni in München an. Es gab sehr viele Menschen am Flughafen. Zuerst verstand ich nur wenig. Aber die Deutschen waren sehr nett, vor allem meine Chefin Frau Volke. Sie half mir sehr bei der Arbeit. Ich fand die Arbeit dann viel leichter. Um 10 Uhr morgens machten wir immer Pause und tranken Kaffee. Manchmal waren unsere Gespräche so interessant, daß wir vergaßen, pünktlich wieder an die Arbeit zu gehen. Aber Frau Volke sagte nichts. Wie Du siehst, kann ich jetzt viel mehr Deutsch. Schreib bald.

Herzliche Grüße

Deine *Peggy*

1. Wann kam Peggy in München an?
2. Was sah sie im Flughafen?
3. Wer war besonders nett?
4. Warum fand Peggy die Arbeit leicht?
5. Was machte man um 10 Uhr morgens?
6. Warum vergaß man manchmal, pünktlich wieder an die Arbeit zu gehen?

◆ *Verbs with past-tense vowel* **ie, u,** *and* **i**

Infinitive	Simple past stem *(ie)*
bleiben	blieb
gefallen	gefiel
halten	hielt
laufen	lief
schlafen	schlief
schreiben	schrieb

Infinitive	Simple past stem *(u or i)*
fahren	fuhr
tragen	trug
gehen	ging

15. Die Reise nach Frankfurt Jürgen has written to Rainer about his trip to Frankfurt. Read his letter and then answer the questions.

Dienstag, den 10. Mai

Lieber Rainer,

Du wolltest wissen, was ich vorige Woche gemacht habe. Nun, ich fuhr mit dem Zug nach Frankfurt. Meine Freundin Julia fuhr natürlich mit. Wir trugen einfach unsere Jeans. Wir liefen ein bißchen in der Fußgängerzone herum und gingen schließlich ins Kino. Wir blieben nur eine halbe Stunde. Der Film gefiel uns nämlich nicht. Dann gingen wir ein Glas Apfelwein trinken. Am Abend fuhren wir dann wieder nach Hause. Julia schrieb Briefe. Aber ich habe den ganzen Weg geschlafen.

Herzliche Grüße

Dein *Jürgen*

1. Wohin fuhren Jürgen und Julia?
2. Was für Hosen trugen sie?
3. Wo liefen sie ein bißchen herum?
4. Warum blieben sie nur eine halbe Stunde im Kino?
5. Was machten sie nach dem Kino?
6. Was tat Julia auf dem Weg nach Hause?
7. Was tat Jürgen?

16. Eine Nacht im Leben von Herrn Zittermann Read the anecdote and answer the questions. Then make up an ending to the story.

Herr Zittermann war allein im Haus. Er lag im Bett, aber er schlief noch nicht. Er hatte die Augen offen. Plötzlich sah er unter der Tür Licht. Starr°   motionless
blieb er liegen. Was war los? Er bekam Angst. Er stand auf und nahm den Revolver, der natürlich neben dem Bett lag. Fest hielt er den Revolver in der Hand. Er ging zur Tür und sah ...

1. Wo lag Herr Zittermann?
2. Wie viele Leute waren im Haus?
3. Schlief Herr Zittermann?
4. Was sah er plötzlich?
5. Was war seine Reaktion?
6. Was lag neben seinem Bett?
7. Wohin ging er?

◆ *Past tense of* **werden**

Infinitive	Simple past stem
werden	wurde

17. Berufe State the occupation of various people. Use the simple past.

▶ Erika wird Ingenieurin.   *Erika wurde Ingenieurin.*

1. Du wirst Lehrer.
2. Wir werden Programmierer.
3. Inge wird Mathematiklehrerin.
4. Klaus wird Sportlehrer.
5. Marion und Monika werden Ärztinnen.
6. Gerd wird Jurist.
7. Karen wird Informatikerin.

18. Alles an einem Tag Write what you did on a particular day last week. Some suggestions are given to get you started

> Telling about activities in the past

    aufstehen ◇ sich duschen ◇ [Deutsch] machen ◇ [zur Uni/in die Stadt] fahren ◇ [in die Bibliothek] gehen ◇ mit [Freunden] reden

▶ *Am Montag stand ich um sieben auf. Dann ...*

8 Past perfect tense

Ich **hatte** vorher noch nie die Wäsche **gewaschen.**	I had never washed clothes before.
Zum Einkaufen **war** ich auch nicht oft **gegangen.**	I had also not gone shopping often.

The English past perfect tense consists of the auxiliary *had* and the past participle of the verb. The German past perfect tense consists of the simple past of **haben** or **sein** and the past participle of the verb. Verbs that use a form of **haben** in the present perfect tense also use a form of **haben** in the past perfect; those that use a form of **sein** in the present perfect also use a form of **sein** in the past perfect.

9 Use of the past perfect tense

Edith **konnte** am Montag nicht **anfangen,** weil sie am Sonntag krank **geworden war.**	Edith couldn't begin on Monday, because she had gotten sick on Sunday.

The past perfect tense is used to report an event or action that took place before another event or action that was itself in the past. The following time-tense line will help you visualize the sequence of tenses.

2nd point earlier in past	1st point in past time	Present time	Future time
Past perfect	Perfect or Simple past		

19. Jetzt hilft die Familie. Give the English equivalents of the sentences below.

1. Frau Wieland fing wieder an zu arbeiten, nachdem sie viele Jahre zu Hause gewesen war.
2. Die Bekannten kritisierten Frau Wieland, nachdem sie wieder mit der Arbeit angefangen hatte.
3. Immer wenn sie abends nach Hause kam, hatte Herr Wieland schon das Essen vorbereitet.
4. Viele Frauen mußten die Hausarbeit machen, nachdem sie den ganzen Tag im Beruf gearbeitet hatten.
5. Die Kinder konnten die Wäsche waschen, weil die Eltern es ihnen gezeigt hatten.
6. Frau Wieland hatte es leichter, nachdem die Familie angefangen hatte zu helfen.

10 Uses of *als, wenn,* and *wann*

Als, wenn, and **wann** are all equivalent to English *when*, but they are not interchangeable in German.

Als Paula gestern in Hamburg war, ging sie ins Theater.	When Paula was in Hamburg yesterday, she went to the theater.
Als Paula ein Teenager war, ging sie gern ins Theater.	When Paula was a teenager, she liked to go to the theater.

Als is used to introduce a clause concerned with a single event in the past or with a block of continuous time in the past.

Wenn Renate in Hamburg ist, geht sie viel ins Kino.	When Renate is in Hamburg, she goes to the movies a lot.
Wenn Erik in Hamburg war, ging er jeden Tag ins Theater.	When (whenever) Erik was in Hamburg, he went (would go) to the theater every day.

In *Kapitel 6* you learned that **wenn** is used to introduce a clause concerned with events or possibilities in present or future time. **Wenn** is also used to introduce a clause concerned with repeated events (whenever) in past time.

Wann gehen wir ins Kino?	When are we going to the movies?
Ich habe keine Ahnung, **wann** wir ins Kino gehen.	I have no idea when we're going to the movies.

Wann is used only for questions. It is used to introduce both direct and indirect questions.

20. Wann ... ?   A friend is asking you a lot of questions. Respond, changing the direct questions into indirect ones. Use one of the phrases listed.

Ich weiß nicht ...   ◇ Ich frage mich auch ...   ◇ Ich möchte auch wissen ...   ◇ Ich habe keine Ahnung ...

▶ Wann beginnt der Film?   *Ich habe keine Ahnung, wann der Film beginnt.*

1. Wann beginnt das Konzert?
2. Wann ruft Moritz an?
3. Wann fährt Anja in die Ferien?
4. Wann wird das Wetter besser?
5. Wann kommt das Taxi?
6. Wann können wir Pause machen?
7. Wann kommt der Briefträger°?   letter carrier

21. Eine berufstätige Mutter Working both outside and inside the home can be difficult. Tell about Frau Wieland's situation by joining the sentences with **als, wenn,** or **wann** as appropriate.

▶ Frauen sind berufstätig. Sie müssen oft noch die ganze Hausarbeit machen.

Wenn Frauen berufstätig sind, müssen sie oft noch die ganze Hausarbeit machen.

1. Frau Wieland fing zu arbeiten an. Klaus lernte die Wäsche zu waschen.
2. Frau Wieland kam abends nach Hause. Sie war oft müde.
3. Klaus wollte gestern essen. Er mußte erst einkaufen gehen.
4. Sie war letzten Sommer viel weg. Ihre Nachbarn kritisierten sie.
5. Ein Mann ist oft weg. Niemand kritisiert ihn.
6. Ihre Nachbarn fragten sie. Hört sie mit der Arbeit auf?

wann → (when) repeat question
ex: when does the train arrive

als → past tense + single event

wenn → as soon as
when(ever)
if (in case)

22. Erzähle von dir. Complete the following statements and share them with a partner. Your partner will then share his/her statements with you. Ask questions for more details.

Recounting events

1. Als ich vier Jahre alt war, …
2. Als ich in die Schule ging, …
3. Als ich das letzte Mal auf einer Party war, …
4. Wenn ich müde/glücklich/deprimiert°/nervös/böse bin
5. Wenn ich Hausarbeit machen muß, …
6. Wenn ich …
7. Als ich …

depressed

WIEDERHOLUNG

1. Neue Erfahrungen An acquaintance of the Fischers (see *Natürlichkeit und Umwelt, Kapitel 7*) wrote a report for a German newspaper on the Fischers' experience with artificial food colors. She wanted to show her German readers how customs in countries can differ. Read the account and answer the questions.

Fischers lebten erst seit einigen Wochen hier in Deutschland. Viele Sachen waren noch neu für sie. Da kamen an einem Sonntag deutsche Bekannte zum Kaffee. Frau Fischer backte den Kuchen selbst. Man saß am Kaffeetisch und sprach über Kinder, Schulen und Geschäfte. Die Gäste tranken den Kaffee, aber sie aßen nur wenig Kuchen. Die Deutschen fanden den Kuchen etwas merkwürdig. Der Kuchen war rot, grün und blau dekoriert. Die Farben waren nicht natürlich und daher schmeckte der Kuchen den Gästen nicht.

1. Wie lange lebten Fischers schon in Deutschland?
2. Warum kamen einige Bekannte?
3. Wo saß man?
4. Worüber sprach man?
5. Warum aßen die Bekannten nur wenig von dem Kuchen?

2. Ergänzen Sie. Be sure to use the correct form of a verb from the list in each sentence.

ansehen ◊ aussehen ◊ sehen

1. Der Kuchen ＿＿＿ gut ＿＿＿ .
2. ＿＿＿ Sie mal das moderne Bild ＿＿＿ . Furchtbar, nicht?
3. Karl ＿＿＿ das Problem nicht.

aufstehen ◊ stehen ◊ verstehen

4. Wir ＿＿＿ sonntags spät ＿＿＿ .
5. Klaus hat das Referat nicht ＿＿＿ .
6. Warum ＿＿＿ die Leute auf dem Fest?

ankommen ◊ bekommen ◊ hereinkommen ◊ kommen

7. Kannst du morgen zu mir ＿＿＿ ?
8. Haben Sie den Brief ＿＿＿ ?
9. Karin und Udo ＿＿＿ heute in München ＿＿＿ .
10. Die Gäste sollen doch ＿＿＿ .

3. Erzählen Sie von gestern. Tell what you did yesterday morning. Use appropriate expressions from the list; add other expressions, if you wish.

aufstehen ◊ sich baden ◊ sich die Haare kämmen ◊ sich anziehen ◊ Kaffee kochen ◊ ein Stück Toast essen ◊ Kaffee trinken ◊ Zeitung lesen ◊ sich die Zähne putzen ◊ zur Vorlesung gehen

4. Was bedeutet das? Form compounds using the following words. Give the English equivalents of the compounds.

1. die Bilder + das Buch
2. die Farb(e) + der Fernseher
3. die Blumen + das Geschäft
4. die Kinder + der Garten
5. die Geschicht(e) + s + der Lehrer
6. die Weihnacht + s + das Geschenk
7. das Hotel + der Gast

Er kocht nach Rezept.

5. **Wie sagt man das?**

1. Helga Nolte is a doctor. Her husband is a lawyer.
2. Christa is an engineer. Her brother is a student.
3. Christine is a programmer. Her father is a butcher.
4. Mrs. Brown is a professor. Her son is a teacher.

6. **Ihre Meinung**   Answer the following questions and then find out how your partner answered them. You may wish to ask additional questions about some of your partner's answers.

1. Wer macht die Hausarbeit bei Ihnen zu Hause?
2. Hat Ihre Mutter einen Beruf?
3. Sind Frauen and Männer in Amerika gleichberechtigt?
4. Finden Sie, daß eine Frau berufstätig sein kann, auch wenn die Kinder noch klein sind?
5. Möchten Sie in einem Flugzeug sitzen, das eine Frau fliegt?

oläne Talk with your partner about several things you wanted
: one of your vacations (Christmas, spring, summer) and why. Be
nclude which of the things you actually were able to do. Remem-
be, .onversation you should use the perfect tense, except for **sein,
haben** and modals, which are in the simple past.

▶ Ich wollte mit Jürgen jeden   *Aber er ist nur drei Mal gekommen,*
   Tag Tennis spielen.   *und so habe ich kaum gespielt.*

   Possible things to talk about are: reisen, ◇ [Tennis] spielen ◇ nach
   (Europa) fliegen ◇ [einem Freund] helfen ◇ eine Arbeit suchen ◇
   [Freunde] besuchen° ◇ einen Film sehen ◇ [ein Buch] lesen ◇   to visit
   spät aufstehen ◇ schwimmen ◇ einkaufen gehen

8. Anregung

1. In German, list five points that describe how the situation for women was
   twenty years ago (**vor zwanzig Jahren**) and how it is today.
2. In German, compare the different status of men and women either as it
   was or as it is now. Are there still areas of inequality today? What are
   they?

GRAMMATIK: ZUSAMMENFASSUNG

Sein and *haben* in simple past

Infinitive	Simple past
sein	war
haben	hatte

sein	
ich war	wir waren
du warst	ihr wart
er/es/sie war	sie waren
Sie waren	

haben	
ich hatte	wir hatten
du hattest	ihr hattet
er/es/sie hatte	sie hatten
Sie hatten	

Modals in the simple past

Infinitive	Simple past
dürfen	durfte
können	konnte
mögen	mochte
müssen	mußte
sollen	sollte
wollen	wollte

(handwritten:) gedurft
gekonnt
gemocht
gemußt
gesollt
gewollt

Simple past of regular weak verbs

Infinitive	Stem	Tense marker	Simple past
glauben	glaub-	-te	glaubte
spielen	spiel-	-te	spielte
baden	bad-	-ete	badete
arbeiten	arbeit-	-ete	arbeitete
regnen	regn-	-ete	regnete

Irregular weak verbs in the simple past

Infinitive	Simple past
bringen	brachte
denken	dachte
kennen	kannte
nennen	nannte
wissen	wußte

In the simple past tense, modals, weak verbs, and irregular weak verbs have the past-tense marker **-te**. In verbs with a stem ending in **-d** or **-t**, and in some verbs ending in **-n** or **-m**, the tense marker **-te** expands to **-ete**. Like **hatte**, all forms except the **ich-** and **er/es/sie-**forms add endings to the past-tense marker **-te**.

Separable-prefix verbs in the simple past

Present tense	Simple past
Sie **kauft** immer im Supermarkt **ein**.	Sie **kaufte** immer im Supermarkt **ein**.
Er **kommt** immer **mit**.	Er **kam** immer **mit**.

In the simple past tense, as in the present tense, the separable prefix is separated from the base form of the verb and is in final position.

Simple past of strong verbs

Infinitive	Simple past
gehen	ging
sehen	sah
schreiben	schrieb

Strong verbs undergo a stem vowel change in the simple past. Like **sein,** they do not take the past tense marker **-te.** The **ich-** and **er/es/sie-** forms have no verb endings.

Selected strong verbs

Below is a table of selected strong verbs that are often used in the simple past tense. For a more complete list see the Grammatical Tables, #23, in the Reference Section.

Infinitive	Simple past stem	*Past participle*
anfangen	fing an	— angefangen
anziehen	zog an	— angezogen
bleiben	blieb	— geblieben
essen	aß	— gegessen
fahren	fuhr	— ist gefahren
finden	fand	— gefunden
geben	gab	— gegeben
gefallen	gefiel	— gefallen
gehen	ging	— gegangen
halten	hielt	— gehalten
helfen	half	— geholfen
kommen	kam	ist gekommen
laufen	lief	— ist gelaufen
lesen	las	— gelesen
liegen	lag	— geliegen
nehmen	nahm	— genommen ~ genommen
schlafen	schlief	— geschlafen
schreiben	schrieb	— geschrieben ~ geschrieben
sehen	sah	— gesehen
sein	war	— gewesen
sitzen	saß	— gesessen
sprechen	sprach	— gesprochen
stehen	stand	— gestanden
tragen	trug	— getragen
treffen	traf	— getroffen
trinken	trank	— getrunken
tun	tat	— getan
vergessen	vergaß	— vergessen
werden	wurde	— geworden

haben hatte gehabt

Past perfect tense

Ich **hatte** vor zwei Tagen **angefangen** zu arbeiten.	I had started working two days before.
Er **war** am Montag **angekommen.**	He had arrived on Monday.

The German past perfect is a compound tense that consists of the simple past of either **haben** or **sein** plus the past participle of the main verb.

Uses of *als, wenn,* and *wann* in the meaning of **when**

1. **Als** Inge Dieter gestern sah, sprachen sie über Politik.	When Inge saw Dieter yesterday, they talked about politics.
2. **Als** Inge jung war, sprach sie gern über Politik.	When Inge was young, she liked to talk about politics.
3. **Wenn** sie Dieter früher sah, redete sie immer über Politik.	When (whenever) she used to see Dieter, she always spoke about politics.
4. **Wenn** wir in München sind, gehen wir ins Konzert.	When (whenever, if) we are in Munich, we go to a concert.
5. **Wann** beginnt das Konzert?	When does the concert begin?
6. Ich weiß nicht, **wann** das Konzert beginnt.	I don't know when the concert begins.

Als, wenn, wann are used as follows.

1. **als** — a single event in past time
2. **als** — a block of continuous time in the past
3. **wenn** — repeated events (whenever) in past time
4. **wenn** — present or future time
5. **wann** — introduces direct questions
6. **wann** — introduces indirect questions

Freizeit im Sommer — Studenten
in Tübingen

Kapitel 12

BAUSTEINE FÜR GESPRÄCHE

Was habt ihr vor?

Dirk: Sagt mal, was macht ihr am Wochenende?

Evi: Keine Ahnung.

Paul: Ich hab' am Freitag Probe mit meiner Band. Am Samstag spielen wir in der Musikfabrik.

Dirk: He, Evi, da könnten wir doch zusammen hingehen. Hättest du Lust?

Evi: Oh ja. Das wäre wirklich super.

Paul: Vielleicht geht auch Gunnar mit, was meint ihr? Würdest du ihn anrufen, Dirk?

Evi: Der muß fürs Examen lernen, der kann nicht.

Dirk: Also gut. Evi, ich hol' dich ab, so gegen neun. O.K.?

Evi: Ist gut.

What are your plans?

Say, what are you doing on the weekend?

No idea.

I've got a rehearsal with my band on Friday. On Saturday we're playing at the Musikfabrik.

Hey, Evi, you know, we could go there together. Feel like it?

Oh yes. That would be really great.

Maybe Gunnar will go along too, what do you think? Would you call him, Dirk?

He has to study for his comprehensives. He can't.

All right then. Evi, I'll pick you up, sometime around nine. O.K.?

That's fine.

Fragen

1. Was hat Paul am Wochenende vor?
2. Wohin möchte Dirk gehen?
3. Warum kann Gunnar wohl nicht mitgehen?
4. Wann holt Dirk Evi ab?

Musiker proben

1. **Was machst du in der Freizeit°?** Find out what a fellow student likes to do for fun. You may wish to refer to the Supplementary Word Sets on Hobbies for *Kapitel 12* and on Sports and Games for *Kapitel 2* in the Reference Section.

Discussing leisure-time activities

Sie	*Gesprächspartner/in*
Was sind deine Hobbys?	**Radfahren.**
	Fußball spielen.
	Musik hören/machen.
	Science Fiction lesen.
	Skilaufen.
	Spazierengehen°.
	Fotografieren°.
	Jogging°.
	Malen°.
	Ins Kino gehen.
	Computer-Programme schreiben.

Was hast du am Wochenende vor?	Ich gehe	**segeln°.**
		schwimmen.
		Ski laufen.
		windsurfen°.
		tanzen.
	Ich mache eine Wanderung°.	
	Ich will	**Musik machen.**
		viel lesen.
		faulenzen°.
		arbeiten.

Was würdest du gern in den Sommerferien machen?	Ich würde gern	**nach Europa fliegen.**
		eine Radtour° machen.
		jobben°.
		faulenzen.
	Ich würde mich gern vom Streß° des Semesters erholen°.	

2. **Was machst du gern?** Choose three answers for each of the questions in 1. Then find fellow students who share your interests.

3. **Was sagen Sie?**   Answer the questions for yourself and then ask a partner for her/his answers. You may wish to ask for more details. Be sure to use **du** with your partner.

1. Was haben Sie am Wochenende gemacht?
2. Was haben Sie dieses Wochenende vor?
3. Möchten Sie eine Radtour machen? Wohin?
4. Spielen Sie ein Musikinstrument°?
5. Möchten Sie in einer Band spielen?

Vokabeln

— Substantive

die **Band, -s** band
das **Examen, -** (comprehensive) examination
die **Freizeit** leisure time
das **Hobby, -s** hobby
das **Jogging** jogging, running
das **Musikinstrument, -e** musical instrument

die **Probe, -n** rehearsal
der **See, -n** lake
der **Streß** stress
die **Tour, -en** tour, trip
die **Wanderung, -en** hike

— Verben

sich erholen (von) to recuperate (from) [an illness, fatigue, etc.]
faulenzen to lounge around, be idle
fotografieren to photograph
jobben (*colloq.*) to have a job (e.g., a summer job)
malen to paint
segeln to sail

spazieren·gehen, ging spazieren, ist spazierengegangen to go for a walk
vor·haben to intend, have in mind
windsurfen gehen to go windsurfing; **surfen** to surf
würde (*subjunctive of* **werden**) would

— Besondere Ausdrücke

Lust haben to feel like; **Dazu habe ich keine Lust.** I don't feel like it; **Hättest du Lust?** Would you feel like it?; **Ich habe keine Lust zu arbeiten.** I don't feel like working.

Ist gut. That's fine (okay) with me.

**Prost Neujahr! —
Feuerwerk in Mittenwald**

Germany celebrates both secular and religious holidays. Among the secular holidays are New Year's Eve (**Silvester**), New Year's Day (**Neujahr**), and **Tag der Arbeit** on May 1, which is celebrated in honor of workers. The newest holiday is the national holiday, **Tag der deutschen Einheit** (Day of Unity), celebrated on October 3 to commemorate the unification of East and West Germany in 1990.

The following Christian holidays are observed throughout the country: Good Friday (**Karfreitag**); Easter (**Ostern**—both **Ostersonntag** and **Ostermontag**); Ascension Day (**Christi Himmelfahrt**), the sixth Thursday after Easter; Pentecost (**Pfingsten**), the seventh Sunday and Monday after Easter; and December 25 and 26 (**erster Weihnachtstag** and **zweiter Weihnachtstag**). Five other Christian holidays are observed in some states, but not all.

FREIZEIT

Vorbereitung auf das Lesen

◆ *Zum Thema*

1. Was ist Ihnen am wichtigsten: Arbeit, Freizeit, Freunde oder Familie?
2. Was meinen Sie? Was ist den typischen Amerikanern am wichtigsten: Arbeit oder Freizeit? Was ist den typischen Deutschen am wichtigsten?
3. Was machen Studenten an Ihrer Uni in der Freizeit?
4. Und was machen andere junge Leute?

◆ *Leitfragen*

1. Manche Leute glauben, daß für die Deutschen die Arbeit zuerst kommt. Wie ist es in Wirklichkeit?
2. Die Deutschen haben viel Freizeit. Wer hat wann frei: Arbeitnehmer, Jugendliche, Studenten?
3. Was machen junge Leute in ihrer Freizeit: Klaus, Susanne, eine Musikgruppe, Susannes Freunde, Susannes Bruder?

DIE DEUTSCHEN ARBEITEN IMMER. SIE SIND SEHR FLEISSIG. UND SIE HABEN NIE ZEIT.

Dieses Bild von den Deutschen war lange Zeit sehr verbreitet°. Der Fleiß° der Deutschen war ebenso sprichwörtlich° wie ihre Ordnung.   *widespread / diligence / proverbial*

In einer Umfrage° des Instituts für Freizeitforschung° in Hamburg zeigten sich die Deutschen aber von einer ganz anderen Seite. Man fragte sie: „Was   *opinion poll / research on leisure time*
5 ist Ihnen von diesen vier Dingen am wichtigsten: Arbeit, Familie und Partnerschaft, Freizeit oder Freunde?" Die Antworten zeigten dieses Bild: Am wichtigsten waren Familie und Partnerschaft. An zweiter Stelle schon stand Freizeit, an dritter Freunde, und erst ganz am Ende folgte Arbeit.

Die Freizeit wird schon aus dem Grund immer wichtiger, weil die Deut-
10 schen immer mehr davon haben. Sonnabends haben die meisten Arbeitnehmer frei. Die Arbeitswoche hat sich in den letzten 15 Jahren von 45 auf 40

Band in einer Würzburger Kneipe

Stunden verkürzt°. In einigen Industrien arbeitet man schon 38,5 Stunden. — shortened

Das Ziel ist die 35-Stunden-Woche. Jugendliche gehen im Durchschnitt° sechs — on the average

Stunden am Tag zur Schule, den ganzen Nachmittag und Abend haben sie

15 frei. Auch Studenten haben relativ viel Zeit, die° sie sich selbst einteilen° — which / arrange

können. Sie sind unabhängiger° in ihrem Studium und nicht so gebunden — more independent

durch den Stundenplan wie amerikanische Studenten.

Klaus geht zum Beispiel morgens für eine Stunde zu einer Vorlesung,

dann noch einmal am späten Nachmittag. Dazwischen° sitzt er fast immer in — in between

20 der Bibliothek und arbeitet, damit er den Abend frei hat. Dann trifft er sich oft

mit Freunden, und sie gehen in eine der Studentenkneipen, um ein Bierchen° — small glass of beer

zu trinken. Er geht am liebsten in Kneipen mit live Musik. Man findet viele

solche Gaststätten im Univiertel. Manchmal spielen dort sogar klassische

Gruppen, aber meistens gibt es Rock. Klaus mag die Atmosphäre da. Gute

25 Musik, gute Gespräche und gutes Bier — was braucht man mehr?

Er geht auch sehr gern ins Kino, meistens in eines der Programmkinos° in — art theaters

der Nähe der Uni. Neulich gab es eine Serie von französischen Filmen. Die

hat ihm gut gefallen. Und die Faßbinder°-Retrospektive fand er auch sehr gut. — [a German movie director]

Susanne würde auch gern öfter ins Kino gehen, wenn sie mehr Zeit hätte.

30 Aber sie studiert Musik und verbringt den größten Teil ihrer Freizeit mit

Musik. So spielt sie in einem Orchester und in einem Streichquartett°. Mit — string quartet

beiden hat sie viele Proben.

Angefangen hat sie in einem Jugendorchester, wo sie vor allem das klas-

sische Repertoire von Komponisten wie Mozart, Bach und Beethoven ken-

35 nenlernte. Seit etwa drei Monaten macht sie bei einer Musikgruppe mit, die° — that

vor allem politische und kritische Lieder singt. Die Gruppenmitglieder schrei-

ben ihre Texte und Lieder selbst, was° Susanne besonderen Spaß macht. — which

Überhaupt ist diese Gruppe eine ganz neue Erfahrung für sie, weil sie bisher

immer nur klassische bzw.° „ernste" Musik gemacht hat. Ein paar Mal haben — bzw. = beziehungsweise: or, rather

40 sie schon auf der Straße gespielt. Und im Moment bereiten sie sich gerade auf

ein Hinterhoffest° in ihrem Stadtviertel vor. Die lokale Bürgerinitiative hat sie — courtyard party

gefragt, ob sie Lust hätten, da mitzumachen, und sie haben natürlich ja

gesagt.

Wenn sie mehr Zeit hätte, würde Susanne gern öfter ein paar Freunde auf

45 dem Lande besuchen. Die haben sich vor kurzem ein Bauernhaus gemietet.

Sie basteln dauernd° an dem Haus herum°. Den Freunden macht das — continually / here and there

Renovieren soviel Spaß, daß sie ihre ganze Freizeit damit verbringen.

Vor kurzem hat Susannes Bruder sie mit dem Motorrad hingefahren. Für

den ist das natürlich nur eine Entschuldigung, wieder eine Tour zu machen,

50 denn er ist begeisterter° Motorradfahrer. Und Susanne fährt gern mit. Peter, — enthusiastic

einer der Freunde, hat ihr ganz stolz den Garten gezeigt. Sie haben Tomaten,

Möhren°, Gurken° und Zwiebeln° gepflanzt, und alles sah sehr gut aus. Peter — carrots / cucumbers / onions

meinte: „Am liebsten würden wir nämlich nur frisches, ungespritztes° — unsprayed

Gemüse aus unserem eigenen Garten essen. Wenn wir ein paar Jahre früher

55 mit diesem Projekt hier angefangen hätten, könnten wir das heute schon. Na

ja, vielleicht können wir das dann im nächsten Jahr."

Fragen zum Lesestück

1. Welches Bild der Deutschen war lange sehr bekannt?
2. Was zeigte sich in der Umfrage?
   a. Was ist den Deutschen am wichtigsten?
   b. Was steht an zweiter (dritter, vierter) Stelle?
3. Warum wird die Freizeit immer wichtiger?
4. Wie viele Stunden am Tag gehen Jugendliche zur Schule?
5. Wann haben sie frei?
6. Wann geht Klaus zur Vorlesung?
7. Was machen er und seine Freunde abends oft?
8. Was gehört zu einem netten Abend für Klaus?
9. In was für Kinos geht Klaus gern?
10. Warum hat Susanne wenig Freizeit?
11. Wo hat Susanne Komponisten wie Bach, Beethoven und Mozart ken-nengelernt?
12. Was macht die Gruppe, bei der° sie seit drei Monaten mitspielt?   whom
13. Was ist für Susanne bei dieser Gruppe neu?
14. Worauf bereiten sie sich gerade vor?
15. Wen würde Susanne gern besuchen?
16. Was machen ihre Freunde mit dem Bauernhaus?
17. Was macht Susannes Bruder gern in seiner Freizeit?
18. Was würden die Freunde gern essen?
19. Warum können sie noch nicht viel Gemüse aus dem eigenen Garten essen?

1. Erzählen Sie.   Select one of the three topics below, A, B or C, to talk about this reading selection. Use the cued words.

A. Klaus in der Freizeit

   Stichworte: Vorlesung ◇ Bibliothek ◇ Kneipen ◇ Kino

B. Susanne in der Freizeit

   Stichworte: klassische Musik ◇ Jugendorchester ◇ Liedergruppe

C. Susannes Fahrt aufs Land

   Stichworte: mit dem Motorrad ◇ Bauernhaus renovieren ◇ Garten

2. In der Freizeit   Ask your partner about his/her leisure-time activities. Develop a conversation using one or two of the questions as a starting point.

Discussing leisure-time activities

Fragen Sie Ihren Partner/Ihre Partnerin,

1. wie viele Stunden er/sie in der Woche arbeitet.
2. wo er/sie meistens arbeitet — in der Bibliothek oder zu Hause.
3. ob er/sie oft in die Kneipe geht.
4. ob er/sie gern ausländische Filme sieht.
5. welchen Film er/sie vor kurzem gesehen hat.
6. ob er/sie gern klassische Musik hört.
7. ob er/sie gern Hard Rock hört.
8. ob er/sie gern ein Bauernhaus renovieren würde.
9. ob er/sie gern bei einer Bürgerinitiative mitmachen würde.
10. was er/sie nicht gern macht.
11. was ihm/ihr wichtiger ist — Arbeit oder Freizeit.

3. Ein Bauernhaus   Assume that you and several friends want to buy an old farmhouse to renovate. You have seen this ad for a house in Affoltern, a village now incorporated into the city of Zürich. A friend wants to know what it says and asks you the following questions. If you need help getting the gist of the ad, see the Vocabulary for Authentic Text Activities in the Reference Section.

1. Wie groß ist das Grundstück?
2. Welche Gebäude gibt es?
3. Was kann man mit den Gebäuden machen?

4. Rollenspiel   After reading the ad, think of what else you must know before you make an offer. Prepare questions you need to ask of the owner (**Eigentümer/in**). You may want to inquire about price, monthly payments, and age and condition of the buildings.

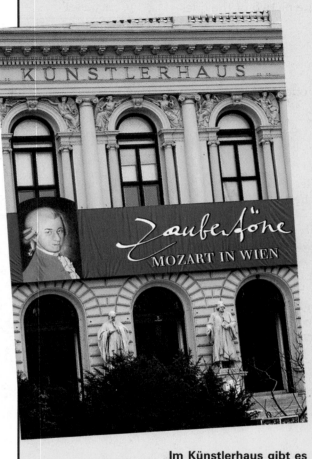

Johann Sebastian Bach (1685–1750) is now considered the great musical genius of the baroque period. During his lifetime, however, he was acknowledged only as an organist. From 1723 on, Bach was the director of music at St. Thomas Church in Leipzig. Bach's reputation as a composer was established as late as 1829, when Felix Mendelssohn revived his "Passion according to St. Matthew" (***Matthäuspassion***). Other famous works by Bach include many of his 300 cantatas (**Kantaten**), his fugues (**Fugen**), the "Mass in B minor" (***Messe in h-moll***), and the "Brandenburg Concertos" (***Brandenburgische Konzerte***).

Wolfgang Amadeus Mozart (1756–1791) was born in Salzburg, Austria. He spent his last ten years in Vienna, where he died in poverty. During his short life, Mozart wrote more than 600 works, including 40 symphonies. Among his best-known operas are "The Marriage of Figaro" (***Le Nozze Di Figaro***), ***Don Giovanni, Cosi fan tutte,*** and "The Magic Flute" (***Die Zauberflöte***).

Ludwig van Beethoven (1770–1827) was born in Bonn, Germany, but moved in 1792 to Vienna. He began to lose his hearing at the age of twenty and was unable to hear his own last compositions. The composer of nine symphonies, concerti, quartets and trios, sonatas, and an opera (***Fidelio***), Beethoven is regarded as one of the founders of musical romanticism.

Im Künstlerhaus gibt es eine Ausstellung: Mozart in Wien.

Vokabeln

— Substantive —

die **Antwort, -en** answer; **die Antwort auf eine Frage** the answer to a question

der **Arbeitnehmer, -**/die **Arbeitnehmerin, -nen** worker, employee der **Bauer, -n, -n**/die **Bäuerin, -nen** farmer; das **Bauernhaus, ̈er** farmhouse

die **Bürgerinitiative, -n** citizens' action group, grassroots movement

die **Entschuldigung, -en** excuse; apology; **Entschuldigung!** Excuse me.

der **Fahrer, -**/die **Fahrerin, -nen** driver

die **Gaststätte, -n** restaurant, pub, bar

der **Grund, ̈e** reason; **aus diesem Grund** for this reason

der **Hof, ̈e** courtyard

die **Industrie, -n** industry

die **Jugend** youth

der/die **Jugendliche** (*noun decl. like adj.*) young person

der **Komponist, -en, -en**/die **Komponistin, -nen** composer

das **Mal, -e** time

das **Mitglied, -er** member (*of group*)

der **Moment, -e** moment; **im Moment** at the moment; **Einen Moment, bitte.** Just a minute, please.

das **Orchester, -** orchestra

die **Ordnung** order

das **Studium** studies

der **Stundenplan, ̈e** schedule

das **Viertel, -** district; das **Stadtviertel** city district

—— Verben

basteln to tinker (with), to work at a hobby

besuchen to visit

binden, band, gebunden to tie

folgen, ist gefolgt (+ *dat.*) to follow

mieten to rent

mit·machen (**bei** + *a group)* to join in, participate; **Sie macht bei einer Musikgruppe mit.** She plays with a music group.

pflanzen to plant

singen, sang, gesungen to sing

sich treffen (trifft), traf, getroffen (mit) to meet; **Ich treffe mich mit Freunden.** I'm meeting friends.

verbringen, verbrachte, verbracht to spend (*time*)

sich vor·bereiten (auf + *acc.*) to prepare (for)

—— Andere Wörter

bisher until now

damit (*conj.*) so that

ebenso just as

französisch French (*adj.*)

höflich polite

neulich recently

sogar even

stolz proud(ly)

—— Besondere Ausdrücke

auf dem Lande in the country; **aufs Land** to the country

immer wichtiger more and more important

in der Nähe (von) nearby, in the vicinity (of)

na ja oh well

noch einmal again, once more

vor kurzem recently

Erweiterung des Wortschatzes

1 *Immer* + comparative

Die Freizeit wird **immer wichtiger,** weil die Deutschen **immer mehr** davon haben.

Leisure time becomes more and more important because the Germans have more and more of it.

The construction **immer** + comparative indicates an increase in the quantity, quality, or degree expressed by the adjective or adverb.

1. Was bedeutet das?

1. Der Lebensstandard der Deutschen wird immer höher.
2. Die Wohnungen werden immer größer.
3. Sie tragen immer bessere Kleidung.
4. Die Arbeitszeit wird immer kürzer.
5. Die Ferien werden immer länger.
6. Immer weniger Leute bleiben während der Ferien zu Hause.
7. Das Leben wird immer schöner.

2 Diminutives *-chen* and *-lein*

das Brot bread   **das Brötchen** roll
das Buch book   **das Büchlein** little book
die Stadt city   **das Städtchen** small town

The diminutive form of nouns is made by adding the suffix **-chen** or **-lein**. The vowels **a, au, o,** and **u** take umlaut. Nouns ending in the suffix **-chen** or **-lein** are neuter, regardless of the gender of the original noun.

2. Hänschen klein Form diminutives by adding **-chen** to the words listed below.

1. die Tochter
2. das Glas
3. die Hand
4. das Haus
5. die Karte
6. Hans
7. der Schlaf
8. der Sohn
9. Katrin

3. Brüderlein und Schwesterlein Form diminutives by adding **-lein** to the words listed below.

1. das Auge
2. die Blume
3. der Brief
4. das Kind
5. der Vogel
6. der Tisch

GRAMMATIK UND ÜBUNGEN

1 Subjunctive mood vs. indicative mood

Indicative	Trudi kommt heute nicht.	Trudi is not coming today.
	Vielleicht kommt sie morgen.	Perhaps she'll come tomorrow.

In *Kapitel 1–11* you have primarily been using verbs in sentences that make statements and ask questions dealing with "real" situations. Verb forms of this type are said to be in the indicative mood. The indicative mood is used to make factual statements *(Trudi is not coming today)*, or statements that may possibly be true or become true *(Perhaps she'll come tomorrow)*.

Subjunctive	Ich **würde** das nicht **tun.**⎫	
	Ich **täte** das nicht. ⎬	I *would* not *do* that.
	Hätte Stefan das **getan?**	*Would* Stefan *have done* that?

When we talk about "unreal" situations we may use verbs in the subjunctive mood. The subjunctive mood indicates a speaker's attitude toward a situation, a feeling that the situation is hypothetical, uncertain, potential, or contrary to fact. When a speaker says "I wouldn't do that," she/he means "I wouldn't do that if I were you (or she, he, or someone else)," because she/he thinks it is not a good idea. When the speaker asks "Would Stefan have done that?", she/he is postulating a hypothetical situation.

You have used subjunctive forms, such as **wäre** (**Wie wäre es ... ?** *How would it be . . . ?*), in earlier chapters.

Wishes	Ich **möchte** eine Tasse Kaffee.	I *would like* a cup of coffee.
Polite Requests	**Würden** Sie das bitte **tun?**	*Would* you *do* that, please?

The subjunctive is also used to express wishes and polite requests. You have been using **möchte** to express wishes since *Kapitel 5*. **Möchte** *(would like)* is the subjunctive form of **mögen** *(to like)*.

German has two ways to express the subjunctive mood. One way is to use the **würde**-construction (Ich **würde** das nicht **tun.**). The other way is to use the subjunctive form of the main verb (Ich **täte** das nicht.). The meaning of both ways is the same (I *would* not *do* that.). In spoken German the **würde**-construction is used much more frequently than the subjunctive form of main verbs, with the exception of a few verbs that are commonly used.

Present-time	Wenn ich heute oder morgen nur Zeit **hätte.**	If I only *had* time today or tomorrow./If I only *would have* time today or tomorrow.
Past-time	Wenn ich gestern nur Zeit **gehabt hätte.**	If I only *had had* time yesterday./If I only *would have had* time yesterday.

Subjunctive forms express two time categories: present time which also can refer to the future (*if I only had time now or in the future*) and past time (*if only I had had time in the past*).

2 The *würde*-construction

Würdest du mir bitte **helfen?**   *Would* you please *help* me?
Ich **würde** das nicht **machen.**   I *would*n't *do* that.

To talk about "unreal" situations in the present, German often uses a **würde**-construction. English uses a *would*-construction.

ich **würde** es **machen**	wir **würden** es **machen**
du **würdest** es **machen**	ihr **würdet** es **machen**
er/es/sie **würde** es **machen**	sie **würden** es **machen**
Sie **würden** es **machen**	

The **würde**-construction consists of a form of **würde** plus an infinitive. **Würde** is the subjunctive form of **werden.** It is formed by adding an umlaut to **wurde,** the simple past of **werden.**

1. Würden Sie mitfahren?   Schmidts are not having much luck in planning an outing. Tell who would not go along. Restate, using each of the cued subjects and the **würde**-construction.

▶   Ich würde nicht mitfahren. (Andrea)   *Andrea würde nicht mitfahren.*

1. Christoph
2. ihr
3. Eva und Hilde
4. du
5. mein Großvater
6. deine Tante
7. Christiane
8. wir

Theater in the German-speaking countries has a long tradition. The present system of theater buildings with resident staffs goes back to the eighteenth century. Many theaters were founded then by local rulers to provide entertainment for the court. Today there are more than 500 theaters in the German-speaking countries. In Germany, most of the theaters are repertory theaters under the jurisdiction of city governments (**Stadttheater**), some are under the jurisdiction of an individual state (**Staatstheater**), and some are private theaters (**Privattheater**).

In addition to the institutionalized theaters there are also many independent theaters (**Freie Theatergruppen**). Some of the private theaters are small stages run in conjunction with a pub (**Kneipe** or **Wirtschaft**) which helps to finance the theater. Many theaters receive government subsidies for their productions, and offer discounted tickets for students. The repertory (**Spielplan**) of German-speaking theaters usually includes a variety of German and foreign classics and modern plays.

**An der Litfaßsäule
erfährt man, wo was los ist.**

3 Uses of the *würde*-construction

Hypothetical conclusions	Ich **würde** ihm **helfen.**	I *would help* him.
Wishes	Wenn er mir nur **helfen würde.**	If only he *would help* me.
Polite requests	**Würden** Sie mir bitte **helfen?**	*Would* you please *help* me?

The **würde**-construction is used in hypothetical conclusions, in wishes, and in polite requests.

2. Sabine würde das auch gern machen. Say that Sabine would like to do things Susanne does. Use the **würde-**construction.

▶ Susanne spielt Gitarre. *Sabine würde auch gern Gitarre spielen.*

1. Susanne studiert Musik.
2. Sie lernt neue Lieder.
3. Susanne macht Musik auf der Straße.
4. Sie besucht Freunde auf dem Land.
5. Sie hilft im Garten.
6. Abends gehen sie in eine Kneipe.

3. Beim Kaffee The Bergers have invited their neighbors for coffee. Restate the sentences below as polite requests, using the **würde-**construction.

▶ Kommen Sie bitte herein. *Würden Sie bitte hereinkommen?*

1. Gehen Sie bitte ins Wohnzimmer.
2. Setzen Sie sich bitte.
3. Nehmen Sie bitte von dem Kuchen.
4. Erzählen Sie bitte von Ihrer Reise.
5. Bleiben Sie bitte noch ein wenig.

4. Was würden Sie gern machen? Answer the following questions for yourself. Then compare your answers with two other members of the class.

▶ Was würden Sie nach der Deutschstunde am liebsten machen?

Ich würde am liebsten nach Hause gehen/einen Kaffee trinken/schlafen.

1. Was würden Sie heute abend gern machen?
2. Was würden Sie am Freitagabend am liebsten machen?
3. Was würden Sie im Sommer gern machen?
4. Was würden Sie nach dem Studium gern machen?
5. Was würden Sie jetzt am liebsten machen?

4 Present-time subjunctive of the main verb

Wenn er mehr **arbeitete,** würde er mehr Geld verdienen.	If he *worked* more, he would earn more money.
Wenn ich das **könnte,** würde ich es tun.	If I *could* (do that), I would (do it).
Wenn sie müde **wäre,** würde sie ins Bett gehen.	If she *were* (colloquial: *was*) tired, she would go to bed.

Notice that in English the subjunctive forms of main verbs are often identical with the past tense [e.g., *worked, could, were* (colloquial: *was*)]. In German the same principle applies. For weak verbs, the present-time subjunctive is identical to the simple past tense (e.g., **arbeitete**); for modals and strong verbs, the subjunctive is based on the simple-past tense form of the verb (e.g., **konnte** > **könnte, war** > **wäre**). German uses the present-time subjunctive to express subjunctive for present and future time.

5 Present-time subjunctive of the main verb vs. the *würde*-construction

Present-time subjunctive	Würde-construction
Wenn er nur besser **spielte**.	Wenn er nur besser **spielen würde**.
Wenn sie nur etwas **täte**.	Wenn sie nur etwas **tun würde**.
Wenn er nur **ginge**.	Wenn er nur **gehen würde**.

In present-time either the **würde**-construction or the subjunctive form of the main verb can be used to express hypothetical conclusions, wishes, and polite requests. However, for the verbs **sein, haben,** and the modals, the present-time subjunctive is generally used instead of the **würde**-construction.

6 Present-time subjunctive of *sein* and *haben*

sein	
ich wär**e**	wir wär**en**
du wär**est**	ihr wär**et**
er/es/sie wär**e**	sie wär**en**
Sie wär**en**	

haben	
ich hätt**e**	wir hätt**en**
du hätt**est**	ihr hätt**et**
er/es/sie hätt**e**	sie hätt**en**
Sie hätt**en**	

The verbs **haben** and **sein** are more commonly used in their subjunctive forms, **wäre** and **hätte,** than as part of the **würde**-construction. Notice that the subjunctive of **haben** is identical to the simple past tense (i.e., **hatte**) except that an umlaut has been added.

In strong verbs like **sein** the endings **-est** and **-et** often contract to **-st** and **-t: wärest** > **wärst, wäret** > **wärt.** Note that the endings above are used on all verbs in the subjunctive.

5. Alle wären froh. Some politicians are talking about a speed limit on the **Autobahn.** Say that the following people would certainly be happy if there were one.

▶ Roland   *Roland wäre sicher froh.*

1. Ria   4. Corinna und Rafael   7. die Grünen
2. du   5. ich   8. Sie
3. wir   6. ihr

6. Alle hätten Angst. A friend asks how the same people would feel if there were a leak in one of the atomic power plants. Say they would all be afraid, of course.

▶ Roland   *Roland hätte natürlich Angst.*

1. Ria   4. Corinna und Rafael   7. die Grünen
2. du   5. ich   8. alle
3. wir   6. ihr

7. Hättest du Lust? Decide what leisure-time activity you would like to do. Then try to find three classmates who would like to do the same thing.

Sie		*Gesprächspartner/in*
Hättest du Lust,	**schwimmen zu gehen?**	Das wäre schön.
	ins Kino zu gehen?	Wenn es nur wärmer wäre.
	eine Party zu geben?	Das würde ich gern machen.
	eine Radtour zu machen?	Das würde Spaß machen.
	Musik zu hören?	Wenn ich nur Zeit hätte.
	fernzusehen?	Dazu hätte ich keine Lust.
	Russisch zu lernen?	

8. Wenn ich nur … You get to make two wishes. Tell your partner what they are and she/he will tell you her/his wishes. Some suggestions are given below.

> Expressing wishes

1. Wenn ich nur […] hätte.

   mehr Geld ◇ Zeit ◇ Freunde ◇ weniger Probleme ◇ Arbeit ◇ keine Hausaufgaben

2. Wenn ich nur […] wäre.

   reich ◇ fleißiger ◇ ruhiger ◇ nicht so müde ◇ nicht so nervös

Am Wochenende ist im Musikcafé immer etwas los.

7 Conditional sentences

A conditional sentence contains two clauses: the condition (**wenn-**clause) and the conclusion. The **wenn-**clause states the conditions under which some event mentioned in the conclusion may or may not take place.

◆ *Conditions of fact*

Wenn ich Zeit **habe, komme** ich **mit.**	If I *have* time (maybe I will, maybe I won't), I'll *come* along.

Conditions of fact are conditions that are capable of fulfillment. Indicative verb forms are used in conditions of fact.

◆ *Conditions contrary to fact*

Wenn ich Zeit **hätte, würde** ich **mitkommen.** Wenn ich Zeit **hätte, käme** ich mit.	If I *had* time [but I don't], I *would come along.*

A sentence with a condition contrary to fact indicates a situation that will not take place. The speaker only speculates on how some things could or would be under certain conditions (if the speaker had time, for example).

To talk about the present, a speaker uses present-time subjunctive of the main verb (e.g., **hätte**) in the condition clause (**wenn-**clause) and generally uses a **würde-**construction (e.g., **würde mitkommen**) in the conclusion clause. In formal usage the conclusion may contain a subjunctive form of the main verb instead (e.g., **käme ich mit**). Formal written German tends to avoid the **würde-**construction in the **wenn-**clause. Subjunctive forms of strong and weak verbs are discussed under headings 9 and 10 in this section.

9. Was wäre, wenn ...? Answer the following questions for yourself, then ask your partner the same questions. Share your answers with the entire class. Remember to use **du** with your partner.

Was würden Sie tun,

1. wenn Sie 10 Jahre älter wären?
2. wenn Sie sehr reich wären?
3. wenn Sie Deutschlehrer/in wären?
4. wenn Sie Präsident/in der USA wären?
5. wenn Sie kein Geld fürs Studium hätten?
6. wenn Ihre Freunde keine Zeit für Sie hätten?
7. wenn Sie morgen frei hätten?
8. wenn Sie kein Auto hätten?
9. wenn Ihr Fernseher kaputt wäre?
10. wenn Sie morgen krank wären?
11. wenn wir morgen 30°C hätten?

Sie	*Gesprächspartner/in*	
Was würdest du tun, wenn du 10 Jahre älter wärest?	Ich würde ein Haus kaufen/ein Buch schreiben/heiraten°.	get married

8 Modals in present-time subjunctive

	Simple past	**Present-time subjunctive**	**Infinitive**
er/es/sie	durfte	**dürfte**	dürfen
	konnte	**könnte**	können
	mochte	**möchte**	mögen
	mußte	**müßte**	müssen
	sollte	**sollte**	sollen
	wollte	**wollte**	wollen

The present-time subjunctive of modals is identical to the simple-past tense except that the modals that have an umlaut in the infinitive also have an umlaut in the subjunctive.

Müßtest du die Arbeit allein machen?　　*Would* you *have to* do the work alone?

Like **sein (wäre)** and **haben (hätte)**, the modals are generally used in their subjunctive form rather than as infinitives with the **würde**-construction.

Dürfte ich auch mitkommen?　　　　　*Might* I come along, too?
Könntest du noch etwas bleiben?　　　*Could* you stay a while?
Müßte sie vor allen Leuten　　　　　*Would* she *have to* speak in front
　sprechen?　　　　　　　　　　　　　of all the people?
Möchten Sie in einer Stunde essen?　　*Would* you *like to* eat in an hour?
Solltet ihr jetzt nicht gehen?　　　　*Should*n't you be going now?

The subjunctive forms of the modals are frequently used to express polite requests or wishes.

Ich wollte, ich hätte Zeit.　　*I wish* I had time.
Ich wollte, sie käme bald.　　*I wish* she would come soon.

The expression **ich wollte** is used frequently to introduce wishes. Note that the verb **wollte** is subjunctive. Thus, strictly, **ich wollte** is equivalent to *I would wish.*

10. Etwas höflicher, bitte!　You and some friends are getting ready to go out for the evening. You express some concerns and some orders. Soften the tone of the statements and questions by using the present-time subjunctive of the modals.

▶　Können wir die Gaststätte allein finden?　　*Könnten wir die Gaststätte allein finden?*

1. Können wir nicht bald gehen?
2. Du mußt noch abwaschen.
3. Kann ich dir helfen?
4. Kann die Musik etwas lauter sein?
5. Dürfen Susi und Christiane mitkommen?
6. Sollen wir Gerd nicht auch einladen?
7. Darf ich für euch alle etwas zu trinken kaufen?

11. **Wenn es nur anders wäre.** Express wishes to a friend about many things in your dormitory you would like to be different.

Expressing wishes

▶ Klaus kocht immer Spaghetti.

Ich wollte, Klaus würde nicht immer Spaghetti kochen.

▶ Michael macht das Zimmer nicht sauber.

Ich wollte, Michael würde das Zimmer saubermachen.

1. Martin lernt nicht für das Examen.
2. Christoph hört immer Musik.
3. Bernd redet so viel.
4. Wolfgang kommt immer zu spät.
5. Stefan macht die Tür nicht zu.

12. **Ich wollte, ich könnte ...** Complete the following sentences for yourself. Then find out from your partner how he/she completed the sentences and what he/she would like to do.

1. Ich wollte, ich könnte _____ .
2. Wenn ich Zeit hätte, _____ .
3. Wenn meine Eltern viel Geld hätten, _____ .
4. Ich sollte _____ .
5. Ich würde gern _____ .

13. **Die Oly Disco** You are visiting a friend in Munich and are discussing what to do during the evening. Your friend suggests dancing at the **Oly Disco.** Get more information by asking the following questions. If you need help getting the gist of the ad, see the Vocabulary for Authentic Text Activities in the Reference Section.

1. Wann ist die Disco geöffnet?
2. Wann ist der Eintritt frei?
3. Wo ist die Disco?
4. Wie kommt man zur Oly Disco?
5. Wer geht zu dieser Disco?
6. Was muß man dabei haben, um in die Disco zu kommen?

14. Rollenspiel Your partner wants to go dancing. You are not so keen on the idea. Discuss options and reach an agreement. You may use some of the sentences below to get started.

Negotiating

Sie	*Gesprächspartner/in*
Möchtest du wirklich tanzen gehen?	Ja, du nicht? Wozu hättest du denn Lust?
Ich würde lieber … .	Das wäre … .
Wir könnten … .	

9 Present-time subjunctive of strong verbs

Infinitive		Simple past	+ umlaut for a, o, u	+ subjunctive ending	Present-time subjunctive
kommen	er/es/sie {	kam	käm	-e	**käme**
bleiben		blieb	blieb	-e	**bliebe**

kommen			
ich **käme**		wir **kämen**	
du **kämest**		ihr **kämet**	
er/es/sie **käme**		sie **kämen**	
	Sie **kämen**		

The present-time subjunctive of strong verbs is formed by adding subjunctive endings to the simple-past stem of the verb. An umlaut is added to the stem vowels **a, o,** or **u.**

Although the **würde-**construction and the subjunctive form of the main verb are equivalent in meaning, the **würde-**construction is more common in spoken German. Only a few strong verbs are used in their subjunctive form in colloquial German. However, you will need to recognize the subjunctive form and understand the meaning of a number of strong verbs in your reading. For a list of subjunctive forms of strong verbs, see #23 of the Grammatical Tables in the Reference Section.

15. Das ginge.   In the list below are a number of expressions using the subjunctive form of strong verbs, followed by a list of English equivalents. Choose the appropriate meaning.

▶   Das ginge.   *That would work.*

1. Das täte ich gern.
2. Wir kämen gern.
3. Das sähe merkwürdig aus.
4. Ich schliefe gern länger.
5. Sie ginge sicher mit.
6. Ich führe gern.
7. So was gäb's bei mir nicht.
8. Sie ließe mich fahren.
9. Wo sonst fänden wir soviel Hilfe?
10. Wenn er nur länger bliebe.
11. Das wäre eine schöne Reise.
12. Und wenn er krank würde?

a. I would do that gladly.
b. I would like to sleep longer.
c. If he would only stay longer.
d. I would like to drive.
e. And (what) if he would get sick?
f. Where else would we find so much help?
g. That would be a nice trip.
h. She would let me drive.
i. Such a thing would never happen with me.
j. She would certainly go along.
k. That would look strange.
l. We would be happy to come.

16. In den Ferien   Frank is thinking about all the things he would do if the conditions were different. Complete Frank's sentences using the general subjunctive of the main verb for the condition and the **würde**-construction for the conclusion.

▶   Leider habe ich kein Auto, aber wenn _____ . (in die Schweiz fahren)

Leider habe ich kein Auto, aber wenn ich ein Auto hätte, würde ich in die Schweiz fahren.

1. Es gibt keinen Schnee, aber wenn _____ . (Ski laufen)
2. Leider habe ich kein Geld, aber wenn _____ . (nach Hawaii fliegen)
3. Es ist nicht warm genug, aber wenn _____ . (zelten)
4. Dieses Buch ist nicht interessant, aber wenn _____ . (lesen)
5. Ich habe keine Lust, aber wenn _____ . (ins Kino gehen)

10 Present-time subjunctive of regular weak verbs

	Simple past	Present-time subjunctive
er/es/sie	spielte	**spielte**
	kaufte	**kaufte**
	arbeitete	**arbeitete**
	badete	**badete**

The present-time subjunctive forms of regular weak verbs are identical to the simple-past forms. For this reason the **würde**-construction is frequently used instead of the subjunctive forms of the weak verbs.

17. Wenn Susanne das nur machte! Susanne's friends at the farm hope she'll come and play for them. Complete their sentences by supplying the present-time subjunctive form of the verb in parentheses. Then translate the sentences for one of the guests who knows no German.

▶ Wenn Frank nicht so oft ____ (telefonieren), könnte Susanne uns anrufen.   *Wenn Frank nicht so oft telefonierte, könnte Susanne uns anrufen. (If Frank wouldn't telephone so often, Susanne would be able to call us.)*

1. Wenn Susanne uns ____ (besuchen), dann könnte sie nicht arbeiten.
2. Wenn ihre Freunde mitkämen, ____ (brauchen) sie nicht allein zu spielen.
3. Wenn ihre Freunde ____ (mitmachen), könnten wir die Nachbarn einladen.
4. Wenn Dieter eine Gitarre ____ (kaufen), müßte er auch mitspielen.
5. Wenn die Gitarre nicht soviel ____ (kosten), könnten wir sie ihm kaufen.

11 Present-time subjunctive of irregular weak verbs

		Simple past	Present-time subjunctive
er/es/sie	{	brachte	br**ä**chte
		dachte	d**ä**chte
		wußte	w**ü**ßte

The present-time subjunctive forms of irregular weak verbs are like the simple-past forms, but with an umlaut added.

18. Ein Picknick Adrian is talking with Stefanie about plans for a picnic. Give the English equivalents.

Adrian: Hättest du Zeit mitzukommen?
Stefanie: Ich dächte schon.
Adrian: Ich wüßte nicht, wen wir sonst einladen sollten.
Stefanie: Vielleicht Onkel Max und Tante Gabi.
Adrian: Vielleicht könnten wir alle zusammen fahren?
Stefanie: Schön. Das könnten wir.
Adrian: Wenn ich nur wüßte, wo die beiden sind!
Stefanie: Was meinst du, was brächte Onkel Max mit?
Adrian: Caviar, wie immer. Ich brächte etwas zu trinken mit.

12 Past-time subjunctive

Wenn sie das **gewußt hätte, hätte**
  sie mir **geholfen.**

If she *had known* that, she *would
have helped* me.

Wenn sie das **gewußt hätte, wäre**
  sie nicht **mitgekommen.**

If she *had known* that, she *would*
not *have come* along.

The past-time subjunctive consists of the subjunctive forms **hätte** or **wäre** +
past participle. The past-time subjunctive is used to express hypothetical conclusions, wishes, and contrary-to-fact conditions in past time.

19. Wenn sie das gewußt hätte ...   Restate the sentences below, telling what
Ursel would or would not have done if only she had known that the weather
was going to be nice over the weekend.

▶ Sie ist übers Wochenende nicht
    weggefahren.

▶ Sie ist zu Hause geblieben.

*Wenn sie das gewußt hätte, wäre
sie übers Wochenende weggefahren.*

*Wenn sie das gewußt hätte,
wäre sie nicht zu Hause geblieben.*

1. Sie ist nicht an den See gefahren.
2. Sie hat ihre Freunde nicht zum Picknick eingeladen.
3. Sie hat nicht gezeltet.
4. Sie ist nicht schwimmen gegangen.
5. Sie ist ins Kino gegangen.
6. Sie hat soviel geschlafen.

20. Sie hätten es anders gemacht.   No one is happy with what they did
yesterday. Complete the sentences below to include what the people would
have rather done.

▶ Karin ist schwimmen gegangen,
    aber _____ (lieber ins Theater
    gegangen).

▶ Marc hat gearbeitet, aber _____
    (lieber geschlafen).

*Karin ist schwimmen gegangen, aber
sie wäre lieber ins Theater
gegangen.*

*Marc hat gearbeitet, aber er
hätte lieber geschlafen.*

1. Ich habe in der Mensa gegessen, aber _____ (lieber in einem eleganten
   Restaurant gegessen).
2. Hanna hat an einem Referat gearbeitet, aber _____ (lieber im Garten
   gearbeitet).
3. Heike und Horst haben Tennis gespielt, aber _____ (lieber gewandert).
4. Klaus hat ferngesehen, aber _____ (lieber ins Kino gegangen).
5. Susanne hat klassische Musik gehört, aber _____ (lieber Hard Rock
   gehört).
6. Dirk hat fürs Examen gelernt, aber _____ (lieber eine Radtour gemacht).

13 Modals in past-time subjunctive

Das **hättest** du **wissen sollen.**	You *should have known* that.
Ich **hätte** dir **helfen können.**	I *could have helped* you.

When a modal is used in the past-time subjunctive with another verb, an alternative past participle of the modal, identical with the infinitive, is used. This is called the "double infinitive" construction. The modal always occurs at the very end of the clause.

21. Was wäre passiert, wenn ... ? Dieter's company had been expecting a foreign visitor. However, the visit did not take place. Dieter explains what would have happened if the visit had taken place. Give the English equivalents of his remarks.

1. Ich hätte Englisch sprechen müssen.
2. Die Besucherin hätte mein Englisch nicht verstehen können.
3. Ich hätte ihr Deutsch nicht verstehen können.
4. Wir hätten einander kaum verstehen können.
5. Ich hätte ihr die Firma zeigen müssen.
6. Wir hätten uns auch die Stadt ansehen können.
7. Wir hätten in einem teuren Restaurant essen dürfen.
8. Wir hätten mit dem Taxi fahren dürfen.
9. Ich hätte sie zum Bahnhof bringen müssen.

22. Was hätte Schiller machen können?   Answer the questions about the ad that invokes the name of Friedrich Schiller (1759–1805), one of the most famous figures in German literature. Schiller was a dramatist, historian and philosopher concerned with the themes of personal and political freedom. You may refer to the Vocabulary for Authentic Text Activities in the Reference Section if you have trouble getting the gist of the ad.

1. Was hätte Schiller gemacht?
2. Wann hätte Schiller sich einschreiben können?
3. Wann hätte er beginnen können?
4. Wo hätte er Auskunft bekommen können?

Schiller hätte geweint vor Freude

über das
Bildungsangebot der
Münchner Volkshochschule...
wollen Sie es nicht nutzen?

Einschreibung
12. bis 16. September (außer
13. September) 9 bis 20 Uhr

Gasteig Kulturzentrum
Troppauer Straße 10
Schlierseestraße 47
Albert-Roßhaupter-Straße 8
Bäckerstraße 14

Semesterbeginn ab
23. September
Auskunft Tel. 4 18 06-0

**Münchner
Volkshochschule**

Herbst

WIEDERHOLUNG

1. Was sagen Sie? Say what you would do under certain conditions. Then think of two more things and ask your partner. Remember to use **du** with your partner.

Was würden Sie tun, …

1. wenn Sie plötzlich viel Geld bekämen?
2. wenn heute Sonntag wäre?
3. wenn Sie heute Geburtstag hätten?
4. wenn Sie jetzt zwei Wochen Ferien hätten?
5. wenn Sie das teure Essen im Restaurant nicht bezahlen könnten?
6. wenn Freunde Sie zu einem Fest nicht einladen würden?

2. Meine Freundin Susanne Complete each sentence below with an appropriate preposition.

1. Erinnerst du dich _____ meine Freundin Susanne?
2. Mit sechs Jahren hat sie _____ Klarinette angefangen.
3. Sie macht _____ einer Volksliedgruppe mit.
4. Sie bereiten sich _____ das Hinterhoffest vor.
5. Susanne erzählt ihrem Freund Dieter _____ ihrer Musik.
6. Er arbeitet _____ Siemens.
7. In seiner Freizeit renoviert er ein Bauernhaus, und er spricht gern _____ Susanne _____ seine Pläne.

3. Was möchten Sie? Tell what you would like by using one or more of the adjectives in parentheses—or by supplying your own—to modify the bold-faced nouns.

1. Wenn ich Geld hätte, würde ich mir ein _____ **Auto** kaufen. (klein, groß, billig, teuer)
2. Ich wollte, man würde mich zu einem _____ **Fest** einladen. (nett, toll, klein, laut, interessant)
3. Ich möchte einen _____ **Pulli** kaufen. (warm, blau, leicht, toll)
4. Ich würde gern mal einen _____ **Film** sehen. (toll, interessant, schön, modern, klassisch, gut)
5. Ich möchte eine _____ **Reise** nach Deutschland machen. (lang, kurz, billig)
6. Ich möchte einen Computer haben, aber es müßte ein _____ **Computer** sein. (billig, teuer, klein, einfach, groß, schnell, bedienungsfreundlich°)   user-friendly

4. Was hat er gemacht? Read the account of what Klaus did yesterday. Then answer the questions.

Klaus ging morgens für eine Stunde zu einer Vorlesung. Nachmittags saß er in der Bibliothek und arbeitete. Den Abend hatte er frei. Er traf sich in einer Kneipe mit Freunden. Da gab es live Musik. Es war eine Volksliedgruppe. Alle Studenten sangen mit. Das hat viel Spaß gemacht.

1. Wohin ging Klaus morgens?
2. Was machte er nachmittags?
3. Mit wem traf er sich abends?
4. Warum traf man sich in der Kneipe?
5. Wer sang mit?

5. Der Lebensstandard in der Schweiz Bärbel makes a few comments about the standard of living in Switzerland. Restate her comments by completing the second sentence in each pair below. Supply **zu** where necessary.

▶ Die Schweizer haben einen hohen Lebensstandard.
Die Schweizer scheinen ———.

Die Schweizer scheinen einen hohen Lebensstandard zu haben.

1. Natürlich arbeiten sie schwer.
   Sie müssen ———.
2. Viele kaufen immer mehr.
   Viele wollen ———.
3. (Man) versteht das.
   Das ist leicht ———.
4. Energie wird teurer.
   Energie fängt an ———.
5. Viele verstehen die Umweltprobleme besser.
   Viele scheinen ———.

6. Wie sagt man das?

1. I have nothing planned on the weekend. (*use* **vorhaben**)
   —Would you like to take a bike trip?
2. Could it be that Erik is ill?
   —I don't know. You could ask him.
3. Would you like to go for a walk?
   —Gladly. How would it be this afternoon?
4. Could you help me, please?
   —I wish I had (the) time.
5. Would you like to watch TV?
   —No. I don't feel like it.

7. Anregung

1. Keep a diary (**Tagebuch**) in German for a week, making entries concerning leisure-time activities.
2. Imagine you are attending a German university for a year. Write a letter in German to a friend, telling what you and your German friends do in your free time.

3. A philanthropic foundation would like to know what you would do with a large sum of money if it were given to you. The foundation is interested in projects to help the environment, to improve education and to assist in charitable endeavors. Write your ideas and explain the reasons for them.

GRAMMATIK: ZUSAMMENFASSUNG

Subjunctive mood

Indicative	Ich **komme** nicht zur Party.	I'm not *coming* to the party.
	Was **hast** du **gemacht?**	What *did* you *do?*
Subjunctive	Ich **käme** nicht zur Party.	I *wouldn't come* to the party.
	Was **hättest** du **gemacht?**	What *would* you *have done?*

In both English and German, the indicative mood is used to talk about "real" conditions or factual situations. The subjunctive mood is used to talk about "unreal," hypothetical, uncertain, or unlikely events.

Present-time subjunctive	Wenn ich heute (oder morgen) nur mehr Zeit **hätte.**	If I *would* only *have* more time today (or tomorrow).
Past-time subjunctive	Wenn ich gestern nur mehr Zeit **gehabt hätte.**	If I only *would have had* more time yesterday.

Subjunctive forms express two time categories: present time (which can refer to the future as well) and past time.

The *würde*-construction

◆ Forms

ich **würde** es **machen**	wir **würden** es **machen**
du **würdest** es **machen**	ihr **würdet** es **machen**
er/es/sie **würde** es **machen**	sie **würden** es **machen**
Sie **würden** es **machen**	

The **würde**-construction consists of a form of **würde** + infinitive. **Würde** is the subjunctive form of **werden.** It is formed by adding an umlaut to **wurde,** the simple past of **werden.**

◆ *Uses*

Ich **würde** das nicht **machen.**	I *would* not *do* that.
Wenn er mir nur **helfen würde.**	If he *would* only *help* me.
Würdest du mir bitte **helfen?**	*Would* you please *help* me?

To talk about "unreal" situations in the present, to express wishes, and to make polite requests, German may use a **würde**-construction. The **würde**-construction is the most common way to express subjunctive mood in spoken German.

Present-time subjunctive of main verbs

Ich **täte** das nicht.	I *would*n't *do* that.
Ich **würde** das nicht **tun.**	

German does have subjunctive forms of main verbs (e.g., **täte**) that may be used in place of the **würde**-construction. Except for a few common verbs, however, the **würde**-construction is more frequent in spoken German. The subjunctive forms of main verbs do appear in formal written German.

Present-time subjunctive of *sein* and *haben*

sein	
ich **wäre**	wir **wären**
du **wärest**	ihr **wäret**
er/es/sie **wäre**	sie **wären**
Sie **wären**	

haben	
ich **hätte**	wir **hätten**
du **hättest**	ihr **hättet**
er/es/sie **hätte**	sie **hätten**
Sie **hätten**	

The verbs **haben** and **sein** are more commonly used in their subjunctive forms, **wäre** and **hätte,** than in the **würde**-construction.

Modals in present-time subjunctive

Infinitive	Simple past	Present-time subjunctive
dürfen	durfte	**dürfte**
können	konnte	**könnte**
mögen	mochte	**möchte**
müssen	mußte	**müßte**
sollen	sollte	**sollte**
wollen	wollte	**wollte**

The modals are generally used in their subjunctive form rather than as infinitives with the **würde**-construction.

Present-time subjunctive of strong verbs

Infinitive	Simple past	Present-time subjunctive
bleiben	blieb	**bliebe**
fahren	fuhr	**führe**
finden	fand	**fände**
geben	gab	**gäbe**
gehen	ging	**ginge**
kommen	kam	**käme**
lassen	ließ	**ließe**
schlafen	schlief	**schliefe**
sehen	sah	**sähe**
tun	tat	**täte**

The present-time subjunctive forms of strong verbs are formed by adding subjunctive endings to the simple-past stem. An umlaut is added to the stem vowels **a, o,** and **u.**

Subjunctive verb endings

ich käm	**e**	wir käm	**en**
du käm	**est**	ihr käm	**et**
er/es/sie käm	**e**	sie käm	**en**
	Sie käm	**en**		

The subjunctive endings above are used for all verbs. The subjunctive verb endings **-est** and **-et** often contract to **-st** and **-t: kämest** > **kämst, kämet** > **kämt.**

Present-time subjunctive of regular weak verbs

Infinitive	Simple past	Present-time subjunctive
kaufen	kaufte	**kaufte**
arbeiten	arbeitete	**arbeitete**

The present-time subjunctive forms of weak verbs are identical to the simple-past forms. For this reason the **würde-**construction is frequently used in place of the subjunctive forms.

Present-time subjunctive of irregular weak verbs

Infinitive	Simple past	Present-time subjunctive
bringen	brachte	**brächte**
denken	dachte	**dächte**
wissen	wußte	**wüßte**

Past-time subjunctive

Wenn ich Zeit **gehabt hätte, wäre** ich **gekommen.**　　If I *had had* time, I *would have come.*

Wenn sie hier **gewesen wäre, hätte** ich sie **gesehen.**　　If she *had been* here, I *would have seen* her.

The past-time subjunctive consists of the subjunctive forms **hätte** or **wäre** + a past participle. A **würde**-construction exists in past-time, but it is not commonly used: **Ich würde es nicht getan haben.**

Modals in past-time subjunctive

Das **hättest** du **wissen sollen.**　　You *should have known* that.

Ich **hätte** dir **helfen können.**　　I *could have helped* you.

When a modal is used in the past subjunctive with another verb, an alternative past participle of the modal, identical with the infinitive, is used. This construction is called the "double infinitive" construction. The modal always occurs at the very end of the clause.

Uses of the *würde*-construction and the subjunctive of the main verb

◆ *Hypothetical conclusions*

Ich **würde** das nicht **tun.**
Ich **täte** das nicht.　　I *would*n't *do* that [if I were you].

Ich **hätte** das auch **getan.**　　I *would have done* that too.

◆ *Wishes*

Wenn Inge das nur **tun würde.**
Wenn Inge das nur **täte.**　　If only Inge *would do* that.

Wenn Gabi das nur **getan hätte.**　　If only Gabi *had done* that.

◆ *Polite requests*

Würden Sie das für mich **tun?** ⎱
Täten Sie das für mich? ⎰   *Would* you *do* that for me?
Könnten Sie das für mich **tun?**   *Could* you *do* that for me?

◆ *Conditions contrary to fact*

Present time	
Wenn ich Zeit **hätte, käme** ich.	If I *had* time [but I don't],
Wenn ich Zeit **hätte, würde** ich **kommen.**	I *would come.*

Past time	
Wenn ich Zeit **gehabt hätte, wäre** ich **gekommen.**	If I *had had* time [but I didn't], I *would have come.*

Contrary-to-fact sentences consist of two clauses: the condition (**wenn**-clause) and the conclusion. Conditions contrary to fact are not capable of fulfillment. Conditions contrary to fact are expressed in the subjunctive mood.

The *würde*-construction vs. present-time subjunctive of the main verb

Wenn Jutta nicht so fleißig   If Jutta *were* not so diligent,
   wäre, hätte sie mehr Freizeit   she *would have* more time and
   und **könnte** ein Hobby **haben.**   *could have* a hobby.

In spoken German the **würde-**construction is used instead of the subjunctive of the main verb for all but a few commonly used verbs. The subjunctive of the main verb is preferred to the **würde-**construction for **sein** (**wäre**), **haben** (**hätte**), and the modals, e.g., **könnte**.

Wenn Gerd täglich Zeitung **läse,**   If Gerd *read* the newspaper daily,
   würde er alles besser verstehen.   he would understand everything better.

Formal written German tends to avoid the **würde-**construction in the **wenn-**clause.

Vasilij Kandinsky, *Winter,* 1909

SchlittenfahreN

Helga M. Novak

Helga Novak was born in 1935 in Berlin. She studied philosophy and journalism in Leipzig and worked in various types of places: factories, a laboratory, and a bookstore. In 1961 she moved to Iceland and returned to Germany in 1967 to live in Frankfurt as a writer. In 1980, the New Literary Society in Hamburg gave her an award for her novel *Die Eisheiligen,* as the best first novel by a German speaker.

In her stories, Helga Novak deals with ordinary people in everyday situations. Through the use of simple sentences and a dry, unemotional style, she suggests much more about human relationships than she actually says. In ''Schlittenfahren,'' taken from her work *Geselliges Beisammensein* (1968), the father does not communicate with his children but simply leaves his retreat long enough to shout the same sentences in their direction, sentences devoid of meaning for them and him. However, the repetition of ''kommt rein'' at the end of the story takes on a new and possibly serious dimension and reveals the problem of using language just to be saying something.

In what sense do the private home (**Eigenheim**) and the garden represent two separate and unrelated scenes of activity? What do the father's actions say about his relationship with the children?

Schlittenfahren

Das Eigenheim° steht in einem Garten. Der Garten ist groß. Durch den Garten fließt° ein Bach°. Im Garten stehen zwei Kinder. Das eine der Kinder kann noch nicht sprechen. Das andere Kind ist größer. Sie sitzen auf einem Schlitten°. Das kleinere Kind weint. Das größere sagt, gib den
5 Schlitten her. Das kleinere weint. Es schreit°.

    Aus dem Haus tritt° ein Mann. Er sagt, wer brüllt°, kommt rein°. Er geht in das Haus zurück. Die Tür fällt hinter ihm zu.

    Das kleinere Kind schreit.

    Der Mann erscheint wieder in der Haustür. Er sagt, komm rein. Na
10 wirds bald°. Du kommst rein. Nix°. Wer brüllt, kommt rein. Komm rein.

    Der Mann geht hinein. Die Tür klappt°.

    Das kleinere Kind hält die Schnur° des Schlittens fest°. Es schluchzt°.

    Der Mann öffnet die Haustür. Er sagt, du darfst Schlitten fahren, aber nicht brüllen. Wer brüllt, kommt rein. Ja. Ja. Jaaa. Schluß jetzt°.
15   Das größere Kind sagt, Andreas will immer allein fahren.

    Der Mann sagt, wer brüllt, kommt rein. Ob er nun Andreas heißt oder sonstwie°.

    Er macht die Tür zu.

    Das größere Kind nimmt dem kleineren den Schlitten weg. Das
20 kleinere Kind schluchzt, quietscht°, jault°, quengelt°.

    Der Mann tritt aus dem Haus. Das größere Kind gibt dem kleineren den Schlitten zurück. Das kleinere Kind setzt sich auf den Schlitten. Es rodelt°.

    Der Mann sieht in den Himmel°. Der Himmel ist blau. Die Sonne ist
25 groß und rot. Es ist kalt.

    Der Mann pfeift° laut. Er geht wieder ins Haus zurück. Er macht die Tür hinter sich zu.

    Das größere Kind ruft°, Vati, Vati, Vati, Andreas gibt den Schlitten nicht mehr her.
30   Die Haustür geht auf. Der Mann steckt° den Kopf heraus. Er sagt, wer brüllt, kommt rein. Die Tür geht zu.

    Das größere Kind ruft, Vati, Vativativati, Vaaatiii, jetzt ist Andreas in den Bach gefallen.

    Die Haustür öffnet sich einen Spalt° breit°. Eine Männerstimme ruft,
35 wie oft soll ich das noch sagen, wer brüllt, kommt rein.

Glosses (right margin):

- private home
- flows / brook
- sled
- screams
- steps / bawls / **rein = herein:** in
- **Na … bald:** hurry up / **Nix = nichts** / slams
- rope / **hält fest:** holds tight / sobs
- **Schluß jetzt:** that's enough
- otherwise
- squeals / howls / whines
- sleds
- sky
- whistles
- calls
- sticks
- crack / wide

Fragen

1. In was für einem Haus wohnt die Familie?
2. Was wissen Sie über den Garten?
3. Was wissen Sie über die Kinder?
4. Warum weint das kleinere Kind?
5. Warum kommt der Mann aus dem Haus? Was sagt er?
6. Wie ist das Wetter?
7. Wer fährt am Ende mit dem Schlitten?
8. Warum ruft das ältere Kind am Ende den Vater?
9. Was antwortet der Vater?

Fragen zur Diskussion

1. Der Mann kommt mehrere Mal zur Tür. Welche Sätze beschreiben das? Was sagen diese Sätze über den Mann?
2. Der Mann geht mehrere Mal ins Haus. Welche Sätze beschreiben das? Was ist damit gesagt?
3. Welchen Satz sagt der Mann immer wieder? Welchen Effekt hat das auf die Kinder? Auf den Leser?
4. Was wird über Jahreszeit und Wetter gesagt? Welche Rolle spielt das?
5. Warum benutzt die Autorin immer wieder das Wort „der Mann"? Welches andere Wort könnte sie benutzen?
6. Wie meint der Mann den letzten Satz? Wie verstehen Sie ihn?

Die Börse ist ein wichtiger Teil des Wirtschaftssystems. (Frankfurt am Main)

Kapitel 13

BAUSTEINE FÜR GESPRÄCHE

Stellenanzeigen

Simon: Na, was gibt's Neues in der Zeitung?
Viktor: Ich weiß nicht. Ich hab' bis jetzt nur die Anzeigen durchgesehen.
Simon: Welche? Die Heiratsanzeigen?
Viktor: Quatsch. Die Stellenanzeigen! Ich such' eine Arbeit, die interessant ist und wo man gut verdient.
Simon: Viel Glück!

Want ads

Well, what's new in the newspaper?
I don't know. Up to now I have only looked through the classified ads.
Which ones? The ones for marriage partners?
Nonsense. The want ads! I'm looking for a job that's interesting and where you can earn a lot.
Lots of luck!

Ein Termin

Viktor: Guten Tag. Graf ist mein Name, Viktor Graf. Ist Frau Dr. Ziegler zu sprechen? Ich habe einen Termin bei ihr.
Sekretärin: Guten Tag, Herr Graf. Ja bitte, gehen Sie doch gleich hinein. Sie erwartet Sie schon.

An appointment

Hello. My name is Graf, Viktor Graf. May I speak to Dr. Ziegler? I have an appointment with her.
Hello, Mr. Graf. Yes, please go right in. She's expecting you.

Fragen

1. Warum weiß Viktor nicht, was in der Zeitung steht?
2. Was für eine Arbeit sucht er?
3. Wen möchte Viktor sprechen?
4. Warum soll Viktor gleich hineingehen?

1. Die Zeitung Ask three fellow students about their newspaper reading habits. Take notes and report on your findings.

Giving factual information

Sie	*Gesprächspartner/in*
Welche Zeitung liest du?	Ich lese [*Die Zeit*].
Warum liest du Zeitung — wofür interessierst du dich?	Für | **Politik.**
	Wirtschaft.
	Sport.
	Musik.
	Theater.
	Literatur.
	Comics.

2. Was ist wichtig? Ask four classmates to name one or two things that are important to them in a job. Some possibilities are given.

Expressing importance

interessante oder leichte Arbeit ◇ gut verdienen ◇ sicherer Arbeitsplatz ◇ den Menschen helfen ◇ viel Freizeit

3. Im Büro Take the role of one of the people involved in a business conversation.

Presenting yourself for an appointment

Frau/Herr Richter	*Sekretärin*
Ist Frau/Herr Dr. Schulze zu sprechen?	Es tut mir leid. Sie/Er ist im Moment beschäftigt°.
	Sie/Er telefoniert gerade, und um drei hat sie/er einen Termin.
	Haben Sie einen Termin?
	Gehen Sie bitte gleich hinein. Sie/Er erwartet Sie.

Mit Erfolg bewerben
Vorstellungsgespräche nutzen
Seminar, 1 1/2 Tage, mit zwei erfahrenen
Trainern (Personalleiter und Dipl.Psychologe)
Großraum Mannheim/ Ludwigshafen

Termine: 29./30. Juni
          27./28. Juli
          5./ 6. Oktober
Preis: DM 450.- + Mwst.

• Organisationsentwicklung
• Beratung • Seminare

human at work
          Hauptstraße 49   6719 Weisenheim

Heiraten/Bekanntschaften

SOS! Wo finde ich eine treue, lustige Partnerin bis 35 J. zum Verlieben, bin 40 J., schlank, jugendl. Erscheinung, etwas schüchtern, reiselustig, selbständig u. Tierliebhaber. Bildzuschr. u. Nr. 764/G an diese Zeitung.

2 junggebliebene Freundinnen, verwitwet. 60 u. 65 J., suchen 2 nette Herrn. mögl. mit Auto, die mit ihnen Tanzen, Schwimmen und gemeinsame, nette Stunden verbringen. Zuschr. mögl. mit Bild unt. Nr. 2/835083/G-Z.

ER, 28 J., 189 cm. schlank, sucht nette SIE, meine Hobbys sind Bodybuilding, Motorrad fahren. Kino u. Essen gehen. Bitte schreibe mir an WT 1/167

Wo ist der liebenswerte, gebildete Mann, großzügig im Denken und Handeln, kein Opatyp, ca. 180 groß? Eine attraktive. symp. Sie. mit Herz. Hirn und Niveau, 47 J., schlk., 167 groß. würde Ihn gerne kennenlernen. Freundl. Zuschr. m. Tel.-Ang. unt. Nr. 2/835181/G-S.

Elfi ist von Beruf Küchenhilfe und ist **21 J.** alt. Sie hat blonde Haare, geht gerne schwimmen und spazieren. Wenn Du sie kennenlernen möchtest, dann schreibe unter AA 2154.

4. **Heiraten/Bekanntschaften** In the dialogue on p. 416 Simon asked Viktor if he was reading the "**Heiratsanzeigen.**" Above are the types of ads Simon was referring to. Answer the questions based on the ads. If you need help with vocabulary, see Vocabulary for Authentic Text Activities in the Reference Section.

1. Wie alt sind die Personen, die die Anzeigen aufgegeben haben?
2. Wie alt sollen die Partner/innen sein?
3. Wer möchte mit der Antwort zusammen ein Bild?
4. Was bedeutet „Opatyp"?
5. In welchen Anzeigen ist das Aussehen wichtig?
6. Welche Anzeige finden Sie sympathisch°?

appealing

Ideal f. Anfänger! Audi 80, 55 PS. 4trg.. 2. Hd.. sehr gut. Zust.. Radio. Veloursaussttg.. Mod. 80. TÜA u. ASU neu. VB 3450.– DM. Tel. (0 64 71) 55 94 od. 5 10 16

Mazda 626 LX, silbermet.. Bj. 3/86, 66 000 km. Garagenwagen. 1. Hd.. 8f. bereift. schadstoffarm. steuerfrei bis 2/92, 2 J. TÜ. zu verk. Tel. 06002/670

DB Kombi 230 TE, Bj. Juni 1990, 107 000 km, ATM 5 000 km mit Garantie. Servo.. ZV. SSD. Dachreling. Technisch und optisch einwandfrei VB 10 500.– DM Tel. (06403) 67931 ab 15.00 Uhr

Golf II, EZ 85. 59 300 km. TÜV neu. 55 PS. unfallfrei. Preis 8950.– DM. Tel. geschäftl. (0 64 41) 6 42 24. privat (0 64 41) 42 10

5. **Gebrauchtwagen** Look at the ads printed here and decide which of the used cars (**Gebrauchtwagen**) you would like to buy. The ad gives you some information. What is it? (If you need help with vocabulary, see Vocabulary for Authentic Text Activities in the Reference Section.) But you still need to ask a number of questions for more details. Assume your partner is the person who placed the ad. Ask your questions of him/her. Negotiate a price and then decide whether you will buy the car.

Negotiating

Vokabeln

___ Substantive ___

die **Anzeige, -n** announcement, ad
die **Heirat** marriage
die **Literatur** literature
die **Politik** politics; political science
der **Quatsch** nonsense; **Quatsch!** nonsense!

der **Termin, -e** appointment
das **Theater, -** (performing arts) theater

___ Verben ___

beschäftigen to occupy, keep busy; **beschäftigt sein** to be busy; **sich beschäftigen (mit)** to be occupied (with)
durch·sehen (sieht durch), sah durch, durchgesehen to look through; glance over; examine

heiraten to marry, to get married
(sich) interessieren (für) to be interested (in)
telefonieren (mit jemandem) to telephone (someone)

___ Andere Wörter ___

hinein in (*as in* **hineingehen** to go in)

___ Besondere Ausdrücke ___

Was gibt's Neues? What's new?

ZUR WIRTSCHAFT IN DEUTSCHLAND

Vorbereitung auf das Lesen

◆ *Zum Thema*

Was wissen Sie über die Wirtschaft in Ihrem Land?

1. Ist der Export oder der Import größer?
2. Was sind wichtige Exportgüter — Maschinen, Autos, Chemikalien, Elektrotechnik, Schuhe, Textilien, Lebensmittel, anderes?
3. Gibt es viele oder wenige Rohstoffe?
4. Gibt es viele Streiks?
5. Sind die Preise stabil? Wie hoch ist die Inflationsrate?
6. Wie ist das soziale Klima? Hilft der Staat den Leuten bei finanziellen Problemen, z.B. im Alter°, bei Krankheit und Arbeitslosigkeit?   old age

◆ *Leitfragen*

1. Import und Export sind für die deutsche Industrie sehr wichtig. Was sind die Gründe dafür?

   Stichworte: Einwohner ◇ Rohstoffe ◇ verdienen

2. Der deutsche Export ist bisher ziemlich erfolgreich gewesen. Was sind die Gründe für diesen Erfolg?

   Stichworte: Qualität ◇ Organisation ◇ Preise ◇ pünktlich liefern

3. Die deutsche Wirtschaft ist eine „soziale Marktwirtschaft". Was bedeutet hier „sozial"? Was bedeutet „Markt"?
4. Was haben die Gewerkschaften erreicht?
5. Die Deutschen halten die Stabilität der Preise für sehr wichtig. Warum?
6. Wie sieht die Zukunft für die deutsche Wirtschaft aus?

   Stichworte: zwei Märkte ◇ z.B. Schuhe — billiger ◇ z.B. Computer — U.S.A. und Japan ◇ konkurrieren

---

Vor der Vereinigung von 1990 gab es eine sozialistische Wirtschaft in der DDR° und eine Marktwirtschaft in der Bundesrepublik. Aus der Vereinigung der beiden Länder resultiert ein ganzes Bündel von wirtschaftlichen Problemen. Zwei Hauptprobleme auf dem Gebiet der früheren DDR sind
5 z.B. die Privatisierung einer weitgehend° staatlichen Wirtschaft und ihre Modernisierung. Wie die Lösungen der vielen Probleme aussehen werden, wird man erst in einigen Jahren sagen können.

Die Marktwirtschaft der alten Bundesrepublik ist für das vereinigte Land die bestimmende° Kraft. Es lohnt sich also, sie etwas genauer anzusehen. In
10 dieser Wirtschaft spielen Import und Export eine besonders große Rolle. Die wichtigsten Exportgüter sind Maschinen, Kraftfahrzeuge°, chemische Produkte und Elektrotechnik°. Diese Industrien hängen etwa zur Hälfte° vom Export ab.

Gründe für die relativ wichtige Rolle des Außenhandels gibt es sicher
15 viele. Aber einer der wichtigsten ist wohl, daß das Land viele Einwohner hat, aber nur wenige Rohstoffe. Wenn die Menschen essen, wohnen und arbeiten wollen, muß das Land Rohstoffe und Lebensmittel einführen°, die es sich durch seine Exporte verdienen muß.

Mit seinen Exporten ist das Land im Lauf der Jahre° ziemlich erfolgreich°
20 gewesen. Ein Außenhandelskaufmann sagt dazu: „Qualitätsprodukte ‚Made in Germany' verkaufen sich immer noch recht gut. Aber sie verkaufen sich natürlich auch nicht von selbst. Man muß einen langen Atem° haben, d.h. man muß über lange Jahre planen und eine Organisation aufbauen°. Man muß den Markt systematisch pflegen°. Außerdem hat es mir natürlich
25 geholfen, daß wir immer eine relativ niedrige Inflationsrate° gehabt haben. So

Deutsche Demokratische Republik: German Democratic Republic (1949–1990)

predominantly

determining

automobiles
electrical engineering products / **zur Hälfte:** by half

import

im ... Jahre: over the years / successful

einen ... haben: to take the long view / build up

foster

rate of inflation

Frankfurt am Main ist das deutsche Bankzentrum.

können meine Kunden mit ziemlich stabilen Preisen rechnen°. Schließlich ist °count on
es wichtig, daß ich meine Waren pünktlich liefern° kann. Das kann ich °deliver
meistens, denn Streiks sind bei uns recht selten."

Dieser Export basiert° auf einer ganz allgemein gut entwickelten °is based
30 Wirtschaft. Die Wirtschaftsform ist die° der „sozialen Marktwirtschaft°". Das °that / socially oriented free market
heißt, man läßt den Markt entscheiden, was und wieviel die Wirtschaft
produziert. Zugleich° ist das soziale Netz° gut entwickelt, das den einzelnen °at the same time / **das … Netz:** social system / old age
bei ihren finanziellen Problemen im Alter°, bei Krankheit, Unfall und
Arbeitslosigkeit hilft. Darüber hinaus° zahlt der Staat z.B. Kindergeld° für °beyond that / child support
35 jedes Kind, Wohngeld° für wirtschaftlich schwache Bürger und Sozialhilfe° °rent supplement / welfare
für Bedürftige°. °needy

Für das soziale Klima des Landes ist es auch sehr positiv, daß Gewerkschaften und Arbeitgeber einander mehr als Partner und weniger als
Gegner° sehen. Streiks sind daher relativ selten. Trotzdem sind die °opponents
40 Gewerkschaften erfolgreich gewesen. Ernst Bruch, Mitglied der IG-Metall°, °metal workers' union
kommentiert: „Wir haben Lohnfortzahlung° bei Krankheit erreicht, sechs °continued payment of wages
Wochen bezahlten Urlaub und die Mitbestimmung°." Zur Frage, was er sich °codetermination
noch wünscht, sagt er: „Da ist vor allem die Arbeitslosigkeit. Es macht mir
große Sorgen, wann und wie wir dieses Problem lösen werden."
45 Schließlich gibt es wohl noch einen Grund für das relativ gute Klima, das
auf dem deutschen Arbeitsmarkt herrscht°: Eine große Mehrheit° des Volkes °prevails / majority

sieht die Stabilität der Preise als eine der wichtigsten, wenn nicht d i e wichtigste wirtschaftliche Aufgabe an. „Daß wir die Stabilität der Preise so ernst nehmen, ist ja kein Wunder°", sagt eine Ärztin von etwa 60 aus Hanno-
50 ver. „Meine Eltern haben schließlich zweimal ihre Ersparnisse° durch die In-flation verloren, nach dem Ersten und nach dem Zweiten Weltkrieg. Und meine Familie war keine Ausnahme°."

wonder
savings

exception

Einige Stichworte zur deutschen Wirtschaft sind also Außenhandel, soziale Marktwirtschaft, Partnerschaft und Stabilität. Wie gut Deutschland
55 damit in Zukunft fahren wird, ist eine andere Sache. E i n e Frage ist, was das Land exportiert und wie die Zukunft für diese Güter auf dem Weltmarkt aussehen wird. Es gibt heute immer mehr Länder, die Waren wie Schuhe und Textilien billiger herstellen°. Mit ihnen wird Deutschland immer weniger konkurrieren können. Neue Jobs wird es dagegen° in den Industrien geben,
60 die Güter wie Computer und Maschinen produzieren. Hier wird Deutschland mit Japan und den USA konkurrieren müssen. Zur gleichen Zeit muß man die Probleme lösen, die aus der Vereinigung von zwei wirtschaftlichen Systemen resultieren. Wie die Resultate aussehen werden, wird die Zukunft zeigen.

produce
on the other hand

Fragen zum Lesestück

1. Warum gibt es nach der Vereinigung von 1990 wirtschaftliche Probleme?
2. Warum lohnt es sich, die Wirtschaft der alten Bundesrepublik genauer anzusehen?
3. Welche wirtschaftlichen Probleme gibt es auf dem Gebiet der früheren DDR?
4. Was für Produkte exportiert die deutsche Industrie vor allem?
5. Wie viele Industrien hängen vom Export ab?
6. Warum ist der Außenhandel so wichtig?
7. Was muß das Land einführen?
8. Warum ist das Land bisher mit seinem Export erfolgreich gewesen? Geben Sie drei Gründe an.
9. Was heißt „Marktwirtschaft"?
10. Geben Sie Beispiele für soziale Hilfen des Staates.
11. Warum heißt die Wirtschaftsform „soziale Marktwirtschaft"?
12. Wie sehen die Gewerkschaften und Arbeitgeber einander vor allem?
13. Worin sind die Gewerkschaften erfolgreich gewesen?
14. Welches Problem ist nicht gelöst?
15. Warum halten viele Deutsche die Stabilität der Preise für so wichtig?
16. Nennen Sie einige Stichworte zur deutschen Wirtschaft. Erklären Sie jedes in einem Satz.
17. Welche großen Gruppen von Exportgütern gibt es für die deutsche Wirtschaft?
18. Auf welchem Markt wird es neue Arbeitsplätze geben?
19. Mit wem wird Deutschland konkurrieren müssen?

1. Erzählen Sie. Give a brief summary of the reading using the following words and phrases as a guide for notetaking.

vor der Vereinigung
Exportgüter
Rohstoffe
Made in Germany
das soziale Netz

Gewerkschaften
Streiks
Stabilität der Preise
die Zukunft

2. Ein Vergleich zwischen Ihrem Land und der Bundesrepublik
Based on the reading and the cultural notes, answer the following questions for yourself; then in a group with two other students compare your opinions on the German economy.

> Making comparisons and discussing current issues

1. Welches Land lebt mehr vom Außenhandel?
2. Welche Rolle spielen die Gewerkschaften bei Ihnen? In Deutschland?
3. Wo ist Arbeitslosigkeit ein größeres Problem?
4. Was halten Sie von dem „sozialen Netz" in Deutschland?
5. Was finden Sie gut an der sozialen Marktwirtschaft? Was finden Sie schlecht oder ungewöhnlich° daran?   *unusual*
6. Wie sieht die Zukunft für die deutsche Wirtschaft aus? Für die Wirtschaft in Ihrem Land?

Metallarbeiter aus Rendsburg (Schleswig-Holstein) bei einer Demo der Industriegewerkschaft Metall in Berlin

Democratic codetermination **(Mitbestimmung)** is a right guaranteed by law in Germany. It allows employees to participate in the industrial decision-making process by sending representatives to special committees and/or supervisory boards.

The employees' councils **(Betriebsrat** or **Personalrat)** perform mainly monitoring functions on behalf of workers and employees. These councils try to ensure that laws, wage agreements, and other regulations are carried out.

For companies with more than 2,000 employees, the law requires that an equal number of representatives of shareholders and of employees sit on the supervisory board **(Aufsichtsrat)**. In Austria, the ratio of workers to shareholders on the supervisory board is 1:3. Switzerland does not require codetermination on boards.

Vokabeln

— Substantive

der **Arbeitgeber, -**/die
   Arbeitgeberin, -nen employer
die **Arbeitslosigkeit** unemployment
der **Außenhandel** foreign trade
der **Fotoapparat, -e** (*also* die
   Kamera, -s) camera
das **Gebiet, -e** area, field
der **Gefrierschrank, ̈e** (*also* die
   Tiefkühltruhe, -n) freezer
die **Gewerkschaft, -en** trade union
die **Güter** (*pl.*) goods
die **Hälfte** half; **mehr als die**
   Hälfte more than half; **eine**
   Hälfte des Brotes one half of
   the bread
Haupt- (*in compounds*) main; das
   Hauptproblem main problem
die **Kauffrau, -en** businesswoman;
   der **Kaufmann, -leute** businessman, merchant
die **Kraft, ̈e** strength; force; power

der **Kunde, -n, -n**/die **Kundin, -nen**
   customer, client
die **Lösung, -en** solution
die **Maschine, -n** machine
der **Preis, -e** price
der **Staubsauger, -** vacuum cleaner
die **Sorge, -n** care, worry; **sich**
   Sorgen machen (um) to worry
   (about)
der **Streik, -s** strike
der **Trockner, -** clothes dryer
der **Unfall, ̈e** accident
der **Urlaub** vacation; **in Urlaub**
   fahren to go on vacation; **in**
   Urlaub sein to be on vacation
die **Vereinigung, -en** unification
die **Videokamera, -s** video camera,
   camcorder
die **Ware, -n** wares, merchandise,
   goods
die **Zukunft** future

— Verben

ab·hängen, hing ab, abgehangen
   (von) to depend on; **es hängt**
   (vom Wetter) ab it depends (on
   the weather)
entscheiden, entschied, entschieden
   to decide; **sich entscheiden** to
   make a decision after reflecting
   on it

sich lohnen to be profitable; **es**
   lohnt sich it is worthwhile
lösen to solve
planen to plan
(sich) wünschen to wish; **Was**
   wünschst du dir zum
   Geburtstag? What do you want
   for your birthday?

— Andere Wörter

einzeln single, individual
früher former
niedrig low

selten seldom, rare(ly)
trotzdem nevertheless

— Besondere Ausdrücke

das heißt (*abbreviation:* **d.h.**) that is
   (i.e.); that means

The foundations of German social legislation were laid during the time that Otto von Bismarck (1815–1898) was chancellor. Statutory health insurance (**Krankenversicherung**), workers compensation (**Unfall- und Invalidenversicherung**), and retirement benefits (**Rentenversicherung**) were introduced at this time. The costs were to be shared by the employer, the employee, and the state. Retirement age was set at 65. Modern Germany has an extensive social "safety net" (**soziales Netz**) which includes child benefits (**Kindergeld**), that is, payments to parents to offset the expenses of child rearing; unemployment insurance (**Arbeitslosenversicherung**); rent subsidies; savings bonuses; and compensation for the victims of war.

Social welfare (**Sozialhilfe**) is provided by the state for those in dire need. The majority of the recipients are in health-care facilities such as nursing homes, rehabilitation centers, or hospitals. Besides providing low-income housing, the government also subsidizes rent payments with **Wohngeld**.

**Eine Kranken-
schwester bei einer Frau im
Alterswohnheim: Die Versicherung bezahlt.**

Erweiterung des Wortschatzes

The suffix *-lich*

der Freund	friend	**freundlich**	friendly
fragen	to ask	**fraglich**	questionable
krank	ill, sick	**kränklich**	sickly

German adjectives and adverbs may be formed from some nouns or verbs by adding the suffix **-lich.** The suffix **-lich** may also be added to other adjectives. Some stem vowels are umlauted: **ä, ö,** and **ü.** The English equivalent is often an adjective or adverb ending in *-ly.*

1. Was bedeutet das?   Give English equivalents of the sentences below. Then identify the verbs, nouns, or adjectives that are related to the bold-faced words.

1. Es ist **fraglich,** ob wir morgen kommen können.
2. Er weiß heute nicht mehr, was er gestern gesagt hat. Er ist sehr **vergeßlich.**
3. Ich kann seinen Brief kaum lesen. Er schreibt immer so **unleserlich.**
4. Daß Eva das gesagt hat, ist wirklich **unglaublich.**
5. Hat Präsident Löwe das wirklich **öffentlich** gesagt?
6. Hans-Jürgen ist gestern abend **schließlich** doch noch gekommen.
7. Die Geschichte ist **sprachlich** sehr schön, aber was bedeutet sie?
8. Ich kann soviel Deutsch, daß ich mich **verständlich** machen kann.

In 1987 the European Community (EC) (**Europäische Gemeinschaft (EG)**) made the commitment to bring about a single internal market for the members of the Community by the end of 1992. The internal market is envisioned as an area without internal borders to ensure the free movement of goods, persons, services, and capital within the member states, without customs checks at the borders. Member states have agreed eventually to standardize their systems of direct and indirect taxes, so that products like alcohol and tobacco will most likely have a similar tax rate and Germany will eliminate its special consumption taxes on coffee, sugar and light bulbs. After the establishment of a single market, the European Community, with a population of more than 320 million, will have an opportunity for significant economic growth and the largest gross domestic product in the world.

The significance of the single internal market reaches beyond economics. In preparing for economic unification the member states have introduced a European passport (**Europaß**). The states are to reevaluate their school curricula to place more emphasis on a European outlook rather than a national perspective, in order to ensure easier relocation within the European Community. Social benefits are being brought to approximately equivalent levels in all member states to prevent mass migration to nations with higher social benefits (e.g., Germany) and to prevent exploitation of workers. Regulations have also been adopted concerning television programs, requiring that 50 percent of the programs be of European origin.

Gradually the member nations are attempting to speak with one voice on issues of foreign policy, a development made possible by the end of the East–West conflict. By close association with countries like Czechoslovakia, Poland and Hungary, the Community will fill the vacuum created by the demise of the Warsaw Pact. Thus, when the single market comes into being, it will not only have economic consequences, but will also bring Europeans closer to the goal of political unification.

Ein Vortrag über Deutschland und die Europäische Gemeinschaft

GRAMMATIK UND ÜBUNGEN

1 Future time: present tense

Ich **komme** morgen bestimmt. I'm going to come tomorrow for sure.

Gehen Sie heute abend ins Kino? Are you going to the movies this evening?

German generally uses the present tense (e.g., **ich komme, gehen Sie?**) to express future time. English often uses a form of *go* in the present (*I'm going to*) to express future time.

1. **Wie sagt man das?** Give the German equivalents of the sentences below. Use the present tense to express future time.

1. Are you going to watch TV tonight?
2. No, I'm going to the movies.
3. What are you going to do tomorrow?
4. My vacation starts tomorrow.
5. Are you going to Zürich again?
6. No, we'll go there next summer.

2 Future time: future tense

Wir **werden** unsere Freunde **einladen.** We will invite our friends.
Jutta **wird** es allein **machen.** Jutta will do it alone.

German, like English, does have a future tense, although in German it is not used as often as the present tense to express future time. Future tense can be used if it is not clear from the context that the events will take place in the future or to express the speaker's determination that the event will indeed take place.

In both English and German, the future is a compound tense. In English, the future is a verb phrase consisting of *will* or *shall* plus the main verb. In German, the future is also a verb phrase and consists of a form of **werden** plus an infinitive in final position.

ich **werde** es **finden**	wir **werden** es **finden**
du **wirst** es **finden**	ihr **werdet** es **finden**
er/es/sie **wird** es **finden**	sie **werden** es **finden**
Sie **werden** es **finden**	

2. Kein Streik   The union leader is reporting the results of a meeting with management. Restate the sentences below in the future tense.

▶ Wir verdienen mehr.   *Wir werden mehr verdienen.*

1. Wir arbeiten 38 Stunden die Woche.
2. Bei Krankheit zahlt die Firma weiter.
3. Wir bekommen sechs Wochen bezahlten Urlaub.
4. Der Arbeitstag fängt um halb acht an.
5. Das Arbeitsklima wird besser.
6. Wir streiken nicht.

Michael weiß nicht, ob Ursel ihn **besuchen wird.**	Michael doesn't know whether Ursel will visit him.
Hans sagt, daß sie sicher **kommen wird.**	Hans says she'll come for sure.

The auxiliary **werden** is in final position in a dependent clause. It follows the infinitive.

3. Ein tolles Wochenende   Inge and Wolf are planning their weekend. Erik asks them about their plans. Restate the sentences below, beginning as shown in the second sentence of each pair.

▶ Inge und Wolf werden zusammen arbeiten.
  Erik fragt sie, ob _____ .

  Erik fragt sie, ob sie zusammen arbeiten werden.

1. Inge wird ihre Notizen durcharbeiten.
   Inge sagt, daß _____ .
2. Wolf wird sein Referat vorbereiten.
   Wolf sagt, daß _____ .
3. Sie werden auch zum Hinterhoffest gehen.
   Erik möchte wissen, ob _____ .
4. Susannes Gruppe wird beim Fest spielen.
   Erik fragt, ob _____ .
5. Sie werden hinterher in eine Gaststätte gehen.
   Inge nimmt an, daß _____ .
6. Sie werden sich in der Gaststätte treffen.
   Erik glaubt, daß _____ .

3 Other uses of the future tense

| Present probability | Inge **wird** wohl zu Hause **sein.** | Inge is probably at home. |
| Supposition | Das **wird** sicher falsch **sein.** | That's surely wrong. |

In addition to expressing future time, the future tense may express probability when it is used with adverbs such as **wohl, sicher** or **schon.** The future tense is also used to express a supposition. You will be able to understand these expressions if you encounter them.

4 Constructions with *lassen*

◆ *Forms of* **lassen**

Present tense
ich lasse wir lassen
du läßt ihr laßt
er/es/sie läßt sie lassen
Sie lassen
Simple past stem: ließ
Past participle: gelassen

◆ *Uses of* **lassen**

| **Laß** den Schlüssel nicht im Auto. | Don't leave the key in the car. |
| **Laß** mich dir helfen. | Let me help you. |

Lassen is a commonly used verb that occurs in a variety of constructions. Like the modals, **lassen** can stand alone or take a dependent infinitive (e.g., **helfen**) without **zu.**

| Hast du deinen Bruder zu Hause **gelassen?** | Did you leave your brother at home? |
| Hast du ihn fahren **lassen?** | Did you let him drive? |

Lassen has two past participles: **gelassen** and **lassen.** The participle **gelassen** is used when the verb occurs without a dependent infinitive. The alternate participle **lassen** is used when the verb occurs with a dependent infinitive. The alternate participle **lassen** is identical with the infinitive; this construction is called the "double infinitive" construction.

◆ *Meanings of* **lassen**

Lassen has four basic meanings.

1. **lassen** = *to leave*

Laß das Buch hier.	Leave the book here.
Ich habe meine Tasche zu Hause **gelassen.**	I've left my bag at home.

2. **lassen** = *to let* or *to permit*

Lassen Sie mich die Arbeit machen.	Let me do the work.
Wie lange **läßt** du ihn arbeiten?	How long are you going to let him work?

3. **lassen** = *let's*

Gerd, **laß** uns jetzt gehen.	Gerd, let's go now.
Freunde, **laßt** uns essen.	Let's eat, folks.

The imperative form of **lassen** plus the pronoun **uns** is often used in place of the first-person plural imperative: **Gehen wir. Essen wir.** In talking to a person you address with **du**, use **laß**; with **ihr** use **laßt**.

4. **lassen** = *to have someone come to do something* or *to have something done*

Frau Lange **läßt** den Elektriker kommen.	Ms. Lange is sending for the electrician.
Wir **lassen** unser Auto reparieren.	We're having our car repaired.

4. Was bedeutet das?   The verb **lassen** can be translated in several different ways. Give all the possible English equivalents for each sentence below.

▶ Er ließ seinen Freund fahren. { *He let his friend drive.* / *He had his friend drive.* }

1. Sie läßt uns allein arbeiten.
2. Ich lasse meinen Chef den Brief schreiben.
3. Sie ließen das Auto reparieren.
4. Weil unser Auto nicht lief, ließen wir ein Taxi kommen.
5. Hast du den Schlüssel im Hotelzimmer gelassen?
6. Laß mich nicht zu lange auf eine Antwort warten!
7. Laßt uns aufs Land fahren.
8. Laßt uns das Wohnzimmer aufräumen.
9. Laß bitte das Fenster offen. Es ist hier sehr heiß.
10. Laßt mich wissen, was ihr für das Wochenende vorhabt.
11. Ich lasse morgen die Waschmaschine reparieren.
12. Ich lasse dich entscheiden, ob wir morgen fahren oder nicht.
13. Darf ich mein Auto über Nacht auf der Straße stehen lassen?

14. Wir wissen nicht, was Dieter vorhat. Wir lassen ihn allein planen.
15. Wo hast du das Fahrrad stehen lassen?
16. Ich habe es in der Garage gelassen.
17. Warum hast du mich so lange schlafen lassen?
18. Hast du dein Kassettendeck reparieren lassen?

5. Noch einmal   Restate the sentences below, using the cued subjects with the verb **lassen.**

▶   Wie lange lassen Sie die Leute da   *Wie lange läßt du die Leute da*
stehen? (du)   *stehen?*

1. Wann lassen Sie uns wissen, wann Sie kommen? (du)
2. Wo habt ihr euer Auto gelassen? (Sabine)
3. Bei wem läßt du deinen Wagen waschen? (ihr)
4. Andrea läßt dich aber lange warten. (deine Eltern)
5. Ich lasse den Geschirrspüler reparieren. (wir)
6. Wann lassen Sie Tanja mit der Arbeit anfangen? (du)
7. Warum hat er uns so lange arbeiten lassen? (du)
8. Ich muß das Auto reparieren lassen. (Sie)

6. Wo lasse ich das?   Discuss your plans for your trip to Europe with a friend. Tell her/him what you will leave with family or friends.

| | Stating intention |

▶   Ich lasse meine Kassetten bei meinem Freund.

7. Was machen wir dann?   Find a partner to do things with. You suggest an activity; your partner will suggest what to do afterward. Then take turns suggesting other activities to each other.

| | Suggesting things to do together |

Sie   *Gesprächspartner/in*
Laß uns schwimmen gehen.   Gut. Dann laß uns Kaffee trinken gehen.

8. Ich lasse alles machen.   Tell your partner three things you will not do for yourself but will have done for you. You may wish to use the following suggestions.

| | Expressing decisions |

Bett machen ◇ [Frühstück] machen ◇ Auto waschen ◇ Hausaufgaben machen ◇ [Fernseher] reparieren ◇ [Briefe] schreiben ◇ (Gartenarbeit) machen

▶   *Ich wasche mein Auto nicht. Ich lasse mein Auto (von meiner Schwester) waschen.*

5 Relative clauses

Ist das **der Mann, den** Sie meinen?	Is that the man (whom) you mean?
Das ist **das Auto, das** ich kaufen möchte.	That's the car (that) I'd like to buy.
Wer ist **die Frau, die** gerade hereinkommt?	Who is the woman (who is) just coming in?

A relative clause provides additional information about a previously mentioned noun or pronoun. The clause is introduced by a relative pronoun (e.g., **den, das, die**) that refers back to the noun, which is the antecedent (e.g., **Mann, Auto, Frau**). Since a relative clause is a dependent clause, the finite verb (e.g., **meinen, möchte, hereinkommt**) stands in last position.

In English, the relative pronoun may or may not be stated. In German, the relative pronoun is always stated. In written German, relative clauses are set off from main clauses by commas.

6 Relative pronouns

	Masculine	Neuter	Feminine	Plural
Nominative	der	das	die	die
Accusative	den	das	die	die
Dative	dem	dem	der	**denen**
Genitive	**dessen**	**dessen**	**deren**	**deren**

The forms of the relative pronoun are the same as the forms of the definite articles, except for the dative plural and all genitive forms.

Masculine	Das ist der Mann, **der** uns gefragt hat.
Neuter	Das ist das Kind, **das** uns gefragt hat.
Feminine	Das ist die Frau, **die** uns gefragt hat.
Plural	Das sind die Leute, **die** uns gefragt haben.

The *gender* (masculine, neuter, or feminine) of the relative pronoun depends on the gender of the noun to which it refers. In the examples above, **der** is masculine because it refers to **der Mann** and **die** is feminine because it refers to **die Frau**. Whether a pronoun is singular or plural also depends on the noun to which it refers. The pronoun **die** that refers to **die Leute** is plural and therefore requires the plural verb **haben**.

Nominative	Ist das der Mann, **der** hier war?
Accusative	Ist das der Mann, **den** Sie meinen?
Dative	Ist das der Mann, **dem** Sie es gesagt haben?
Genitive	Ist das der Mann, **dessen** Auto Sie gekauft haben?

The *case* (nominative, accusative, dative, or genitive) of a relative pronoun depends on its grammatical function in the relative clause. In the examples above, **der** is nominative because it is the subject of its clause; **den** is accusative because it is the direct object of the verb **meinen** in that clause; **dem** is dative because it is an indirect object in the clause; and **dessen** is genitive because it shows possession.

Ist das die Frau, **für die** Sie arbeiten?	Is that the woman for whom you work?
Ist das die Firma, **bei der** Sie arbeiten?	Is that the firm (that) you work for?

A preposition followed by a relative pronoun may introduce a relative clause. The case of the relative pronoun then depends on what case the preposition takes. In **für die**, **die** is accusative because of **für**; in **bei der**, **der** is dative because of **bei**.

In German, whenever a relative pronoun is the object of a preposition, the preposition precedes the pronoun. In colloquial English the preposition is usually in last position [(*that*) *you work for*].

9. Die deutsche Wirtschaft Below are sentences on the German economy. Identify the relative pronouns. Indicate the case and function of each relative pronoun, and name its antecedent.

▶ Die Regierung arbeitet für einen Welthandel, der wirklich frei ist.   *der = nominative, subject, Welthandel*

1. Ein Land wie Deutschland, das wenig Rohstoffe hat, lebt vom Handel.
2. Die Produkte, die man produziert, müssen von bester Qualität sein.
3. Denn es gibt mehrere Länder, mit denen Deutschland konkurrieren muß.
4. In der Zukunft ändert sich der Markt, für den Deutschland produzieren muß.
5. Einige Firmen, die Sachen produzieren, die man nicht mehr kauft, werden pleite machen.
6. Das bedeutet, daß die Arbeitnehmer, deren Firmen pleite sind, arbeitslos werden.
7. Die Arbeitslosigkeit ist ein Problem, das nur schwer zu lösen ist.
8. Die Gewerkschaften, die sich vor allem als Partner der Arbeitgeber sehen, werden auch im neuen Markt eine große Rolle spielen.

10. Die sind doch gar nicht kaputt. Your friend is good at fixing electrical things and audio equipment, only he can't seem to find the right ones. Tell him the things he wants to fix for you aren't the broken ones. Use the nominative of the relative pronoun.

▶ Ich repariere jetzt diese Schreibmaschine, ja? *Das ist doch nicht die Schreibmaschine, die kaputt ist.*

1. Ich repariere jetzt diesen Fernseher, ja?
2. Ich repariere jetzt diesen Kassettenrecorder, ja?
3. Ich repariere jetzt diese Stereoanlage, ja?
4. Ich repariere jetzt dieses Kassettendeck, ja?
5. Ich repariere jetzt dieses Radio, ja?
6. Ich repariere jetzt diese Lampen, ja?
7. Ich repariere jetzt diese Uhren, ja?

11. Die Sachen sind toll. Gabi shows you various articles of clothing. Show your interest by asking whether they are the ones she got for her birthday. Use the accusative of the relative pronoun.

▶ Wie gefällt dir diese Jacke? *Toll. Ist das die Jacke, die du zum Geburtstag bekommen hast?*

1. Wie gefällt dir diese Hose?
2. Wie gefällt dir dieses Hemd?
3. Wie gefällt dir dieser Rock?
4. Wie gefällt dir diese Bluse?
5. Wie gefällt dir dieser Pulli?
6. Wie gefallen dir diese Jeans?
7. Wie gefallen dir diese Schuhe?

12. Wem gehören diese Sachen? Say to whom the things belong. Use the dative of the relative pronoun.

▶ der Mann / das rote Auto. *Das ist der Mann, dem das rote Auto gehört.*

1. die Frau / der große Hut
2. der Professor / der Computer
3. die Journalistin / die Kamera
4. das kleine Kind / der Ball
5. der Student / die Büchertasche
6. das Mädchen / das Fahrrad
7. die Leute / das Haus an der Ecke
8. die Kaufleute / das neue Geschäft

13. Informationen für Touristen   Combine each pair of sentences, using a preposition and a relative pronoun.

▶ Meyers ist ein Lebensmittelgeschäft. Man kann alles in dem
Lebensmittelgeschäft finden.

Meyers ist ein Lebensmittelge-
schäft, in dem man alles finden
kann.

1. Die „Krone" ist ein gutes Restaurant. Man kann billig in diesem Restaurant essen.
2. Dinkelsbühl ist ein interessantes Städtchen. Man hört oft von diesem Städtchen.
3. Frankfurt ist eine wichtige Stadt. Man hört oft von dieser Stadt.
4. Der „Peterhof" ist ein großer Biergarten. Man hört gute Musik in diesem Biergarten.
5. Heidelberg ist eine alte und gute Universität. Jeder möchte auf diese Universität gehen.
6. München ist eine attraktive Stadt. Jeder möchte in dieser Stadt leben.

14. Wer sind diese Leute?   Veronika is a guest at a party where she knows no one. Your friend tells her something about the people. But since she knows no German you must translate.

▶ Das ist die Frau, deren Sohn in
Marburg studiert.

That is the woman whose son is
studying in Marburg.

1. Das ist der Mann, dessen Tochter bei Volkswagen arbeitet.
2. Das sind die Leute, deren Kinder gut Englisch können.
3. Das ist der Mann, dessen Sohn arbeitslos ist.
4. Das ist der Mann, dessen Frau Chefärztin ist.
5. Das ist die junge Frau, deren Vater ein bekannter Jurist ist.
6. Das ist der junge Mann, dessen Eltern sehr reich sind.

Ende gut, alles gut.

**Eine türkische Familie
in Berlin**

Historically, Germany has not encouraged immigration, and there is some discussion whether it is an immigration country (**Einwanderungsland**) or not. Nonetheless, there are approximately five million foreigners (6.5 percent of the population) living in Germany. Like new inhabitants of any country, these foreigners have many problems to face, such as coming to terms with a new culture and a new language and some prejudice from Germans.

The majority of these foreigners came as foreign workers (**Gastarbeiter** or **ausländische Arbeitnehmer**) and are permanent residents of Germany. More than 70 percent have lived in Germany for more than 10 years and many were born in Germany. These workers often hold low-paying jobs with little seniority, although they receive the same social benefits as Germans. In western Germany, the largest number of foreigners is from Turkey, followed by Yugoslavians, Italians, Greeks, and Poles. In eastern Germany, the largest number is from Vietnam, followed by Mozambique, Cuba, the Soviet Union, Poland, and Hungary.

Another large group of foreigners is made up of people applying for political asylum (**Asyl**). Because of the persecution under the National Socialists in the Third Reich, the framers of the Constitution (**Grundgesetz**) of the Federal Republic of Germany included an article that guarantees the right to asylum to all persons persecuted on political grounds. They thus created one of the most liberal asylum laws in the world. These asylum seekers (**Asylanten**) receive financial aid from the government while waiting for their cases to be heard. If asylum is granted, they receive help to integrate them into German society. In recent years the number of people applying for asylum has grown dramatically, but only about 4.4 percent of the applications are approved. In 1990 the largest number of asylum seekers came from Rumania, followed by Yugoslavia and Turkey. Applicants from Third World groups came from Lebanon and Vietnam among others. There has been much discussion in Germany about changing the policy on asylum seekers to limit the number. However, the issue may be settled by the introduction of a European asylum law which is now under discussion within the European Community.

A special category of "foreigners" are the ethnic German resettlers (**Aussiedler**) who come to Germany. In recent years many have come from German enclaves in the Soviet Union. Although of German heritage, these migrants speak their own dialect, and Germany has an extensive system of special programs to integrate these people into German society.

15. Erzähl mal. In groups of three take turns completing each of the sentences.

▶ Wien ist eine Stadt, …   *[die sehr alt ist].*
                               [die ich besuchen möchte].
                               [in der ich leben möchte].

1. Die Schweiz ist ein Land, …
2. Österreich ist ein Land, …
3. Volkswagen ist eine Firma, …
4. Ich hätte gern einen Präsidenten/eine Präsidentin, …
5. Ich habe einen Freund, …
6. Ich habe eine Freundin, …
7. Ich habe einen Professor/eine Professorin, …
8. Der Juli ist ein Monat, …

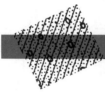

WIEDERHOLUNG

1. Eine bekannte Autorin Read the following account about Kirsten Elsner's start as an author. Answer the questions.

Herr Elsner bekam eine neue Stelle in einer anderen Stadt. Weil Frau Elsner dort keine Arbeit fand, blieb sie zu Hause und sorgte für die Kinder. Am Anfang machte sie alles gern. Sie kochte, putzte, ging einkaufen und half den Kindern bei den Schulaufgaben. Um etwas für die Kinder zu tun, fing sie an, kurze Geschichten für sie zu schreiben. Sie wurde durch die Kindergeschichten bald bekannt. Jetzt nennt man sie nicht mehr Kirsten Elsner, die Frau von Herrn Elsner. Jetzt heißt sie Kirsten Wiener, und Herr Elsner ist der Mann von der bekannten Autorin.

1. Warum wohnten Elsners in einer neuen Stadt?
2. Warum blieb Frau Elsner zu Hause?
3. Was machte sie zu Hause?
4. Warum fing sie an, Kindergeschichten zu schreiben?
5. Wie nennt man Herrn Elsner jetzt?

2. Gabi weiß jetzt mehr.   Tanja wants to know whether you helped Gabi understand some facts about the economic situation in Germany. Answer the questions below. Replace the boldfaced words with a pronoun or use a **da**-compound.

▶   Wollte Gabi etwas über **die**   *Ja, sie wollte etwas darüber wis-*
   deutsche Wirtschaft wissen?   *sen.*
   Ja, sie _____ .

1. Hast du ihr von **der Rolle des Außenhandels** erzählt?
   Ja, ich _____ .
2. Hat sie **die Rolle** verstanden?
   Ja, sie _____ .
3. Ein Land wie Deutschland lebt vom **Handel,** nicht?
   Ja, es _____ .
4. Interessiert sich Gabi auch für **die Rolle der Gewerkschaften?**
   Ja, sie _____ .
5. Weiß sie etwas über **die Ziele der Gewerkschaften?**
   Ja, sie _____ .
6. Haben die Deutschen große Angst vor **Inflation?**
   Ja, sie _____ .
7. Findet Gabi **den Lebensstandard der Deutschen** hoch?
   Ja, sie _____ .

3. Ein Student an der Uni Bernd wonders how Peter is getting along at the university. Tell him things are not going well, but that Peter doesn't seem to mind. Complete the sentences below with adjective endings, where necessary. Then answer the questions in the negative, using adjectives from the list as antonyms for the adjectives in the questions.

alt ◇ dumm ◇ dunkel ◇ faul ◇ groß ◇ lustig ◇ leicht ◇ schlecht ◇ teuer

▶ *Geht Peter auf eine klein_____ Universität?*   *Geht Peter auf eine kleine Universität? Nein, auf eine große.*

1. Ist er ein fleißig_____ Student?
2. Ist er intelligent_____?
3. Liest er gern ernst_____ Geschichten?
4. Wohnt er in einer modern_____ Wohnung?
5. Wohnt er in einem hell_____ Zimmer?
6. Führt er ein schwer_____ Leben?
7. Hat er einen gut bezahlt_____ Studentenjob?
8. Findet er Wohnen und Essen billig_____?

4. Markus schreibt über Frauen. Markus has written some brief comments about **Frauen in Deutschland.** Complete his work by supplying appropriate relative pronouns.

1. Viele Frauen ärgern sich über das Frauenbild, _____ in vielen Schulbüchern noch zu finden ist.
2. In diesen Büchern ist es immer ein Junge, _____ etwas baut oder Fußball spielt.
3. Und es ist immer ein Mädchen, _____ zusieht und weniger gefährliche Sachen macht.
4. Die Frauen, _____ Berufe wie Elektrikerin und Mechanikerin gelernt haben, haben es besonders schwer.
5. Man nennt eine Frau, _____ wegen der Arbeit vier Tage von zu Hause weg ist, eine Rabenmutter.
6. Ein Mann, _____ dieselbe Arbeit macht, ist aber kein Rabenvater.
7. Es gibt also noch traditionelle Rollen, von _____ Männer und Frauen sich emanzipieren müssen.

5. Was sagen Sie?

1. Arbeiten Sie während der Ferien oder während des Semesters bei einer Firma?
2. Wo arbeiten Sie? Wie gefällt Ihnen Ihre Arbeit?
3. Wie ist das Arbeitsklima da, wo Sie arbeiten?
4. Gehören Sie zu einer Gewerkschaft?
5. Was ist für Sie wichtig? (Möchten Sie mehr verdienen? Möchten Sie längere Ferien haben?)
6. Wie könnten die Gewerkschaften mehr gegen die Arbeitslosigkeit tun?

In Germany young people who want a career that requires special skills in business or industry serve an apprenticeship (**Lehre**) after graduating at the 9th- or 10th-grade level from a secondary school called the **Hauptschule.** They are generally called **Lehrlinge,** although the official term is **Auszubildender** for a boy, **Auszubildende** for a girl. They work 3 to 4 days a week while taking related courses at a specialized continuation school. After 2½ to 3½ years as apprentices, upon passing an examination they become journeymen or journeywomen (**Gesellen**) in the trades and assistants (**Gehilfen**) in office jobs. The master's examination (**Meisterprüfung**) may be taken after five more years of work and additional schooling. With a diploma (**Meisterbrief**), which is displayed much as a doctor's or lawyer's license, the successful candidate is qualified to train **Auszubildende** (**Azubis**) and/or to open her or his own business in the chosen occupation.

Azubis in einer Berufsschule in Stuttgart

6. Erzählen Sie mal.

1. Erzählen Sie mal über ein Buch, das Sie gern kaufen würden.
2. Erzählen Sie mal über eine Reise, die Sie gern machen würden.
3. Erzählen Sie mal über Ferien, die Sie gern machen würden.
4. Erzählen Sie mal über Politiker, die Sie gern reden hören würden.
5. Erzählen Sie mal über einen Film, den Sie gern sehen würden.

> Talking about personal preferences

7. Anregung   Write a paragraph in German about some of the differences between the economies of your country and Germany. Use the questions below as a guideline.

In welchem Land spielt der Außenhandel eine größere Rolle? Warum?
Welches Land hat mehr Rohstoffe?
Welche Produkte exportieren die Länder vor allem?
In welchem Land sehen die Chancen für eine gesunde Wirtschaft besser aus?
    Warum?
In welchem Land sind die Gewerkschaften stärker?

GRAMMATIK: ZUSAMMENFASSUNG

The future tense

ich **werde** es **machen**	wir **werden** es **machen**
du **wirst** es **machen**	ihr **werdet** es **machen**
er/es/sie **wird** es **machen**	sie **werden** es **machen**
	Sie **werden** es **machen**

The German future tense consists of the auxiliary **werden** plus an infinitive in final position.

Erika sagt, daß sie es **machen wird.**

In a dependent clause, the auxiliary **werden** is in final position. It follows the infinitive.

Future time

Ich **komme** morgen bestimmt.	I'll come tomorrow for sure.
Fahren Sie nächstes Jahr nach Deutschland?	Are you going to Germany next year?

German uses the future tense less frequently than English. German generally uses the present tense to express future time if the time reference is clearly future.

Wir **werden** unsere Freunde **einladen.**	We will invite our friends.
Jutta **wird** es allein **machen.**	Jutta will do it alone.

The future tense is used if the time reference is not clear from the context of the sentence or to express the speaker's determination that an event will indeed take place.

Constructions with *lassen*

Present tense	
ich lasse	wir lassen
du läßt	ihr laßt
er/es/sie läßt	sie lassen
Sie lassen	
Simple past stem:	ließ
Past participle:	gelassen

◆ *Uses of* **lassen**

Inge **ließ** ihren Bruder zu Hause.	Inge left her brother at home.
Inge **ließ** ihre Schwester fahren.	Inge let her sister drive.

Lassen behaves like the modals, in that it can stand alone or take a dependent infinitive without **zu.**

Hast du deinen Bruder zu Hause **gelassen?**	Did you leave your brother at home?
Hast du ihn fahren **lassen?**	Did you let him drive?

Lassen has two past participles: **gelassen** and **lassen.** The participle **gelassen** is used when the verb occurs without a dependent infinitive. The alternate participle **lassen** is used when the verb occurs with a dependent infinitive. The participle **lassen** is identical with the infinitive; this construction is called the "double infinitive" construction.

◆ *Meanings of* **lassen**

Lassen is one of the most commonly used verbs in German. **Lassen** has four basic meanings.

1. **lassen** = *to leave*

Uwe **hat** seinen Freund allein **gelassen.**	Uwe left his friend alone.
Hast du deine Jacke zu Hause **gelassen?**	Did you leave your jacket at home?

2. **lassen** = *to let* or *to permit*

Wir **lassen** euch arbeiten.	We'll let you work.
Lassen Sie mich Ihnen helfen.	Let me help you.

3. **lassen** = *let's*

Inge, **laß** uns jetzt lesen.	Inge, let's read now.
Kinder, **laßt** uns singen.	Children, let's sing.

   In talking to a person you address with **du,** use **laß;** with **ihr,** use **laßt.**

4. **lassen** = *to have something done* or *to have someone come to do something*

Uschi **läßt** ihr Radio reparieren.	Uschi is having her radio repaired.
Haben Sie den Elektriker kommen **lassen?**	Did you send for the electrician?

Relative clauses

Wie teuer ist **der Fernseher, den** du kaufen willst?	How expensive is the television (that) you want to buy?
Wie alt ist **das Auto, das** du verkaufen möchtest?	How old is the car (that) you want to sell?
Ist das **die Schallplatte, die** du gestern gekauft hast?	Is that the record (that) you bought yesterday?

A relative clause provides additional information about a previously mentioned noun or pronoun. The clause is introduced by a relative pronoun, which refers back to the noun or pronoun (called an antecedent). A relative clause is a dependent clause, and the verb is in final position.

Relative pronouns

	Masculine	Neuter	Feminine	Plural
Nominative	der	das	die	die
Accusative	den	das	die	die
Dative	dem	dem	der	**denen**
Genitive	**dessen**	**dessen**	**deren**	**deren**

Nominative	Ist das der Mann, **der** immer so viel fragt?
Accusative	Ist das der Mann, **den** Sie meinen?
	für den Sie arbeiten?
Dative	Ist das der Mann, **dem** Sie oft helfen?
	von dem Sie erzählt haben?
Genitive	Ist das der Mann, **dessen** Auto Sie gekauft haben?

The *gender* (masculine, neuter, or feminine) and *number* (singular or plural) of the relative pronoun are determined by its antecedent, i.e., the noun to which it refers. The *case* (nominative, accusative, dative, or genitive) of the relative pronoun is determined by its function within its clause (subject, direct object, object of a preposition, etc.).

DER KOPIERER, DER
BEWEGUNG INS BÜRO
BRINGT.

TA TRIUMPH-ADLER

Wenn Sie
das »Schlange stehen«
am Kopierer leid sind.
TA 215 Z, der Vielseitige
unter den Kompakten.
Von TA.

Kokoschka, *Porträt Gino Schmidt*

Als ich noch junq war

Werner Schmidli

Werner Schmidli was born in 1939 in Basel, Switzerland. He has been publishing short stories, novels, and poetry since 1966.

In his writings, Werner Schmidli explores the relationship of language to the reality it represents. He writes in a clear, matter-of-fact prose style. Through language he tries to help the reader see the familiar in a new light. The narrator of "Als ich noch jung war," taken from the collection of prose *Sagen Sie nicht: beim Geld hört der Spaß auf* (1971), contrasts the time of his/her youth with the present day. The narrator's judgments consist of statements commonly heard among the "older" generation. By piling comment upon comment and mixing judgments with observations the narrator lets readers see the exaggeration of the claims and forces them to think carefully about all the statements. Upon close examination many of them turn out to say nothing.

Which statements have some concrete substance to them? Which statements imply judgments that are hard to prove? Which statements say nothing at all?

Als ich noch jung war

Als ich noch jung war, da hatten wir Respekt vor den Alten. Als ich jung war, da waren die Kinder noch Kinder und haben zugehört°, wenn man ihnen etwas sagte. Man hat gehorcht° und den Mund gehalten°, wenn die Erwachsenen redeten. Als ich jung war, hat man nicht soviel Wert° aufs
5 Äußere° gelegt, die Mädchen waren noch Mädchen und die Frauen wußten, wo ihr Platz ist. Die jungen Männer waren noch Männer und wußten, was sie wollten. Da hat man die Nachbarn gekannt. Da war nicht alles so hygienisch, und wir leben immer noch.

Als ich jung war, mußte man nicht Angst haben, überfahren zu
10 werden°, wenn man auf die Straße ging. Die Luft war nicht verpestet°, die Flüsse° waren noch sauber, der Sommer war noch ein richtiger Sommer, im Winter hatten wir Schnee und das Holz° verfaulte° nicht in den Wäldern.

Als ich jung war, hatten wir noch Anstand°. In der Straßenbahn
15 standen wir auf, am Sonntagmorgen ging die Familie in die Kirche°, am Nachmittag spazieren und wenn einer krank war, dann war er wirklich krank.

Als ich jung war, da war der Franken° noch ein Franken und wenn wir etwas wollten, haben wir zuerst gefragt. Als ich jung war, da waren
20 wir nicht so verweichlicht°. Wir hatten gute Zähne. Das Obst war gesund und die Milch fetter°. Wir lebten gesünder. Da hat man noch Kartoffeln gegessen und Huhn° gab es nur am Sonntag.

Als ich jung war, war alles anders!
Die Bauern waren noch Bauern.
25 Die Leute hatten Zeit.
Eine Familie war eine Familie.
Handarbeit° wurde geschätzt°.
An Weihnachten hatten wir immer Schnee.
In den Städten konnte man wohnen.
30 Kinder waren ein Segen°.
Die Zimmer waren größer.
Man wußte, was man den Eltern schuldig ist°.

listened
*obeyed / **den ... gehalten:** kept one's mouth shut*
value
appearances

***überfahren ... werden:** to be run over / polluted*
rivers
wood / rotted

good manners
church

(Swiss unit of currency)

pampered
higher fat content
chicken

manual work / appreciated

blessing

***schuldig ist:** owes*

446

Fragen

Früher war alles anders.

1. Geben Sie Beispiele für die Kinder. Wie waren sie früher? Wie sind sie heute?
2. Und die Mädchen, Frauen und Männer?
3. Was hat „man" früher alles anders gemacht?
4. Und die Umwelt? Wie war die früher, und wie ist sie heute?
5. Und die Jahreszeiten?
6. Und das Geld?

Fragen zur Diskussion

Hier spricht ein anonymes Ich. Dieses Ich findet viele Unterschiede zwischen früher und heute.

1. Finden Sie, daß das Ich einige Unterschiede ganz richtig sieht? Welche?
2. Welche Unterschiede finden Sie weniger richtig gesehen?
3. In welchen Unterschieden zeigt sich der Sprecher als reaktionär?
4. Warum verfaulte früher das Holz nicht in den Wäldern?
5. Wie war es früher mit Hygiene und Krankheiten? Und heute? Was ist besser?
6. Ist aus dem jungen Ich wirklich ein Erwachsener geworden? Warum (nicht)?
7. Kennen Sie Menschen, die so reden wie dieses Ich? Was sagen sie?

November 1989 in Berlin —
die Mauer fällt.

Kapitel 14

BAUSTEINE FÜR GESPRÄCHE

Was wird gespielt?

Adrian: Hättest du Lust, heute abend ins Theater zu gehen?
Bettina: In welches?
Adrian: Ins Berliner Ensemble.
Bettina: Vielleicht ja. Was wird gespielt?
Adrian: Ein Brecht-Stück. „Leben des Galilei".
Bettina: Oh gut! Das würde ich mir gern ansehen.

What's playing?

Would you feel like going to the theater tonight?
Which one?
The Berliner Ensemble.
Maybe. What's playing?

A play by Brecht. "Galileo."

Oh good! I'd love to see that.

Hast du Karten?

Bettina: Hast du denn schon Karten für heute abend?
Adrian: Ja, ganz gute sogar. Von meinen Eltern. Die können nicht.
Bettina: So ein Glück! Weißt du, wer den Galilei spielt?
Adrian: Der Klaus Martens.
Bettina: Oh wirklich? Da bin ich ja gespannt.

Have you got tickets?

Have you already got tickets for tonight?
Yes, very good ones as a matter of fact. From my parents. They can't go.
What luck! Do you know who's playing Galileo?
Klaus Martens.
Oh really? I wonder how he'll be.

Fragen

1. Wohin gehen Bettina und Adrian heute abend?
2. Was wird gespielt?
3. Warum geht Bettina mit?
4. Woher bekommen sie die Karten?
5. Warum ist Bettina gespannt?

1. **Kommst du mit?** Find out from a fellow student what kind of entertainment she/he likes and then invite her/him to join you in attending an event.

Talking about cultural events

Sie

Gehst du gern	ins	**Musical?**
		Theater?
		Konzert°?
		Kino?
	in die	Oper°?

Gesprächspartner/in

Natürlich.
Wenn ich Zeit habe.
Wenn etwas Gutes gespielt wird.
Ja, sehr gern.
Nein, das interessiert mich nicht.
Nicht besonders.

Gehst du mit	ins	**Theater** heute abend?
		Kino
		Konzert
		Pop-Konzert
		Open-Air-Konzert
	in die	Oper

Ja, gern.
In welche(s)?
Oh ja, das interessiert mich sehr.
Wenn du mich einlädst, schon.
Hast du Karten?
Es ist leider ausverkauft°.

| Wer | **spielt?** |
| | singt |

Nein, ich habe leider keine Zeit.
Nein, ich habe keine Lust.

Gesprächspartner/in

Was wird gespielt?

Sie

Die Dreigroschenoper [The Threepenny Opera].
Goethes *Faust.*
Ende gut, alles gut.
Die Zauberflöte [The Magic Flute].
Fidelio.
Lohengrin.
Beethovens *Neunte.*
Schumanns *Klavierkonzert°.*

2. **Gehst du mit?** In a group of four decide what you want to do on the weekend (go to the theater, a concert, the opera, or a musical). After you agree on what to see, decide how much you want to spend for a ticket. Then decide what you want to do afterwards. You may wish to use the following sentences to get you started.

Making plans

Ich möchte ins […].
Ich würde lieber […].
Das ist […].

3. Interview Interview a fellow student about his/her taste in entertainment. Keep track of your findings and report them.

Fragen Sie Ihren Partner/Ihre Partnerin,

1. ob er/sie oft ins Theater geht.
2. was für Theaterstücke er/sie gern sieht.
3. ob er/sie lieber ins Kino geht.
4. wie oft er/sie ins Kino geht — einmal in der Woche, zweimal im Monat.
5. welche neuen Filme er/sie gut findet.
6. ob er/sie manchmal in die Oper geht.
7. welche Opern er/sie kennt.
8. ob er/sie oft ins Konzert geht.
9. was für Musik er/sie gern hört.
10. welche Rockbands er/sie gut findet.
11. welche Fernsehsendung er/sie gut findet.

Vokabeln

___ Substantive _____

die **Karte, -n** ticket
das **Klavier, -e** piano
das **Konzert, -e** concert; concerto
das **Musical, -s** musical
die **Oper, -n** opera
das **Stück, -e** (das **Theaterstück**)
  play (live theater)

___ Andere Wörter _____

ausverkauft sold out
einmal: einmal in der Woche once
  a week
gespannt eager, anxious; **gespannt
  sein** to be in suspense, anxious
  to know; to wonder about

Bertolt Brecht
BAAL
Regie: Manfred Karge, Bühnenbild und
Kostüme: Heidi Brambach

BURGTHEATER

SPIELZEIT

PREMIEREN   PLÄNE

**August 1961:
Bau der Berliner Mauer**

Two German states existed from 1949–1990. In the later years of the separation, West Germany (The Federal Republic of Germany/**Die Bundesrepublik Deutschland**) referred to this situation as "two states, but one nation" (**zwei Staaten, eine Nation**), and its constitution assumed a future reunification. East Germany (The German Democratic Republic/**Die Deutsche Demokratische Republik**), in contrast, was increasingly dedicated to building an independent, separate country. While West Germany developed a market economy, East Germany followed an economic system of central planning wherein 220 state conglomerates (**Kombinate**) controlled 85 percent of the economy and farms were collectivized (1960). While the citizens of East Germany liked the fact that there was no unemployment, that government subsidies kept rents and prices of food staples low, and that the government provided health care and a pension system, they found that the political system restricted individual freedom, and the scarcity of non-staple consumer goods was a daily irritant.

The construction of the Berlin Wall (**Mauerbau**) in 1961 was the most dramatic attempt to stop the wave of people leaving East Germany. In addition, the gradual build-up of the border system of fences, dogs, and minefields between the two states had made the border practically impenetrable.

In the early seventies, Willy Brandt, Chancellor of the Federal Republic of Germany, made the first open overtures to East Germany (part of his **Ostpolitik**) and thereby laid the groundwork for cooperation with East Germany. West Germany supplemented diplomacy with hard currency by establishing special trade regulations for importing East German goods and granting credits (**Kredite**) to East Germany. In the course of the years the climate between the two countries improved. At first retirees (**Rentner**) and later others from East Germany were allowed to visit West Germany, permanent representations similar to embassies (**ständige Vertretungen**) were established, and West Germans living in border areas were allowed to travel more freely across the border (**grenznaher Verkehr**).

In 1989, the overall political climate in the eastern bloc countries began to change. Hungary was the first to open the Iron Curtain by taking down the barbed wire and letting East Germans cross into Austria. A democratic movement spread throughout the Warsaw Pact countries, of which East Germany was a member. Throughout East Germany there were large demonstrations and in November 1989, the government opened the Berlin Wall and subsequently resigned. The freedom movement culminated in free elections in March 1990.

Am Tag nach der Maueröffnung am Checkpoint Charlie, dem alten Grenzübergang für Ausländer (10. November 1989)

Article 2 of the Unification Treaty (**Einigungsvertrag**) states that "Berlin is the capital city of Germany." But from the end of World War II until the unification of Germany, Berlin had a special status under international law. Legally, it belonged neither to the **Bundesrepublik** nor to the **Deutsche Demokratische Republik (DDR).** In practice both parts of Berlin were closely connected to their respective systems. Many countries recognized Berlin as the capital of the **DDR.**

After World War II, the four Allies divided Germany into four zones of occupation, and its capital Berlin into four sectors: American, British, French, and Soviet. Currency reforms in the Western zones and then in the Soviet zone in 1948, the blockade of Berlin by the Soviets, and the establishment of the **Bundesrepublik** and the **Deutsche Demokratische Republik** in 1949 led to the separation of Berlin into two parts: a western and an eastern part. However, since there was an open border between the two, Berlin provided an escape route for East Germans who wanted to go to the West. By 1961 between 2 and 3.5 million East Germans (an estimated 15 percent of the work force) had left the **DDR** for the West. To prevent further loss of workers, the **DDR** gradually sealed its border with the **Bundesrepublik.** In 1961, the **DDR** permanently halted emigration with the construction of the Berlin Wall (**die Mauer**), thus completing the division of Berlin, which lasted until November 9, 1989, when the wall was opened. On that day people streamed across the border and celebrated night and day. As of October 3, 1990, Berlin is again one city. It is the largest city in Germany with a population of 3.4 million and is one of the sixteen **Bundesländer** (federal states). With unification Berlin reclaimed its historical role as capital of Germany.

DEUTSCHLAND—ELF PLUS FÜNF

Vorbereitung auf das Lesen

◆ *Zum Thema*

Was wissen Sie schon über das vereinigte Deutschland?

1. Wie viele Einwohner hat das vereinigte Deutschland? 20, 40, 60, 80 Millionen?
2. Wie viele Länder in der Europäischen Gemeinschaft° sind größer als Deutschland?   *European Community*
3. Die alte Bundesrepublik hatte eine Marktwirtschaft. Was für eine Wirtschaft hatte die DDR?
4. Wie lange haben die Deutschen in zwei getrennten Staaten gelebt? Von wann bis wann?
5. Wer war während der Teilung reicher, die Ostdeutschen oder die Westdeutschen? Was für Konsequenzen hat es, wenn ein reicheres und ein weniger reiches Land vereinigt werden? Was meinen Sie?
6. Was wissen Sie über Probleme bei der Vereinigung? Welche Probleme gab es? Welche gibt es immer noch?

◆ *Leitfragen*

1. Was wird über das vereinigte Deutschland gesagt?

   Stichworte: Einwohner ◇ Bundesländer ◇ Hauptstadt

2. Welche Gedanken hat der Bundespräsident geäußert°?   *expressed*

   Stichworte: Wirtschaft ◇ tägliche Erfahrungen

3. Wo lagen die wirtschaftlichen Probleme?

   Stichworte: Kapital, Know-how brauchen ◇ investieren ◇ frühere Eigentümer, Vermögen, zurückhaben

   Stichworte: Infrastruktur ◇ Telefonsystem: veraltet, 15 Prozent der Haushalte; Modernisierung: 7–10 Jahre; auf der Post telefonieren

4. Die Menschen im Osten und die Menschen im Westen haben 45 Jahre getrennt gelebt. Was für Folgen hat das gehabt?

   Stichworte: Westdeutsche, „Deutschland" ◇ Ostdeutsche, nur „die DDR" ◇ westdeutsche Mannschaft, „deutsche Mannschaft"

   Stichworte: Ostdeutsche ◇ relativ arm; vergessen, zurückgesetzt

   Stichworte: Zusammenwachsen ◇ Zeit brauchen

Am 3. Oktober 1990 hörte die DDR auf zu existieren. Sie trat der Bundesrepublik bei°. Die Bundesrepublik wurde so mit 78,8 Millionen Einwohnern der größte Staat in der Europäischen Gemeinschaft. Die Zahl der Bundesländer wuchs auf sechzehn: Zu den elf westdeutschen Ländern
5 kamen fünf neue ostdeutsche. Berlin wurde wieder Hauptstadt.

trat bei: joined

An diesem 3. Oktober 1990 sagte Bundespräsident Richard von Weizsäcker in einer Rede: „ … Die Vereinigung Deutschlands ist etwas anderes als eine bloße Erweiterung° der Bundesrepublik. Der Tag ist gekommen, an dem zum ersten Mal in der Geschichte das ganze Deutschland
10 seinen dauerhaften° Platz im Kreis der westlichen Demokratien findet. Dies ist für uns selbst wie für alle unsere Nachbarn ein Vorgang° von fundamentaler Bedeutung." Der Präsident beschrieb, wie es zur Vereinigung gekommen war. Dann sagte er, daß man aber nicht vergessen dürfe, wieviel die Westdeutschen und die Ostdeutschen noch voneinander trenne. Er
15 sprach nicht nur von den wirtschaftlichen Unterschieden, sondern auch von den 45 Jahren, in denen die täglichen Erfahrungen der Menschen im Osten und im Westen ganz verschieden gewesen seien.

expansion

permanent

process

Die wirtschaftlichen Unterschiede waren am 3. Oktober 1990 in der Tat gewaltig°. Nur wenige Zweige° der früheren DDR-Wirtschaft waren auf dem
20 Weltmarkt konkurrenzfähig°. Die ostdeutsche Industrie brauchte also massiv Kapital und Know-how aus dem Westen. Aber nur wenige Firmen wollten zu dieser Zeit investieren und so die dringend° benötigten° Arbeitsplätze schaffen. Warum waren es nicht mehr? Es gab dafür eine ganze Reihe von Gründen. Ein wichtiger Grund war, daß in den fünf neuen Ländern am
25 Anfang kaum jemand wußte, was wem gehörte. In der DDR waren nämlich viele Häuser, Grundstücke° und Fabriken enteignet° worden. Die früheren Eigentümer° waren zum Teil in die Bundesrepublik geflohen°. Nach der Vereinigung begannen sie, ihr Eigentum° zurückzufordern°. In den Rathäusern Ostdeutschlands lagen mehr als eine Million Anträge° auf
30 Vermögensrückgabe°. Wer will aber in einer solchen Situation etwas kaufen, von dem er nicht weiß, ob es ihm am Ende auch gehört?

enormous / branches

able to compete

urgently / needed

lots (real estate) / expropriated

owners / fled

property / demand back

applications

return of assets

Ein weiterer wichtiger Grund war der desolate Zustand der Infrastruktur. Straßen und Schienen° mußten dringend repariert und modernisiert werden. Das Telefonnetz war hoffnungslos veraltet°. Es war seit 1945 so gut wie nicht
35 modernisiert worden. Man schätzte°, daß nur 15% der Haushalte 1990 ein Telefon hatten. Es fehlten etwa 90 000 öffentliche Telefonzellen°. Modernisierung und Ausbau° sollten sieben bis zehn Jahre dauern. Natürlich wollte kaum jemand in einem Gebiet investieren, wo man nur auf der Post telefonieren kann und wo man vielleicht mit vielen anderen Schlange stehen
40 muß.

tracks (railroad)

obsolete

estimated

telephone booths

expansion

Es gab am 3. Oktober 1990 aber nicht nur wirtschaftliche Unterschiede und Schwierigkeiten. Man muß auch an die Tatsache denken, daß die Menschen im Osten und die Menschen im Westen 45 Jahre anders gelebt, andere Erfahrungen gemacht, sich auseinander gelebt haben°. Die Westdeutschen

sich … haben grew apart

**Renovierung alter
Häuser in Berlin-Pankow**

45 lernten im Lauf der Zeit°, die Bundesrepublik als einen funktionierenden demokratischen Staat zu sehen. Die DDR erschien ihnen dagegen als eine Fehlkonstruktion°. Drei Millionen Zuwanderer° aus der DDR schienen das zu bestätigen°. Die Westdeutschen glaubten, daß sie „Deutschland" seien, die Ostdeutschen nur „die DDR". Die „deutsche Botschaft°" war überall die

50 Botschaft der Bundesrepublik. Die „deutsche Mannschaft°" war die westdeutsche. Auch die Ostdeutschen glaubten das. Eine Nürnberger Familie brachte es auf den Punkt°, als sie am 4. Oktober 1990 zu einem Bekannten aus Leipzig sagten: „Nun seid ihr auch Deutsche."

Die Westdeutschen lebten zwischen Helmstedt und Mallorca. Der Westen

55 war ihre Welt. Die DDR war weit weg, uninteressant und weitgehend° unbekannt. Die Ostdeutschen waren die relativ Armen, die Provinziellen°, die Eingesperrten°, die Deutschen zweiter Klasse. Die Westdeutschen konnten ohne die Ostdeutschen gut leben, die Ostdeutschen aber nur schwer ohne die Westdeutschen. Die Sachsen, Thüringer, Brandenburger,

60 Mecklenburger orientierten sich am Westen, waren auf ihn fixiert°. Von daher kamen Moden, Maßstäbe° und Träume. In dieser Situation fühlten die Ostdeutschen sich vergessen, abgeschrieben°, zurückgesetzt°. Und 40 Jahre Zurücksetzung° sind schwer zu verkraften°, schwer zu überwinden°.

Es ist also klar, daß das Zusammenwachsen von Ostdeutschen und

65 Westdeutschen seine Zeit brauchen wird. Fünfundvierzig Jahre Teilung, d.h. 45 Jahre verschiedene wirtschaftliche Entwicklung und 45 Jahre Entfremdung° sind eben nicht in ein oder zwei Jahren zu überwinden.

---

im ... Zeit in the course of time

faulty construction / immigrants / confirm

embassy

team

brachte ... Punkt expressed it to a T

largely

provincials

prisoners

fixated

standards

written off / slighted

neglect / deal with / overcome

alienation

Fragen zum Lesestück

1. Wann hörte die DDR auf zu existieren? Wie viele Jahre hatte sie existiert?
2. Der Bundespräsident sprach von einem „Vorgang von fundamentaler Bedeutung". Warum ist dieser Vorgang so fundamental?
3. Der Präsident sprach von wirtschaftlichen Unterschieden, die die Menschen trennten. Was trennte sie außerdem?
4. Warum brauchte die ostdeutsche Industrie Kapital und Know-how?
5. Warum wollten in dieser Zeit nur relativ wenige westdeutsche Firmen in Ostdeutschland investieren?
6. Was taten viele frühere Eigentümer von Grundstücken und Häusern?
7. Welche Schwierigkeiten gab es bei der Infrastruktur?
8. Wieviel Prozent der Haushalte hatten ein Telefon?
9. Wie lange sollten Ausbau und Modernisierung des Telefonnetzes dauern?
10. Wohin mußten viele Leute gehen, wenn sie telefonieren wollten?
11. Was war in 45 Jahren im Westen anders als im Osten gewesen?
12. Wie sahen die Westdeutschen die alte Bundesrepublik? Wie sahen sie die DDR?
13. Welche Mannschaft war „die deutsche Mannschaft", die westdeutsche oder die ostdeutsche?
14. Wo fühlten sich die Westdeutschen zu Hause?
15. Woran orientierten sich die Ostdeutschen?
16. Welche Gefühle wuchsen in den Ostdeutschen?
17. Warum wird das Zusammenwachsen seine Zeit brauchen?

Erzählen Sie. Talk about one aspect of German unification. Use the cues as they appear in the *Leitfragen* on p. 455 in addition to your own.

Vokabeln

__ Substantive _____

die **Bedeutung, -en** meaning, significance

die **DDR (Deutsche Demokratische Republik)** German Democratic Republic

die **Demokratie, -n** democracy

die **Fabrik, -en** factory

die **Hoffnung, -en** hope

der **Kreis, -e** circle

die **Mode, -n** fashion

die **Post** post office; mail; postal service

der **Punkt, -e** point; period

das **Rathaus, ̈er** city hall

die **Rede, -n** speech

die **Reihe, -n** series; row

die **Tat, -en** deed; **in der Tat** indeed

die **Tatsache, -n** fact

der **Zustand, ̈e** condition, shape

Verben

dauern to last; require (time)
fehlen (+ *dat.*) to lack, to be absent or missing

schaffen, schuf, geschaffen to create, set up
trennen to separate, divide

Andere Wörter

arm (ä) poor
bloß only; mere(ly)
hoffnungslos hopeless

vereinigt unified
wirtschaftlich economic

Besondere Ausdrücke

Schlange stehen to stand in line

Erweiterung des Wortschatzes

City names used as adjectives

Die **Nürnberger** Familie kommt aus der früheren GDR.

The Nürnberg family is from the former GDR.

Waren Sie je auf der **Leipziger** Messe?

Have you ever been to the Leipzig Trade Fair?

Names of cities used as adjectives end in **-er.** The **-er** ending is never declined and no additional adjective endings are used to indicate gender or case.

GRAMMATIK UND ÜBUNGEN

1 The passive voice

Active voice	
Helga Klein schreibt das Buch.	Helga Klein is writing the book.
Hoffentlich lesen **viele** das Buch.	Let's hope that many read the book.

Passive voice	
Das Buch wird von Helga Klein geschrieben.	The book is being written by Helga Klein.
Hoffentlich wird **es** gelesen.	Let's hope it will be read.

In the active voice, the subject is "active": the subject is the agent that performs the action expressed by the verb. Active voice focuses attention on the agent. The attention in the active sentences on page 459 is focused on Helga Klein, who is writing a book, and on the many people who will read it.

In the passive voice, the subject is "passive": the subject is acted upon by an expressed or unexpressed agent. Passive voice focuses attention on the receiver of the action. The attention in the passive sentences above is focused on the book, which is being written by Helga Klein or read by the public.

The subject (e.g., **Buch**) of a passive sentence corresponds to the accusative object of an active sentence. The agent (e.g., **Helga Klein**) of a passive sentence corresponds to the subject of an active sentence. The agent is often omitted in a passive sentence, as if the corresponding active sentence had no subject.

In everyday conversation, speakers of German use the active voice much more often than the passive voice. The passive is very often used in technical and scientific writing, however, where an impersonal style is frequently preferred.

2 Tenses in the passive voice

Present	Das Buch **wird geschrieben.**	The book is being written.
Simple past	Das Buch **wurde geschrieben.**	The book was being written.
Perfect	Das Buch **ist geschrieben worden.**	The book has been written.
Past perfect	Das Buch **war geschrieben worden.**	The book had been written.

In English, a passive verb phrase consists of a form of the auxiliary verb *to be* and the past participle of the verb. In German, the passive verb phrase consists of a form of the auxiliary **werden** and the past participle of the main verb (e.g., **geschrieben**). In active voice, the present perfect and past perfect tenses of **werden** are **ist geworden** and **war geworden,** respectively. In the passive voice, **geworden** is replaced by **worden.** The past participle of the main verb remains unchanged (e.g., **geschrieben**).

While passive voice can occur in all tenses, the ones listed above are the most common. The future tense is rarely used (**Das Buch wird geschrieben werden.** *The book will be written.*).

3 *Von* + agent

Die Ingenieurin wurde **von ihren Nachbarn** kritisiert.	The engineer was criticized by her neighbors.
Die Hausarbeit wird **von ihrem Mann** gemacht.	The housework is (being) done by her husband.

In the passive voice, the role of the agent (e.g., **Nachbarn, Mann**) is secondary in importance to the receiver of the action (e.g., **Ingenieurin, Hausarbeit**). The agent is the object of the preposition **von** and thus in the dative case.

4 *Durch* + means

Das Geld wurde **durch schwere Arbeit** verdient.	The money was earned through hard work.
Die Nachbarn wurden **durch die laute Musik** gestört.	The neighbors were disturbed by the loud music.

The means by which something is brought about (e.g., **Arbeit, Musik**) is most often the object of the preposition **durch** and therefore in the accusative case.

1. Ein Theaterabend   Bettina has written a letter to a friend about her evening at the theater with Adrian. Give the English equivalent.

Ich wurde von Adrian wieder ins Theater eingeladen. Wir haben *Leben des Galilei* gesehen. Du weißt, das Stück ist von Brecht und wurde 1938 geschrieben. Ich wurde ziemlich früh von Adrian abgeholt, und wir konnten vorher ein bißchen spazierengehen. Da Galilei von Klaus Martens gespielt wurde, war das Theater voll. Der war ausgezeichnet.

2. Von wem wird das gemacht?   State by whom the following things are done in your family. Use the passive voice.

▶ Von wem wird das Essen gekocht?   *Das Essen wird von [meinem Vater] gekocht.*

1. Von wem wird das Auto gewaschen?
2. Von wem wird das Brot gekauft?
3. Von wem wird das Haus saubergemacht?
4. Von wem wird das Geschirr abgewaschen?
5. Von wem wird die Wäsche gewaschen?
6. Von wem wird Kuchen oder Brot gebacken?
7. Von wem wird die Gartenarbeit gemacht?

**Am 3. Oktober 1990
feiert man den Tag der deutschen
Einheit — Feststimmung am Berliner Reichstag.**

When the Berlin Wall fell (9 November 1989), few observers believed that East and West Germany would be unified less than a year later. Unification came about in two major stages. In July 1990, economic union occurred when the

Deutsche Mark became the common currency of East and West Germany. On 3 October 1990, political unification was completed, followed by the first all-German elections in December 1990. For the most part, unification meant that West German laws took effect in the new states. However, for a transition time, some laws will co-exist. An amendment to the Basic Law (**Grundgesetz**) requires that all-German laws must be passed by December 1995.

Economic unification revealed that the economy of East Germany, the strongest in the Eastern Bloc and supporting the highest living standard in that area, was by western standards in a shambles. Unemployment grew rapidly. To facilitate the conversion to a market economy, the German government established a trustee agency (**Treuhandanstalt**). It is charged with privatizing some 8,000 state-owned companies, deciding which ones would be viable in a market economy, and arranging for new or restructured ownership.

Unification also called for coordination of social and governmental services in the east and west. Often the result was lower social benefits and fewer services in the east while at the same time prices rose. Rents which had been subsidized in East Germany increased substantially. The rent for a dormitory room in eastern Berlin increased from DM 10 per month to DM 50 in a short period of time.

In addition to these political and economic considerations, the two parts of Germany are faced with the necessity of adjusting to each other on a personal level. The social division is reflected in the terms **"Ossis"** (eastern Germans) and **"Wessis"** (western Germans). **Wessis** accuse the **Ossis** of being lazy while the **Ossis** perceive the **Wessis** as unfeeling and less friendly. German society will be challenged to synthesize these two groups and systems into one.

3. **Wer war das?** Think of five trivia questions. Ask your partner the questions; she/he will answer them and then ask you five questions. Use the passive voice.

Von wem wurde der Film _____ gedreht°?
Von wem wurde _____ erfunden°?
Von wem wurde _____ entdeckt°?
Von wem wurde _____ gebaut?
Von wem wurde _____ komponiert°?

Film gedreht: was the movie made / invented
discovered

composed

4. **Gleichberechtigung gab es damals nicht.** Mark listened to a discussion about the former position of women in society. Give the English equivalents of his notes.

1. Warum wurde Frau Meier denn eigentlich immer schlechter bezahlt als ihr Mann?
   — Na ja, eine Erklärung ist, daß die besseren Stellen immer den Männern gegeben wurden.
2. Die Kinder von Speemanns sind durch die Vorurteile° der Kinderbücher beeinflußt worden, nicht?
   — Ja, in ihren Büchern ist eben immer nur das traditionelle Frauenbild gezeigt worden.
3. Von wem wurde denn bei Gardes das Geld verdient?
   — Von Herrn Garde. Und die Hausarbeit wurde natürlich von Frau Garde gemacht.
   — Ja, für sie war das immer ein langer Tag. Nachdem abends die Kinder ins Bett gebracht worden waren, war ihr Tag immer noch nicht zu Ende.
4. Und bei den jungen Kortes, von wem wird da die Wäsche gewaschen und das Haus geputzt?
   — Oft von der ganzen Familie. Schließlich wird ja ein Teil des Geldes auch von Frau Korte verdient.
5. Ganz allgemein kann man sagen, daß früher die Probleme der Gleichberechtigung anders gesehen wurden als heute.
   — Schon die Kinder wurden auf eine traditionelle Rolle als Mann oder Frau vorbereitet.

prejudices

vote" (**Erststimme**) and a "second vote" (**Zweitstimme**), which permits them to vote for a particular candidate as well as for a political party. The representative one votes for need not belong to the party one votes for. The constitution (**Grundgesetz**) of the Federal Republic stipulates that a political party has to have a minimum of 5% of all the votes cast to be represented in the **Bundestag.**

The **Bundestag** is the only federal body elected directly by the people. The Federal Council (**Bundesrat**) consists of delegates of the states. The Federal President (**Bundespräsident**) is elected by the Federal Convention, a constitutional body that convenes only for this purpose. The President's tasks are mainly ceremonial in nature.

The head of the government in the Federal Republic of Germany is the Federal Chancellor (**Bundeskanzler**), who is nominated by the President and elected by the **Bundestag.** The Chancellor nominates a head (**Bundesminister**) for each Federal Ministry. They are then formally appointed by the President. The Federal Ministers and the Chancellor together form the Federal Government (**Bundesregierung**) until new elections are called.

Nach der ersten gesamtdeutschen Wahl tagt der Bundestag am 20. Dezember 1990 im Berliner Reichstag.

In the Federal Republic of Germany each state (**Bundesland**) maintains a constitution. However, the central government holds a strong position.

National elections of the House of Representatives (**der Bundestag**) take place every four years. All German citizens over 18 have a "first

5 Modals and the passive infinitive

Unser Computer kann nicht mehr **repariert werden.**

Müssen die Disketten neu **gemacht werden?**

Our computer can't be fixed anymore.

Do the diskettes have to be redone?

Modals are frequently used with a passive infinitive. The passive infinitive (e.g., **repariert werden** and **gemacht werden**) consists of a past participle plus **werden.**

5. Die deutsche Wirtschaft   Give the English equivalents of the observations below about the German economy.

1. Rohstoffe müssen importiert werden.
2. Von den Firmen sollen Qualitätsprodukte produziert werden.
3. Qualitätsprodukte können meistens gut verkauft werden.
4. Die Inflationsrate soll niedrig gehalten werden.
5. Das Problem der Arbeitslosigkeit darf nicht vergessen werden.
6. Arbeit soll für alle Leute gefunden werden.

6. Das muß gemacht werden.   Compare your "to do" list with that of a fellow classmate. Use the cues provided and add your own.

▶   Referat schreiben   *Mein Referat muß noch geschrieben werden.*

1. Hausaufgaben machen
2. Fernseher reparieren
3. Briefe schreiben
4. Auto bezahlen
5. Garage aufräumen

7. Das Leben in der früheren DDR   Give the English equivalents of the statements below about the former **DDR.**

1. Die Leute wurden nach dem Leben in der früheren DDR gefragt.
2. Manche Arbeiter waren dafür, daß überall etwa gleich viel verdient wurde.
3. Viele Firmen sollten modernisiert werden.
4. Es mußte sehr viel getan werden.
5. Einige Arbeiter wurden durch den Computer ersetzt°.   replaced
6. Für die Umwelt wurde oft nicht genug gesorgt.

6 Summary of the uses of *werden*

◆ *Active voice: main verb*

Herr Heller **wird** alt.	Mr. Heller is growing old.
Die Kinder **wurden** müde.	The children were getting tired.
Frau Ullmann **ist** Chefin der Firma **geworden.**	Ms. Ullmann has become head of the company.

Werden as a main verb is equivalent to English *to grow, get,* or *become.*

◆ *Auxiliary verb in future tense*

Er **wird** hoffentlich mehr **arbeiten.**	I hope he will work more.
Du **wirst** das wohl **wissen.**	You probably know that.

Werden is used with a dependent infinitive to form the future tense.

◆ *Passive voice: auxiliary verb*

Die Industrie der neuen Bundesländer **wird modernisiert.**	The industry of the new federal states is being modernized.
In einigen Firmen **sind** viele Arbeiter durch Computer **ersetzt worden.**	In some firms many workers have been replaced by computers.

Werden is used with a past participle to form the passive voice. The passive voice can occur in any tense. The participle **worden** is used in place of **geworden** in the perfect and past perfect tenses.

8. **Was bedeutet das?** Identify the verb phrase with **werden** in each sentence below. Tell whether **werden** is being used (a) as a main verb in the active voice (give the tense), (b) to express future, or (c) as a tense of the passive voice (give the tense). Then give English equivalents for the sentences.

▶ Das Problem ist gelöst worden.   *perfect passive / The problem has been solved.*

1. Hier muß noch viel gemacht werden.
2. Die Situation wird im nächsten Jahr sicher besser.
3. Der Export wird langsam weniger.
4. Wer wird dem Land helfen?
5. Werden die Waren auf dem Weltmarkt eine Zukunft haben?
6. Es ist bekannt, daß das Land immer weniger Rohstoffe haben wird.
7. Das Leben ist in letzter Zeit teurer geworden.
8. Die Industrie wird sich wohl neue Märkte suchen.
9. Das Wetter wird hoffentlich in den nächsten Tagen besser.
10. Erik will einfach nicht arbeiten. Was soll aus ihm werden?
11. Die Arbeit muß noch gemacht werden.
12. Jörg ist krank, aber er wird wohl bald wieder gesund.

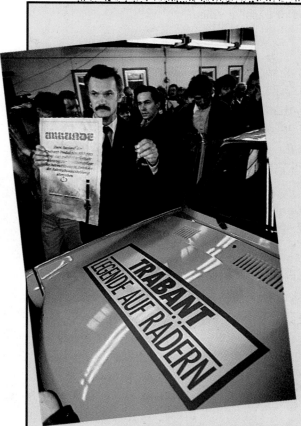

Der letzte Trabant (Zwickau)

Eisenach in Thüringen is famous for the Wartburg Castle, built in the eleventh century. Here Martin Luther translated the New Testament into German, and tourists can visit the room where, according to legend, Luther hurled his inkwell at the devil.

Eisenach is also a center of the German car industry. Since 1898 cars have been manufactured in the city, but in 1991 the trustee agency (**Treuhandanstalt**) decided to close the factory because it believed that the factory would never be profitable.

The history of this factory under socialism illustrates why the eastern economy was not competitive when unification came. Initially a BMW factory, the works were nationalized in 1952 and dedicated to producing the Wartburg car. At its peak the Wartburg factory produced 50,000 cars per year; in the last year of its existence it produced 7,200 cars, each subsidized with approximately DM 7000 by the German government. Like the other automobile produced in the GDR, the simpler Trabant, the Wartburg had a two-stroke engine and the same basic design for almost 40 years. Ideas for new designs were thwarted by the government's central economic planners who believed that one design was sufficient. Not surprisingly, eastern consumers quickly abandoned these cars when they could buy high-powered and stylish western models.

In addition to design problems, there was the problem of low productivity in the factory. Approximately 190 cars were manufactured on a "good day." Modern western factories produce two to three times as many cars with half the employees. The Wartburg factory employed 6,200 workers and its suppliers employed an additional 15,000. Some of these people attempted to relocate to car manufacturing centers in the west like Wolfsburg (Volkswagen) and Munich (BMW). Others remained. The **Treuhandanstalt** has announced plans for extensive retraining of Eisenach workers. Nonetheless, the closing has had an impact on the entire region. This situation is not unique but repeated in other regions. But there is hope for Eisenach: although the Wartburg has disappeared, the western car manufacturer Opel has invested DM 27 million in a new assembly plant which will employ 2,600 workers. Thus the tradition of car manufacturing will not disappear from Eisenach.

7 Alternatives to the passive voice

In German, other constructions are frequently used instead of passive voice. Three possible alternatives follow.

◆ man *as subject*

Man sagt das oft.	One often says that.
(Das wird oft gesagt.)	That's often said.
Wie kann **man** das machen?	How can people do that?
(Wie kann das gemacht werden?)	How can that be done?

In German, the pronoun **man** is used frequently instead of the passive voice, whenever there is no expressed agent. English has several possible equivalents of **man**: *one, you, we, they,* or *people.*

9. Die Universität in der Schweiz Diane has many questions about universities in Switzerland. Give the English equivalents of the sentences below.

1. Wie lange geht man auf die Universität?
2. Wieviel bezahlt man dafür?
3. Muß man viel lernen?
4. Wie lange darf man studieren?
5. Was kann man später machen?
6. Wie viele Klausuren muß man im Semester schreiben?
7. Soll man mehrere Fächer auf einmal studieren?

10. Noch einmal Restate the sentences below, using **man.**

▶ Wie wird das gemacht? *Wie macht man das?*

1. Wann wird Kaffee getrunken?
2. Wie wird das Wort geschrieben?
3. Wann wird mit der Arbeit aufgehört?
4. Hier wird gearbeitet.
5. Hier darf nicht geredet werden.
6. Die Schreibmaschine soll benutzt werden.

◆ sein ... zu + *infinitive*

Das **ist** leicht **zu verstehen.**	That's easy to understand.
(Das kann leicht verstanden werden.)	That can be understood easily.
Die Arbeit **ist** noch **zu machen.**	The work is still to be done.
(Die Arbeit muß noch gemacht werden.)	The work must still be done.

A form of **sein ... zu** + infinitive is often used in German instead of a passive verb phrase. The **sein ... zu** + infinitive construction expresses the possibility or necessity of doing something.

11. Dieter geht ins Theater. Dieter asks questions about the play you want to see. Respond as suggested, using **sein ... zu** + infinitive.

▶ Kann man das Theater leicht finden? (Ja) *Ja, das Theater ist leicht zu finden.*

1. Kann man das Theater mit dem Bus erreichen? (Ja)
2. Muß man die Karten vorher kaufen? (Ja)
3. Kann man noch gute Plätze haben? (Ja)
4. Kann man noch billige Karten bekommen? (Ja)
5. Kann man das Stück leicht verstehen? (Nein)

12. Was ist zu tun? Using the cues below, tell someone what things must be done in the former **DDR.**

▶ viele Probleme lösen *Viele Probleme sind zu lösen.*

1. die Industrie modernisieren
2. die Straßen reparieren
3. Umweltprobleme lösen
4. neue Arbeitsplätze schaffen
5. Kapital importieren
6. das Telefonnetz ausbauen°   expand

◆ **sich lassen +** *infinitive*

Das **läßt sich** machen. (Das kann gemacht werden.)	That can be done.
Läßt sich dieses Auto überhaupt bezahlen? (Kann dieses Auto überhaupt bezahlt werden?)	Can this car be paid for at all?

A form of **sich lassen** + infinitive can be used in place of a passive verb phrase. This construction expresses the possibility of something being done.

13. Läßt sich das Auto reparieren? Daniel is telling Anna that they have to do something about their old car. Translate his remarks into English.

1. Hoffentlich läßt sich der Motor noch reparieren.
2. Aber es läßt sich noch nicht sagen, wieviel das kostet.
3. Leider lassen sich die Türen nicht so gut öffnen.
4. Vielleicht läßt sich ein Weg finden, wenigstens die linke Tür zu reparieren.
5. Ich weiß nicht, wie sich das Problem mit unserem alten Auto lösen läßt.
6. Wenn das Auto repariert ist, läßt es sich sicher verkaufen.

14. Alles läßt sich machen. In a business conference, Ms. Hohner asks whether most matters are taken care of. Answer her questions, using a form of **sich lassen** + infinitive.

▶ Kann man einen Weg finden?   *Oh ja! Ein Weg läßt sich finden.*

1. Kann man die Ware billig produzieren?
2. Kann man das Problem lösen?
3. Kann man darüber reden?
4. Kann man das bezahlen?
5. Kann man das leicht erklären?
6. Kann man die Ware gut verkaufen?

8 Indirect discourse

Direct discourse	Erika sagte: „Ich bin müde."	Erika said, "I'm tired."
Indirect discourse	Erika sagte, **daß sie müde wäre.**	Erika said that she was (*colloquial:* is) tired.
	Erika sagte, **sie wäre müde.**	Erika said she was (*colloquial:* is) tired.

Direct discourse (also called direct quotation) is used to repeat the exact words of another person. In writing, the direct quotation is set off by quotation marks. Indirect discourse (also called indirect quotation) is used to report what someone else has said.

The pronouns change in indirect discourse to correspond to the perspective of the speaker. Erika speaks of herself and says **"ich."** You report her message and refer to Erika as **"sie."**

The conjunction **daß** may or may not be stated in indirect discourse. When **daß** is stated, the finite verb (e.g., **wäre**) is in last position; when it is omitted, the finite verb is in second position.

Subjunctive	Karin sagte, sie **könnte** nicht mitkommen.	Karin said she couldn't come along.
Indicative	Karin sagt, sie **kann** nicht mitkommen.	Karin says she can't come along.

The verb in indirect discourse (e.g., **könnte**) is in the subjunctive. While subjunctive is always used in formal writing, indicative (e.g., **kann**) is used more and more in colloquial German.

◆ *Present time*

Direct discourse	Volkmar sagte: „Man **kann** da gut Geld verdienen."	Volkmar said, "One can earn good money there."
	Laura fragte: „**Haben** sie eine freie Stelle?"	Laura asked, "Do they have an opening?"
Indirect discourse	Volkmar sagte, man **könnte** da gut Geld verdienen.	Volkmar said one could (*colloquial:* can) earn good money there.
	Laura fragte, ob sie eine freie Stelle **hätten.**	Laura asked whether they had (*colloquial:* have) an opening.

In German, when the present tense (e.g., **kann, haben**) is used in a direct quotation, the present-time subjunctive (e.g., **könnte, hätten**) is used in the corresponding indirect quotation. Present-time subjunctive is used to express present and future time. The verb in the introductory statement can be in any tense. In the above sentences the verbs in the introductory statements (**sagte, fragte**) are in the simple past.

15. Ja, das hat sie gesagt.   Confirm that Gabi really said the things mentioned below about Christiane, a new student she met in Bonn. Begin the indirect quotation with **daß.**

▶   Hat Gabi gesagt, Christiane wäre nett?   *Ja, Gabi hat gesagt, daß Christiane nett wäre.*

1. Hat sie gesagt, Christiane wohnte im Studentenheim?
2. Hat sie gesagt, Christiane studierte Informatik?
3. Hat sie gesagt, Christiane käme aus der Schweiz?
4. Hat sie gesagt, Christiane hätte schwarzes Haar?
5. Hat sie gesagt, Christiane spielte gut Gitarre?
6. Hat sie gesagt, Christiane arbeitete viel?

Glücklich ist, wer vergißt, was nicht mehr zu ändern ist.

◆ *Past time*

Direct discourse	Lucy sagte: „Ich **habe** den Brief gestern **geschrieben.**"	Lucy said, "I wrote the letter yesterday."
Indirect discourse	Lucy sagte, sie **hätte** den Brief gestern **geschrieben.**	Lucy said she had written (*colloquial:* she wrote) the letter yesterday.

In German, when a past tense (simple past, perfect, past perfect) is used in a direct quotation, the past-time subjunctive (e.g., **hätte geschrieben**) is used in an indirect quotation to express past time. Using the past-time subjunctive shows that the action or event happened at a time prior to the moment when the statement was being made. In the example above, Lucy wrote the letter the day before she talked about it. The verb in the introductory statement (e.g., **sagte**) can be in any tense.

16. Die neue Stelle   Sigrid is telling what Christoph said about his new job. Translate what she said.

1. Christoph sagte, er hätte Schreibmaschine schreiben gelernt.
2. Er sagte, er hätte um 8 Uhr morgens angefangen.
3. Er sagte weiter, er hätte 20 DM in der Stunde verdient.
4. Christoph sagte, er hätte Briefe auf englisch geschrieben.
5. Er erzählte weiter, die Kollegen wären nett gewesen.
6. Er sagte, die Chefin wäre mit der Arbeit zufrieden gewesen.
7. Er sagte, das Wochenende hätte ihm trotzdem am meisten Spaß gemacht.

9 Special subjunctive

Special subjunctive	Uwe sagte, er **habe** eine gute Stelle.⎱	Uwe said he had (*colloquial:* he has)
General subjunctive	Uwe sagte, er **hätte** eine gute Stelle.⎰	a good position.

German also has a special subjunctive which is used for indirect discourse. This form is usually used in formal writing such as newspapers and literature. The subjunctive form that you have been using up to now for indirect discourse and "unreal" conditions (see *Kapitel 12*) is sometimes called the general subjunctive. When used for indirect discourse, the *meaning* of special and general subjunctive is the same.

◆ *Present-time special subjunctive*

schreiben	
ich schreib**e**	wir schreib**en**
du schreib**est**	ihr schreib**et**
er/es/sie schreib**e**	sie schreib**en**
Sie schreib**en**	

The present-time special subjunctive is composed of the infinitive stem (e.g., **schreib-**) plus the subjunctive endings. Most of the forms of the special subjunctive are basically the same as the indicative forms. Use of the special subjunctive is generally limited to the **er/es/sie**-form, since it is the only form that is clearly different from the indicative.

Infinitive	Special subjunctive: *er/es/sie*-form	Indicative: *er/es/sie*-form
fahren	**fahre**	fährt
lesen	**lese**	liest
werden	**werde**	wird
können	**könne**	kann
haben	**habe**	hat
sein	**sei**	ist

Verbs that have a vowel change in the **du-** and **er/es/sie**-forms of the indicative do not undergo a vowel change in the special subjunctive.

◆ *Special subjunctive of* **sein**

ich **sei**	wir **seien**
du **seiest**	ihr **seiet**
er/es/sie **sei**	sie **seien**
Sie **seien**	

Sei occurs frequently in its several forms in indirect discourse, since the forms are clearly different from the indicative. **Sei** does not have the **-e** ending characteristic of the **ich** and **er/es/sie**-forms in the special subjunctive.

◆ *Past-time special subjunctive*

Heike sagte, sie **habe** einen Job **gefunden.**	Heike said she had found (*colloquial:* she found) a job.
Uwe sagte, er **sei** allein **gefahren.**	Uwe said he had driven (*colloquial:* he drove) alone.

Past-time special subjunctive is composed of the special subjunctive forms of the auxiliaries **haben** (e.g., **habe**) or **sein** (e.g., **sei**) plus the past participle of the main verb.

10 Special vs. general subjunctive

Indicative and special subjunctive	Sie sagte, die Kinder **haben** es **gemacht.**	She said the children had done (*colloquial:* the children did) it.
General subjunctive	Sie sagte, die Kinder **hätten** es **gemacht.**	

The special subjunctive is generally used only in the **er/es/sie-**form, which is clearly different from the indicative. The special subjunctive is always replaced by general subjunctive when the special subjunctive forms are identical to the indicative forms.

17. Ferienpläne It is the end of the semester. Frank tells about his friends' conversations regarding their vacation plans. Translate his comments.

1. Kirstin fragte, ob Andreas nach Amerika fliegen wolle. Andreas meinte, er wisse es noch nicht genau.
2. Beate fragte Bärbel, warum sie jetzt so wenig Zeit habe. Bärbel antwortete, sie müsse ihr Referat noch fertig machen.
3. Christian fragte Beate, ob sie schon einen Ferienjob gefunden habe. Beate sagte, sie habe einen guten Job gefunden.
4. Kirstin meinte, sie suche Arbeit in einem Supermarkt. Barbel erzählte, sie fahre für drei Wochen in die Schweiz.
5. Martin meinte, er und Sara könnten dieses Jahr nicht wegfahren. Christian sagte, er finde das schade.

WIEDERHOLUNG

1. Ein Fest wird vorbereitet. Tell about the party Christiane and Stefan are preparing. Form sentences in the present tense, using the cues below.

1. Stefan / abwaschen / Geschirr
2. Christiane / einkaufen / noch / für / Fest
3. wann / Gäste / sollen / kommen / ?
4. dann / Volker / müssen / saubermachen / Wohnzimmer / schnell
5. Gerd / mitbringen / sein Kassettenrecorder
6. Michael / können / mitbringen / neu / Kassetten / ?
7. hoffentlich / Monika / finden / Haus
8. Fest / machen / alle / Spaß

2. Der Theaterabend Tell about Stefanie's and Christian's night at the theater. Restate the sentences below in the perfect tense.

▶ Stefanies Eltern geben ihr zwei *Stefanies Eltern haben ihr zwei*
Theaterkarten. *Theaterkarten gegeben.*

1. Sie lädt Christian ein mitzugehen.
2. Er holt Stefanie um sieben Uhr ab.
3. Sie sehen ein Stück von Bertolt Brecht.
4. Nach dem Theater gehen sie etwas trinken.
5. Sie entscheiden sich für eine Studentenkneipe.
6. Da treffen sie einige Freunde.
7. Sie hören eine Jazzgruppe.
8. Sie reden über die letzten Sommerferien.

3. Interviews in den neuen Bundesländern A journalist tells about several interviews in the new federal states (the former German Democratic Republic). Complete the sentences by adding relative pronouns and appropriate word endings where needed.

1. Die Journalistin erzählt von ihr＿＿ Reise durch die neu＿＿ Bundesländer.
2. In Halle sprach sie mit ein＿＿ älter＿＿ Rentner°.   retiree
3. Er sprach über sein＿＿ alt＿＿ Arbeit in der Chemieindustrie.
4. Er ist zufrieden mit sein＿＿ neu＿＿ Leben.
5. Er kann jed＿＿ Sommer ein＿＿ schön＿＿ Urlaub in Frankreich machen, denn da hat er gut＿＿ Bekannt＿＿ .
6. Das ist ein Land, d＿＿ ihm unbekannt＿＿ ist.
7. Die Journalistin sprach auch mit ein＿＿ jung＿＿ verheiratet＿＿ Frau, d＿＿ voll berufstätig＿＿ ist.
8. Die Frau erzählte, daß der Staat in der früher＿＿ DDR viel für die Familie getan hätte.
9. Ihr＿＿ Wohnung und der Kindergarten waren zum Beispiel sehr billig＿＿ .
10. Aber für ein＿＿ neu＿＿ Auto mußte man sehr viel＿＿ Geld bezahlen.
11. Sie mußten auch einig＿＿ Jahre darauf warten.
12. Ihr＿＿ neu＿＿ Leben gefällt ihr eigentlich besser＿＿ .

VERANSTALTUNGEN

· ·
9. Samstag
· ·
Teilhabekongreß · Sozialer und kultureller Rückschritt bei gigantischem ökonomischen Fortschritt: Nicht nur die drei Mil-lionen registrierten und nicht registrierten Erwerbslosen sind von neuer sozialer Existenzunsicherheit betroffen, auch ein immer größerer Teil der Erwerbstätigen. Ökonomischer und technischer Fortschritt ist nur dann wünschenswert, wenn er die Lage aller verbessert. Ungesicherte Beschäftigte fordern daher ökonomische Teilhabe und rufen auf zum Kongreß im · *Haus der Jugend, Deutschherrnufer 12, 10 h; auch am Sonntag, 10. Juni*

Studenten aus Nicaragua und Syrien an der Humboldt Universität (April 1991)

4. Wandern und Zelten   Andreas and Tanja discuss plans to go hiking and camping. Complete the sentences below with the cued infinitives. Use **zu** where appropriate.

1. Wann hört es endlich auf _____? (regnen)
2. Wir können dann _____. (wandern)
3. Hättest du Lust _____? (mitkommen)
4. Es ist schön, im Wald _____. (spazierengehen)
5. Hast du auch vor _____? (zelten)
6. Wir können uns um neun Uhr _____. (treffen)
7. Es ist leider schwer, so früh bei dir _____. (sein)
8. Kannst du dann um zehn bei mir _____? (sein)
9. Wir brauchen nicht gleich _____. (wegfahren)
10. Ich muß mir noch neue Schuhe kaufen. Meine alten sind nicht mehr _____. (tragen)

5. Ein Schulexperiment   Read the following report about an investigation conducted by a teacher and give the English equivalents.

Eine Lehrerin erzählte von einem Schulexperiment mit Kindern. Die Kinder hätten berichtet, daß die Mutter berufstätig sei, den ganzen Tag arbeite, und dann noch zu Hause das Essen koche, einkaufe, putze und die Wäsche wasche. Vater dagegen lese Bücher und Zeitungen, sehe fern, trinke Bier und spiele Fußball. Es habe sich also gezeigt, daß die Frauen in vielen Familien zwei Berufe hätten. Vielleicht sei das einer der Gründe, warum es seit einigen Jahren in vielen Familien weniger Kinder gebe.

6. Die Wirtschaft heute   Dieter Meier has taken notes on a report about modern industrial society. Give the English equivalents.

1. Hoffentlich kann ein Weg gefunden werden, die Arbeitslosen wieder zu beschäftigen.
2. Das läßt sich aber nicht von heute auf morgen machen.
3. Ältere Arbeiter sind oft nur schwer in moderne Industriefirmen zu integrieren.
4. Einige Probleme können nicht leicht gelöst werden.
5. Bei diesen Problemen läßt sich nicht sagen, was die Zukunft bringen wird.
6. Man kann auch nicht sagen, ob der Staat all das bezahlen kann.

7. Wie sagt man das?

Ingrid: What would you like to do this evening?
Thomas: I'd go to the theater if I had money.
Ingrid: Could I invite you?
Thomas: That would be nice.
Ingrid: Could you drive?
Thomas: I'd drive if I had my car. My brother has it.
Ingrid: We could go by streetcar.
Thomas: For that I have enough money.
Ingrid: Good.

8. Ihre Meinung

1. Sollte der Staat Kindergartenplätze für Kinder berufstätiger Eltern bezahlen oder subventionieren°?   subsidize
2. Sollte es in Amerika ein Recht auf Arbeit geben? Warum (nicht)?
3. Sind Sie dafür, daß Frauen in „Männerberufen" arbeiten?
4. Sollten amerikanische Frauen eine größere Rolle in der Politik spielen?
5. Tut der Staat genug für alte Leute in Amerika?

GRAMMATIK: ZUSAMMENFASSUNG

Tenses in the passive voice

Present	Der Brief **wird geschrieben.**	The letter is being written.
Simple past	Der Brief **wurde geschrieben.**	The letter was being written.
Perfect	Der Brief **ist geschrieben worden.**	The letter has been written.
Past perfect	Der Brief **war geschrieben worden.**	The letter had been written.

NOTE: In the perfect and past-perfect tenses the participle **worden** is used in place of **geworden.**

Agent or means expressed

***von* + agent**	
Das Geld wurde **von den Arbeitern** verdient.	The money was earned *by the workers.*

***durch* + means**	
Das Geld wurde **durch schwere Arbeit** verdient.	The money was earned *through hard work.*

In passive voice the agent is the object of the preposition **von** and thus in the dative case. The means is the object of the preposition **durch** and therefore in the accusative case. The agent or means may be omitted (**Viel Geld wurde verdient.**)

Modals + passive infinitive

Der Brief muß **geschrieben werden.**　The letter must be written.
Kann diese Arbeit schnell　　　　　　 Can this work be done quickly?
　gemacht werden?

The passive infinitive consists of the past participle of a verb plus **werden.** Modals are often used with a passive infinitive.

Alternatives to the passive voice

Passive Voice	Deutsch **kann** leicht **gelernt werden.**	German can be learned easily.
1. *man*	Deutsch kann **man** leicht lernen.	One can learn German easily.
2. *sein ... zu* + **infinitive**	Deutsch **ist** leicht **zu lernen.**	German is easy to learn.
3. *sich lassen* + **infinitive**	Deutsch **läßt sich** leicht **lernen.**	German can be learned easily.

Indirect discourse

Direct discourse	Uwe sagte: „Ich habe keine Zeit."	Uwe said, "I have no time."
Indirect discourse	Uwe sagte, daß er keine Zeit hätte. Uwe sagte, daß er keine Zeit habe.	Uwe said that he had (*colloquial:* has) no time.

Direct discourse is used to repeat the exact words of another person. Indirect discourse is used to report what someone else has said. The conjunction **daß** may or may not be stated in indirect discourse: **Uwe sagte, er hätte/habe keine Zeit.** In German, indirect discourse is quite often in the subjunctive (general subjunctive: **hätte,** special subjunctive: **habe**). While the subjunctive is always used in formal writing, indicative is often used in colloquial German.

Present-time general subjunctive

Erika sagte, sie **schriebe** einen Brief.

Erika said she was (*colloquial:* is) writing a letter.

Past-time general subjunctive

Erika sagte, sie **hätte** den Brief gestern **geschrieben.**

Erika said she had written (*colloquial:* she wrote) the letter yesterday.

Special subjunctive

Frau Schiller sagte, sie **habe** keine Zeit.

Ms. Schiller said she had (*colloquial:* has) no time.

German has a special subjunctive that is usually used in formal writing. The meaning of the special and general subjunctive in indirect discourse is the same. In an informal situation the above sentence could be expressed with the general subjunctive: **Frau Schiller sagte, sie hätte keine Zeit.**

Present time of special subjunctive

gehen	
ich geh**e**	wir geh**en**
du geh**est**	ihr geh**et**
er/es/sie geh**e**	sie geh**en**
Sie geh**en**	

Usually only the **er/es/sie**-form of the special subjunctive is used, since it is the only form that is clearly different from the indicative.

Infinitive	Special subjunctive: *er/es/sie*-form	Indicative: *er/es/sie*-form
schlafen	**schlafe**	schläft
essen	**esse**	ißt
sehen	**sehe**	sieht
werden	**werde**	wird
müssen	**müsse**	muß
haben	**habe**	hat
sein	**sei**	ist

Special subjunctive of *sein*

ich **sei**	wir **seien**
du **seiest**	ihr **seiet**
er/es/sie **sei**	sie **seien**
Sie **seien**	

Past-time special subjunctive

Erika sagte, sie **habe** den Brief gestern geschrieben.

Hans sagte, er **sei** allein gefahren.

Erika said she had written (*colloquial:* she wrote) the letter yesterday.

Hans said he had driven (*colloquial:* he drove) alone.

Past-time special subjunctive is composed of the special subjunctive form of the auxiliary **haben** or **sein** plus the past participle of the main verb.

REFERENCE SECTION

PRONUNCIATION AND WRITING GUIDE

The best way to learn to pronounce German is to imitate speakers of German, as completely and accurately as you can. Some of the sounds of German are just like those of English and will cause you no trouble. Others may sound strange to you at first and be more difficult for you to pronounce. With practice, you will be able to master the unfamiliar sounds as well as the familiar ones.

Though imitation is the one indispensable way of learning to pronounce any language, there are two things that should help you in your practice. First, you should learn how to manipulate your vocal organs so as to produce distinctly different sounds. Second, you should learn to distinguish German sounds from the English sounds that you might be tempted to substitute for them.

As you learn to pronounce German, you will also start to read and write it. Here a word of caution is in order. The writing system of German (or any language) was designed for people who already know the language. No ordinary writing system was ever designed to meet the needs of people who are learning a language. Writing is a method of reminding us on paper of things that we already know how to say; it is not a set of directions telling us how a language should be pronounced.

This Pronunciation and Writing Guide will give you some help with the German sound system. Further practice with specific sounds will be given in the Lab Manual section of the *Arbeitsheft*.

Stress

Nearly all native German words are stressed on the "stem syllable," that is, the first syllable of the word, or the first syllable that follows an unstressed prefix.

Without prefix		*With unstressed prefix*	
den'ken	to think	**beden'ken**	to think over
kom'men	to come	**entkom'men**	to escape

In the end vocabulary of this book, words that are not stressed on the first syllable are marked. A stress mark follows the stressed syllable.

German vowels

German has short vowels, long vowels, and diphthongs. The short vowels are clipped, and are never "drawled" as they often are in English. The long vowels are monophthongs ("steady-state" vowels) and not diphthongs (vowels that "glide" from one vowel sound toward another). The diphthongs are similar to English diphthongs except that they, like the short vowels, are never drawled. Compare the English and German vowels in the words below.

English (with off-glide)	*German (without off-glide)*
bait	**Beet**
vein	**wen**
tone	**Ton**
boat	**Boot**

Spelling as a reminder of vowel length

By and large, the German spelling system clearly indicates the difference between long and short vowels. German uses the following types of signals:

1. A vowel is long if it is followed by an **h** (unpronounced): **ihn, stahlen, Wahn.**
2. A vowel is long if it is double: **Beet, Saat, Boot.**
3. A vowel is generally long if it is followed by one consonant: **den, kam, Ofen, Hut.**
4. A vowel is generally short if it is followed by two or more consonants: **denn, Sack, offen, Busch, dick.**

Pronunciation of vowels

Long and short a

Long [ā] = **aa, ah, a (Saat, Bahn, kam, Haken):** like English *a* in *spa*, but with wide-open mouth and no off-glide.
Short [a] = **a (satt, Bann, Kamm, Hacken):** between English *o* in *hot* and *u* in *hut*.

Long and short e

Long [ē] = **e, ee, eh, ä, äh (wen, Beet, fehlen, gähnt):** like *ay* in English *say*, but with exaggeratedly spread lips and no off-glide.
Short [e] = **e, ä (wenn, Bett, fällen, Gent):** Like *e* in English *bet*, but more clipped.

Unstressed [ə] *and* [ər]

Unstressed [ə] = **e (bitte, endet, gegessen):** like English *e* in *begin, pocket.*
Unstressed [ər] = **er (bitter, ändert, vergessen):** When the sequence [ər] stands at the end of a word, before a consonant, or in an unstressed prefix, it sounds much like the final -*a* in English *sofa;* the **-r** is not pronounced.

Long and short i

Long [ī] = **ih, ie (ihn, Miete, liest):** like *ee* in *see*, but with exaggeratedly spread lips and no off-glide.
Short [i] = **i (in, Mitte, List):** like *i* in *mitt*, but more clipped.

Long and short o

Long [ō] = **oh, o, oo (Moos, Tone, Ofen, Sohne):** like English *o* in *so*, but with exaggeratedly rounded lips and no off-glide.
Short [o] = **o (Most, Tonne, offen, Sonne):** like English *o* often heard in the word *gonna.*

Long and short u

Long [ū] = **uh, u (Huhne, schuf, Buße, Mus):** like English *oo* in *too*, but with more lip rounding and no off-glide.
Short [u] = **u (Hunne, Schuft, Busse, muß):** like English *u* in *bush*, but more clipped.

Diphthongs

[ai] = **ei, ai, ey, ay (Nein, Kaiser, Meyer, Bayern):** like English *ai* in *aisle*, but clipped and not drawled.
[oi] = **eu, äu (neun, Häuser):** like English *oi* in *coin*, but clipped and not drawled.
[au] = **au (laut, Bauer):** like English *ou* in *house*, but clipped and not drawled.

Long and short ü

Long [ū] = üh, ü (**Bühne, kühl, lügen**): To pronounce long [ū], keep your tongue in the same position as for long [ī], but round your lips as for long [ū].
Short [ü] = ü (**Küste, müssen, Bünde**): To pronounce short [ü], keep your tongue in the same position as for short [i], but round your lips as for short [u].

Long and short ö

Long [ō] = ö, öh (**Höfe, Löhne, Flöhe**): To pronounce long [ō], keep your tongue in the same position as for long [ē], but round your lips as for long [ō].
Short [ö] = ö (**gönnt, Hölle, Knöpfe**): To pronounce short [ö], keep your tongue in the same position as for short [e], but round your lips as for short [o].

Consonants

Most of the German consonant sounds are similar to English consonant sounds. There are four major differences.

1. German has two consonant sounds without an English equivalent: [x] and [ç]. Both are spelled **ch**.
2. The German pronunciation of [l] and [r] differs from the English pronunciation.
3. German uses sounds familiar to English speakers in unfamiliar combinations, such as [ts] in an initial position: **zu**.
4. German uses unfamiliar spellings of familiar sounds.

The letters b, d, *and* g

The letters **b, d,** and **g** generally represent the same consonant sounds as in English. German **g** is usually pronounced like English *g* in *go*. When the letters **b, d,** and **g** occur at the end of a syllable, or before an **s** or **t**, they are pronounced like [p], [t], and [k] respectively.

b = [b] (**Diebe, gaben**)   b = [p] (**Dieb, Diebs, gab, gabt**)
d = [d] (**Lieder, laden**)   d = [t] (**Lied, Lieds, lud, lädt**)
g = [g] (**Tage, sagen**)   g = [k] (**Tag, Tags, sag, sagt**)

The letter j

The letter **j** (**ja, jung**) represents the sound *y* as in English *yes*.

The letter l

English [l] typically has a "hollow" sound to it. When an American pronounces [l], the tongue is usually "spoon-shaped": It is high at the front (with the tongue tip pressed against the gum ridge above the upper teeth), hollowed out in the middle, and high again at the back. German [l] (**viel, Bild, laut**) never has the "hollow" quality. It is pronounced with the tongue tip against the gum ridge, as in English, but with the tongue kept flat from front to back. Many Americans use this "flat" [l] in such words as *million, billion,* and *William*.

The letter r

German [r] can be pronounced in two different ways. Some German speakers use a "tongue-trilled [r]," in which the tip of the tongue vibrates against the gum ridge above the upper teeth—like the *rrr* that children often use in imitation of a telephone bell or police whistle. Most German speakers, however, use a "uvular [r]," in which the back of the tongue is raised toward the uvula, the little droplet of skin hanging down in the back of the mouth.

You will probably find it easiest to pronounce the uvular [r] if you make a gargling sound before the sound [a]: ra. Keep the tip of your tongue down and out of the way; the tip of the tongue plays no role in the pronunciation of the gargled German [r].

r = [r] + vowel (Preis, Jahre, Rose): When German [r] is followed by a vowel, it has the full "gargled" sound.

r = vocalized [r] (Tier, Uhr, Tür): When German [r] is not followed by a vowel, it tends to become "vocalized," that is, pronounced like the vowel-like glide found in the final syllable of British English *hee-uh* (here), *thay-uh* (there).

The letters s, ss, ß

s = [ș] (sehen, lesen, Gänse): Before a vowel, the letter **s** represents the sound [ș], like English *z* in *zoo*.

s = [s] (das, Hals, fast): In most other positions, the letter **s** represents the sound [s], like English [s] in *so*.

[s] = ss, ß (wissen, Flüsse, weiß, beißen, Füße): The letters **ss** and **ß** (called **ess-tsett**) are both pronounced [s]. When they are written between vowels, the double letters **ss** signal the fact that the preceding vowel is short, and the single letter **ß** signals the fact that the preceding vowel is long (or a diphthong). The letter **ß** is also used before a consonant and at the end of a word.

The letter v

v = [f] (Vater, viel): The letter **v** is generally pronounced like English [f] as in *father*.

v = [v] (Vase, November): In words of foreign origin, the letter **v** is pronounced [v].

The letter w

w = [v] (Wein, Wagen, wann): Many centuries ago, German **w** (as in **Wein**) represented the sound [w], like English *w* in *wine*. Over the centuries, German **w** gradually changed from [w] to [v], so that today the **w** of German **Wein** represents the sound [v], like the *v* of English *vine*. German no longer has the sound [w]. The letter **w** always represents the sound [v].

The letter z

z = final and initial [ts] (Kranz, Salz, Zahn, zu): The letter **z** is pronounced [ts], as in English *rats*. In English, the [ts] sound occurs only at the end of a syllable; in German, [ts] occurs at the beginning as well as at the end of a syllable.

The consonant clusters gn, kn, pf, qu

To pronounce the consonant clusters **gn, kn, pf, qu** correctly, you need to use familiar sounds in unfamiliar ways.

gn: pronunciation is [gn]   **pf:** pronunciation is [pf]
kn: pronunciation is [kn]   **qu:** pronunciation is [kv]

gn = [gn-] (Gnade, Gnom)
kn = [kn-] (Knie, Knoten)
pf = [pf-] (Pfanne, Pflanze)
qu = [kv-] (quälen, Quarz, quitt)

The combination ng

ng = [ŋ] (Finger, Sänger, Ding): The combination ng is pronounced [ŋ], as in English *singer*. It does not contain the sound [g] that is used in English *finger*.

The combinations sch, sp, *and* st

sch = [š] (Schiff, waschen, Fisch)
sp = [šp] (Spaten, spinnen, Sport)
st = [št] (Stein, Start, stehlen)

Many centuries ago, both German and English had the combinations sp, st, sk, pronounced [sp], [st], [sk]. Then two changes took place. First, in both languages, [sk] changed to [š], as in English *ship, fish,* and German Schiff, Fisch. Second, in German only, word-initial [sp-] and [st-] changed to [šp-] and [št-]. The *sp* in English *spin* is pronounced [sp-], but in German spinnen it is pronounced [šp-]. The *st* in English *still* is pronounced [st-], but in German still it is pronounced [št-]. Today, German sch always represents [š] (like English *sh,* but with more rounded lips); sp- and st- at the beginning of German words or word stems represent [šp-] and [št-].

The letters ch

The letters ch are usually pronounced either [x] or [ç]. The [x] sound is made in the back of the mouth where [k] is produced.

   If you have ever heard a Scotsman talk about "Lo*ch* Lomond," you have heard the sound [x]. The sound [x] is produced by forcing air through a narrow opening between the back of the tongue and the back of the roof of the mouth (the soft palate). Notice the difference between [k], where the breath stream is stopped in this position and [x], where the breath stream is forced through a narrow opening in this position.

   To practice the [x] sound, keep the tongue below the lower front teeth and produce a gentle gargling sound, without moving the tongue or lips. Be careful not to substitute the [k] sound for the [x] sound.

ck, k = [k] (Sack, pauken, Pocken, buk)
ch = [x] (Sache, hauchen, pochen, Buch)

The [ç] sound is similar to that used by many Americans for the *h* in such words as *hue, huge, human.* It is produced by forcing air through a narrow opening between the front of the tongue and the front of the roof of the mouth (the hard palate). Notice the difference between [š], where the breath stream is forced through a wide opening in this position and the lips are rounded, and [ç], where the breath stream is forced through a narrow opening in this position and the lips are spread.
To practice the [ç] sound, round your lips for [š], then use a slit-shaped opening and spread your lips. Be careful not to substitute the [š] sound for [ç].

sch = [š] (misch, fischt, Kirsche, Welsch, Menschen)
ch = [ç] (mich, ficht, Kirche, welch, München)

Note two additional points about the pronunciation of ch:

   1. ch = [x] occurs only after the vowels a, o, u, au.
   2. ch = [ç] occurs only after the other vowels and n, l, and r.

The combination **chs**

chs = [ks] **(sechs, Fuchs, Weichsel)**
chs = [xs] or [çs] **(des Brauchs, du rauchst, des Teichs)**

The fixed combination **chs** is pronounced [ks] in words such as **sechs, Fuchs,** and **Ochse.** Today, **chs** is pronounced [xs] or [çs] only when the **s** is an ending or part of an ending **(ich rauche, du rauchst; der Teich, des Teichs).**

The suffix **-ig**

-ig = [iç] **(Pfennig, König, schuldig):** In final position, the suffix **-ig** is pronounced [iç] as in German **ich.**
-ig = [ig] **(Pfennige, Könige, schuldige):** In all other positions, the **g** in **-ig** has the sound [g] as in English *go.*

The glottal stop

English uses the glottal stop as a device to avoid running together words and parts of words; it occurs only before vowels. Compare the pairs of words below. The glottal stop is indicated with an *.

an *ice man   a nice man
not *at *all   not a tall
an *ape   a nape

German also uses the glottal stop before vowels to avoid running together words and parts of words.

Wie *alt *ist *er?
be*antworten

The glottal stop is produced by closing the glottis (the space between the vocal cords), letting air pressure build up from below, and then suddenly opening the glottis, resulting in a slight explosion of air. Say the word *uh-uh,* and you will notice a glottal stop between the first and second *uh.*

The Writing System

German punctuation

Punctuation marks in German are generally used as in English. Note the following major differences.

1. In German, dependent clauses are set off by commas.
   German   Der Mann, der hier wohnt, ist alt.
   English   The man who lives here is old.

2. In German, independent clauses joined by **und** *(and)* or **oder** *(or)* are set off by commas if the second clause contains both a different subject and a different verb.
   German   Robert singt, und Karin tanzt.
   English   Robert is singing and Karin is dancing.

3. In German, a comma is not used in front of **und** in a series as is often done in English.

German   Robert, Ilse und Karin singen.

English   Robert, Ilse, and Karin are singing.

4. In German, opening quotation marks are placed below the line.

German   Er fragte: „Wie heißen Sie?"

English   He asked, "What is your name?"

Note that a colon is used in German before a direct quotation.

5. In German commas stand outside of quotation marks.

German   „Meyer", antwortete sie.

English   "Meyer," she answered.

German capitalization

1. In German, all nouns are capitalized.

German   Wie alt ist der Mann?

English   How old is the man?

2. Adjectives are not capitalized, even if they denote nationality.

German   Ist das ein amerikanisches Auto?

English   Is that an American car?

3. The pronoun **ich** is not capitalized, unlike its English counterpart *I*.

German   Morgen spiele ich um zwei Uhr Tennis.

English   Tomorrow I am playing tennis at two o'clock.

GRAMMATICAL TABLES

1. Personal pronouns

Nominative	ich	du	er	es	sie	wir	ihr	sie	Sie
Accusative	mich	dich	ihn	es	sie	uns	euch	sie	Sie
Dative	mir	dir	ihm	ihm	ihr	uns	euch	ihnen	Ihnen

2. Reflexive pronouns

	ich	du	er/es/sie	wir	ihr	sie	Sie
Accusative	mich	dich	sich	uns	euch	sich	sich
Dative	mir	dir	sich	uns	euch	sich	sich

3. Interrogative pronouns

Nominative	wer	was
Accusative	wen	was
Dative	wem	
Genitive	wessen	

4. Relative and demonstrative pronouns

	Masculine	Neuter	Feminine	Plural
Nominative	der	das	die	die
Accusative	den	das	die	die
Dative	dem	dem	der	denen
Genitive	dessen	dessen	deren	deren

5. Definite articles

	Masculine	Neuter	Feminine	Plural
Nominative	der	das	die	die
Accusative	den	das	die	die
Dative	dem	dem	der	den
Genitive	des	des	der	der

6. *Der*-words

	Masculine	Neuter	Feminine	Plural
Nominative	dieser	dieses	diese	diese
Accusative	diesen	dieses	diese	diese
Dative	diesem	diesem	dieser	diesen
Genitive	dieses	dieses	dieser	dieser

The **der**-words are **dieser, jeder, mancher, solcher,** and **welcher.**

7. Indefinite articles and *ein*-words

	Masculine	Neuter	Feminine	Plural
Nominative	ein	ein	eine	keine
Accusative	einen	ein	eine	keine
Dative	einem	einem	einer	keinen
Genitive	eines	eines	einer	keiner

The **ein**-words include **kein** and the possessive adjectives: **mein, dein, sein, ihr, unser, euer, ihr,** and **Ihr.**

8. Plural of nouns

Type	Plural signal	Singular	Plural	Notes
1	Ø (no change)	das Zimmer	**die Zimmer**	Masculine and neuter nouns
	¨ (umlaut)	der Garten	**die Gärten**	ending in **el, -en, -er**
2	-e	der Tisch	**die Tische**	
	¨e	der Stuhl	**die Stühle**	
3	-er	das Bild	**die Bilder**	Stem vowel **e** or **i** cannot take umlaut
	¨er	das Buch	**die Bücher**	Stem vowel **a, o, u** takes umlaut
4	-en	die Uhr	**die Uhren**	
	-n	die Lampe	**die Lampen**	
	-nen	die Freundin	**die Freundinnen**	
5	-s	das Radio	**die Radios**	Mostly foreign words

9. Masculine *N*-nouns

	Singular	Plural
Nominative	der Herr	die Herren
Accusative	den Herrn	die Herren
Dative	dem Herrn	den Herren
Genitive	des Herrn	der Herren

Some other masculine N-nouns are **der Bauer, der Journalist, der Junge, der Jurist, der Kollege, der Komponist, der Mensch, der Nachbar, der Pilot, der Student.**

A few masculine N-nouns add **-ns** in the genitive: **der Name > des Namens.**

10. Preceded adjectives

	Singular			Plural
	Masculine	**Neuter**	**Feminine**	
Nom.	der **alte** Tisch ein **alter** Tisch	das **alte** Buch ein **altes** Buch	die **alte** Uhr eine **alte** Uhr	die **alten** Bilder keine **alten** Bilder
Acc.	den **alten** Tisch einen **alten** Tisch	das **alte** Buch ein **altes** Buch	die **alte** Uhr eine **alte** Uhr	die **alten** Bilder keine **alten** Bilder
Dat.	dem **alten** Tisch einem **alten** Tisch	dem **alten** Buch einem **alten** Buch	der **alten** Uhr einer **alten** Uhr	den **alten** Bildern keinen **alten** Bildern
Gen.	des **alten** Tisches eines **alten** Tisches	des **alten** Buches eines **alten** Buches	der **alten** Uhr einer **alten** Uhr	der **alten** Bilder keiner **alten** Bilder

11. Unpreceded adjectives

	Masculine	**Neuter**	**Feminine**	**Plural**
Nominative	kalt**er** Wein	kalt**es** Bier	kalt**e** Milch	alt**e** Leute
Accusative	kalt**en** Wein	kalt**es** Bier	kalt**e** Milch	alt**e** Leute
Dative	kalt**em** Wein	kalt**em** Bier	kalt**er** Milch	alt**en** Leuten
Genitive	kalt**en** Weines	kalt**en** Bieres	kalt**er** Milch	alt**er** Leute

12. Nouns declined like adjectives

◆ *Nouns preceded by definite articles or* **der-words**

	Masculine	Neuter	Feminine	Plural
Nominative	der Deutsche	das Gute	die Deutsche	die Deutschen
Accusative	den Deutschen	das Gute	die Deutsche	die Deutschen
Dative	dem Deutschen	dem Guten	der Deutschen	den Deutschen
Genitive	des Deutschen	des Guten	der Deutschen	der Deutschen

◆ *Nouns preceded by indefinite article or* **ein-words**

	Masculine	Neuter	Feminine	Plural
Nominative	ein Deutscher	ein Gutes	eine Deutsche	keine Deutschen
Accusative	einen Deutschen	ein Gutes	eine Deutsche	keine Deutschen
Dative	einem Deutschen	einem Guten	einer Deutschen	keinen Deutschen
Genitive	eines Deutschen	—	einer Deutschen	keiner Deutschen

Other nouns declined like adjectives are **der/die Bekannte, Erwachsene, Fremde, Jugendliche, Verwandte.**

13. Irregular comparatives and superlatives

Base form	bald	gern	gut	hoch	nah	viel
Comparative	eher	lieber	besser	höher	näher	mehr
Superlative	ehest-	liebst-	best-	höchst-	nächst-	meist-

14. Adjectives and adverbs taking umlaut in the comparative and superlative

alt	jung	oft
arm	kalt	rot
blaß (blasser *or* blässer)	krank	schwach
dumm	kurz	schwarz
gesund (gesünder *or* gesunder)	lang	stark
groß	naß (nässer *or* nasser)	warm

)sitions

accusative	With dative	With either accusative or dative	With genitive
bis	aus	an	(an)statt
durch	außer	auf	trotz
für	bei	hinter	während
gegen	mit	in	wegen
ohne	nach	neben	
um	seit	über	
	von	unter	
	zu	vor	
		zwischen	

16. Verbs and prepositions with special meanings

abhängen von
anfangen mit
anrufen bei
antworten auf (+ *acc.*)
arbeiten bei (*at a company*)
aufhören mit
beginnen mit
sich beschäftigen mit
danken für
denken an (+ *acc.*)
sich erinnern an (+ *acc.*)
erzählen über (+ *acc.*) *or* von
fahren mit (*by a vehicle*)
sich freuen auf (+ *acc.*)
sich freuen über (+ *acc.*)
sich fürchten vor (+ *dat.*)
halten von
helfen bei
hoffen auf (+ *acc.*)
sich interessieren für

sich kümmern um
lächeln über (+ *acc.*)
mitmachen bei (*with a group*)
reden über (+ *acc.*) *or* von
riechen nach
schicken nach
schreiben an (+ *acc.*)
schreiben über (+ *acc.*)
sorgen für
sprechen über (+ *acc.*), von *or* mit
studieren an *or* auf (+ *dat.*)
suchen nach
teilnehmen an (+ *dat.*)
vergleichen mit
sich vorbereiten auf (+ *acc.*)
warnen vor (+ *dat.*)
warten auf (+ *acc.*)
wissen über (+ *acc.*) *or* von
wohnen bei
zeigen auf (+ *acc.*)

17. Dative verbs

The number indicates the chapter in which each verb is introduced.

antworten 9	gefallen 7	helfen 7	schmecken 7
danken 6	gehören 6	leid tun 5	weh tun 10
fehlen 14	glauben 2	passen 9	

The verbs **glauben, erlauben** (to permit), and **schmecken** may take an impersonal accusative object: **ich glaube es; ich erlaube es.**

18. Present tense

	lernen[1]	arbeiten[2]	tanzen[3]	geben[4]	lesen[5]	fahren[6]	laufen[7]	auf·stehen[8]
ich	lern**e**	arbeit**e**	tanz**e**	geb**e**	les**e**	fahr**e**	lauf**e**	steh**e** ... auf
du	lern**st**	arbeit**est**	tan**zt**	g**i**bst	l**ie**st	f**ä**hrst	l**äu**fst	stehst ... auf
er/es/sie	lern**t**	arbeit**et**	tan**zt**	g**i**bt	l**ie**st	f**ä**hrt	l**äu**ft	steht ... auf
wir	lern**en**	arbeit**en**	tanz**en**	geb**en**	les**en**	fahr**en**	lauf**en**	stehen ... auf
ihr	lern**t**	arbeit**et**	tanz**t**	geb**t**	les**t**	fahr**t**	lauf**t**	steht ... auf
sie	lern**en**	arbeit**en**	tanz**en**	geb**en**	les**en**	fahr**en**	lauf**en**	stehen ... auf
Sie	lern**en**	arbeit**en**	tanz**en**	geb**en**	les**en**	fahr**en**	lauf**en**	stehen ... auf
Imper. sg.	lern(e)	arbeite	tanz(e)	g**i**b	l**ie**s	fahr(e)	lauf(e)	steh(e) ... auf

1. The endings are used for all verbs except the modals, **wissen, werden,** and **sein.**
2. A verb with stem ending in **-d, -t, Cm,** or **Cn** (where **C** = any consonant other than l or r, e.g., **atmen** and **regnen**) has an **e** before the **-st** and **-t** endings.
3. The **-st** ending of the **du**-form contracts to **-t** when the verb stem ends in a sibilant (**-s, -ss, -ß, -z,** or **-tz**). Thus the **du**- and **er/es/sie**-forms are identical.
4. Some strong verbs have a stem-vowel change **e > i** in the **du**- and **er/es/sie**-forms and the imperative singular.
5. Some strong verbs have a stem-vowel change **e > ie** in the **du**- and **er/es/sie**-forms and the imperative singular. The strong verbs **gehen** and **stehen** do not change their stem vowel.
6. Some strong verbs have a stem-vowel change **a > ä** in the **du**- and **er/es/sie**-forms.
7. Some strong verbs have a stem-vowel change **au > äu** in the **du**- and **er/es/sie**-forms.
8. In the present tense, separable prefixes are separated from the verbs and are in last position.

19. Simple past tense

	Weak verbs		Strong verbs
	lernen[1]	arbeiten[2]	geben[3]
ich	lernte	arbeitete	gab
du	lerntest	arbeitetest	gabst
er/es/sie	lernte	arbeitete	gab
wir	lernten	arbeiteten	gaben
ihr	lerntet	arbeitetet	gabt
sie	lernten	arbeiteten	gaben
Sie	lernten	arbeiteten	gaben

1. Weak verbs have the past-tense marker **-te** + endings.
2. A weak verb with stem endings in **-d, -t, Cm,** or **Cn** (where **C** = any consonant other than l or r) has a past-tense marker **-ete** + endings.
3. Strong verbs have a stem-vowel change + endings.

20. Auxiliaries *haben, sein, werden*

ich	habe	bin	werde
du	hast	bist	wirst
er/es/sie	hat	ist	wird
wir	haben	sind	werden
ihr	habt	seid	werdet
sie	haben	sind	werden
Sie	haben	sind	werden

21. Modal auxiliaries: present, simple past, and past participle

	dürfen	**können**	**müssen**	**sollen**	**wollen**	**mögen**	**(möchte)**
ich	darf	kann	muß	soll	will	mag	(möchte)
du	darfst	kannst	mußt	sollst	willst	magst	(möchtest)
er/es/sie	darf	kann	muß	soll	will	mag	(möchte)
wir	dürfen	können	müssen	sollen	wollen	mögen	(möchten)
ihr	dürft	könnt	müßt	sollt	wollt	mögt	(möchtet)
sie	dürfen	können	müssen	sollen	wollen	mögen	(möchten)
Sie	dürfen	können	müssen	sollen	wollen	mögen	(möchten)
Simple past	durfte	konnte	mußte	sollte	wollte	mochte	
Past participle	gedurft	gekonnt	gemußt	gesollt	gewollt	gemocht	
Past part. with dependent inf.	dürfen	können	müssen	sollen	wollen	mögen	

22. Verb conjugations: strong verbs *sehen* and *gehen*

◆ *Indicative*

	Present		**Simple past**	
ich	sehe	gehe	sah	ging
du	siehst	gehst	sahst	gingst
er/es/sie	sieht	geht	sah	ging
wir	sehen	gehen	sahen	gingen
ihr	seht	geht	saht	gingt
sie	sehen	gehen	sahen	gingen
Sie	sehen	gehen	sahen	gingen

	Present Perfect				Past perfect			
ich	habe		bin		hatte		war	
du	hast		bist		hattest		warst	
er/es/sie	hat		ist		hatte		war	
wir	haben	gesehen	sind	gegangen	hatten	gesehen	waren	gegangen
ihr	habt		seid		hattet		wart	
sie	haben		sind		hatten		waren	
Sie	haben		sind		hatten		waren	

	Future				
ich	werde		werde		
du	wirst		wirst		
er/es/sie	wird		wird		
wir	werden	sehen	werden	gehen	
ihr	werdet		werdet		
sie	werden		werden		
Sie	werden		werden		

◆ *Imperative*

Imperative		
Familiar singular	sieh	geh(e)
Familiar plural	seht	geht
Formal	sehen Sie	gehen Sie

◆ *Subjunctive*

Present-time subjunctive			
General subjunctive		**Special subjunctive**	
ich	sähe	ginge	sehe	gehe
du	sähest	gingest	sehest	gehest
er/es/sie	sähe	ginge	sehe	gehe
wir	sähen	gingen	sehen	gehen
ihr	sähet	ginget	sehet	gehet
sie	sähen	gingen	sehen	gehen
Sie	sähen	gingen	sehen	gehen

Past-time subjunctive							
General subjunctive				**Special subjunctive**			
ich	hätte		wäre		habe		sei
du	hättest		wärest		habest		seiest
er/es/sie	hätte		wäre		habe		sei
wir	hätten	gesehen	wären	gegangen	haben	gesehen	seien	gegangen
ihr	hättet		wäret		habet		seiet
sie	hätten		wären		haben		seien
Sie	hätten		wären		haben		seien

◆ *Passive voice*

	Present passive		**Past passive**	
ich	werde		wurde	
du	wirst		wurdest	
er/es/sie	wird		wurde	
wir	werden	gesehen	wurden	gesehen
ihr	werdet		wurdet	
sie	werden		wurden	
Sie	werden		wurden	

	Present perfect passive		**Past perfect passive**	
ich	bin		war	
du	bist		warst	
er/es/sie	ist		war	
wir	sind	gesehen worden	waren	gesehen worden
ihr	seid		wart	
sie	sind		waren	
Sie	sind		waren	

23. Principal parts of strong and irregular weak verbs

The following list includes all the strong and irregular verbs used in this book. Compound verbs like **hereinkommen** and **hinausgehen** are not included, since the principal parts of compound verbs are identical to the basic forms: **kommen** and **gehen**. Separable-prefix verbs like **einladen** are included only when the basic verb **(laden)** is not listed elsewhere in the table. Basic English meanings are given for all verbs in this list. For additional meanings, consult the German-English vocabulary on pages R-43–R-68. The number indicates the chapter in which the verb was introduced.

Infinitive	Present-tense vowel change	Simple past	Past participle	General subjunctive	Meaning
anfangen	fängt an	fing an	angefangen	finge an	*to begin* 7
backen		backte	gebacken	backte	*to bake* 7
beginnen		begann	begonnen	begönne *or* begänne	*to begin* 10
binden		band	gebunden	bände	*to bind, tie* 12
bleiben		blieb	ist geblieben	bliebe	*to stay* 3
bringen		brachte	gebracht	brächte	*to bring* 5
denken		dachte	gedacht	dächte	*to think* 3
einladen	lädt ein	lud ein	eingeladen	lüde ein	*to invite; to treat* 8
entscheiden		entschied	entschieden	entschiede	*to decide* 13
essen	ißt	aß	gegessen	äße	*to eat* 4
fahren	fährt	fuhr	ist gefahren	führe	*to drive, travel* 6
finden		fand	gefunden	fände	*to find* 4
fliegen		flog	ist geflogen	flöge	*to fly* 6
geben	gibt	gab	gegeben	gäbe	*to give* 4
gefallen	gefällt	gefiel	gefallen	gefiele	*to please* 7
gehen		ging	ist gegangen	ginge	*to go* 2
haben	hat	hatte	gehabt	hätte	*to have* 3
halten	hält	hielt	gehalten	hielte	*to hold; to stop* 7
hängen		hing	gehangen	hinge	*to hang* 8
heißen		hieß	geheißen	hieße	*to be called, named* 1
helfen	hilft	half	geholfen	hülfe *or* hälfe	*to help* 7
kennen		kannte	gekannt	kennte	*to know* 4
kommen		kam	ist gekommen	käme	*to come* 2
lassen	läßt	ließ	gelassen	ließe	*to let, allow* 7
laufen	läuft	lief	ist gelaufen	liefe	*to run* 6
leihen		lieh	geliehen	liehe	*to borrow* 5
lesen	liest	las	gelesen	läse	*to read* 5
liegen		lag	gelegen	läge	*to lie* 3
nehmen	nimmt	nahm	genommen	nähme	*to take* 4
nennen		nannte	genannt	nennte	*to name* 11
riechen		roch	gerochen	röche	*to smell* 4

Infinitive	Present-tense vowel change	Simple past	Past participle	General subjunctive	Meaning
schaffen		schuf	geschaffen	schüfe	*to create, set up* 14
scheinen		schien	geschienen	schiene	*to shine* 3; *to seem* 10
schlafen	schläft	schlief	geschlafen	schliefe	*to sleep* 6
schließen		schloß	geschlossen	schlösse	*to close* 4
schreiben		schrieb	geschrieben	schriebe	*to write* 1
schwimmen		schwamm	ist geschwommen	schwömme *or* schwämme	*to swim* 2
sehen	sieht	sah	gesehen	sähe	*to see* 5
sein	ist	war	ist gewesen	wäre	*to be* 2
singen		sang	gesungen	sänge	*to sing* 12
sitzen		saß	gesessen	säße	*to sit* 7
sprechen	spricht	sprach	gesprochen	spräche	*to speak* 5
stehen		stand	gestanden	stände *or* stünde	*to stand* 4
tragen	trägt	trug	getragen	trüge	*to wear; to carry* 7
treffen	trifft	traf	getroffen	träfe	*to meet; to hit* 8
treiben		trieb	getrieben	triebe	*to engage in* 2
trinken		trank	getrunken	tränke	*to drink* 4
tun		tat	getan	täte	*to do* 7
unterscheiden		unterschied	unterschieden	unterschiede	*to distinguish* 10
vergessen	vergißt	vergaß	vergessen	vergäße	*to forget* 7
verlieren		verlor	verloren	verlöre	*to lose* 4
wachsen	wächst	wuchs	ist gewachsen	wüchse	*to grow* 7
waschen	wäscht	wusch	gewaschen	wüsche	*to wash* 10
werden	wird	wurde	ist geworden	würde	*to become* 5
wissen	weiß	wußte	gewußt	wüßte	*to know* 5

SUPPLEMENTARY EXPRESSIONS

1. Expressing skepticism

Red' keinen Unsinn/Stuß. Don't talk nonsense.

Ist das dein Ernst? Are you serious?

Hier ist was faul. There's something fishy here.

Meinst du? Wirklich? Meinst du das wirklich? Do you think so? Really? Do you really mean that?

Das ist ja komisch/eigenartig/merkwürdig. That's funny/strange.

Irgendetwas stimmt hier nicht. Something's wrong here.

Ist das wahr? Is that true?

Wer sagt das? Wer hat das gesagt? Who says that? Who said that?

Woher weißt du das? Wo/Von wem hast du das gehört? How do you know that? Where/From whom did you hear that?

2. Expressing insecurity or doubt

Das ist unwahrscheinlich. That's unlikely.

Das glaub' ich nicht. I don't believe that.

Es ist unwahrscheinlich, daß [sie das gesagt hat]. It's unlikely that [she said that].

Das ist zweifelhaft. That's doubtful.

Ich glaube nicht/ich bezweifle, daß [er das gesagt hat]. I don't believe [he said that].

Ich glaube das nicht. I don't believe that.

Das kann nicht sein. That can't be.

3. Expressing annoyance

Quatsch! / Unsinn! / Blödsinn! Nonsense!

Blödmann! / Dussel! / Idiot! Idiot!

Der hat wohl nicht alle Tassen im Schrank. He doesn't have all his marbles.

Bei der ist wohl eine Schraube los/locker. She's got a screw loose.

Hör mal. Listen.

Geh. Go on.

Also, wissen Sie. / Wirklich. / Tsk, tsk, tsk. Well, you know. / Really. / Tsk,tsk,tsk.

(Das ist doch) nicht zu glauben. (That is) not to be believed.

(Das ist) unerhört/unglaublich. (That is) unheard of/unbelievable.

(Das ist eine) Schweinerei. That's a mess, a dirty trick.

Das tut/sagt man nicht. One doesn't do/say such a thing.

Das kannst du doch nicht machen/sagen. You can't do/say that.

So eine Gemeinheit. That's mean.

Frechheit! The nerve!; She's/He's/You've got some nerve!

Also komm. Come on.

4. Stalling for time

Also. / Na ja. / Ja nun. Well. / Well, of course. / Well, now.

hmmmmmmmmmm hmmmmmmmmmm

Laß mich mal nachdenken. Let me think about it.

Darüber muß ich (erst mal) nachdenken. I have to think about that (first).

Das kann ich so (auch) nicht sagen. I can't say that (either).

Das muß ich mir erst mal überlegen. I have to think about it.

Da muß ich erst mal überlegen. Let me think.

5. Being noncommittal

(Das ist ja) interessant. (That is) interesting.

hmmmmmmmmmm hmmmmmmmmmm

Wirklich? Really?

Ach ja? Oh really?

So so. Oh yes, I see.

6. Expressing good wishes

Ich halte/drücke [dir] die Daumen. I'll cross my fingers [for you].

Gesundheit! Bless you!

(Ich wünsche) guten Appetit/gesegnete Mahlzeit. (I hope you) enjoy your meal.

Prost! / Auf Ihr Wohl! / Zum Wohl! Cheers! / To your health!

Herzlichen Glückwunsch! Congratulations!

Herzlichen Glückwunsch zum Geburtstag! Happy birthday!

Ich wünsche Ihnen gute Reise! / Gute Reise! Bon voyage! Have a nice trip!

Gute Besserung. Get well soon.

Viel Glück! Good luck!

Viel Vergnügen/Spaß! Have fun!

Alles Gute! All the best! Best wishes!

Hals- und Beinbruch! Good luck! Break a leg!

7. *Courtesy expressions*

Bitte (sehr/schön).   Please.
Danke (sehr/schön).   Thanks (very much).

8. *Saying ''you're welcome''*

Bitte (sehr/schön).   You're (very) welcome.
Gern geschehen.   Glad to do it.
Nichts zu danken.   Don't mention it.

9. *Expressing surprise*

Ach nein!   Oh no!
(Wie) ist das (nur) möglich?   (How) is that possible?
Das hätte ich nicht gedacht.   I wouldn't have thought that.
Das ist ja prima/toll/klasse/stark/Wahnsinn!   That's great/fantastic/terrific, etc.!
Ich werd' verrückt.   I must be crazy.
(Das ist ja) nicht zu glauben!   (That's) unbelievable!
Kaum zu glauben.   Hard to believe.
Ich bin von den Socken/sprachlos.   I'm bowled over/speechless.
Um Himmels willen!   For heaven's sake!
Sag' bloß.   You don't say.
Was für 'ne Überraschung!   What a surprise!
Das haut/wirft mich um.   That bowls me over/knocks me out/blows me away.; *(neg.)* That's a bummer.

10. *Expressing agreement (and disagreement)*

Natürlich (nicht)! / Selbstverständlich (nicht)!   Naturally, of course (not)!
Klar.   Sure.
Warum denn nicht?   Why not?
Das kann (nicht) sein.   That can(not) be.
(Das) stimmt (nicht).   (That's) (not) right.
Richtig. / Falsch.   Right. / Wrong.
Das finde ich auch/nicht.   I think so, too./I don't think so.
Genau. / Eben.   Exactly. / That's right.
Du hast recht.   You're right.

11. *Responding to requests*

Bitte. / Selbstverständlich. / Natürlich. / Klar.   Glad to. / Of course. / Naturally.
Gern. / Machen wir. / Mit Vergnügen.   Glad to. / We'll do it. / With pleasure.
(Es tut mir leid, aber) das geht nicht.   (I'm sorry but) that won't work.

Das kann ich nicht [reparieren].   I can't [repair that].
Das habe ich nicht.   I don't have it.
Das ist zu schwer/groß/teuer.   That's too difficult/big/expensive.

12. *Expressing regret*

(Das) tut mir leid.   I'm sorry.
(Es) tut mir leid, daß [ich nicht kommen kann].   I'm sorry [I can't come].
Leider [kann ich morgen nicht].   Unfortunately [I can't tommorow].
(Es) geht leider nicht.   That won't work, unfortunately.
Schade.   That's a shame. / Too bad.
(So ein) Pech.   That's tough luck.

13. *Excusing oneself*

Bitte entschuldigen Sie mich.   Please excuse me. / I beg your pardon.
Bitte verzeihen Sie mir [die Verspätung].   Please pardon [my delay].
Entschuldigung. / Verzeihung. / Entschuldigen Sie.   Excuse (pardon) me.
Entschuldigen Sie bitte, daß [ich erst jetzt komme].   Please excuse me [for arriving so late].
Das ist keine Entschuldigung.   That's no excuse.

14. *Expressing indifference*

(Das) ist mir egal.   That's all the same to me.
Es ist mir egal, ob [er kommt].   I don't care whether [he comes].
Das macht mir nichts aus.   It doesn't matter to me.
Das ist nicht meine Sorge.   That's not my problem.
Es macht mir nichts aus, daß [sie mehr verdient].   I don't care that [she earns more].
Macht nichts.   Doesn't matter.
Das ist mir wurscht.   I couldn't care less.
Das kannst du machen, wie du willst.   You can do as you please.
Das kannst du halten wie der Dachdecker.   You can do/take that as you wish.
Ich habe nichts dagegen. / Meinetwegen.   I have nothing against it.

15. *Expressing admiration*

Ach, wie schön! / Klasse! Oh, how nice! / Great! / Terrific!

Phantastisch! / Toll! / Super! / Stark! / Irre! / Einsame spitze! Fantastic! / Great! / Super! / Incredible!, Really great!, etc.

Erstklassig! / Ausgezeichnet! First-rate! / Excellent!

Das ist aber nett [von Ihnen/dir]. That's really nice [of you].

Der/Die ist nett. He/She is nice.

Das sind nette Leute. Those are nice people.

16. *Expressing rejection*

(So ein) Mist! (What) rubbish!

(Das ist) schrecklich! (That is) awful!

Das ärgert mich. That annoys me.

Der/Das/Die gefällt mir (gar) nicht. I don't like him/that/her (at all).

Ich mag ihn/sie nicht. I don't like him/her.

Ich kann ihn/sie nicht leiden. I don't like him/her.

Ich finde, er/sie ist langweilig/doof/uninteressant. I think he/she is boring/stupid/uninteresting.

Ich finde das schlecht/langweilig. I think that is bad/boring.

Ich finde ihn/sie nicht sympathisch/nett. I don't find him/her likeable/nice.

17. *Expressing joy and pleasure*

Wir freuen uns. We're pleased.

Wir freuen uns auf [seinen Besuch/die Ferien]. We're looking forward to [his visit/our vacation].

Wir sind begeistert. We are enthusiastic.

Wir sind froh (darüber), daß [er wieder arbeitet]. We're happy (about the fact) that [he's working again].

Es freut mich, daß [sie gekommen ist]. I'm happy that [she has come].

Das tun/kochen/essen wir gern. We like to do/cook/eat that.

Das macht mir/uns Spaß. I/We enjoy that./That's fun.

Das machen wir zum Vergnügen. We do that for fun.

18. *Expressing sadness*

Ach (nein)! Oh (no)!

Wie schrecklich! How awful/horrible!

Mein Gott/O je! My God!

Ich bin traurig, weil [er/sie nicht hier ist]. I am unhappy, because [he/she isn't here].

Ich bin sehr traurig darüber. I am very unhappy about that.

Ich bin deprimiert/frustriert. I am depressed/frustrated.

19. *Making requests*

Hättest du/Hätten Sie Lust [mitzukommen]? Would you like [to come along]?

Hättest du/Hätten Sie Zeit, [uns zu besuchen]? Would you have time [to come see us]?

Hättest du/Hätten Sie etwas [Zeit] für mich? Would you have some [time] for me?

Ich hätte gern [ein Pfund Äpfel]. I'd like [a pound of apples].

Könntest du/Könnten Sie [mein Auto reparieren]? Could you [repair my car]?

Würdest du/Würden Sie mir bitte helfen? Would you please help me?

Hättest du/Hätten Sie etwas dagegen? Would you mind?

Hast du/Hätten Sie etwas dagegen, wenn [ich mitkomme]? Would you mind if [I come along]?

Dürfte ich [ein Stück Kuchen haben]? May I/Is it OK if I [have a piece of cake]?

Macht es dir/Ihnen etwas aus? Do you mind?

Sei/Seien Sie so gut. Be so kind.

Ich möchte fragen, ob ich [mitkommen] darf/kann. I'd like to ask if I may/can [come along].

Könnte ich [um neun Uhr zu dir/Ihnen kommen]? Could I [come see you at nine o'clock]?

Ist es dir/Ihnen recht? Is it OK with you?

20. *Asking for favors*

Könntest du/Könnten Sie mir einen Gefallen tun und [mich mitnehmen]? Could you do me a favor and [take me along]?

Ich hätte eine Bitte: könntest/würdest du (könnten/würden Sie) [mich mitnehmen]? I have a request: could/would you [take me along]?

21. *Making surmises*

Ich glaube schon. / Ich denke ja. I think so.

Ich glaube (schon), daß [sie das gesagt hat]. I do believe [she said that].

Das dürfte/könnte wahr/richtig sein. That might/could be true/right.

Wahrscheinlich [stimmt das]. Probably [that's right].

Sicher. / Ich bin sicher. / Ich bin ziemlich sicher, daß [er das gesagt hat]. Sure / I'm sure. / I'm quite sure that [he said that].

Ich vermute. / Ich nehme das an. I assume so.

Ich nehme an, daß [das stimmt]. I assume that [that's right].

Das scheint [nicht zu stimmen]. That appears [not to be right].

22. *Expressing expectation*

Hoffentlich. / Hoffentlich [kommt sie]. I hope. / I hope [she comes].

Ich hoffe (es) (sehr). I hope (so) (very much).

Ich hoffe, daß [er das Paket bekommen hat]. I hope [he received the package].

Ich freue mich auf [die Ferien]. I'm looking forward to [my vacation].

Ich kann es kaum erwarten. I can hardly wait.

23. *Expressing fears*

Ich befürchte/ich fürchte, daß [sie nicht kommt]. I'm afraid [she's not coming].

Ich habe Angst, [nach Hause zu gehen]. I'm afraid [to go home].

Davor habe ich Angst. I'm afraid of that.

Ich habe Angst vor [dem Hund]. I'm afraid of [the dog].

[Der Hund] jagt mir Angst ein. [The dog] scares me.

Das ist mir unheimlich. It scares me.

24. *Giving advice*

Ich schlage vor, daß [wir um acht anfangen]. I suggest that [we begin at eight].

Ich rate dir/Ihnen, [zu Hause zu bleiben]. I advise you [to stay home].

Das würde ich dir/Ihnen (nicht) raten. I would (not) advise that.

Das würde ich (nicht) machen/sagen. I would (not) do/say that.

Das würde ich anders/so machen. I would do that differently/this way.

Das mußt du/Müssen Sie so machen. You have to do it this way.

Ich zeige dir/Ihnen, [wie man das macht]. I'll show you [how one does that].

An [deiner/seiner/ihrer] Stelle würde ich [zu Hause bleiben]. If I were [you/him/her], I'd [stay home].

25. *Correcting misunderstandings*

Das habe ich nicht so gemeint. I didn't mean it that way.

Das habe ich nur aus Spaß gesagt. I only said that in fun/jest.

Das war doch nicht so gemeint. It wasn't meant that way.

Das war nicht mein Ernst. I wasn't serious.

Nimm doch nicht alles so ernst. Don't take everything so seriously.

The following word lists will help you to increase the number of things you can say and write.

Kapitel 1

Classroom objects

der **Filzstift** felt-tip pen
das **Klassenzimmer** classroom
die **Kreide** chalk
der **Kurs** course
die **Landkarte; die Wandkarte** map; wall map
der **Papierkorb** wastebasket
das **Ringbuch** loose-leaf binder
der **Schwamm** sponge
das **Sprachlabor** language lab
die **(Wand)tafel** chalkboard

Colors

dunkel[blau] dark [blue]
hell[blau] light [blue]
lila lilac
orange orange
purpur purple
rosa pink

Kapitel 2

Adjectives for mood or personality

ausgezeichnet excellent
elend miserable
erstklassig first-rate
furchtbar horrible
kaputt worn out, tired
klasse terrific
miserabel miserable
phantastisch fantastic
prima excellent
schrecklich dreadful
toll great

Adjectives for personality

clever clever
fies disgusting; unfair
freundlich friendly
klug smart

lahm slow, sluggish
langsam slow
praktisch practical
verrückt crazy

Physical description of people

blond blond
dick fat
dunkel brunette
fett fat
gut aussehend handsome
häßlich ugly
hübsch pretty
mager thin
normal normal
schön beautiful
schwach weak
stark strong
vollschlank full-figured

Sports and Games

das **Ballonfahren** ballooning
das **Billard** billiards
das **Bodybuilding** bodybuilding
die **Dame** checkers
das **Drachenfliegen** hang gliding
das **Eishockey** hockey
das **Fallschirmspringen** parachute jumping
der **Federball** badminton
der **Flipper** pinball machine; **ich flippere** I play the pinball machine
das **Gewichtheben** weightlifting
die **Gymnastik** calisthenics
der **Handball, Hallenhandball** handball
das **Hockey** field hockey
das **Jogging; joggen** jogging; to jog
die **Leichtathletik** track and field
der **Radsport,** das **Radfahren** bicycling
das **Segelfliegen** glider flying
das **Turnen** gymnastics
der **Wasserball** water polo
das **Windsurfen** wind surfing

boxen to box
fechten to fence
jagen to hunt
kegeln to bowl
ringen to wrestle
rudern to row
schießen to shoot

Farewells (and Greetings)
Adé. 'Bye. *(used in southern Germany and Austria)*
Auf Wiederhören. Good-by. *(on the telephone)*
Bis bald. See you soon.
Bis dann! See you later.
Ciao. So long.
Grüezi. Hello. *(used in Switzerland)*
Grüß Gott. Good-by. Hello. *(used in southern Germany and Austria)*
Mach's gut. Take it easy.
Servus. Good-by! Hello! *(used in southern Germany and Austria)*
Tschüß. 'Bye.

Kapitel 3

Weather expressions
der **Blitz** lightning
Celsius centigrade
der **Donner** thunder
das **Gewitter** thunderstorm
das **Grad** degree; **Wieviel Grad sind es?** What's the temperature?
der **Hagel** hail
das **Hoch** high-pressure system
die **Kaltfront** cold front
der **Landregen** all-day rain
die **Luft** air
der **Luftdruck** air pressure
der **Nebel** fog
der **Niederschlag** precipitation
der **Nieselregen** drizzle
der **Schauer** shower
der **Schneefall** snowfall
der **Sprühregen** drizzle
der **Tau** dew
die **Temperatur** temperature
das **Tief** low-pressure system
die **Warmfront** warm front

der **Wetterbericht** weather report; **Was steht im Wetterbericht?** What's the weather report?
die **Wettervorhersage** weather prediction
die **Windrichtung** wind direction

bedeckt overcast
bewölkt cloudy; **stark bewölkt** very cloudy
eisig icy cold
heiter fair
klar clear, cloudless
neb(e)lig foggy
schwül humid
sonnig sunny
stürmisch stormy
wolkenlos cloudless
wolkig cloudy

Es gießt (in Strömen). It's pouring.
Es regnet Bindfäden. It's raining cats and dogs.
Es ist naßkalt. It's damp and cold.

Kapitel 4

Small specialty shops
die **Apotheke** pharmacy
die **Bäckerei** bakery
das **Blumengeschäft** florist shop
die **Buchhandlung** bookstore
die **chemische Reinigung** dry cleaning shop
die **Drogerie** drugstore
das **Eisenwarengeschäft** hardware store
das **Elektrogeschäft** appliance store
das **Feinkostgeschäft** delicatessen
das **Fotogeschäft** camera store
der **Juwelier** jeweler's; jewelry store
das **Kaffeegeschäft** store selling coffee
der **Kiosk** kiosk, stand
der **Klempner** plumber
die **Konditorei** coffee and pastry shop
der **Metzger** butcher shop
das **Möbelgeschäft** furniture store
der **Optiker** optician's shop
das **Schreibwarengeschäft** stationery store
das **Schuhgeschäft** shoe store
der **Schuhmacher;** der **Schuster** shoe repair (shop)
das **Sportgeschäft;** die **Sportausrüstungen** sporting goods store; sporting goods
der **Waschsalon** laundromat

Breakfast

das **Ei (weich gekocht)** egg (soft-boiled)
das **Graubrot** light rye bread
der **Honig** honey
der **Joghurt** yogurt
der **Kakao** cocoa
die **Marmelade** jam, marmalade
der **Orangensaft** orange juice
der **Pumpernickel** pumpernickel bread
die **Schokolade** hot chocolate
das **Schwarzbrot** dark rye bread
der **Tee** tea
der **Tomatensaft** tomato juice
das **Vollkornbrot** coarse, whole-grain bread
das **Weißbrot** white bread

Main meal

das **Getränk** drink
die **Suppe** soup
der **gemischte Salat** vegetable salad plate
der **grüne Salat** tossed (green) salad

der **Fisch** fish
der **Braten** roast
das **Hähnchen** chicken
das **Kalbfleisch** veal
das **Kotelett** chop
das **Rindfleisch** beef
die **Roulade** roulade
der **Schinken** ham
das **Schnitzel** cutlet
das **Schweinefleisch** pork
der **Speck** bacon
der **Truthahn** turkey

die **Bohnen** *(pl.)* beans
der **Champignon** mushroom
die **Erbsen** *(pl.)* peas
die **Karotten, gelbe Rüben** *(pl.)* carrots
die **Kartoffeln** *(pl.)* potatoes
der **Kohl** cabbage
der **Mais** corn

die **(gefüllte) Paprikaschote** (stuffed) pepper
die **Pilze** *(pl.)* mushrooms
der **Reis** rice
das **Sauerkraut** sauerkraut
der **Spargel** asparagus
die **Tomate** tomato
die **Zwiebel** onion

die **Nudeln** *(pl.)* noodles

das **Salz** salt
der **Pfeffer** pepper
der **Zucker** sugar

Lunch/supper

der **Käse** cheese
die **(saure) Gurke** (half-sour) pickle
das **Spiegelei** fried egg
der **Thunfisch** tuna fish
die **Wurst/der Aufschnitt** sausage/cold cuts
das **Würstchen** frankfurter

Desserts and fruit

das **Eis** ice cream
der **Karamelpudding** custard
das **Kompott** stewed fruit
die **Schokoladencreme** chocolate mousse
der **Vanillepudding** vanilla pudding

die **Sahne** cream
die **Schlagsahne** whipped cream

die **Ananas** pineapple
der **Apfel** apple
die **Banane** banana
die **Erdbeeren** *(pl.)* strawberries
die **Himbeeren** *(pl.)* raspberries
die **Orange, Apfelsine** orange
der **Pfirsich** peach
die **Pflaume** plum
der **Rhabarber** rhubarb
die **Zitrone** lemon
die **Zwetsch(g)e** plum

Kapitel 5

Professions

ein **Angestellter**/eine **Angestellte** employee
der **Apotheker**/die **Apothekerin** pharmacist
der **Arzt**/die **Ärztin** physician
der **Betriebswirt**/die **Betriebswirtin** manager
der **Dolmetscher**/die **Dolmetscherin** translator
der **Elektriker**/die **Elektrikerin** electrician
der **Flugbegleiter**/die **Flugbegleiterin** flight attendant
der **Ingenieur**/die **Ingenieurin** engineer
der **Journalist**/die **Journalistin** journalist
der **Krankenpfleger**/die **Krankenschwester** nurse
der **Lehrer**/die **Lehrerin** teacher
der **Mechaniker**/die **Mechanikerin** mechanic
der **Pfarrer**/die **Pfarrerin** clergyperson
der **Physiotherapeut**/die **Physiotherapeutin** physiotherapist
der **Rechtsanwalt**/die **Rechtsanwältin** lawyer
der **Sekretär**/die **Sekretärin** secretary
der **Sozialarbeiter**/die **Sozialarbeiterin** social worker
der **Sozialpädagoge**/die **Sozialpädagogin** social worker (with college degree)
der **Steward**/die **Stewardeß** flight attendant
der **Verkäufer**/die **Verkäuferin** salesperson
der **Volkswirt**/die **Volkswirtin** economist
der **Wissenschaftler**/die **Wissenschaftlerin** scientist

Film and literature

der **Abenteuerfilm** adventure movie
der **Action-Film** action movie
der **Horrorfilm** horror film
der **Liebesfilm** romance
der **Science-Fiction-Film** science fiction movie

die **Außenaufnahme** location shot
das **Drehbuch** (film) script
die **Filmfestspiele** *(pl.)* film festival
die **Filmkomödie** comedy film
die **Filmkritik** movie criticism
die **(Film)leinwand** (movie) screen
der **(Film)schauspieler**/die **(Film)schauspielerin** movie actor/actress
die **(Film)szene** (movie) scene
das **(Film)studio** (movie) studio
der **Kameramann** cameraman
der **Regisseur**/die **Regisseurin** director

die **Anthologie** anthology
das **Drama** drama, play
das **Gedicht** poem
die **Kurzgeschichte** short story
der **Roman** novel
die **Zeitschrift** magazine
die **Illustrierte** illustrated magazine

der **Autor**/die **Autorin** author
der **Dichter**/die **Dichterin** poet
der **Dramatiker**/die **Dramatikerin** dramatist
der **Schriftsteller**/die **Schriftstellerin** writer

Family

der **Neffe** nephew
die **Nichte** niece
die **Oma** grandma
der **Opa** grandpa
die **Stiefmutter** stepmother
der **Stiefvater** stepfather
die **Schwiegermutter** mother-in-law
der **Schwiegervater** father-in-law
die **Schwägerin** sister-in-law
der **Schwager** brother-in-law

geschieden divorced
ledig single
verheiratet married

College majors

Amerikanistik American studies
Anglistik English language and literature
Betriebswirtschaft business administration
Biologie biology
Chemie chemistry
Chinesisch Chinese
Englisch English
Französisch French
Gemeinschaftskunde social studies
Germanistik German language and literature
Informatik computer science
Ingenieurwesen engineering
Italienisch Italian
Japanisch Japanese
Jura law
Kommunikationswissenschaft communications
Kunstgeschichte art history
Medizin medicine

Philosophie philosophy
Physik physics
Politik political science
Psychologie psychology
Publizistik journalism
Religionswissenschaft/Theologie religion
Rechnungswesen accounting
Romanistik Romance languages and literature
Russisch Russian
Soziologie sociology
Spanisch Spanish
Sprachwissenschaft/Linguistik linguistics
Theaterwissenschaft theater studies
Volkswirtschaft economics

Kapitel 6

Geographic terms

die **Anhöhe;** der **Hügel** hill
der **Atlantik** Atlantic (Ocean)
der **Bach** brook
der **Berg** mountain
das **(Bundes)land** (federal) state in Germany and
    Austria
der **(Bundes)staat** (federal) state in the U.S.A.
die **Ebbe/die Flut** low tide/high tide
der **Fluß** river
das **Gebirge** mountain range
die **Gezeiten** (*pl.*) tide
der **Gipfel** peak
der **Gletscher** glacier
die **Hauptstadt** capital
die **Insel** island
der **Kanal** canal; channel
der **Kanton** canton (Switzerland)
die **Küste** coast
das **Meer** sea
der **Pazifik** Pacific (Ocean)
der **See** lake
die **See** sea
der **Strand** beach

das **Tal** valley
der **Teich** pond
das **Ufer** shore
der **Wald** woods
die **Wiese** meadow
die **Wüste** desert

Modes of transportation

die **Kutsche** carriage
der **Pferdewagen** horse-drawn wagon

der **LKW (= Lastkraftwagen)**/der **Laster** truck
der **PKW (= Personenkraftwagen)** passenger car
der **Anhänger** trailer
der **Campingwagen,** der **Wohnwagen** camper
    (pulled by a car)
der **Caravan** camper (recreational vehicle)
der **Combi** station wagon

die **Bergbahn** mountain railway; cable car
die **Eisenbahn** train, railway
der **Güterzug** freight train

das **Boot** boat
das **Containerschiff** container ship
die **Fähre** ferry
der **Frachter** freighter
das **Kanu** canoe
das **Motorboot** motorboat
der **Passagierdampfer** passenger ship
das **Ruderboot** rowboat
der **Schleppkahn** barge
das **Segelboot** sailboat
das **Segelschiff** sailing ship
der **Tanker** tanker

der **Hubschrauber** helicopter
der **Jet** jet
der **Jumbojet** jumbo jet
das **(Propeller)flugzeug** propeller plane
das **Raumschiff** spaceship
das **Segelflugzeug** glider; sailplane

Buildings and other landmarks

die **Autobahnauffahrt (-ausfahrt)** expressway on-
ramp (off-ramp)
der **Bahnhof** train station
die **Bahnlinie** railroad line
der **Bauernhof** farm
die **Brücke** bridge
die **Bundesstraße** federal highway
die **Burg** fortress
das **Denkmal** monument
die **Fabrik** factory
der **Fernsehturm** TV tower
der **Flughafen** airport
der **Friedhof** cemetery
der **Funkturm** radio and TV tower
der **Fußweg** footpath
die **Kapelle** chapel
die **Kirche**/die **Kathedrale** church/cathedral
das **Kloster** monastery
die **Mühle** mill
das **Museum** museum
das **Parkhaus** parking garage
die **Polizei** police
die **Post** post office
die **Ruine** ruin
das **Schloß** castle
die **Tiefgarage** underground garage
der **Tunnel** tunnel

Asking directions

Wo ist [der Bahnhof]? Where is the [train station]?
Wie weit ist es [zum Bahnhof]? How far is it [to
the train station]?
Wie komme ich am schnellsten [zum Bahnhof]?
What is the quickest way [to the train station]?
Wo ist hier in der Nähe [ein Café]? Is there [a café]
around here?
Wissen Sie den Weg nach [Obersdorf]? Do you
know the way to [Obersdorf]?
**Wir wollen nach [Stuttgart]. Wie fahren wir am
besten?** We're going to [Stuttgart]. What is the
best route?

Giving directions

Da fahren Sie am besten mit [der U-Bahn]. It's
best if you go by [subway].
Fahren Sie mit der [Drei]; Nehmen Sie die [Drei].
Take number [3].
**[Dort/An der Ecke/An der Kreuzung] ist die
Haltestelle.** [Over there/on the corner/at the
intersection] is the [bus] stop.
An der [ersten] Kreuzung gehen Sie [rechts]. At
the [first] intersection turn [right].
Gehen Sie die [erste] Straße [links]. Take the [first]
street [to the left].
Gehen Sie geradeaus. Go straight ahead.
Bei der Ampel biegen Sie [rechts] ab. At the traffic
light turn [right].

Kapitel 7

Table setting

das **Besteck** flatware
die **Butterdose** butter dish
der **Eierbecher** egg cup
der **Eßlöffel** tablespoon
das **Gedeck** table setting
das **Gericht** dish (food)
die **Kaffeekanne**/die **Teekanne** coffeepot/teapot
das **Milchkännchen** creamer (small pitcher for
cream or milk)
die **Schüssel** bowl
die **Serviette** napkin
die **Speise** dish (food)
der **Teelöffel** teaspoon
der **Teller** plate
die **Untertasse** saucer
die **Zuckerdose** sugar bowl

Clothing for men and women

der **Anorak** jacket with hood, parka
der **Blazer** blazer
die **Daunenjacke** down jacket
der **Hut** hat
die **Kniestrümpfe** (*pl.*) knee socks
die **Latzhose** bib overalls
der **Mantel** coat
die **Mütze** cap

der **Overall** jumpsuit
der **Parka** parka
das **Polohemd** polo shirt
der **Regenmantel** raincoat
der **Rollkragenpullover** turtleneck
die **Sandalen** (*pl.*) sandals
der **Schal** scarf
der **Schlafanzug** pajamas
die **Shorts** (*pl.*) shorts
die **Sportschuhe** (*pl.*) sneakers
die **Strickjacke** (cardigan) sweater
das **Sweatshirt** sweatshirt
das **T-Shirt** t-shirt
der **Trainingsanzug** sweat suit
die **Turnschuhe** (*pl.*) fitness/workout shoes
die **Weste** vest
der **Wintermantel** winter coat

Clothing for women

das **Abendkleid** evening dress/gown
der **Badeanzug** bathing suit
der **Hosenrock** culottes
das **Kostüm** suit
das **Trägerkleid** jumper

Clothing for men

der **Anzug** suit
die **Badehose** bathing trunks
das **Freizeithemd** casual shirt

Kapitel 8

TV Programs

das **Familiendrama,** die **Seifenoper** soap opera
die **Fernsehserie** serial
die **Fernsehkömodie** sitcom (situation comedy)
die **Fernsehshow,** die **Unterhaltungsshow** game show
der **Krimi** detective or crime drama
die **Nachrichten** news
die **Quizsendung,** das **Fernsehquiz** quiz show
die **Seifenoper** soap opera
der **Spielfilm** feature (film)
die **Sportschau** sports program
der **Zeichentrickfilm** cartoon

Kapitel 9

Stereo and audio-visual equipment

die **Boxen** speakers
die **Compact Disk** compact disc
der **CD-Player**/der **CD-Spieler** compact disc player
der **Farbfernseher** color television
der **Kassettenrecorder** cassette recorder
der **Kopfhörer** headphone
der **Lautsprecher** loudspeaker
das **Mikrophon** microphone
der **Plattenspieler** record player
der **Radiorecorder** cassette radio
der **Schwarzweißfernseher** black-and-white television
das **Tonband,** das **Band** tape
das **Tonbandgerät** (reel-to-reel) tape recorder
der **Tuner** tuner
der **Verstärker** amplifier
der **Videorecorder** video recorder
der **Walkman** personal stereo

Chores

abstauben to dust
Fenster putzen to clean windows
(das) **Abendessen vorbereiten, machen** to prepare supper
(das) **Mittagessen kochen** to cook dinner
(die) **Wäsche bügeln** to iron the wash, laundry
Wäsche, Kleider flicken to mend clothes

(die) **Bäume beschneiden/pflanzen/fällen** to prune/ to plant/to cut down trees
das **Haus**/den **Zaun**/das **Boot streichen** to paint the house/the fence/the boat
die **Hecke schneiden** to trim the hedge
(das) **Holz sägen/spalten/hacken** to saw/to split/to chop wood
(den) **Rasen mähen** to mow the lawn
(den) **Schnee fegen, kehren/schippen** to sweep/to shovel snow
(das) **Unkraut jäten** to pull out weeds

Kapitel 10

Body care and hygiene

der **Haartrockner,** der **Föhn** hair dryer
die **Haarbürste** hair brush
das **Handtuch** hand towel
der **Kamm** comb
das **Make-up** makeup
der **Rasierapparat** razor
die **Schere** scissors
die **Seife** soap
die **Sonnenbrille** sun glasses
der **Spiegel** mirror
das **Taschentuch** handkerchief
die **Zahnbürste** toothbrush
die **Zahnpasta** toothpaste

Kapitel 11

Computer terminology

der **Anwender** program user
anzeigen to display
mit dem Computer arbeiten to work on the
   computer
auswählen to select a program
der **Bildschirm** screen
der **Computer** computer
der **Personalcomputer** personal computer
die **Diskette** diskette
das **Diskette-Laufwerk** diskette drive
der **Drucker** printer
der **Matrixdrucker** matrix printer
der **Typendrucker** letter-quality printer
das **Typenrad** daisy wheel
laden to load
ein **Programm laufen lassen** to run a program
der **Monitor** monitor
der **Positionsanzeiger** cursor
programmieren to program
die **Programmiersprache** computer language
die **Software;** das **Softwarepacket** software;
   software package
speichern to store
auf Diskette speichern to store on diskette
ein **30 MB Speicher** a 30 megabyte memory
die **Tastatur** keyboard
die **Taste;** die **Funktionstaste** key; function key
der **Textverarbeiter,** der **Wortprozessor** word
   processor

Kapitel 12

Musical instruments

das **Akkordeon** accordion
die **Blockflöte** recorder
die **Bratsche** viola
das **Cello** cello
das **Fagott** bassoon
die **Flöte** flute
die **Geige, Violine** violin
die **Gitarre** guitar
die **Harfe** harp
die **Klarinette** clarinet
das **Klavier** piano
der **Kontrabaß** double bass
die **Oboe** oboe
die **Orgel** organ
die **Posaune (+ blasen)** trombone (to play)
die **Pauke** kettle drum
das **Saxophon** saxophone
das **Schlagzeug** percussion (instrument)
die **Trommel** drum
die **Trompete (+ blasen)** trumpet (to play)
die **Tuba (+ blasen)** tuba (to play)
das **(Wald)horn (+ blasen)** French horn (to play)

Hobbies

angeln to fish
Blumen (z.B. Rosen, Dahlien, Lilien, Nelken)
   flowers (*e.g.*, roses, dahlias, lilies, carnations)
campen to go camping
die **Gartenarbeit** gardening
malen to paint
schreiben [Gedichte, Geschichten, Romane,
   Dramen] to write [poems, stories, novels, plays]
zeichnen to draw

Collectibles

sammeln to collect
alte Flaschen old bottles
Briefmarken stamps
Glas glass
Münzen coins
Pflanzen (getrocknet) plants (dried)
Puppen dolls
Silber silver
Streichholzschachteln matchboxes
Zinn pewter

Kapitel 14

Music and theater

das **Theaterstück;** die **Tragödie;** die **Komödie;** der
  Einakter play; tragedy; comedy; one-act play
das **Musical** musical comedy
die **Oper** opera
die **Operette** operetta

der **Dirigent**/die **Dirigentin** conductor
der **Regisseur**/die **Regisseurin** director
der **Sänger**/die **Sängerin** singer
der **Schauspieler**/die **Schauspielerin** actor/actress
der **Zuschauer**/der **Zuschauerin** spectator

der **Beifall,** der **Applaus** applause
die **Bühne** stage
das **Foyer** hallway, lobby
die **Inszenierung** mounting of a production
das **Orchester** orchestra
die **Pause** intermission
das **Programmheft** program
die **Vorstellung** performance

Kapitel 4

Preisring-Markt

Fanta name of a popular softdrink
die **Gurke** cucumber
der **Rinderbraten** beef roast
das **Rindergulasch** beef for stew
Sarotti name of a brand of chocolate
die **Schokolade** chocolate
der **Sekt** champagne
Söhnlein name of a brand of champagne
das **Sonderangebot** special
die **Theke** counter

Kapitel 5

Kino-Programm

die **Anzeige** advertisement
AZ = Abendzeitung name of newspaper
die **Begierde** desire
das **Ereignis** event
fabelhaft fabulous
die **Flucht** flight, escape
die **Fremdsprache** foreign language
hassen to hate
die **Hexe** witch
hervorragend outstanding
klimatisiert air-conditioned
kucken to look
die **Nonne** nun
Hör zu name of a TV magazine
namens by the name of
die **Spur** trace
der **Stein** stone
der **Stern** star
SZ = Süddeutsche Zeitung name of a newspaper in
   Munich
Verlieben: zum Verlieben for falling in love
die **Zukunft** future

Kapitel 6

Restop Altea Motel

die **Ausflugsfahrt** excursion
der **Ausgangspunkt** starting point
äußerst extremely
der **Badestrand** beach
Bergsteigen mountain climbing
bzw. (= beziehungsweise) respectively
einladen to invite
die **Erholung** relaxation
erreichbar accessible
die **Fahrtrichtung** direction
hoteleigner private (hotel's own)
die **Kulturstätte** place of cultural interest (e.g.,
   castle, museum)
die **Lage** site, location
das **Loch** hole
Mondsee the name of a lake and a town on the
   lake in Austria, about 30 km east of Salzburg
Salzkammergut area in Austria, famous for its
   many lakes and alpine landscape
die **Schiffsrundfahrt** boat excursion
überraschen to surprise
die **Umgebung** environs, the area
die **Veranstaltung** event (e.g., concert)
das **Vergnügen** fun

3 Tage Budapest

die **Ankunft** arrival
das **Bad** bath
ca (= circa.) approximately
die **Dusche** shower
die **Ecke** corner
der **Einbettzuschlag** additional charge for single
   room
die **Halbpension** halfboard, i.e., including breakfast
   and one other meal
inbegriffen included
die **Leistung** service
lt. (= laut) according to
die **Nächtigung** overnight stay

der **Pauschalpreis** all-inclusive price
die **Reiseleitung** tour guide
die **Stadtrundfahrt** city tour
der **Stornoschutz** cancellation insurance
Verfügung: zur freien Verfügung free time
das **WC (= Wasserklosett)** toilet

Kapitel 7

Cafe an der Uni

die **Ananas** pineapple
die **Beilage** side dish
der **Champignon** mushroom
Fanta name of a popular soft drink
Faß: vom Faß on tap
das **Gebäck** cake and pastries
gebrühter Tee brewed tea
das **Gericht** dish (food)
geöffnet open
das **Getränk** beverage
die **Gurke** pickle
die **Johannisbeere** currant
die **Kugel** scoop of ice cream
der **Pilz** mushroom
die **Preiselbeere** cranberry
die **Remoulade** a kind of mayonnaise (dressing)
die **Sahne** cream
der **Schinken** ham
die **Schlagsahne** whipped cream
das **Schnitzel** slice, cutlet
die **Schüssel** bowl
das **Spiegelei** fried egg
die **Speise** dish (food)
der **Thunfisch** tuna
der **Truthahn** turkey
Wahl: nach Wahl of your choice
Wiener Art Viennese style
**Bitte treffen Sie an unserer Schauvitrine Ihre Wahl
und bestellen Sie bei Ihrer Bedienung!** Please
make your selection at the display case and order
it from your server.
**Alle Preise sind Inklusivpreise und enthalten
Bedienungsgeld und Mehrwertsteuer.** All prices
include service charge and sales tax.

Karstadt

aktuell current, "the latest"
das **Erdgeschoß** ground floor

geöffnet open
die **Kapuze** hood; **Kapuzen-** hooded
Karstadt a German department store chain
leben to live
mod. (= modische) fashionable
die **Riesenauswahl** gigantic selection
versch. (= verschiedene) various
der **Wendeblouson** reversible light jacket,
windbreaker

Kapitel 8

Fernseh-Programm

Abendschau evening news
**ARD (= Arbeitsgemeinschaft der öffentlich-
rechtlichen Rundfunkanstalten der
Bundesrepublik Deutschland (= erstes
Programm)** T.V. channel 1
Ausgeliefert Deliverance
Auweia! Woe is me!
Baumeister . . . Rokoko Builder of the Bavarian Rococo
die **Betriebswirtschaftslehre** course in business
administration
BR (= Bayrischer Rundfunk) Bavarian Radio
der **Forstinspektor** forest inspector
der **Fürst** prince
Gas geben to step on the gas
Das Gespensterhaus The Haunted House
das **Gruselkabinett** horror room
das **Jubiläum** anniversary
der **Koffer** suitcase
die **Macht** power
der **Massentourismus** tourism for the masses
Nachtgedanken Night Thoughts
Nix für ungut! Don't Take it Wrong!
Presseschau current issues in the press
Regie direction
Rundschau TV magazine program
der **Spielfilm** feature (film)
Tagesschau daily news
Umschau Review
die **Wirtschaft** economy
Die Zauberfischgräte Magic Fish Bone
ZDF (= Zweites Deutsches Fernsehen) T.V.
channel 2
der **Zeichentrickfilm** cartoon

Kapitel 9

Wohnlandschaft mit Garten

das **Baugrundstück** building site
beraten lassen to get (professional) advice
ca. (= **circa**) approximately
das **Dachgeschoß** attic story, loft
die **Diele** hall
einzeln individual
Gard. (= **Garderobe**) front hall with space for
  hanging coats
der **Gartenanteil** share of the yard
großzügig spacious
günstig favorable
der **Hinweispfeil** direction sign
die **Loggia**, *pl.* **Loggien** recessed balcony
m² square meter
der **Quadratmeter** square meter
Whg (= **Wohnung**) apartment
die **Wohnlandschaft** "home scape"
Zi. (= **Zimmer**) room

Kapitel 10

Bootsgarage am Luganersee

der **Anteil** share
das **Außenbad** outdoor pool
der **Aufzug** hoist
Cheminee (*French*) fireplace
die **Einstellhalle** parking garage
das **Hallenbad** indoor pool
inkl. (= **inklusive**) inclusive
der **Lift** elevator
Luganersee . Lake Lugano
die **Pergola** (*Italian*) arbor
die **Zahlung** payment

Occasion unique a Yverdon Unique opportunity in
Yverdon

A luxury villa, early 19th century, including
  adjoining property of 16,317 square meters, as
  well as a farm requiring renovation. Unmatched
  view overlooking Neuchatel and lake, two
  minutes by car from center of city.
For more information, write: 22-120-5843, Est
  Vaudois. 1820 Montreux.

Pian San Giacomo

For sale: Chalet, consisting of 1 apartment with large
  living room, fireplace, 3 bedrooms, bathroom,
  large terrace.
1 apartment with living room, bedroom, bathroom,
  wood storage, laundry room, electric heating.
Beautiful garden with granite table, parking space,
  serene and sunny, open view, completely
  furnished.
5 minutes from the S. Bernardino racetrack. 40
  minute drive on the expressway N13 from
  Lugano or Locarno.
Price: 395,000 francs. Call during evening hours
  (091) 54 20 21

Kapitel 11

Stellenangebote or Stellenanzeigen

ab sofort beginning immediately
aufgeschlossen out-going
die **Ausbildung** training
die **Aushilfe** temporary job
die **Bewerbung** application
der **Elektroinstallateur** electrician
f. = **für**
der **Festfahrer** permanent employee (driver)
das **Fotofachlabor** photo lab
die **Gräfin** countess
jhr. (= **-jährig**) year-old
der **Kundenbereich** customer service
der **Lebenslauf** a short biography in narrative form
od. = **oder**
der **Raum** area
der **Schichtdienst** shift work
der **Schnellkurs** concentrated crash course
selbständig independent
Sprachkenntnisse proficiency in a foreign language
das **Stellenangebot** job offer
su. = **suchen**
tüchtig capable and hard-working
u. = **und** *or* **unter**
Wunsch: auf Wunsch as you wish (your choice)
Zuschr. (= **Zuschriften**) replies

Kapitel 12

Älteres Bauernhaus

bäuerliche Verhältnisse farming
die **Chiffre** code
die **Grundstückfläche** size of property
m² (Quadratmeter) square meter
die **Inseratenabteilung** ad department
das **Nebengebäude** outbuilding
die **Offerten** offers
das **Postfach** post office box
die **Scheune** barn
der **Stall** stable
Umbauobjekt suitable for remodeling

City Disco

der **Einlaß** entry
der **Eintritt** admittance
Olympiazentr. (= das Olympiazentrum) the name of subway stop
schauen to look, *here:* to stop in at
die **Stube** room
der **Treff** meeting place
U3/U2 (= U-Bahnlinien 3 und 2) subway lines 3 and 2

Schiller hätte geweint

die **Auskunft** information
das **Bildungsangebot** courses offered
die **Einschreibung** registration
Freude: vor Freude weinen to weep with joy
nutzen to use
die **Volkshochschule** adult education

Kapitel 13

Heiraten/Bekanntschaften

die **Bekanntschaft** acquaintance
Bildzuschr. (= Bildzuschriften) picture included with replies
ca. (= circa) approximately
cm (= Zentimeter) centimeter
die **Erscheinung** appearance
freundl. = freundlich
gebildet educated, cultured
gemeinsam joint, together
großzügig generous

das **Herz** heart
das **Hirn** brain; *here:* brains *(colloq.)*, mind
J. = Jahre
jugendl. (= jungendlich) youthful
liebenswert lovable, amiable
m. = mit
mögl. (= möglichst) if at all possible
das **Niveau** class
reiselustig fond of travel
schlk. (= schlank) slim, slender
schüchtern shy
selbständig independent
symp. (= sympathisch) likeable
der **Tierliebhaber** a person fond of animals
Tel.-Ang. (= Telefonangabe) telephone
Treffpunkt Wagner ... *the name and address of a partner service*
treu loyal, faithful
u. = und *or* **unter**
unt. = unter
Verlieben: zum Verlieben to fall in love with
verwitwet widowed
Zuschr. (= Zuschriften) replies

Gebrauchtwagen

ASU (= Abgasuntersuchung) emissions control inspection
ATM (= Austauschmotor) (factory) rebuilt engine
Bj. (= Baujahr) model year
die **Dachreling** luggage carrier, roof rack
DB = Daimler Benz
einwandfrei perfect, faultless
EZ (= Erstzulassung) first registration
f. = für
8f. bereift (8fach) eight tires (i.e., summer and winter)
gebraucht used
geschäftl. (= geschäftlich) business, work
1. Hd. (= erster Hand) original owner
2. Hd. (= zweiter Hand) second hand
der **Kombi** station wagon
Mod. (= Modell) model
PS (= Pferdestärke) horsepower
schadstoffarm low emission
Servo power (brakes/steering)
silbermet. (= silbermetallic) silver metallic
SSD (= Stahlschiebedach) steel sun roof

steuerfrei tax exempt
4trg. (= viertürig) with four doors
TÜ (= technische Überwachung) federal car
   inspection
TÜA (= technische Überwachung Abnahme)
   federal car inspection (i.e., when next due)
unfallfrei accident free

VB (= Verhandlungsbasis) negotiable asking price
Verloursaussttg. (= Veloursausstattung) velour
   interior
verk. = verkaufen
Zust. (= Zustand) condition
ZV (= Zentralverriegelung) automatic door locks

SUPPLEMENTARY DIALOGUES

The following dialogues contain phrases that may be particularly useful to you if you ever have the opportunity to travel or live in a German-speaking country.

Was steht in der Zeitung?

Thomas: Was steht Neues in der Zeitung?
Ulf: Keine Ahnung. Mich interessieren nur die Anzeigen.
Thomas: Was suchst du denn?
Ulf: Einen Job und eine Wohnung.

Auf einer Party

Frau Schwarz: Frau Schiller, darf ich bekannt machen? Herr Busch.
Frau Schiller: Guten Tag, Herr Busch.
Herr Busch: Guten Tag, Frau Schiller.

Auf Wohnungssuche

Volker: (*nimmt Hörer ab*) Volker Hornung.
Martin: Ja, guten Tag. Ich rufe wegen der Anzeige im Tagesblatt an. Ist das Zimmer noch frei?
Volker: Nein, es tut mir leid. Wir haben es gestern abend vermietet. Aber die Leute in der Wohnung unter uns haben auch ein Zimmer zu vermieten.
Martin: Wissen Sie, wie hoch die Miete ist?
Volker: Nein, da sprechen Sie besser mit den Leuten selbst. Ihre Telefonnummer ist 781 66 54. Die Leute heißen Grüning. Das Zimmer ist auf jeden Fall groß, und es hat einen Balkon.
Martin: Das hört sich ja toll an. Also, vielen Dank. Ich rufe bei Grünings jetzt gleich an. Auf Wiederhören.

In der Tankstelle

Kunde: Volltanken, bitte.
Tankwart: Super oder Normal?
Kunde: Normal. Und kontrollieren Sie bitte Ölstand und Reifendruck.

What's in the newspaper?

What's new in the newspaper?
No idea. I'm only interested in the classifieds.

What are you looking for?
A job and an apartment.

At a party

Ms. Schiller, I'd like you to meet Mr. Busch.

How do you do, Mr. Busch.
How are you, Ms. Schiller?

Apartment hunting

(*lifts the receiver*) Volker Hornung.
Yes, hello. I'm calling about the advertisement in the daily newspaper. Is the room still available?
No, I'm afraid not. We rented it out yesterday evening. But the people in the apartment downstairs also have a room for rent.
Do you know how much the rent is?
No, you'd better speak to them about that. Their telephone number is 781 66 54. Their name is Grüning. In any case the room is large, and it has a balcony.
That sounds great. Well thanks very much. I'll call Grünings right away. Good-by.

At the service station

Fill it up, please.
Super or regular?
Regular. And please check the oil and tires.

Auf der Post

Kundin: Ich möchte diesen Brief per Luftpost
 schicken.
Beamter: Nach Amerika? Bis 5 Gramm kostet er DM
 1,65.
Kundin: Geben Sie mir bitte 5 Briefmarken zu 20
 Pfennig und 5 zu 50 Pfennig. Kann ich dieses
 Paket hier aufgeben?
Beamter: Nein, die Paketannahme ist am Schalter
 nebenan.

Auf der Bank

Kunde: Ich möchte gern Reiseschecks einlösen,
 Dollarschecks.
Angestellte: Bitte schön. Wieviel möchten Sie wech-
 seln?
Kunde: Fünfzig. Wie steht der Dollar heute?
Angestellte: Der Kurs für Reiseschecks ist 1,60 (eins
 sechzig). Das sind also 80 Mark minus 1 Mark
 Gebühren.

Im Kaufhaus

Kundin: Darf ich bitte diese Jacke anprobieren?
Verkäuferin: Selbstverständlich ... Das Blau steht
 Ihnen gut, wirklich.
Kundin: Leider ist sie etwas zu eng.
Verkäuferin: Hier habe ich die gleiche Jacke eine
 Nummer größer. Die müßte Ihnen passen.

Im Café

1. Dame: Sind diese zwei Plätze noch frei?
Gast: Ja, bitte.
Ober: Was wünschen die Damen?
2. Dame: Was können Sie uns denn empfehlen?
Ober: Der Apfelstrudel ist ausgezeichnet.
1. Dame: Zwei Stück bitte. Mit Sahne. Und zwei
 Kännchen Kaffee.
Ober: Aber gern.

At the post office

I'd like to send this letter air mail.

To America? The cost is 1 mark 65 for up to
 5 grams.
Please give me five 20-Pfennig stamps and five
 50-Pfennig ones. Can I mail this package here?

No, the package window is the next one over.

At the bank

I'd like to cash some traveler's checks, dollar checks.

Fine. How much would you like to change?

Fifty dollars' worth. What's the exchange rate today?
The rate for traveler's checks is 1,60 (one sixty). So
 that comes to 80 marks, minus 1 mark fee.

In the department store

May I please try on this jacket?
Of course ... Blue looks good on you, really.

I'm afraid it's somewhat too tight.
Here, I have the same jacket a size larger. It should
 fit you.

In the Café

Are these two seats taken [unoccupied]?
Yes, please sit down.
What would you like, ladies?
What would you recommend?
The apple strudel is excellent.
Two pieces, please. With whipped cream. And two
 pots of coffee.
Certainly.

Bei der Ärztin

Patient: Frau Doktor, ich habe immer solche Rückenschmerzen.
Ärztin: Wie lange haben Sie die Schmerzen denn schon?
Patient: Seit zwei Wochen.
Ärztin: Zeigen Sie mir mal genau, wo es weh tut.

At the doctor's

Doctor, my back aches all the time.

How long have you had the pain?

Two weeks.
Show me exactly where it hurts.

Im Hotel

Touristin: Haben Sie noch ein Einzelzimmer frei?
Empfangschefin: Ja. Wir haben eins mit Dusche (im sechsten Stock).
Touristin: Wieviel kostet es?
Empfangschefin: Sechzig Mark. Mit Frühstück, natürlich.
Touristin: Schön. Ich nehme es für eine Nacht.
Empfangschefin: Bitte sehr. Tragen Sie sich hier ein, bitte. Hier ist der Schlüssel.

In the hotel

Do you still have a single room available?
Yes. We have one with a shower (on the sixth floor).
How much is it?
Sixty marks. Breakfast is included, of course.

Fine. I'll take it for one night.
Fine. Please register here. Here's the key.

An der Theaterkasse

Student: Ich möchte gern zwei Karten für den ersten Rang, für heute abend.
Angestellte: Tut mir leid. Ich habe nur noch Karten fürs Parkett.
Student: Wie teuer sind die Karten? Ich habe einen Studentenausweis.
Angestellte: Dann bekommen Sie Ihre Karte fünfzig Prozent billiger.

At the theater box office

I'd like two tickets in the first balcony for this evening.

I'm sorry. I only have orchestra tickets left.

How much are the tickets? I have a student I.D.

Then you get a fifty percent discount.

Am Flughafen

Fluggast: Fliegt die Maschine direkt nach Istanbul?
Angestellter: Nein, sie macht eine Zwischenlandung in Athen. Möchten Sie Raucher oder Nichtraucher?
Fluggast: Nichtraucher, bitte.
Angestellter: Gang- oder Fensterplatz?
Fluggast: Ich hätte gern einen Fensterplatz.

At the airport

Does the plane go directly to Istanbul?
No, it makes a stop in Athens. Would you like smoking or non-smoking?

Non-smoking, please.
Aisle or window seat?
I would like a window seat.

Im Flugzeug

Flugbegleiter: Wir bitten Sie, sich jetzt anzuschnallen und die Rückenlehnen senkrecht zu stellen.

In the airplane

Please fasten your seat belts and place your seat backs in the upright position.

Bei der Zugauskunft

Tourist: Können Sie mir sagen, wann der nächste
  Zug nach München fährt?
Beamtin: Um 14 Uhr 20 fährt ein Intercity ab.

Am Fahrkartenschalter

Reisender: Einmal erster Klasse München, bitte.
Beamter: Hin und zurück oder einfach?
Reisender: Einfach, bitte. Von welchem Bahnsteig
  fährt mein Zug ab?
Beamter: Gleis elf.

Im Zug

Reisende: Warten Sie. Ich hebe den Koffer ins
  Gepäcknetz. (*Schaffnerin macht die Tür auf.*)
Schaffnerin: (Ist) hier noch jemand zugestiegen?
  (*Reisende reicht ihr die Fahrkarte.*)
Schaffnerin: Sie müssen in München umsteigen. Der
  Anschlußzug wartet auf Gleis 7.
Reisende: Können Sie mir sagen, wo der
  Speisewagen ist?
Schaffnerin: Ja, in der Mitte des Zuges.

At the railway station information desk

Can you tell me when the next train leaves for
  Munich?
An Intercity-train leaves at 2:20 p.m.

At the ticket window

One ticket to Munich, please. First class.
Round trip or one-way?
One-way, please. From which platform does my
  train leave?
Track eleven.

In the train

Just a minute, I'll put the suitcase up on the rack.
  (*The conductor opens the door.*)
Has anyone here just gotten on? (*Passenger hands her
  the ticket.*)
You have to change trains in Munich. The connect-
  ing train will be waiting on Track 7.
Can you tell me where the dining car is?

Yes, in the middle of the train.

This vocabulary includes all the words used in *Deutsch heute* except numbers. The definitions given are limited to the context in which the words are used in this book. Chapter numbers are given for all words and expressions occurring in the chapter vocabularies and in the *Erweiterung des Wortschatzes* sections to indicate where a word or expression is first used. Passive vocabulary does not have a chapter reference. The symbol ~ indicates repetition of the key word (minus the definite article, if any).

Nouns are listed with their plural forms: **der Abend, -e.** No plural entry is given if the plural is rarely used or nonexistent. If two entries follow a noun, the first one indicates the genitive and the second one indicates the plural: **der Herr, -n, -en.**

Strong and irregular weak verbs are listed with their principal parts. Vowel changes in the present tense are noted in parentheses, followed by simple-past and past-participle forms. All verbs take **haben** in the past participle unless indicated with **sein.** For example: **fahren (ä), fuhr, ist gefahren.** Separable-prefix verbs are indicated with a raised dot: **auf·stehen.**

Adjectives and adverbs that require an umlaut in the comparative and superlative forms are noted as follows: **warm (ä).** Stress marks are given for all words that are not accented on the first syllable. The stress mark follows the accented syllable: **Amerika'ner.** In some words, either of two syllables may be stressed.

The following abbreviations are used:

abbr.	abbreviation	*dat.*	dative	*p.p.*	past participle
acc.	accusative	*decl.*	declined	*part.*	participle
adj.	adjective	*f.*	feminine	*pl.*	plural
adv.	adverb	*fam.*	familiar	*sg.*	singular
colloq.	colloquial	*gen.*	genitive	*subj.*	subjunctive
comp.	comparative	*m.*	masculine	*sup.*	superlative
conj.	conjunction	*n.*	neuter		

A automobile symbol for Austria

ab away; from; ~ **und zu** now and then 11

der **Abend, -e** evening; **Guten ~.** Good evening. 2; **zu ~ essen** to have supper/dinner 4

abend: gestern ~ last night 7; **heute ~** this evening 2

das **Abendessen** dinner, supper 4; **zum ~** for supper 4

abends evenings, in the evening 4

aber *(conj.)* but, however 2; *(flavoring particle)* really, certainly 3

ab·fahren (ä), fuhr ab, ist abgefahren to depart, leave (by some means of transportation) 8

der/die **Abgeordnete** *(noun declined like adj.)* representative, member of Bundestag

abgeschrieben dismissed, written off

ab·hängen, hing ab, abgehangen (+ **von**) to depend on 13

ab·holen to pick up 6

das **Abitur'** *Gymnasium* diploma 5

absolut' absolute(ly)

die **Abstimmung** voting

ab·trocknen to dry dishes, wipe dry 9

ab·waschen (ä), wusch ab, abgewaschen to wash (dishes) 9

ab·werten to discredit

ach oh 1

Ach so.' Oh, I see.

achten (auf + *acc.***)** to watch

die **Adres'se, -en** address 1; **Wie ist deine/Ihre ~?** What is your address? 1

ah oh 1

ähnlich (+ *dat.*) similar 7

die **Ähnlichkeit, -en** similarity

die **Ahnung, -en** hunch, idea; **keine ~** no idea 11

akzepta'bel acceptable

akzeptie'ren to accept 10

alle all 7

allein' alone 6

alles everything 4

allgemein general 8

die **Alltagssprache** colloquial speech

die **Alpen** *(pl.)* Alps 6

das **Alpenland** alpine country

das **Alphabet'** alphabet 1

als (*conj.*) when 11; (*after a comp.*) than 3

also therefore, well, so 1

alt (ä) old 1; **Wie ~ bist du?** How old are you? 1; **Ich bin 19 Jahre ~.** I am 19 years old. 1

das **Alter** (old) age

alternativ' alternative (*adj.*)

die **Alternati've, -n** alternative (noun)

das **Altersheim, -e** retirement home, rest home

die **Altstadt** old part of city or town

(das) **Ame'rika** America 3

der **Amerika'ner, -/**die **Amerika'nerin, -nen** American (person) 3

amerika'nisch American (*adj.*) 3

das **Amt, ⸚er** office; agency

die **Amtssprache, -n** official language

an (+ *acc./dat.*) on; at; to 8

an·bieten, bot an, angeboten to offer

ander (-er, -es, -e) other 3

anderem: unter ~ among other things

anderes: etwas ~ something else, anything else

(sich) ändern to change

anders different(ly) 3

anderswo elsewhere

an·deuten to indicate

der **Anfang, ⸚e** beginning 7

an·fangen (ä), fing an, angefangen to begin 7; **mit [der Arbeit] ~** to begin [(the) work] 7

an·fassen to touch

angebaut (*p.p. of* **an·bauen**) grown (crops)

angenehm pleasant 8

die **Angli'stik** English studies (language and literature) 5

die **Angst, ⸚e** fear 8; **~ haben** to be afraid 8; **~ machen** to cause fear; **~ um** fear for 8

an·kommen, kam an, ist angekommen to arrive 8

an·nehmen (nimmt an), nahm an, angenommen to assume; to accept

an·rufen, rief an, angerufen to call, telephone; **bei [dir] ~** to call [your] home 7

an·sehen (ie), sah an, angesehen to look at, to watch; **ich sehe es mir an** I'll look it over 5

(an)statt' (+ *gen.*) instead of 9

anstrengend strenuous

der **Antrag, ⸚e** application

die **Antwort, -en** answer; **die ~ auf eine Frage** the answer to a question 12

antworten [auf eine Frage] to answer [a question] (*as in* **ich antworte auf die Frage**) 9; (+ *dat. of person*) to answer (*as in* **ich antworte der Frau**) 9

die **Anzeige, -n** advertisement 13

an·zeigen to indicate, show

(sich [acc.]) an·ziehen, zog an, angezogen to dress 10; **ich ziehe mich an** I get dressed 10

(sich [dat.]) an·ziehen, zog an, angezogen to put on 10; **ich ziehe mir [die Schuhe] an** I put on [my shoes] 10

der **Anzug, ⸚e** man's suit 7

die **Apothe'ke, -n** pharmacy; **in die ~** to the pharmacy 4

der **Apothe'ker, -/**die **Apothe'kerin, -nen** pharmacist

der **Apparat', -e** apparatus, appliance 10

der **April'** April 3

die **Arbeit, -en** work; (school or academic) paper 5

arbeiten to work; to study 2; **bei [einer Firma] ~** to work at [a company] 2

der **Arbeiter, -/**die **Arbeiterin, -nen** worker

der **Arbeitgeber, -/**die **Arbeitgeberin, -nen** employer 13

der **Arbeitnehmer, -/**die **Arbeitnehmerin, -nen** worker 12

die **Arbeitskräfte** (*pl.*) workers

der **Arbeitslohn, ⸚e** wage

arbeitslos unemployed

die **Arbeitslosigkeit** unemployment 13

der **Arbeitsmarkt, ⸚e** job market

der **Arbeitsplatz, ⸚e** job, position

die **Arbeitsproduktivität** worker productivity

die **Arbeitswelt** work world

die **Arbeitswoche, -n** work week

sich ärgern (über + *acc.*) to feel angry (about) 11

das **Argument'** argument

arm (ä) poor 14

der **Arm, -e** arm 10

die **Armut** poverty, scarcity

das **Aro'ma** aroma

arrangie'ren to arrange

arrogant' arrogant

die **Art, -en** way, manner 8

der **Arti'kel, -** article 5

der **Arzt, ⸚e/**die **Ärztin, -nen** doctor, physician 7

der **Aspekt', -e** aspect

das **Aspirin'** aspirin 4

der **Atem** breath

der **Atlan'tische Ozean** Atlantic Ocean

atmen to breathe 8

die **Atmosphä're** atmosphere

das **Atom'kraftwerk, -e** nuclear power plant

attraktiv' attractive

auch also 2; **ich ~** me, too 2; **~ wenn** even if

auf (+ *acc./dat.*) on; at; to 8; **Auf Wiedersehen.** Good-by. 2; **~ [englisch]** in [English]

auf·bauen to build (up)

die **Aufenthaltserlaubnis** residence permit

die **Aufführung, -en** performance

die **Aufgabe, -n** assignment, task, set of duties 11; **die Hausaufgaben** (*pl.*) homework 11

auf·geben (gibt auf), gab auf, aufgegeben to give up 11

auf·hören (mit) to stop 7; **mit [der Arbeit] ~** to stop [work]

auf·machen to open 5
auf·nehmen (nimmt auf), nahm auf, aufgenommen to accept, to take in
auf·passen to watch out; ~ (**auf** + *acc.*) to take care of 11
auf·räumen to straighten up (a room) 9
auf·stehen, stand auf, ist aufgestanden to stand up 5; to get up
auf·wachsen, wuchs auf, ist aufgewachsen to grow up
auf·wärmen to warm up
das **Auge, -n** eye 10
der **August'** August 3
aus (+ *dat.*) out of; from (is a native of) 6
der **Ausbau** enlargement, improvement
aus·bauen to expand
aus·bilden to train, educate 11
die **Ausbildung** training, development
der **Ausdruck, ⁼e** expression
auseinan'der apart, separate; **sich ~ leben** to drift apart, grow apart
der **Ausflug, ⁼e** excursion
aus·füllen to fill out, complete (a form)
die **Ausgangsbasis** starting point
aus·geben (i), gab aus, ausgegeben to spend (money)
ausgesprochen definitely, clearly
ausgezeich'net excellent(ly) 7
aus·kommen, kam aus, ist ausgekommen to get by (manage)
das **Ausland** foreign country; **ins ~ gehen** to go abroad
der **Ausländer, -**/die **Ausländerin, -nen** foreigner 8
ausländisch foreign
die **Ausnahme, -n** exception
aus·schließen, schloß aus, ausgeschlossen to exclude
aus·sehen (ie), sah aus, ausgesehen to look like, seem 7
der **Außenhandel** foreign trade 13

die **Außenpolitik** foreign policy
außer (+ *dat.*) besides, except for 6
außerdem in addition; as well 7
das **Äußere** external appearance
außergewöhnlich extraordinary
außerhalb (+ *gen.*) outside of, beyond
die **Äußerlichkeit, -en** superficiality
äußern to express
die **Aussprache** pronunciation
aus·steigen, stieg aus, ist ausgestiegen to get off (a vehicle)
der **Austauschstudent, -en, -en**/die **Austauschstudentin, -nen** exchange student
(das) **Austra'lien** Australia
aus·trinken, trank aus, ausgetrunken to drink up
ausverkauft sold out 14
die **Auswahl** choice
(sich [+ *acc.*]) **aus·ziehen, zog aus, ausgezogen** to get undressed; **Ich ziehe mich aus.** I get undressed. 10
(sich [+ *dat.*]) **aus·ziehen, zog aus, ausgezogen** to take off; **Ich ziehe mir [die Schuhe] aus.** I take off [my shoes]. 10
das **Auto, -s** automobile, car 6
die **Autobahn, -en** freeway, expressway 8
das **Autokennzeichen, -** abbreviation for country of registry for automobiles
automa'tisch automatic(ally)
autonom' autonomous
die **Autonomie'** autonomy
der **Autor, -en**/die **Autorin, -nen** author
der/die **Azu'bi, -s** (*abbr. for* der/die **Auszubildende**) apprentice

das **Baby, -s** baby
der **Bach, ⁼e** brook
backen, backte, gebacken to bake 7
der **Bäcker, -**/die **Bäckerin, -nen** baker 4; **beim Bäcker** at the bakery 4; **zum Bäcker** to the bakery 4
die **Bäckerei', -en** bakery 4
der **Backstein** brick
das **Bad, ⁼er** bath; bathroom 9
baden to bathe 7
das **Baden** bathing
die **Badewanne, -n** bathtub
das **Badezimmer, -** bathroom 9
das **BAFöG = das Bundesausbildungsförderungsgesetz** national law to support education in Germany
die **Bahn, -en** train, railroad 6
der **Bahnhof, ⁼e** train station 8
bald (eher, ehest-) soon 3
der **Balkon', -s** balcony 9
der **Ball, ⁼e** ball
die **Bana'ne, -n** banana
die **Band, -s** (music) band 12
die **Bank, -en** bank 11
basie'ren (auf + *dat.*) to be based (on)
die **Basis, Basen** basis
der **Basketball** basketball 2
basteln to tinker (with), to work at a hobby 12
die **Batterie', -n** battery
der **Bau, -ten** building, construction
bauen to build 9
der **Bauer, -n, -n**/die **Bäuerin, -nen** farmer, 12
das **Bauernhaus, ⁼er** farmhouse 12
der **Baum, ⁼e** tree 8
die **Baumwolle** cotton 7
der **Baustein, -e** building block
(das) **Bayern** Bavaria
der **Beam'te** (*noun decl. like adj.*) (government) official (*m.*)
die **Beam'tin, -nen** (government) official (*f.*)
beant'worten to answer
bedau'erlich regrettable
bedeckt' overcast
bedeu'ten to mean, imply; **Was bedeutet das?** What does that mean? 8; to indicate
bedeu'tend significant

die **Bedeu'tung, -en** meaning, significance 14

sich **bedie'nen** to serve oneself

die **Bedin'gung, -en** condition

beein'flussen to influence 3

begei'stert enthusiastic

begin'nen, begann, begonnen to begin 10; **mit [der Arbeit]** ~ to begin [(the) work]

begrei'fen, begriff, begriffen to grasp, understand

begrün'den to support; give reasons for

die **Begrü'ßung, -en** greeting

behaup'ten to declare

bei (+ *dat.*) at (a place of business); with (at the home of) 4; ~ **uns** in our country; ~ **[dir]** at [your] place 6; near (in the proximity of) 6; while, during (*indicates a situation*); **beim Fernsehen** while watching TV

beide both 5

beides both 6

das **Bein, -e** leg 10

das **Beispiel, -e** example 3; **zum** ~ (*abbrev.* z.B.) for example 3

bei·treten (tritt bei), trat bei, ist beigetreten to join, become a member of

bekannt' familiar; well known 7

der/die **Bekann'te** (*noun declined like adj.*) acquaintance 7

die **Bekannt'schaft, -en** acquaintance

(das) **Belgien** Belgium

bekom'men, bekam, bekommen to receive 4

beliebt' favorite; popular

bemer'ken to notice 7

sich **beneh'men (benimmt), benahm, benommen** to behave oneself

benö'tigt needed, required

benut'zen to use 8

das **Benzin'** gasoline, fuel

beob'achten to observe 8

bequem' comfortable

der **Berg, -e** mountain 6

bergsteigen mountain climbing; ~ **gehen** to go mountain climbing

der **Bergsteiger, -/die Bergsteigerin, -nen** mountain climber

der **Bericht', -e** report 8

berich'ten to report

der **Beruf', -e** profession, occupation 11

die **Berufs'schule, -n** vocational school

berufs'tätig employed (in a profession) 11

(sich) **beschäf'tigen (mit)** to occupy (oneself) (with), to keep busy 13

beschäf'tigt sein to be busy 13

beschlie'ßen, beschloß, beschlossen to decide

beschrei'ben, beschrieb, beschrieben to describe 10

die **Beschrei'bung, -en** description

der **Besitz'** property

beson'der- particular 6; **nichts Besonderes** nothing special 2

beson'ders especially, particularly 4

bespre'chen (i), besprach, besprochen to discuss, talk about

besser (*comp. of* **gut**) better 4

(die) **Besserung: (Ich wünsche dir) gute** ~. I wish you a speedy recovery. Get well soon.

bestätigen to confirm

beste'hen, bestand, bestanden to exist

bestel'len to order 5

bestim'mend determining

bestimmt' certain(ly) 3

die **Bestimmt'heit** certainty

der **Besuch', -e** visit 4; ~ **haben** to have company 4

besu'chen to visit 12

der **Besu'cher, -/die Besu'cherin, -nen** visitor, guest 9

beto'nen to reinforce, emphasize

der **Betrieb', -e** company

das **Bett, -en** bed 1; **zu (ins)** ~ **gehen** to go to bed

die **Bevöl'kerung** population

bevor' (*conj.*) before

sich **bewe'gen** to move

die **Bewe'gung, -en** movement

der **Bewoh'ner, -/die Bewoh'nerin, -nen** inhabitant, resident

bewölkt' cloudy

der **Bewer'ber, -/die Bewer'berin, -nen** applicant

bewußt' aware of, conscious

bezah'len to pay (for) 4

die **Bezie'hung, -en** relation(ship)

bezie'hungsweise (*abbr.* **bzw.**) that is to say; respectively

der **Bezirk', -e** district

die **Bibliothek', -en** library 2; **in der** ~ in/at the library 2

das **Bier** beer 4

das **Bierchen** small glass of beer

der **Biergarten, ÷** beer garden 8

das **Bild, -er** picture; photograph; image 1

das **Bilderbuch, ÷er** picture book

billig cheap 4

binden, band, gebunden to tie 12

der **Bio-Laden, ÷** health food store

die **Biologie'** biology

biolo'gisch biological(ly)

bis (+ *acc.*) until 2; ~ **zu** up to; ~ **dann** see you then 2

bisher' until now 12

bißchen: ein ~ a little 5

bitte please; you're welcome 1; ~ **schön.** You're welcome. ~ **sehr.** (*said when handing someone something*) Here you are; **Wie** ~? I beg your pardon. 1

bitten, bat, gebeten (+ **um**) to request, ask (for) 6

blaß pale 10

blau blue 1

bleiben, blieb, ist geblieben to remain, to stay 3

der **Bleistift, -e** pencil 1
der **Blick, -e** glance, look; view
der **Blitz** lightning
blond blond
bloß only, mere(ly) 14
die **Blume, -n** flower 4
das **Blumengeschäft, -e** flower shop
der **Blumenmarkt** flower market 4
die **Bluse, -n** blouse 7
der **Boden, ⸚** floor
der **Bodensee** Lake Constance
bombardie'ren to bombard
die **Börse** stock exchange
böse angry 8; **Sei mir nicht ~.** Don't be angry with me. 8
die **Botschaft, -en** message; embassy
brauchen to need 4
braun brown 1
die **BRD (= Bundesrepublik Deutschland)** Federal Republic of Germany 3
brechen (i), brach, gebrochen to break
der **Brei** porridge; stew
breit wide
der **Brief, -e** letter 8
die **Briefmarke, -n** postage stamp
bringen, brachte, gebracht to bring 5
das **Brot, -e** bread; sandwich 4
das **Brötchen, -** hard-crusted (breakfast) roll 4
die **Brücke, -n** bridge
der **Bruder, ⸚** brother 5
brüllen to bawl
das **Buch, ⸚er** book 1
das **Bücherregal, -e** bookcase 1
die **Büchertasche, -n** book bag 1
die **Buchhandlung, -en** bookstore 4
buchstabie'ren to spell
bummeln to stroll
der **Bund** federation
das **Bündel, -** bundel
der **Bundeskanzler, -** Federal Chancellor

(das) **Bundesland** federal state in Germany and Austria
die **Bundespost** German Federal Postal Service
der **Bundespräsident, -en, -en/die Bundespräsidentin, -nen** President of the Federal Republic
die **Bundesrepublik Deutschland (BRD)** Federal Republic of Germany (FRG) 3
der **Bundesstaat, -en** federal state (in the U.S.A.)
der **Bundestag** lower house of Parliament in Germany
bunt colorful
die **Burg, -en** castle
der **Bürger, -/die Bürgerin, -nen** citizen 10
die **Bürgerinitiative, -n** citizens' action group, grassroots movement 12
das **Büro', -s** office 6
die **Bürokratie'** bureaucracy
der **Bus, -se** bus 6
die **Butter** butter 4
das **Butterbrot** bread-and-butter sandwich
bzw. (= bezie'hungsweise) that is to say; respectively

das **Café', -s** café 5
campen to camp
das **Camping** camping
der **Campus** campus
die **CD, -s (Compact Disk)** compact disk 9
der **CD-Spieler, -** (also der **CD-Player, -**) CD player 9
CH (= Confoederatio Helvetica) automobile symbol for Switzerland
die **Chance, -n** opportunity, chance
die **Chancengleichheit** equal opportunity
der **Charak'ter** character
der **Chef, -s/die Chefin, -nen** boss 11

der **Chefarzt, ⸚e/die Chefärztin, -nen** chief [doctor] of staff
die **Chemie'** chemistry 5
chemie'frei free of chemicals
die **Chemika'lien** (*pl.*) chemicals
chemisch chemical
der **Chor, ⸚e** choir
circa (*abbr.* **ca.**) approximately
das **Cockpit, -s** cockpit
die **Cola** cola drink 7
das **College, -s** college
die **Comics** (*pl.*) comics
der **Compu'ter, -** computer 1; **mit dem ~ arbeiten** to work (at) a computer 11
ČS automobile symbol for Czechoslovakia

D automobile symbol for Germany
da there 1; (*conj.*) since, because 9; then 10
das **Dach, ⸚er** roof 9
der **Dachboden, ⸚** attic 9
dadurch thereby, by this means
dafür' for that
dafür', da'für for that; but instead
dage'gen against it; on the other hand
daher therefore, for that reason 5
dahin' there (to that place)
damals at that time
damit' so that 12
danach' after that
(das) **Dänemark** Denmark
der **Dank** thanks 9; **vielen ~** many thanks, thanks a lot 9
danke thanks 1; **Danke sehr.** Thank you very much.
danken (+ *dat. of person*) to thank 6
dann then 1
darauf' on
darf (dürfen): Was darf es sein? What would you like?
darin' in (it)
das **Darlehen, -** loan
dar·stellen to present
darü'ber over, above
darü'ber hinaus' beyond that

darum therefore, for that reason

das that; the (*n.*) 1

daß (*conj.*) that 6

das **Datum**, *pl.* **Daten** date

dauerhaft permanent

dauern to last, to require time 14; **dauernd** continuously

da'zu for that, to that

dazu' in addition, with it

dazwi'schen in between

die **DDR** (= **Deutsche Demokra'tische Republik'**) German Democratic Republic 14

dein your (*fam. sg.*) 1

dekorie'ren to decorate 7

die **Demokratie'**, **-n** democracy 14

die **Demonstration'**, **-en** (*abbr.* **Demo**) demonstration

demonstrie'ren to demonstrate

denken, dachte, gedacht (**an** + *acc.*) to think (of), believe 3

denn (*conj.*) because, for 3; (*flavoring particle adding emphasis to questions*) 4

deprimiert' depressed

der the (*m.*) 1

deshalb therefore 5

deswegen therefore, for that reason

deutsch German (*adj.*) 3

(das) **Deutsch** German (language) 2; ~ **machen** to do German (homework) 5; **auf deutsch** in German; **ich mache** ~ I'm doing German homework 2

die **Deutsche Demokra'tische Republik'** (**DDR**) German Democratic Republic (GDR) 14

der/die **Deutsche** (*noun decl. like adj.*) German person 3

(das) **Deutschland** Germany 3

deutschsprachig German-speaking

der **Dezem'ber** December 3

d.h. = **das heißt** i.e., that is

der **Dialekt'**, **-e** dialect

dicht dense(ly)

die the (*f.*) 1

dienen (+ *dat.*) to serve

der **Dienstag** Tuesday 1

dies (**-er, -es, -e**) this, these 5; the latter

diesmal this time

diktie'ren to dictate

die **Dimension'**, **-en** dimension

das **Ding**, **-e** thing 6

dir (*dat.* of **du**) (to) you 6; **Und dir?** How about you? (*as part of response to* **Wie geht's?**) 2

direkt' direct(ly)

der **Direk'tor, Direkto'ren** (*pl.*)/die **Direkto'rin**, **-nen** director

die **Disket'te**, **-n** diskette 5

die **Diskussion'**, **-en** discussion

DM (= **Deutsche Mark**) unit of currency used in Germany

D-Mark (= **Deutsche Mark**) German mark

doch (*flavoring particle*) after all, indeed 4; Yes, of course; on the contrary (*response to negative statement or question*) 4

der **Dom**, **-e** cathedral

der **Donnerstag** Thursday 1

doof silly, stupid

doppelt double

das **Dorf**, **⁺er** village

dort there 11

drastisch drastic(ally)

draußen outside 8

drin (= **darin**) in it

dringend urgent

das **Drittel**, **-** third

die **Drogerie'**, **-n** drugstore 4

der **Drogeriemarkt**, **⁺e** self-service drugstore

du you (*fam. sg.*) 1; **Du!** Hey! (*used to get someone's attention*) 5

dumm (**ü**) dumb, stupid 2; **etwas Dummes** something dumb 7

die **Dummheit**, **-en** stupidity

dunkel (**dunkler, dunkelst-**) dark 9

durch (+ *acc.*) divided by 1; through 4; by (means of which) 14

durch·arbeiten to work through, to study 5

der **Durchschnitt** average; **im ~** on the average

durch·sehen (**ie**), **sah durch, durchgesehen** to look through; glance over; examine 13

durchsichtig transparent

dürfen (**darf**), **durfte, gedurft** to be permitted or allowed 5

der **Durst** thirst 7; ~ **haben** to be thirsty 7

die **Dusche**, **-n** shower

(sich) **duschen** to shower 10; **Ich dusche. Ich dusche mich.** I take a shower. 10

duzen to use informal address: (**du**)

eben just 5; (*flavoring particle denoting finality*) 5

ebenso just as 12; likewise, the same

echt real, genuine 8; (*slang*) very 6; ~ **toll** really neat

die **Ecke**, **-n** corner 7

effektiv' effective(ly)

die **EG** (*abbr. for* **Europä'ische Gemein'schaft**) EC (European Community)

egal' equal; the same 6; **Das ist mir ~.** It's all the same to me. 6

der **Ehemann**, **⁺er** husband

eher (*comp. of* **bald**) rather, sooner

das **Ei**, **-er** egg 4

die **Eidgenossenschaft** confederation

eigen own 8

eigenartig strange

das **Eigenheim**, **-e** private home

eigentlich actually 5

das **Eigentum** property

der **Eigentümer**, **-**/die **Eigentümerin**, **-nen** owner

ein(e) a, an 2;

einan'der one another 8

eindeutig unequivocal; clear

der **Eindruck**, **⁺e** impression

einfach simple; simply 8

die **Einfachheit** simplicity
ein·fallen (ä), fiel ein, ist eingefallen (+ *dat.*) to occur (in one's mind) 10
das **Einfamilienhaus, ⁼er** single-family home 9
ein·führen to import
einheitlich unified
einige some, several 5
einiges something
ein·kaufen to shop 4
die **Einkaufstasche, -n** shopping bag 4
ein·laden (ä), lud ein, eingeladen to invite 7; to treat 8
die **Einladung, -en** invitation
einmal once, one time 8; **noch ~** again, once more 12; **~ die Woche** once a week 8; **~ in der Woche** once a week 14
ein·packen to pack up
ein·richten to furnish
das **Einsatzgebiet, -e** area of application
ein·schließen, schloß ein, eingeschlossen to include
ein·stecken to pack, to take along
die **Einstellung, -en** attitude
ein·teilen to arrange
einverstanden agreed
die **Einwegflasche, -n** disposable bottle
der **Einwohner, -/die Einwohnerin, -nen** inhabitant 3
das **Einwohnermeldeamt** residence registration office
einzeln single, individual 13
einzig only, sole
das **Eis** ice; ice cream 7
elegant' elegant
der **Elek'triker, -/die Elek'trikerin, -nen** electrician
elek'trisch electrical
der **Elek'troingenieur, -e/die Elek'troingenieurin, -nen** electrical engineer
die **Elek'trotechnik** electrical engineering products
elend miserable
die **Eltern** (*pl.*) parents 5

die **Emanzipation'** emancipation
emanzipie'ren to emancipate
empfeh'len (ie), empfahl, empfohlen to recommend
das **Ende, -n** end, conclusion; **am ~** in/at the end 5
endlich finally 4
die **Energie'** energy
eng close; tight, narrow 6
(das) **England** England 11
(das) **Englisch** English (language) 5; **auf englisch** in English
englisch English (*adj.*)
der **Enkel, -/die Enkelin, -nen** grandson/granddaughter
enorm' enormous(ly)
entde'cken to discover
enteig'net expropriated
die **Entfrem'dung** alienation
entschei'den, entschied, entschieden to decide 13; **sich entscheiden** to make a decision (after reflecting on it) 13
die **Entschei'dung, -en** decision
die **Entschul'digung, -en** excuse; apology 12
Entschul'digung! Excuse me! 12
entste'hen, entstand, ist entstanden to arise, to come about
(sich) **entwi'ckeln** to develop 10
die **Entwi'cklung, -en** development 11
er he; it 1
die **Erbse, -n** pea
die **Erde** earth
das **Erdgeschoß** ground floor 9
das **Ereig'nis, -se** event
erfah'ren (ä), erfuhr, erfahren to come to know
die **Erfah'rung, -en** experience 11
der **Erfolg'** success
erfolg'reich successful
erfül'len to fulfill
die **Erhö'hung, -en** increase
sich **erho'len (von)** to recover (from), recuperate (from) 12
(sich) **erin'nern (an** + *acc.*) to remember [someone or something] 11

die **Erin'nerung, -en** remembrance
sich **erkäl'ten** to catch a cold 10
erkältet: Ich bin ~. I have a cold.
die **Erkäl'tung, -en** cold (illness) 10
erklä'ren to explain 5
die **Erklä'rung, -en** explanation 8
erlau'ben to allow
ernst serious 2; **Ist das dein Ernst?** Are you serious?
errei'chen to reach, attain 11
erschei'nen, erschien, ist erschienen to appear 8
erset'zen to replace
die **Erspar'nisse** (*pl.*) savings
erst only, just, not until 5; first 8; first of all 10; once; **~ einmal** first, sometime
erstaunt' astonished 9
der **Erste Weltkrieg** World War I
erstens first of all
der/die **Erwach'sene** (*noun decl. like adj.*) adult
erwäh'nen to mention
erwar'ten to expect 11
die **Erwei'terung** expansion, extension
erzäh'len (von/ über + *acc.*) to tell (about) 3
die **Erzäh'lung, -en** story, narrative
es it 1; **~ gibt** (+ *acc.*) there is, there are 4
das **Essen** meal; prepared food; eating 5; **~ und Wohnen** board and room
essen (ißt), aß, gegessen to eat 4
der **Eßtisch** dining table
das **Eßzimmer, -** dining room 9
etwa about, approximately 3
etwas some, somewhat 4; **~ anderes** something different 8
euch: bei ~ in your country
euer (*fam. pl.*) your 3
(das) **Euro'pa** Europe 3
der **Europä'er, -/die Europä'erin, -nen** European (person)

die **Europä'ische Gemein'schaft (EG)** European Community (EC)

eventuell' possibly

das **Exa'men, -** comprehensive examination 5

existie'ren to exist

experimentie'ren to experiment

der **Export'** export

exportie'ren to export

der **Extrakt', -e** extract

F automobile symbol for France

die **Fabrik', -en** factory 14

das **Fach, ̈er** (academic) subject 5

das **Fachgeschäft, -e** specialty store

fahren (ä), fuhr, ist gefahren to drive; to travel; **mit [dem Auto] ~** to go by [car] 6

der **Fahrer, -/die Fahrerin, -nen** driver 12

das **Fahrrad, ̈er** bicycle 6

die **Fahrschule** driving school

der **Fahrschulkurs** driving-school course

die **Fahrt, -en** trip 8

die **Fakten** (*pl.*) facts

fallen (ä), fiel, ist gefallen to fall

falsch wrong 7

die **Fami'lie, -n** family 5

die **Farbe, -n** color; **Welche ~ hat . . . ?** What color is . . . ? 1

der **Farbfernseher, -** color television (set)

fast almost 6

faszinie'rend fascinating

faul lazy 2

faulenzen to lounge around, be idle 12

der **Februar** February 3

fehlen (+ *dat.*) to lack; be absent or missing 14

die **Fehlkonstruktion** faulty construction

die **Feier, -n** party, celebration

feiern to celebrate 7

der **Feiertag, -e** holiday

fein fine 8

das **Fenster, -** window 1

der **Fensterladen, ̈** shutter

die **Ferien** (*pl.*) vacation 6; **in den ~** on vacation, during vacation 6

die **Ferienreise** vacation trip

das **Fernsehen** television 8

fern·sehen (ie), sah fern, ferngesehen to watch TV 8

der **Fernseher, -** TV (set) 1

die **Fernsehsendung, -en** TV program

fertig finished; ready 5

fest firm

das **Fest, -e** celebration; feast; party 9

fest·halten (ä), hielt fest, festgehalten to hold tight

die **Feststimmung** festive spirit

die **Fete, -n** party

fett thick, fat

das **Feuerwerk** fireworks

das **Fieber** fever 10

die **Figur', -en** figure; statue

der **Film, -e** film, movie 5

der **Filmemacher, -/die Filmemacherin, -nen** film maker

finanziell' financial(ly)

finden, fand, gefunden to find 4; **Wie ~ du das?** What do you think of that? How do you like that ? 4

der **Finger, -** finger 10

finster dark

die **Firma, *pl.* Firmen** company 6

der **Fisch, -e** fish 4

der **Fischmann, ̈er /die Fischfrau, -en** fish seller

fit fit, trim

fixiert' fixated

FL automobile symbol for Liechtenstein

das **Flachland** lowland

die **Flasche, -n** bottle 9; **eine ~ Mineralwasser** a bottle of mineral water

das **Fleisch** meat 4

der **Fleiß** diligence

fleißig industrious, hard-working 2

fliegen, flog, ist geflogen to fly 6

fliehen, floh, ist geflohen to flee

fließen, floß, ist geflossen to flow

fließend fluent(ly)

flirten to flirt

der **Flüchtling, -e** refugee

der **Flughafen, ̈** airport 8

die **Flugkarte, -n** plane ticket

das **Flugzeug, -e** airplane 6

der **Flur, -e** entrance (hall) 9

der **Fluß, *pl.* Flüsse** river

der **Föderalis'mus** federalism

folgen, ist gefolgt (+ *dat.*) to follow 12

folgend following

die **Form, -en** form

das **Formular', -e** form

die **Forschung** research

fort·fahren (ä), fuhr fort, ist fortgefahren to continue

der **Fotoapparat, -e** camera 13

fotografie'ren to photograph 12

die **Frage, -n** question 5; **eine Frage stellen** to ask a question

fragen to ask 4

fraglich questionable

der **Franken** Swiss unit of currency

(das) **Frankreich** France

der **Franzose, -n, -n/die Französin, -nen** Frenchman/Frenchwoman

franzö'sisch French (*adj.*) 12

(das) **Franzö'sisch** French (language)

die **Frau, -en** woman; **Frau** (*term of address for adult women*) Mrs.; Ms. 1

der/die **Frauenbeauftragte, -n** (*noun declined like adj.*) commissioner for women's affairs

die **Frauenbewegung** women's movement

das **Frauenbild** image of women

das **Frauenhaus, ̈er** women's shelter

das **Fräulein, -** term of address for very young unmarried women; also for waitress 1

frei free; frank, open 5

das Freie the open; **im Freien** out in the open

die Freiheit, -en freedom

der Freitag Friday 1

die Freizeit leisure time 12

fremd foreign

der Fremdenverkehr tourism

die Fremdsprache, -n foreign language

sich freuen (über + acc.) to be pleased (about); ~ **auf** (+ acc.) to look forward to

der Freund, -e/die Freundin, -nen friend 4

freundlich friendly 2

die Freundlichkeit friendliness

frisch fresh 4

froh glad, happy 2

früh early 6

früher formerly 13

das Frühjahr spring

der Frühling spring 3

das Frühstück, -e breakfast 4; **zum ~** for breakfast 4

frühstücken to eat breakfast

sich fühlen to feel [ill, well, etc.] 10

führen to lead 9

fundamental' fundamental

die Funktion', -en function

funktionie'ren to function; **funktionie'rend** functioning

für (+ acc.) for 3

furchtbar horrible, horribly 2

(sich) fürchten (vor + dat.) to fear, be afraid (of)

fürchterlich horrible, horribly 10

der Fuß, -̈e foot 6; **zu ~** on foot 6

der Fußball soccer 2

der Fußgänger, -/die Fußgängerin, -nen pedestrian

die Fußgängerzone, -n pedestrian mall 8

die Gabel, -n fork 8

ganz complete, whole; very; ~ **gut** not bad, O.K. 2; ~ **schön** really quite pretty; ~ **schön blaß** pretty pale 10

das Ganze the whole thing

gar: ~ **nicht** not at all 9

die Gara'ge, -n garage 9

garantie'ren to guarantee

garantiert' guaranteed

der Garten, -̈ garden 1

die Gasse, -n small, narrow street

der Gast, -̈e guest 7

der Gastarbeiter, -/die Gastarbeiterin, -nen foreign worker

das Gasthaus, -̈er restaurant, pub, bar

die Gaststätte restaurant, pub, bar 12

geben (i), gab, gegeben to give 4; **es gibt** (+ acc.) there is, there are 4; **Was gibt's zum Essen?** What's for lunch? 4; **Was gibt's Neues?** What's new? 13

das Gebiet', -e area, field 13

gebrau'chen to use 9

gebraucht' used, second-hand

gebraut' (p.p. of brauen) brewed

der Geburts'tag, -e birthday 3; **zum ~** for one's birthday 3; **Wann hast du ~?** When is your birthday? 3 **Herzlichen Glückwunsch zum ~!** Happy Birthday! 9

die Geburts'tagsfeier birthday celebration

die Geduld' patience 11

gefähr'lich dangerous 11

gefal'len (ä), gefiel, gefallen (+ dat.) to please; to be pleasing (to) 7

der Gefrier'schrank, -̈e freezer 13

das Gefühl', -e feeling 8

gegen (+ acc.) against 4; ~ **Ende des Jahres** around the end of the year

gegenü'ber (+ dat.) opposite; on the opposite side; opposed to; in relation to

der Gegner, -/die Gegnerin, -nen opponent

das Gehalt', -̈er salary

gehen, ging, ist gegangen to go 2; **Es geht (nicht).** It will (it won't) do, it's (not) O.K. 2; It's (not) possible. 3; **Mir geht's schlecht.** I'm not well.; **Wie geht es Ihnen?** How are you? (formal) 2; **Wie geht's?** How are you? (informal) 2; **Geht das?** (Is it) OK? 6

gehö'ren (+ dat.) to belong to 6

gelb yellow 1

das Geld money 4

die Gele'genheit, -en opportunity

gelernt' skilled, trained

gelten (i), galt, gegolten to be worth, valid; prevail

die Gemein'de, -n community

das Gemü'se vegetable 4

gemüt'lich comfortable, informal

genau' exact(ly), that's right; careful 5

genau'so exactly (as)

Genf Geneva

genug' enough 4

die Geographie' geography

geopolitisch geopolitical

gera'de just; straight 7

die Gera'nien (pl.) geraniums

das Gerät', -e appliance; tool; utensil 9

geräu'chert smoked

die Germani'stik German studies (language and literature) 5

gern (lieber, liebst-) gladly, willingly; used with verbs to indicate liking for, as in **Ich spiele gern Tennis.** I like to play tennis. 2; ~ **haben** to like, as in **Ich habe sie ~.** I like her. 4

gesamt' whole, entire

das Geschäft', -e store; business 7

die Geschäfts'frau, -en businesswoman 11

der Geschäfts'mann, Geschäfts'-leute businessman 11

das Geschenk', -e present, gift 9

die Geschich'te, -n story; history 5

geschicht'lich historic(al)

der **Geschichts'lehrer, -/**die
   Geschichts'lehrerin, -nen
   history teacher
das **Geschirr'**   dishes 9
der **Geschirr'spüler, -**   dishwasher
   9
der **Geschmack'**   taste
die **Geschwi'ster** (*pl.*)   brothers
   and sisters 5
die **Gesell'schaft, -en**   society;
   company
das **Gesetz', -e**   law
das **Gesicht', -er**   face 10
das **Gespräch', -e**   conversation 7
gespannt'   to be in suspense; to
   wonder about; to be anxious
   to know 14
gestern   yesterday 3; **~ abend**
   last night 7
gesund'   healthy 7
die **Gesund'heit**   health 7
das **Gesund'heitsamt**   public
   health office
geteilt' (durch)   divided (by) 1
das **Getränk', -e**   drink, beverage
die **Gewalt'**   violence, force
gewal'tig   enormous
die **Gewerk'schaft, -en**   trade
   union 13
gewin'nen, gewann, gewonnen
   to win; to acquire
das **Gewit'ter, -**   thunderstorm
sich **gewöh'nen (an** + *acc.*)   to become accustomed (to) 11
gewohnt'   accustomed to
ginge (*subj.* of **gehen**)**: das ~**
   (nicht)   that would (not) be
   possible, that would (not) work
die **Gitar're, -n**   guitar 1
das **Glas, ⸚er**   glass 4
glauben (*dat. of person*)   to believe
   2; **Ich glaube [schon** or **ja/**
   nicht].   I think [so/not]. 2
gleich   same; **~** (+ *dat.*)   similar
   (to) 4; immediately 4
gleichberechtigt   having equal
   rights
die **Gleichberechtigung**   equal
   rights 11

gleichzeitig   simultaneously
die **Glocke, -n**   bell
das **Glück**   luck 5; **viel ~**   good
   luck 5; **~ haben**   to be lucky
   5; **zum ~**   luckily
glücklich   happy
der **Glückwunsch, ⸚e**
   congratulations; **Herzlichen ~**
   (zum Geburtstag)!   Happy
   Birthday! 9
graben (ä), grub, gegraben   to dig
das **Gramm** (*abbr.* **g**)   gram 4
die **Gramma'tik**   grammar
gramma'tisch   grammatical
das **Gras**   grass
gratulie'ren (+ *dat.*)   to congratulate 9; **Ich gratuliere**
   (zum Geburtstag)!   Happy
   Birthday!
grau   gray 1
die **Grenze, -n**   border 6
der **Grenzübergang, ⸚e**   border
   crossing
(das) **Griechenland**   Greece
groß (ö)   large, big; tall (of people)
   1
großartig   first-rate, splendid,
   great 8
die **Großeltern** (*pl.*)   grandparents
   5
die **Großmutter, ⸚**   grandmother
   5
die **Großstadt, ⸚e**   (large) city
der **Großvater, ⸚**   grandfather 5
die **Grube, -n**   hole, ditch
grün   green 1; **ins Grüne**   out
   into the country 12
der **Grund, ⸚e**   reason; basis, back-
   ground; **aus diesem ~**   for
   this reason 12
das **Grundgesetz**   constitution of
   Germany
die **Grundlage, -n**   base, basic element
das **Grundstück, -e**   property (real
   estate); plot of land
die **Grünen** (*pl.*)   environmentalist
   political party in Germany
die **Gruppe, -n**   group 10

die **Grup'penpsychologie'**   group
   psychology
der **Gruß, ⸚e**   greeting
grüßen: Grüß dich.   Hello. (*informal*) 2
die **Gurke, -n**   cucumber
gut (besser, best-)   good, well;
   fine 2; **sei so ~**   be so kind 5;
   ist ~ dran   is well off; **ist ~**
   that's OK 12
Güte: Du meine ~!   Good gracious! Good Heavens! 9
die **Güter** (*pl.*)   goods 13
das **Gymna'sium,** *pl.* **Gymnasien**
   German secondary school 5

H   automobile symbol for Hungary
das **Haar, -e**   hair 10
haben (hat), hatte, gehabt   to
   have 3; **Was hast du?**   What is
   wrong with you? What's the
   matter? 10
der **Hafen, ⸚**   harbor, port
halb   half 2; **halb [zwei]**   half
   past [one], [one-thirty]
halbtags   half-days
die **Hälfte**   half 13; **zur ~**   half;
   eine ~ des Brotes   one half of
   the bread
hallo   hello; hey 2
der **Hals, ⸚e**   throat, neck 10
halten (ä), hielt, gehalten   hold; **~**
   von (+ *dat.*)   to think of, have
   an opinion of 7; **sich fit ~**   to
   keep fit
die **Hand, ⸚e**   hand 10
die **Handarbeit**   manual work
der **Handel**   trade 6
handeln von   to be about
der **Handschuh, -e**   glove 7
die **Handtasche, -n**   handbag,
   purse 7
hängen, hing, (hat) gehangen   to
   be suspended, be hanging 8
hängen, gehängt   to hang, put 8
Haupt . . .   (in compounds)   main
   . . . ; **das Hauptproblem**
   main problem 13

das **Hauptfach, ⁻er** major (subject) 5
die **Hauptstadt, ⁻e** capital (city) 3
das **Haus, ⁻er** house 4; **nach Hause** [to go] home 4; **zu Hause** [to be] at home 6
die **Hausarbeit** housework, chore 9; homework
die **Hausaufgaben** *(pl.)* homework 11
der **Haushalt** household; housekeeping
die **Haut** skin
die **Hautcreme, -s** skin cream
He! Hey! 9; **~ Mann!** Hey, man! 9
die **Hecke, -n** hedge 9
das **Heft, -e** notebook 1
die **Heimat** native land
die **Heirat, -en** marriage 13
heiraten to marry, to get married 13
die **Heiratspolitik** arrangement of marriages for political reasons
heiß hot 3
heißen, hieß, geheißen to be named 1; **Wie heißt du?** What is your name? *(informal)*; **Wie heißen Sie?** What is your name? *(formal)* 1; **Du heißt [Mark], nicht?** Your name is [Mark], isn't it? 1; **das heißt (d.h.)** that is to say (i.e.); **es heißt** it says 13
heiter cheerful; (weather) clear, fair
der **Held, -en, -en**/die **Heldin, -nen** hero/heroine
helfen (i), half, geholfen (+ *dat.*) to help 7; **bei [der Arbeit] ~** to help with [work] 7
hell bright; light (color) 9
das **Hemd, -en** shirt 7
her (to) here 8
die **Heraus'forderung, -en** challenge
der **Herbst** autumn, fall 3; **im ~** in the fall 3
der **Herd, -e** kitchen range 9

herein' into (a building)
herein'·schauen to look in
der **Herr, -n, -en** gentleman; **Herr** Mr. 1
herrschen to prevail; to rule
herum' around 9; **Sie basteln an dem Haus ~.** They're tinkering around on the house.
das **Herz, -ens, -en** heart 10
herzlich warm(ly), cordial(ly); **~ willkommen** welcome
heute today 1; **~ abend** this evening 2; **~ morgen** this morning 2; **~ nachmittag** this afternoon 2
heutig present(-day)
hier here 3
die **Hilfe** help
der **Himmel** sky; heaven; **um Himmels willen** for heaven's sake
hin (to) there 8
hinein' in(to) (*as in* **hinein'gehen**) 13
hin·fahren (ä), fuhr hin, ist hingefahren to drive there
hinter (+ *acc./dat.*) behind, in back of 8
hinterher afterwards
das **Hinterhoffest** courtyard party
histo'risch historic
das **Hobby, -s** hobby 12
hoch (höher, höchst-) high 10; **hoh-** *before nouns, as in* **ein hoher Preis** a high price
das **Hochdeutsch** High German, standard German 10
das **Hochgebirge** high mountains
die **Hochschule, -n** institution of higher learning (e.g. university)
der **Hof, ⁻e** courtyard 12
hoffen (auf + *acc.*) to hope (for) 7
hoffentlich hopefully 3
die **Hoffnung, -en** hope 14
hoffnungslos hopeless 14
höflich polite(ly) 12
holen to get, fetch 5
das **Holz** wood

horchen to listen
hören to hear; listen to 2
der **Hörsaal, Hörsäle** university classroom, lecture hall
die **Hose, -n** pants 7; **die kurze ~** shorts 7
das **Hotel, -s** hotel
das **Huhn, ⁻er** chicken
der **Hund, -e** dog
der **Hunger** hunger 7; **~ bekommen/kriegen** to get hungry 7; **~ haben** to be hungry 7
husten to cough 10
der **Hut, ⁻e** hat 7
das **Hügelland** hilly country

I automobile symbol for Italy
ich I 1; **~ auch** me, too
die **Idee', -n** idea 9
identifizie'ren to identify
die **Identität'** identity
IG-Metall' (IG = Industriegewerkschaft) metal workers' union
Ihnen (*dat. of* **Sie**) (to) you; **und ~?** and you? (*as part of response to* **Wie geht's?**) 2
ihr you (*fam. pl.*) 2; her; their 3
Ihr your (*formal*) 1
der **Imbißstand, ⁻e** snack bar, hot dog stand
die **Immatrikulation'** enrollment (university)
immer always 4; **~ noch** still 5; **noch ~** still 11; **~ wieder** again and again 5; **wie ~** as always 4; **~ wichtiger** increasingly more important 12; **~ mehr** more and more 11
der **Import'** import
importie'ren to import
in (+ *acc./dat.*) in 3; into; to 4
die **Industrie', -n** industry 12; **die Industrie'stadt, ⁻e** industrial city
die **Inflation'** inflation
die **Inflations'rate** rate of inflation

die **Informa'tik** computer science 5

der **Informa'tiker, -/die Informa'tikerin, -nen** computer scientist 11

die **Information'** information

die **Infrastruktur** infrastructure

der **Ingenieur', -e/die Ingenieu'rin, -nen** engineer 11

die **Innenstadt** town or city center

das **Insektizid', -e** insecticide

insgesamt altogether

das **Institut', -e** institute

das **Instrument', -e** instrument

integrie'ren to integrate

intelligent' smart, intelligent 2

interessant' interesting 5

das **Interes'se, -n** interest

(sich) **interessie'ren (für)** to be interested (in) 13

interessiert' sein (an + dat.) to be interested (in)

international' international

das **Interview', -s** interview

investie'ren to invest

intervie'wen to interview

inwiefern' in what way

irgendwann sometime, at some point 10

(das) **Ita'lien** Italy

italie'nisch Italian (adj.)

ja yes 1; (as a flavoring particle) indeed, of course 4

die **Jacke, -n** jacket 7

das **Jahr, -e** year 1; **Ich bin [19] Jahre alt.** I'm [19] years old. 1; **vor [10] Jahren** [10] years ago 10

die **Jahreszeit, -en** season 3

das **Jahrhun'dert, -e** century 10

-jährig -year-old

der **Januar** January 3

(das) **Japan** Japan

jaulen to howl

der **Jazz** jazz

je: O ~! Oh my!

die **Jeans** (pl.) jeans 7

jed- (er, es, e) each; every; everyone 5

jedoch' nonetheless, however

jemand someone, anyone 7

jen- (er, es, e) that; the former

jetzt now 3

der **Job, -s** job 5

jobben (colloq.) to have a temporary job (e.g., a summer job) 12

das **Jogging** jogging, running 12

der **Journalist', -en, -en/die Journali'stin, -nen** journalist, reporter 13

die **Jugend** youth 12

die **Jugendherberge, -n** youth hostel

der/die **Jugendliche** (noun decl. like adj.) young person 12

(das) **Jugosla'wien** Yugoslavia

der **Juli** July 3

jung (ü) young 5

der **Junge, -n, -n** boy 1

der **Juni** June 3

der **Jurist', -en, -en/die Juri'stin, -nen** lawyer 11

der **Kaffee** coffee 4; **zum ~** for (afternoon) coffee 7

das **Kaffeehaus, ⸚er** coffee house

die **Kaffeemaschine, -n** coffee machine

kalt (ä) cold 3

die **Kamera, -s** camera

die **Kamil'le** camomile

der **Kamm, ⸚e** comb 4

(sich) **kämmen** to comb 10; **Ich kämme mich./Ich kämme mir die Haare.** I comb my hair. 10

der **Kampf, ⸚e** fight, battle

kämpfen to fight

(das) **Kanada** Canada

der **Kana'dier, -/die Kana'dierin, -nen** Canadian (person)

der **Kanton', -e** canton

die **Kapel'le, -n** chapel; band, orchestra

das **Kapital'** capital, funds, assets

das **Kapi'tel, -** chapter

kaputt' broken; exhausted (slang) 6

der **Karrie'remacher, -/die Karrie'remacherin, -nen** (pronounced Ka-ri-e'-re) person interested only in a career

die **Karte, -n** card; postcard 2; die **Karten** (pl.) playing cards 2; ticket 14; **Karten spielen** to play cards

die **Kartof'fel, -n** potato 4

der **Karton', -s** cardboard box

der **Käse** cheese 4

die **Käserei'** cheese dairy

die **Kasset'te, -n** (tape) cassette 9

das **Kasset'tendeck, -s** cassette deck 9

der **Kasset'tenrecorder** cassette recorder 9

die **Katze, -n** cat

der **Kauf, ⸚e** purchase

kaufen to buy 4

das **Kaufhaus, ⸚er** department store 4

der **Kaufmann, -leute/die Kauffrau, -en** merchant 13

kaum hardly 5

kein not a, not any 4; **~ ... mehr** no more . . . 4

der **Keller, -** basement 9

der **Kellner, -/die Kellnerin, -nen** waiter/waitress

kennen, kannte, gekannt to know [people, places, or things] 4

kennen·lernen to get to know, make the acquaintance of 5

die **Kerze, -n** candle

die **Kfz-Steuer, -n** automobile tax

das **Kilo(gramm)'** (abbr. **kg**) kilo(gram) 4

der **Kilome'ter, -** kilometer 3

das **Kind, -er** child 1

das **Kinderbuch, ⸚er** children's book

der **Kindergarten, ⸚** kindergarten, nursery school

das **Kindergeld** government subsidy for children
die **Kinderkrippe** day nursery
das **Kino, -s** movie theater; **ins ~** to the movies 2
die **Kirche, -n** church
das **Kissen, -** pillow
klappen to slam
klar clear; of course; naturally 5
die **Klarinet'te, -n** clarinet
die **Klasse, -n** class 10; die **Deutschklasse** German class 10
klasse! first-rate, great!
das **Klassenzimmer, -** classroom
der **Klassiker, -** author of a standard or classic work
klassisch classic(al) 8
die **Klausur', -en** test 5; **eine ~ schreiben** to take a test
das **Klavier', -e** piano 14
das **Kleid, -er** dress; (pl.) clothing 7
die **Kleidung** clothing 7
klein small; short (of people) 1
die **Kleinigkeit, -en** detail, trifle
die **Kleinkinder** (pl.) small children, toddlers
die **Kleinstadt, ⁼e** small town
das **Klima** climate 3
die **Kneipe, -n** pub, bar 8
der **Koch, ⁼e**/die **Köchin, -nen** cook
das **Kochbuch, ⁼er** cookbook
kochen to cook 4
der **Koffer, -** suitcase
die **Kohle, -n** coal
Köln Cologne
der **Kolle'ge, -n, -n**/die **Kolle'gin, -nen** colleague 11
kommen, kam, ist gekommen to come 2; **~ auf** to come up to
der **Kommentar', -e** commentary
kommentie'ren to comment
komplett' complete
kompliziert' complicated
die **Komponen'te, -n** component

der **Komponist', -en, -en**/die **Komponi'stin, -nen** composer 12
die **Konfession', -en** creed, confession
der **Konflikt', -e** conflict
konkurrenz'fähig able to compete
konkurrie'ren to compete 10
können (kann), konnte, gekonnt can, to be able to 5; **Ich kann [Deutsch].** I know [German].
konservativ' conservative
das **Konservie'rungsmittel** preservative
konspirie'ren to conspire
der **Konsum'** consumption
der **Kontakt', -e** contact 6
kontakt'freudig able to make friends easily
kontrollie'ren to control
das **Konzept', -e** concept; rough copy
das **Konzert', -e** concert; concerto 14
der **Kopf, ⁼e** head 10
die **Kopfschmerzen** (pl.) headache 4
kosten to cost 7
das **Kostüm', -e** costume; woman's suit
die **Kraft, ⁼e** strength; power; force 13
das **Kraftfahrzeug** (abbr. **Kfz**) automobile
der **Kraftfahrzeugmechaniker, -**/die **Kraftfahrzeugmechanikerin, -nen** auto mechanic
krank (ä) ill, sick 2
das **Krankenhaus, ⁼er** hospital
die **Krankenkasse** health insurance
der **Krankenpfleger, -**/die **Krankenpfegerin, -nen** nurse
die **Krankenschwester, -n** nurse (female) 11
der **Krankenwagen** ambulance
die **Krankheit, -en** illness 10
der **Kreis, -e** circle 14
das **Kreuz, -e** cross

der **Krieg, -e** war 6
kriegen to get, obtain 7
der **Krimi, -s** mystery (novel or film) 5
die **Krise** crisis
die **Kritik', -en** criticism; review
kritisch critical
kritisie'ren to criticize 11
die **Küche, -n** kitchen 9
der **Kuchen, -** cake 4
die **Küchenmaschine, -n** mixer and food processor combined 9
der **Kugelschreiber, -** (der **Kuli, -s** colloq.) ballpoint pen 1
kühl cool 3
der **Kühlschrank, ⁼e** refrigerator 9
der **Kuli, -s** (colloq. for **Kugelschreiber**) ballpoint pen 1
die **Kultur'** culture
kulturell' cultural
sich **kümmern um** to take care of
der **Kunde, -n, -n**/die **Kundin, -nen** customer, client 13
die **Kunst** art; skill
der **Kunstdünger, -** chemical fertilizer
der **Künstler, -**/die **Künstlerin, -nen** artist
künstlich artificial 7
die **Kur** cure (at a spa)
der **Kurs, -e** course 5
kurz (ü) short, brief 6; **vor kurzem** recently 6
die **Kürze** brevity
die **Kurzgeschichte, -n** short story
kürzlich recent(ly)
die **Kusine, -n** cousin (f.) 5

lächeln (über + acc.) to smile (about) 7
lachen to laugh
der **Laden, ⁼** store, shop 4
die **Lage, -n** situation
die **Lampe, -n** lamp 1
das **Land, ⁼er** country; land 3; state (Germany and Austria) 11; **auf dem Lande** in the country; **aufs Land** to the country 12

die **Landkarte, -n** map 6
lang (ä) (*adj.*) long 6
lange (ä) (*adv.*) for a long time 8
langsam slow(ly) 9
längst long ago
langweilig boring 8
der **Lärm** noise 11
lassen (läßt), ließ, gelassen to leave; to let, permit; to have something done 7
(das) **Latein'** Latin
latei'nisch Latin (*adj.*)
der **Lauf** course; **im ~** (+ *gen.*) during the course (of)
laufen (ä), lief, ist gelaufen to run; to go on foot 6
laut loud(ly) 8
die **Lawi'ne, -n** avalanche
leben to live 6; **für sich ~** to keep to oneself
das **Leben, -** life 7
leben'dig lively
der **Lebenslauf** a short biography in narrative form
die **Lebensmittel** (*pl.*) food; groceries 4
der **Lebensstandard** standard of living 10
das **Leberwurstbrot** liverwurst sandwich
lebhaft lively
lecker tasty 7
legen to lay 8
die **Lehre, -n** apprenticeship
der **Lehrer, -/die Lehrerin, -nen** teacher 11
der **Lehrgang** course of instruction
der **Lehrgangsleiter, -/die Lehrgangsleiterin, -nen** course director
leicht easy; light 5
das **Leichtmetall** light metal
leid: (es) tut mir ~ I'm sorry 5
leider unfortunately 3
leihen, lieh, geliehen to lend; to borrow 5
lernen to learn; to study 5
das **Lernziel, -e** learning objective

das **Lesebuch, ⁼er** primer, reader
lesen (ie), las, gelesen to read 5
der **Leserbrief, -e** letter from a reader
das **Lesestück, -e** reading selection
die **Lesung, -en** reading
letzt last 5
die **Leute** (*pl.*) people 4
das **Licht, -er** light
lieb (*adj.*) dear; **Liebe [Barbara], Lieber [Paul] ...** Dear [Barbara], Dear [Paul] (*used at the beginning of a letter*)
die **Liebe** love 5
lieber (*comp. of* **gern**) preferably, rather 10
der **Liebesroman, -e** romance (novel) 5
der **Liebling, -e** favorite; darling 8; die **Lieblingssendung, -en** favorite (TV or radio) program 8
das **Lied, -er** song 8
liefern to deliver
liegen, lag, gelegen to lie; to be situated, located 3
die **Limona'de, -n** soft drink 4
die **Linde, -n** linden or lime tree
links left
der **Lippenstift, -e** lipstick
der **Liter, -** (*abbr.* **l**) liter (= 1.056 U.S. quarts) 4
die **Literatur'** literature 13
die **Litfaßsäule, -n** advertising pillar
live live, *as in* **live Musik**
der **Löffel, -** spoon 8
logisch logical
der **Lohn, ⁼e** wage; reward
sich **lohnen** to be profitable; **Es lohnt sich.** It is worthwhile. 13
die **Lohnfortzahlung** continued payment of wages
lokal' local
los: Was ist ~? What's wrong? 2
lösen to solve 13; to loosen
die **Lösung, -en** solution 13

die **Luft** air 7
die **Lufthansa** German Airline
die **Lust** pleasure, enjoyment 12; **~ haben** to feel like 12; **Ich habe keine ~ zu arbeiten.** I don't feel like working.; **Dazu habe ich keine ~.** I don't feel like it. 12
lustig funny; merry, cheerful 2

machen to do; to make 2; **(es) macht nichts** (it) doesn't matter 8; **Deutsch ~** to do/study German homework 5
die **Macht** power
mag (*present tense of* **mögen**) to like 5; **Das ~ wohl sein.** That may be. 8
das **Mädchen, -** girl 1
der **Magen, ⁼** stomach 10
die **Magenschmerzen** (*pl.*) stomach-ache 10
mahlen, mahlte, gemahlen to grind
der **Mai** May 3; **im ~** in May 3
mal time; times (*in multiplication*) 1; **dreimal** three times; **mal (= einmal)** once, sometime 7; (*flavoring particle that softens a command and leaves the time indefinite*) 8
das **Mal, -e** time 12; **zum ersten ~** for the first time
malen to paint 12
man one, people, (*impersonal* you) 1
manch (-er, -es, -e) many a (*sg.*); some (*pl.*) 5
manchmal sometimes 4
der **Mann, ⁼er** man; husband 1
die **Männerstimme, -n** man's voice
männlich masculine
die **Mannschaft, -en** team
der **Mantel, ⁼** coat
die **Mark** mark; die **Deutsche ~** (basic monetary unit in Germany) 4
der **Markt, ⁼e** market 4;

die **Marktwirtschaft** market economy

die **Marmela'de** marmalade, jam 4

der **März** March 3

die **Maschi'ne, -n** machine 13

die **Massa'ge, -n** massage

massiv' massive

der **Maßstab** yardstick, standard

die **Mathe** math

die **Mathematik'** mathematics 5

die **Mauer, -n** wall

die **Maus, ⁼e** mouse

der **Mecha'niker, -/die Mecha'nikerin, -nen** mechanic

das **Medikament', -e** medicine 7

mediterran' Mediterranean

die **Medizin'** medicine

das **Meer, -e** ocean

mehr (*comp. of* **viel**) more 3; **~ oder weniger** more or less 6; **kein... ~** no . . . more 4; **nicht ~** no longer 5

mehrere several

die **Mehrheit** majority

die **Mehrwegflasche, -n** returnable bottle

die **Meile, -n** mile

mein my 1

meinen to mean; to think, have an opinion 8; **Was meinst du?** What do you think? 8

die **Meinung, -en** opinion 9; **[meiner] ~ nach** in [my] opinion 9

meist (= meistens) mostly 6

meist (*sup. of* **viel**) most 5; **die meisten [Leute]** most of [the people] 5

meistens mostly, most of the time 9

der **Meister, -/die Meisterin, -nen** master (craftsperson); foreperson, champion

meistern to master

die **Mensa, -s** *or* **Mensen** university cafeteria 8

Mensch! Man! Wow!

der **Mensch, -en, -en** person, human being 2

die **Mentalität', -en** mentality

merken to notice

merkwürdig strange 7

die **Messe, -n** trade fair

das **Messer, -** knife 8

der **Meter, -** (*abbr.* **m**) meter (= 39.37 inches)

der **Metzger, -** butcher 4; **beim ~** at the butcher shop 4; **zum ~** to the butcher shop 4

die **Metzgerei', -en** butcher shop, meat market 4

die **Miete, -n** rent

mieten to rent 12

die **Mietwohnung, -en** rental apartment

der **Mikrowellenherd, -e** (*also* das **Mikrowellengerät, -e**) microwave oven 9

die **Milch** milk 4

das **Milchglas** frosted glass

mild mild

die **Million', -en** million 3

das **Mineral'wasser** mineral water 7

der **Mini'ster, -/die Mini'sterin, -nen** minister

der **Mini'sterpräsident, -en, -en/die Mini'sterpräsidentin, -nen** Prime Minister

die **Minu'te, -n** minute 2

der **Minu'tenzeiger, -** the minute hand (on a clock or watch)

mir (*dat. of* **ich**) (to) me 5

mischen to mix

die **Mischung, -en** mixture

der **Mist** manure

mit (+ *dat.*) with 5; **~ [dem Auto]** by [car] 6

die **Mitbestimmung** codetermination

mit·bringen, brachte mit, mitgebracht to bring along 5

miteinan'der with one another

mit·fahren (fährt mit), fuhr mit, ist mitgefahren to drive/ride along/with 6

das **Mitglied, -er** member 12

mit·kommen, kam mit, ist mitgekommen to come along/with

mit·machen (bei + a group) to participate in, join in 12

mit·nehmen (nimmt mit), nahm mit, mitgenommen to take along

der **Mittag, -e** noon; **zu ~ essen** to have lunch or midday meal 4

das **Mittagessen** lunch, midday meal 4; **zum ~** for lunch 4

die **Mittel** (*pl.*) means

der **Mittwoch** Wednesday 1

die **Möbel** (*pl.*) furniture; das **Möbelstück** piece of furniture

möchte (*subj. of* **mögen**) would like 5

die **Mode, -n** fashion 14

das **Modell', -e** model

moderie'ren to moderate

modern' modern 9

modernisie'ren to modernize

die **Modernisie'rung** modernization

mögen (mag), mochte, gemocht to like 5; **Das mag wohl sein.** That may well be. 8

möglich possible 11

die **Möglichkeit, -en** possibility

die **Möhre, -n** carrot

der **Moment', -e** moment 12; **im ~** at the moment 12; **Einen Moment, bitte.** Just a minute, please. 12

der **Monat, -e** month 3

der **Montag** Monday 1; **am ~** on Monday 2; **~ in acht Tagen** a week from Monday

morgen tomorrow 3

der **Morgen** morning; **Guten ~.** Good morning. 2; **heute morgen** this morning 2

morgens mornings, every morning 4

der **Motor, Moto'ren** motor

das **Motorboot, -e** motor boat
das **Motorrad, ⁼er** motorcycle 6
müde tired 2
der **Müll** garbage, trash
die **Mülldeponie, -n** garbage
dump
der **Mund, ⁼er** mouth 10; **den ~
halten** to keep one's mouth
shut
munter merry, lively
das **Muse'um,** (*pl.*) **Muse'en**
museum
das **Musical, -s** musical 14
die **Musik'** music 2; **Musik'hören**
listening to music 2
der **Musiker, -/die Musikerin, -nen**
musician 11
das **Musik'instrument, -e** musical
instrument 12
die **Musik'stunde, -n** music lesson
müssen (muß), mußte, gemußt
must, to have to 5
der **Mut** courage
die **Mutter, ⁼** mother 5
die **Mutti, -s** mom 5

na: ~ gut all right 2; well (*interjection*) 5; **~ ja** well now 7;
oh well 12
nach (+ *dat.*) after 2; to (*with cities
and masc. and neuter countries,
e.g.,* **nach Berlin**) 3; **~ Hause**
(to go) home 4
der **Nachbar, -n, -n/die Nachbarin,
-nen** neighbor 3
das **Nachbarland, ⁼er** neighboring
country
nachdem' (*conj.*) after 11
**nach·gehen, ging nach, ist nach-
gegangen** to be slow (*said of a
clock*)
nachher afterwards 5
der **Nachmittag, -e** afternoon 2
nachmittag: heute ~ this afternoon 2
nachmittags afternoons 4
die **Nachricht, -en** a piece of
news; **Nachrichten** (*pl.*)
newscast 8

**nach·schlagen (ä), schlug nach,
nachgeschlagen** to look up
nächst next 5
die **Nacht, ⁼e** night 2; **Gute Nacht**
Good night
der **Nachteil, -e** disadvantage
der **Nachtisch** dessert 7
nah (näher, nächst-) near, close
die **Nähe: in der ~** nearby, in the
vicinity 12
der **Name, -ns, -n** name 5
nämlich after all; that is (to say);
you know; you see 7
die **Nase, -n** nose 10
naß (ä) wet 3
die **Nation', -en** nation
die **Nationalität', -en** nationality
die **Natur', -en** nature 7
natür'lich natural(ly); of course 4
die **Natür'lichkeit** naturalness 7
N.C. = der Numerus clausus
(Latin) limited number of
students admitted to certain
degree programs
der **Nebel** fog, mist
neben (+ *acc./dat.*) beside, next to
8
nebenan' next door
das **Nebenfach, ⁼er** minor (subject) 5
der **Neffe, -n, -n** nephew
**nehmen (nimmt), nahm, genom-
men** to take 4; **Nimmst du
Kaffee?** Are you having coffee? 4
nein no 1
nennen, nannte, genannt to call;
to name 11
der **Nerv, -en** nerve; **Er geht mir
auf die Nerven.** He gets on
my nerves.
nervös' nervous 2
nett nice 2
das **Netz, -e** net
neu new 1; **Was gibt's Neues?**
What's new? 13
(das) **Neubraun'schweig** New
Brunswick
Neues: Was gibt's Neues? What's
new? 13

neugierig curious 9
neulich recently 12
(das) **Neuschott'land** Nova Scotia
neutral' neutral
die **Neutralität'** neutrality
nicht not 2; **nicht?** (*tag question*)
don't you? isn't it? 1; **~
wahr?** isn't that so? 2; **Du
heißt [Monika], nicht?** Your
name is [Monika], isn't it? 1;
~ mehr no longer 5; **~ nur
... sondern auch** not only
. . . but also . . . 6
die **Nichte -n** niece
nichts nothing 2; **(es) macht ~**
(it) doesn't matter 8; **~ Besonderes** nothing special 2
nie never 7
niederdeutsch North German;
low German
die **Niederlande** Netherlands
Niedersachsen Lower Saxony
der **Niederschlag** precipitation
niedrig low 13
niemand no one 7
niesen to drizzle
der **Nieselregen** drizzle
noch still, in addition 3; **~ ein**
another, additional 5; **~ einmal** again, once more 12; **~
immer** still
die **Nonchalance'** nonchalance
der **Norden** north 3
nördlich to the north 3
normal' normal
(das) **Norwegen** Norway
der **Notfall** emergency
die **Notiz', -en** note 5
der **Novem'ber** November 3
die **Numerus clausus** limited
admission to study certain
subjects
die **Nummer, -n** number 1
nun now; well (*interjection*) 7
nur only, nothing but, solely, just
2

O je! Oh my! (*interjection*)
ob (*conj.*) whether, if 6

der **Ober** waiter; **Herr Ober!**
  Waiter!
das **Oberland** highlands
das **Obst** fruit 4
obwohl' (*conj.*) although 6
oder or 2
offen open 8
öffentlich public(ly), openly 13
offiziell' official(ly)
öffnen to open 9
die **Öffnung** opening
oft (ö) often 2
oh oh 2
ohne (+ *acc.*) without 4
das **Ohr, -en** ear 10
ökono'misch economic
der **Okto'ber** October 3
das **Öl** oil
die **Oma, -s** grandma 5
der **Onkel, -** uncle 5
der **Opa, -s** grandpa 5
die **Oper, -n** opera 14
die **Oran'ge, -n** orange 4
der **Oran'gensaft** orange juice 4
das **Orche'ster, -** orchestra 12
die **Ordnung** order 12
die **Organisation', -en**
  organization
sich **orientie'ren** to orient oneself
der **Ort, -e** place (geographical)
  10
ostdeutsch eastern German
der **Osten** east 3
(das) **Österreich** Austria 3
der **Österreicher -/die Österreicherin, -nen** Austrian person 3
österreichisch Austrian (*adj.*)
östlich easterly, eastern
der **Ozean, -e** ocean 3

paar: ein ~ a few, some; **ein
  Paar, -e** a pair 9
das **Paar, -e** pair; couple
das **Papier', -e** paper 1
das **Papier'geschäft, -e** stationery
  store
der **Park, -s** park 8
parken to park
das **Parlament', -e** parliament

parlamenta'risch parliamentary
die **Partei', -en** (political) party
der **Partner, -/die Partnerin, -nen**
  partner
die **Partnerschaft** partnership
partout' at all (French)
die **Party, -s** party
der **Paß**, *pl.* **Pässe** passport
der **Passagier', -e** passenger
passen (+ *dat.*) to fit; to suit 9
passie'ren, ist passiert (+ *dat.*) to
  happen
passiv passive
der **Pensionär' -e/die Pensionärin,
  -nen** retiree
die **Person', -en** person
das **Personal'** personnel
persön'lich personal(ly)
die **Persön'lichkeit** personality
das **Pestizid, -e** pesticide
das **Pfand, ⁻er** (bottle) deposit
pfeifen to whistle
der **Pfennig, -e** 1/100 of a German mark
die **Pflanze, -n** plant 1
pflanzen to plant 12
pflegen to care for; to foster
das **Pferd, -e** horse
das **Pfund** (*abbr.* **Pfd.**) pound
  (= 1.1 U.S. pounds) 4
phanta'stisch fantastic
die **Philosophie'** philosophy 5
die **Physik'** physics 5
das **Picknick, -s** picnic 5
der **Pilot', -en, -en/die
  Pilotin, -nen** pilot
das **Pils** pilsner beer
der **Pkw (der Personenkraftwagen)**
  car, auto
plädie'ren (für) to plead (for)
das **Plakat', -e** poster
der **Plan, ⁻e** plan 6
planen to plan 13
das **Plastik** plastic
die **Platte, -n** record
der **Plattenspieler, -** record player
der **Platz, ⁻e** space; place; seat 5;
  ~ nehmen to take a seat 13
das **Plätzchen** snug little place;
  cookie

platzen to burst
plausi'bel plausible
pleite broke (out of money) 8
plötzlich suddenly 11
plump clumsy; tactless
die **Podiumsdiskussion, -en**
  panel discussion
(das) **Polen** Poland
die **Politik'** politics, political
  science 13
der **Poli'tiker, -/die Poli'tikerin,
  -nen** politician
poli'tisch political 8
die **Polizei'** police 8
die **Pommes frites** (*pl.*) French
  fries 7
das **Pop-Konzert, -e** pop concert
positiv positive
die **Post** post office; postal service; mail 14
das **Poster, -** poster 1
praktisch practical(ly) 9
der **Präsident', -en, -en/die
  Präsiden'tin, -nen** president
die **Präzision'** precision
der **Preis, -e** price 13
prima excellent, fine, great
der **Prinzip', -ien** principle
privat' private 5
die **Privatisie'rung** privatization
pro per; **~ Woche** per week
  11
die **Probe, -n** rehearsal 12
proben to rehearse
probie'ren to try; to taste 7
das **Problem', -e** problem 6
das **Produkt', -e** product
der **Produzent', -en, -en** producer
produzie'ren to produce
professionell' professional(ly)
der **Profes'sor, Professo'ren/die
  Professo'rin, -nen** professor 2
das **Programm', -e** program 8; TV
  channel 8; **das Fernsehprogramm** TV guide
der **Programmie'rer, -/die
  Programmie'rerin, -nen**
  programmer 11
die **Programmier'sprache, -n**
  computer language

das **Programm'kino, -s** art cinema, theater
progressiv' progressive
das **Projekt', -e** project
prost (prosit)! cheers!; **Prost Neujahr!** Happy New Year!
protestie'ren to protest
der/die **Provinziel'le** (*noun declined like adj.*) provincial person
das **Prozent', -e** percent 11
der **Prozeß',** (*pl.*) **Prozesse** process; trial
prüfen to examine; to test
prüfend scrutinizingly
die **Prüfung, -en** examination 5
die **Psychologie'** psychology 5
der **Pulli, -s** sweater 7
der **Punkt, -e** point; period 14
pünktlich punctual(ly) 8
die **Pünktlichkeit** punctuality
die **Puppe, -n** doll
putzen to clean 9; **Ich putze mir die Zähne.** I'm brushing my teeth. 10

der **Quadrat'kilometer, -** (*abbr.* **km²** or **qkm**) square kilometer
die **Qualität', -en** quality
der **Quatsch** nonsense; **Quatsch!** Nonsense! 13
quengeln to whine
quietschen to squeal

die **Rabenmutter** unfit mother
das **Rad, ⁼er** bike (short for **Fahrrad** = bicycle) 6; wheel; **Rad fahren** to bicycle
das **Radio, -s** radio 1
der **Rand, ⁼er** edge; **am Rande** on the edge
(sich) **rasie'ren** to shave 10
das **Rathaus, ⁼er** city hall 14
rationalisie'ren to make improvements that increase efficiency
der **Ratskeller, -** town hall restaurant
der **Rauch** smoke 8
der **Raum, ⁼e** room; space

rauschen to rustle
rechnen to calculate; **~ mit** to count on
recht right 6; **Du hast immer ~.** You're always right 8; **Ist es dir ~?** Is it all right/O.K. with you?; **~ haben** to be right 7; rather, quite
das **Recht, -e** (**auf** + *acc.*) right (to)
die **Rede, -n** speech; **die ~ ist von ...** the topic under discussion is . . .
reden (**über** + *acc.*/**von**) to talk (about) 8
reduzie'ren to reduce
das **Referat', -e** report 5
reformie'ren to reform
das **Reform'haus, ⁼er** health (food) store
regelmäßig regular(ly)
die **Regelstudienzeit** limit on time spent at university
der **Regen** rain 3
der **Regenmantel, ⁼** raincoat 7
die **Regie'rung, -en** government 11
regnen to rain 3
reich rich, wealthy 5
der **Reichstag** parliament building in Berlin
die **Reihe, -n** series; row 14
rein pure, clean 7
rein (= herein) in
die **Reinheit** purity
die **Reise, -n** trip 5
reisen, ist gereist to travel
reiten, ritt, ist geritten to ride (on horseback)
reizend charming
die **Rekla'me, -n** advertisement, commercial 7; **~ machen** to advertise
relativ' relative(ly)
die **Religion'** religion
renovie'ren to renovate, restore
die **Renovie'rung** renovation
der **Rentner, -/die Rentnerin, -nen** retiree, pensioner

die **Reparatur', -en** repair
reparie'ren to repair 9
das **Repertoire'** repertoire
die **Republik', -en** republic
respektie'ren to respect
das **Restaurant', -s** restaurant 8
das **Resultat', -e** result
die **Retrospekti've** retrospective
der **Revol'ver, -** revolver
das **Rezept', -e** recipe; prescription
richtig correct, right; real; really 3
die **Richtigkeit** accuracy; correctness
riechen, roch, gerochen (nach) to smell (of) 4
der **Rock, ⁼e** skirt 7; rock (music)
die **Rockband, -s** rock band
die **Rockmusik** rock music
rodeln to sled, go tobogganing
der **Rohstoff, -e** raw material 9
der **Rolladen, ⁼** shutter, blind
die **Rolle, -n** role 6; **eine ~ spielen** to play a part; to be important 6
der **Roman, -e** novel 5
rot (ö) red 1
rufen, rief, gerufen to call
die **Rückmeldung** a registration subsequent to the first one (university)
die **Ruhe** calm; peace and quiet
ruhig calm, easy-going, quiet 1; **Sei ~.** Be quiet.
(das) **Rumä'nien** Rumania
(das) **Russisch** Russian (language)
(das) **Rußland** Russia

die **Sache, -n** thing 7; affair, concern; (*pl.*) clothes
(das) **Sachsen** Saxony
der **Saft, ⁼e** juice 4
sagen to say, tell 3
die **Sahne** cream; whipped cream
der **Sakko, -s** sport coat 7
sammeln to collect, gather 11
die **Sammlung, -en** collection
der **Samstag** (*in southern Germany*) Saturday 1

samstags on Saturdays 4
der **Sandstein** sandstone
der **Sänger, -**/die **Sängerin, -nen** singer
der **Satz, ⁼e** sentence 9
sauber clean 8
das **Schach** chess 2
schade too bad; a pity, a shame 10
das **Schaf, -e** sheep
schaffen, schuf, geschaffen to create, set up 14
die **Schallplatte, -n** record
schätzen to appreciate; estimate
die **Schau, -en** show
schauen to look at
der **Schauer, -** (rain) shower
die **Scheibe, -n** pane
scheinen, schien, geschienen to shine 3; to appear, seem 10
der **Schenkel, -** thigh
schenken to give (a gift) 6
schicken (nach) to send (for)
schief distorted, false; sloping; crooked 11
das **Schiff, -e** ship 6
die **Schiffsreise** ship cruise
das **Schild, -er** sign
der **Schilling, -e** Austrian unit of currency
der **Schirm, -e** umbrella
schlafen (ä), schlief, geschlafen to sleep 6
das **Schlafzimmer, -** bedroom 9
schlagen (ä), schlug, geschlagen to hit, slap
die **Schlagsahne** whipped cream
die **Schlange: ~ stehen** to stand in line 14
schlecht bad, badly 2; **Mir geht's ~.** I don't feel well.; **Mir ist ~.** I feel nauseated. 10
schließen, schloß, geschlossen to close 4
schließlich finally, after all 8
schlimm bad, terrible
der **Schlitten, -** sled
das **Schloß,** *pl.* **Schlösser** lock 9; castle

schluchzen to sob
der **Schluß, Schlüsse** end, conclusion
der **Schlüssel, -** key 9
schmecken (+ *dat. of person*) to taste 7
der **Schmerz, -en** pain 10
schmutzig dirty
der **Schnee** snow 3
schneien to snow 3
schnell fast, quick(ly) 9; **Mach ~!** Hurry up!
die **Schnur, ⁼e** rope, line
die **Schokola'de** chocolate
schon already 3
schön nice, beautiful 3; O.K. 4
schonen to protect
die **Schönheit** beauty
der **Schrebergarten, ⁼** small garden plot on outskirts of city
schrecklich terrible, frightful 8
schreiben, schrieb, geschrieben to write 1; **Wie schreibt man das?** How do you spell that? 1; **~ (an + acc.)** to write (to); **~ (über + acc.)** to write (about)
die **Schreibmaschine, -n** typewriter 11; **~ schreiben können** to be able to type 11
schreien, schrie, geschrie(e)n to cry; to scream
schriftlich in writing
der **Schriftsteller, -**/die **Schriftstellerin, -nen** writer, author 6
der **Schritt, -e** step 10
der **Schuh, -e** shoe 7
der **Schulabschluß** formal completion of schooling
schuldig: ~ sein (+ *dat.*) to owe
die **Schule, -n** school 5
der **Schüler, -**/die **Schülerin, -nen** pupil
die **Schulwelt** school environment
schützen to protect against, shelter from
schwach (ä) weak 10

der **Schwager, ⁼**/die **Schwägerin, -nen** brother-/sister-in-law
schwarz black 1
(das) **Schweden** Sweden
schweigen, schwieg, geschwiegen to be silent
die **Schweiz** Switzerland 3
der **Schweizer, -**/die **Schweizerin, -nen** Swiss person 3
Schweizer Swiss (*adj.*) 3
(das) **Schweizerdeutsch** Swiss German (language)
die **Schwelle, -n** threshold, sill
schwer heavy; difficult 4
die **Schwester, -n** sister 4
schwierig difficult
die **Schwierigkeit, -en** difficulty 8
das **Schwimmbad, ⁼er** swimming pool
schwimmen, schwamm, ist geschwommen to swim 2
die **Science Fiction** science fiction
der **See, -n** lake 12
die **See, -n** ocean, sea
segeln, ist gesegelt to sail 12
der **Segen** blessing
sehen (ie), sah, gesehen to see 5
sehr very (much) 2
sei (du-*imperative of* **sein**): **~ so gut** be so kind, do me a favor 4; **~ mir nicht böse.** Don't be angry with me. 8
die **Seife** soap 7
sein his; its 3
sein (ist), war, ist gewesen to be 2; **gut dran ~** to be well off
seit (+ *dat.*) since, for [time] 6; **~ wann** (for) how long, since when 5; **~ kurzer Zeit** recently 7
die **Seite, -n** side; page 6
der **Sekretär', -e**/die **Sekretä'rin, -nen** secretary 1
selbst oneself, myself, etc. 4
selbständig independent
selbstverständ'lich of course; natural(ly); obvious(ly)
selten seldom, rare(ly) 13
seltsam strange

das **Seme′ster, -** semester 5
das **Seminar′, -e** seminar, seminar room 5
die **Seminar′arbeit, -en** seminar report 5
der **Senat′** senate
die **Sendung, -en** radio or TV program 8
der **Septem′ber** September 3
die **Serie** series
die **Serviet′te, -n** napkin 8
setzen to set, put 8
das **Shampoo′** shampoo 7
die **Shorts** (*pl.*) shorts 7
sicher safe; certain(ly) 8
Sie you (*formal*) 1; **Sie!** (*used to get someone's attention*) Hey! 5
sie she, it 1; they 2
das **Silber** silver
singen, sang, gesungen to sing 12
der **Sinn, -e** sense; mind; purpose
die **Situation′, -en** situation, condition
der **Sitz, -e** seat; headquarters
sitzen, saß, gesessen to sit 7
der **Ski, -er** ski 6
Ski laufen (ä), lief Ski, ist Ski gelaufen; *also* **Ski fahren** (**Ski** *pronounced* **Schi**) to ski 6
das **Skilaufen/Skifahren** skiing 6
so so, thus, this way 2; **~ ... wie** as . . . as 3; **~ [ein]** such [a], that kind of 5; **So?** Is that so? 5
so was something (like that)
die **Socke, -n** sock 7
sofort immediately
die **Software** software 5
sogar′ even 12
sogenannt so-called
der **Sohn, ⁻e** son 5
solch (-er, -es, -e) such a (*sing.*); such (*pl.*) 5
soli′de solid
sollen (soll), sollte, gesollt to be supposed to 5

der **Sommer** summer 3
sondern (*conj.*) but, on the contrary 6; **nicht nur ... , ~ auch ...** not only . . . , but also . . . 6
der **Sonnabend** (*in northern Germany*) Saturday 1
die **Sonne** sun 3
der **Sonntag** Sunday 1
sonntags on Sundays 4
sonst otherwise 4; **~ noch (et)was?** Anything else? 4
sonstwie otherwise
die **Sorge, -n** care, worry 13; **sich Sorgen machen [um]** to worry [about] 13
sorgen für to care for; see to it; arrange for (*a thing to be done*) 11
die **Sorte, -n** sort, kind
soviel so much
die **Sowjet′union** Soviet Union
sozial′ social; for the common good
die **Sozial′hilfe** welfare
soziali′stisch socialist
sozusa′gen so to speak
die **Spaghet′ti** (*pl.*) spaghetti 4
der **Spalt** crack
(das) **Spanien** Spain
(das) **Spanisch** Spanish (language)
sparen to save
der **Spaß** fun 8; **Es/Das macht ~.** That's fun 8; **~ an [+ dat.] haben** to enjoy [something] 7; **Späße** (*pl.*) jokes 8
spät late 2; **Wie ~ ist es?** What time is it? 2; **später** later 2
der **Spatz, -en** sparrow
spazie′ren, ist spaziert to take a walk, stroll
spazie′ren·fahren (ä), fuhr spazieren, ist spazierengefahren to go for a pleasure drive 10
spazie′ren·gehen, ging spazieren, ist spazierengegangen to go for a walk 12
der **Spazier′gang, ⁻e** walk, stroll

die **Sphäre, -n** sphere
das **Spiegelbild, -er** reflection
das **Spiel, -e** game
spielen to play 2
spitze (*colloq.*) first-rate
der **Sport** sport 2; **~ treiben** to engage in sports 2
der **Sportler, -/die Sportlerin, -nen** athlete
der **Sportschuh, -e** athletic shoe, tennis shoe 7
die **Sprache, -n** language 6
sprachlich linguistically; as far as the language is concerned
sprachlos speechless 9
sprechen (i), sprach, gesprochen to speak 5; **~ über** (+ *acc.*) to speak about; **~ von** to speak of; **~ mit** to speak to (someone)
der **Sprecher, -/die Sprecherin, -nen** speaker
die **Sprechstunde, -n** office hour
sprichwörtlich proverbial
spülen to rinse; to wash; **Geschirr ~** to wash dishes 9
der **Staat, -en** country, state 6
staatlich public, state-owned 5
stabil′ stable
die **Stabilität′** stability
die **Stadt, ⁻e** city 3
das **Städtchen, -** little town
städtisch city (*adj.*)
stark (ä) strong 10; **~ bewölkt** cloudy
sich stärken to fortify oneself
starr blank
statt (+ *gen.*) instead of 9
der **Status** status
Staub saugen to vacuum 9
der **Staubsauger, -** vacuum cleaner 13
das **Steak, -s** steak 7
stecken to stick, put into 8; to be (inserted) 8
stehen, stand, gestanden to stand, to be located 4
stehlen (ie), stahl, gestohlen to steal

steigen, stieg, ist gestiegen to rise

der **Stein, -e** stone

die **Stelle, -n** position, job; place 11

stellen to place 8

das **Stellenangebot, -e** job ad

die **Stellung, -en** position, job

die **Stereoanlage, -n** stereo system, stereo unit 1

das **Steuer** steering wheel

die **Steuer, -n** tax 10

das **Stichwort, ⸚er** key word

still still, quiet

die **Stimme, -n** voice; vote 11

die **Stimmung** atmosphere, mood

die **Stirne** forehead

der **Stock,** (*pl.*) **Stockwerke** floor/story (of building) 9

stolz proud(ly) 12

stoppen to stop

stören to bother, to disturb 8

die **Straße, -n** street 1

die **Straßenbahn, -en** streetcar 6

der **Strauß, ⸚e** bouquet

das **Streichquartett** string quartet

der **Streik, -s** strike 13

streiken to strike

der **Streß** stress 11

der **Strumpf, ⸚e** stocking

die **Strumpfhose, -n** pantyhose 7

die **Stube, -n** room

das **Stück, -e** piece 4; theater play 14

der **Student', -en, -en**/die **Studen'tin, -nen** student 1

der **Studen'tenausweis, -e** student identification card

der **Studen'tenjob, -s** job for students

die **Studen'tenkneipe, -n** pub frequented by students

das **Studen'ten(wohn)heim, -e** dormitory 5

die **Studiengebühren** (*pl.*) tuition

der **Studienplatz, ⸚e** available space for student in a course of study

studie'ren to study; to go to college 5; ~ **an/auf** (+ *dat.*) to study at (*a college*)

das **Studium** studies 12

der **Stuhl, ⸚e** chair 1

die **Stunde, -n** hour; lesson; class 9; die **Deutschstunde** German class

der **Stundenplan, ⸚e** class schedule 12

der **Stundenzeiger, -** hour hand (of a clock)

subatomar subatomic

suchen to look for 4

der **Süden** south 3

super super

der **Supermarkt, ⸚e** supermarket 4; **in den** ~ to the supermarket 4

die **Suppe** soup

surfen to surf 12

süßlich sweet

sympathisch likeable, engaging

das **System', -e** system

systema'tisch systematical(ly)

die **Szene, -n** scene

die **Tablette, -n** pill, tablet 4

der **Tag, -e** day 1; **Guten** ~./**Tag.** Hello. Hi. 2; **eines Tages** one day 7

tagen to meet (*parliament, conference*)

täglich daily 7

die **Tante, -n** aunt 5

der **Tante-Emma-Laden, ⸚** mom-and- pop store

tanzen to dance 2

die **Tasche, -n** bag; pocket 4

das **Taschenbuch, ⸚er** paperback

die **Tasse, -n** cup 4

die **Tat, -en** deed; **in der** ~ indeed 14

die **Tatsache, -n** fact 14; **Tatsachen** (*pl.*) data

tatsächlich really

die **Taube, -n** dove, pigeon

das **Taxi, -s** taxi

technisch technical

der **Tee** tea 4

der **Teenager, -** teenager

der **Teil, -e** part, portion 6; **zum** ~ in part 10

teil·nehmen (nimmt teil), nahm teil, teilgenommen (an + *dat.*) to take part (in); **Ich habe an dem Gespräch teilgenommen.** I took part in the conversation.

die **Teilung** partition

das **Telefon', -e** telephone 1

das **Telefon'netz** telephone network

die **Telefon'zelle, -n** telephone booth

telefonie'ren to telephone 13; **mit [jemandem]** ~ to telephone [someone]

die **Telefon'nummer** telephone number 1; **Wie ist die** ~ **von ... ?** What is the telephone number of . . . ? 1

die **Temperatur', -en** temperature

die **Tendenz'** tendency

das **Tennis** tennis 2

der **Termin', -e** appointment 13

die **Terras'se, -n** terrace, patio 9

der **Test, -s** test

teuer (teurer, teuerst-) expensive 5

der **Text, -e** text

die **Texti'lien** (*pl.*) textiles

das **Thea'ter, -** (performing arts) theater 13

das **Thea'terstück, -e** play 14

das **Thema,** (*pl.*) **Themen** theme; topic

tief low; deep; **das Tief** depression (*weather*)

die **Tiefkühltruhe, -n** (also der **Gefrierschrank, ⸚e**) freezer 13

der **Tisch, -e** table 1

das **Tischtennis** table tennis, Ping-Pong 2

der **Titel, -** title

der **Toast** toast

die **Tochter, ⸚** daughter 5

der **Tod, -e** death

die **Toilette** bathroom 9
toll great; fantastic 7
die **Toma'te, -n** tomato
tot dead
total' complete, total
die **Torte, -n** fancy (multi-layer) cake 4
die **Tour, -en** tour, trip 12
der **Touris'mus** tourism
traditionell' traditional
tragen (ä), trug, getragen to carry; to wear 7
trampen (*colloq.*) to hitchhike
die **Träne, -n** tear
der **Transport', -e** transportation; transport
das **Transportmittel, -** means of transportation
der **Traum, ⁺e** dream
träumen to dream 9
traurig sad 2
(sich) **treffen (i), traf, getroffen** meet 8; **Ich treffe mich mit Freunden.** I'm meeting friends. 12
treiben, trieb, getrieben to engage in 2; to drive
trennen to separate, divide 14
die **Treppe, -n** step; stairway
treten (tritt), trat, ist getreten to step
das **Triebwerk** gear (drive); engine
sich **trimmen** to get into shape
trinken, trank, getrunken to drink 4; **Was gibt's zum Trinken?** What's there to drink?
trocken dry 3
die **Trockenheit** dryness
der **Trockner, -** dryer 13
trotz (+ *gen.*) in spite of 9
trotzdem nevertheless 13
die **Tschechoslowakei'** Czechoslovakia
Tschüß. (*informal*) So long. Good-by. 1
das **T-Shirt, -s** T shirt 7
tun, tat, getan to do 7; **Es tut mir leid.** I'm sorry. 5

die **Tür, -en** door 1
der **Türke, -n, -n**/die **Türkin, -nen** Turk
die **Türkei'** Turkey
der **Turm, ⁺e** tower
der **Türrahmen, -** door frame
die **Tüte, -n** bag
typisch typical(ly) 8

die **U-Bahn** (*abbr.* for **Untergrundbahn**) subway 6
üben to practice
über (+ *acc./dat.*) over, above 4; across; about; by way of
überall everywhere 8
überfah'ren (ä), überfuhr, überfahren to run over
überflüssig superfluous
überhaupt' in general; at all 7
überle'ben to survive
(sich) **überle'gen** to reflect, think about
übermorgen day after tomorrow
überra'schen to surprise 6
überra'schend surprising
die **Überra'schung, -en** surprise
überset'zen to translate
die **Überset'zung, -en** translation 10
überwin'den, überwand, überwunden to overcome
übrig left over, remaining 11
die **Übung, -en** exercise; practice
die **Uhr, -en** clock, watch 1; **Wieviel ~ ist es?** What time is it? 2
um (+ *acc.*) around; at 2; **~ zwei Uhr** at two o'clock 2; **~ wieviel Uhr?** at what time? 2; **~ ... zu** (+ *inf.*) in order to . . . 10; **~ Himmels willen!** For heaven's sake!
die **Umfrage, -n** opinion poll
die **Umgangssprache, -n** colloquial language
umgekehrt in reverse, backwards
um·schalten to switch over
umsonst' gratis, for free, in vain
der **Umstand, ⁺e** circumstance

die **Umwelt** environment 7
umweltfreundlich good for the environment
der **Umweltminister, -**/die **Umweltministerin, -nen** Secretary for Environmental Affairs
der **Umweltschutz** protection of the environment
die **Umweltverschmutzung** pollution of the environment
unabhängig independent 10
die **Unabhängigkeit** independence
unbedingt necessarily
unbekannt unknown
und (*conj.*) and; plus 1; **~ so weiter** (*abbr.* **usw.**) and so on, (etc.) 7
der **Unfall, ⁺e** accident 13
unfreundlich unfriendly 2
ungarisch Hungarian
(das) **Ungarn** Hungary
ungefähr approximately
ungelernt unskilled
ungemahlen unground
ungespritzt unsprayed
ungewohnt unaccustomed, unusual
unglaub'lich unbelievable 8
das **Unglück** misfortune
die **Universität', -en** (**die Uni, -s** *colloq.*) university 5
das **Univiertel** university district
unkultiviert uncultured
unleserlich illegible 13
UNO United Nations (Organization)
unordentlich disorganized, disorderly
die **Unordnung** disorder
unschuldig innocent(ly); not guilty
unser our 3
unsozial socially unjust
unten below, beneath; downstairs 6
unter (+ *acc./dat.*) under, beneath; among 8; **~ anderem** among other things

sich **unterhal'ten (ä), unterhielt, unterhalten** to converse, chat

unterrich'ten to inform; to instruct, to teach

(sich) **unterschei'den, unterschied, unterschieden** to distinguish, differ 10

der **Unterschied, -e** difference 5

unverschämt impertinent

der **Urlaub** vacation 13; **in ~ fahren** to go on vacation; **in ~ sein** to be on vacation 13

die **USA** (*pl.*) U.S.A. 8

usw. (= und so weiter) etc. (and so on) 7

die **Varian'te, -n** variant

der **Vater, ~** father 5

der **Vati, -s** dad 5

veral'tet obsolete, antiquated

die **Veran'staltung, -en** event; rally

verant'wortlich responsible

die **Verant'wortung, -en** responsibility 11

die **Verbes'serung, -en** improvement

verbin'den, verband, verbunden to connect, associate

verbrei'tet (*p.p. of* **verbrei'ten**) widespread

verbrin'gen, verbrachte, verbracht to spend (time) 12

verder'ben (i), verdarb, verdorben to spoil

verdie'nen to earn 11

der **Verdienst', -e** earnings

verei'nigen to unify

verei'nigt unified 14

die **Verei'nigung** unification 11

die **Verfas'sung, -en** constitution

verfau'len to rot

verges'sen (vergißt), vergaß, vergessen to forget 7

vergeß'lich forgetful

der **Vergleich', -e** comparison

verglei'chen, verglich, verglichen (mit) to compare (to/with)

das **Vergnü'gen** enjoyment, fun; **Viel ~!** Have a good time!

verhan'deln to negotiate

sich **verhei'raten (mit)** to marry

verhei'ratet (mit) married (to) 6

verkau'fen to sell 7

der **Verkäu'fer, -/die Verkäu'ferin, -nen** salesperson

das **Verkehrs'mittel** means of transportation

verkraf'ten to handle, deal with

verkür'zen to shorten

verlet'zen to injure; to violate 9

verliebt' in love

verlie'ren, verlor, verloren to lose 4

vermit'teln to mediate

die **Vermö'gensrückgabe** return of property or assets

die **Verpa'ckung, -en** packaging, wrapping

verpe'stet polluted

verra'ten to betray

verschie'den different 6

verschö'nern to beautify

verschrei'ben, verschrieb, verschrieben to prescribe

verschwen'den to waste

die **Versi'cherung** insurance

verspre'chen (verspricht), versprach, versprochen (*dat. of person*) to promise

verständ'lich understandable; **sich ~ machen** to make oneself understood

verste'hen, verstand, verstanden to understand 5

versu'chen to try 6

der/die **Verwand'te** (*noun decl. like adj.*) relative

verweich'lichen to pamper

der **Vetter, -n** cousin (*m.*) 5

die **Videokamera, -s** video camera 13

das **Videospiel, -e** video game

viel (mehr, meist-) much 2; **viele** many 4

vielleicht' maybe, perhaps 2

der **Vielvölkerstaat** multi-ethnic state

das **Viertel, -** quarter 2; **~ nach [zwei]** quarter after [two]; **~ vor [drei]** quarter to [three] 2; district 12; **das Stadtviertel** city district 12

vietnamesisch Vietnamese

die **Vitamin'tablette, -n** vitamin pill

die **Voka'bel, -n** vocabulary word

das **Volk, ~er** people, folk 6

das **Volkslied, -er** folk song

voll full; complete(ly) 8

der **Volleyball** volleyball 2

von (+ *dat.*) from; of 1; by (the person doing something)

vor (+ *acc./dat.*) before 2; in front of 8; **~ allem** above all 6; **~ [einer Woche]** [a week] ago 8; **~ kurzem** recently 12

voraus'·sehen (ie), sah voraus, vorausgesehen to anticipate

vorbei'·kommen, kam vorbei, ist vorbeigekommen to come by 6; **bei mir ~** to come by my place 6

vor·bereiten to prepare 5; **sich ~ (auf** + *acc.*) to prepare oneself (for) 12

die **Vorbereitung, -en** preparation

der **Vorgang, ~e** process, proceeding

vor·gehen, ging vor, ist vorgegangen to be fast (*said of a clock*)

vor·haben (hat vor), hatte vor, vorgehabt to intend, have in mind 12

vorher before 7

vorig last, previous

die **Vorlesung, -en** lecture 5

die **Vorlesungsnotizen** (*pl.*) lecture notes

der **Vorname, -ns, -n** first name 8

vor·schlagen (ä), schlug vor, vorgeschlagen to suggest

sich (*dat.*) **vor·stellen** to imagine

die **Vorstellung, -en** idea, concept; performance (of a play) das **Vorstellungsgespräch, -e** job interview

der **Vorteil, -e** advantage

der **Vortrag, ̈e** lecture

das **Vorurteil, -e** prejudice

vorwurfsvoll reproachfully

das **Vorzimmer, -** outer office, anteroom

wachsen (ä), wuchs, ist gewachsen to grow 7

das **Wachstum** growth

wagen to dare

der **Wagen, -** car 6

die **Wahl, -en** choice; election

das **Wahlrecht** right to vote

das **WC (das Wasserklosett)** toilet

während (+ *gen.*) during 9; *(conj.)* while, whereas

wahrschein'lich probably

der **Wald, ̈er** forest 8

die **Wand, ̈e** wall 1

der **Wanderer, -/die Wanderin, -nen** hiker

das **Wanderlied, -er** hiking song

die **Wanderlust** wanderlust

wandern, ist gewandert to hike; to go walking 2

die **Wanderung, -en** hike 12

wann when 2

war (*past tense of* **sein**) was 3

die **Ware, -n** merchandise; commodity, goods 13

warm (ä) warm 3; **schön ~** nice and warm

warnen (vor + *dat.*) to warn (against)

warten (auf + *acc.*) to wait (for) 6

warum' why 2

was what 2; = **etwas** something; **~ anderes** something different 8; **~ für (ein)** what kind (of) (a) 2; **~ ist los?** What's wrong?

die **Wäsche** wash, laundry 9

(sich) **waschen (ä), wusch, gewaschen** to wash 9; **Ich wasche mich.** I'm washing

(myself); **Ich wasche mir [die Hände].** I'm washing my [hands]. 10

die **Waschmaschine, -n** washing machine 9

der **Waschsalon, -s** laundromat

das **Wasser** water 7

der **Wasserski, -er** water ski 6; **Wasserski fahren (ä), fuhr Wasserski, ist Wasserski gefahren** to waterski 6

wechseln to change (e.g., money); exchange (e.g., letters); switch 11

weg away, gone 7

der **Weg, -e** way 4; **auf dem ~** on the way 4

weg·bleiben, blieb weg, ist weggeblieben to stay away; to stay out

wegen (+ *gen.*) on account of, because of 9

weg·fahren (ä), fuhr weg, ist weggefahren to leave; to drive away

weg·nehmen (nimmt weg), nahm weg, weggenommen to take away

die **WG, -s** (*abbrev. for* die **Wohngemeinschaft, -en**) group of people sharing an apartment

weh tun (+ *dat.*) to hurt 10

weiblich feminine

das **Weihnachten** Christmas; *(used often in pl.)* 8; **Fröhliche Weihnachten!** Merry Christmas!

das **Weihnachtsgeschenk, -e** Christmas present

der **Weihnachtsmann, ̈er** Santa Claus

weil *(conj.)* because 6

der **Wein** wine 4

weinen to cry

die **Weise: auf diese ~** in this way

weiß white 1

weit far 11

weiter farther; further 3; **und so ~** and so on 7

weitergehend extensive

welch (-er, -es, -e) which 1; **Welche Farbe hat ... ?** What color is . . . ? 1

die **Welt, -en** world 6

der **Weltkrieg, -e** world war 6

der **Weltmarkt, ̈e** world market

wem (*dat.* of **wer**) (to) whom 6

wenig little; **wenige** few 4; **ein ~** a little

weniger minus (*in subtraction*) 1

wenigstens at least

wenn (*conj.*) when; if 6

wer who 2

die **Werbung** advertising

werden (i), wurde, ist geworden to become 5

werfen (i), warf, geworfen to throw

das **Werkzeug, -e** tool

der **Werkzeugmacher, -/die Werkzeugmacherin, -nen** toolmaker

der **Wert** value

wert worth; worthwhile

der **Westen** west 3

westlich western, westward

das **Wetter** weather 3

der **Wetterbericht, -e** weather report 8

wichtig important 6

die **Wichtigkeit** importance

wie how 1; like 3; as 4; **~ immer** as always 4; **~ wär's mit ... ?** How about . . . ? 8; **~ alt bist du?** How old are you? 1

wieder again 3; **immer ~** again and again 5

wieder·haben to have back

das **Wiedersehen: Auf ~.** Good-by. 2

wiederum again, in turn

die **Wiedervereinigung** reunification

Wien Vienna 6

das **Wienerschnitzel** wiener schnitzel, breaded veal cutlet

wieviel' how much; **wie viele** how many 1

die **Wiese, -n** meadow
wild wild
die **Wilden** *(pl.)* the wild ones
willkom'men welcome
der **Wind** wind 3
windsurfen: ~ gehen to go windsurfing 12
der **Winter** winter 3
winzig tiny
wir we 2
wirklich really 3
die **Wirklichkeit** reality
wirksam effective
die **Wirtschaft** economy 10; **~, -en** inn, pub, tavern 2
wirtschaftlich economic 14
die **Wirtschaftswissenschaft** economics
das **Wirtshaus, ⁼er** inn
wischen to wipe
wissen (weiß), wußte, gewußt to know (a fact) 5; **~ über** (+ *acc.*) to know about; **~ von** (+ *dat.*) to know of
der **Wissenschaftler, -/**die **Wissenschaftlerin, -nen** scientist
wo where 3
die **Woche, -n** week 1
das **Wochenende, -n** weekend 4; **Schönes ~.** Have a nice weekend. 4
woher' where from 8
wohin' where to 6
wohl probably, indeed 8; well 10
der **Wohlstand** affluence
der **Wohnblock, -s** block of flats, apartment building
wohnen (bei) to live, reside (at a place) 5
Wohnen: ~ und Essen room and board
das **Wohngeld** (government) rent supplement
die **Wohngemeinschaft, -en** a group of people sharing an apartment
das **Wohnhaus, ⁼er** apartment building

die **Wohnung, -en** dwelling; apartment 8
der **Wohnwagen, -** camper, trailer
das **Wohnzimmer, -** living room 9
die **Wolke, -n** cloud
wolkenlos cloudless
wolkig cloudy
wollen (will), wollte, gewollt to want to, intend to 5
das **Wort, ⁼er** word 1; **das ~ haben** to have the floor
der **Wortprozessor, -en** word processor 11; **mit dem ~ arbeiten** to do word processing 11
der **Wortschatz** vocabulary
das **Wunder, -** miracle; wonder
wunderbar wonderful
wünschen to wish 13
würde *(subj. of* **werden***)* would 12
die **Wurst, ⁼e** sausage, lunch meat 4
das **Wurstbrot, -e** cold meat sandwich
die **Würze, -n** spice

z.B. = zum Beispiel e.g. = for example 5
die **Zahl, -en** number, numeral 1
zahlen to pay 5
der **Zahn, ⁼e** tooth 10; **sich die Zähne putzen** to brush one's teeth
der **Zahnarzt, ⁼e/**die **Zahnärztin, -nen** dentist 11
die **Zahnpasta** toothpaste
die **Zahnschmerzen** *(pl.)* toothache 10
Die Zauberflöte The Magic Flute *(opera by Mozart)*
der **Zaun, ⁼e** fence 9
zeigen to show 9; **~ auf** (+ *acc.*) to point to
die **Zeit, -en** time 6; **seit kurzer ~** recently; **zur gleichen ~** at the same time 11; **zur ~ (z.Zt.)** at the time; currently; **zu dieser ~** at this time

die **Zeitschrift, -en** magazine
die **Zeitung, -en** newspaper 10
das **Zelt, -e** tent
zelten to camp in a tent 6
die **Zensur', -en** grade, mark 5
zentral' central
das **Zentrum, *(pl.)* Zentren** center
die **Zerstö'rung** destruction
ziehen, zog, gezogen to pull
das **Ziel, -e** goal 11
ziemlich quite, rather 3
die **Zigaret'te, -n** cigarette
das **Zimmer, -** room 1
zu too 3; **~** (+ *dat.*) to *(with people and some places)* 4
zueinan'der to each other
zuerst' at first 7
zufrie'den satisfied
der **Zug, ⁼e** train 6
zugleich' at the same time
zu·hören to listen
die **Zukunft** future 13
zuletzt' last
zu·machen to close 9
zu·nehmen (nimmt zu), nahm zu, zugenommen to increase
die **Zunge: auf der ~ liegen** to be on the tip of one's tongue
zurück' back, in return 5
zurück'·fordern to demand back
zurück'·gesetzt neglected, slighted
zurück'·zahlen to pay back 5
zusam'men together 2
die **Zusam'menarbeit** cooperation
zusam'men·arbeiten to cooperate
zusam'menhängen, hing zusammen, zusammengehangen to hang together; to be connected
der **Zusatz, ⁼e** supplement
zu·sehen (ie), sah zu, zugesehen to watch
der **Zustand, ⁼e** condition; shape 14
die **Zuverlässigkeit** dependability, reliability
zuviel' too much, too many 5
der **Zuwanderer, -/**die **Zuwanderin, -nen** immigrant

zuwe'nig   too little, too few 5
zwar   indeed; no doubt
der **Zweck, -e**   purpose
das **Zweifamilienhaus, ̈er**   two-family house, duplex
zweifeln   to doubt

der **Zweig, -e**   branch
zweimal   twice
zweit-   second
zweitgrößt (-er, -es, -e)   second largest
der **Zweite Weltkrieg**   World War II

die **Zwiebel, -n**   onion
zwischen (+ *acc./dat.*)   between, among 8
die **Zwischenprüfung, -en**   qualifying exam

ENGLISH-GERMAN VOCABULARY

The English-German end vocabulary contains the words included in the active vocabulary lists and the *Erweiterung des Wortschatzes* section of the chapters. Not included from the active lists are numbers, articles, and pronouns. The plural forms of nouns are given. Strong and irregular weak verbs are indicated with a raised degree mark (°). Their principal parts can be found in the Reference Section. Separable-prefix verbs are indicated with a raised dot: **mit·bringen.**

able: to be ~ to können°
absent: to be ~ fehlen
about über
above all vor allem
accident der Unfall, ⸚e
account: on ~ of wegen
acquaintance der/die Bekannte (*noun decl. like adj.*); **to make the ~ of** kennen·lernen
actually eigentlich
addition: in ~ noch
address die Adresse, -n; **What is your ~ ?** Wie ist deine/Ihre Adresse?
advertisement die Reklame, -n; die Anzeige,-n
afraid: to be ~ Angst haben, (sich) fürchten
after nach (*prep.*); nachdem (*conj.*); **~ all** schließlich
afternoon der Nachmittag, -e; **this ~** heute nachmittag
afternoons nachmittags
afterwards nachher
again wieder; noch einmal
against gegen
ago: [ten years] ~ vor [zehn Jahren]
air die Luft
airplane das Flugzeug, -e
airport der Flughafen, ⸚
all alle; **at ~** überhaupt; **~ day** den ganzen Tag
allowed: to be ~ to dürfen°
almost fast
alone allein
already schon
also auch

although obwohl
always immer
America (das) Amerika
American (*adj.*) amerikanisch; **~ (person)** der Amerikaner, -/ die Amerikanerin, -nen
among unter
and und; **~ so on** und so weiter
angry böse; **Don't be ~ with me.** Sei mir nicht böse; **to feel ~** sich ärgern
answer die Antwort, -en; **~ [the woman]** [der Frau] antworten; **(to) ~ the question** auf die Frage antworten
any einige; etwas; **I don't have any . . .** Ich habe kein …
anyone jemand
anything: ~ else? Sonst noch etwas?
apartment die Wohnung, -en
apology die Entschuldigung, -en
appear scheinen°; erscheinen°
appliance das Gerät, ⸚e
appointment der Termin, -e
approximately ungefähr
April der April
arm der Arm, -e
arrive an·kommen°
article der Artikel, -
artificial künstlich
as als; wie; **~ . . . ~** so … wie; **~ always** wie immer
ask fragen; **~ for** bitten° um
aspirin das Aspirin
assignment die Aufgabe, -n
astonished erstaunt

at an; auf; **~ (a place)** bei; **~ [seven]** um [sieben]
attic der Dachboden
August der August
aunt die Tante, -n
Austria (das) Österreich
Austrian österreichisch (*adj.*); **~ (person)** der Österreicher, -/ die Österreicherin, -nen
author der Autor, -en/die Autorin, -nen
automobile das Auto, -s
autumn der Herbst
away weg; ab

back (*adv.*) zurück
bad schlecht; schlimm; **not ~** ganz gut; **too ~** schade
badly schlecht
bag die Tasche, -n
bake backen°
baker der Bäcker, -/die Bäckerin, -nen
bakery die Bäckerei, -en; **at the ~** beim Bäcker; **to the ~** zum Bäcker
balcony der Balkon, -s
ball-point pen der Kugelschreiber, - [der Kuli, -s (*colloq.*)]
band die Band, -s
bank die Bank
basement der Keller, -
basketball der Basketball
bath das Bad, ⸚er
bathe (sich) baden
bathroom das Bad, ⸚er; die Toilette, -n

R-69

be sein°; ~ **so kind.** Sei/Seien Sie so gut.

beautiful schön

because weil; denn; ~ **of** wegen

become werden°

bed das Bett, -en; **to make the ~** das Bett machen

bedroom das Schlafzimmer, -

beer das Bier; ~ **garden** der Biergarten, ⁻

before vor; vorher

begin an·fangen°; beginnen°; ~ **the work** mit der Arbeit anfangen

beginning der Anfang, ⁻e

behind hinter

believe glauben; **I ~ so.** Ich glaube schon/ja.

belong to gehören

beside bei; neben; außer; außerhalb

besides außerdem; außer

best best; ~ **of all** am besten

better besser

between zwischen

bicycle das Fahrrad, ⁻er; **to ride a ~** mit dem Fahrrad fahren

big groß

bike das Rad, ⁻er; ~ **trip** die Radtour, -en

birthday der Geburtstag, -e; **When is your ~ ?** Wann hast du Geburtstag?; **for one's ~** zum Geburtstag

black schwarz

blouse die Bluse, -n

blue blau

body der Körper, -

book das Buch, ⁻er

book bag die Büchertasche, -n

bookcase das Bücherregal, -e

bookstore die Buchhandlung, -en

border die Grenze, -n

boss der Chef, -s/die Chefin, -nen

both beide; beides

bother stören

bottle die Flasche, -n

boy der Junge, -n, -n; ~ **friend** der Freund, -e

bread das Brot, -e

breakfast das Frühstück; **for ~** zum Frühstück; **to eat ~** frühstücken

bright hell

bring bringen°; ~ **along** mit·bringen°

broke (out of money) pleite

broken: ~ down kaputt

brother der Bruder, ⁻; **brothers and sisters** die Geschwister (pl.)

brown braun

brush: to ~ my teeth mir die Zähne putzen

build bauen

bus der Bus, -se

business das Geschäft, -e; ~ **man** der Kaufmann, -leute; ~ **woman** die Kauffrau, -en

busy: to be ~ beschäftigt sein; **to keep ~** (sich) beschäftigen

but aber; sondern

butcher der Metzger, -/die Metzgerin, -nen

butcher shop die Metzgerei, -en; **at the ~** beim Metzger; **to the ~** zum Metzger

butter die Butter

buy kaufen

by: ~ [car] mit [dem Auto]

café das Café, -s

cafeteria (university) die Mensa, -s or Mensen

cake der Kuchen, -; die Torte, -n

call nennen°; an·rufen°; ~ **[your] home** bei [dir] anrufen

called: it's ~ (es) heißt

calm ruhig

camera der Fotoapparat, -e; die Kamera, -s

camp campen; **to ~ in a tent** zelten

can können°

Canadian (person) der Kanadier, -/die Kanadierin, -nen

capital die Hauptstadt, ⁻e

car das Auto, -s; der Wagen, -

card die Karte, -n; **(playing) cards** die Karten (pl.)

care die Sorge, -n; **(to) ~ for** sorgen für

carry tragen°

cassette die Kassette, -n

cassette deck das Kassettendeck, -s

castle das Schloß, Schlösser

CD player der CD-Spieler, -; der CD-Player, -

celebration die Feier, -n; das Fest, -e

cellar der Keller, -

century das Jahrhundert, -e

certain(ly) bestimmt; sicher

chair der Stuhl, ⁻e

change wechseln

cheap billig

check: The ~, please. Zahlen, bitte.

cheerful lustig

cheese der Käse

chemistry die Chemie

chess das Schach

child das Kind, -er

chocolate die Schokolade, -n

Christmas (das) Weihnachten

cigarette die Zigarette, -n

circle der Kreis, -e

citizens' action group die Bürgerinitiative

city die Stadt, ⁻e; **old part of the ~** die Altstadt; ~ **hall** das Rathaus, ⁻er

class die Klasse, -n; **German ~** die Deutschklasse, -n

classical klassisch

clean sauber; **to ~** putzen; auf·räumen; sauber machen

clear klar

climate das Klima

clock die Uhr, -en

close eng; nah(e)

close: to ~ schließen°; zu·machen
clothing die Kleidung; **article of ~** das Kleidungsstück, -e
coat der Mantel, ¨; **sport ~** der Sakko, -s
coffee der Kaffee; **for (afternoon) ~** zum Kaffee; **to go for ~** Kaffee trinken gehen
cola drink die Cola
cold kalt; die Erkältung, -en; **to catch a ~** sich erkälten
colleague der Kollege, -n, -n/die Kollegin, -nen
collect sammeln
college das College, -s; **to go to ~** studieren; auf/an die Universität gehen
color die Farbe, -n; **What ~ is . . . ?** Welche Farbe hat ... ?
comb: to ~ (one's hair) (sich) kämmen
come kommen°; **~ along** mit·kommen°; **~ by** vorbei·kommen°
commercial (TV or radio) die Reklame, -n
compact disc die Compact Disk, -s, die CD, -s
company die Gesellschaft, -en; die Firma, Firmen; **have ~** Besuch haben
compete konkurrieren
complete(ly) ganz; voll
computer der Computer, -; **~ science** die Informatik; **~ language** die Programmiersprache, -n
concept die Vorstellung, -en
concert das Konzert, -e
concerto das Konzert, -e
condition der Zustand, ¨e
contrary: on the ~ sondern; doch
cook kochen
cool kühl
corner die Ecke, -n
correct richtig
cost kosten
cough husten

could könnte
country das Land, ¨er; der Staat; **in our ~** bei uns; **in the ~** auf dem Land(e); **out into the ~** ins Grüne; **to the ~** aufs Land
course der Kurs, -e; die Vorlesung, -en
course: of ~ natürlich; klar; selbstverständlich
courtyard der Hof, ¨e
cousin (female) die Kusine, -n; **~** (male) der Vetter, -n
create schaffen°
crooked schief
curious neugierig
customer der Kunde, -n, -n/die Kundin, -nen

dad der Vati, -s
daily täglich
dance: to ~ tanzen
dancing: I'm going ~. Ich gehe tanzen.
dangerous gefährlich
dark dunkel
darling der Liebling, -e
data die Tatsachen (pl.)
date das Datum; **What's the ~ today?** Den wievielten haben wir heute?; Der wievielte ist heute?
daughter die Tochter, ¨
day der Tag, -e; **one/some ~** eines Tages; **all ~** den ganzen Tag; **days of the week** die Wochentage (pl.)
December der Dezember
decide (sich) entscheiden°; beschließen°; **to make a decision (after reflecting on it)** sich entscheiden
decorate dekorieren
deed die Tat, -en
dentist der Zahnarzt, ¨e/die Zahnärztin, -nen
department store das Kaufhaus, ¨er

depend on ab·hängen von
describe beschreiben°
dessert der Nachtisch, -e
develop (sich) entwickeln
development die Entwicklung, -en
different verschieden; anders; **something ~** (et)was anderes
difficult schwer; schwierig
difficulty die Schwierigkeit, -en
dining room das Eßzimmer, -
dinner das Abendessen, -; **for ~** zum Abendessen; **to eat ~** zu Abend essen
discussion die Diskussion, -en
diskette die Diskette, -n
dishwasher der Geschirrspüler, -
distorted schief
district das Viertel, -; **city ~** das Stadtviertel, -
disturb stören
divided by [in mathematics] geteilt durch
do machen; tun°; **to ~ a task** eine Arbeit machen
doctor der Arzt, ¨e/die Ärztin, -nen; **to go to the ~** zum Arzt gehen
doll die Puppe, -n
done fertig; **to have something ~** etwas machen lassen
door die Tür, -en
dormitory das Studentenheim, -e
downstairs unten
dream: (to) ~ träumen
dress das Kleid, -er; **to ~** (sich) an·ziehen°; **I get dressed.** Ich ziehe mich an.
drink trinken°
drive fahren°; **to ~ away** weg·fahren°; **to ~ along** mit·fahren
driver der Fahrer, -/die Fahrerin, -nen
dry trocken; **to ~ (dishes)** ab·trocknen
dumb dumm; **something ~** etwas Dummes

during während
dwelling die Wohnung, -en

each jed- (er, es, e)
ear das Ohr, -en
early früh
earn verdienen
east der Osten
easy-going ruhig
eat essen°
economy die Wirtschaft
educate aus·bilden
education die Erziehung; die
  Ausbildung; das Schulwesen
egg das Ei, -er
employer der Arbeitgeber, -/die
  Arbeitgeberin, -nen
employee der Arbeitnehmer, -/die
  Arbeitnehmerin, -nen
employed berufstätig
end das Ende, -n; **in/at the ~**
  am Ende
engage treiben°; **~ in sports**
  Sport treiben
engineer der Ingenieur, -e/die
  Ingenieurin, -nen
England (das) England
English(adj.) englisch; **~ language** (das) Englisch
enjoyment die Lust; das Vergnügen
enough genug
entrance hall der Flur, -e
environment die Umwelt
especially besonders
etc. usw.
even sogar; **~ if** auch wenn
evening der Abend, -e; **Good ~**
  Guten Abend.; **this ~** heute
  abend
evenings abends
every jed- (er, es, e)
everyone jed- (er, es, e)
everything alles
everywhere überall
exactly genau
examination die Klausur, -en; die
  Prüfung, -en; **comprehensive**

~ das Examen, -; **to take an
~** eine Klausur schreiben
examine durch·sehen°; prüfen
example das Beispiel, -e; **for ~**
  zum Beispiel (z.B.)
excellent(ly) ausgezeichnet
except außer
excuse die Entschuldigung, -en;
  ~ me! Entschuldigung!
expect erwarten
expensive teuer
experience die Erfahrung, -en
explain erklären
explanation die Erklärung, -en
expressway die Autobahn
eye das Auge, -n

face das Gesicht, -er
fact die Tatsache, -n
fairly ganz; ziemlich
fall der Herbst
familiar bekannt
family die Familie, -n
famous bekannt
fantastic phantastisch; toll
far weit
farmhouse das Bauernhaus, ¨er
farmer der Bauer, -n, -n/die Bäuerin, -nen
farther weiter
fast schnell
father der Vater, ¨
favorite der Liebling, -e; **~ (program)** die Lieblings(sendung)
fear die Angst, ¨e; **(to) ~** sich
  fürchten; **(to) ~ for** Angst
  haben um
feast das Fest, -e
February der Februar
Federal Republic of Germany die
  Bundesrepublik Deutschland
  (BRD)
feel sich fühlen; **~ like** Lust
  haben; **I don't ~ like working.** Ich habe keine Lust zu
  arbeiten.; **I don't ~ like it.**
  Dazu habe ich keine Lust.

feeling das Gefühl, -e
fence der Zaun, ¨e
fever das Fieber
few wenig(e); **a ~** ein paar
fight kämpfen
film der Film, -e
finally schließlich
find finden°
fine fein; gut; **I'm ~.** Es geht
  mir gut.
finger der Finger,
finished fertig
first erst; **at ~** zuerst; **~ of all**
  erst einmal, erstens
first name der Vorname, -ns, -n
first-rate klasse, spitze, ausgezeichnet
fish der Fisch, -e
fit passen
floor der Boden, ¨; **~ (of a
  building)** der Stock, (pl.)
  Stockwerke; **first ~** das
  Erdgeschoß
flower die Blume, -n
fluent(ly) fließend
fly fliegen°
food das Essen; die Lebensmittel
  (pl.)
foot der Fuß, ¨e; **to go on ~** zu
  Fuß gehen°; laufen°
for für (prep.); denn (conj.); **(time)**
  seit; **~ a year** seit einem
  Jahr
foreigner der Ausländer, -/die
  Ausländerin, -nen
forest der Wald, ¨er
forget vergessen°
forgetful vergeßlich
fork die Gabel, -n
(the) former jen- (er, es, e)
formerly früher
fourth das Viertel, -
France (das) Frankreich
free frei; **for ~** umsonst, gratis
freeway die Autobahn, -en
freezer der Gefrierschrank, ¨e
French (adj.) französisch; **~ (language)** (das) Französisch

French fries die Pommes frites
(pl.)
fresh frisch
Friday der Freitag
friend der Freund, -e/die Freundin, -nen
friendliness die Freundlichkeit
friendly freundlich
from von; (native of) aus; **Where do you come ~?** Woher kommst du?
fruit das Obst
full voll
fun das Vergnügen; der Spaß; **That's ~.** Es macht Spaß.
funny lustig
furnished möbliert
furniture die Möbel *(pl.);* **piece of ~** das Möbelstück, -e
further weiter

game das Spiel, -e
garage die Garage, -n
garden der Garten, ⸚
gasoline das Benzin
general: in ~ überhaupt, allgemein
gentleman der Herr, -n, -en
genuine echt
German *(adj.)* deutsch; **~ (person)** der/die Deutsche *(noun decl. like adj.);* **~ (language)** (das) Deutsch; **to do ~ (homework)** Deutsch machen; **I'm doing ~.** Ich mache Deutsch.; **~ Mark** D-Mark; **~ studies (language and literature)** die Germanistik; **~ secondary school** das Gymnasium, *(pl.)* Gymnasien
German Democratic Republic die Deutsche Demokratische Republik (DDR)
Germany (das) Deutschland
get bekommen°; kriegen; **~ up** auf·stehen°; **to ~ together** zusammen·kriegen, sich treffen°

girl das Mädchen, -; **~ friend** die Freundin, -nen
give geben°; **~ (as a gift)** schenken; **~ up** auf·geben°
glad froh
gladly gern
glove der Handschuh, -e
go gehen°; **~ by [car]** mit [dem Auto] fahren°
goal das Ziel, -e
gone weg
good gut; **~ Gracious/Heavens!** Du meine Güte!
good-by Auf Wiedersehen.; Tschüß. *(colloq.)*
government die Regierung, -en
grade die Zensur, -en
grandfather der Großvater, ⸚
grandmother die Großmutter, ⸚
grandparents die Großeltern *(pl.)*
gray grau
great toll, ausgezeichnet
green grün
groceries die Lebensmittel *(pl.)*
group die Gruppe, -n
grow wachsen°
guest der Gast, ⸚e; der Besucher, -/die Besucherin, -nen
guilty schuldig; **not ~** unschuldig
guitar die Gitarre, -n

hair das Haar, -e
half die Hälfte, -n; halb
hall der Flur, -e
hand die Hand, ⸚e
handbag die (Hand)tasche, -n
hang hängen°
happy froh, glücklich
hardly kaum
hard-working fleißig
has hat
hat der Hut, ⸚e
have haben°; **to ~ to** müssen°; **to ~ something done** etwas machen lassen°; **~ some cake.** Nehmen Sie etwas Kuchen.

head der Kopf, ⸚e
headache die Kopfschmerzen *(pl.)*
healthy gesund
hear hören
heavy schwer
hello Guten Tag.; Grüß dich.; Hallo. *(informal)*
help helfen°; **~ with [work]** bei [der Arbeit] helfen
here hier, da; **~ [toward the speaker]** her; **~ you are** bitte sehr
Hey! Du!; He!
Hi! Tag!
high hoch
hike die Wanderung, -en; **(to) ~** wandern
history die Geschichte
hobby das Hobby, -s
hold halten°
holiday der Feiertag, -e
home: at ~ zu Hause; **(to go) ~** nach Hause; **at the ~ of** bei
homework die Hausaufgaben *(pl.)*
hope die Hoffnung, -en; **(to) ~** hoffen; **~ for** hoffen auf *(+acc.);* **I ~** hoffentlich
horrible furchtbar; fürchterlich; schrecklich
horribly furchtbar; fürchterlich; schrecklich
hot heiß
hour die Stunde, -n
house das Haus, ⸚er
how wie; **~ are you?** Wie geht es Ihnen?/Wie geht's?
however aber
human being der Mensch, -en, -en
hunger der Hunger
hungry: to be ~ Hunger haben; **to get ~** Hunger bekommen/kriegen
hurt weh tun°
husband der (Ehe)mann, ⸚er

ice das Eis
ice cream das Eis

idea die Idee, -n; die Vorstellung, -en; die Ahnung; **No ~ !** Keine Ahnung!
idle: be ~ faulenzen
if wenn; ob; **even ~** wenn auch
ill krank
illegible unleserlich
illness die Krankheit, -en
image das Bild, -er; die Vorstellung, -en
immediately gleich
important wichtig; **be ~** eine Rolle spielen
impression der Eindruck, ⁻e
improve vebessern
in(to) in; hinein
indeed in der Tat
independent unabhängig
individual einzeln
industrious fleißig
industry die Industrie, -n
inflation die Inflation
influence beeinflussen°
inhabitant der Einwohner, -/die Einwohnerin, -nen
innocent(ly) unschuldig
in order to um … zu
in spite of trotz
instead of (an)statt
intelligent intelligent
intend to wollen°
interested: to be ~ (in) (sich) interessieren (für)
interesting interessant
international international
invite ein·laden°
is ist; **isn't it?** nicht? *(tag question);* **Your name is [Monica], isn't it?** Du heißt [Monika], nicht?

jacket die Jacke, -n
January der Januar
jeans die Jeans *(pl.)*
job der Beruf, -e; der Job, -s; die Stelle, -n; **to have a ~** jobben *(colloq.)*
jogging das Jogging
join in mit·machen (bei + *dat.*)

journalist der Journalist, -en/die Journalistin, -nen
July der Juli
juice der Saft ⁻e
June der Juni
just eben; erst; gerade

key der Schlüssel, -
kilogram das Kilo(gramm)
kilometer der Kilometer, -
kind: be so ~ sei/seien Sie so gut/nett; **what ~ of person** was für ein Mensch
kindergarten der Kindergarten
kitchen die Küche, -n; **~ range** der Herd, -e
knife das Messer, -
know (a fact) wissen°; **~ (be acquainted)** kennen°; **to get to ~** kennen·lernen; **to ~ [German]** Deutsch können

lack fehlen
lake der See, -n
lamp die Lampe, -n
land das Land, ⁻er
language die Sprache, -n
large groß
last letzt; **~ night** gestern abend; **to ~** dauern
late spät
later später; **until ~** bis später, tschüß, bis dann, bis bald
laundry die Wäsche
lawyer der Jurist, -en, -en/die Juristin, -nen; der Rechtsanwalt, ⁻e/die Rechtsanwältin, -nen
lay legen
lazy faul
lead führen
learn lernen
least: at ~ wenigstens
leave lassen°; weg·fahren°; ab·fahren°
lecture die Vorlesung, -en
leg das Bein, -e
leisure time die Freizeit

lend leihen°
lesson die Stunde, -n; **piano ~** die Klavierstunde, -n
let lassen°
letter der Brief, -e
library die Bibliothek, -en
lie liegen°
life das Leben, -
light *(adj.)* leicht ; **~ (in color)** hell
like wie; **would ~ to** möchte; **to ~** gern haben; mögen; gefallen°; **What do you ~ to do?** Was machst du gern? **I ~ to swim.** Ich schwimme gern. **How do you ~ the cheese?** Wie findest du den Käse?
likewise ebenso; auch
listen: to ~ to music Musik hören
literature die Literatur
little klein; wenig; **a ~** ein bißchen, ein wenig
live leben; wohnen
living room das Wohnzimmer, -
living standard der Lebensstandard
located: to be ~ liegen°
lock das Schloß, Schlösser
long lang; lange; **a ~ time** lange
longer: no ~ nicht mehr
look: ~ at an·sehen°, an·schauen; **~ like . . .** wie … aus·sehen°; **~ for** suchen; **~ forward to** sich freuen auf
lose verlieren°
lot: a ~ viel
loud laut
lounge around faulenzen
love die Liebe; **to ~** lieben; **in ~** verliebt
low niedrig
luck das Glück; **Good ~!** Viel Glück!; **to be lucky** Glück haben
lunch das Mittagessen; **for ~** zum Mittagessen; **to have ~** zu Mittag essen°
lunch meat die Wurst, ⁻e

magazine die Zeitschrift, -en
major subject das Hauptfach, ⸚er
main Haupt-
make machen
man der Mann, ⸚er; ~ ! Mensch!
manner die Art
many viele; **how ~** wie viele; **too ~** zu viele
map die Landkarte, -n
March der März
market der Markt, ⸚e
marmalade die Marmelade
marriage die Heirat, -en
married verheiratet
marry heiraten
mathematics die Mathematik
matter: it doesn't ~ (es) macht nichts
May der Mai
may dürfen°; **that ~ well be** das mag wohl sein
maybe vielleicht
meal das Essen
mean meinen; bedeuten; **What does that ~ ?** Was bedeutet das?
meaning die Bedeutung, -en
meat das Fleisch
meat market die Metzgerei, -en
medicine das Medikament, -e
meet (sich) treffen°; kennen·lernen; **I'm meeting friends.** Ich treffe mich mit Freunden.
member das Mitglied, -er
merchandise die Ware, -n
merchant der Kaufmann, -leute/ die Kauffrau, -en
mere(ly) bloß
merry lustig
microwave oven der Mikrowellenherd, -e
milk die Milch
million die Million, -en
mind: to have in ~ vor·haben°
mineral water das Mineralwasser
minor subject das Nebenfach, ⸚er
minute die Minute, -n; **Just a ~, please!** Einen Moment, bitte!

Miss Fräulein
missing: to be ~ fehlen
mixer (+food processor) die Küchenmaschine, -n
modern modern
mom die Mutti, -s
moment der Moment, -e; **at the ~** im Moment
Monday der Montag
Mondays montags
money das Geld
month der Monat, -e
more mehr; **no ~** . . . kein ... mehr; **~ and ~** immer mehr; **~ or less** mehr oder weniger
morning der Morgen; **Good ~.** Guten Morgen.; **this ~** heute morgen
mornings morgens
most of the time meistens
mostly meistens
mother die Mutter, ⸚
motorcycle das Motorrad, ⸚er
mountain der Berg, -e
mouth der Mund, ⸚er
movie der Film, -e; **~ theater** das Kino, -s
movies das Kino, -s; **to the ~** ins Kino
Mr. Herr
Mrs. Frau
Ms. Frau
much viel; **how ~** wieviel; **too ~** zuviel
music die Musik
music lesson die Musikstunde, -n
musical das Musical, -s
musical instrument das Musikinstrument, -e
musician der Musiker, -/die Musikerin, -nen
must müssen°
mystery (novel or film) der Krimi, -s

name Name, -ns, -n; **What is your ~?** Wie heißen Sie?; **to ~** nennen°; **Your ~ is**

[Mark], isn't it? Du heißt [Mark], nicht?
named: to be ~ heißen°
napkin die Serviette, -n
narrow eng
nature die Natur
natural(ly) klar; natürlich; selbstverständlich
near bei; **~ by** in der Nähe, nah(e)
neck der Hals, ⸚e
need brauchen
neighbor der Nachbar, -n, -n/die Nachbarin, -nen
neighboring country das Nachbarland, ⸚er
nervous nervös
never nie
nevertheless trotzdem
new neu; **What's ~?** Was gibt's Neues?
newspaper die Zeitung, -en
next nächst
nice nett; schön
night die Nacht, ⸚e; **last ~** gestern abend; **Good ~.** Gute Nacht.
no nein; kein; nicht; **~ longer** nicht mehr; **~ more** . . . kein ... mehr
no one niemand
nonsense der Quatsch
north der Norden
nose die Nase, -n
not nicht; **isn't that so?** nicht?; **~ at all** gar nicht; **~ any, no** kein; **~ only . . . but also . . .** nicht nur ... sondern auch ...
note die Notiz, -en
notebook das Heft, -e
nothing nichts; **~ special** nichts Besonderes
notice bemerken
novel der Roman, -e
November der November
now jetzt; nun; **~ and then** ab und zu
number die Zahl, -en

numeral die Zahl, -en
nurse der Krankenpfleger, -/die
   Krankenpflegerin, -nen; **(female only)** die Krankenschwester, -n
nursery school der Kindergarten, ⸚

observe beobachten
obtain kriegen
occupy beschäftigen
occupied: to be ~ beschäftigt sein
occur (one's mind) einfallen°
ocean der Ozean, -e
October der Oktober
of von
offer an·bieten°
office das Büro, -s
often oft
oh ach, ah; **~ I see** ach so; **~
   my** o je; **~ well** naja
OK okay (O.K.); ganz gut; **It's
   (not) ~.** Es geht (nicht).
old alt; **I'm [19] years ~.** Ich bin
   [19] Jahre alt. **How ~ are you?**
   Wie alt bist du?
on an; auf; **~ account of**
   wegen
once einmal; mal; **~ more** noch
   einmal
one (*pronoun*) man; **~ another**
   einander
oneself selbst
only nur; erst; bloß
open offen; **(to) ~** auf·machen
opera die Oper, -n
opinion die Meinung, -en; **What's
   your ~?** Was hältst du
   davon?
or oder
orange die Orange, -n; **~ juice**
   der Orangensaft
orchestra das Orchester, -
order die Ordnung; **(to) ~**
   bestellen
organize organisieren
organization die Organisation, -en

other ander- (er, es, e)
otherwise sonst; anders
out of aus
outside draußen
own eigen

page die Seite, -n
paint malen
pale blaß
pants die Hose, -n
pantyhose die Strumpfhose, -n
paper das Papier; **(theme, essay)**
   die Arbeit, -en
paperback das Taschenbuch, ⸚er
pardon: I beg your ~? Wie bitte?
parents die Eltern (*pl.*)
park der Park, -s
part der Teil, -e; **in ~** zum Teil;
   to play a ~ eine Rolle spielen
participate (in) mit·machen (bei);
   I ~ in a game. Ich mache bei
   einem Spiel mit.
particular besonder-
particularly besonders
party die Party, -s; die Feier, -n;
   das Fest, -e; die Fete, -n; **at a
   ~** auf einem Fest
patio die Terrasse, -n
pay: ~ for bezahlen; zahlen; **~
   back** zurückzahlen
pen der Kugelschreiber,- [der
   Kuli, -s (*colloq.*)]
pencil der Bleistift, -e
people die Leute (*pl.*); die Menschen (*pl.*); die Einwohner
   (*pl.*); man
per pro
perhaps vielleicht
period der Punkt, -e
permit lassen°
permitted: to be ~ dürfen°
person der Mensch, -en, -en; die
   Person, -en
pharmacy die Apotheke, -n; **to
   the ~** in die Apotheke
philosophy die Philosophie
photograph fotografieren
physics die Physik

piano das Klavier, -e
pick up ab·holen
picnic das Picknick, -s
picture das Bild, -er
piece das Stück, -e
Ping-Pong das Tischtennis
pity: what a ~ schade
place der Platz, ⸚e; die Stelle, -n;
   der Ort, -e; **to my ~** zu mir;
   at my ~ bei mir
plan der Plan, ⸚e; **to ~**
   vor·haben°
plant die Pflanze, -n; **(to) ~**
   pflanzen
play das Theaterstück, -e; **(to) ~**
   spielen
please bitte; **(to) ~** gefallen°
pleased: to be ~ (about) sich
   freuen (über)
pleasure die Lust; das Vergnügen
pocket die Tasche, -n
point der Punkt, -e
police die Polizei
politician der Politiker, -/die
   Politikerin, -nen
portion der Teil, -e
position die Stelle, -n
possible möglich; **It's (not) ~.**
   Es geht (nicht).; **That would
   (not) be ~.** Das ginge nicht.
postcard die Postkarte, -n
potato die Kartoffel, -n
pound das Pfund
practical(ly) praktisch
prefer: I ~ to work. Ich arbeite
   lieber.
prejudice das Vorurteil, -e
prepare (for) (sich) vor·bereiten
   (auf)
present das Geschenk, -e
pretty schön; **~ pale** ganz
   schön blaß
price der Preis, -e
private(ly) privat
probably wahrscheinlich
product das Produkt, -e
profession der Beruf, -e
professor der Professor, -en/die
   Professorin, -nen

program das Programm, -e; **TV**
or radio ~ die Sendung, -en
programmer der Programmierer,-/
die Programmiererin, -nen
promise versprechen°
proud(ly) stolz
psychology die Psychologie
pub die Kneipe, -n; die Gaststätte, -n; die Wirt-
schaft, -en
public öffentlich; staatlich
pullover der Pulli, -s; der Pullover, -
punctual(ly) pünktlich
pure rein
purse die Handtasche, -n
put legen; stellen; stecken; setzen;
hängen

quality die Qualität, -en
quarter das Viertel, -
question die Frage, -n
questionable fraglich
quick schnell
quiet ruhig; still
quite ziemlich

radio das Radio, -s
railroad die Bahn, -en
rain der Regen; **(to)** ~ regnen
raincoat der Regenmantel, ⸚
range (kitchen) der Herd, -e
rare(ly) selten
rather ziemlich; ~ **than** lieber
als
raw material der Rohstoff, -e
reach erreichen
read lesen°
ready fertig
real echt; richtig
really wirklich; richtig; echt
(slang); ~ **neat** echt toll
reason der Grund, ⸚e; **for that** ~
daher; darum; aus diesem
Grund
receive bekommen°
recently vor kurzem; neulich; seit
kurzer Zeit

record die Platte, -n
record player der Plattenspieler, -
recover (from) sich erholen (von)
recuperate sich erholen
red rot
refrigerator der Kühlschrank, ⸚e
rehearsal die Probe, -n
remain bleiben°
remaining übrig
remember (someone/something)
sich erinnern (an +
jemand/etwas)
rent die Miete, -n; **(to)** ~
mieten; vermieten
repair reparieren
report das Referat, -e; **(to)** ~
berichten
reporter der Journalist, -en, -en/
die Journalistin, -nen
request bitten° (+um)
responsibility die Verantwortung, -en
responsible verantwortlich
restaurant das Restaurant, -s; die
Gaststätte, -n; **town hall** ~
der Ratskeller, -
return zurück·fahren°; zurück·ge-
hen°; zurück·kommen°
rich reich
ride: to ~ **a bike** mit dem Fahrrad fahren, Rad fahren
right das Recht, -e; **Is it all** ~
with you? Ist es dir recht?; **to
be** ~ recht haben; **you're** ~
du hast recht; **that's** ~ genau;
richtig; ~ **to** Recht (auf +
acc.)
role die Rolle, -n
roll das Brötchen, -
romance (novel) der Liebesroman, -e
room das Zimmer, -
run laufen°
running das Jogging

sad traurig
safe sicher
sail: (to) ~ segeln

salary das Gehalt, ⸚er
same gleich; **It's all the** ~ **to me.**
Das ist mir egal.
sandwich das [Wurst] Brot, -e
satisfied zufrieden
Saturday der Samstag; der Sonnabend
Saturdays samstags
sausage die Wurst, ⸚e
say sagen
schedule der Stundenplan, ⸚e
school die Schule, -n
season die Jahreszeit, -en
seat der Platz, ⸚e; **Is this** ~
taken? Ist hier frei?
secretary der Sekretär, -e/die Sekretärin, -nen
see sehen°
seem scheinen°
seldom selten
sell verkaufen
semester das Semester, -
seminar das Seminar, -e; ~
room das Seminar, -e; ~
report die Seminararbeit, -en
send schicken
sentence der Satz, ⸚e
separate: (to) ~ trennen
September der September
serious ernst; **Are you** ~? Ist
das dein Ernst?
serve dienen
set setzen
several einige; mehrere
shampoo das Shampoo
shave (sich) rasieren
shine scheinen°
ship das Schiff, -e
shirt das Hemd, -en
shoe der Schuh, -e
shop das Geschäft, -e; der Laden, ⸚; **(to)** ~ ein·kaufen
shopping: to go ~ ein·kaufen
gehen
shopping bag die Einkaufstasche, -n
short kurz; ~ **(people)** klein
shorts die Shorts *(pl.)*
show zeigen

shower die Dusche, -n; **(to)** ~
  (sich) duschen
sick krank
side die Seite, -n
significance die Bedeutung
similar ähnlich; gleich
simple einfach
simply einfach
since seit *(prep.)*; da *(conj.* =
  because); ~ **when** seit wann
sing singen°
singer der Sänger, -/
  die Sängerin, -nen
single einzeln
single-family home das Einfamilienhaus, ̈-er
sister die Schwester, -n
sit sitzen° **to** ~ **down** sich setzen
situated: to be ~ liegen°
situation die Situation, -en
ski der Ski, -er; **(to)** ~ Ski lau-
  fen°, Ski fahren°
skirt der Rock, ̈-e
sleep schlafen°; **to** ~ **at [a**
  friend's] house bei [einem
  Freund] schlafen
slow(ly) langsam
small klein
smart intelligent
smell riechen°
smile (about) lächeln (über +
  acc.)
smoke der Rauch; **(to)** ~ rauchen
snow der Schnee; **(to)** ~
  schneien
so so; also; **Isn't that** ~**?** Nicht?;
  ~ **that** damit; ~ **long.**
  Tschüß. **I believe** ~. Ich
  glaube schon/ja.
soap die Seife
soccer der Fußball
sock die Socke, -n
soft drink die Limonade, -n
software die Software
solution die Lösung, -en
some etwas; einige; manch (-er,
  -es, -e); **at** ~ **point**
  irgendwann
someone jemand

something etwas/was; ~ **like**
  that so was
sometime irgendwann
sometimes manchmal
somewhat etwas
son der Sohn, ̈-e
song das Lied, -er
soon bald
sorry: I'm ~ (es) tut mir leid
south der Süden
space der Platz, ̈-e
spaghetti die Spaghetti *(pl.)*
Spanish (language) (das) Spanisch
speak sprechen°
speechless sprachlos
spell buchstabieren; **How do you**
  ~ **that?** Wie schreibt man
  das?
spend (money) aus·geben°; ~
  (time) verbringen°
splendid großartig
spoon der Löffel, -
sport der Sport; **to engage in**
  sports Sport treiben°
spring der Frühling
stairs die Treppe, -n
stand stehen°; ~ **up**
  auf·stehen°;
  ~**/put upright** stellen
standard German (das) Hochdeutsch
state (in Germany) das Land, ̈-er;
  ~ **(in the USA)**
  der Staat, -en
state-owned staatlich
stay: (to) ~ bleiben°
steak das Steak, -s
step der Schritt, -e;
  die Treppe, -n
steps die Treppe, -n
stereo system die Stereoanlage, -n
still noch; immer noch; noch
  immer
stomach der Magen
stomachache die Magenschmerzen *(pl.)*
stop auf·hören (mit); halten°
store das Geschäft, -e;
  der Laden, ̈-

story die Geschichte, -n
straight gerade
straighten up auf·räumen
strange merkwürdig
street die Straße, -n; ~ **car** die
  Straßenbahn, -en
stress der Streß
strike der Streik, -s; **(to)** ~
  streiken
stroll spazieren
strong stark
student der Student, -en, -en/die
  Studentin, -nen
studies das Studium
study studieren; lernen; arbeiten;
  durch·arbeiten
stupid dumm
subject (academic) das Fach, ̈-er
subway die U-Bahn
such solch (-er, -es, -e); ~ **a** so
  ein
suddenly plötzlich
suit (man's) der Anzug, ̈-e;
  (woman's) ~ das Kostüm, -e;
  (to) ~ passen
summer der Sommer
sun die Sonne, -n
Sunday der Sonntag
Sundays sonntags
supermarket der Supermarkt, ̈-e
  to the ~ in den Supermarkt;
  at the ~ im Supermarkt
supper das Abendessen; **for** ~
  zum Abendessen; **to have** ~
  zu Abend essen
supposed: to be ~ **to** sollen°
sure sicher; bestimmt; (agreement)
  ~**! Natürlich!**
surf surfen
surprise überraschen
suspense: to be in ~ gespannt
  sein
swim schwimmen°
swimming: to go ~ schwimmen
  gehen°
Swiss *(adj.)* Schweizer; ~ **(per-**
  son) der Schweizer, -/die
  Schweizerin, -nen
switch (to change) wechseln

Switzerland die Schweiz

table der Tisch, -e
table tennis das Tischtennis
take nehmen°
take along mit·nehmen°
take care of (someone) auf·passen (auf + *acc.*)
take off sich (*dat.*) [etwas] aus·ziehen°; **I take off my shoes.** Ich ziehe mir die Schuhe aus.
talk: ~ (about) reden (über); sprechen° (von/über + *acc.*)
tall (people) groß
task die Aufgabe, -n
taste schmecken; probieren
tasty lecker
tax die Steuer, -n
teacher der Lehrer, -/die Lehrerin, -nen
telephone das Telefon, -e; **to ~** telefonieren; an·rufen°
telephone number die Telefonnummer, -n; **What is your ~?** Wie ist deine/Ihre Telefonnummer?
television das Fernsehen; **~ set** der Fernseher, -; **color ~** der Farbfernseher; **~ program** die Fernsehsendung, -en; **to watch ~** fern·sehen°
tell sagen; erzählen; **to ~ (about)** erzählen (von + *dat.* /über + *acc.*)
tennis das Tennis
terrace die Terrasse, -n
terrible schlimm; furchtbar; schrecklich
test die Klausur, -en; **(to) take a ~** eine Klausur schreiben°
than als (after a comparison)
thank danken; **~ you very much** danke sehr/schön
thanks danke; der Dank; **~ a lot, many ~** vielen Dank
that daß; jen- (er, es, e)
theater das Theater, -; **to go to the ~** ins Theater gehen; **~ play** das Theaterstück, -e; **movie ~** das Kino, -s

then dann; da
there da; dort; dahin; **~ is/are** es gibt
thereby dadurch
therefore also; deshalb; daher; darum
these diese
they sie
thing das Ding, -e; die Sache, -n
think denken°; meinen; **What do you ~?** Was meinst du? **What do you ~ of the cake?** Was hältst du von dem Kuchen?; **I don't ~ so.** Ich glaube nicht.
third das Drittel, -
thirst der Durst
thirsty: to be ~ Durst haben°
this dies (-er, -es, -e)
throat der Hals, ¨e
throw werfen°
Thursday der Donnerstag
thus also
ticket die Karte, -n
tie binden°; **neck ~** die Krawatte, -n
tight eng
time die Zeit, -en; das Mal, -e; mal; **at this ~** zur Zeit; **at that ~** damals; **at the same ~** zur gleichen Zeit; **for a long ~** lange; **a short ~ ago** vor kurzem, neulich; **What ~ is it?** Wieviel Uhr ist es?/Wie spät ist es?; **At what ~?** Um wieviel Uhr?; **Have a good ~!** Viel Vergnügen!
times mal; **[three] ~** [drei] mal
tinker basteln
tired müde; kaputt
to an; auf, in; nach; zu
today heute; **What day is it ~?** Welcher Tag ist heute?
together zusammen
tomorrow morgen; **day after ~** übermorgen
tonight heute abend
too zu; **me ~** ich auch; **~ little** zu wenig; **~ much** zuviel

tool das Gerät, -e; das Werkzeug, -e
tooth der Zahn, ¨e; **to brush [my] teeth** [mir] die Zähne putzen
toothache die Zahnschmerzen (*pl.*)
tour die Tour, -en
town hall restaurant der Ratskeller, -
trade der Handel
train der Zug, ¨e; die Bahn; **~ station** der Bahnhof,¨e
translation die Übersetzung, -en
travel fahren°; reisen
tree der Baum, ¨e
trip die Reise, -n, die Fahrt, -en; die Tour, -en; **bike ~** die Radtour, -en
trousers die Hose, -n
try versuchen; probieren
T-shirt das T-Shirt, -s
Tuesday der Dienstag
Tuesdays dienstags
TV das Fernsehen; **~ set** der Fernseher, -; **~ program** die Fernsehsendung, -en
type: (to) ~ tippen; **to be able to ~** Schreibmaschine schreiben können
typewriter die Schreibmaschine, -n

unbelievable unglaublich
uncle der Onkel, -
under unter
understand verstehen°
undress (sich) aus·ziehen°; **I get undressed.** Ich ziehe mich aus.
unfortunately leider
unification die Vereinigung
unified vereinigt
union die Gewerkschaft, -en
university die Universität, -en; die Uni, -s; **to attend a ~** an/auf die Universität gehen; **at the ~** an/auf der Universität
until bis; **~ now** bisher; **until later** bis später; tschüß; bis dann; bis bald

up to bis zu

USA die USA *(pl.)*; **to the ~** in die USA

use benutzen; gebrauchen

utensil das Gerät, -e

vacation der Urlaub; die Ferien *(pl.)*; **on/during ~** in den Ferien; **to go on ~** in Urlaub fahren°; **to be on ~** in Urlaub sein°

vacuum der Staubsauger, -; **to ~** Staub saugen

vain: in ~ umsonst

vegetable das Gemüse

very sehr; ganz

vicinity: in the ~ in der Nähe

video camera die Videokamera, -s

video game das Videospiel, -e

village das Dorf, ¨er

visit der Besuch; **(to) ~** besuchen

visitor der Besucher, -/die Besucherin, -nen

volleyball der Volleyball

washing machine die Waschmaschine, -n

wait (for) warten (auf)

walk der Spaziergang, ¨e; **(to) take a ~** einen Spaziergang machen; spazieren; **(to) go for a ~** spazieren·gehen°; **walking: to go ~** wandern

wall die Wand, ¨e; die Mauer, -n

want (to) wollen°

war der Krieg, -e; **world ~** der Weltkrieg, -e

warm warm

was war

wash die Wäsche; **(to) ~** (sich) waschen°; **(to) ~ dishes** ab·waschen°; Geschirr spülen

watch die (Armband)uhr, -en; **(to) ~** an·sehen°; **(to) ~ TV** fern·sehen°; **~ out** auf·passen

water das Wasser

water ski der Wasserski, -er; **to ~** Wasserski fahren

way der Weg, -e; **on the ~** auf dem Weg; die Art

weak schwach

wear tragen°

weather das Wetter; **~ report** der Wetterbericht, -e

Wednesday der Mittwoch

week die Woche, -n; **a ~ from [Monday]** [Montag] in acht Tagen

weekend das Wochenende; **on the ~** am Wochenende

welcome: you're ~ bitte (sehr)

well gut; wohl; **I'm not ~** Mir geht's schlecht.; **~** (interjection) na!, nun!; **~ now, oh ~** na

well known bekannt

west der Westen

wet naß

what was; **~ kind (of), ~ a** was für (ein)

when wann; wenn; als

where wo; **~ (to)** wohin; **~ do you come from?** Woher kommst du?

whether ob

which welch (-er, -es, -e)

while während

white weiß

who wer

whole ganz

whom wen *(acc. of* wer); wem *(dat. of* wer)

why warum

willingly gern

wind der Wind

window das Fenster, -

windsurfing: to go ~ windsurfen gehen°

wine der Wein, -e

winter der Winter

wish wünschen; **I ~ I had . . .** Ich wollte, ich hätte ...

with mit; **~ it** damit; **~ me** mit mir; **to live ~ a family** bei einer Familie wohnen

woman die Frau, -en

wonder: to ~ about gespannt sein

woods der Wald, ¨er

word das Wort, ¨er

word processor der Wortprozessor, -en; **to do word processing** mit dem Wortprozessor arbeiten

work die Arbeit; **(to) do the ~** die Arbeit machen; arbeiten; **to ~ through** durch·arbeiten; **It doesn't ~.** Es geht nicht.; **It works.** Es geht.

worker der Arbeiter, -/die Arbeiterin, -nen; der Arbeitnehmer, -/die Arbeitnehmerin, -nen

world die Welt, -en

worry die Sorge, -n; **(to) ~ about** sich kümmern um

worth wert

worthwhile wert; **to be ~** sich lohnen

would würde; **~ like** möchte; **How ~ it be?** Wie wär's?

wow Mensch!

write schreiben°

writer der Schriftsteller, -/die Schriftstellerin, -nen

wrong falsch; **What's ~?** Was ist los?; **What is ~ with you?** Was hast du?

year das Jahr, -e

yellow gelb

yes ja

yesterday gestern

yet noch; schon; **not ~** noch nicht

you: (to) ~ dir *(dat. of* du)

young jung

your *(fam. pl.)* euer

youth die Jugend; der/die Jugendliche, -n

PERMISSIONS AND CREDITS

The authors and editors of *Deutsch heute, Fifth Edition* would like to thank the following authors and publishers for granting permission to use copyrighted material:

Mani Matter, "Heidi," from *Us emer lääre Gygechaschte*, Zürich: Benziger Verlag, 1972, and LP Zyt 24, *I han es Zündhölzli azünd*, Produktion + Copyright: Zytglogge Verlag, Gümligen.

Helga M. Novak, "Schlittenfahren," from *Palisaden. Erzählungen*, © 1980 by Luchterhand Literaturverlag, Darmstadt und Neuwied.

Werner Schmidli, "Als ich noch jung war," from *Sagen Sie nicht, beim Geld hört der Spaß auf*, Zürich: Benziger Verlag, 1971. Reprinted by permission of the author.

The authors and editors would also like to thank the following companies and organizations for granting permission to use copyrighted material:

Realia

p. 9: Courtesy of Jochen Grobholz.
p. 84: Courtesy of Dallmayr, München.
p. 101: Courtesy of Preisring-Markt.
p. 149: Mit Genehmigung des DE-VAU-GE Gesundkostwerk GmbH, Lüneburg.
p. 168: Bundeskanzleramt, *Österreich, Tatsachen und Zahlen*, 1986/87, Seite 6.
p. 174: Courtesy of Restop Altea Mondsee.
p. 177 left: Courtesy of Itallingua; center: Courtesy of Step In Dance Studio; right: Courtesy of Taekwon-do Black-Belt-Center.
p. 197: Courtesy of Staatl. Mineralbrunnen Siemens Erben, Mainz.
p. 205: Courtesy of OKA.
p. 208: Courtesy of Erdgarten Naturkost, München.

p. 216: Karstadt AG, Essen.
p. 217: Oetker Haushaltgeräte Gesellschaft, Bielefeld.
p. 261: Courtesy of Girmes GmbH.
p. 273: Courtesy of Philips Industries, N.V.; Siemens AG; Electrolux; Bosch Domestic Appliances.
p. 282: Courtesy of Baywobau, München.
p. 290: Verkehrsgemeinschaft Hochschwarzwald e.V.
p. 312: Schweizer Bankverein/Swiss Bank Corporation, Basel.
p. 325: "Der kleine Herr Jakob", © Hans Jürgen Press.
p. 337: Sport-Billy Productions R. Deyle.
p. 342: Hannes Keller AG Computer-Zentrum, Zürich.
p. 361: Courtesy of Ingenieurbüro Thor Elektrobau.

p. 396: Studenten im Olympiazentrum e.V.
p. 402: Courtesy of Münchner Volkshochschule, München.
p. 417: Courtesy of Kasubek/Schramm, 1989.
p. 438: Hapag-Lloyd AG, Hamburg; J.A. Henckels Zwillingswerk AG, Solingen; KHD Humboldt Wedag AG, Köln; Lufthansa German Airlines; MAN GHH Corp., New York, NY; Mobay Corp., Pittsburgh, PA; Pfaff and Co., Köln; Poggenpohl, Inc., Alandale, NJ; Thyssen Inc., New York, NY.
p. 443: Triumph Adler AG, Nürnberg.
p. 461: © Manfred von Papen.
p. 475: Courtesy of *Pflasterstrand*, Frankfurt a/M.

Photos

facing p. 1: © Ulrike Welsch
p. 4: © Andrew Brilliant
pp. 5, 10: © Ulrike Welsch
p. 18: © Carol Palmer
p. 21: © Kathy Squires
pp. 23, 33: © Beryl Goldberg
p. 38: Courtesy of German Information Center
pp. 50, 58: © Andrew Brilliant
p. 63: © H. Mark Weidman
p. 67: © Ulrike Welsch
p. 71: Bildarchiv Foto Marburg/Art Resource
p. 78 left and right: Focus on Sports
p. 82: © Andrew Brilliant
p. 85 left and right: © Beryl Goldberg
p. 89: © Carol Palmer

p. 92: © Kathy Squires
p. 94: © Andrew Brilliant
p. 96, 99: © Carol Palmer
p. 100: © Stevens/Sipa Press
p. 110: © Ulrike Welsch
p. 124: © Beryl Goldberg
p. 127 top: Courtesy of German Information Center; bottom: © Kathy Squires
p. 131: © H. Mark Weidman
p. 133: © Beryl Goldberg
p. 137: © Ulrike Welsch
p. 139: © Beryl Goldberg
p. 151: © AFP/Scott Flynn
p. 154: © Beryl Goldberg
p. 158: © Judy Poe
p. 162: © Kathy Squires

pp. 164, 166: © Carol Palmer
p. 168: Courtesy of Austrian Tourist Office
p. 171: © Judy Poe
p. 172: © Carol Palmer
p. 194: © Beryl Goldberg
p. 199: © Andrew Brilliant
p. 202: © Beryl Goldberg
p. 204: © Andrew Brilliant
p. 213: © dpa/Photoreporters
p. 215: © Beryl Goldberg
p. 220: © Andrew Brilliant
p. 227: © Fredrik D. Bodin
p. 232: © Beryl Goldberg
pp. 235, 237: © Andrew Brilliant
p. 241: © H. Mark Weidman
p. 242: © Andrew Brilliant

R-85

pp. 262, 268, 277: © Kathy Squires
p. 283: © Andrew Brilliant
pp. 287, 297: © Kathy Squires
p. 302: Courtesy of Swiss National
 Tourist Office
p. 304 left and right: © dpa/
 Photoreporters
p. 306: © Schumann/dpa/
 Photoreporters
p. 310: © Abramson/Stock Boston
p. 311: © Judy Poe
p. 314: © David Parker/Science Photo
 Library/Photo Researchers
pp. 315, 316, 321, 332: Courtesy of
 Swiss National Tourist Office
p. 340: © Kathy Squires
p. 345 left and right: Courtesy of
 German Information Center

p. 348: © dpa/Photoreporters
p. 350: © Ulrike Welsch
p. 351: © Kathy Squires
p. 352: © H. Mark Weidman
p. 355: © Bernd Lammel/Time Inc.
p. 369: © Kathy Squires
p. 374: © H. Mark Weidman
p. 376: © Kathy Squires
p. 379: © Bildarchiv Huber
p. 380: © Andrew Brilliant
p. 384: © Carol Palmer
p. 389: © Andrew Brilliant
p. 393: © Kathy Squires
p. 401: © Beryl Goldberg
p. 410: Art Resource
p. 411: Courtesy of Luchterhand
 Literaturverlag Verlag
p. 414: © Ulrike Welsch

p. 421: © Beryl Goldberg
p. 423: © Andrew Brilliant
p. 425: © Schulte/dpa/Photoreporters
p. 426: © Kathy Squires
pp. 436, 440: © Beryl Goldberg
p. 444: Art Resource
p. 445: Courtesy of Benziger Verlag
p. 448: © Alfred/Sipa Press
p. 453: © Sipa Press
p. 454: © Witt/Sipa Press
p. 457: © Kathy Squires
p. 462: © Gibod/Sipa Press
p. 464: © Boning-Exys Fotos/Sipa Press
p. 467: © Adenis/Sipa Press
p. 476: © Beryl Goldberg

Illustrations

Illustrations by Penny Carter: pp. 13, 24–25, 54, 91, 112, 138, 163, 165, 209, 246–247,
 249, 280, 307, 308–309, and 395.
Illustrations by Chris Demarest: pp. 31, 64, 107, 173, 210, 259, 293, 329, 435, and 471.